Learning to Use VP-Planner Plus

GARY B. SHELLY

THOMAS J. CASHMAN

JAMES S. QUASNEY

Boyd & Fraser

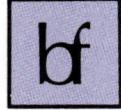

The Shelly and Cashman Series
Boyd & Fraser Publishing Company

SHELLY AND CASHMAN TITLES FROM BOYD & FRASER

Computer Concepts

Computer Concepts with BASIC

    ClassNotes and Study Guide to Accompany Computer Concepts and Computer Concepts with BASIC

Computer Concepts with Microcomputer Applications (Lotus® version)

Computer Concepts with Microcomputer Applications (VP-Planner Plus® version)

    ClassNotes and Study Guide to Accompany Computer Concepts with Microcomputer Applications
(VP-Planner Plus® and Lotus® versions)

Learning to Use WordPerfect® Lotus 1-2-3® and dBASE III PLUS®

    ClassNotes and Study Guide to Accompany Learning to Use WordPerfect® Lotus 1-2-3® and dBASE III PLUS®

Learning to Use WordPerfect® VP-Planner Plus® and dBASE III PLUS®

    ClassNotes and Study Guide to Accompany Learning to Use WordPerfect® VP-Planner Plus® and dBASE III PLUS®

Learning to Use WordPerfect®

    ClassNotes and Study Guide to Accompany Learning to Use WordPerfect®

Learning to Use VP-Planner Plus®

    ClassNotes and Study Guide to Accompany Learning to Use VP-Planner Plus®

Learning to Use Lotus 1-2-3®

    ClassNotes and Study Guide to Accompany Learning to Use Lotus 1-2-3®

Learning to Use dBASE III PLUS®

    ClassNotes and Study Guide to Accompany Learning to Use dBASE III PLUS®

Computer Fundamentals with Application Software

    Workbook and Study Guide to Accompany Computer Fundamentals with Application Software

Learning to Use SuperCalc®3 dBASE III® and WordStar® 3.3: An Introduction

Learning to Use SuperCalc®3: An Introduction

Learning to Use dBASE III®: An Introduction

Learning to Use WordStar® 3.3: An Introduction

BASIC Programming for the IBM Personal Computer

Turbo Pascal Programming

FORTHCOMING SHELLY AND CASHMAN TITLES

RPG II and III   Systems Analysis and Design

© 1990 by Boyd & Fraser Publishing Company

Developed and produced by Solomon & Douglas
Manufactured in the United States of America

VP-Planner Plus® is a registered trademark of Paperback Software International

Library of Congress Cataloging-in-Publication Data

```
Shelly, Gary B.
    Learning to use VP-Planner Plus / Gary B. Shelly, Thomas J.
  Cashman, James S. Quasney.
       p.   cm. -- (Shelly and Cashman series)
    Includes index.
    ISBN 0-87835-343-7
    1. VP-planner (Computer program)  2. Business--Data processing.
  I. Cashman, Thomas J.  II. Quasney, James S.  III. Title.
  IV. Series: Shelly, Gary B.  Shelly and Cashman series.
  HF5548.4.V65S44   1989
  005.36'9--dc19                                88-38594
                                                   CIP
```

10 9 8 7 6 5 4 3 2 1

CONTENTS IN BRIEF

PREFACE x

INTRODUCTION TO COMPUTERS COM 1

INTRODUCTION TO DOS DOS 1

SPREADSHEETS USING VP-PLANNER PLUS VP 1

    PROJECT 1 Building a Worksheet VP 2

    PROJECT 2 Formatting and Printing a Worksheet VP 46

    PROJECT 3 Enhancing Your Worksheet VP 96

    PROJECT 4 Building Worksheets with Functions and Macros VP 146

    PROJECT 5 Graphing with VP-Planner Plus VP 184

    PROJECT 6 Sorting and Querying a Worksheet Database VP 213

CONTENTS

Introduction to Computers

OBJECTIVES

WHAT IS A COMPUTER? COM 3

WHAT IS DATA AND INFORMATION? COM 3

WHAT ARE THE COMPONENTS OF A COMPUTER? COM 3

Input Devices COM 4

The Processor COM 6

Output Devices COM 6

Computer Screens COM 8

Auxiliary Storage COM 8

SUMMARY OF THE COMPONENTS OF A COMPUTER COM 12

WHAT IS COMPUTER SOFTWARE? COM 12

Application Software COM 13

System Software COM 13

SUMMARY OF INTRODUCTION TO COMPUTERS COM 14

SUMMARY COM 14

STUDENT ASSIGNMENTS COM 14

INTRODUCTION TO COMPUTERS INDEX COM 16

Introduction to DOS

OBJECTIVES   DOS 2
INTRODUCTION   DOS 2
Operating Systems for IBM PCs   DOS 2
DOS Versions   DOS 3
USING THE DISK OPERATING SYSTEM (DOS)   DOS 3
Starting the Computer   DOS 3
   The Cold Start   DOS 4
   The Warm Start or Reset   DOS 4
   Loading DOS   DOS 4
Setting the Date and Time   DOS 4
The DOS Prompt   DOS 5
The Default Drive   DOS 5
ENTERING DISK OPERATING SYSTEM (DOS) COMMANDS   DOS 6
Internal and External Commands   DOS 6
DIRECTORY COMMAND (DIR)   DOS 7
Displaying Directories of Other Disks   DOS 7
Pausing Directory Listings   DOS 8
   Pause Screen (Control S)   DOS 8
   DIR Command Options   DOS 8
   /P—The Pause Option   DOS 8
   /W—The Wide Display Option   DOS 9
Canceling a Command (Break)   DOS 9
FORMATTING A DISKETTE   DOS 9
The FORMAT Command   DOS 10
Formatting a System Disk (/S Option)   DOS 12
Assigning a Volume Label (/V Option)   DOS 12
CLS COMMAND   DOS 13
MANAGING DATA AND PROGRAM FILES ON DISKS   DOS 13
Assigning File Specifications   DOS 13
   Filenames   DOS 14
   Filename Extensions   DOS 14

COPY COMMAND   DOS 14
Using the COPY Command   DOS 14
Copying Files from One Diskette to Another   DOS 15
Copying to the Default Disk   DOS 16
Copying a File to the Same Diskette   DOS 16
Global Filename Characters ("Wildcards") DOS 17
   The * Character   DOS 17
   Copying All Files from One Diskette to Another   DOS 19
   The ? Character   DOS 19
Using Wildcards with DOS Commands   DOS 19
RENAME COMMAND   DOS 19
ERASE AND DEL COMMANDS   DOS 21
Removing Files   DOS 21
USING DIRECTORIES AND SUBDIRECTORIES   DOS 21
Directory Entries and Subdirectories   DOS 21
The PROMPT Command   DOS 22
Making Subdirectories   DOS 22
Changing Directories   DOS 24
   The Current Directory   DOS 24
Specifying a Path to Subdirectories and Files   DOS 25
   Specifying Paths in Commands   DOS 25
Managing Files Within Subdirectories   DOS 25
Removing Subdirectories   DOS 25
   Erasing Subdirectory Files   DOS 25
   Removing a Subdirectory   DOS 26
LOADING A PROGRAM   DOS 26
SUMMARY   DOS 27
STUDENT ASSIGNMENTS   DOS 28
True/False Questions   DOS 28
Multiple/Choice Questions   DOS 29
Projects   DOS 31

Spreadsheets Using VP-Planner Plus

PROJECT 1   BUILDING A WORKSHEET   VP 2

OBJECTIVES   VP 2
STARTING VP-PLANNER PLUS   VP 2
Computer with One or Two Floppy Disks and No Fixed Disk   VP 3
Computer with a Fixed Disk   VP 3
THE WORKSHEET   VP 4
Cell, Cell Cursor, and Window   VP 4

The Control Panel and the Current-Mode Line   VP 5
   Status Line   VP 5
   Input Line   VP 5
   Prompt Line   VP 5
   Current-Mode Line   VP 5

MOVING THE CELL CURSOR ONE CELL AT A TIME   VP 6
ENTERING LABELS   VP 6
Labels That Begin with a Letter   VP 7
Labels Preceded by a Special Character   VP 10

ENTERING NUMBERS   VP 13
Whole Numbers   VP 13
Decimal Numbers   VP 15

MOVING THE CELL CURSOR MORE THAN ONE CELL AT A TIME   VP 15
The GOTO Command   VP 15
Summary of Ways to Move the Cell Cursor   VP 17

ENTERING FORMULAS   VP 17
Assigning Formulas to Cells   VP 18
Order of Operations   VP 21

SAVING A WORKSHEET   VP 21
The Command Mode   VP 22
Backing Out of the Command Mode   VP 23
The File Save Command (/FS)   VP 23
Saving Worksheets to a Different Disk Drive   VP 26

PRINTING A SCREEN IMAGE OF THE WORKSHEET   VP 26
CORRECTING ERRORS   VP 27
Correcting Errors While the Data Is on the Input Line   VP 27
Editing Data in a Cell   VP 28
Erasing the Contents of a Cell (/RE)   VP 32

Erasing the Entire Worksheet (/WE)   VP 32
ONLINE HELP FACILITY   VP 32
QUITTING VP-PLANNER PLUS (/Q)   VP 33
PROJECT SUMMARY   VP 34
STUDENT ASSIGNMENTS   VP 36
Student Assignment 1: True/False Questions   VP 36
Student Assignment 2: Multiple Choice Questions   VP 36
Student Assignment 3: Understanding the Worksheet   VP 37
Student Assignment 4: Understanding VP-Planner Plus Commands   VP 38
Student Assignment 5: Correcting Formulas in a Worksheet   VP 40
Student Assignment 6: Correcting Worksheet Entries   VP 40
Student Assignment 7: Entering Formulas   VP 41
Student Assignment 8: Building an Inventory Listing Worksheet   VP 42
Student Assignment 9: Building a Yearly Personal Expenses Comparison Worksheet   VP 43
Student Assignment 10: Building a Quarterly Income and Expense Worksheet   VP 44
Student Assignment 11: Using the Online Help Facility   VP 44
Student Assignment 12: Changing Data in the Quarterly Income and Expense Worksheet   VP 44

PROJECT 2   FORMATTING AND PRINTING A WORKSHEET   VP 46

OBJECTIVES   VP 46
RETRIEVING A WORKSHEET (/FR)   VP 47
CHANGING THE WIDTH OF THE COLUMNS   VP 49
Changing the Width of All the Columns (/WGC)   VP 50
Changing the Width of One Column at a Time (/WCS)   VP 52

DEFINING A RANGE   VP 53
FORMATTING NUMERIC VALUES   VP 54
Invoking the Format Command (/RF or /WGF)   VP 54
Selecting a Range by Pointing   VP 56
Summary of Format Commands   VP 58
Determining the Format Assigned to a Cell   VP 59

REPEATING CHARACTERS IN A CELL   VP 60
REPLICATION—THE COPY COMMAND (/C)   VP 61
Source Range   VP 62
Destination Range   VP 62

SAVING AN INTERMEDIATE COPY OF THE WORKSHEET   VP 65
USING BUILT-IN FUNCTIONS   VP 66
The SUM Function   VP 66
Copying Functions   VP 67
Alternative Ways to Sum Cells   VP 70

DETERMINING A PERCENT VALUE   VP 71
FORMATTING TO PERCENT AND CURRENCY   VP 72
The Percentage Format (/RFP)   VP 72
The Currency Format (/RFC)   VP 74

SAVING THE WORKSHEET A SECOND TIME   VP 76
PRINTING THE WORKSHEET   VP 77
The Print Printer Command (/PP)   VP 78
Quitting the Print Command   VP 80
Printing a Section of the Worksheet   VP 80
Printing the Cell-Formulas Version of the Worksheet (/PPOOCQAC)   VP 82
Printing a Worksheet to a File (/PF)   VP 83
Summary of Commands in the Print Menu   VP 83

DEBUGGING THE FORMULAS IN A WORKSHEET USING THE TEXT FORMAT   VP 84
PROJECT SUMMARY   VP 85
STUDENT ASSIGNMENTS   VP 87
Student Assignment 1: True/False Questions   VP 87
Student Assignment 2: Multiple Choice Questions   VP 87
Student Assignment 3: Understanding Ranges   VP 88

Student Assignment 4: Understanding Formats   VP 89
Student Assignment 5: Correcting the Range in a Worksheet   VP 90
Student Assignment 6: Correcting Functions in a Worksheet   VP 91
Student Assignment 7: Modifying an Inventory Worksheet   VP 92
Student Assignment 8: Building an Employee Payroll Comparison Worksheet   VP 93
Student Assignment 9: Building a Monthly Expense Worksheet   VP 94
Student Assignment 10: Building a Monthly Sales Analysis Worksheet   VP 94
Student Assignment 11: Changing Data in the Monthly Expense Worksheet   VP 95
Student Assignment 12: Changing Data in the Monthly Sales Analysis Worksheet   VP 95

PROJECT 3   ENHANCING YOUR WORKSHEET   VP 96

OBJECTIVES   VP 96
VARYING THE WIDTH OF THE COLUMNS   VP 97
FORMATTING THE WORKSHEET GLOBALLY (/WGF)   VP 99
DISPLAYING THE DATE AND TIME   VP 100
The NOW Function   VP 100
Formatting the Date (/RFD)   VP 102
Formatting the Time (/RFD)   VP 102
Updating the Time—Recalculation   VP 103
Date and Time Formats   VP 103
ENTERING THE QUARTERLY BUDGET LABELS   VP 104
INSERTING AND DELETING ROWS AND COLUMNS   VP 105
The Insert Command (/WI)   VP 105
The Delete Command (/WD)   VP 108
COPYING CELLS WITH EQUAL SOURCE AND DESTINATION RANGES   VP 108
ENTERING NUMBERS WITH A PERCENT SIGN   VP 110
FREEZING THE TITLES   VP 110
The Titles Command (/WT)   VP 111
Unfreezing the Titles (/WTC)   VP 112

MOVING THE CONTENTS OF CELLS (/M)   VP 112
DISPLAYING FORMULAS AND FUNCTIONS IN THE CELLS (/RFT)   VP 114
ABSOLUTE VERSUS RELATIVE ADDRESSING   VP 116
Relative Addressing   VP 116
Absolute and Mixed Cell Addressing   VP 117
Copying Formulas with Mixed Cell Addresses   VP 117
Switching from Text Format to the Comma Format   VP 119
POINTING TO A RANGE OF CELLS TO SUM   VP 119
Pointing versus Entering a Range of Cells   VP 121
Copying the Total Expenses and Net Income for Each Month   VP 121
Summing Empty Cells and Labels   VP 121
SAVING AND PRINTING THE WORKSHEET   VP 123
Printing the Worksheet (/PP)   VP 124
Changing the Printer Margin Settings (/PPOM)   VP 125

Printing the Worksheet in Condensed Mode
(/PPOS)   VP 126
Other Printer Options (/PPO)   VP 127
WHAT-IF QUESTIONS   VP 127
Manual versus Automatic Recalculation
(/WGR)   VP 129
**CHANGING THE WORKSHEET DEFAULT
SETTINGS (/WGD)   VP 130**
**CHANGING THE SCREEN SO THAT IT LOOKS
LIKE THE LOTUS 1-2-3 SCREEN   VP 131**
THE UNDO AND REDO KEYS   VP 133
INTERACTING WITH DOS   VP 133
PROJECT SUMMARY   VP 134
STUDENT ASSIGNMENTS   VP 136
Student Assignment 1: True/False
Questions   VP 136
Student Assignment 2: Multiple Choice
Questions   VP 136
Student Assignment 3: Understanding Absolute,
Mixed, and Relative Addressing   VP 137

Student Assignment 4: Writing VP-Planner Plus
Commands   VP 138
Student Assignment 5: Correcting the Range in a
Worksheet   VP 139
Student Assignment 6: Correcting Errors in a
Worksheet   VP 140
Student Assignment 7: Building a Projected Price
Increase Worksheet   VP 141
Student Assignment 8: Building a Payroll Analysis
Worksheet   VP 142
Student Assignment 9: Building a Book Income
Worksheet   VP 143
Student Assignment 10: Building a Salary Budget
Worksheet   VP 144
Student Assignment 11: Changing Manufacturing
Costs and Royalty Rates in the Book Income
Worksheet   VP 145
Student Assignment 12: Changing Sales
Allocation Percent Values and Salary Increase
Percent in the Salary Budget Worksheet
VP 145

PROJECT 4   BUILDING WORKSHEETS WITH FUNCTIONS AND MACROS   VP 146

OBJECTIVES   VP 146
**PROJECT 4A—ANALYZING STUDENT TEST
SCORES   VP 148**
Assigning a Name to a Range of Cells (RNC)
VP 150
Statistical Functions—AVG, COUNT, MIN, MAX,
STD, and VAR   VP 152
Saving and Printing the Worksheet   VP 154
Erasing the Worksheet from Main Computer
Memory (/WE)   VP 154
**PROJECT 4B—DETERMINING THE MONTHLY
PAYMENT FOR A CAR LOAN   VP 154**
Assigning a Label Name to an Adjacent Cell
(/RNL)   VP 155
Determining the Loan Payment—PMT   VP 157
The Data Fill Feature (/DF)   VP 157
Determining the Yearly Ending Balance—PV
VP 159
Making Decisions—The IF Function   VP 159
Saving the Worksheet   VP 162

Using a Data Table to Answer What-If Questions
(/DT)   VP 162
MACROS   VP 165
Designing a Sample Macro   VP 165
Documenting Macros   VP 165
Entering and Naming a Macro   VP 165
Invoking a Macro   VP 166
Adding More Macros to the Worksheet   VP 166
Guarding Against Macro Catastrophes   VP 167
/X Macro Commands and Macro Words   VP 168
Interactive Macros   VP 169
WINDOWS (/WW)   VP 169
Synchronizing Windows (/WWS)   VP 171
Clearing the Windows (/WWC)   VP 171
CELL PROTECTION (/WGPE)   VP 171
Saving and Printing the Worksheet   VP 171
**OBTAINING A SUMMARY OF ALL THE
VP-PLANNER PLUS FUNCTIONS   VP 172**
PROJECT SUMMARY   VP 172

STUDENT ASSIGNMENTS   VP 175

Student Assignment 1: True/False
Questions   VP 175

Student Assignment 2: Multiple Choice
Questions   VP 175

Student Assignment 3: Understanding
Functions   VP 176

Student Assignment 4: Understanding
Macros   VP 177

Student Assignment 5: Using the Data Fill
Command   VP 178

Student Assignment 6: Using the Data Table
Command   VP 178

Student Assignment 7: Building a Weekly Payroll
Worksheet   VP 180

Student Assignment 8: Building a Future Value
Worksheet   VP 181

Student Assignment 9: Building a Data Table for
the Future Value Worksheet   VP 182

Student Assignment 10: Building Macros for the
Future Value Worksheet   VP 182

Student Assignment 11: Building Macros for the
Weekly Payroll Worksheet   VP 183

PROJECT 5   GRAPHING WITH VP-PLANNER PLUS   VP 184

OBJECTIVES   VP 184
THE GRAPH COMMAND (/G)   VP 185
PIE CHARTS (/GTP)   VP 186
Selecting the A Range   VP 187
Selecting the X Range   VP 187
Selecting the B Range   VP 188
Adding a Title to the Pie Chart   VP 188
Naming the Pie Chart   VP 189
Saving and Printing the Pie Chart   VP 190
The Effect of What-If Analyses on the Pie
Chart   VP 190
PIC Files   VP 191

LINE GRAPHS (/GTL)   VP 191
Selecting the X Range   VP 192
Selecting the A Range   VP 193
Adding Titles to the Line Graph   VP 193
Viewing the Line Graph   VP 193
Naming the Line Graph   VP 194
Saving and Printing the Line Graph   VP 194
Multiple-Line Graphs   VP 194
Assigning Legends to the Data Ranges   VP 196
Viewing the Multiple-Line Graph   VP 196
Naming the Multiple-Line Graph   VP 196
Saving and Printing the Multiple-Line Graph
VP 196
Scatter Graphs   VP 196
Changing the Multiple-Line Graph to a Scatter
Graph   VP 197
Viewing the Scatter Graph   VP 197
Naming, Saving, and Printing the Scatter
Graph   VP 197
BAR GRAPHS (/GTB) or (/GTS)   VP 197

Simple Bar Graphs (/GTB)   VP 198
Using a Named Graph   VP 198
Changing the Line Graph to a Bar Graph   VP 198
Viewing the Simple Bar Graph   VP 198
Naming, Saving, and Printing the Simple Bar
Graph   VP 199
Side-by-Side Bar Graphs (/GTB)   VP 199
Using a Named Graph   VP 199
Changing the Multiple-Line Graph to a Side-by-Side
Bar Graph   VP 200
Viewing the Side-by-Side Bar Graph   VP 200
Naming, Saving, and Printing the Side-by-Side Bar
Graph   VP 200
Stacked-Bar Graphs (/GTS)   VP 200
Changing the Side-by-Side Bar Graph to a Stacked-
Bar Graph   VP 201
Viewing the Stacked-Bar Graph   VP 201
Naming, Saving, and Printing the Stacked-Bar
Graph   VP 201

ADDITIONAL GRAPH OPTIONS (/GO)   VP 201
Data-Labels (/GOD)   VP 201
Scale Command (/GOS)   VP 202
Color/B&W Commands (/GOC or /GOB)   VP 203
XY GRAPHS (/GTX)   VP 203
PROJECT SUMMARY   VP 204
STUDENT ASSIGNMENTS   VP 207
Student Assignment 1: True/False
Questions   VP 207
Student Assignment 2: Multiple Choice
Questions   VP 208
Student Assignment 3: Understanding Graph
Commands   VP 208

Student Assignment 4: Understanding the Graph Options   VP 208

Student Assignment 5: Drawing a Pie Chart   VP 209

Student Assignment 6: Drawing a Multiple-Line Graph and Side-by-Side Bar Graph   VP 210

Student Assignment 7: Drawing a Stacked-Bar Graph   VP 211

Student Assignment 8: Building a Table of Coordinates and Drawing the Corresponding XY Graph   VP 212

PROJECT 6   SORTING AND QUERYING A WORKSHEET DATABASE   VP 213

OBJECTIVES   VP 213

SORTING A DATABASE   VP 214

The Sort Menu (/DS)   VP 215

Sorting the Records by Employee Name   VP 216

Sorting the Records by Years of Seniority within Sex Code   VP 217

QUERYING A DATABASE   VP 219

The Query Menu (/DQ)   VP 220

The Find Command (/DQF)   VP 221

More About the Criterion Range   VP 223

No Conditions   VP 223

Conditions with Labels   VP 224

Conditions with Numbers   VP 225

Conditions with Formulas   VP 225

Mixing Conditions with Formulas and Labels   VP 226

The Extract Command (/DQE)   VP 226

THE DATABASE FUNCTIONS   VP 229

THE LOOKUP FUNCTIONS   VP 230

The CHOOSE Function   VP 231

The VLOOKUP and HLOOKUP Functions   VP 231

PROJECT SUMMARY   VP 232

STUDENT ASSIGNMENTS   VP 235

Student Assignment 1: True/False Questions   VP 235

Student Assignment 2: Multiple Choice Questions   VP 235

Student Assignment 3: Understanding Sorting   VP 236

Student Assignment 4: Understanding Criteria   VP 236

Student Assignment 5: Understanding Database and Lookup Functions   VP 237

Student Assignment 6: Building and Sorting a Database of Prospective Programmers   VP 237

Student Assignment 7: Finding Records in the Prospective Programmer Database   VP 238

Student Assignment 8: Extracting Records from the Prospective Programmer Database   VP 238

Student Assignment 9: Property Tax Rate Table Lookup   VP 238

INDEX   VP 239

PREFACE

Today there are over 20 million microcomputers in businesses, schools, and homes throughout the world. To use the power of these computers, a new generation of software, commonly called application software, has been developed. One of the most widely used types of application software is called a spreadsheet program. Spreadsheet programs are used for financial, accounting, and management planning and decision making.

This textbook is designed to be used in an introductory course on the use of spreadsheet programs. It assumes no previous experience with computers and is written with continuity, simplicity, and practicality in mind—characteristics we consider essential for students who are learning about application software for the first time. This textbook provides an introduction to computer concepts, an introduction to the use of the IBM Personal Computer Disk Operating System (PC-DOS), and detailed instructions on the use of VP-Planner Plus, an industry-leading application software package. After completing this textbook, students will be able to implement a wide variety of applications using VP-Planner Plus.

ORGANIZATION OF THE TEXTBOOK

his textbook consists of two introductory chapters and six projects using VP-Planner Plus.

An Introduction to Computers

Many students taking a course in the use of spreadsheet software will have had little previous experience using microcomputers. For this reason this textbook begins with *Introduction to Computers*—coverage of computer hardware and software concepts important to first-time microcomputers users. These concepts include the functions of the computer and the components of a typical microcomputer system—the keyboard, the display, the processor unit, and the printer, as well as discussions of diskettes and hard disks as forms of auxiliary storage.

An Introduction to DOS

To use a computer effectively, students need a practical knowledge of operating systems. The second chapter in this text, therefore, is *Introduction to DOS*—an introduction to the most commonly used DOS commands—such as loading DOS, formatting a diskette, and copying files.

Six Problem-Oriented Projects

After presenting the basic microcomputer and DOS concepts, this textbook provides detailed instruction on how to use VP-Planner Plus. (VP-Planner Plus emulates Lotus 1-2-3. For example, every sequence of VP-Planner Plus keystrokes in this textbook is exactly the same for Lotus 1-2-3.)

The instruction on how to use VP-Planner Plus is divided into 6 projects. In each of the projects students learn how to use VP Planner-Plus by way of the unique Shelly and Cashman problem-oriented approach, in which various problems are presented and then *thoroughly* explained in a step-by-step manner. Numerous carefully labeled screens and keystroke sequences illustrate the exact sequence of operations necessary to solve the problems presented. Using this approach, students are visually guided as they enter the various commands and can quickly become familiar with important concepts and techniques.

The material instructing students how to use VP-Planner Plus is divided among the six projects as follows:

Project 1—Building a Worksheet The first project introduces students to worksheet terminology and the basic characteristics of a worksheet. Topics include moving the cell cursor; entering labels, numbers, and formulas; saving a worksheet; printing the screen image of the worksheet; correcting errors; and using the online help facility of VP-Planner Plus. In this project, students apply this know-how to create a company's first quarter sales report.

Project 2—Formatting and Printing a Worksheet In Project 2 students add summary totals to the worksheet built in Project 1 and format the worksheet so that it is easier to read. Topics discussed in Project 1 are reinforced. New topics include retrieving a worksheet from disk, changing column widths, formatting numeric values, replication, printing the as-is and cell-formulas versions of the worksheet, and debugging methods.

Project 3—Enhancing Your Worksheet In Project 3 students create a more complex quarterly total report. New topics include what-if analyses, moving cell contents, inserting and deleting rows and columns, freezing titles, changing worksheet default settings, printing a worksheet in the condensed mode, copying absolute cell addresses, temporarily returning control to DOS, and changing the screen to make it look like a Lotus 1-2-3 screen. This project also strengthens students' understanding of copying cells from one range to another and the formatting capabilities of a spreadsheet program.

Project 4—Building Worksheets with Functions and Macros In Project 4 students build two worksheets. The first is a grading report. Emphasis is placed on naming ranges and using statistical functions. The second worksheet determines the monthly payment and amortization schedule for a car loan, and a data table is incorporated for what-if analyses. Several macros are also incorporated into the worksheet. In this project students also learn to use the IF function, the Data Fill command, labels for naming adjacent cells, multiple windows, and the cell protection scheme.

Project 5—Graphing with VP-Planner Plus In Project 5 students create several graphics to illustrate worksheet data. These graphics are pie chart, line graph, multiple-line graph, scatter graph, simple bar graph, side-by-side bar graph, stacked bar graph, and XY graph.

Project 6—Sorting and Querying a Worksheet Database In Project 6 students build a worksheet database and then manipulate the data to generate information. Basic database terminology is discussed. Topics include sorting, finding records, extracting records, database functions, and lookup functions.

The Three Integrated Parts of VP-Planner Plus

VP-Planner Plus, as Lotus 1-2-3, is made up of three highly integrated parts—spreadsheet, data management, and graphics. All three parts are covered in this textbook.

Spreadsheet—The spreadsheet feature of VP-Planner Plus is particularly useful for manipulating data that can be organized into rows and columns to create a worksheet, also called a spreadsheet. Easy to use commands and functions can generate valuable information with little effort and no detailed programming.

Data Management—This part of VP-Planner Plus allows a user to sort worksheet data that has been organized as records in a file. In addition to the sort capability, records can be found and extracted on the basis of meeting some requirement, such as extracting sales for one particular month from a worksheet containing sales for a total year.

Graphics—This part of VP-Planner Plus allows users to easily generate elaborate graphs of the worksheet data. Six types of graphs can be generated: line, bar, pie, XY, stacked-bar, and scatter plot. (A color/graphics adapter is required to view graphs on the computer screen or to print the graphs.)

FEATURES

Companion Software

A free educational version of VP-Planner Plus is available to adopters of this text. Note that this software is *not* a tutorial but is the *actual* application software package in its commercial form. This educational version provides a worksheet of 64 columns by 256 rows. It does not allow creation of multidimensional arrays, but otherwise has the same capabilities as the commercial version of VP-Planner Plus. Schools using this textbook may copy the free software as required for classroom use at no charge. This software is available for IBM Personal Computers and PS/2 series, and for IBM compatible computers.

For information on how you can receive this free software refer to page xv.

End-of-Project Summaries

Two helpful learning and review tools are included at the end of each project—the Project Summary and the Keystroke Summary. The Project Summary lists the key concepts covered in the project. The Keystroke Summary is an exact listing of each keystroke used to build the worksheet presented in the project.

Student Assignments

An important feature of this textbook is the numerous and wide variety of Student Assignments provided at the end of each project. These assignments include the following: true/false questions; multiple choice questions; assignments that require students to write and/or explain various commands; assignments that require students to identify common errors on screen displays; and perhaps most important of all, a series of realistic problems for students to analyze and solve by applying what they have learned in the project.

THE SUPPLEMENTS TO ACCOMPANY THIS TEXT

I n addition to the educational software, six teaching and learning materials supplement this textbook. They are the Instructor's Materials, Data Diskette, ProTest, HyperGraphics, Instructor's Manual to accompany HyperGraphics, and ClassNotes and Study Guide.

Instructor's Materials

This manual includes four items to help improve instruction and learning. These items are Lesson Plans, Answers/Solutions, Test Bank, and Transparency Masters.

Lesson Plans—Each project lesson plan begins with chapter or project behavioral objectives. Next an overview of each chapter or project is included to help the instructor quickly review the purpose and key concepts. Detailed outlines of each chapter and/or project follow. These outlines are annotated with the page number of the textbook on which the outlined material is covered; notes, teaching tips, and additional activities that the instructor might use to embellish the lesson; and a key for using the Transparency Masters.

Answers/Solutions—Complete answers and solutions for the Student Assignments are included to ease course administration.

Test Bank—This is a hard copy version of the test questions. It is comprised of three types of questions—true/false, multiple choice, and fill-in. Each project has approximately 50 true/false, 25 multiple choice, and 35 fill-ins. Answers to all of these test questions are included.

Transparency Masters—A Transparency Master is included for *every* figure in the textbook.

Data Diskette

This free supplement contains the project worksheets and Student Assignment worksheet solutions for Projects 1 through 6.

ProTest

This is Boyd & Fraser's computerized test generating system that is available free to adopters of this textbook. It includes all of the questions from the Test Bank included in the Instructor's Materials for this book. ProTest is an easy-to-use menu-driven package that provides testing flexibility and allows customizing of testing documents. For example, a user of ProTest can enter his or her own questions into the ProTest and can generate review sheets and answer keys. ProTest will run on any IBM PC, IBM PS/2, or IBM compatible system with two diskette drives or a hard disk.

HyperGraphics®

How instructors teach has changed very little in the last few decades. After all the flag waving about computer tutorials, CAI, and the like, we have learned that the human instructor is neither replaceable by a machine nor by someone who is untrained. HyperGraphics is a tool that acknowledges these facts.

What Is HyperGraphics? HyperGraphics is an instructional delivery system; it is a piece of software that presents all of the Shelly and Cashman textbook content with the use of graphics, color, animation, and interactivity. It is a powerful software tool that enhances classroom instruction. It is a state-of-the-art, computer-based teaching and learning environment that promotes interactive learning and self-study.

What Hardware Do You Need for HyperGraphics? You need three pieces of hardware to run HyperGraphics; two additional pieces are optional.

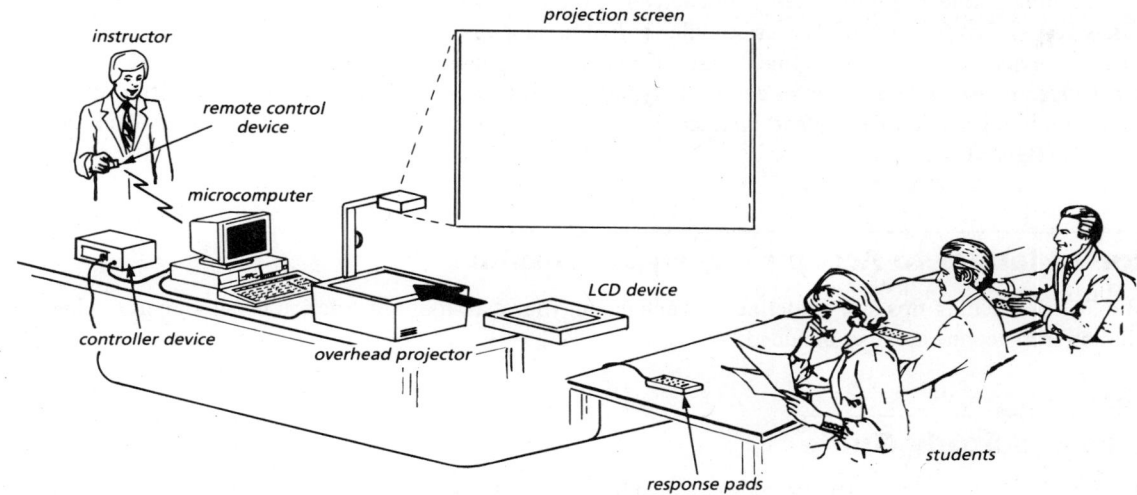

1. An IBM Personal Computer or PS/2 Series computer (or compatible) with a standard CGA graphics card.
2. A standard overhead projector and projection screen.
3. A standard projection device, such as a color projector or a liquid crystal display (LCD), that fits on the projection area of the overhead projector. The projection device is connected to the personal computer, resulting in the projection of the computer's screen.
4. A hand-held remote control device (*optional*), that allows the instructor to navigate throughout the presentation materials and still move freely around the classroom.
5. A set of at least eight response pads (*optional*), small pads consisting of 10 digit keys, that can be pressed to indicate a student's response. (These pads are linked to the microcomputer by a controller device.)

How Does the Instructor Use HyperGraphics? HyperGraphics is very easy to use. The instructor presses the appropriate keys on the hand-held remote control device or the keyboard and thereby controls the screen display. This display is projected through the LCD to the overhead projector. The instructor has complete control over the order and pacing of how the lessons are taught. By pushing one or more keys he or she can do such things as:

- View and select from the lesson menu
- Deliver the lesson's instructional materials in sequence
- Repeat any portion of a lesson to reinforce or review material
- Move ahead to specific portions of the lesson
- View the chapter objectives at any time
- View one or more questions about the lesson at any time
- Have students respond to one or more questions via the response pads
- Log students' responses to questions
- Randomly select students to respond to a question

- End a lesson
- Return directly to that point in the lesson where he or she stopped in the previous class meeting

What Are the Benefits of Using the Student Response Pads? Instructors have never before had the opportunity to assess student comprehension and retention of class instruction immediately and accurately. They can now do so if they use Hyper-Graphics with the student response pads.

For example, suppose the instructor presents a multiple choice question on the screen at the end of a segment of a lesson. Students will see an indication light illuminate on their response pads, and they'll have a period of time (controlled by the instructor) to press the button corresponding to the answer of their choice. The answers are tabulated by the microcomputer, and an optional aggregate bar chart of the answers selected is immediately available for viewing by the entire class. Each student's answer is also available on disk for later analysis or review. Thus, the progress of the entire class as well as each student can be tracked throughout the course.

Using these response pads results in substantial and *measurable* benefits to instructors as well as to students. The pads provide a rich teaching and learning experience and actively promote student participation.

What Does HyperGraphics Cost? HyperGraphics is *free* to adopters of this textbook. The only cost is for the computer and the projection device and screen, equipment that most educational institutions already possess. (Student response pads and the controller device are available at an extra charge.) HyperGraphics revolutionizes classroom instruction. It brings classroom instruction alive through graphic imagery and interactivity, and it can provide immediate and direct feedback to students and instructors.

Instructor's Manual to Accompany HyperGraphics

This manual contains teaching tips and guidelines for enhancing your classroom instruction using HyperGraphics. Easy-to-follow installation instructions are also included.

ClassNotes and Study Guide

The active learning experience of HyperGraphics can also be promoted if students purchase this supplement. As its title suggests, the *ClassNotes and Study Guide* serves three purposes. First, it relieves students from laborious and tedious notetaking responsibilities, freeing them to concentrate on the instruction. Second, if used with HyperGraphics, it provides an active learning experience for students to fill in key terms and key concepts during classroom instruction. Third, used without HyperGraphics this supplement provides a chance for students to review and study independently, as they can with traditional study guides.

ACKNOWLEDGMENTS

*L*earning to Use VP-Planner Plus would not be the quality textbook it is without the help of many people. We would like to express our appreciation to the following people, who worked diligently to assure a quality publication: Jeanne Huntington, typesetter; Michael Broussard and Ken Russo, artists; Becky Herrington, production and art coordinator; Sheryl Rose, manuscript editor; Scott Alkire, Kathy McCann, and Martha Simmons, production assistants; Mary Douglas, director of production; Susan Solomon, director of development; and Tom Walker, Publisher and Vice President of Boyd & Fraser.

For more Information about the Shelly and Cashman Series

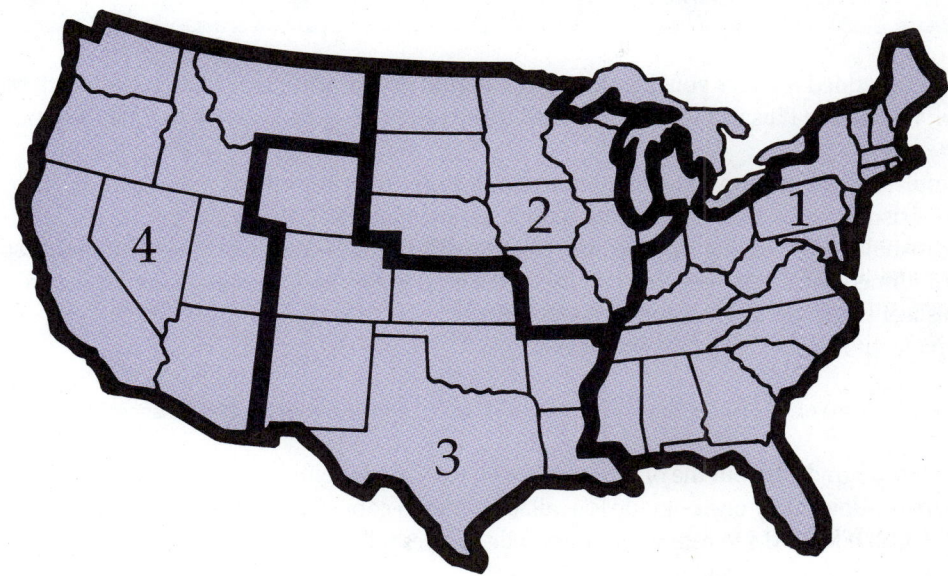

1 ORDER INFORMATION
5101 Madison Road
Cincinnati, OH 45227-1490
General Telephone–513-527-6945
Telephone: 1-800-543-8440
FAX: 513-527-6979
Telex: 214371

FACULTY SUPPORT INFORMATION
5101 Madison Road
Cincinnati, OH 45227-1490
General Telephone–513-527-6950
Telephone: 1-800-543-8444

Alabama	Massachusetts	Pennsylvania
Connecticut	Michigan (Lower)**	Rhode Island
Delaware	Mississippi	South Carolina
Florida	New Hampshire	Tennessee
Georgia	New Jersey	Vermont
Indiana*	New York	Virginia
Kentucky	North Carolina	West Virginia
Maine	Ohio	District of Columbia
Maryland		

*Except for ZIP Code Areas 463, 464. These areas contact Region 2 Office.
**Except for the Upper Peninsula. This area contacts Region 2 Office.

2 ORDER INFORMATION and FACULTY SUPPORT INFORMATION
355 Conde Street
West Chicago, IL 60185
General Telephone–312-231-6000
Telephone: 1-800-543-7972

Illinois	Minnesota	North Dakota
Indiana*	Missouri	South Dakota
Iowa	Nebraska	Wisconsin
Michigan (Upper)**		

*Only for ZIP Code Areas 463, 464. Other areas contact Region 1 office.
**Only for Upper Peninsula. Other areas contact Region 1 office.

3 ORDER INFORMATION
13800 Senlac Drive
Suite 100
Dallas, TX 75234
General Telephone–214-241-8541
Telephone: 1-800-543-7972

FACULTY SUPPORT INFORMATION
5101 Madison Road
Cincinnati, OH 45227-1490
General Telephone–513-527-6950
Telephone: 1-800-543-8444

Arkansas	Louisiana	Texas
Colorado	New Mexico	Wyoming
Kansas	Oklahoma	

4 ORDER INFORMATION and FACULTY SUPPORT INFORMATION
6185 Industrial Way
Livermore, CA 94550
General Telephone–415-449-2280
Telephone: 1-800-543-7972

Alaska	Idaho	Oregon
Arizona	Montana	Utah
California	Nevada	Washington
Hawaii		

Introduction to Computers

Introduction to Computers

OBJECTIVES

- Define computer and discuss the four basic computer operations: input, processing, output and storage.
- Define data and information.
- Explain the principal components of the computer and their use.
- Describe the use and handling of diskettes and hard disks.
- Discuss computer software and explain the difference between application software and system software.

The computer is an integral part of the daily lives of most individuals. Small computers, called microcomputers or personal computers (Figure 1), have made computing available to almost everyone. Thus, your ability to understand and use a computer is rapidly becoming an important skill. This book teaches you how to use a computer by teaching you how to use software applications. Before you learn about the application software, however, you must understand what a computer is, the components of a computer, and the types of software used on computers. These topics are explained in this Introduction.

FIGURE 1
Microcomputers: The IBM PS/2 Model 30 (left) and Compaq Deskpro 386S (right) are two examples of popular microcomputer systems.

WHAT IS A COMPUTER?

A **computer** is an electronic device, operating under the control of instructions stored in its own memory unit, that accepts input or data, processes data arithmetically and logically, produces output from the processing, and stores the results for future use. All computers perform basically the same four operations:

1. **Input operations**, by which data is entered into the computer for processing.
2. **Arithmetic operations**, are addition, subtraction, multiplication, and division. **Logical operations** are those that compare data to determine if one value is less than, equal to, or greater than another value.
3. **Output operations**, which make the information generated from processing available for use.
4. **Storage operations**, which store data electronically for future reference.

FIGURE 2
This microprocessor is shown "packaged" and ready for installation in a microcomputer.

These operations occur through the use of electronic circuits contained on small silicon chips inside the computer (Figure 2). Because these electronic circuits rarely fail and the data flows along these circuits at close to the speed of light, processing can be accomplished in millionths of a second. Thus, the computer is a powerful tool because it can perform these four operations reliably and quickly.

WHAT IS DATA AND INFORMATION?

The four operations that can be performed using a computer all require data. **Data** is raw facts, the numbers and words that are suitable for processing in a predetermined manner on a computer to produce information. Examples of data include the hours posted to a payroll time card or the words comprising a memo to the sales staff. A computer accepts data, processes data and, as a result of the processing, produces output in the form of useful information. **Information** can therefore be defined as data that has been processed into a form that has meaning and is useful.

WHAT ARE THE COMPONENTS OF A COMPUTER?

To understand how computers process data into information, it is necessary to examine the primary components of the computer. The four primary components of a computer are:

1. input devices   3. output devices
2. processor unit   4. auxiliary storage units

Figure 3 illustrates the relationship of the various components to one another.

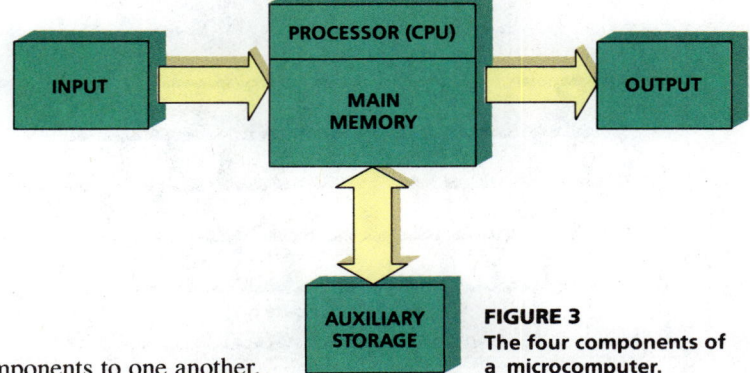

FIGURE 3
The four components of a microcomputer.

Input Devices

Input devices enter data into main memory. Several input devices exist. The two most commonly used are the keyboard and the mouse.

The Keyboard. The input device you will most commonly use on computers is the **keyboard** on which you manually "key in" or type the data (Figures 4a and b). The keyboard on most computers is laid out in much the same manner as a typewriter. Figures 4a and b show two styles of IBM keyboards: the original standard keyboard and a newer enhanced keyboard. Although the layouts are somewhat different, the use of the keys is the same.

FIGURE 4a The IBM standard keyboard

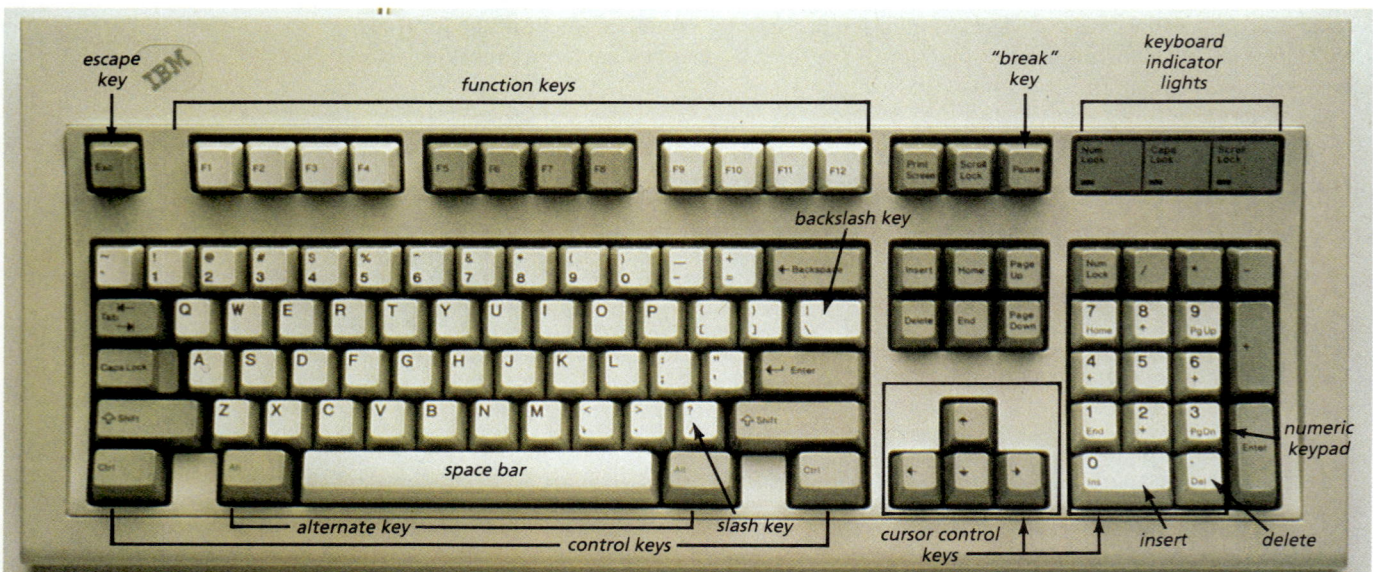

FIGURE 4b The enhanced IBM PS/2 keyboard. Note the different placement of the function and cursor keys.

A **numeric keypad** in the 10-key adding machine or calculator key format is located on the right side of both keyboards. This arrangement of keys allows you to enter numeric data rapidly. To activate the numeric pad on the keyboards you press the Num Lock key, located above the numeric keys. On the enhanced keyboard, a light turns on at the top right of the keyboard to indicate that the numeric keys are in use. You may also invoke the number keys by using the shift key together with the number keys located across the top of the typewriter keys.

Cursor control keys determine where data is displayed on the screen. The **cursor** is a symbol, such as an underline character, which indicates where on the screen the next character will be entered. On the keyboards in Figures 4a and b the cursor control keys or arrow keys are included as part of the numeric keypad. The enhanced keyboard has a second set of cursor control keys located between the typewriter keys and the numeric keypad. If you press the **Num Lock** key at the top of the numeric keypad, numeric characters appear on the screen when you press the numeric key pad keys. You can still use the cursor control keys by pressing the Shift key together with the desired cursor control key. If the Num Lock key is engaged (indicated by the fact that as you press any numeric key pad key, a number appears on the screen) you can return to the standard mode for cursor control keys by pressing the Num Lock key.

The cursor control keys allow you to move the cursor around the screen. Pressing the **Up Arrow** key ↑ causes the cursor to move upward on the screen. The **Down Arrow** key ↓ causes the cursor to move down; the **Left** ← and **Right** → **Arrow** keys cause the cursor to move left and right on the screen.

The other keys on the keypad—(PgUp), (PgDn), Home, and End—have various uses depending on the microcomputer software you use. Some programs make no use of these keys; others use the **(PgUp)** and **(PgDn)** keys, for example, to display previous or following pages of data on the screen. Some software uses the **Home** key to move the cursor to the upper left corner of the screen. Likewise, the **End** key may be used to move the cursor to the end of a line of text or to the bottom of the screen, depending on the software.

Function keys on many keyboards can be programmed to accomplish specific tasks. For example, a function key might be used as a help key. Whenever that key is pressed, messages appear that give instructions to help the user. Another function key might be programmed to cause all data displayed on the CRT screen to be printed on a printer whenever the key is pressed. In Figure 4a, ten function keys are on the left portion of the standard keyboard. In Figure 4b, twelve function keys are located across the top of the enhanced keyboard.

Other keys have special uses in some applications. The **Shift** keys have several functions. They work as they do on a typewriter, allowing you to type capital letters. The Shift key is always used to type the symbol on the upper portion of any key on the keyboard. Also, to use the cursor control keys temporarily as numeric entry keys, you can press the Shift key to switch into numeric mode. If, instead, you have pressed the Num Lock key to use the numeric keys, you can press the Shift key to shift temporarily back to the cursor mode.

The keyboard has a Backspace key, a Tab key, an Insert key and a Delete key that perform the functions their names indicate.

The **Escape (Esc)** key also has many different uses. In some microcomputer software it is used to cancel an instruction but this use is by no means universally true.

As with the Escape key, many keys are assigned special meaning by the microcomputer software. Certain keys may be used more frequently than others by one piece of software but rarely used by another. It is this flexibility that allows the computer to be used in so many different applications.

The Mouse   An alternative input device you might encounter is a mouse. A **mouse** (Figure 5) is a pointing device that can be used instead of the cursor control keys. You lay the palm of your hand over the mouse and move it across the surface of a table or desk. The

mouse detects the direction of your movement and sends this information to the screen to move the cursor. You push buttons on top of the mouse to indicate your choices of actions from lists displayed on the computer screen.

FIGURE 5
A mouse can be used as a cursor control device.

The Processor

The **processor unit** is composed of the central processing unit (CPU) and main memory (see Figure 3). The **central processing unit** contains the electronic circuits that actually cause processing to occur. The CPU interprets instructions to the computer, performs the logical and arithmetic processing operations, and causes the input and output operations to occur.

    Main memory consists of electronic components that store numbers, letters of the alphabet, and characters such as decimal points or dollar signs. Any data to be processed must be stored in main memory.

    The amount of main memory in microcomputers is typically measured in **kilobytes** (K or KB), which equal 1,024 memory locations. A memory location, or byte, usually stores one character. Therefore, a computer with 640K can store approximately 640,000 characters. The amount of main memory for microcomputers may range from 64K to several million characters, also called a **megabyte (MB)**, or more.

FIGURE 6
This dot matrix printer, the IBM Proprinter II, is often used to print documents from an IBM PC and other popular microcomputers.

Output Devices

Output devices make the information resulting from processing available for use. The output from computers can be presented in many forms, such as a printed report or color graphics. When a computer is used for processing tasks, such as word processing, spreadsheets, or database management, the two output devices most commonly used are the **printer** and the televisionlike display device called a **screen**, **monitor**, or **CRT** (cathode ray tube).

    Printers   Printers used with computers can be either impact printers or nonimpact printers.

    An **impact printer** prints by striking an inked ribbon against the paper. One type of impact printer often used with microcomputers is the dot matrix printer (Figure 6). To print a character, a **dot matrix printer** generates a dot pattern representing a particular character. The printer then activates vertical wires in a print head contained on the printer, so that selected wires press against the ribbon and paper, creating a character. As you see in Figure 7, the character consists of a series of dots produced by the print head wires. In the actual size created by the printer, the characters are clear and easy to read.

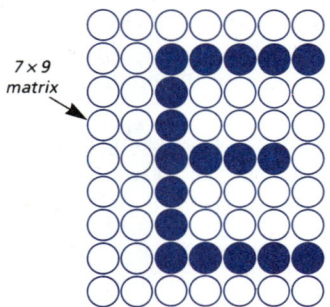

7 × 9 matrix

Dot matrix printers vary in the speed with which they can print characters. These speeds range from 50 characters per second to over 300 characters per second. Generally, the higher the speed, the higher the cost of the printer.

Many dot matrix printers also allow you to choose two or more sizes and densities of character. Typical sizes include condensed print, standard print, and enlarged print. In addition, each of the three print sizes can be printed with increased density, or darkness (Figure 8).

FIGURE 8
These samples show condensed, standard, and enlarged print. These can all be produced by a dot-matrix printer.

```
This line of type is in CONDENSED Print
AaBbCcDdEeFfGgHhIiJjKkLlMmNnOoPpQqRrSsTtUuVvWwXxYyZz 0123456789

This line of type is in STANDARD Print
AaBbCcDdEeFfGgHhIiJjKkLlMmNnOoPpQqRrSsTtUuVvWwXxYyZz 0123456789

This line of type is in ENLARGED Pr
AaBbCcDdEeFfGgHhIiJjKkLlMmNnOoPpQqR
UuVvWwXxYyZz 0123456789
```

Another useful feature of dot matrix printers is their ability to print graphics. The dots are printed not to form characters, but rather to form graphic images. This feature can be especially useful when working with a spreadsheet program in producing graphs of the numeric values contained on the worksheet.

When users require printed output of high quality, such as for business or legal correspondence, a letter-quality printer is often used. The term **letter quality** refers to the quality of the printed character that is suitable for formal or professional business letters. A letter-quality printed character is a fully formed, solid character like those made by typewriters. It is not made up of a combination of dots, as by a dot matrix printer.

The letter-quality compact printer most often used with microcomputers is the **daisy wheel printer**. It consists of a type element containing raised characters that strike the paper through an inked ribbon.

Nonimpact printers, such as ink jet printers and laser printers, form characters by means other than striking a ribbon against paper (Figure 9). An **ink jet printer** forms a character by using a nozzle that sprays drops of ink onto the page. Ink jet printers produce relatively high-quality images and print between 150 and 270 characters per second.

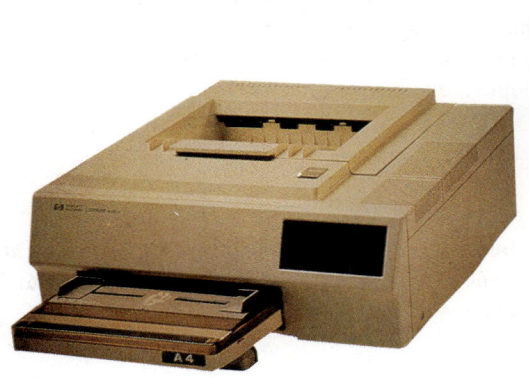

FIGURE 9
Two nonimpact printers: a laser printer (left) and inkjet printer (right)

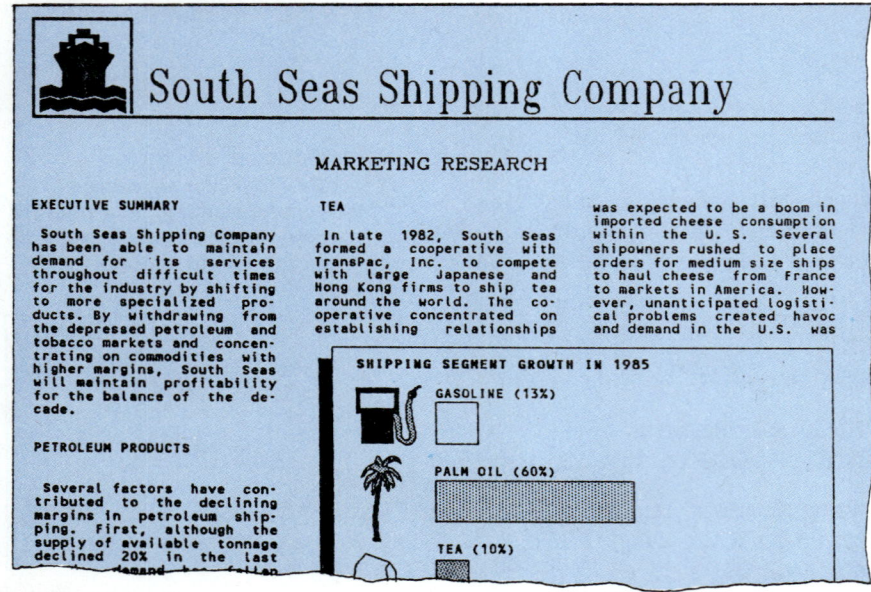

FIGURE 10
Sample output from a laser printer

Laser printers convert data from the personal computer into a beam of laser light that is focused on a photoconductor, forming the images to be printed. The photoconductor attracts particles of toner that are fused onto paper to produce an image. An advantage of the laser printer is that numbers and alphabetic data can be printed in varying sizes and type styles. The output produced is very high quality (Figure 10), with the images resembling professional printing rather than typewritten characters. Laser printers for microcomputers can cost from $1,500 to over $8,000. They can print six to eight pages of text and graphics per minute.

Computer Screens

The computer you use probably has a screen sometimes called a **monitor** or **CRT** (cathode ray tube). The **screen** displays the data entered on the keyboard and messages from the computer.

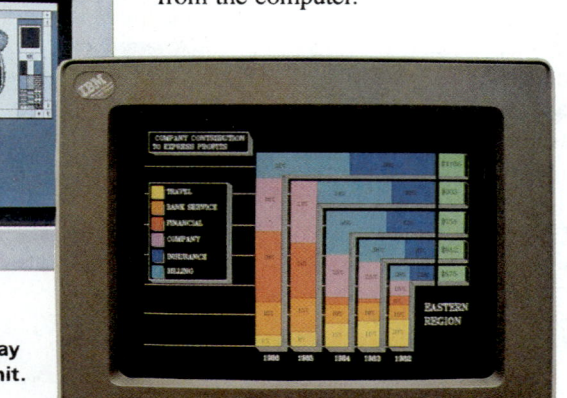

FIGURE 11
A computer display screen may be a monochrome or color unit.

Two general types of screens are used on computers. A **monochrome** screen (Figure 11) uses a single color (green, amber, or white) to display text against a dark background. Some monochrome screens are designed to display only characters; others can display both characters and graphics. Although they cannot display multiple colors, some monochrome screens simulate full color output by using up to 64 shades of the screen's single color.

The second type of screen is a color display. These devices are generally able to display 256 colors at once from a range of more than 256,000 choices.

Computer graphics, charts, graphs, or pictures, can also be displayed on a screen so that the information can be easily and quickly understood. Graphics are often used to present information to others, for example, to help people make business decisions.

Auxiliary Storage

Main memory is not large enough to store the instructions and data for all your applications at one time, so data not in use must be stored elsewhere. **Auxiliary storage** devices are used to store instructions and data when they are not being used in main memory.

Diskettes   One type of auxiliary storage you will use often with microcomputers is the **diskette**. A diskette is a circular piece of oxide-coated plastic that stores data as magnetic spots. Diskettes are available in various sizes. Microcomputers most commonly use diskettes that are 5¼ inches or 3½ inches in diameter (Figure 12).

To read data stored on a diskette or to store data on a diskette, you insert the diskette in a diskette drive (Figure 13). You can tell that the computer is reading data on the diskette or writing data on it because a light on the disk drive will come on while read/write operations are taking place. Do not try to insert or remove a diskette when the light is on. You could easily cause permanent damage to the data stored on it.

The storage capacities of diskette drives and the related diskettes can vary widely (Figure 14). The number of characters that can be stored on a diskette by a diskette drive depends on three factors: (1) the number of sides of the diskette used; (2) the recording density of the bits on a track; and (3) the number of tracks on the diskette.

Early diskettes and diskette drives were designed so that data could be recorded only on one side of the diskette. These drives are called **single-sided drives**. **Double-sided diskettes**, the typical type of diskette used now, provide increased storage capacity because data can be recorded on both sides of the diskette. Diskette drives found on many microcomputers are 5¼-inch, double-sided disk drives that can store approximately 360,000 bytes on the diskette. Another popular type is the 3½-inch diskette, which, although physically smaller, stores from 720,000 to 1.44 million bytes—over twice the capacity of the 5¼-inch diskette. An added benefit of the 3½-inch diskette is its rigid plastic housing, which protects the magnetic surface of the diskette.

The second factor affecting diskette storage capacity is the **recording density** provided by the diskette drive. (The recording density is stated in technical literature as the bpi—the number of bits that can be recorded on a diskette in a one-inch circumference of the innermost track on the diskette.) For the user, the diskettes and diskette drives are identified as being **single density**, **double density**, or **high density**. You need to be aware of the density of diskettes used by your system because data stored on high-density diskettes, for example, cannot be processed by a computer that has only double-density diskette drives.

The third factor that influences the number of characters that can be stored on a diskette is the number of tracks on the diskette. A **track** is a very narrow recording band forming a full circle around the diskette (Figure 15 on the following page). The width of this recording band depends on the number of tracks on the diskette. The recording bands are separated from each other by a very narrow blank gap. The tracks are established by the diskette drive using the diskette, and they are not visible.

FIGURE 12
Diskettes come in both 5 1/4-inch and 3 1/2-inch sizes. One advantage of the 3 1/2-inch type is its rigid plastic housing, which helps prevent damage to the diskette.

FIGURE 13
To read from a diskette or to store data on it, you must insert the diskette into the computer's diskette drive.

DIAMETER SIZE (INCHES)	DESCRIPTION	CAPACITY (BYTES)
5.25	Single-sided, double-density	160KB/180KB
5.25	Double-sided, double-density	320KB/360KB
5.25	High-capacity, double-density	1.25MB
3.5	Double-sided	720KB
3.5	Double-sided, double-density	1.44MB

FIGURE 14
Types of diskettes and their capacities

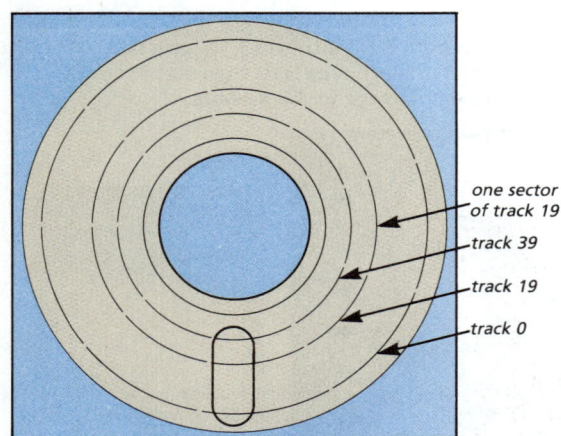

one sector
of track 19

track 39

track 19

track 0

FIGURE 15
How a diskette is formatted

Each track on a diskette is divided into sectors. **Sectors** are the basic units for diskette storage. When data is read from a diskette, a minimum of one full sector is read. When data is stored on a diskette, one full sector is written at one time. The number of sectors per track and the number of characters that can be stored in each sector are defined by a special formatting program that is used with the computer.

Data stored in sectors on a diskette must be retrieved and placed into main memory to be processed. The time required to access and retrieve data, called the **access time**, can be important in some applications. The access time for diskettes varies from about 175 milliseconds (one millisecond equals 1/1000 of a second) to approximately 300 milliseconds. On average, data stored in a single sector on a diskette can be retrieved in approximately 1/5 to 1/3 of a second.

Diskette care is important to preserve stored data. Properly handled, diskettes can store data indefinitely. However, the surface of the diskette can be damaged and the data stored can be lost if the diskette is handled improperly. A diskette will give you very good service if you follow a few simple procedures (Figure 16):

Don't touch the disk surface. It is easily contaminated, which causes errors.

Don't use near magnetic field including a telephone. Data can be lost if exposed.

Keep disk in protective envelope when not in use.

Don't bend or fold the disk.

Don't place heavy objects on the disk.

Don't use rubber bands or paper clips on the disk.

Insert disk carefully. Grasp upper edge and place it into the disk drive.

Don't expose the disk to excessive heat for sunlight.

Don't write on the index label with pencil or ballpoint. Use felt-tip pen only.

Don't use erasers on the disk label.

FIGURE 16
How to care for and handle diskettes

1. Store the diskette in its protective envelope when not in use. This procedure is especially necessary for the 5¼-inch diskette that has an oval opening, the **access window**, which permits the read/write heads to access the diskette but also allows the diskette to be easily damaged or soiled.

2. Keep diskettes in their original box or in a special diskette storage box to protect the diskette from dirt and dust and prevent it from being accidentally bent. Store the container away from heat and direct sunlight. Magnetic and electrical equipment, including telephones, radios, and televisions, can erase the data on a diskette so do not place diskettes near such devices. Do not place heavy objects on the diskette, because the weight can pinch the covering, causing damage when the disk drive attempts to rotate the diskette.

3. To affix one of the self-adhesive labels supplied with most diskettes, write or type the information on the label *before* placing the label on the diskette. If the label is already on the diskette, *do not* use an eraser to change the label. If you must write on the label after it is on the diskette, use only a felt-tip pen, *not* a pen or pencil, and press lightly.

4. To use the diskette, carefully remove it from the envelope by grasping the diskette on the side away from the side to be inserted into the disk drive. Slide the diskette carefully into the slot on the disk drive. If the disk drive has a latch or door, close it. If it is difficult to close the disk drive door, do not force it—the diskette may not be inserted fully, and forcing the door closed may damage the diskette. Reinsert the diskette if necessary, and try again to close the door.

The diskette **write-protect** feature (see Figure 17) prevents the accidental erasure of the data stored on a diskette by preventing the diskette drive from writing new data or erasing

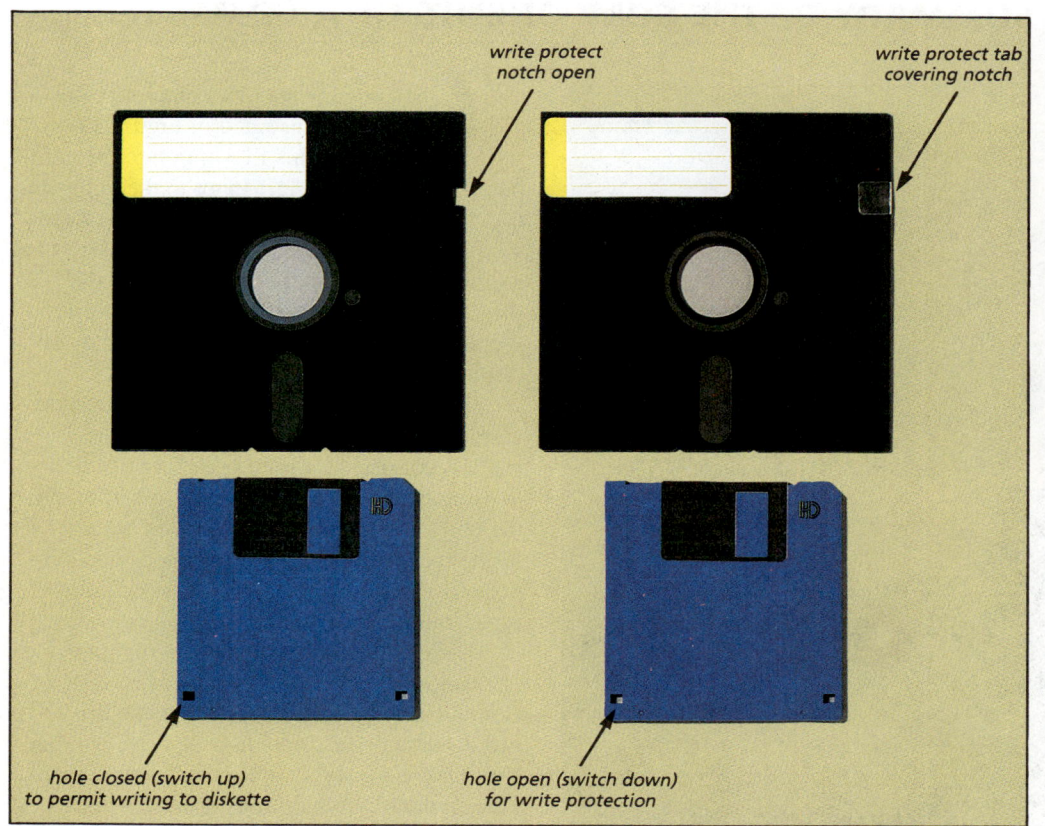

write protect
notch open

write protect tab
covering notch

hole closed (switch up)
to permit writing to diskette

hole open (switch down)
for write protection

FIGURE 17
The write-protect notch of the 5 1/4-inch disk on the left is open and therefore data could be written to the disk. The notch of the 5 1/4-inch disk on the right, however, is covered. Data could not be written to this disk. The reverse situation is true for the 3 1/2-inch disk. Data cannot be written on the 3 1/2-inch disk on the right because the small black piece of plastic is not covering the window in the lower left corner. Plastic covers the window of the 3 1/2-inch disk on the left, so data can be written on this disk.

existing data. On a 5¼-inch diskette, a **write-protect notch** is located on the side of the diskette. A special **write-protect label** is placed over this notch whenever you want to protect the data. On the 3½-inch diskette, a small switch can slide to cover and uncover the write protection notch. On a 3½-inch diskette, when the notch is uncovered the data is protected.

Hard Disk   Another form of auxiliary storage is a hard disk. A **hard disk** consists of one or more rigid metal platters coated with a metal oxide material that allows data to be magnetically recorded on the surface of the platters (Figure 18). Although hard disks are available in cartridge form, most hard disks cannot be removed from the computer and thus are called "fixed disks." As with diskettes, the data is recorded on hard disks on a series of tracks. The tracks are divided into sectors when the disk is formatted.

The hard disk platters spin at high rate of speed, typically 3,600 revolutions per minute. When reading data from the disk, the read head senses the magnetic spots that are recorded on the disk along the various tracks and transfers that data to main memory. When writing, the data is transferred from main memory and is stored as magnetic spots on the tracks on the recording surface of one or more of the disks. Unlike diskette drives, the read/write heads on a fixed disk drive do not actually touch the surface of the disk.

The number of platters permanently mounted on the spindle of a hard disk varies from one to four. On most drives each surface of the platter can be used to store data. Thus, if a hard disk drive uses one platter, two surfaces are available for data. If the drive uses two platters, four sets of read/write heads read and record data from the four surfaces. Storage capacities of fixed disks for microcomputers range from five million characters to over 100 million characters.

FIGURE 18
Cutaway of typical hard disk construction.

SUMMARY OF THE COMPONENTS OF A COMPUTER

*T*he components of a complete computer are illustrated in Figure 19. (Compare this illustration to the computer you will be using.) Input to the computer occurs through the keyboard. As data is keyed on the keyboard, the data is transferred to main memory. In addition, the keyed data is displayed on the computer display screen. The output may be printed on a printer or may be displayed on the computer screen.

The processor unit, which contains main memory and the central processing unit (CPU), consists of circuit boards inside a housing called the **system unit**. In addition to the CPU and main memory, circuit boards inside the system unit contain electronic components that allow communication with the input, output, and auxiliary storage devices.

Data can be transferred from main memory and stored on a diskette or a hard disk. Computers may have a single diskette drive, two diskette drives, one diskette drive and one hard disk drive, or several other combinations. The keyboard, system unit, printer, screen, and auxiliary storage devices are called **computer hardware**.

FIGURE 19
A computer system

WHAT IS COMPUTER SOFTWARE?

A computer's input, processing, output, and storage operations are controlled by instructions collectively called a **computer program** or **software**. A computer program specifies the sequence in which operations are to occur in the computer. For example, a person may give instructions that allow data to be entered from a keyboard and stored in main memory. Another time the program might issue an instruction to perform a calculation using data in main memory. When a task has been completed, a program could give instructions to direct the computer to print a report, display information on the screen, draw a color graph on a color display unit, or store data on a diskette. When directing the operations to be performed, a program must be stored in main memory. Computer programs are written by computer programmers.

Most computer users purchase the software they need for their computer systems. The two major categories of computer software are (1) application software and (2) system software.

Application Software

Application software allows you to perform an application-related function on a computer. A wide variety of programs is available, but for microcomputers the three most widely used types of application software are word processing, spreadsheet, and database management.

Word Processing Software   **Word processing software** such as WordPerfect enables you to use a computer to create documents.

As you use a word processing program, words are keyed in, displayed on the screen, and stored in main memory. If necessary, you can easily correct errors by adding or deleting words, sentences, paragraphs, or pages. You can also establish margins, define page lengths, and perform many other functions involving the manipulation of the written word.

After you have created and corrected your text, you can print it and store it on auxiliary storage for reuse or future reference.

Spreadsheet Software   **Spreadsheet software** is used for reporting and decision making within organizations. At home, you can use a spreadsheet program for budgeting, income tax planning, or tracking your favorite team's scores. You might choose VP Planner or Lotus 1-2-3 to enter the values and formulas needed to perform the desired calculations.

One of the more powerful features of spreadsheet application software is its ability to handle "what-if" questions such as, "What would be the effect on profit if sales increased 12% this year?" The values on the worksheet could easily be recalculated to provide the answer.

Database Software   **Database software** is used to store, organize, update, and retrieve data. Packages such as **dBASE III Plus** store data in a series of files. A **file** is a collection of related data. The data can be organized in the manner you select for your particular application. Once stored in the database, data can be retrieved for use in a variety of ways. For example, data can be retrieved based on the name of an employee in an employee file and full reports can be generated.

System Software

System software consists of programs that start up the computer—load, execute, store, and retrieve files—and perform a series of utility functions. A part of the system software available with most computers is the operating system. An **operating system** is a collection of programs that provides an interface between you or your application programs and the computer hardware itself to control and manage the operation of the computer.

System software, including operating systems, available on computers performs the following basic functions: (1) booting, or starting, the computer operation, (2) interfacing with users, and (3) coordinating the system's access to its various devices.

"Booting" the Computer   When a computer is turned on, the operating system is loaded into main memory by a set of instructions contained internally within the hardware of the computer. This process is called **booting** the computer. When the operating system is loaded into main memory, it is stored in a portion of main memory.

Interface with Users   To communicate with the operating system, the user must enter commands that the operating system can interpret and act upon. The commands can vary from copying a file from one diskette to another, to loading and executing application software.

Coordinating System Devices Computer hardware is constructed with electrical connections from one device to another. The operating system translates a program's requirements to access a specific hardware device, such as a printer. The operating system can also sense whether the devices are ready for use, or if there is some problem in using a device, such as a printer not being turned on and, therefore, not ready to receive output.

SUMMARY OF INTRODUCTION TO COMPUTERS

s you learn to use the software taught in this book, you will also become familiar with the components and operation of your computer system. You can refer to this introduction when you need help understanding how the components of your system function.

SUMMARY

1. A **computer** is an electronic device operating under the control of instructions stored in its memory unit.
2. All computers perform basically the same four operations: input, processing, output, and storage.
3. **Data** may be defined as the numbers, words, and phrases that are suitable for processing on a computer to produce information. The production of information from data is called **information processing**.
4. The four basic components of a computer are input unit, processor unit, output unit, and auxiliary storage units.
5. The **keyboard** is the most common input unit. It consists of typewriterlike keys, a numeric keypad, cursor control keys, and programmable function keys.
6. The computer's **processing unit** consists of the central processing unit (CPU) and main memory.
7. Output units consist primarily of displays and printers. **Displays** may be single color (monochrome) or full color. **Printers** may be impact or nonimpact printers.
8. A **dot matrix printer**, the type most commonly used for personal computing, forms characters by printing series of dots to form the character.
9. **Auxiliary storage** on a personal computer is generally disk storage. Disk storage may be on a 5¼-inch or 3½-inch **diskette**, or it may be on an internal **hard disk**.
10. New diskettes must be formatted before they can be used to store data.
11. Computer software can be classified as either **system software**, such as the **operating system**, or as **application software**, such as a word processing, spreadsheet, or database program.

STUDENT ASSIGNMENTS

True-False Questions

Instructions: Circle T if the statement is true or F if the statement is false.

T F 1. The basic operations performed by a computersystem are input operations, processing operations, output operations, and storage operations.
T F 2. Data may be defined as numbers, words, or phrases suitable for processing to produce information.
T F 3. A commonly used input unit on most personal computers is the keyboard.
T F 4. A mouse is a hand-held scanner device for input.
T F 5. The central processing unit contains the processor unit and main memory.
T F 6. Typical personal computer memory is limited to a range of approximately 256,000 to 512,000 bytes of main memory.
T F 7. Auxiliary storage is used to store instructions and data when they are not being used in main memory.
T F 8. The diskette or floppy disk is considered to be a form of main memory.

T F   9. A commonly used 5¼-inch double-sided double-density diskette can store approximately 360,000 characters.
T F 10. Diskettes can normally store more data than hard disks.
T F 11. A computer program is often referred to as computer software.
T F 12. A computer program must be permanently stored in main memory.
T F 13. Programs such as database management, spreadsheet, and word processing software are called system software.
T F 14. The cursor is a mechanical device attached to the keyboard.
T F 15. PgUp, PgDn, Home, and End are Function keys.
T F 16. A laser printer is one form of impact printer.
T F 17. A dot matrix printer forms characters or graphics by forming images as a closely spaced series of dots.
T F 18. Application software is the type of program you will use to perform activities such as word processing on a computer.
T F 19. The operating system is a collection of programs that provides an interface between you and the computer.

Multiple Choice Questions

1. Which of the following activities will a personal computer *not* be able to perform?
   a. word processing
   b. taking orders in a restaurant
   c. making airline reservations
   d. replacing human decision making
2. The four operations performed by a computer include
   a. input, control, output, storage
   b. interface, processing, output, memory
   c. input, output, arithmetic/logical, storage
   d. input, logical/rational, arithmetic, output
3. Data may be defined as
   a. a typed report   c. a graph
   b. raw facts   d. both a and c
4. PgUp, PgDn, Home, and End keys are
   a. word processing control keys
   b. function keys
   c. optional data entry keys
   d. cursor control keys
5. A hand-held input device that controls the cursor location is
   a. the cursor control keyboard
   b. a mouse
   c. a scanner
   d. the CRT
6. A printer that forms images without striking the paper is
   a. an impact printer   c. an ink jet printer
   b. a nonimpact printer   d. both b and d
7. A screen that displays only a single color is
   a. a multichrome monitor
   b. an upper-lower character display
   c. a 7-by-9 matrix screen
   d. a monochrome screen

8. Auxiliary storage is the name given to
   a. the computer's main memory
   b. diskette drives
   c. instruction storage buffers
   d. none of the above
9. A diskette
   a. is a nonremovable form of storage
   b. is available in 5¼- and 3½-inch sizes
   c. is a form of magnetic data storage
   d. both b and c
10. The amount of storage provided by a diskette is a function of
    a. whether the diskette records on one or both sides
    b. the recording pattern or density of bits on the diskette
    c. the number of recording tracks used on the track
    d. all of the above
11. Some diskettes have an access window that is used to
    a. pick up and insert the diskette into a diskette drive
    b. provide access for cleaning
    c. provide access for the read/write head of the diskette drive
    d. verify data stored on the diskette
12. When not in use, diskettes
    a. should be placed in their protective envelopes
    b. should be stored away from heat, magnetic fields, and direct sunlight
    c. should be stored in a diskette box or cabinet
    d. all of the above
13. A hard disk is
    a. an alternate form of removable storage
    b. a rigid platter with magnetic coating
    c. a storage system that remains installed in the computer
    d. both a and b

14. Storage capacities of hard disks
    a. are about the same as for diskettes
    b. range from 80,000 to 256,000 bytes
    c. range from five million to over 100 million
    d. vary with the type of program used

15. Software is classified as
    a. utility and applied systems
    b. operating systems and application programs
    c. language translators and task managers
    d. word processing and spreadsheet programs

Projects

1. Popular computer magazines contain many articles and advertisements that inform computer users of the latest in computing trends. Review a few recent articles and report on the apparent trends you have noted. Discuss which hardware features seem to be the most in demand. What are the differences between the alternative hardware choices? Discuss the implications these choices may have on the type of software chosen by a computer owner.

2. Software changes as computer users become more knowledgeable. According to your reading of computer magazines, what software innovations seem to have the greatest promise? Which specific features or styles of user interfaces seem to offer new computing capabilities? Discuss any particular program that seems to be a style setter in its field.

3. Visit local computer retail stores to compare the various types of computers and supporting equipment available. Ask about warranties, repair services, hardware setup, training, and related issues. Report on the knowledge of the sales staff assisting you and their willingness to answer your questions. Does the store have standard hardware "packages," or are they willing to configure a system to your specific needs? Would you feel confident about buying a computer from this store?

INDEX

Access time, **COM 10**
Access window, **COM 10**
Application software, **COM 13**
Arithmetic operations, **COM 3**
Auxiliary storage devices, **COM 8**
Booting, **COM 13**
Byte, **COM 6**
Central processing unit (CPU), **COM 6**
Color screen, COM 8
Computer
  components of, COM 3-12
  defined, **COM 3**
Computer graphics, **COM 8**
Computer hardware, **COM 12**, COM 14
Computer program, **COM 12**
Computer software, **COM 12**
  application, COM 13
  system, COM 13-14
CRT (cathode ray tube), **COM 6, COM 8**
Cursor, **COM 5**
Cursor control keys, **COM 5**
Daisy wheel printer, **COM 7**
Data, **COM 3**
Database software, **COM 13**
dBASE III Plus, **COM 13**
Diskette, **COM 9**
Dot matrix printer, **COM 6**
Double density drives, **COM 9**
Double-sided diskettes, **COM 9**
Down Arrow key, **COM 5**
End key, **COM 5**
Escape (Esc) key, **COM 5**

File, **COM 13**
Fixed disks, COM 11
Function keys, **COM 5**
Graphics
  monitors and, COM 8
  printers and, COM 7
Hard disk, **COM 11**
High density drives, **COM 9**
Home key, **COM 5**
Impact printer, **COM 6**
Information, **COM 3**
Ink jet printer, **COM 7**
Input devices, **COM 4**
  keyboard, 4-5
  mouse, 6
Input operations, **COM 3**
Keyboard, **COM 4**
Kilobytes (KB), **COM 6**
Laser printer, **COM 8**
Left Arrow key, **COM 5**
Letter quality printer, **COM 7**
Logical operations, **COM 3**
Main memory, **COM 6**
Megabyte (MB), **COM 6**
Memory, COM 6
Microcomputers (See Personal
  computers)
Monitor, **COM 6, COM 8**
Monochrome screen, **COM 8**
Mouse, **COM 6**
Nonimpact printers, **COM 7**
Numeric keypad, **COM 5**

Num Lock key, **COM 5**
Operating system, **COM 13**
Output devices
  monitors, 8
  printers, 6-8
Output operations, **COM 3**
Personal computers, COM 2
PgDn key, **COM 5**
PgUp key, **COM 5**
Printers, **COM 6**
  impact, COM 6-7
  nonimpact, COM 7-8
Processor unit, **COM 6**
Recording density, **COM 9**
Right Arrow key, **COM 5**
Screen, **COM 6, 8**
Sectors, **COM 10**
Shift key, **COM 5**
Single density drives, **COM 9**
Single-sided drives, **COM 9**
Spreadsheet software, **COM 13**
Storage operations, **COM 3**
System software, **COM 13**
System unit, **COM 12**
Track, **COM 9**
Up Arrow key, **COM 5**
User interface, COM 13
Word processing software, **COM 13**
Write-protect, **COM 10-11**
Write-protect label, **COM 11**
Write-protect notch, **COM 11**

Photo Credits: **Opening Page**, International Business Machines Corp.; **Figure 1**, International Business Machines Corp.; Compaq Computer Corp.; **Figure 2**, Intel Corp.; **Figure 4**, (a) Curtis Fukuda, (b) International Business Machines Corp.; **Figure 5**, Logitech, Inc.; **Figure 6**, International Business Machines Corp.; **Figure 9 and 10**, Hewlett-Packard Company; **Figure 11**, (left) Wyse Technology; (right) International Business Machines Corp.; **Figures 12, 13, and 17**, Curtis Fukuda; **Figure 18**, Seagate Technology; **Figure 19**, International Business Machines Corp.

Introduction to DOS *

Introduction to DOS

OBJECTIVES

You will have mastered the basics of using DOS when you can:

- "Boot" your microcomputer
- Enter the time and date, if required
- Establish the system default disk drive
- List a disk directory
- Cancel commands
- Format diskettes, using /S and /V
- Use file specifications to address files on various disks
- Copy files on the same disk and from one disk to another
- Rename and erase files
- Organize and manage file subdirectories on a hard disk
- Start application programs

INTRODUCTION

An operating system is one or more programs that control and manage the operation of the computer. These programs provide an interface among the user, the computer equipment, and the application programs. For instance, to use a computer to print a memo, you'd first use the operating system to start the computer. Next, you would enter a keyboard command that the operating system processes to activate the word processing program. When the word processing program instructs the computer to print the memo, the operating system finds the proper file on the disk, retrieves the data from the disk, and routes the output to the printer. The operating system is not part of the application program itself, but it provides essential services that the application program uses to perform its functions.

Operating Systems for IBM PCs

Microsoft Corporation joined forces with IBM to develop the program known as **DOS**, an acronym for **Disk Operating System**, used since 1981 in IBM PC and IBM-compatible computers. **PC-DOS** is the name for versions of DOS distributed by IBM for its Personal Computer and Personal System/2 lines. All IBM-compatible computers use versions of this operating system distributed by Microsoft as **MS-DOS**. This book uses the term DOS to refer to any of the various editions of PC- or MS-DOS and covers information applicable to all versions of DOS, unless otherwise noted.

DOS Versions

The numbers following the abbreviation DOS indicate the specific version and release of the product (Figure 1). The version number is the whole number and signifies a major improvement of the product. The release number is the decimal number and identifies minor corrections or changes to a version of the product. For example, DOS 1.1 corrected some minor problems with DOS 1.0.

Software developers try to maintain **upward compatibility**, that is, that all the features of an earlier version remain supported by a later one. However, "downward" compatibility is not common. Programs or equipment that require the features of DOS 3.3, for example, will not function with DOS 3.2 or earlier versions.

DOS VERSION RELEASE	MAJOR FEATURE SUPPORTED	YEAR
3.3	Introduction of PS/2	1987
3.2	Token-Ring Networks, 3.5'' Diskette	
3.1	Addition of Networking, 1.2 mb 5.25 Diskette	
3.0	Introduction of PC/AT	1985
2.1	Enhancements to 2.0	
2.0	Introduction of PC/XT	1983
1.1	Enhancements to 1.0	
1.0	Introduction of IBM/PC	1981

FIGURE 1

USING THE DISK OPERATING SYSTEM (DOS)

Starting the Computer

DOS programs are normally stored on a diskette or on a hard disk. To begin using the operating system, it must be read into main memory, a process known as booting. If you are using a system with two diskette drives, insert the diskette containing DOS into drive A of the computer and turn on the computer (Figure 2). If you are using a system with a hard disk, DOS is already available on the hard disk. Turn on the computer (Figure 3) and be certain you do not insert a diskette before the system has completed its startup process. If the computer is already on and your DOS diskette is in drive A (or DOS is on the hard disk and drive A is empty), you can restart the system by pressing the CTRL, ALT, and DEL keys simultaneously (Figure 4).

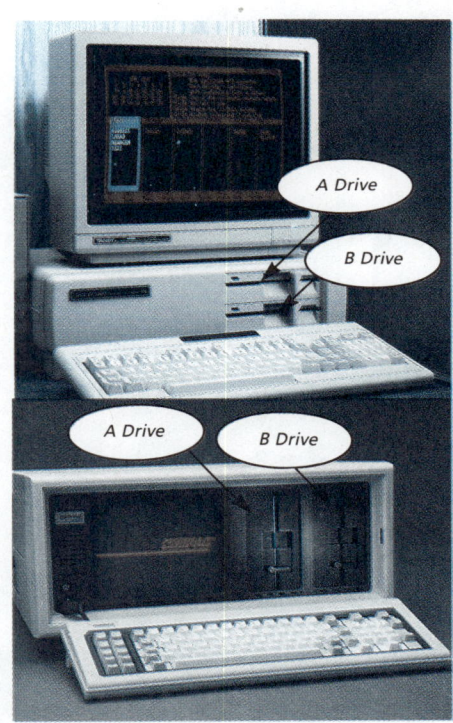

A Drive

B Drive

A Drive

B Drive

FIGURE 2

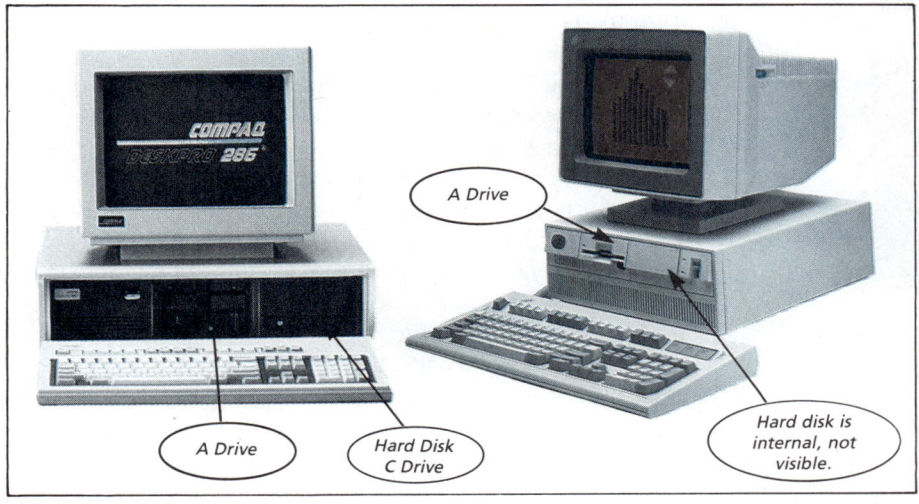

A Drive

A Drive

Hard Disk C Drive

Hard disk is internal, not visible.

FIGURE 3

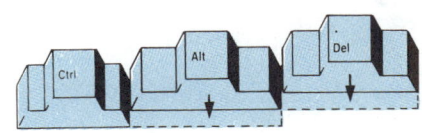

Ctrl   Alt   Del

FIGURE 4

The Cold Start.   Starting the computer by turning on the power switch is known as a ==cold start== or ==cold boot==. The computer will first run some tests to diagnose its own circuitry (known on some computers as a **power-on self-test**, or **POST** process). After running this test, the computer will begin to read the DOS diskette.

The Warm Start or Reset.   Restarting the operating system by pressing the CTRL, ALT, and DEL keys simutaneously is called a ==warm start==, or ==warm boot==, because the computer has already been turned on. This procedure does not repeat the POST process, but it does erase all programs and data from main memory and reloads DOS. Do not worry about losing data from diskettes during this process, however, because data properly stored on diskettes will remain there.

Loading DOS.   While the system is being booted, the status light on the disk drive flashes on and off, and the disk drive whirls for a few seconds. During this time, the program from the operating system is being loaded into main memory. When DOS has been loaded into main memory, an image similar to Figure 5 appears on the screen. When DOS has been loaded into main memory, the system will perform various activities depending upon how the startup procedure has been tailored for the specific computer.

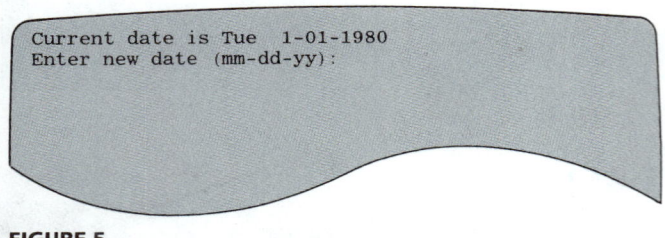

FIGURE 5

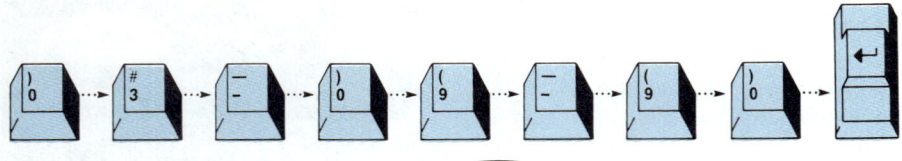

Setting the Date and Time

Although not required, it is a good practice to enter the date and time so that files you create are accurately documented. Enter the current date when the computer screen displays the message shown in Figure 6. To enter the date, always enter the month, day, and year separated by hyphens (-), slashes (/), or, in DOS 3.30 and later versions, periods (.). For example, assume that today is March 9, 1990. Type 03-09-90. Then press the Enter key (Figure 7).

If the date displayed is already correct—which it may be if your computer has an internal clock—you do not need to enter the date. Instead, press the Enter key when the message "Enter new date:" appears on the screen.

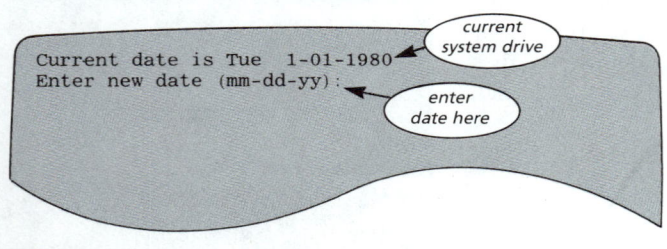

FIGURE 6

You enter the time in the format hh:mm:ss.xx, where hh stands for hours, mm stands for minutes, ss stands for seconds, and xx stands for hundredths of a second. As with the date, you are not required to enter the time, although it is a good practice to do so. For practice, type the time as 11:50 and press the Enter key (Figure 8). (If you do not include seconds and hundredths of seconds, the operating system assumes a value of zero for them.)

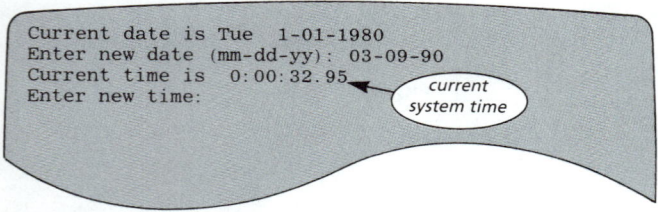

FIGURE 7

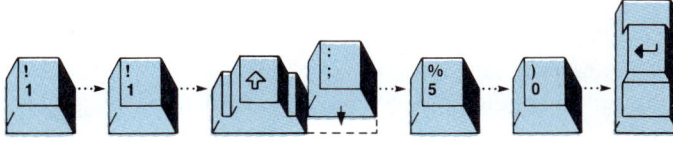

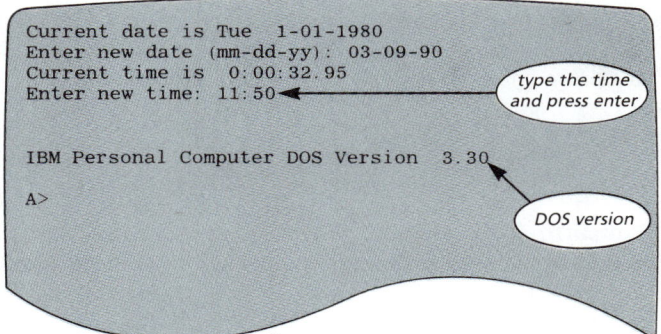

```
Current date is Tue  1-01-1980
Enter new date (mm-dd-yy): 03-09-90
Current time is  0:00:32.95
Enter new time: 11:50

IBM Personal Computer DOS Version  3.30

A>
```

type the time and press enter

DOS version

FIGURE 8

The Default Drive

The default drive assignment will vary depending upon the specific hardware you are using. A two-diskette system typically assigns drive A as the default drive (Figure 9). If your computer has a hard disk, the default drive will initially be drive C, and the prompt will appear as it is shown in Figure 10.

At times you will need to change the default drive assignment. Before you do so, be certain that the new drive is ready. A hard disk is always installed, but in a two-diskette system the disk drive must have a diskette inserted before it can be assigned as the default drive. If the drive does not have a diskette in it, the computer will give you an error message.

To change the drive assignment, type the letter of the new drive to be used, followed by a colon, and then press the Enter key. For example, to change the default to drive B, type the letter B, followed by a colon (:), and then press the Enter key (Figure 11, step 1). The prompt will display drive B as the default drive. Now, change the default drive back to drive A by typing A:↵ (Figure 11, step 2).

The DOS Prompt

After the messages are displayed, the **system prompt** indicates that the operating system is ready to receive your commands (Figures 9 and 10). The letter displayed within the prompt > indicates which drive has been assigned as the default disk drive. The **default drive** is the disk drive in which the operating system assumes the disk or diskette containing the operating system and other programs is located. Another term used for the default drive is **current drive**, because it is the drive that is assumed to be in current use.

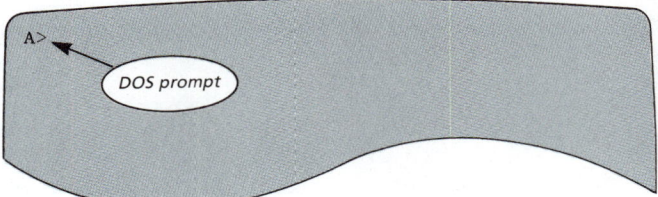

A>

DOS prompt

FIGURE 9

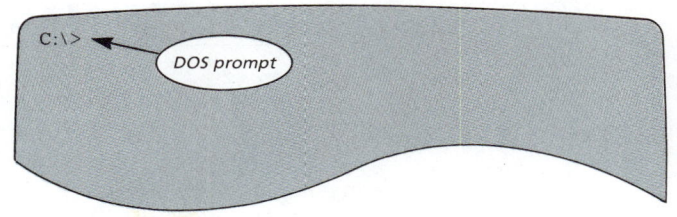

C:\>

DOS prompt

FIGURE 10

FIGURE 11

```
A>B:

B>A:

A>
```

default drive returned to A

indicates default drive is B

Step 1: Change the default drive from A to B.   **Step 2: Change the default drive from B to A.**

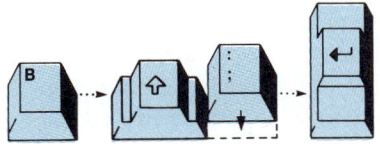

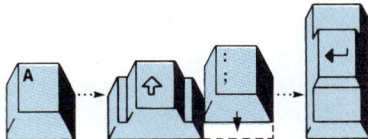

In most of the examples in this text, the default drive will be drive A. You will be told when the procedures for a hard disk are different than those for a diskette system. Figure 12 shows how to change the default drive for a hard disk system from drive C to drive A (step 1) and back to drive C (step 2).

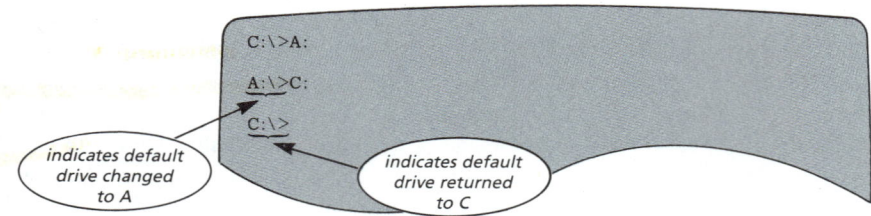

C:\>A:

A:\>C:

C:\>

indicates default drive changed to A

indicates default drive returned to C

Step 1: Change the default drive from C to A.   **Step 2: Change the default drive from A to C.**

FIGURE 12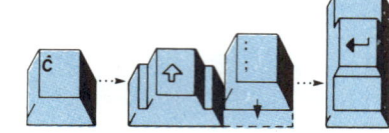

ENTERING DISK OPERATING SYSTEM (DOS) COMMANDS

Now that you have booted the DOS system, you are able to enter commands to instruct the computer. DOS includes a variety of commands to assist you in using the computer. Some of the commands might be called "status" or "informative" commands because they instruct DOS to give you information about the system's operation. The directory command, DIR, is one such informative command. It lists the names of files stored on a disk. Other commands support DOS functions, helping you use the computer. FORMAT, for instance, prepares a new disk for use in storing files.

The DOS commands you have entered so far have been typed in capital letters. You can type capital letters either by pressing the Caps Lock key or by holding down one of the two shift keys. However, you do not have to enter all DOS commands in capital letters. Commands, drive specifiers, and other entries to the operating system can be entered in any combination of uppercase and lowercase letters.

Internal and External Commands

An **internal command** is part of the operating system program. Once you have loaded DOS into main memory, an internal command is always started there. You can enter an internal command at any time. It does not matter whether the DOS system diskette is in the default drive. DIR, COPY, CLS, ERASE, RENAME, and DEL are examples of internal commands.

External commands, on the other hand, are stored on the DOS system disk as program files. They must be read from the disk into main memory before they can be executed. This means that the DOS system disk must be in the default drive or the specified drive so that the program can be found on the disk and loaded into main memory for execution. FORMAT and CHKDSK are examples of external commands. Another easy way to identify external commands is to look for the extensions .BAT, .COM, or .EXE following the filename, such as FORMAT.EXE.

DIRECTORY COMMAND (DIR)

*O*ne of the functions of the operating system is to store files containing both programs and data on diskettes. To facilitate that storage, the operating system maintains a directory of all the files stored on a diskette. To display the directory of the diskette you have placed in drive A of your computer, use the **DIR command**. At the A> prompt, type DIR and press the Enter key (Figure 13).

The directory of the diskette in the default drive will then be displayed as in Figure 14. Because the default drive is drive A (as specified by the system's A> prompt), the directory of the diskette in drive A is displayed. If you are using a hard disk and your default disk is drive C, the DIR command will display the directory of your hard disk.

The directory itself consists of the names of the files on the diskette, the number of bytes required to store the file on the diskette, the date of the last change of the file, and for some files, the time of the last change of the file. The message at the end of the directory listing indicates the number of files on the diskette (in Figure 14 there are 15 files on the diskette) and the remaining space available on the diskette (181248 unused bytes remain on the diskette in Figure 14). At the end of the directory display, the system prompt reappears on the screen, indicating that the system is ready for your next command.

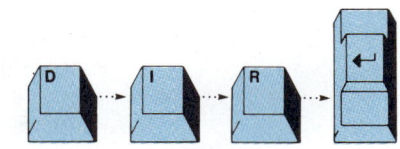
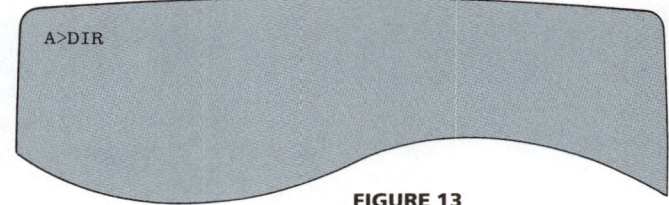

FIGURE 13

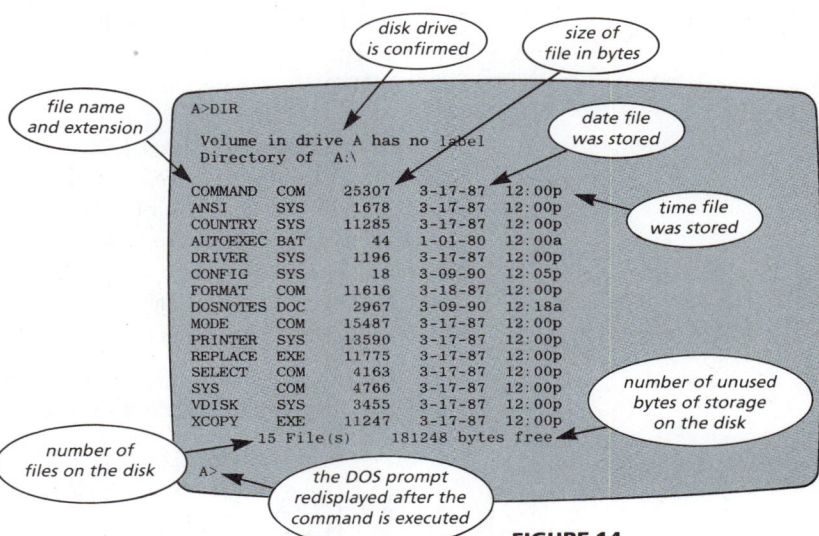

FIGURE 14

Displaying Directories of Other Disks

The directories of files on diskettes in other disk drives of the computer can be displayed as well. For practice, remove your system diskette from drive A and move it to drive B. To display the directory, type the command DIR B: and press the Enter key, as in Figure 15. You have directed the operating system to display the directory of the diskette located in drive B. The entry B: specifies that drive B is to be used.

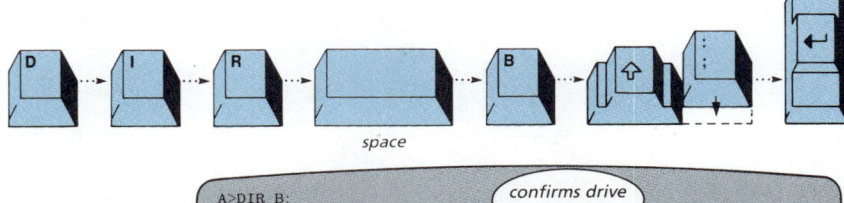

space

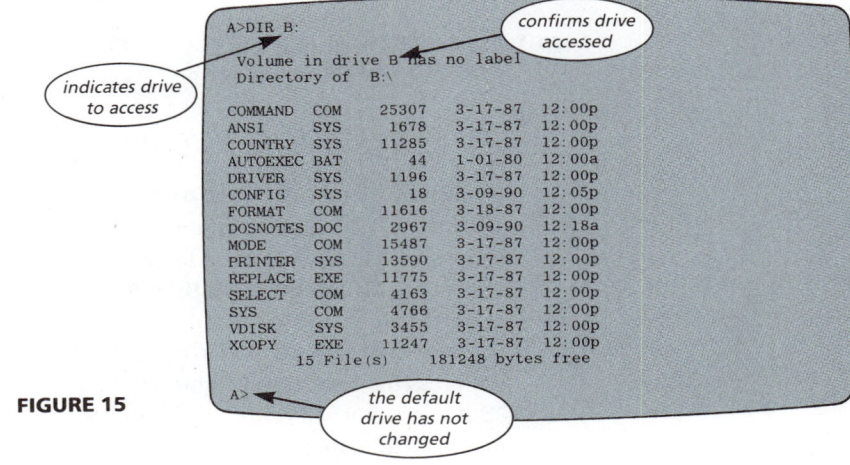

FIGURE 15

If your computer has a hard disk and you have been using drive C as the default drive, you can insert a diskette into drive A and then list the directory of that diskette drive by typing DIR A: and pressing the Enter key (Figure 16).

FIGURE 16

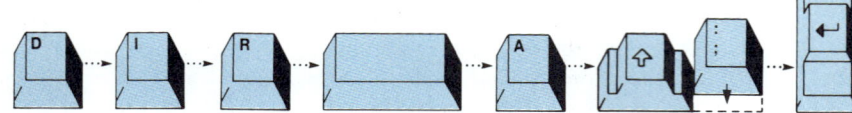

Note the use of the **colon**, **:**, with the disk drive letter. Whenever you refer to a specific disk drive, type the letter designating the drive followed by the colon, such as A:, B:, or C:.

Pausing Directory Listings

The directory of your diskette will often contain more files than can be displayed on the screen at one time. DOS has two methods of handling this situation: the pause screen option and the DIR command options.

Pause Screen (Control S).   To use a **pause screen** function, first make certain that your DOS diskette is in drive A. Type DIR and press the Enter key (Figure 17, step 1). When approximately one screenful of information is displayed, press Control-S. The directory display immediately halts (Figure 17, step 2). You can then examine the screen for any information you require. To continue the display, press any character key on the keyboard. The directory display will continue to scroll as if it had never halted. This pause screen operation can be used with many DOS commands.

Step 1: Display a directory of the default drive.

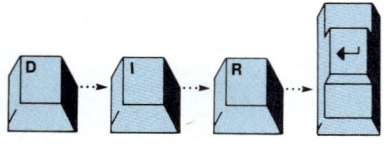

Step 2: Halt the directory listing.

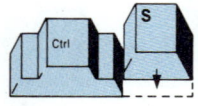

Step 3: Continue the display by pressing any character key.

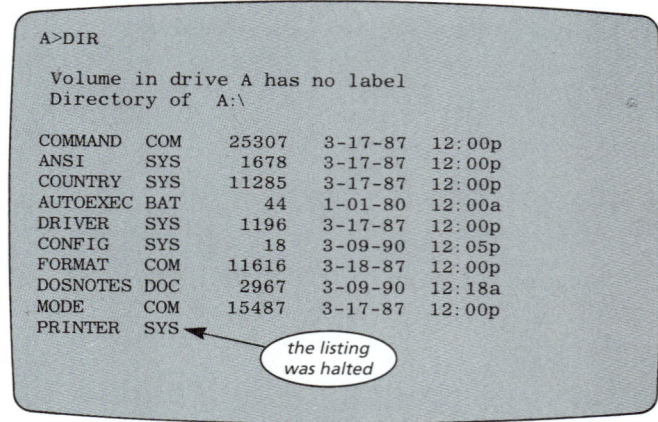

FIGURE 17

DIR Command Options.   It is not always easy to pause the directory listing where you want it. Therefore, you might want to use two other options with the DIR command. One option, /P, causes the screen to pause. The second option, /W, displays more data on the screen by increasing the **width** of the display area.

/P—the Pause Option.   To demonstrate the pause option, type DIR followed by /P and press the Enter key (Figure 18). When the screen is full, the listing stops and the message "Strike a key when ready . . ." appears at the bottom of the screen. When you are ready to continue the listing, press any character key.

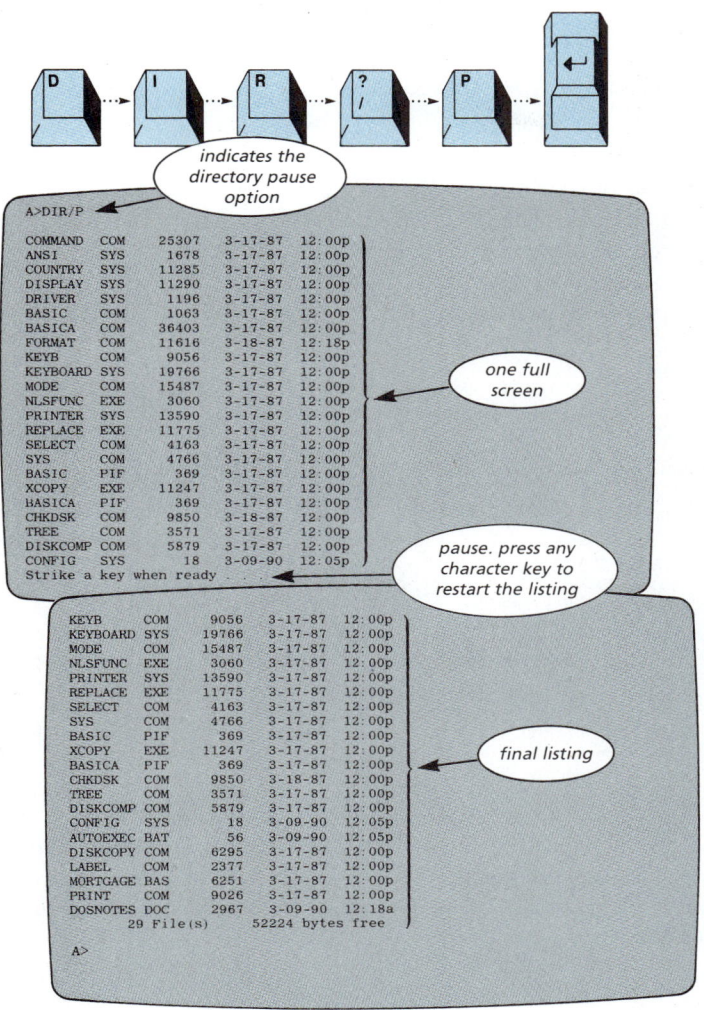

```
A>DIR/P

COMMAND   COM   25307   3-17-87   12:00p
ANSI      SYS    1678   3-17-87   12:00p
COUNTRY   SYS   11285   3-17-87   12:00p
DISPLAY   SYS   11290   3-17-87   12:00p
DRIVER    SYS    1196   3-17-87   12:00p
BASIC     COM    1063   3-17-87   12:00p
BASICA    COM   36403   3-17-87   12:00p
FORMAT    COM   11616   3-18-87   12:18p
KEYB      COM    9056   3-17-87   12:00p
KEYBOARD  SYS   19766   3-17-87   12:00p
MODE      COM   15487   3-17-87   12:00p
NLSFUNC   EXE    3060   3-17-87   12:00p
PRINTER   SYS   13590   3-17-87   12:00p
REPLACE   EXE   11775   3-17-87   12:00p
SELECT    COM    4163   3-17-87   12:00p
SYS       COM    4766   3-17-87   12:00p
BASIC     PIF     369   3-17-87   12:00p
XCOPY     EXE   11247   3-17-87   12:00p
BASICA    PIF     369   3-17-87   12:00p
CHKDSK    COM    9850   3-18-87   12:00p
TREE      COM    3571   3-17-87   12:00p
DISKCOMP  COM    5879   3-17-87   12:00p
CONFIG    SYS      18   3-09-90   12:05p
Strike a key when ready . . .
```

indicates the directory pause option

one full screen

pause. press any character key to restart the listing

```
KEYB      COM    9056   3-17-87   12:00p
KEYBOARD  SYS   19766   3-17-87   12:00p
MODE      COM   15487   3-17-87   12:00p
NLSFUNC   EXE    3060   3-17-87   12:00p
PRINTER   SYS   13590   3-17-87   12:00p
REPLACE   EXE   11775   3-17-87   12:00p
SELECT    COM    4163   3-17-87   12:00p
SYS       COM    4766   3-17-87   12:00p
BASIC     PIF     369   3-17-87   12:00p
XCOPY     EXE   11247   3-17-87   12:00p
BASICA    PIF     369   3-17-87   12:00p
CHKDSK    COM    9850   3-18-87   12:00p
TREE      COM    3571   3-17-87   12:00p
DISKCOMP  COM    5879   3-17-87   12:00p
CONFIG    SYS      18   3-09-90   12:05p
AUTOEXEC  BAT      56   3-09-90   12:05p
DISKCOPY  COM    6295   3-17-87   12:00p
LABEL     COM    2377   3-17-87   12:00p
MORTGAGE  BAS    6251   3-17-87   12:00p
PRINT     COM    9026   3-17-87   12:00p
DOSNOTES  DOC    2967   3-09-90   12:18a
        29 File(s)     52224 bytes free

A>
```

final listing

FIGURE 18

FORMATTING A DISKETTE

You cannot use a brand new diskette to store files. The diskette must first be formatted using the DOS FORMAT program. The **formatting** process establishes sectors on the diskette and performs other functions that allow the diskette to store files. Be careful when selecting disks to be used with the FORMAT command. Formatting a diskette destroys all files previously stored on the diskette. Therefore, you must be extremely careful to place the correct diskette in the drive and to make the correct drive letter designation. With a hard disk, extra precaution is necessary to avoid losing files by formatting the hard disk accidentally. DOS versions 3.0 and later provide some protection against accidental formatting of a hard disk, but your own precautions are still the best insurance.

/W—the Wide Display Option. The second option for displaying a long list of files is the /W option, which displays the information in a wide format. To use the /W option, type DIR /W, then press the Enter key (Figure 19). Note that only the file and directory names are listed, not the size, time, or date of the files.

Canceling a Command (Break)

In some cases, you only need to see a portion of the directory and so you might want to cancel the DIR command after you have seen that portion. To cancel a command you use the Break key. Locate this key on your keyboard; on many keyboards it is on the side of a key, often on the Scroll Lock key or the Pause key. When you press Ctrl-Break the characters ^C appear on the screen and the system prompt reappears. You will often hear this keystroke combination referred to as **Control-Break** or the **Break key**. The characters ^C indicate that you canceled the command by using the Break key. In general, you can cancel any DOS command that has been initiated by pressing Control-Break. An alternate method of canceling DOS commands is pressing Control-C (Figure 20).

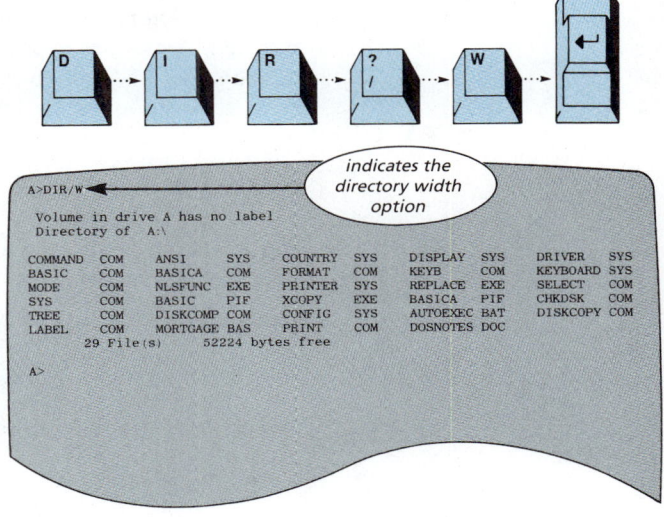

indicates the directory width option

```
A>DIR/W

 Volume in drive A has no label
 Directory of  A:\

COMMAND  COM   ANSI     SYS   COUNTRY  SYS   DISPLAY  SYS   DRIVER   SYS
BASIC    COM   BASICA   COM   FORMAT   COM   KEYB     COM   KEYBOARD SYS
MODE     COM   NLSFUNC  EXE   PRINTER  SYS   REPLACE  EXE   SELECT   COM
SYS      COM   BASIC    PIF   XCOPY    EXE   BASICA   PIF   CHKDSK   COM
TREE     COM   DISKCOMP COM   CONFIG   SYS   AUTOEXEC BAT   DISKCOPY COM
LABEL    COM   MORTGAGE BAS   PRINT    COM   DOSNOTES DOC
        29 File(s)       52224 bytes free

A>
```

FIGURE 19

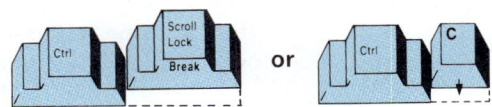

FIGURE 20

The FORMAT Command

To initiate the FORMAT program, select a new diskette, or one that may be erased. (Use the DIR command to check the contents of your diskette if you are not certain it may be erased.) Because FORMAT is an external DOS command, the FORMAT.COM program file must be on the system disk in the computer when you use this command.

To format a diskette on a two-diskette system, place the DOS diskette in drive A. Type the command FORMAT B: and press the Enter key (Figure 21).

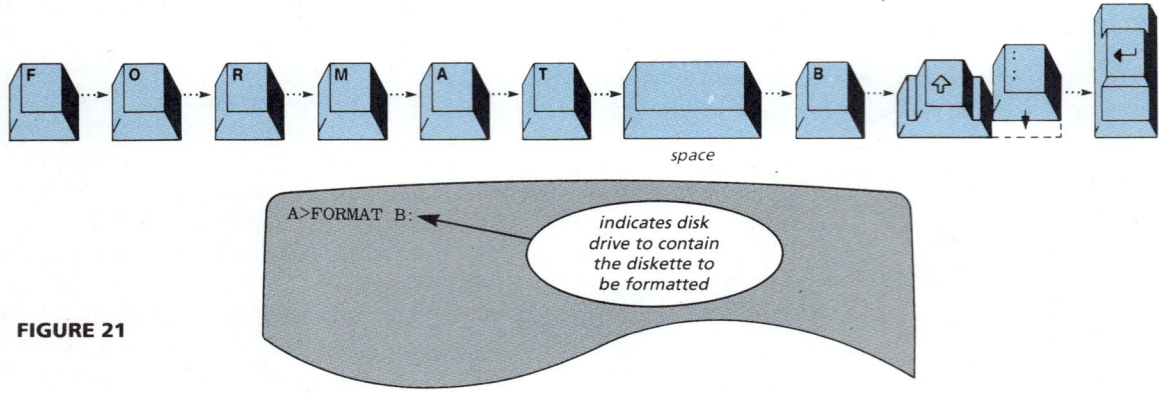

space

A>FORMAT B:

indicates disk drive to contain the diskette to be formatted

FIGURE 21

When you press the Enter key, the FORMAT program is loaded into main memory and is executed. A message appears on the screen instructing you to "Insert new diskette for drive B: and strike ENTER when ready" (Figure 22). If the disk you want to format is already in drive B, simply press the Enter key.

Step 1: View the message and insert diskette.

Step 2: Press Enter.

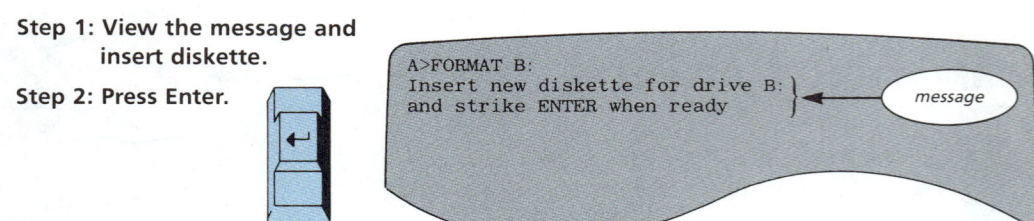

A>FORMAT B:
Insert new diskette for drive B:
and strike ENTER when ready

message

FIGURE 22

The FORMAT procedure on a hard-disk system is essentially the same as for a two-diskette system, except that the FORMAT program is stored on drive C, the hard disk. Be careful NOT to format drive C accidentally. To format a diskette in drive A at the C> prompt, type FORMAT A: and press the Enter key (Figure 23). The program will instruct you when to place the diskette to be formatted into drive A (Figure 24).

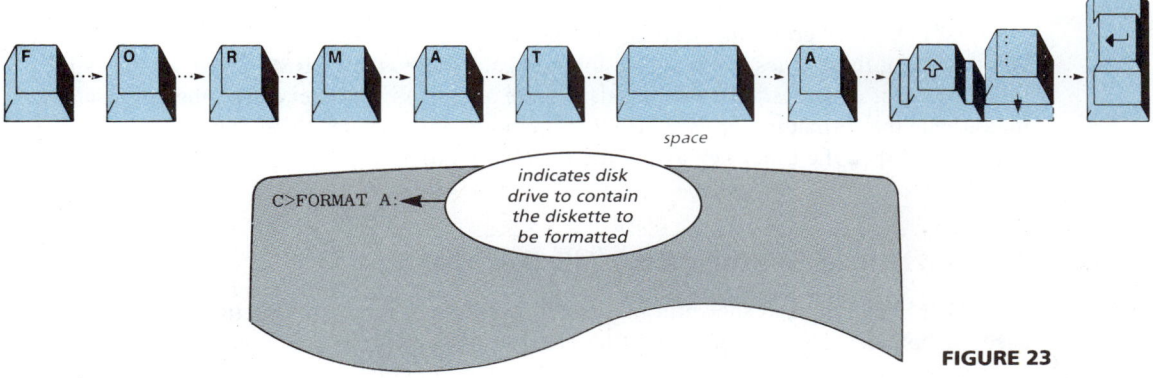

```
C>FORMAT A:
```

indicates disk
drive to contain
the diskette to
be formatted

space

FIGURE 23

To complete the format process, place the diskette to be formatted into the appropriate drive (drive B for a two-diskette system; drive A for a computer with a hard-disk) and press the Enter key. While formatting occurs, a message appears indicating that the process is underway. Figure 25 shows the message from a two diskette system and Figure 26 illustrates the message on a computer with a hard-disk. Messages may differ slightly depending upon the version of DOS you are using. When the formatting process is complete, the messages shown in Figure 27 or 28 appear.

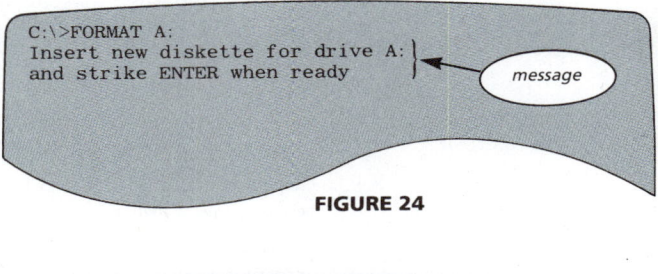

```
C:\>FORMAT A:
Insert new diskette for drive A:
and strike ENTER when ready
```

message

FIGURE 24

```
A>FORMAT B:
Insert new diskette for drive B:
and strike ENTER when ready

Head: 0 Cylinder: 16
```

indicates area
of diskette currently
being formatted

FIGURE 25

```
C:\FORMAT A:
Insert new diskette for drive B:
and strike ENTER when ready
Head: 0 Cylinder: 16
```

indicates area
of diskette being
formatted

FIGURE 26

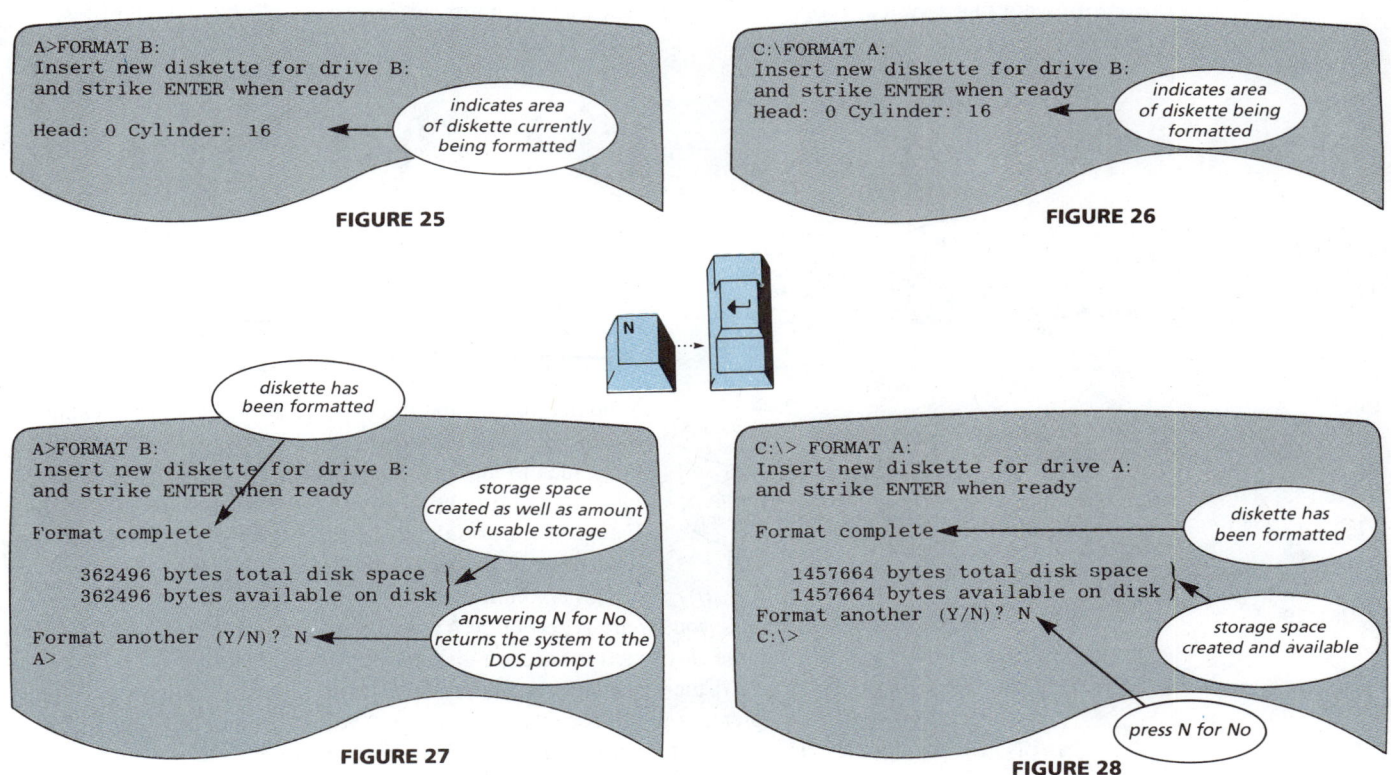

diskette has
been formatted

```
A>FORMAT B:
Insert new diskette for drive B:
and strike ENTER when ready

Format complete

    362496 bytes total disk space
    362496 bytes available on disk

Format another (Y/N)? N
A>
```

storage space
created as well as amount
of usable storage

answering N for No
returns the system to the
DOS prompt

FIGURE 27

```
C:\> FORMAT A:
Insert new diskette for drive A:
and strike ENTER when ready

Format complete

    1457664 bytes total disk space
    1457664 bytes available on disk
Format another (Y/N)? N
C:\>
```

diskette has
been formatted

storage space
created and available

press N for No

FIGURE 28

The FORMAT program specifies that the diskette is formatted for a total number of bytes and that all of these bytes are available for storage. Finally, the FORMAT program asks if there are other diskettes to be formatted. If there are, press the letter Y and then the Enter key to continue the formatting process. If there are not more diskettes to be formatted, press the letter N and then the Enter key to end the FORMAT program.

Formatting a System Disk (/S Option)

The FORMAT command shown in Figures 26 and 27 will format a diskette so that it can be used for both data files and program files. However, the diskette cannot be used to boot the system because it does not contain the special system programs that are required for booting. To format a diskette so that it contains these special programs, thus creating what is called a **system disk**, you must use the **/S option**.

Use the same diskette you used in the last exercise. If you are using a two-diskette system, use the following commands. If you are using a hard-disk system, use drive C as the default drive and place the diskette to be formatted in drive A. Be very certain NOT to format drive C accidentally.

To create a system disk on a two-diskette system, type FORMAT B:/S and press the Enter key (Figure 29). On a hard-disk system, type FORMAT A:/S. You will be prompted to insert a new diskette in drive B (or A); if the diskette you formatted earlier is still in the disk drive, simply press the Enter key. After the diskette is formatted, the "System transferred" message appears. In general, if you are formatting a diskette to be used only for storing data files, do not place system programs on the diskette so that more space is available for the data files.

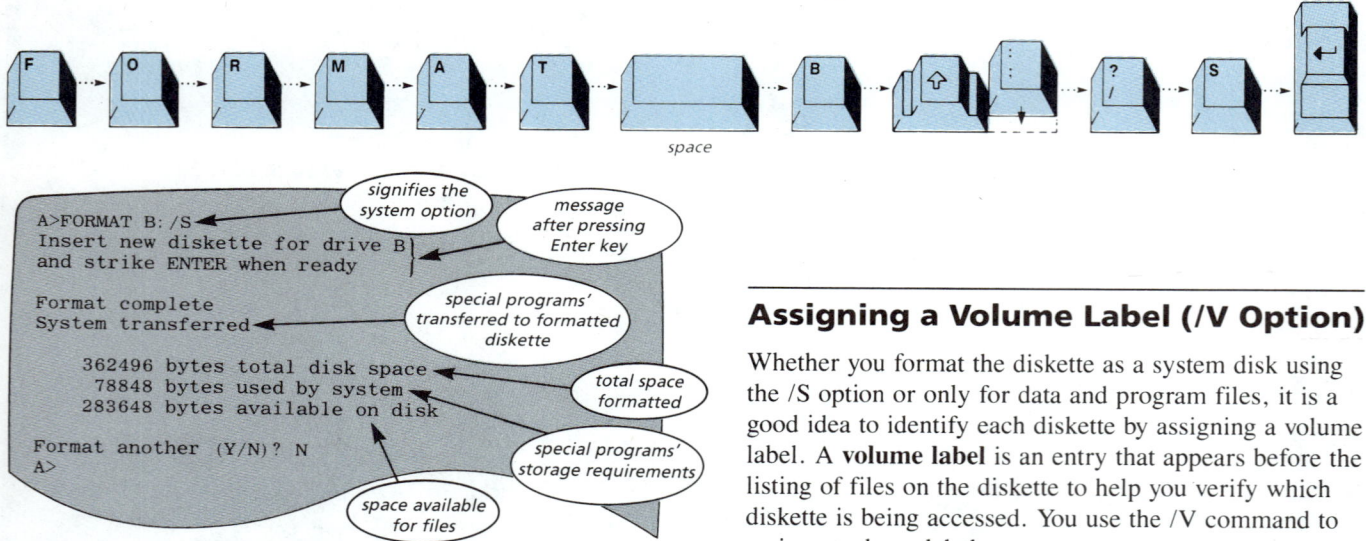

A>FORMAT B: /S   *signifies the system option*
Insert new diskette for drive B   *message after pressing Enter key*
and strike ENTER when ready

Format complete
System transferred   *special programs' transferred to formatted diskette*

   362496 bytes total disk space   *total space formatted*
    78848 bytes used by system
  283648 bytes available on disk   *special programs' storage requirements*

Format another (Y/N)? N   *space available for files*
A>

FIGURE 29

Assigning a Volume Label (/V Option)

Whether you format the diskette as a system disk using the /S option or only for data and program files, it is a good idea to identify each diskette by assigning a volume label. A **volume label** is an entry that appears before the listing of files on the diskette to help you verify which diskette is being accessed. You use the /V command to assign a volume label.

To assign a volume label, you would type FORMAT B:/V and press the Enter key (Figure 30). You will again be instructed to insert a diskette into drive B. Insert a new diskette, or press the Enter key if the diskette from the previous exercise is still in drive B. When the format process is complete, you will receive the message "Volume label (11 characters, ENTER for none)?" as a prompt to enter your label. You may use 11 characters—letters, numbers, or spaces—but not punctuation or special characters. After you enter a label and press the Enter key, a message appears asking if you want to format another diskette. You would press N and the Enter key to return to the DOS prompt.

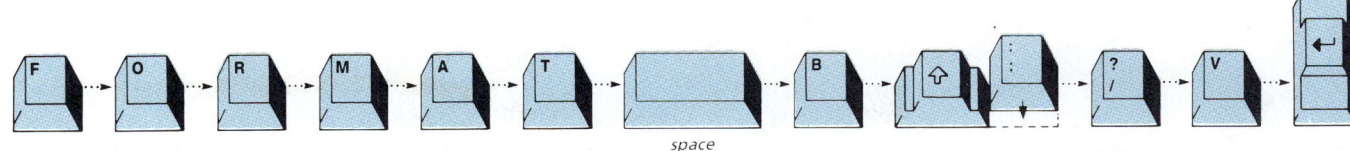

FIGURE 30

CLS COMMAND

Quite often, as you issue several commands or perform lengthy processes, the display screen will become crowded and difficult to read and interpret (Figure 31). To clear the screen and place the system prompt on the first line of the screen, you can use the CLS (Clear Screen) command. Type the letters CLS, then press the Enter key to execute the Clear Screen command.

MANAGING DATA AND PROGRAM FILES ON DISKS

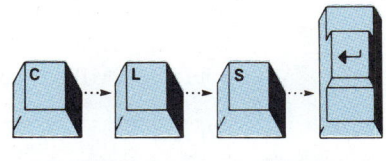

A data file is a collection of data created by application or system programs and used by the programs. The data can be the figures used for a spreadsheet showing sales revenues, names and addresses in a database file, or a word processing document announcing the arrival of a new employee. A **program file** contains machine-readable instructions that the computer follows to perform its tasks. The program might be an operating system program or one of the application programs such as word processing that uses data files. Both data files and program files require your attention to be stored on a disk correctly.

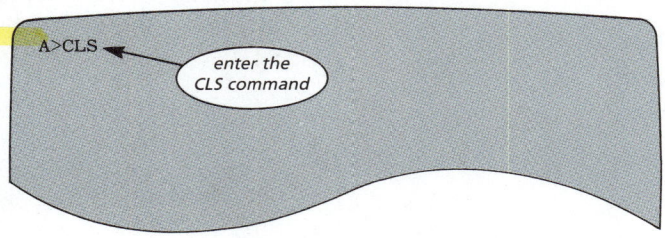

A>CLS

enter the CLS command

FIGURE 31

Assigning File Specifications

DOS identifies the files on a disk by a combination of several specifications (Figure 32). A **file specification** lets DOS know exactly where to search for a file and gives its exact name. There are four parts to a DOS file specification: (1) the drive specifier, which you already know as drive A: or B: or C:, if there is a hard disk; (2) a directory specification (explained later); (3) the filename; (4) the filename extension.

FIGURE 32

LEGEND	DEFINITION
d:	The disk drive letter specifies the drive containing the file you are requesting. For example, A: specifies disk drive A. If you omit the drive letter, DOS assumes the file is located on the default drive. A disk drive letter is always followed by a colon (:).
\path	A path is an optional reference to a subdirectory of files on the specified disk. It is preceded, and sometimes followed, by a backslash (\).
filename	The filename consists of from one to eight characters.
.ext	A filename may contain an optional extension of a period followed by from one to three characters. The extension is used to add further identity to files.

Filenames.   Regardless of the type of data in the file, you must assign a filename to every data file, as well as to every program file. A **filename** consists of one to eight characters and is used by DOS to identify a specific file. You may use any combination of characters except: period (.), quotation mark ("), slash (/), backslash (\), brackets ([ ]), colon (:), less than (<), greater than (>), plus (+), equals (=), semicolon (;), and comma (,).

In general, your filename should reflect the data stored in it. For example, if your file contains employee records, it is more meaningful to use the filename EMPLOYEE than to use the filename FILE1, even though DOS will accept either filename.

Filename Extensions.   A filename can be made more specific by an optional extension. A **filename extension** consists of a period followed by one to three characters. The same characters that are permitted for a filename are permitted for a filename extension. The filename extension can identify a file more specifically or describe its purpose (Figure 33). For example, if you wish to create a copy of the EMPLOYEE file, you could use the filename extension .CPY to identify the file as a copied file. The entire file specification for the file would be EMPLOYEE.CPY.

FIGURE 33

.COM Files		.EXE Files		.BAT Files	
COMMAND	COM	APPEND	EXE	AUTOEXEC	BAT
ASSIGN	COM	ATTRIB	EXE	WP	BAT
BACKUP	COM	FASTOPEN	EXE	INSTALL	BAT
BASIC	COM	FIND	EXE		
BASICA	COM	JOIN	EXE		
CHKDSK	COM	NLSFUNC	EXE		
COMP	COM	REPLACE	EXE		
DEBUG	COM				
DISKCOMP	COM				
DISKCOPY	COM				
FORMAT	COM				
LABEL	COM				

Certain programs associated with the Disk Operating System use special filename extensions. All files with the filename extensions .COM or .EXE are executable programs. Files with the extension .BAT are **DOS batch files** and contain a series of DOS commands to be executed in sequence. Any DOS command with one of these filename extensions is an external command. You can execute any external command simply by typing the filename (the extension is not required) and pressing the Enter key.

COPY COMMAND

Once you have formatted a diskette and are ready to use it to store data or program files, you will need a method of placing these files on the diskette. Use the **COPY command** to copy one file or a series of files to the same or a different diskette. As a DOS internal command, COPY may be used at any time, with or without the system disk.

Using the COPY Command

The COPY command is often used to make working copies of program and data diskettes. Copying original files from one diskette creates a second diskette that can be used for everyday work to protect the original disk from damage. A similar use for COPY is to make a **backup copy** of a diskette to guard against accidental loss of data. One frequently used technique is to make a backup copy of a file whenever you work on revisions to an existing file. In fact, some application programs will make a backup file automatically, using the filename extension .BAK or .BAC to indicate that it is a backup file.

Copying Files from One Diskette to Another

In the following examples of the COPY command, you will copy files from drive A to drive B. Check to see that you have the practice diskette provided with this book in drive A and your formatted diskette in drive B. If you are using a hard disk system, use drive C as the default drive, copying the files to drive A.

For practice, copy the file DOSNOTES.DOC from drive A to drive B. Your instructor will make the DOSNOTES.DOC file available to you or will give you the name of another file to copy. Type COPY DOSNOTES.DOC B: and press the Enter key. Note that after the word COPY you leave one or more spaces, then state the file specification of the file to be copied. In DOS terminology, this file is called the **source file**. In Figure 34, the filename DOSNO-TES.DOC is specified as the source file. Since no drive specification is included, the operating system assumes the file is located on the default drive, drive A.

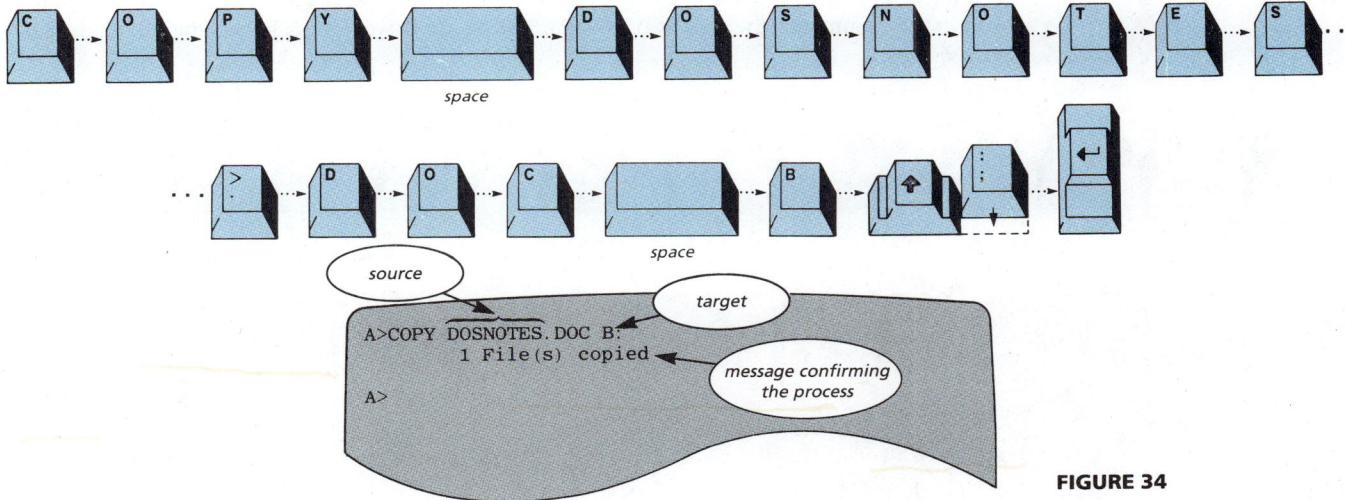

FIGURE 34

Following the source file is one or more blank spaces. Then, the **file specification**, which can include the drive specification, and the name of the **target file**, that is, the filename and filename extension of the source file after it is copied, is specified. In Figure 34, the drive specification B: states that the file is to be copied to a diskette in drive B. Because no filename is specified for the target file on drive B, DOS defaults to the same name as the source file, and so the name of the file on drive B will be DOSNOTES.DOC. The message "1 File(s) copied" signals that the command is completed.

When you copy a file from a diskette in one drive to a diskette in another drive, you can assign a new name to the target file. To copy the file DOSNOTES.DOC from the diskette in drive A to the diskette in drive B, giving the new file the name NOTECOPY on drive B, type COPY DOSNOTES.DOC B:NOTECOPY and press the Enter key (Figure 35). Again, the message "1 File(s) copied" appears when the task is completed, as in Figure 34.

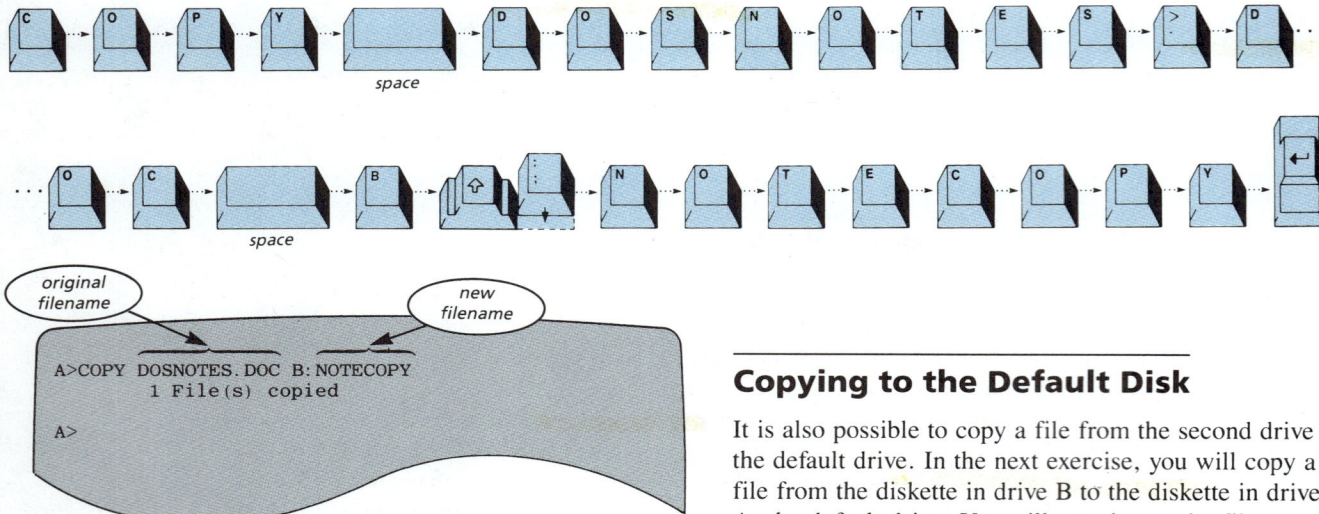

original filename

new filename

```
A>COPY  DOSNOTES.DOC  B:NOTECOPY
      1 File(s) copied

A>
```

FIGURE 35

Copying to the Default Disk

It is also possible to copy a file from the second drive to the default drive. In the next exercise, you will copy a file from the diskette in drive B to the diskette in drive A, the default drive. You will not change the filename. To accomplish this procedure, type COPY B:NOTE-COPY A: and press the Enter key. This command copies the file named NOTECOPY from the diskette in drive B to the diskette in drive A. When the message "1 File(s) copied" appears, as in Figure 36, the copying process is completed. Because no target filename was given in the command, the file NOTECOPY will be on drive A under the same name as it is on drive B.

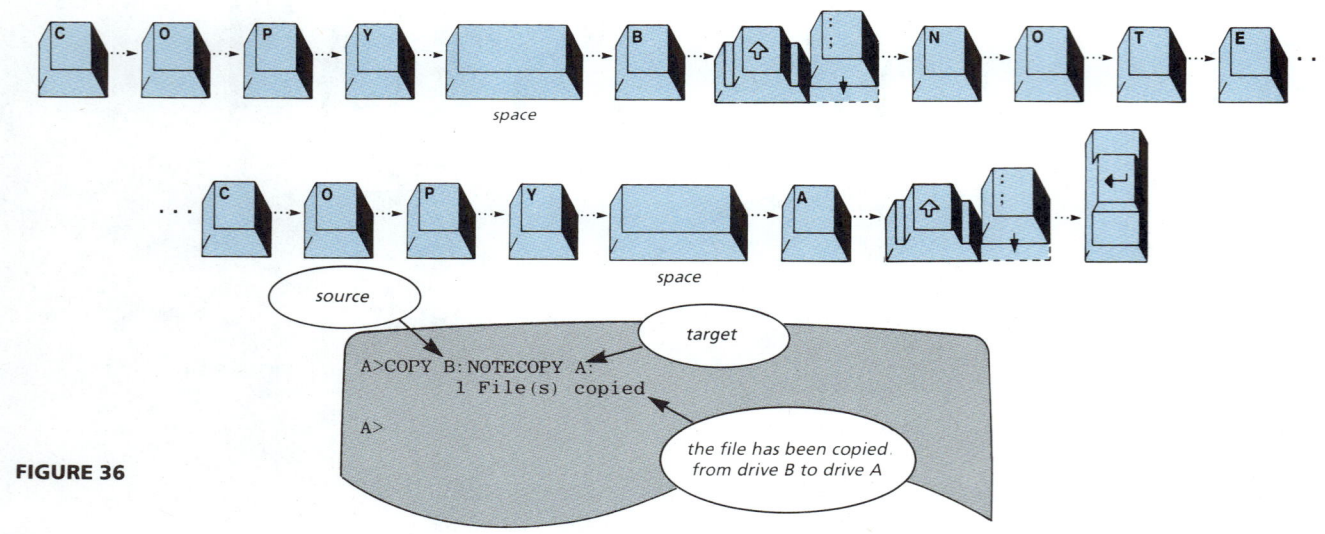

source

target

```
A>COPY B:NOTECOPY A:
      1 File(s) copied

A>
```

the file has been copied from drive B to drive A

FIGURE 36

Copying a File to the Same Diskette

It is possible to copy a file to the same diskette, but you must use a different filename. For practice, copy the file named DOSNOTES.DOC stored on drive A onto the same diskette. Give the filename DOSNOTES.BAK to the target file. Type the command COPY DOSNO-TES.DOC DOSNOTES.BAK and press the Enter key.

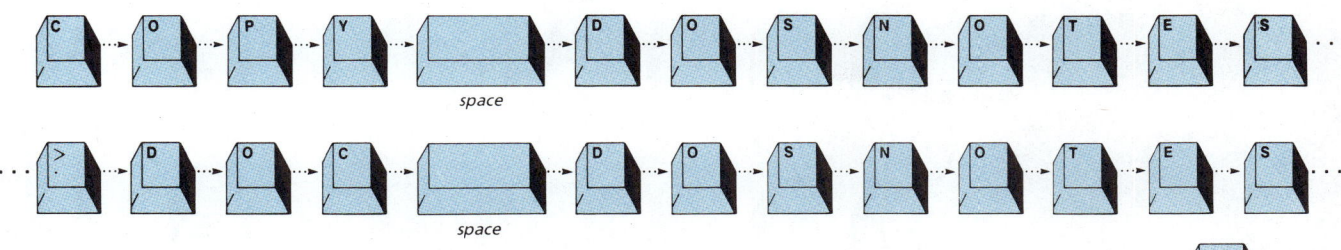

space

space

When your COPY command is executed, the file DOSNO-TES.DOC in drive A is copied to the same diskette on drive A as DOSNOTES.BAK (Figure 37). The file extension .BAK is used to distinguish the files. If you had used the same filename to designate both the target and source files on the same diskette, an error message would be displayed, stating that a file cannot be copied into itself. You would then have to reenter the COPY command using a different name for the target file.

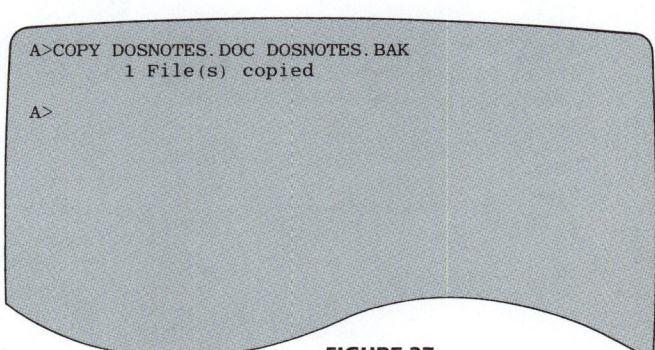

```
A>COPY DOSNOTES.DOC DOSNOTES.BAK
        1 File(s) copied

A>
```

FIGURE 37

Global Filename Characters (''Wildcards'')

You can copy more than one file at a time using a single COPY command. To copy more than one file, you use **global characters, or wildcards**. These are special characters indicating that any character may occupy that specific location in the filename. The two global characters are the ***** (asterisk) and the **?** (question mark).

To use wildcards, you need to know the files stored on the diskette. Figure 38 shows the directory of the diskette in drive A. Notice that the files DOSNOTES.BAK and NOTECOPY appear, a result of the COPY commands you used earlier. Notice also that several files have the same filename extensions. It is not uncommon, on any disk with many files, to find several files with similarities in filenames or extensions. These similarities can be exploited by using wildcard characters.

The * Character.   You can use the global character ***** (asterisk) to indicate a portion of the filename or extension. When the * global character appears, any character can occupy that position and all the remaining positions in the filename or the filename extension.

For example, let us use the wildcard asterisk (*) to copy files with the filename extension .COM from the diskette in drive A to the diskette in drive B. Type COPY *.COM B: and press the Enter key. In Figure 39, the source files are specified by the entry *.COM. The asterisk (*) in the filename portion of the specification means that any filename can be used. The file extension .COM states that the file specification must include the file extension .COM. In Figure 38, five filenames satisfy this criterion: COMMAND.COM, FORMAT-.COM, MODE.COM, SELECT.COM, and SYS.COM.

```
Volume in drive A has no label
Directory of  A:\

COMMAND   COM    25307    3-17-87   12:00p
ANSI      SYS     1678    3-17-87   12:00p
COUNTRY   SYS    11285    3-17-87   12:00p
AUTOEXEC  BAT       44    1-01-80   12:00a
DRIVER    SYS     1196    3-17-87   12:00p
CONFIG    SYS       18    3-09-90   12:05p
NOTECOPY          2967    3-09-90   12:18a
FORMAT    COM    11616    3-18-87   12:00p
COPYNOTE          2967    3-09-90   12:18a
DOSNOTES  DOC     2967    3-09-90   12:18a
MODE      COM    15487    3-17-87   12:00p
DOSNOTES  BAK     2967    3-09-90   12:18a
PRINTER   SYS    13590    3-17-87   12:00p
REPLACE   EXE    11775    3-17-87   12:00p
SELECT    COM     4163    3-17-87   12:00p
SYS       COM     4766    3-17-87   12:00p
VDISK     SYS     3455    3-17-87   12:00p
XCOPY     EXE    11247    3-17-87   12:00p
       18 File(s)    172032 bytes free

A>
```

FIGURE 38

FIGURE 39

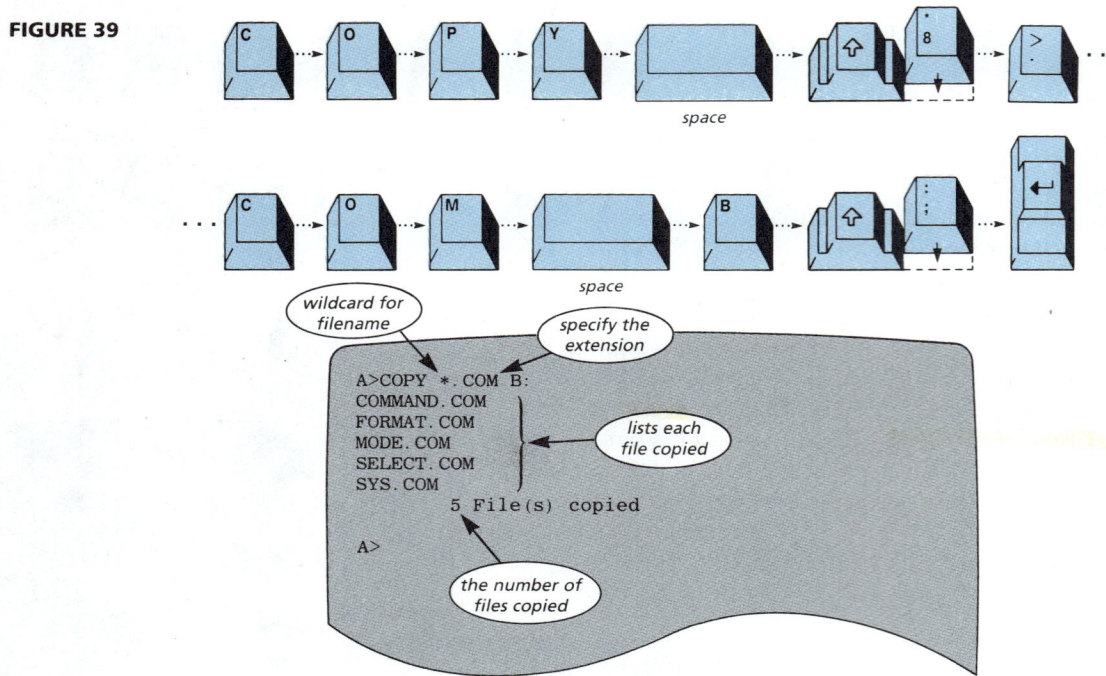

These files are copied to the diskette in disk drive B. The filenames for the copied files on the diskette in drive B remain the same as the source filenames on the diskette in drive A because you specified no new names in the copy command. When you copy files with a COPY command using the * global character, all files copied are listed by the COPY command. Figure 39 lists the five copied files.

You can also specify the global character * as the filename extension to copy a specific filename with any extension. For example, the diskette contains two files with the name DOSNOTES, DOSNOTES.BAK and DOSNOTES.DOC. Type the command COPY DOS-NOTES.* B: as in Figure 40 and press the Enter key to copy both the files with the filename DOSNOTES to drive B.

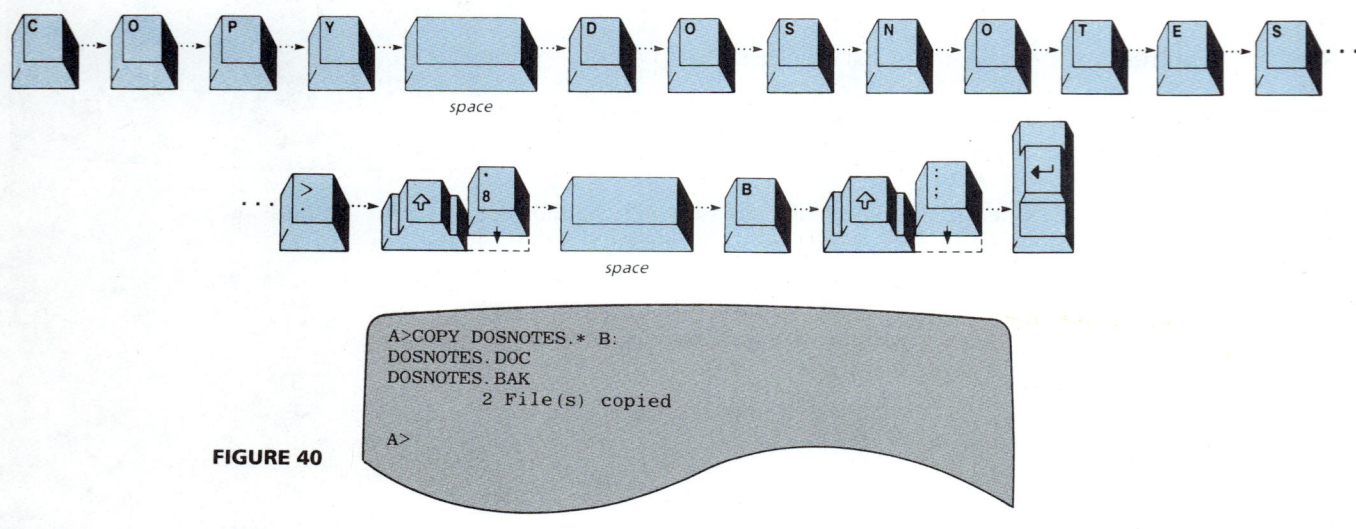

FIGURE 40

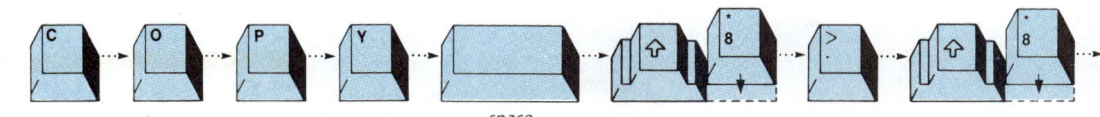

space

Copying All Files from One Diskette to Another.

You can also use the COPY command to copy all of the files on
one diskette to another diskette by using the * global character.
This technique is useful in making backup or working copies of
entire diskettes. You use the * wildcard in both the filename and
extension positions to signify "all filenames.all extensions" in the
command. Practice by typing COPY *.* B: and pressing the
Enter key to copy all files on drive A to drive B (Figure 41).

The ? Character.

The ? (question mark) global charac-
ter can also be used to represent any character occupying the
position in which the wildcard character appears. However, the ?
represents only a single character replacement, whereas the *
can represent one or more characters. You can use a single ? or
several in a command to identify files. Practice this option by
typing COPY DOSNOTES.BA? B: and pressing the Enter key
to copy DOSNOTES.BAK to drive B (Figure 42).

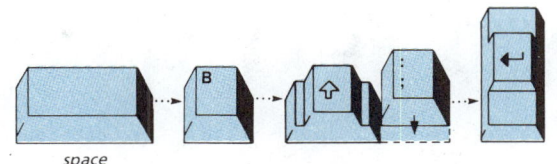

space

```
A>COPY *.* B:
COMMAND.COM
ANSI.SYS
COUNTRY.SYS
AUTOEXEC.BAT
DRIVER.SYS
CONFIG.SYS
NOTECOPY
FORMAT.COM
COPYNOTE
DOSNOTES.DOC
MODE.COM
DOSNOTES.BAK
PRINTER.SYS
REPLACE.EXE
SELECT.COM
SYS.COM
VDISK.SYS
XCOPY.EXE
        18 File(s) copied

A>
```

FIGURE 41

Using Wildcards with DOS Commands

You have learned to use the wildcard characters with the COPY command. Many DOS commands support the use of global replacement characters. For example, you can use the wildcards with the DIR command to look for files of a common type. To look at all DOS batch
files on a diskette, you would type the command DIR *.BAT and press the Enter key to display all files with the filename extension .BAT.

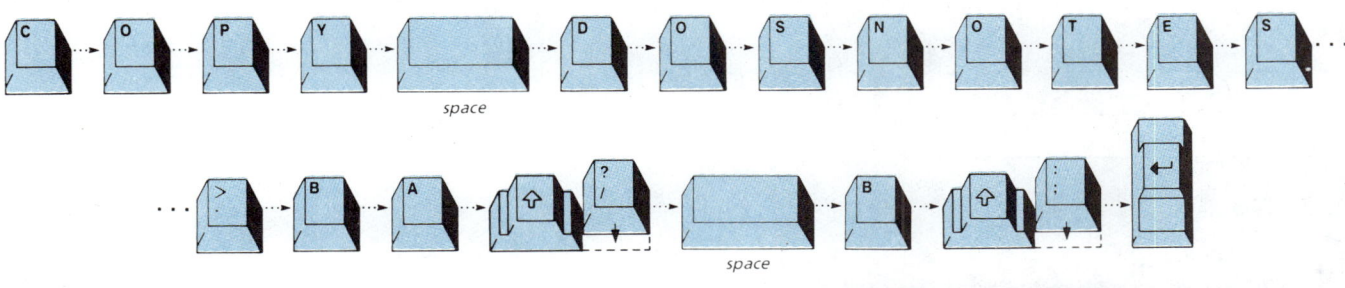

space

RENAME COMMAND

Use the **RENAME command** when you want to
rename a file on a diskette. If you assign a filename already used by a file currently on the disk-
ette, DOS creates the new file on the diskette and destroys the previously existing file with that
name. You will not receive any warning that this has happened. Thus, you should periodically
check the filenames on a diskette to avoid accidental replacement of files. If you discover a filename you might reuse, you can use the RENAME command to change the name of the file.

```
A>COPY DOSNOTES.BA? B:
DOSNOTES.BAK  ◄───────      the ? is replaced
        1 File(s) copied          by the letter K

A>
```

FIGURE 42

In the example in Figure 43, the file with the filename NOTECOPY on drive A is to be renamed DOSFILE. Type the command RENAME NOTECOPY DOSFILE immediately after the system prompt and press the Enter key. When you press the Enter key, the filename on the diskette in drive A is changed from NOTECOPY to DOSFILE.

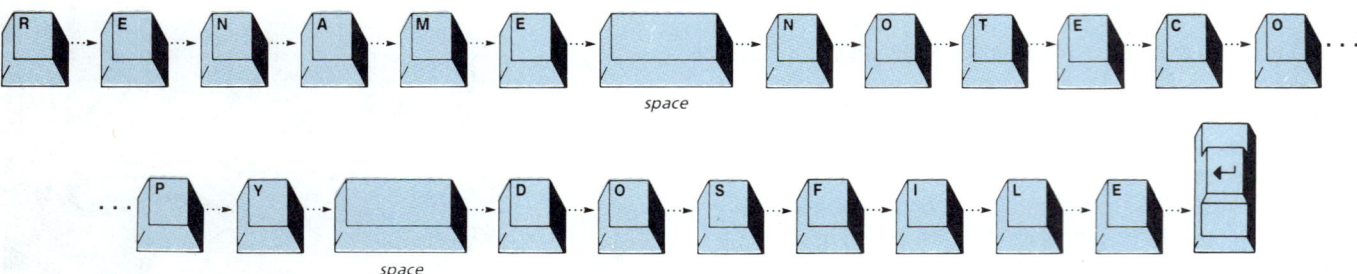

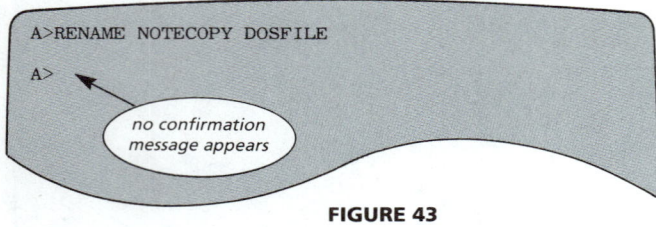

```
A>RENAME NOTECOPY DOSFILE

A>
```
no confirmation
message appears

FIGURE 43

You can use the global characters * and ? with the RENAME command. In Figure 44, all files with the file extension .BAK are renamed with a file extension .BAC. Type the wildcard character * with the command RENAME *.BAK *.BAC and press the Enter key. All characters represented by the * will remain the same in the new filename. Thus, in Figure 44, all the filenames in the renamed files will remain the same, but the file extensions will change from .BAK to .BAC. RENAME does not confirm the operation on the screen, so you should use the DIR command before and after you use the RENAME command to assure the command was executed (Figure 45).

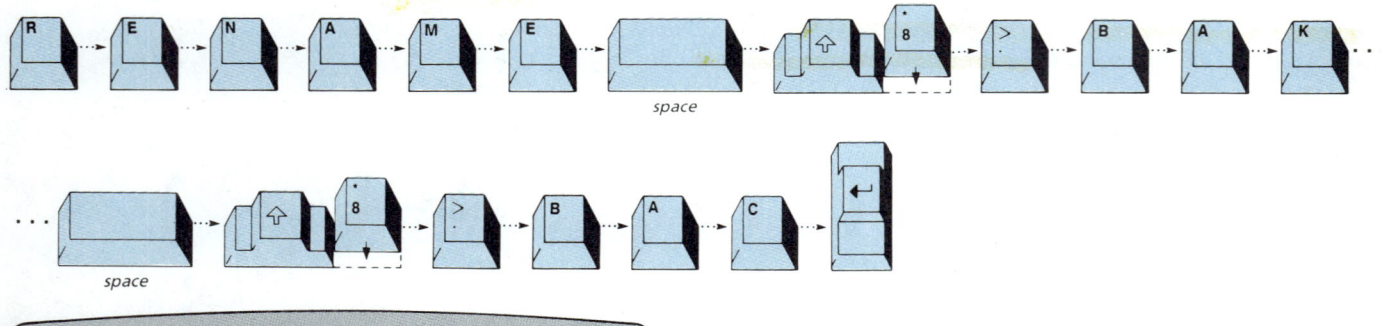

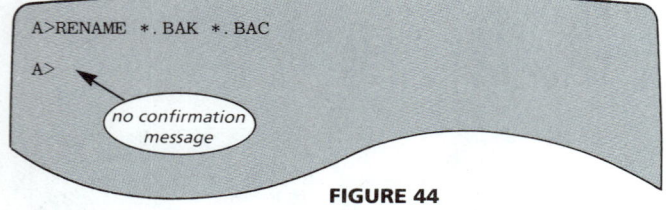

```
A>RENAME *.BAK *.BAC

A>
```
no confirmation
message

FIGURE 44

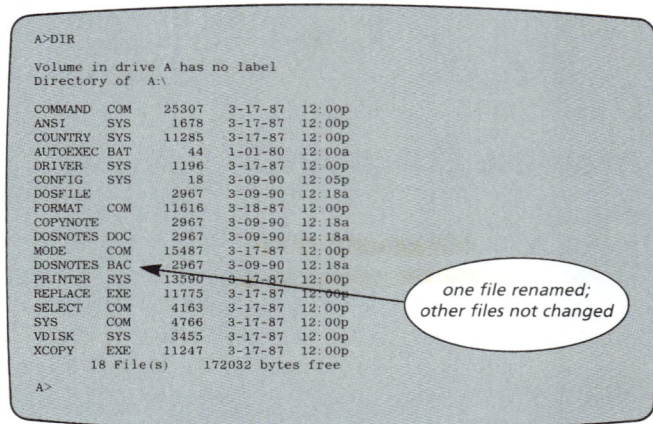

```
A>DIR

Volume in drive A has no label
Directory of  A:\

COMMAND   COM    25307   3-17-87   12:00p
ANSI      SYS     1678   3-17-87   12:00p
COUNTRY   SYS    11285   3-17-87   12:00p
AUTOEXEC  BAT       44   1-01-80   12:00a
DRIVER    SYS     1196   3-17-87   12:00p
CONFIG    SYS       18   3-09-90   12:05p
DOSFILE           2967   3-09-90   12:18a
FORMAT    COM    11616   3-18-87   12:00p
COPYNOTE          2967   3-09-90   12:18a
DOSNOTES  DOC     2967   3-09-90   12:18a
MODE      COM    15487   3-17-87   12:00p
DOSNOTES  BAC     2967   3-09-90   12:18a
PRINTER   SYS    13590   3-17-87   12:00p
REPLACE   EXE    11775   3-17-87   12:00p
SELECT    COM     4163   3-17-87   12:00p
SYS       COM     4766   3-17-87   12:00p
VDISK     SYS     3455   3-17-87   12:00p
XCOPY     EXE    11247   3-17-87   12:00p
     18 File(s)     172032 bytes free

A>
```
one file renamed;
other files not changed

FIGURE 45

ERASE AND DEL COMMANDS

As a part of diskette file management, you should periodically remove unneeded files from your diskette. The **ERASE command** will erase, or remove, a file from a diskette. An alternative command that functions like the erase command is the **DEL** (delete) command. Take care when using the ERASE or DEL commands, because once a file has been erased from the directory, it cannot be easily recovered. Such inadvertent erasing of a file is another reason for keeping backup files.

Removing Files

We will begin by removing a single file, DOSFILE, from drive A. Type ERASE DOSFILE and press the Enter key, as shown in Figure 46. (You could use the DEL command instead, typing DEL DOSFILE and pressing the Enter key.) Use the DIR command to assure that the file has been removed from the diskette.

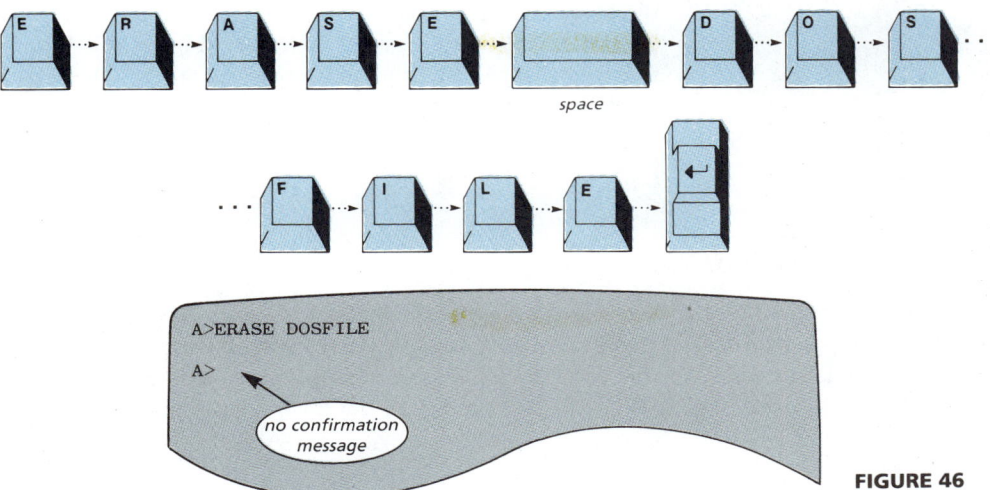

A>ERASE DOSFILE

A>

no confirmation message

FIGURE 46

USING DIRECTORIES AND SUBDIRECTORIES

Directory Entries and Subdirectories

When you need to view the files on any disk, the computer does not actually read the entire disk looking for the file. Instead, a **file directory** or listing of each of the filenames on the disk is searched. This directory, created when the diskette is formatted, is called the **root directory**. Entries for subdirectories are made in the root directory. The root directory is the highest level directory of a disk (Figure 47).

You can make three types of entries into a disk directory: (1) the filename and extension, (2) the volume label, (3) a subdirectory entry. We have previously discussed (1) and (2).

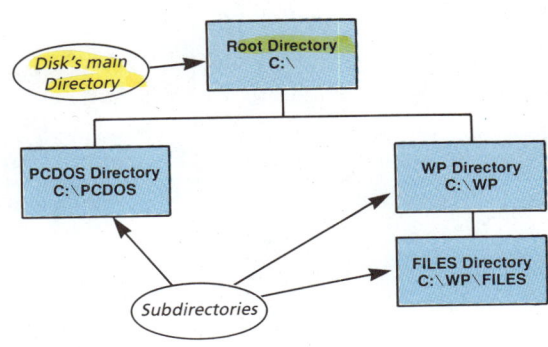

FIGURE 47

You can create a **subdirectory** to group all files of a similar type together (Figure 47). For example, you can create a subdirectory containing all the files related to DOS.

There are at least two good reasons to use subdirectories. First, the operating system provides a limited number of entries in the file directory. A diskette has room for only 112 entries; a hard disk allows up to 512 entries. This capacity may be sufficient on a diskette, but a hard disk with many millions of bytes of storage may have more files than the directory permits.

It is also easier to find files that are organized by related groups than to search randomly through all the files on a disk.

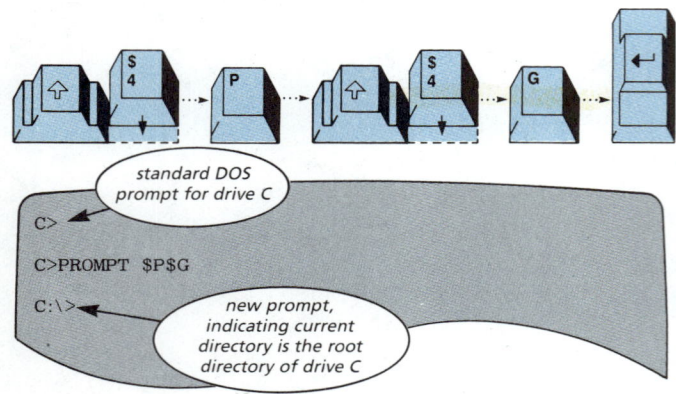

FIGURE 48

The PROMPT Command

The standard DOS prompt, A >, B >, or C >, does not tell you what subdirectories you are using. DOS provides a way for you to monitor which directory is in use through the **PROMPT command**. To have DOS include the subdirectory information as a part of the DOS prompt, type PROMPT PG and press the Enter key (Figure 48). Whenever you change disk drive addresses, you will see the subdirectory information as a part of the prompt.

Making Subdirectories

To create a subdirectory, use the **MKDIR command,** usually abbreviated as **MD**. If you have a hard disk, and *if your instructor approves*, create a subdirectory on drive C. Otherwise, practice the command on a diskette in drive A. To create a subdirectory called "PCDOS" on your diskette or disk drive, type MD A:\PCDOS and press the Enter key (Figure 49).

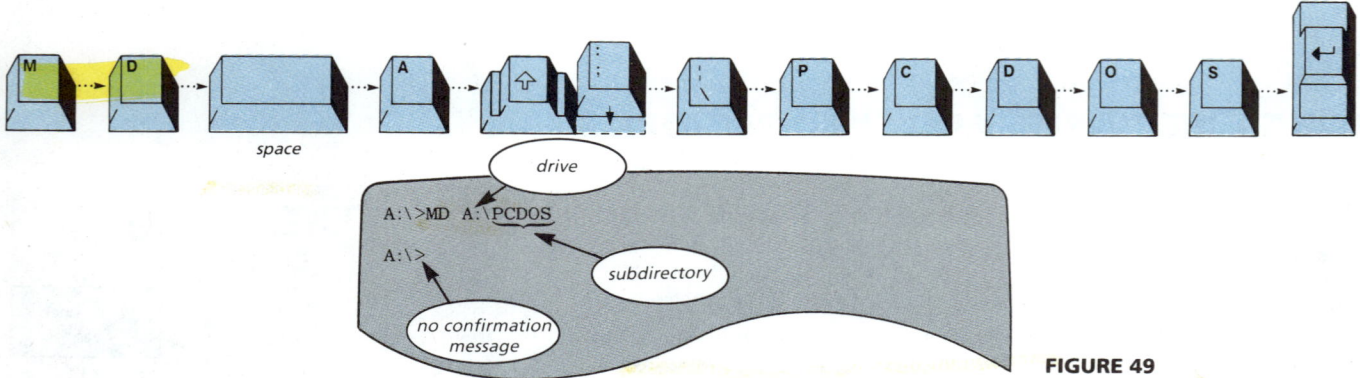

FIGURE 49

There are specific steps to the MD command. (1) Start a subdirectory entry with the drive designation. If the directory is to be on drive C, enter C: immediately after the MD command. Use the command MD A:\PCDOS to use drive A on a diskette. You can omit the drive specification if you are creating the directory on the default drive.

(2) Begin a subdirectory entry with the **backslash** character, \. The root directory for your hard disk is designated by a backslash alone. For example, C:\ designates the root

directory of drive C. The subdirectory made for the DOS files is C:\PCDOS. Notice that because you have issued the PROMPT command, the DOS prompt now includes the root or subdirectory name, C:\> or C:\PCDOS>.

(3) The subdirectory name, like any filename, can contain one to eight characters, followed optionally by a period and one to three characters in an extension. (Generally, subdirectory names do not include extensions.)

(4) You can assign a subdirectory entry to an existing subdirectory. For instance, you can create a subdirectory for a word processing program and a subordinate subdirectory for the data files created by the program. To create the word processing subdirectories shown in Figures 50 and 51, make the word processing subdirectory by typing MD A:\WP and press the Enter key. To make the subordinate subdirectory, type MD A:\WP\FILES and press the Enter key. The program subdirectory is A:\WP, and the word processing files can be stored in a second subdirectory, A:\WP\FILES. These two operations result in a series of related directories. Refer back to Figure 47 to see the relationships among the directories and subdirectories we have created.

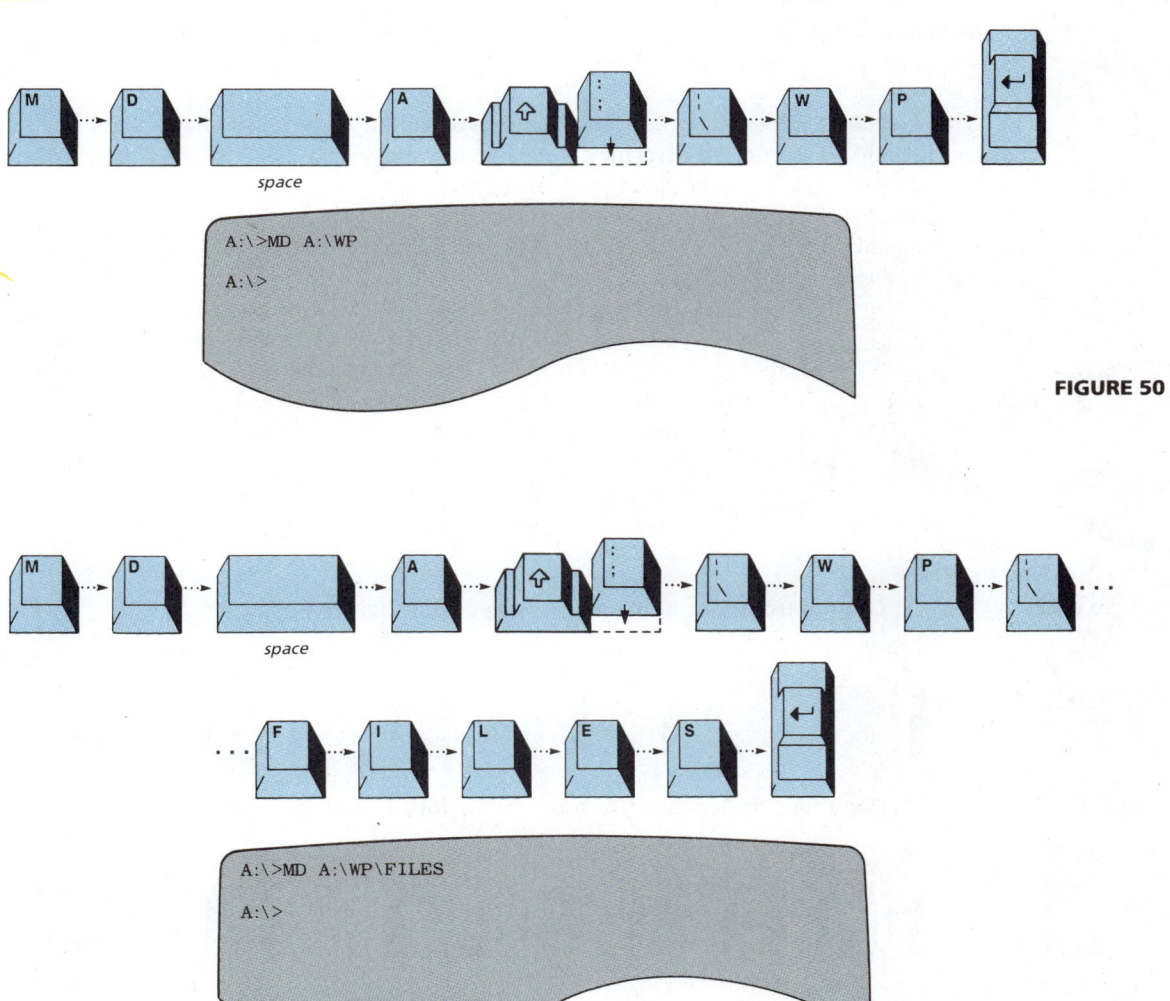

```
A:\>MD A:\WP

A:\>
```

FIGURE 50

```
A:\>MD A:\WP\FILES

A:\>
```

FIGURE 51

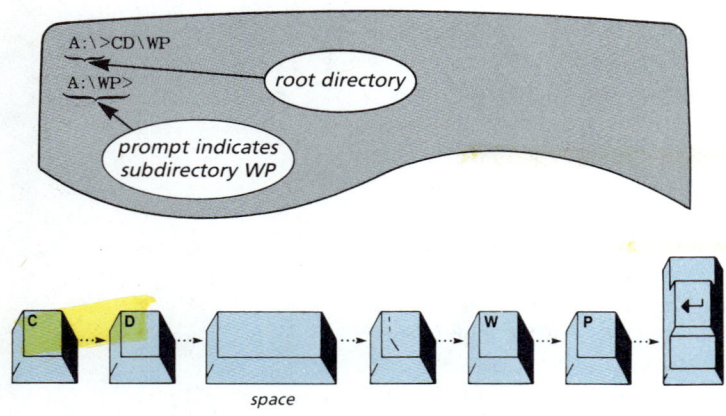

FIGURE 52

Changing Directories

Use the **CHDIR command** to move from one directory to another. Enter the letters **CD** immediately following the DOS prompt. Then type the backslash character and the subdirectory name and press the Enter key. To change from the root directory to the WP directory, for instance, type the entry CD \WP and press the Enter key. The result shown in Figure 52 should appear on your screen. To move to a lower subdirectory, such as the FILES subdirectory, type CD \WP\FILES and press the Enter key.

If you are moving to a directory that is subordinate to the current subdirectory, you can simply type CD and the subdirectory name. For instance, if your current directory is WP, you can move to the FILES subdirectory by entering CD FILES. Note that the entry omits both the reference to WP (the current directory) and the backslash character.

To return to the root directory simply type CD\ and press the Enter key. The backslash character entered by itself signifies the root directory.

The Current Directory.   Just as there is a default or current disk drive, there is a current directory. The **current directory** is the one in which you are currently working. When you first access a disk, the root directory is the current directory. You can, however, direct DOS to a subdirectory, which then becomes the current directory for that disk. If you temporarily set another drive as the default drive, the named directory remains the current directory for the first disk.

FIGURE 53

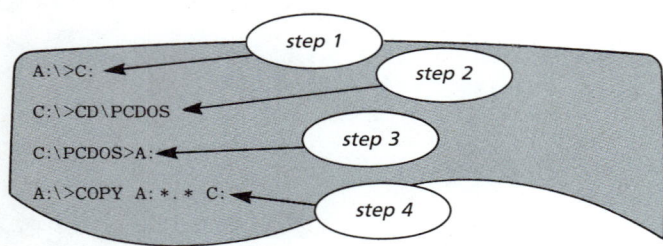

For practice, set your default drive to drive C by entering C: (Figure 53, step 1). Then set PCDOS as the current subdirectory for drive C by entering CD \PCDOS (step 2). Switch to drive A as the default drive (step 3) and copy files from drive A to drive C: type the copy command COPY A:*.* C: (step 4). Files are copied from the A drive to the PCDOS subdirectory on drive C even though the subdirectory is not specified in the copy command.

Step 1: Change default to drive C.   **Step 2: Change from root directory of drive C to PCDOS directory.**

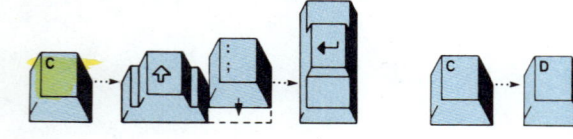

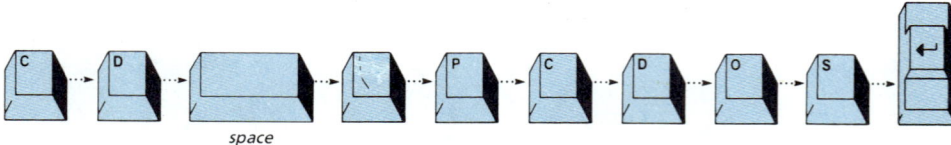

Step 3: Return to A drive.   **Step 4: Copy files from drive A to the subdirectory PCDOS on drive C.**

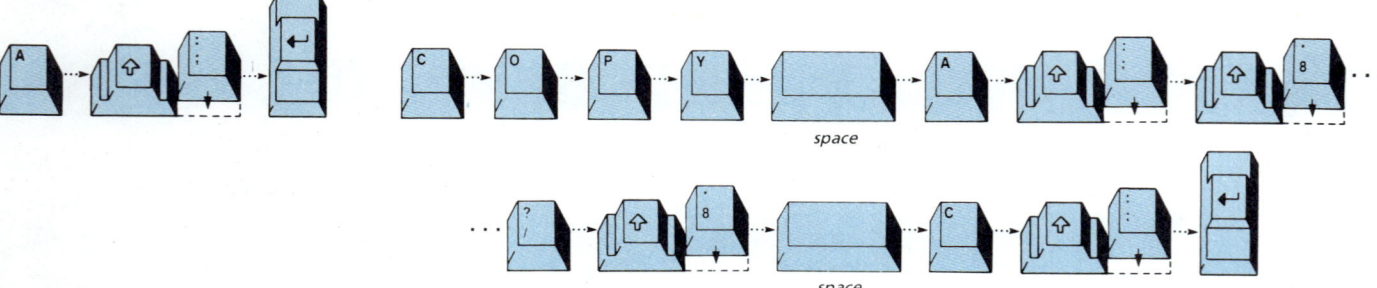

Specifying a Path to Subdirectories and Files

You will find it very convenient to group files in subdirectories. To use the technique you must learn to specify the path to a file. The **path** includes three components: (1) the drive, (2) the name of the subdirectories, (3) the name of the file. The path specifies the route DOS is to take from the root directory through subdirectories leading to a file. Specify the path whenever you wish to access a file for DIR, COPY, or similar commands. Unless you specify a path, DOS may not find the file you desire because it would search only the current directory of the default drive.

Specifying Paths in Commands.   One way to specify the path is to include it in the command you are using. For example, to make a backup copy on a diskette of a file named DOSNOTES.DOC stored in the FILES subdirectory under the WP subdirectory, type the command COPY C:\WP-\FILES\DOSNOTES.DOC A:. The COPY command includes the source drive (C:), both directories specified together (\WP\FILES), and the filename preceded by a backslash (\DOSNOTES.DOC). On drive A, the file is stored simply as DOSNOTES.DOC under the root directory, because no subdirectory has been made or referenced on that disk.

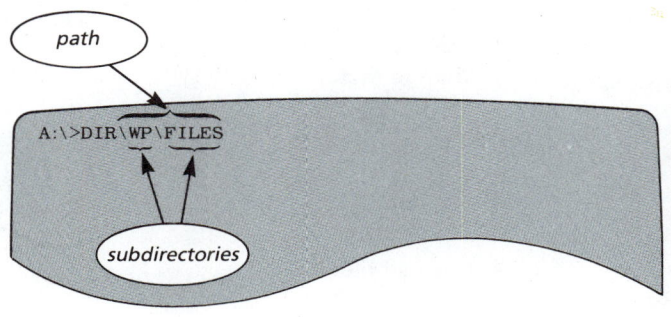

FIGURE 54

You can use this style with other DOS commands and when specifying files in many programs. For example, to display the file contents of the FILES subdirectory, enter DIR \WP\FILES and press the Enter key (Figure 54). Enter DIR \WP to list the program files for the word processing software stored under the WP subdirectory.

Managing Files Within Subdirectories

To copy files or data to subdirectories, you can use the COPY command or any file storage techniques offered by your application program. Some programs may not recognize the subdirectory structure on your diskette, so you may need to set the current directory before you use the program. The RENAME, DIR, ERASE, and other DOS commands work in subdirectories in nearly the same way as they do in the main directory.

Removing Subdirectories

When you no longer need a subdirectory, you can remove it. Use the **RMDIR command**, abbreviated to **RD**, to remove a specified directory from a disk.

Erasing Subdirectory Files.   To remove a subdirectory, you must first remove all files stored within it. You can do so by using the global character * with the ERASE command. You can issue this command from the subdirectory to be removed or from another directory if you give the full path specification. If you issue the command from another directory, make certain to use the correct subdirectory and path information or you might inadvertently erase files from another part of the disk.

For practice, delete the FILES subdirectory (Figure 55). First, enter the FILES subdirectory by typing the command CD\WP\FILES and pressing the Enter key. Next, empty the subdirectory of files by typing ERASE *.* and pressing the Enter key. You will receive the message "Are you sure (Y/N)?", to which you must press Y and then the Enter key.

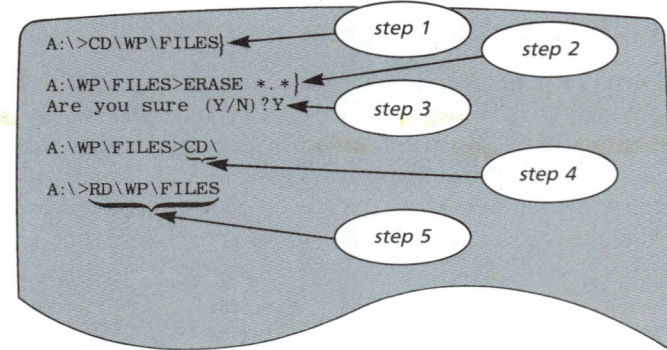

Step 1: Change the directory to WP\FILES.

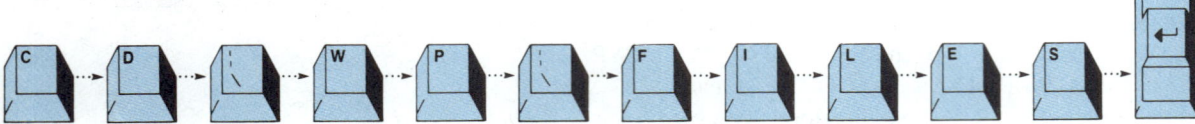

Step 2: Erase all files.

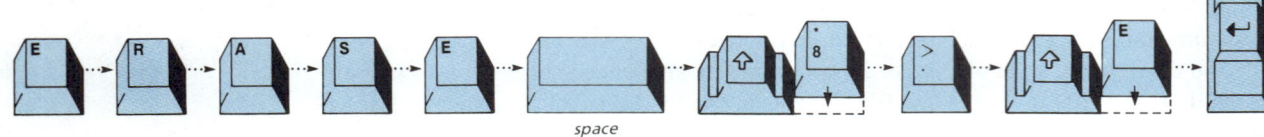

space

Step 3: Respond "Yes" to the prompt.   **Step 4: Change to the root directory.**

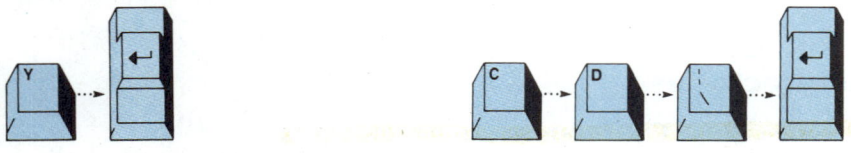

Step 5: Remove the FILES subdirectory.

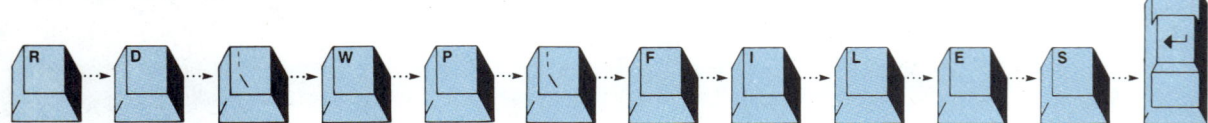

FIGURE 55   **Removing a Subdirectory.**   After you have emptied the subdirectory files, you can remove the subdirectory. Enter the root directory by typing the command CD\ and pressing the Enter key. To remove the FILES subdirectory, enter RD \WP\FILES and press the Enter key. Note that you must specify the full path, even though the WP directory is to remain. You must specify the full path so that DOS follows the path from the root directory, where the WP directory entry is stored, through the WP directory to find and remove the FILES entry.

LOADING A PROGRAM

 **program** is a series of instructions that specifies the steps your computer must perform to accomplish a specific purpose. To execute a program, you must first load the program into main memory from diskette or disk storage. The program must be

stored either on a diskette, which you have inserted into one of the disk drives, or on the internal hard disk. If you are using a two-diskette system, place the diskette containing the program to be executed in the default drive, usually drive A. Then type the program name (or name abbreviation) and press the Enter key. (Notice that loading and executing an application program is essentially the same as issuing an external DOS command.)

SUMMARY

1. An **operating system** is one or more programs that control and manage the operation of a computer.
2. The operating system for an IBM Personal Computer is **PC-DOS**. Other compatible computers use a similar program called **MS-DOS**.
3. The **version** number of a program is the whole number and signifies a major improvement of the product. The **release** number is the decimal number and identifies minor corrections or changes to a version of the product.
4. "**Booting**" the computer refers to loading the operating system from a disk into main memory.
5. The computer can be "booted" by turning it on with the operating system located on a disk in the computer. This is called a "cold start."
6. To reload the operating system when the computer is already switched on, hold down the **Control** and **Alternate** keys and press the **Delete** key. This process is called a "warm start" or "reset."
7. The operating system will **prompt** you for its commands. DOS has two general types of commands: (1) **internal commands** that are executed from the program stored in the main memory; (2) **external commands** that are programs loaded from a disk as the command is executed.
8. After the operating system has been loaded into main memory, you may be prompted to enter the date or time. Some systems have an internal clock that provides this information for you.
9. The **DOS prompt** includes the letter address of the **default disk drive**, the disk that is currently in use for data or program access.
10. The default drive of a two-diskette computer is usually drive A. A computer with a hard disk drive will generally use drive C as its default drive.
11. You can change the default drive by entering a valid drive letter, followed by a colon, and pressing the Enter key.
12. To examine files on a disk, issue the **DIR** (directory) command. Use the /P option to pause a long directory listing when the screen is full. Use the /W option to list files across the width of the screen.
13. Give the **pause-screen** command by holding down the Control key and pressing the S key.
14. Many commands can be canceled by holding down the **Control** key and pressing the **Break** key or by pressing Control-C.
15. Use the **FORMAT** command to prepare diskettes for storing data or program files. Several options are available for various types of diskettes. Use /S to format the diskette as a **system disk**. The /V option prompts a **volume label**.
16. Filenames must be created by following specific rules. A **filename** may consist of up to eight letters, numbers, or certain symbols. The filename **extension** is an optional one- to three-character addition, separated from the filename by a period.
17. Files with the extensions **.BAT**, **.COM**, or **.EXE** are external, executable command files.
18. Use the COPY command to transfer a file to another diskette or to create a backup file on the same diskette.
19. **Wildcards**, the * and ? characters, can be used in conjunction with many DOS commands to replace specific characters.
20. A file to be copied is the **source** file. The resulting copy is called the **target** file.
21. You can change a file's name by specifying the target file used during the COPY command or by using the **RENAME** command.
22. To remove a file from a diskette, execute the **ERASE** or the **DELETE** command.
23. Disks can be better organized through the use of **subdirectories**. A disk's primary directory is the **root** directory, signified by a **backslash** following the drive letter, such as C:\.
24. Use the **MKDIR** or the **MD** command to create a subdirectory. The entry includes the drive, backslash, and directory name, such as C:\WP.
25. To switch from one directory to another, use the **CHDIR** or **CD** command, for example, CD\WP.
26. A directory can be removed by first erasing all the files in the directory, then using the REMOVE DIRECTORY command, **RD**.
27. To **load a program** for execution, type the name of the program file at the DOS prompt.

STUDENT ASSIGNMENTS

True/False Questions

Instructions: Circle T if the statement is true or F if the statement is false.

T   F   1. PC-DOS and MS-DOS are essentially the same operation system.

T   F   2. When DOS is updated for a new version, programs operating in prior versions may not work under the newer edition.

T   F   3. The programs comprising an operating system such as PC-DOS can be stored on a diskette.

T   F   4. "Booting" the computer refers to the procedure of starting the operating system.

T   F   5. DOS commands are divided into two types: internal and external commands.

T   F   6. As a part of the system startup procedures, you are requested to enter the computer's serial number.

T   F   7. After the operating system has been loaded, you can type the command DIR and press the Enter key to display a directory of the diskette in the default drive.

T   F   8. The computer may have a built-in clock that the operating system automatically accesses to input the date and time.

T   F   9. The symbol A:>, which appears on the computer screen, is called the DOS Interlock.

T   F   10. A default disk drive is one that improperly stores data.

T   F   11. To change the disk drive assignment to drive C, type C:↵.

T   F   12. All DOS commands must be entered in uppercase characters.

T   F   13. You can list the directory of the default disk drive by typing DIR and pressing the Enter key.

T   F   14. The option /P used with the DIR command will cause the listing to pause when the screen is full.

T   F   15. Holding down the Control key and then pressing the Break key will cancel a command function.

T   F   16. To format a diskette, put the diskette to be formatted in disk drive A and enter the command FORMAT B:.

T   F   17. The command Copy A: can be used to copy all files from one disk drive to another.

T   F   18. The ERASE command can be used to remove a file from the file directory.

T   F   19. To include the operating system on a formatted disk, use the command FORMAT B:/S.

T   F   20. When you use the FORMAT option /V, the system will prompt you to enter a volume label.

T   F   21. To cancel a command, hold down the ALT key and press the END key.

T   F   22. A DOS filename may contain from 1 to 11 characters plus an optional extension of 1 to 3 characters.

T   F   23. The disk containing the file to be copied is known as the source disk.

T   F   24. Global replacement characters include *, ?, and \.

T   F   25. Hard disk drives are generally addressed as drive C.

T   F   26. Subdirectories on disks are used to group filename entries for convenient storage and retrieval.

T   F   27. A disk's main file directory is called the root directory.

T   F   28. The current directory is the one in which you are currently working.

T   F   29. To move from one current directory to another, use the MD command.

T   F   30. A file address contains the disk drive letter, the subdirectory path, and the filename.

T   F   31. A program cannot be loaded from a disk unless the program disk is in the current drive.

Multiple-Choice Questions

1. "Booting" the computer refers to
   a. loading the operating system
   b. placing covers over the disk drives
   c. using application programs to access disk drives
   d. the system interface
2. "DOS" stands for
   a. Digital Organizing Software
   b. Data Output Stream
   c. Disk Operating System
   d. Dielectric Orthanographic Startup
3. PC-DOS is used on IBM Personal Computers and Personal System/2 systems. IBM-compatible computers generally use
   a. PC-OMD
   b. MS-DOS
   c. XD-DOS
   d. CP/DUZ
4. A term describing your ability to use newer editions of software while retaining features and data used in earlier ones is
   a. software generation
   b. compatibility curve
   c. upward compatibility
   d. version control
5. When you start up the computer, you load the operating system
   a. from a diskette in drive A
   b. from the computer's internal memory
   c. from the fixed disk if the computer is so equipped
   d. both a and c
6. The term for restarting the operating system in a computer already powered on is
   a. warm start
   b. cold start
   c. warm boot
   d. both a and c
7. The symbol A>
   a. is called a DOS prompt
   b. indicates the name of a program
   c. indicates the default disk drive
   d. both a and c
8. Listing the files on a disk is accomplished by
   a. typing DIR and pressing the Enter key
   b. typing LIST and pressing the Enter key
   c. typing CHKDSK and pressing the Enter key
   d. typing RUN FILES and pressing the Enter key

9. To pause a listing on the screen, press
   a. Control and Break
   b. Alternate, Control, and Delete
   c. Control and S
   d. either b or c
10. To cancel a command, press
   a. Control and Break
   b. Alternate, Control, and Delete
   c. Control and S
   d. either c or d
11. The _____ command establishes sectors on a diskette and performs other functions that allow the diskette to store files.
   a. CHKDSK
   b. DIR
   c. REUSE
   d. FORMAT
12. A valid DOS filename specification consists of
   a. 10 alphanumeric characters
   b. a 9-character filename
   c. an 11-character name, separated by a period at any position within the name
   d. an 8-character filename plus an optional extension of a period followed by 3 characters
13. A common use of the COPY command is to make working copies of program and data disks, producing
   a. file disks
   b. backup copies
   c. extension disks
   d. authorized disks
14. To copy the file PROGRAM.EXE from drive A to drive B, type the command
   a. COPY PROGRAM.EXE TO DRIVE B
   c. COPY A:PROGRAM.EXE TO B:PROGRAM.EXE
   d. COPY A:PROGRAM.EXE B:
   3. either b or c
15. To copy all files on drive A to drive C, type the command
   a. COPY DRIVE A TO DRIVE C
   b. COPY ALL FILES TO C
   c. COPY A:?.* C:?.*
   d. COPY A: C:
16. To change the name of a file from FILEX.DOC to FILEA.DOC, enter
   a. ALTER FILEX.DOC TO FILEA.DOC
   b. CHANGE FILEX.DOC TO FILEA.DOC
   c. ASSIGN FILEX.DOC AS FILEA.DOC
   d. RENAME FILEX.DOC FILEA.DOC
17. To remove a file from a disk, type
   a. REMOVE FILE
   b. DELETE FILEX.DOC
   c. ERASE FILEX.DOC
   d. either b or c
18. Filenames are grouped on disks into
   a. index lists
   b. directories and subdirectories
   c. subject and filename entries
   d. internally labeled entries

19. The MKDIR, or MD, command will
    a. manage directory files
    b. make a directory on a disk
    c. create a file copy
    d. either a or b
20. To shift from the root directory to a directory of files under a word processing directory, type the command
    a. CH /FILES
    b. GOTO WP FILES
    c. CD \WP\FILES
    d. C:\WP\FILES*.*

Projects

1. Start your computer without a DOS disk in drive A. What is the display on the screen? Why did this display appear? Insert a DOS disk in drive A and restart the computer by pressing the Ctrl Alt Del keys simultaneously.
2. Start your computer with the DOS disk in the default disk drive. If permitted in your computer lab, prepare a new diskette as a system disk using the proper FORMAT command options for the task at hand and for the specific diskette your computer uses.
3. Prepare a diskette to be a file disk using the FORMAT command. Give the diskette a volume label using your own name. Determine the proper type of diskette to use on the computer and, after formatting, determine the amount of free space remaining on the diskette.
4. If permitted in your computer lab, create a working copy of your application program diskettes.
    a. First, format a new diskette. Will there be enough room on the diskette to contain both the operating system and the program? How can you know?
    b. Using one command, copy all files from the master copy of the disk to your newly prepared diskette.
5. Create a subdirectory named SUB1 on your diskette.
6. Make subdirectory SUB1 the current directory. Copy all .DOC files into SUB1 and display the directory.
7. Remove the subdirectory created in Assignment 8.

DOS Index

* (asterisk) character, **DOS 17**
? (question mark) character, **DOS 19**
: (colon), **DOS 8**

Asterisk (*) character, **DOS 17**

Backslash, DOS 22
Booting, **DOS 3**
Break key (^C), **DOS 9**

^C (break key), **DOS 9**
CHDIR (change directory) command, **DOS 24**
CLS (clear screen) command, **DOS 13**
Cold boot, **DOS 4**
Colon (:), **DOS 8**
Commands (See DOS commands)
Control-Break, **DOS 9**
COPY command, **DOS 14** (See also Copying)
Copying
  all files from one diskette to another, DOS 19
  to default disk, DOS 16
  global characters and, DOS 17–19
  from one diskette to another, DOS 15
  to same diskette, DOS 16–17
Current directory, **DOS 24**
Current drive (See Default drive)

Data file, **DOS 13**
Date, setting, DOS 4
Default drive, **DOS 5**
  changing, DOS 5–6
  copying to, DOS 16
DEL (delete) command, **DOS 21**
DIR (directory) command, **DOS 7**
Directories
  changing, DOS 24
  current, DOS 24
  file, DOS 7–9, DOS 21
  in other disk drives, DOS 7
  pausing display of, DOS 8
  root, DOS 21
  using, DOS 21–24
  wide display of, DOS 9
Diskette, formatting, DOS 9–12
Disk Operating System (See DOS)
DOS, **DOS 2**
  batch files (.BAT), **DOS 14**

file specification, DOS 13–14
loading, DOS 4
prompt in, DOS 5
using, DOS 3–6
versions of, DOS 3
DOS commands
  canceling, DOS 9
  CHDIR, DOS 24
  CLS, DOS 13
  COPY, DOS 14–19
  DEL, DOS 21
  DIR, DOS 7–9
  entering, DOS 6
  ERASE, DOS 21
  external, DOS 6
  FORMAT, DOS 10–12
  internal, DOS 6
  paths in, DOS 25
  RENAME, DOS 19–20
  RMDIR, DOS 25
  using wildcards with, DOS 19

ERASE command, **DOS 21**
External command, **DOS 6**

File(s)
  data, DOS 13
  naming, DOS 14
  path to, DOS 25
  program, DOS 13
  source, DOS 15
  in subdirectories, DOS 25
  target, DOS 15
File directory, DOS 7–9, **DOS 21**
Filename, **DOS 14**
  renaming, DOS 19–20
Filename extension, **DOS 14**
File specification, **DOS 13, DOS 15**
FORMAT command, DOS 10–12
Formatting, **DOS 9**
  system disk, DOS 12
  volume label, DOS 12

Global characters, **DOS 17**

Hard disk
  booting, DOS 3
  directories, DOS 7, 8
  formatting, DOS 10
  prompt, DOS 5

IBM PCs, operating systems for, DOS 2–3
Internal command, **DOS 6**

MKDIR command, (MD), **DOS 22**
MS-DOS, **DOS 2** (See also DOS)

Operating system, **DOS 2** (See also DOS)

/P (pause) option, **DOS 8**
Path, **DOS 25**
Pause (/P) option, **DOS 8**
PC-DOS, **DOS 2** (See also DOS)
Power-on self-test (POST) process, **DOS 4**
Program, **DOS 26**
Program file, **DOS 13**
PROMPT command, **DOS 22**

Question mark (?) character, **DOS 19**

Release number, **DOS 3**
RENAME command, **DOS 19**
RMDIR (remove directory) command, **DOS 25**
Root directory, **DOS 21**

/S (system) option, **DOS 12**
Software compatibility, DOS 3
Source file, **DOS 15**
Subdirectories, DOS 22
  file management in, DOS 25
  path to, DOS 25
  removing, DOS 25–26
  using, DOS 25–26
System disk (/S), **DOS 12**
System prompt, **DOS 5**

Target file, **DOS 15**
Time, setting, DOS 4

Upward compatibility, **DOS 3**
User interface, DOS 2

/V (volume label) option, **DOS 12**
Version number, **DOS 3**
Volume label (/V), **DOS 12**

/W (wide) option, **DOS 9**
Warm boot, **DOS 4**
Wide display (/W) option, **DOS 9**
Wildcards, **DOS 17**

Photo Credits: **Opening Page and Figure 2a**, Radio Shack, a division of Tandy Corp.; **Figures 2b and 3a**, Compaq Computer Corp.; **Figure 3b**, International Business Machines Corp.

Spreadsheets Using VP-Planner Plus

PROJECT 1
Building a Worksheet
STARTING VP-PLANNER PLUS
THE WORKSHEET
MOVING THE CELL CURSOR ONE
CELL AT A TIME
ENTERING LABELS
ENTERING NUMBERS
MOVING THE CELL CURSOR MORE
THAN ONE CELL AT A TIME
ENTERING FORMULAS
SAVING A WORKSHEET
PRINTING A SCREEN IMAGE OF THE
WORKSHEET
CORRECTING ERRORS
ONLINE HELP FACILITY
QUITTING VP-PLANNER PLUS (/Q)
PROJECT SUMMARY
STUDENT ASSIGNMENTS

PROJECT 2
**Formatting and Printing a
Worksheet**
RETRIEVING A WORKSHEET (/FR)
CHANGING THE WIDTH OF THE
COLUMNS
DEFINING A RANGE
FORMATTING NUMERIC VALUES
REPEATING CHARACTERS IN A CELL
REPLICATION—THE COPY
COMMAND (/C)
SAVING AN INTERMEDIATE COPY OF
THE WORKSHEET
USING BUILT-IN FUNCTIONS
DETERMINING A PERCENT VALUE
FORMATTING TO PERCENT AND
CURRENCY
SAVING THE WORKSHEET A SECOND
TIME
PRINTING THE WORKSHEET
DEBUGGING THE FORMULAS IN A
WORKSHEET USING THE TEXT
FORMAT
PROJECT SUMMARY
STUDENT ASSIGNMENTS

PROJECT 3
Enhancing Your Worksheet
VARYING THE WIDTH OF THE
COLUMNS
FORMATTING THE WORKSHEET
GLOBALLY (/WGF)
DISPLAYING THE DATE AND TIME
ENTERING THE QUARTERLY BUDGET
LABELS
INSERTING AND DELETING ROWS
AND COLUMNS
COPYING CELLS WITH EQUAL
SOURCE AND DESTINATION
RANGES
ENTERING NUMBERS WITH A
PERCENT SIGN
FREEZING THE TITLES
MOVING THE CONTENTS OF CELLS
(/M)
DISPLAYING FORMULAS AND
FUNCTIONS IN THE CELLS (/RFT)
ABSOLUTE VERSUS RELATIVE
ADDRESSING
POINTING TO A RANGE OF CELLS TO
SUM
SAVING AND PRINTING THE
WORKSHEET
WHAT-IF QUESTIONS
CHANGING THE WORKSHEET
DEFAULT SETTINGS (/WGD)
CHANGING THE SCREEN SO THAT IT
LOOKS LIKE THE LOTUS 1-2-3
SCREEN
THE UNDO AND REDO KEYS
INTERACTING WITH DOS
PROJECT SUMMARY
STUDENT ASSIGNMENTS

PROJECT 4
**Building Worksheets with
Functions and Macros**
PROJECT 4A—ANALYZING STUDENT
TEST SCORES
PROJECT 4B—DETERMINING THE
MONTHLY PAYMENT FOR A CAR
LOAN
MACROS
WINDOWS (/WW)
CELL PROTECTION (/WGPE)
OBTAINING A SUMMARY OF ALL
THE VP-PLANNER PLUS
FUNCTIONS
PROJECT SUMMARY
STUDENT ASSIGNMENTS

PROJECT 5
Graphing with VP-Planner Plus
THE GRAPH COMMAND (/G)
PIE CHARTS (/GTP)
LINE GRAPHS (/GTL)
BAR GRAPHS (/GTB or /GTS)
ADDITIONAL GRAPH OPTIONS (/GO)
XY GRAPHS (/GTX)
PROJECT SUMMARY
STUDENT ASSIGNMENTS

PROJECT 6
**Sorting and Querying a Worksheet
Database**
SORTING A DATABASE
QUERYING A DATABASE
THE DATABASE FUNCTIONS
THE LOOKUP FUNCTIONS
PROJECT SUMMARY
STUDENT ASSIGNMENTS

PROJECT 1

Building a Worksheet

Objectives

You will have mastered the material in this Project when you can:

- Start VP-Planner Plus
- Describe the worksheet
- Move the cell cursor around the worksheet
- Enter labels, numbers, and formulas into a worksheet
- Save a worksheet
- Print the screen image of the worksheet
- Correct errors in a worksheet
- Answer your questions regarding VP-Planner Plus using the online help facility
- Quit VP-Planner Plus

n Project 1 we will develop the worksheet illustrated in Figure 1-1. It contains a company's first quarter sales report. To build this worksheet, we will enter the revenues and costs for January, February, and March. VP-Planner Plus calculates the profit for each month by subtracting the cost from the revenue.

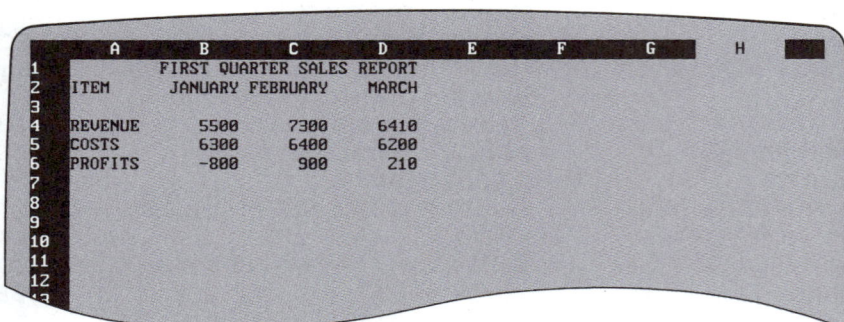

FIGURE 1-1
The worksheet we will build in Project 1.

STARTING VP-PLANNER PLUS

Boot the computer following the procedures presented earlier in the Introduction to DOS. Next, follow the steps listed on the next page for your type of computer system. Several seconds will elapse while the VP-Planner Plus program is loaded from the disk into main computer memory. The red light on the disk drive turns on during this loading process. After VP-Planner Plus is loaded into main computer memory, it is automatically executed. The first screen displayed by VP-Planner Plus is the worksheet with the copyright message, shown in Figure 1-2. Press the Enter key and the copyright message disappears, leaving the worksheet illustrated in Figure 1-3.

Computer with One or Two Floppy Disks and No Fixed Disk

To start VP-Planner Plus from a computer with one or two floppy disks and no fixed disk, do the following:

1. Replace the DOS disk in drive A with the VP-Planner Plus program disk. If you have two floppy disks, place your data disk in drive B.
2. At the A > prompt, enter the letters VPP (or vpp) and press the Enter key.
3. If you have only one floppy disk, replace the program disk in drive A with your data disk after the program is loaded.

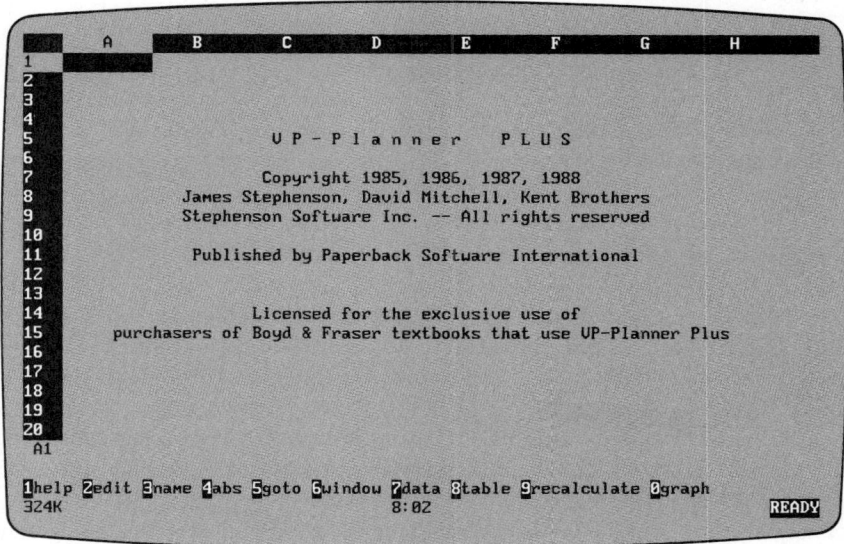

FIGURE 1-2 The copyright screen displays when you load VP-Planner Plus.

Computer with a Fixed Disk

To start VP-Planner Plus from a fixed disk, do the following:

1. Use the DOS command CD to change to the subdirectory containing the VP-Planner Plus program.
2. Place your data disk in drive A.
3. At the DOS prompt, enter the letters VPP (or vpp) and press the Enter key.

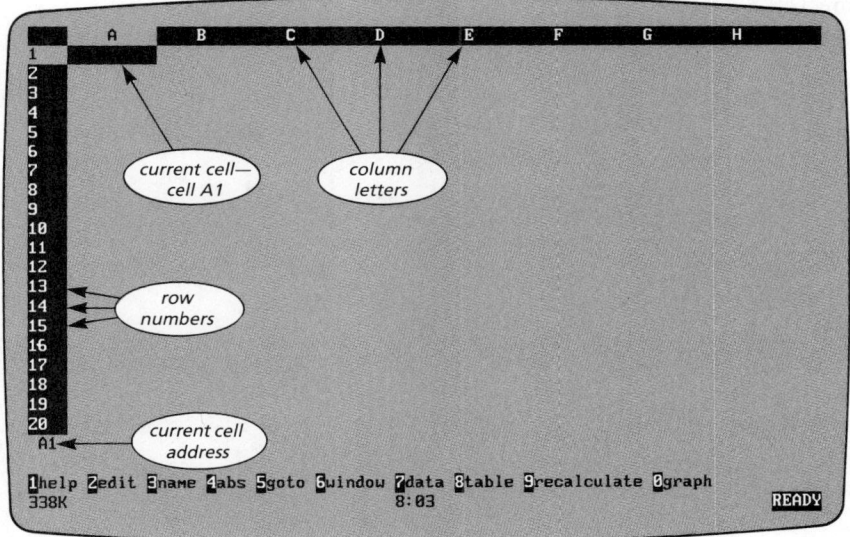

FIGURE 1-3 The worksheet.

THE WORKSHEET

**T**he worksheet is organized into a rectangular grid containing columns (vertical) and rows (horizontal). In the border at the top, each **column** is identified by a column letter. In the border on the left side, each **row** is identified by a row number. As shown in Figure 1-3, eight columns (A to H) and twenty rows (1 to 20) of the worksheet appear on the screen.

Cell, Cell Cursor, and Window

Within the borders is the worksheet. It has three parts: cell, cell cursor and window. A **cell** is the intersection of a column and a row. It is referred to by its **cell address**, the coordinates of the intersection of a column and a row. When you specify a cell address, you must name the column first, followed by the row. For example, cell address D3 refers to the cell located at the intersection of column D and row 3.

One cell on the worksheet is designated the current cell. The **current cell** is the one in which you can enter data. The current cell in Figure 1-3 is A1. It is identified in two ways. First, a reverse video rectangle called the **cell cursor** displays over the current cell. Second, the **current cell address** displays on the first of four lines at the bottom of the screen. It is important to understand the layout of the worksheet and how to identify all cells, including the current cell.

The educational version of VP-Planner Plus has 64 columns and 256 rows for a total of 16,384 cells, while the complete version of VP-Planner Plus has 256 columns and 9,999 rows for a total of 2,559,744 cells. In either case, only a small portion of the rectangular worksheet displays on the screen at any one time. For this reason, the area between the borders on the screen is called a **window**. Think of your screen as a window through which you can see parts of the worksheet as illustrated in Figure 1-4.

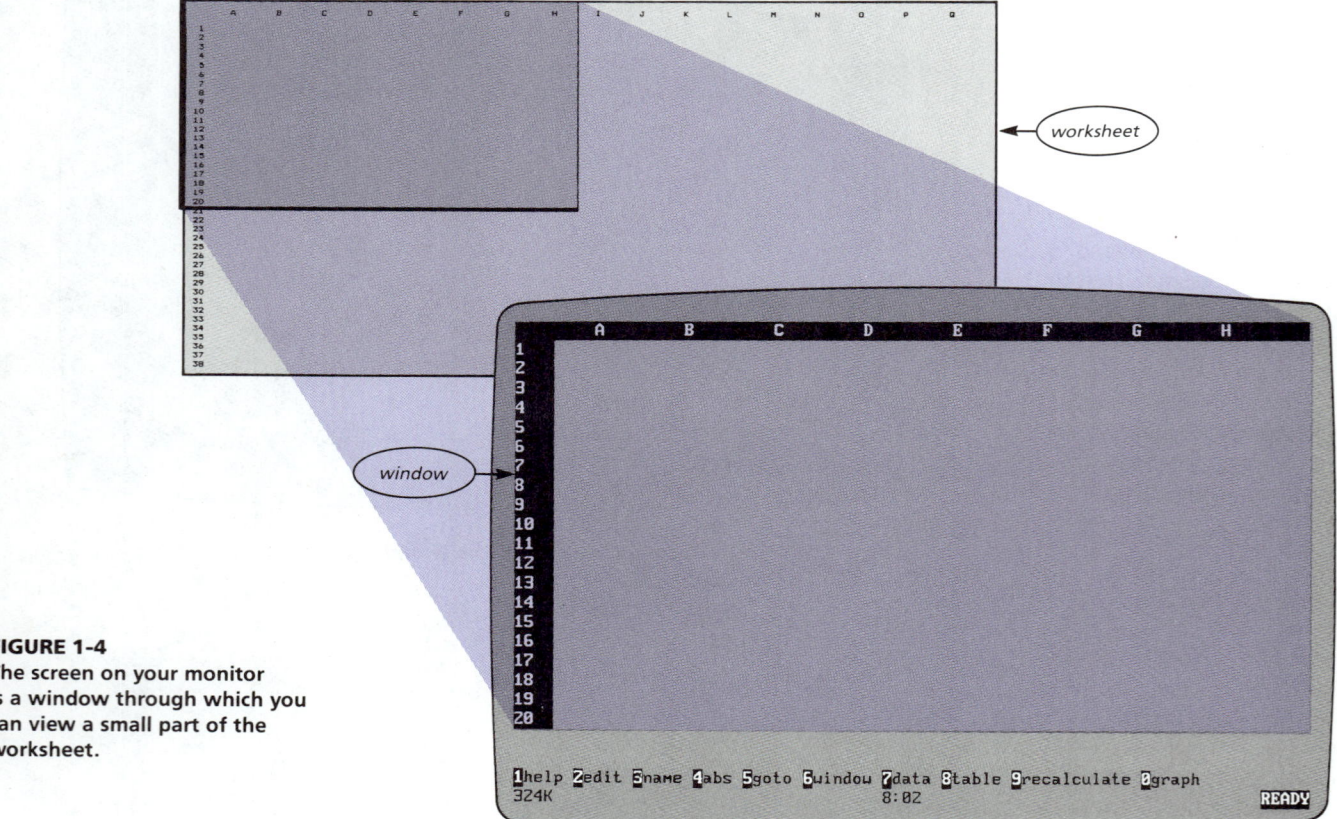

FIGURE 1-4
The screen on your monitor
is a window through which you
can view a small part of the
worksheet.

The Control Panel and the Current-Mode Line

Below the window are four lines that display important information about the worksheet. The first three lines—status line, input line, and prompt line—are collectively called the **control panel**. The bottom line is called the current-mode line. These four lines are illustrated in Figure 1-5.

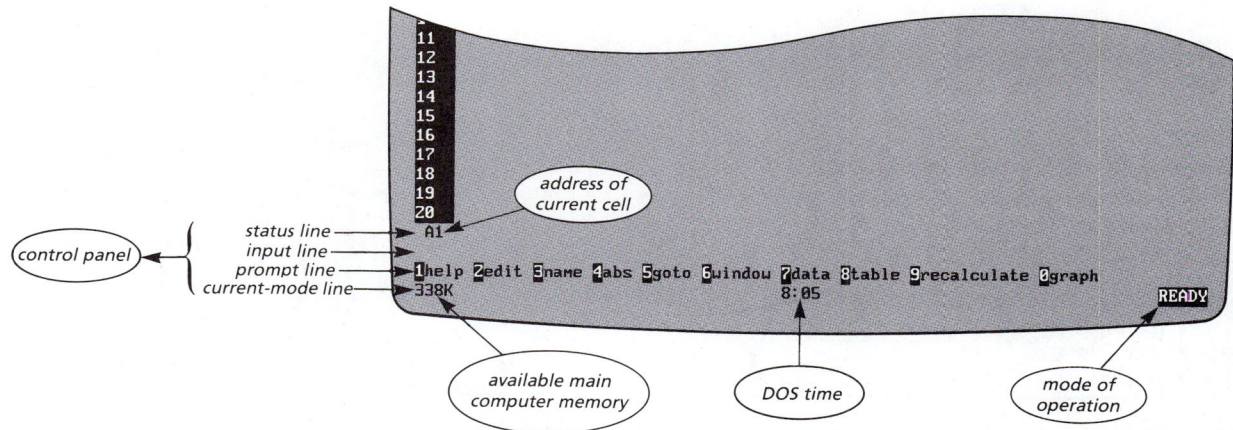

FIGURE 1-5 The control panel and the current-mode line at the bottom of the screen.

Status Line   The status line, the first line below the window, identifies the current cell address. If data is already in the current cell, the status line also shows the type of entry and its contents.

Input Line   Just below the status line is the input line. The input line shows what you are typing as you enter data into a cell.

Prompt Line   The prompt line, the third line, displays a menu that describes the purpose of the function keys. For example, the word "help" follows the digit 1 on the prompt line. Therefore, if you press function key F1 (see Figure 1-6 on the next page), VP-Planner Plus displays a screen of helpful information relating to the current program mode or command. The function keys may be located at the far left side or at the top of the keyboard. In either case, the function keys work the same. For these projects, we assume that the function keys are located at the far left side of the keyboard.

Current-Mode Line   The line at the very bottom of the screen is the **current-mode line**. It displays four items: the amount of main computer memory that remains for your worksheet, the time of day as maintained by DOS, status indicators, and the current mode of VP-Planner Plus. Status indicators, like CAPS, CIRC, END, ERROR, NUM, SCROLL, and WAIT, tell you which keys are engaged and alert you to special worksheet conditions.

Current-mode indicators, like EDIT, LABEL, MENU, POINT, and READY, tell you the current mode of operation of VP-Planner Plus. For now you should know that when the mode indicator READY displays (see Figure 1-5), VP-Planner Plus is ready to accept your next command or data entry. When the status indicator WAIT displays in place of READY, VP-Planner Plus is busy performing some operation that is not instantaneous, like saving a worksheet to disk.

MOVING THE CELL CURSOR ONE CELL AT A TIME

Before you can build a worksheet, you must learn how to move the cell cursor to the cells in which you want to make entries. Several methods let you easily move to any cell in the worksheet. The most popular method is to use the four arrow keys located on the numeric keypad. Figure 1-7 illustrates a numeric keypad on a computer keyboard.

FIGURE 1-6 The function keys on the keyboard.

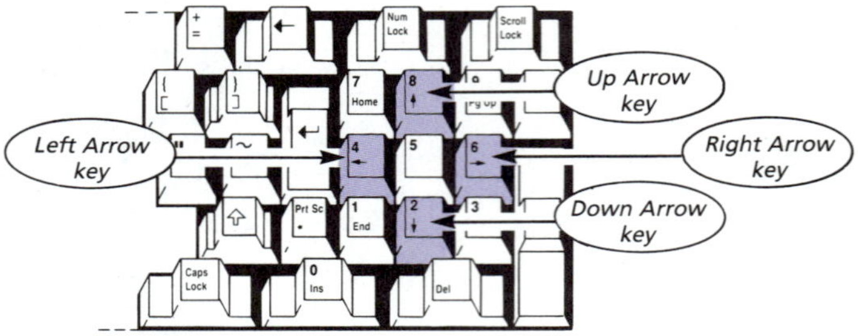

FIGURE 1-7 The arrow keys on the keyboard.

On some computers, you have a choice of two sets of arrow keys. One set, as shown in Figure 1-7, is part of the numeric keypad. The other set is located just to the left of the numeric keypad. If you have two sets of arrow keys, use the **Num Lock key** to activate one set or the other. When the Num Lock key is on, a red light on the key indicates that the arrow keys to the left are active. When the red light is off, the arrow keys on the numeric keypad are active.

For these projects we use the arrow keys located on the numeric keypad. The arrow keys on the numeric keypad work as follows:

1. **Down Arrow key** (↓) moves the cell cursor directly down one cell.
2. **Left Arrow key** (←) moves the cell cursor one cell to the left.
3. **Right Arrow key** (→) moves the cell cursor one cell to the right.
4. **Up Arrow key** (↑) moves the cell cursor directly up one cell.

In the sample worksheet in Figure 1-1, the title FIRST QUARTER SALES REPORT begins in cell B1. Therefore, we must move the cell cursor from cell A1, where it is when VP-Planner Plus starts, to cell B1 so we can enter the title. Do this by pressing the Right Arrow key one time, as shown in Figure 1-8. Notice that the current cell address on the status line in the lower left corner of the screen changes from A1 to B1. Remember, the current cell address on the status line always identifies the current cell—the one where the cell cursor is.

ENTERING LABELS

With the cell cursor on the proper cell (B1), we can enter the title of the worksheet. In the title FIRST QUARTER SALES REPORT, all the letters are capitals. While it is possible to enter capital letters by holding down one of the Shift keys on the keyboard each time you type a letter, a more practical method is to press the **Caps Lock key** one time (Figure 1-9).

The word CAPS on the current-mode line in Figure 1-9 indicates that the Caps Lock key is engaged. Therefore, all subsequent letters you type will be accepted by VP-Planner Plus as capital letters. Note, however, that both uppercase and lowercase letters are valid in a worksheet, and that the letters appear in the same case as they are entered. The Caps Lock key affects only the keys representing letters. Digit and special-character keys continue to transmit the lower character on the key when you press them, unless you hold down a Shift key while pressing the key. To enter a lowercase letter when the Caps Lock key is engaged, hold down the Shift key while typing the letter.

Labels That Begin with a Letter

Entering the title is simple. Just type the required letters on the computer keyboard. Type the words FIRST QUARTER SALES REPORT on the keyboard to get the display shown in Figure 1-10.

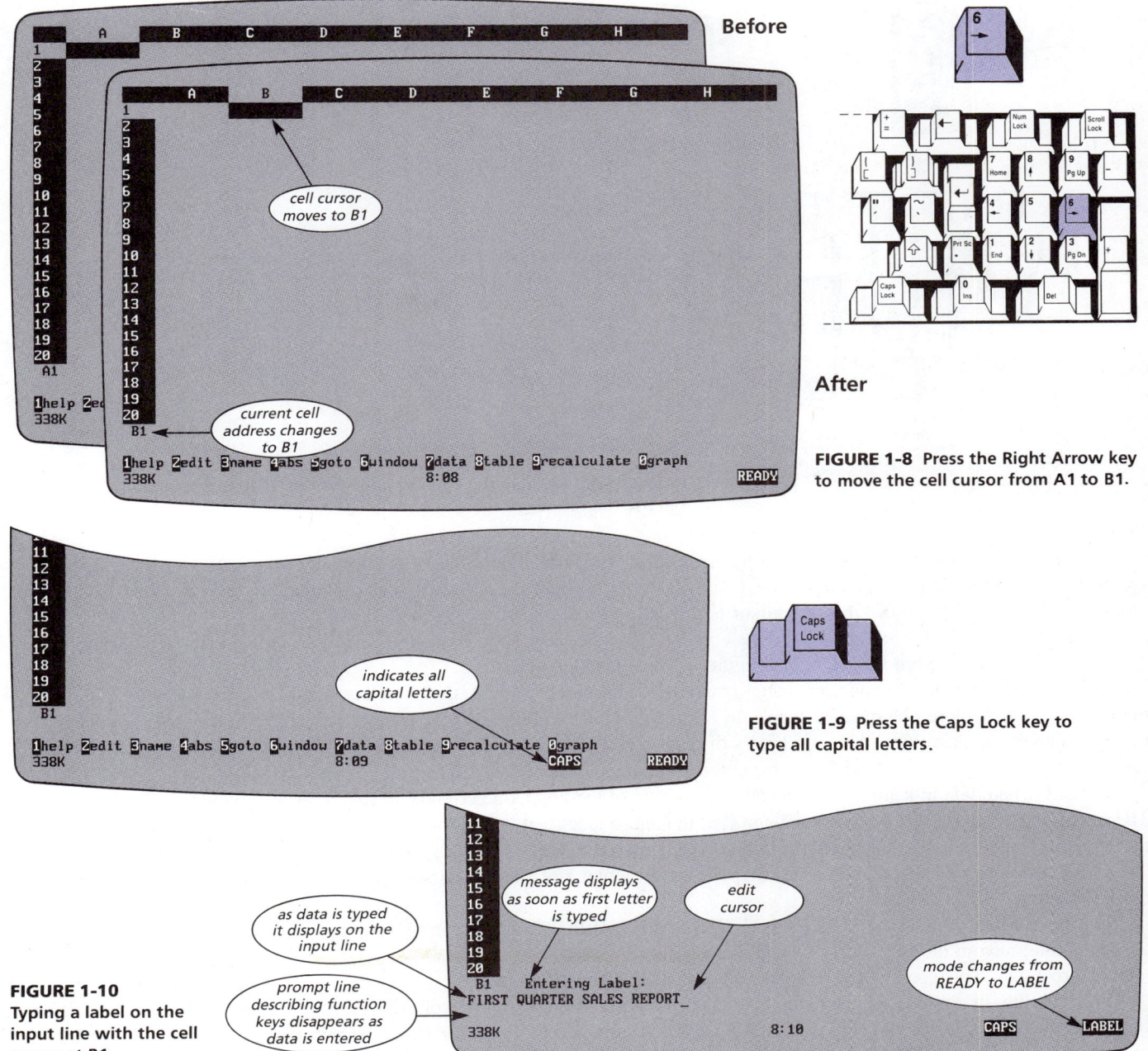

Before

cell cursor moves to B1

current cell address changes to B1

FIGURE 1-8 Press the Right Arrow key to move the cell cursor from A1 to B1.

After

indicates all capital letters

FIGURE 1-9 Press the Caps Lock key to type all capital letters.

FIGURE 1-10
Typing a label on the input line with the cell cursor at B1.

as data is typed it displays on the input line

prompt line describing function keys disappears as data is entered

message displays as soon as first letter is typed

edit cursor

mode changes from READY to LABEL

Entering Label:
FIRST QUARTER SALES REPORT_

Figure 1-10 shows three important features. First, as soon as we enter the first character of the report title, the message "Entering Label:" displays next to the cell address in the lower left corner of the screen. VP-Planner Plus determines that the entry is a **label** because the first character typed is a letter. Second, the status indicator in the lower right corner of the screen changes from READY to LABEL.

Third, as we type the report title, it displays on the input line followed immediately by the edit cursor. The **edit cursor** is a small, blinking underline symbol. It indicates where the next character typed will be placed on the input line.

Although the data appears at the bottom of the screen on the input line, it still is not in cell B1. To assign the title to cell B1, press the Enter key as shown in Figure 1-11. This causes the report title displayed on the input line to be placed in the worksheet beginning at cell B1, the cell identified by the cell cursor.

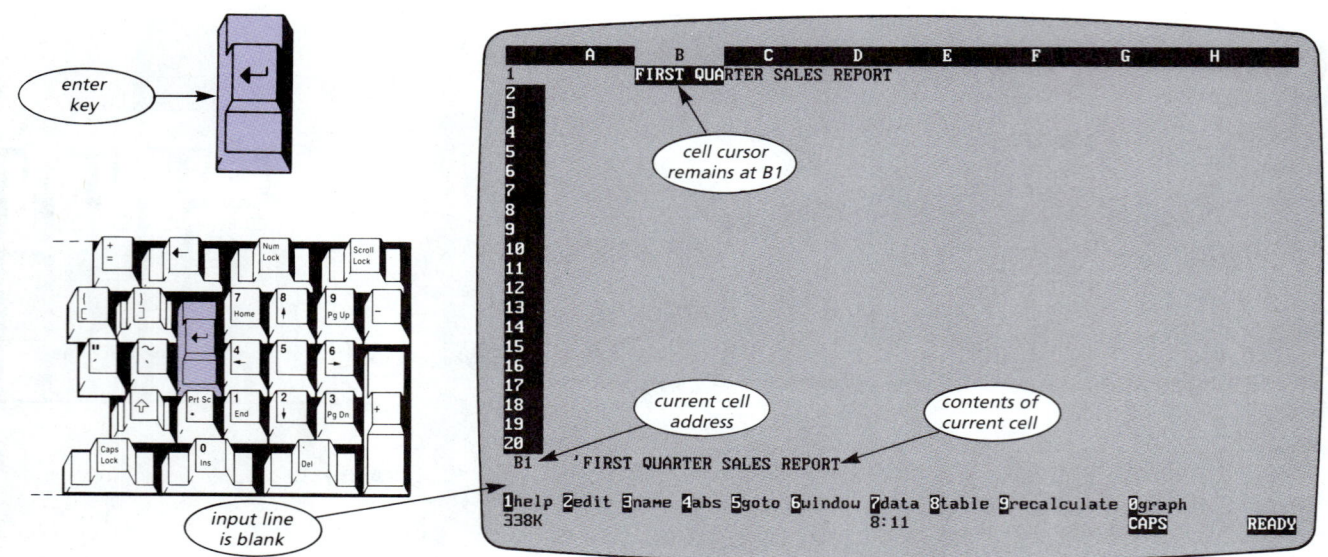

FIGURE 1-11   Pressing the Enter key assigns the label on the input line to cell B1. The cell cursor remains at B1.

If you type the wrong letter and notice the error while it is on the input line at the bottom of the screen, use the **Backspace key** (above the Enter key on the keyboard) to erase all the characters back to and including the ones that are wrong. If you see an error in a cell, move the cell cursor to the cell in question and retype the entry.

When you enter a label, a series of events occurs. First, the label is positioned left-justified in the cell where it begins. Therefore, the F in the word FIRST begins in the leftmost position of cell B1.

Second, when a label has more characters than the width of the column, the characters are placed in adjacent columns to the right so long as these columns are blank. In Figure 1-11, the width of cell B1 is nine characters. The words we entered have 26 characters. Therefore, the extra letters display in cell C1 (nine characters) and cell D1 (eight characters), since both cell C1 and cell D1 were blank when we made the 26-character entry in cell B1.

If cell C1 had data in it, only the first nine characters of the 26-character entry in cell B1 would show on the worksheet. The remaining 17 characters would be hidden, but the entire label that belongs to the cell displays in the lower left corner of the screen on the status line whenever the cell cursor is moved to B1.

Third, when you enter data into a cell by pressing the Enter key, the cell cursor remains on the cell (B1) in which you make the entry.

Fourth, a label, in this case FIRST QUARTER SALES REPORT, appears in two places on the screen: in the cell and on the status line, next to the cell address. Note that VP-Planner Plus adds an apostrophe (`) before the label on the status line (see Figure 1-11). This apostrophe identifies the data as a left-justified label.

With the title in cell B1, the next step is to enter the column titles in row 2 of the worksheet. Therefore, move the cell cursor from cell B1 to cell A2 by using the arrow keys (see Figure 1-12). Press the Down Arrow key and then the Left Arrow key. Pressing the Down Arrow key once causes the cell cursor to move to cell B2. Then pressing the Left Arrow key once causes the cell cursor to move to cell A2. Remember that pressing an arrow key one time moves the cell cursor one cell in the direction of the arrow. The current cell address changes on the status line from B1 to A2.

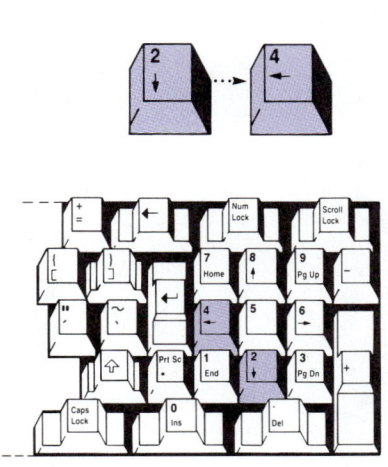

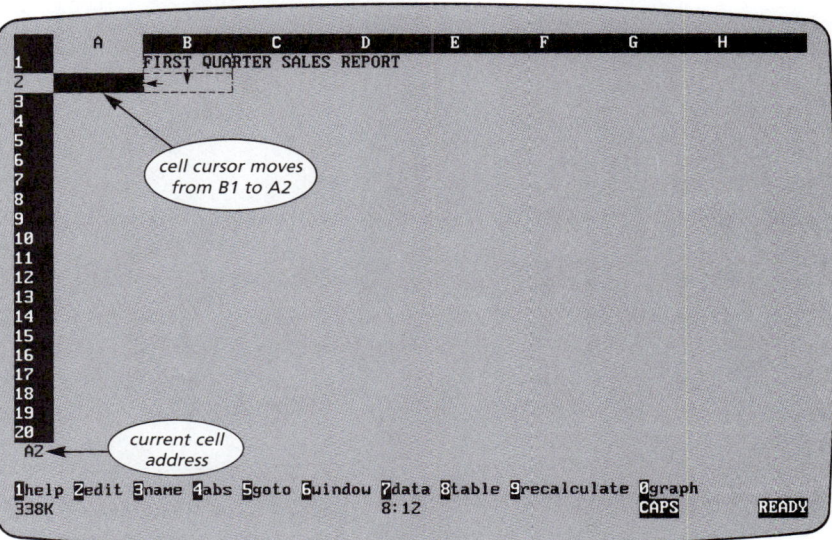

With the cell cursor on A2, enter the label ITEM as shown on the input line in Figure 1-13. Since the entry starts with a letter, VP-Planner Plus will position the label left-justified in the current cell. To enter the label in cell A2 we could press the Enter key as we did for the report title in cell B1. But another way is to press any one of the four arrow keys, as shown in Figure 1-14 on the next page. Press the Right Arrow key. This is the better alternative because not only is the data entered into the current cell, but the cell cursor also moves one cell to the right. The cell cursor is at cell B2, the location of the next entry.

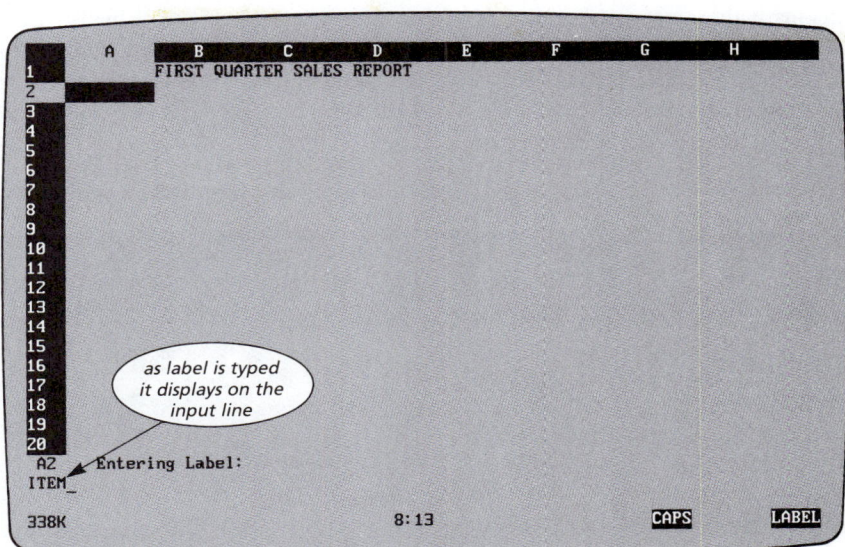

FIGURE 1-13
Typing a label on the input line.

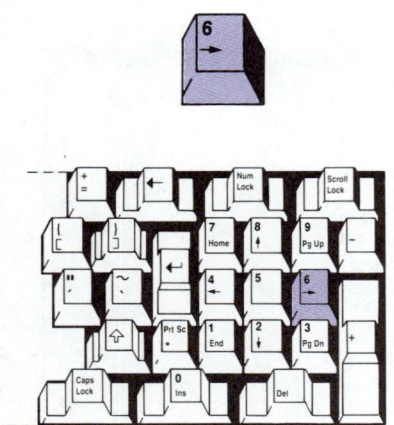

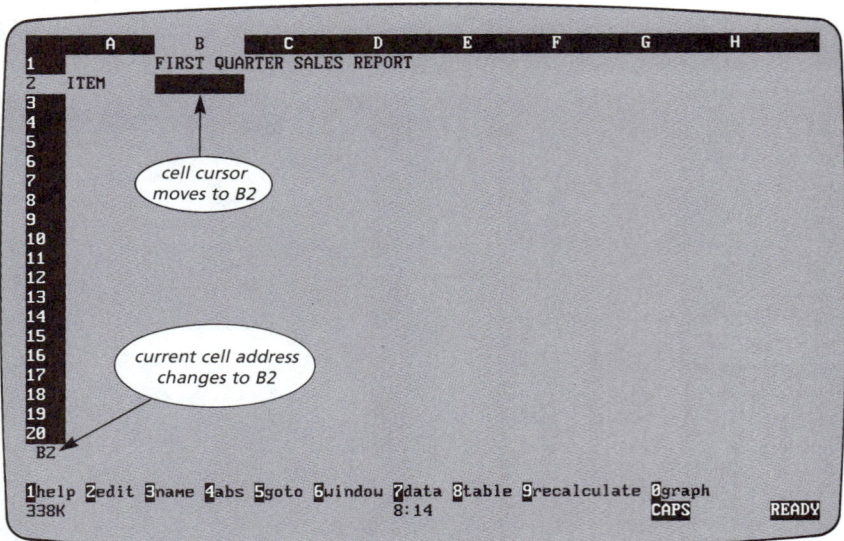

FIGURE 1-14 Pressing the Right Arrow key rather than the Enter key assigns the label on the input line to cell A2 and moves the cell cursor one cell to the right to B2.

Labels Preceded by a Special Character

The worksheet in Figure 1-1 that we are in the process of building requires that the column headings JANUARY, FEBRUARY, and MARCH be positioned right-justified in the cell, rather than left-justified. There are three different ways to position labels in a cell: left-justified, right-justified, or centered. Remember that the first character of the entry instructs VP-Planner Plus how to place the label in the cell.

If a label begins with a letter or apostrophe ('), VP-Planner Plus positions the label left-justified in the current cell. If a label begins with a quotation mark ("), it is positioned right-justified. Finally, if a label begins with a circumflex (^), it is centered within the cell. When the first character is an apostrophe, quotation mark, or circumflex, VP-Planner Plus does not consider the special character to be part of the label and it will not appear in the cell. However, the special character will precede the label on the status line when the cell cursor is on the cell in question. Table 1-1 summarizes the positioning of labels in a cell.

TABLE 1-1   Positioning Labels within a Cell

FIRST CHARACTER OF DATA	DATA ENTERED	POSITION IN CELL	REMARK
1. Letter	ITEM	ITEM	Left-justified in cell.
2. Apostrophe (')	'9946	9946	Left-justified in cell. The label 9946 is a name, like the address on a house, and not a number.
3. Quotation Mark (")	"MARCH	MARCH	Right-justified in cell. This always results in one blank character at the end of the label in the cell.
4. Circumflex (^)	^MARCH	MARCH	Centered in the cell.

With the cell cursor located at cell B2, enter the column heading JANUARY preceded by a quotation mark (") as shown in Figure 1-15, and then press the Right Arrow key. The word JANUARY appears, right-justified, in cell B2 and the cell cursor moves to cell C2 in preparation for the next entry. This procedure is shown in Figure 1-16.

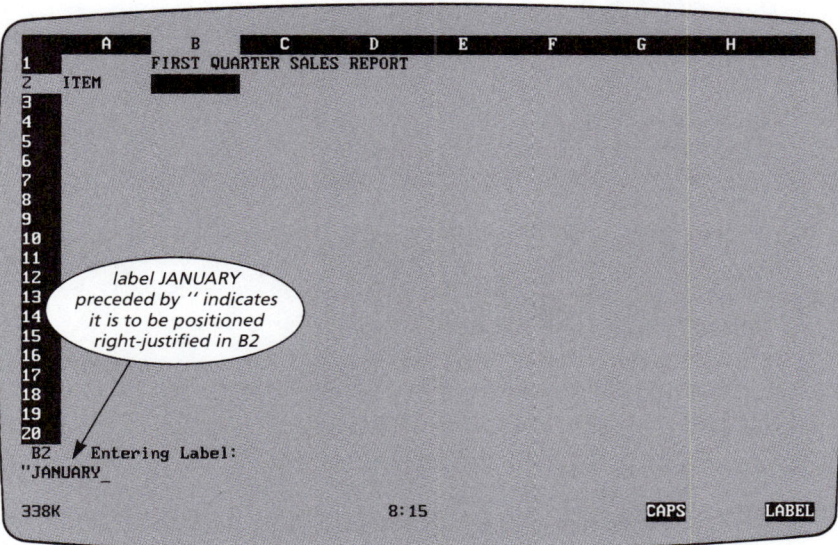

FIGURE 1-15 Begin a label with a quotation mark (") to make it right-justified.

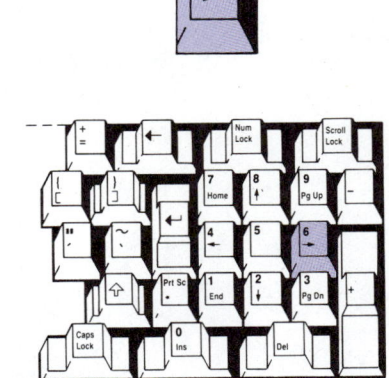

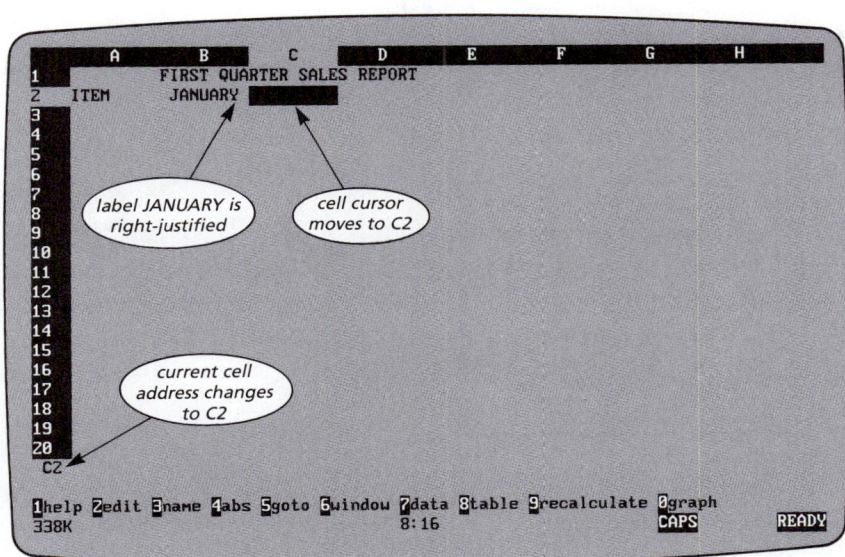

FIGURE 1-16 Pressing the Right Arrow key assigns the label on the input line to cell B2 and moves the cell cursor one cell to the right to C2.

Next, enter the month name FEBRUARY in cell C2 and the month name MARCH in cell D2. Enter both labels right-justified. That is, precede each month name with the quotation mark ("). Press the Right Arrow key after typing each label. With these latest entries, the worksheet appears as illustrated in Figure 1-17.

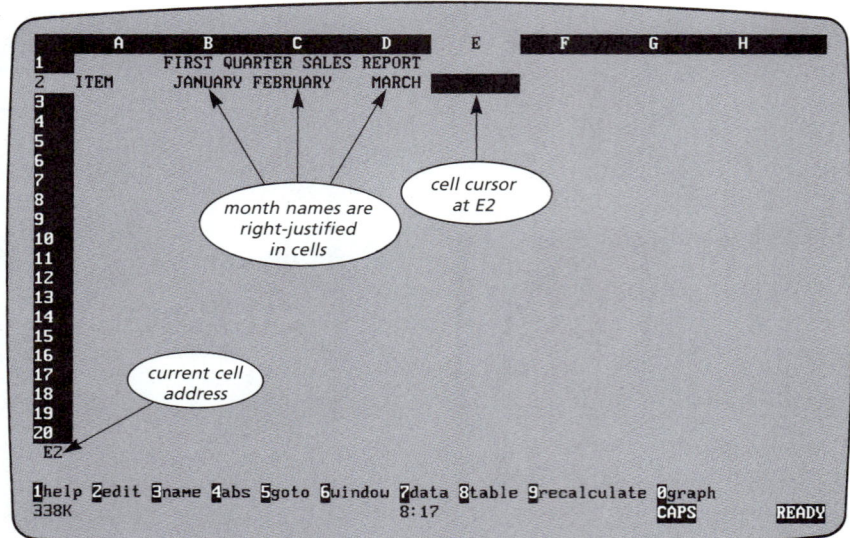

FIGURE 1-17
The three month names entered right-justified.

The cell cursor is now located at cell E2, but according to Figure 1-1 no data is to be entered into cell E2. The next entry is the label REVENUE in cell A4. Therefore, move the cell cursor from cell E2 to cell A4. Press the Down Arrow key twice and the Left Arrow key four times, as shown in Figure 1-18.

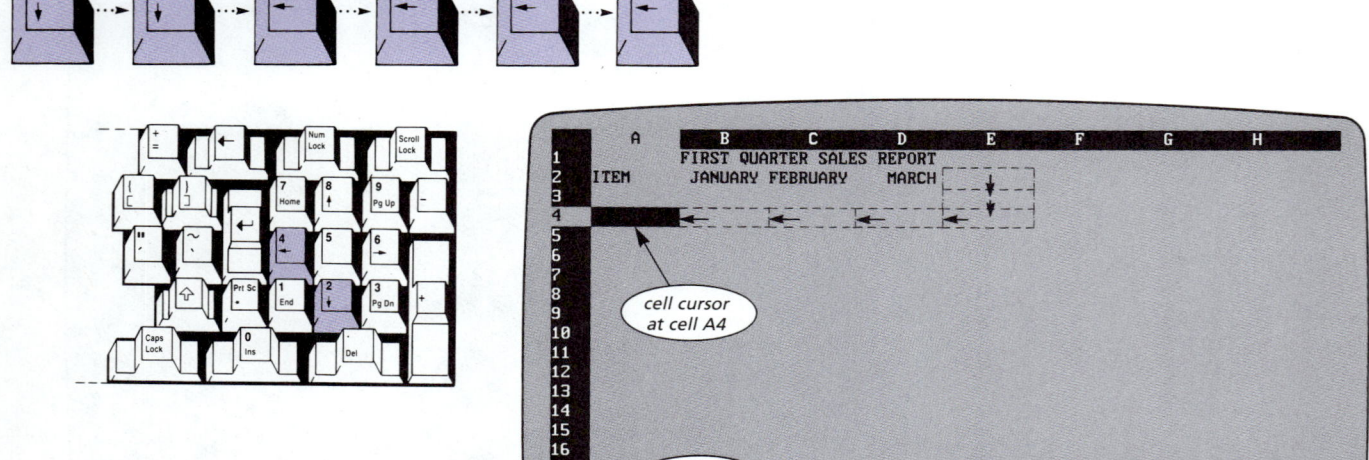

FIGURE 1-18
Using the arrow keys to move the cell cursor from E2 to A4.

With the cell cursor at A4, type the label REVENUE and press the Right Arrow key. The cell cursor moves to cell B4 as shown in Figure 1-19.

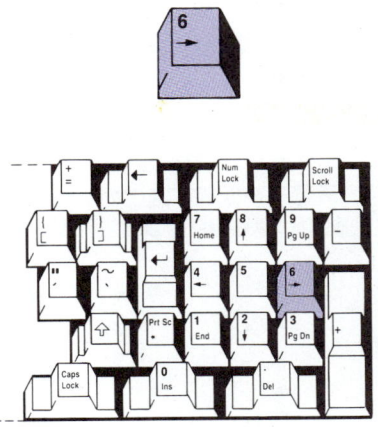

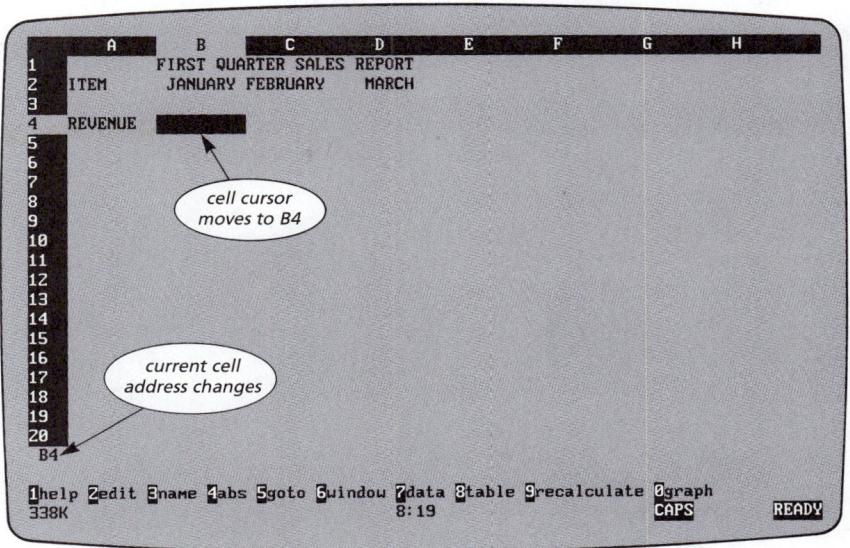

FIGURE 1-19
Pressing the Right Arrow key
assigns the label on the input line to cell A4
and moves the cell cursor to B4.

ENTERING NUMBERS

 umbers are entered into cells to represent amounts. Numbers are also called **values**. VP-Planner Plus assumes that an entry for a cell is a number or a formula if the first character you type is one of the following:

0 1 2 3 4 5 6 7 8 9 (@ + − . # $

Whole Numbers

With the cell cursor located in cell B4, enter the revenue amount for January. As shown in Figure 1-1, this amount is 5500. Type the amount 5500 on the keyboard without any special character preceding the number (see Figure 1-20). Remember, the CAPS indicator affects only the keys that represent letters on the keyboard. Therefore, never hold down a Shift key to enter a number.

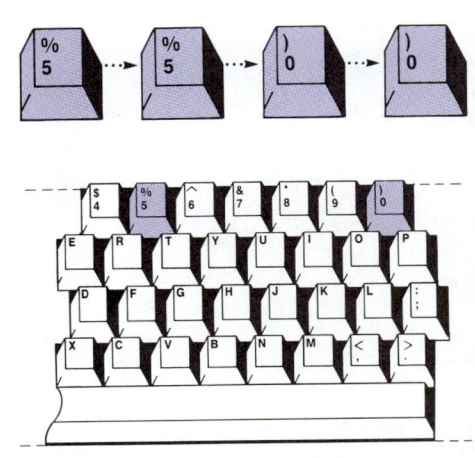

FIGURE 1-20
Entering a number on the input line.

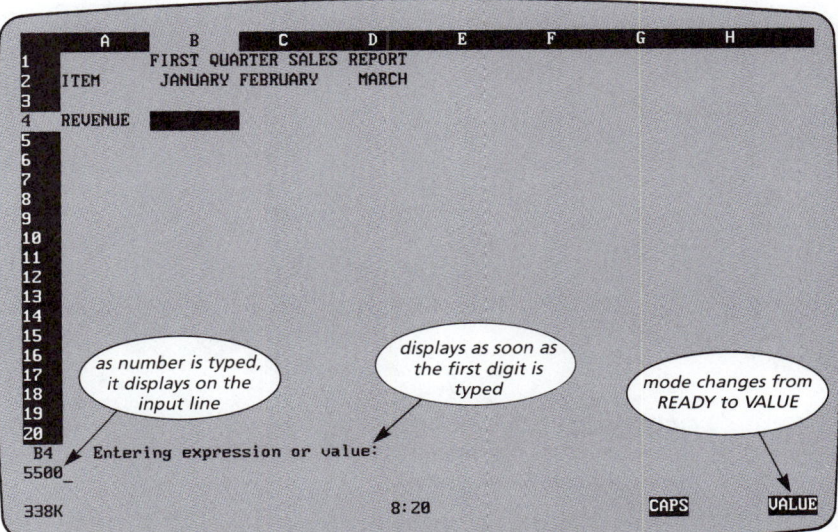

As soon as we enter the first digit, 5, the message "Entering expression or value:" displays on the status line next to the cell address. Also, the status indicator on the current-mode line changes from READY to VALUE. As we type the value 5500, it displays in the lower left corner of the screen on the input line followed immediately by the edit cursor.

Press the Right Arrow key to enter the number 5500 in cell B4 and move the cell cursor one cell to the right. The number 5500 displays right-justified in cell B4 as shown in Figure 1-21. Numbers always display right-justified in a cell. As with right-justified labels, a blank is added to the right of a number when it is assigned to a cell (see Table 1-1).

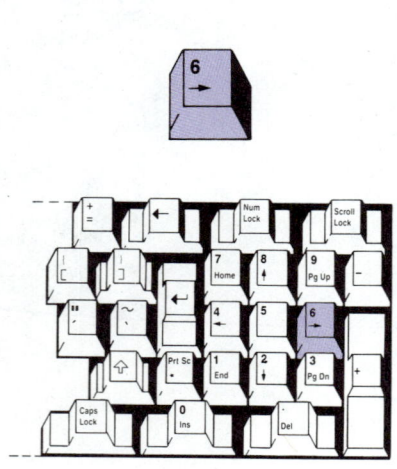

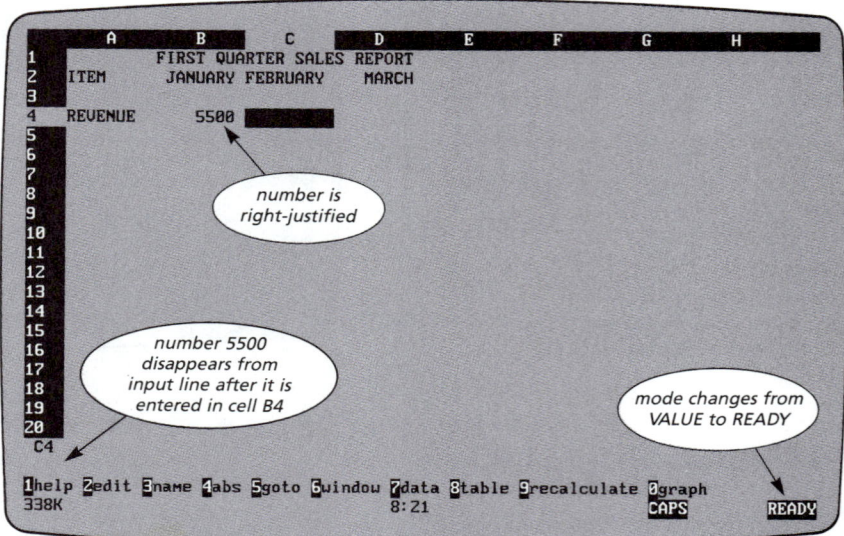

FIGURE 1-21 Pressing the Right Arrow key assigns the number on the input line to cell B4 and moves the cell cursor to C4.

After we enter the data in cell B4, the cell cursor moves to cell C4. At this point, enter the revenue values for February (7300) and March (6410) in cells C4 and D4 in the same manner as we entered the number 5500 into cell B4. After we make the last two revenue entries, the cell cursor is located in cell E4 as shown in Figure 1-22.

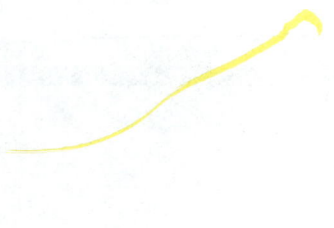

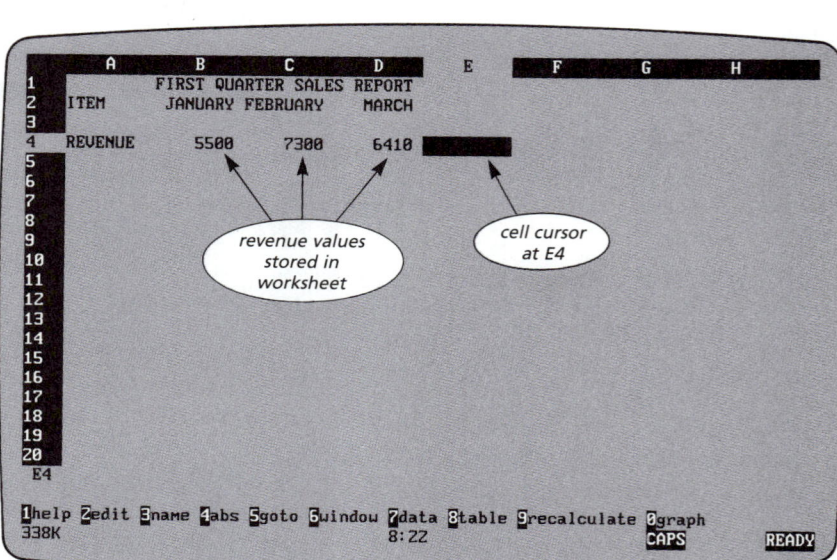

FIGURE 1-22
The revenues for the three months entered into cells B4, C4, and D4.

Decimal Numbers

Although the numeric entries in this project are all whole numbers, you can enter numbers with a decimal point, a dollar sign, and a percent sign. However, the dollar sign and percent sign will not appear in the cell. Other special characters, like the comma, are not allowed in a numeric entry. Table 1-2 gives several examples of numeric entries.

TABLE 1-2 Valid Numeric Entries

NUMERIC DATA ENTERED	CELL CONTENTS	REMARK
1.23	1.23	Decimal fraction numbers are allowed.
32.20	32.2	Insignificant zero dropped.
320.	320	Decimal point at the far right is dropped.
$67.54	67.54	Dollar sign dropped.
47%	.47	Percent converted to a decimal fraction.

MOVING THE CELL CURSOR MORE THAN ONE CELL AT A TIME

After we enter the revenue values for the three months, the cell cursor resides in cell E4. Since there are no more revenue values to enter, move the cell cursor to cell A5 to enter the next line of data. While we can use the arrow keys on the right side of the keyboard to move the cell cursor from E4 to A5, there is another method that is faster and involves fewer keystrokes. This second method uses the GOTO command.

The GOTO Command

The **GOTO command** moves the cell cursor directly to the cell you want. Issue the GOTO command by pressing function key F5. The message "Enter destination cell: E4" displays in the lower left corner of the screen on the input line and the mode changes from READY to POINT. This is illustrated in Step 1 of Figure 1-23. When the mode is POINT, VP-Planner Plus is requesting a cell address.

FIGURE 1-23 (Step 1 of 3)
Press function key F5 to issue the GOTO command to move the cell cursor from E4 to A5.

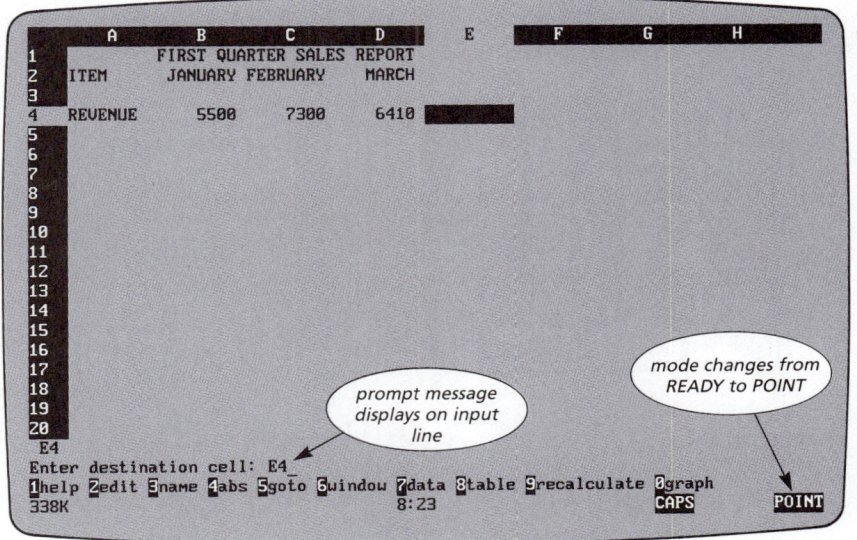

Enter the cell address A5 as shown in Step 2 of Figure 1-23. Remember to enter the column letter first, followed by the row number. Now press the Enter key. The cell cursor immediately moves to cell A5 as shown in Step 3 of Figure 1-23. Note that not only does the cell cursor move, but also the current cell address on the status line in the lower left corner changes from E4 to A5.

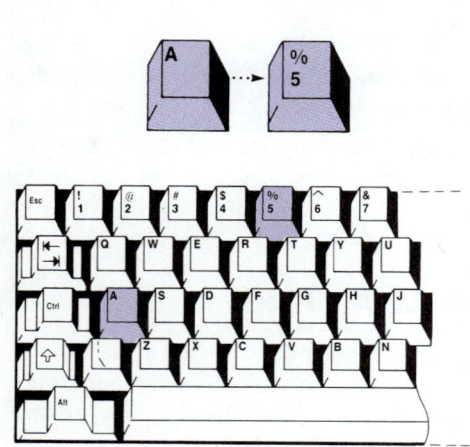

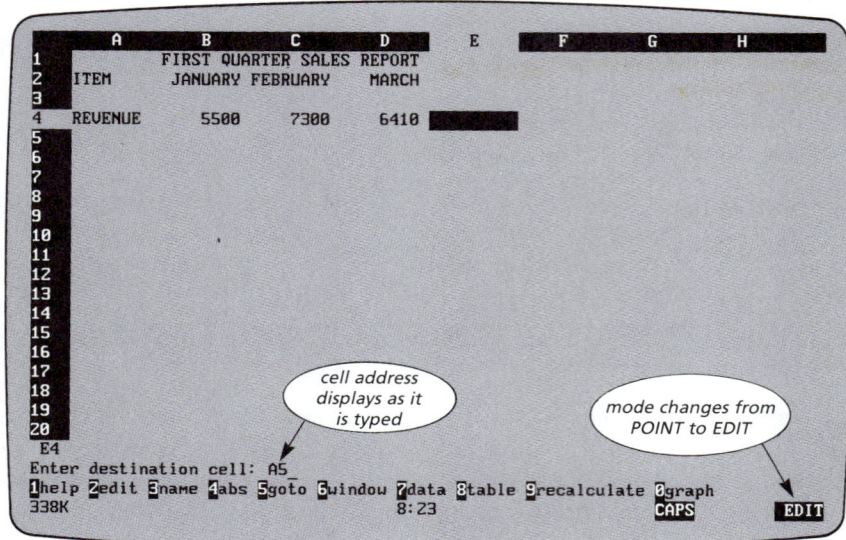

FIGURE 1-23 (Step 2 of 3) Enter the cell address A5.

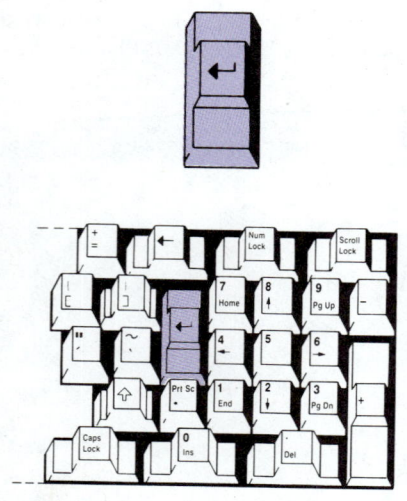

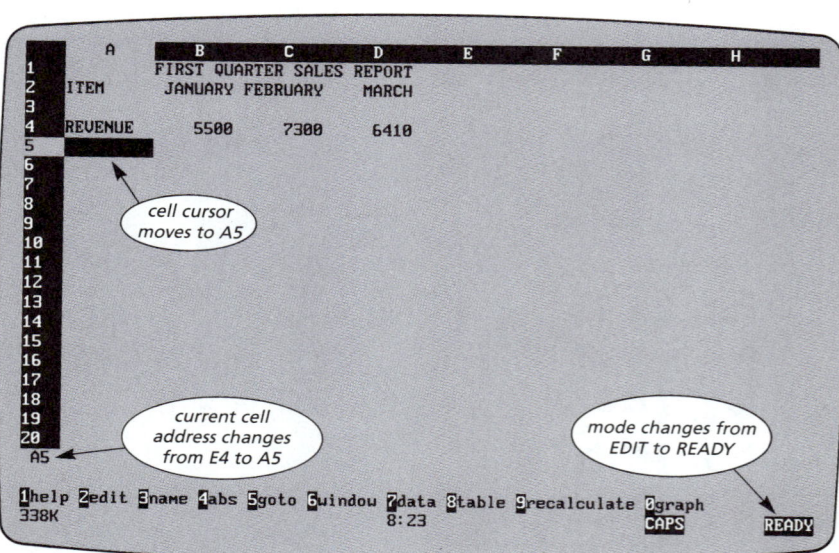

FIGURE 1-23 (Step 3 of 3) Press the Enter key and the cell cursor moves to A5.

With the cell cursor at cell A5, enter the label COSTS followed by the costs for January, February, and March in the same manner as for the revenues on the previous row. After entering the costs, enter the label PROFIT in cell A6. Figure 1-24 illustrates these entries.

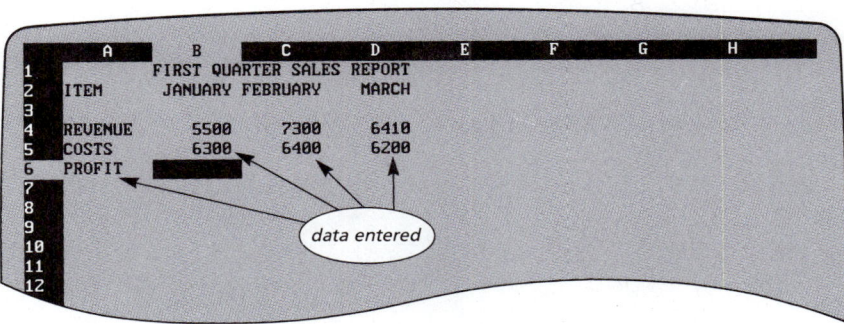

FIGURE 1-24
Costs for the three months entered into cells B5, C5, and D5 and the label PROFIT entered into cell A6.

Summary of Ways to Move the Cell Cursor

Table 1-3 summarizes the various ways you can move the cell cursor around the worksheet. As we proceed through the projects in this book, this table will be a helpful reference. Practice using each of the keys described in Table 1-3.

TABLE 1-3   Moving the Cell Cursor Around the Worksheet

KEY(S)	RESULT
↓	Moves the cell cursor directly down one cell.
←	Moves the cell cursor one cell to the left.
→	Moves the cell cursor one cell to the right.
↑	Moves the cell cursor directly up one cell.
Home	Moves the cell cursor to cell A1 no matter where the cell cursor is located on the worksheet.
End	Used in conjunction with the arrow keys to move to the border columns and rows of the worksheet.
F5	Moves the cell cursor to the designated cell address.
PgDn	Moves the worksheet under the cell cursor 20 rows down.
PgUp	Moves the worksheet under the cell cursor 20 rows up.
Tab	Moves the worksheet under the cell cursor one screenful of columns to the left.
Shift and Tab	Moves the worksheet under the cell cursor one screenful of columns to the right.
Scroll Lock	Causes the worksheet to move under the cell cursor when the cell cursor movement keys are used.

ENTERING FORMULAS

The profit for each month is calculated by subtracting the costs for the month from the revenue for the month. Thus, the profit for January is obtained by subtracting 6300 from 5500. The result, –800, belongs in cell B6. The negative sign preceding the number indicates that the company lost money and made no profit in January.

One of the reasons why a spreadsheet program is such a valuable tool is because you can assign a formula to a cell and it will be calculated automatically. In this example, the formula subtracts the value in cell B5 from the value in cell B4 and assigns the result to cell B6.

Assigning Formulas to Cells

In Figure 1-25, the cell cursor is located at cell B6. Type the formula +B4–B5 on the input line. This formula instructs VP-Planner Plus to subtract the value in cell B5 from the value in cell B4 and place the result in the cell to which the formula is assigned.

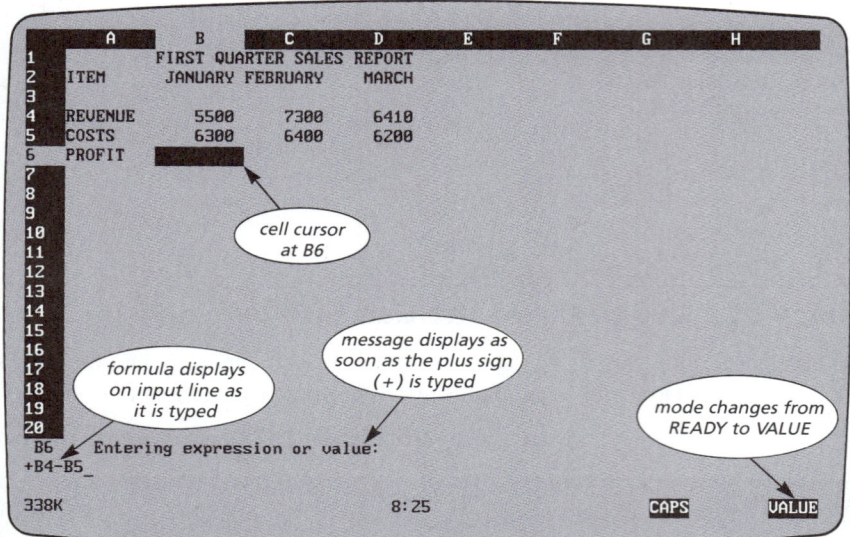

FIGURE 1-25
Entering a formula on the input line.

The plus sign (+) preceding B4 is an important part of the formula. It alerts VP-Planner Plus that you are entering a formula and not a label. The minus sign (–) following B4 is the **arithmetic operator**, which directs VP-Planner Plus to perform the subtraction operation. Other valid arithmetic operators include addition (+), multiplication (∗), division (/) and exponentiation (^).

Pressing the Right Arrow key assigns the formula +B4–B5 to cell B6. Instead of displaying the formula in cell B6, however, VP-Planner Plus completes the arithmetic indicated by the formula and stores the result, –800, in cell B6. This is shown in Figure 1-26. Note that the negative number displays in cell B6 with the minus sign on the left side of the number. Positive numbers display without any sign.

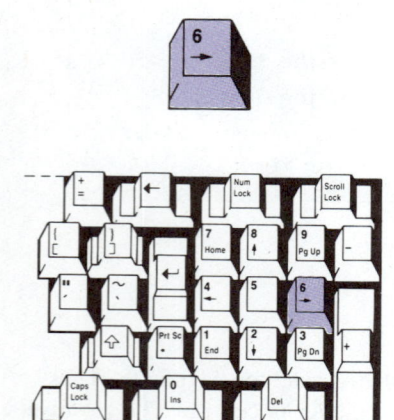

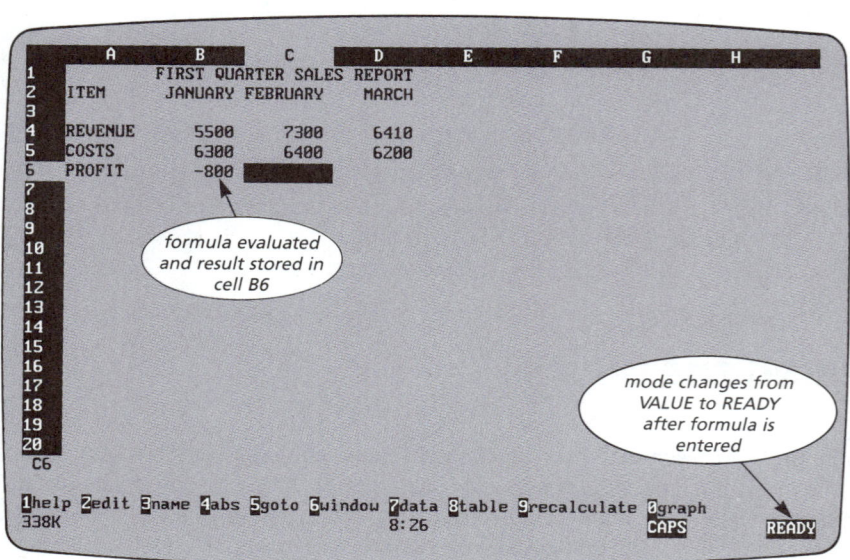

FIGURE 1-26 Pressing the Right Arrow key assigns the formula to cell B6 and moves the cell cursor to C6.

Formulas may be entered in uppercase or lowercase. That is, +b4–b5 is the same as +B4–B5. Like a number, a valid formula begins with one of the following characters:

0 1 2 3 4 5 6 7 8 9 (@ + – . # $

Otherwise, the formula is accepted as a label. Therefore, an alternative to the formula +B4–B5 is (B4–B5). The entry B4–B5 is a label and not a formula, because it begins with the letter B.

To be sure that you understand the relationship of a formula, the associated cell, and the contents of the cell, move the cell cursor back to cell B6. This procedure is shown in Figure 1-27. In the lower left corner of the screen, the status line shows the assignment of the formula +B4–B5 to cell B6. However, in the cell itself, VP-Planner Plus displays the result of the formula (–800).

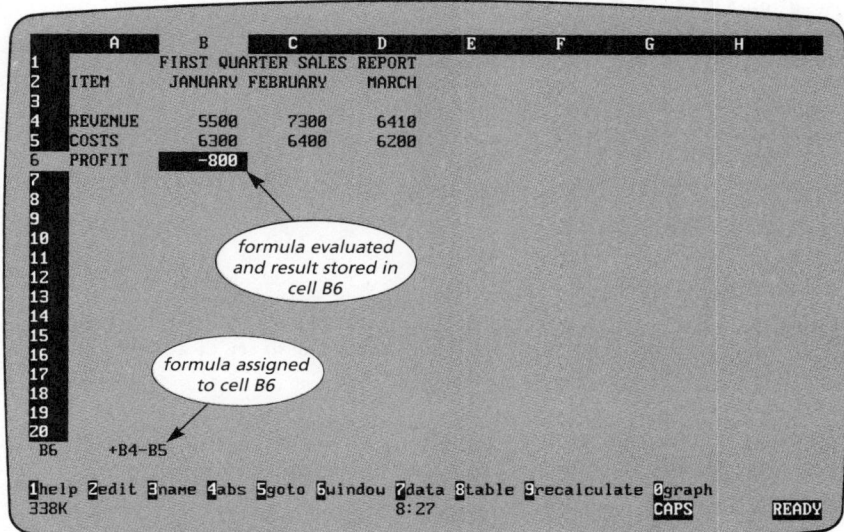

FIGURE 1-27
When the cell cursor is moved to a cell assigned a formula, the formula displays on the status line.

Next move the cell cursor to C6 and type the formula +C4–C5. As shown in Figure 1-28, the formula for determining the profit for February displays on the input line.

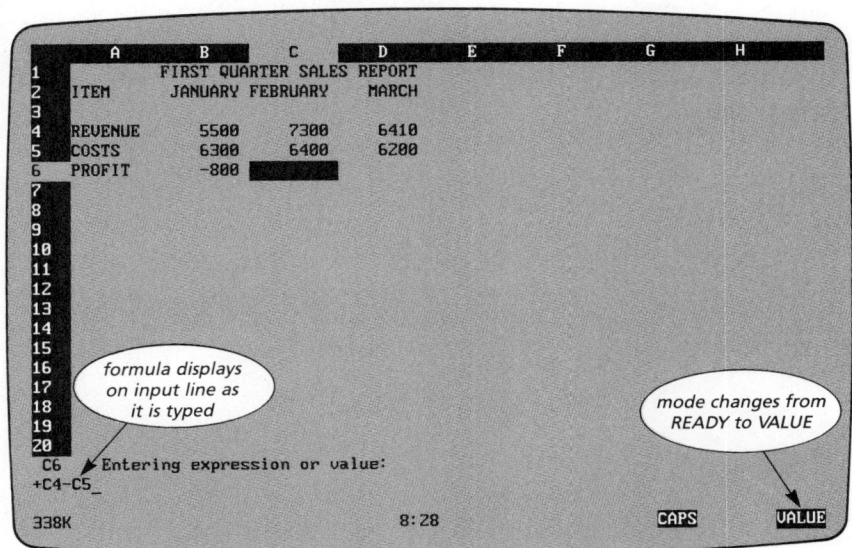

FIGURE 1-28
Entering the profit formula for February on the input line.

Press the Right Arrow key. The value in cell C5 (February costs) is subtracted from the value in cell C4 (February revenue) and the result of the computation displays in cell C6 (February profit). The cell cursor also moves to cell D6, as shown in Figure 1-29. As you can see, the process for entering a formula into a cell is much the same as for entering labels and numbers.

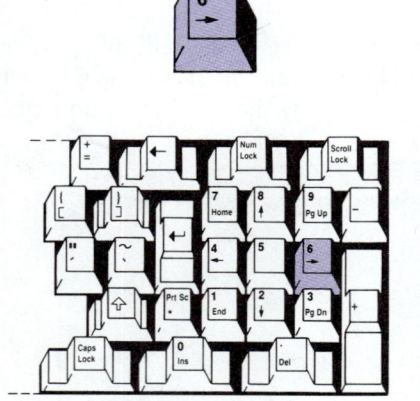

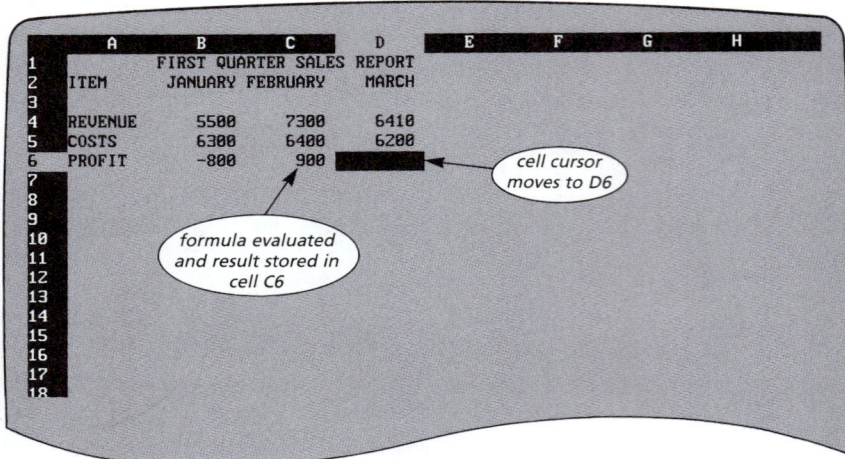

FIGURE 1-29 Pressing the Right Arrow key assigns the formula on the input line to cell C6 and the cell cursor moves to D6.

The same technique can be used to assign the formula +D4–D5 to cell D6. After you press the Right Arrow key to conclude the entry in D6, the worksheet is complete, as illustrated in Figure 1-30.

FIGURE 1-30
Worksheet for Project 1 is complete.

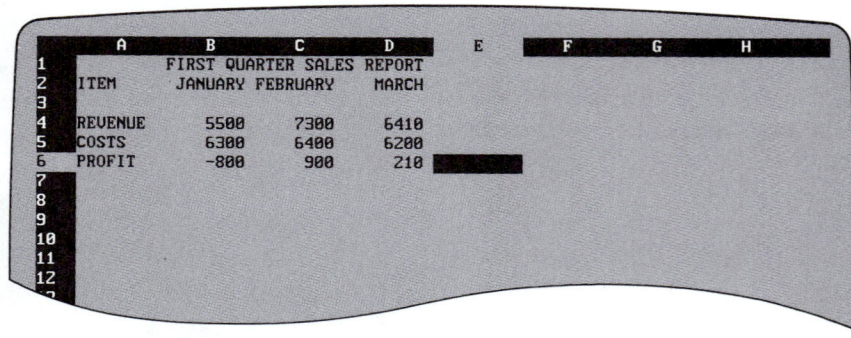

Order of Operations

The formulas in this project involve only one arithmetic operator, subtraction. But when more than one operator is involved in a formula, the same order of operations is used as in algebra. Moving from left to right in a formula, the **order of operations** is as follows: first all exponentiations ($\wedge$), then all multiplications ($*$) and divisions ($/$), and finally all additions ($+$) and subtractions ($-$). You can use parentheses to override the order of operations. Table 1-4 illustrates several examples of valid formulas.

TABLE 1-4   Valid Formula Entries

FORMULA	REMARK
+ E3 or (E3)	Assigns the value in cell E3 to the current cell.
7*F5 or +F5*7 or (7*F5)	Assigns 7 times the contents of cell F5 to the current cell.
–G44*G45	Assigns the negative value of the product of the values contained in cells G44 and G45 to the current cell.
2*(J12–F2)	Assigns the product of 2 and the difference between the values contained in cells J12 and F2 to the current cell. It is invalid to write this formula as 2(J12–F2). The multiplication sign (*) between the 2 and the left parenthesis is required.
+ A1/A1–A3*A4 + A5 $\wedge$ A6	From left to right: exponentiation ($\wedge$) first, followed by multiplication (*) and division (/), and finally addition (+) and subtraction (–).

SAVING A WORKSHEET

You use VP-Planner Plus either to enter data into the worksheet, as we did in the last section, or to execute a command. In this section we discuss the first of a series of commands that allows you to instruct VP-Planner Plus to save, load, modify, and print worksheets.

When a worksheet is created, it is stored in main computer memory. If the computer is turned off or if you quit VP-Planner Plus, the worksheet is lost. Hence, it is mandatory to save to disk any worksheet that will be used later.

The Command Mode

To save a worksheet, place VP-Planner Plus in **command mode**. Do this by pressing the **Slash key** (/) as illustrated in Figure 1-31. First note in Figure 1-31 that the mode at the bottom of the screen is MENU. This means that VP-Planner Plus is now in the command mode. Next, notice the menus in the middle of the screen. A **menu** is a list from which you can choose. The **command menu** appears in a single-lined box on the left side of the screen. A second-level menu appears in a double-lined box to the right of the box containing the command menu.

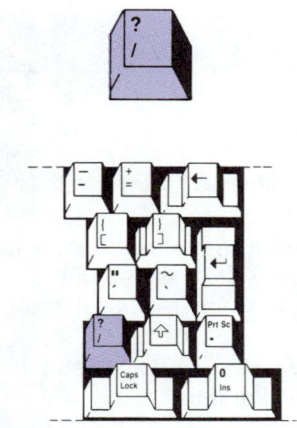

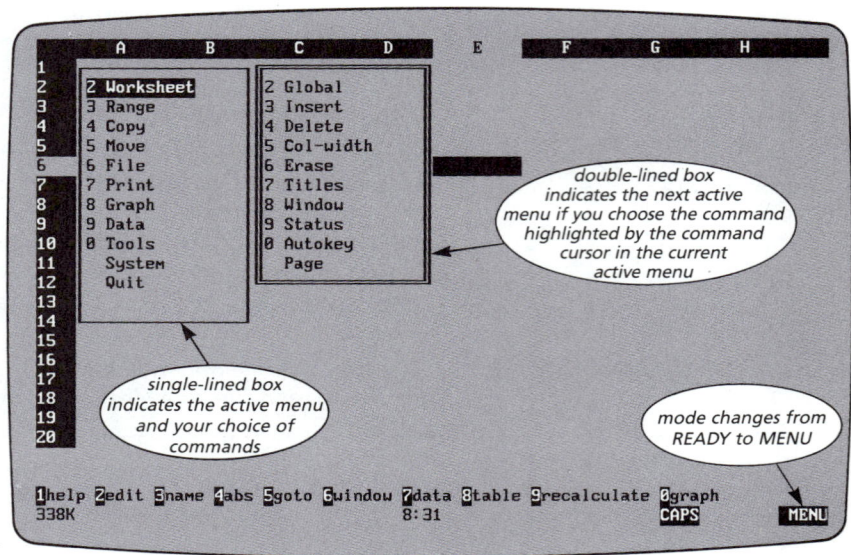

FIGURE 1-31
To save a worksheet to disk, press the Slash key (/) to switch VP-Planner Plus to command mode.

The second-level menu lists the secondary commands that are available if you select the command highlighted by the command cursor in the command menu. The **command cursor** is a reverse video rectangle that can be moved from command to command in the active menu, using the Up Arrow and Down Arrow keys. Although there are two menus on the screen, only one of them is active. The command menu is always the active one when you first press the Slash key. If you press the Down Arrow key four times, the command cursor rests on the File command. This procedure is shown in Figure 1-32. Now compare Figure 1-31 to Figure 1-32. Note that the second level of commands has changed in Figure 1-32 to show the list of secondary commands that are available if you select the File command.

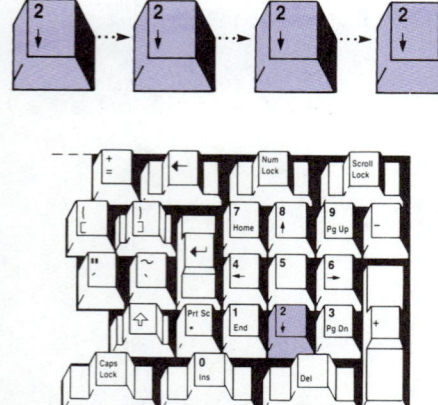

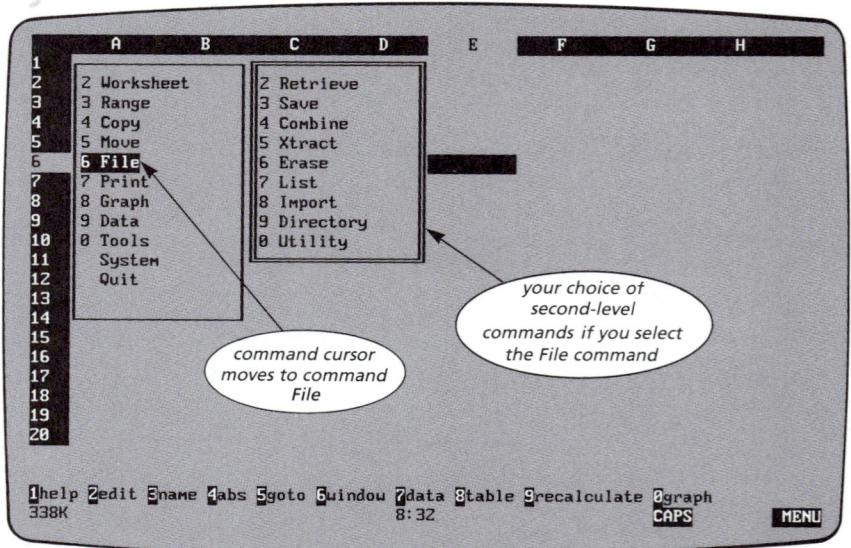

FIGURE 1-32 As you move the command cursor to each command, the double-lined box on the right side of the active menu indicates what the command can do.

Don't be concerned that these *pop-up* menus have overwritten the worksheet on the screen. Press and hold down one of the Shift keys and the worksheet reappears (see Figure 1-33). Release the Shift key and the command menu reappears.

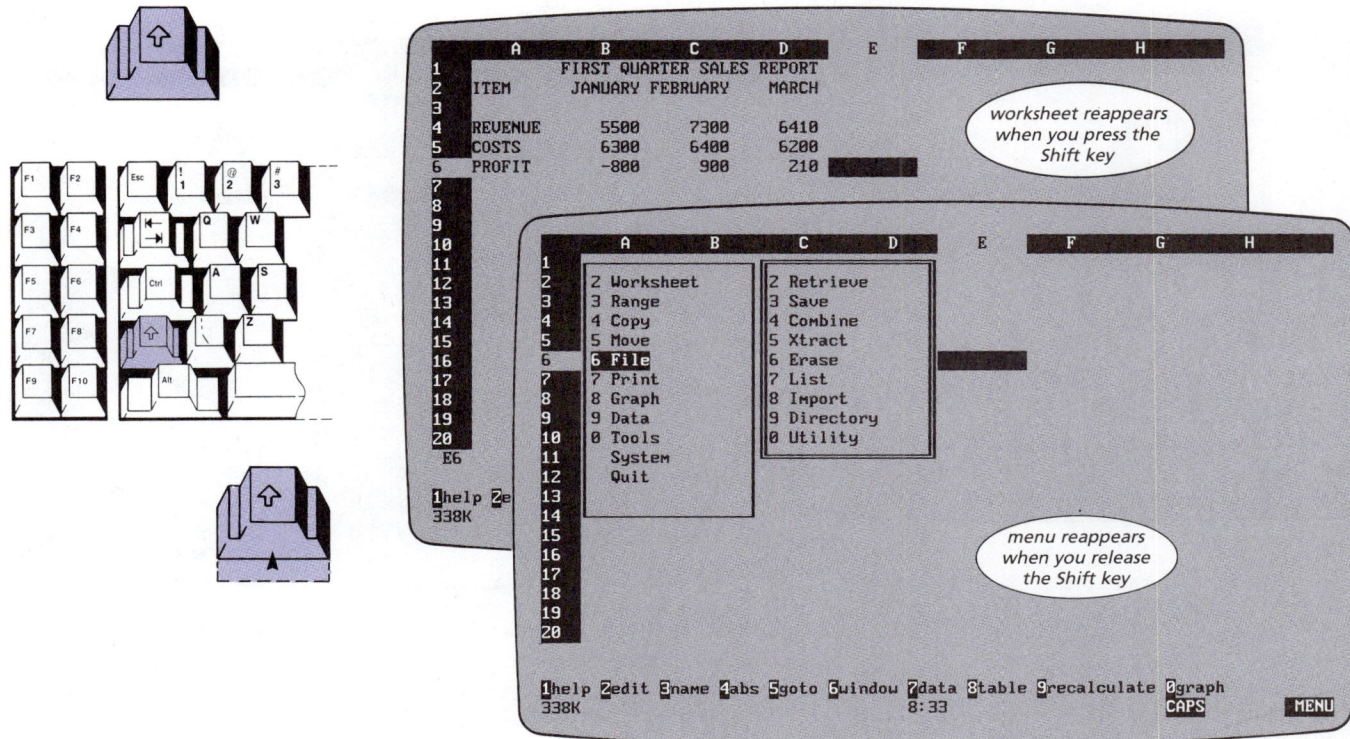

FIGURE 1-33 Press the Shift key to view the worksheet when VP-Planner Plus is in command mode.

Backing Out of the Command Mode

If you decide that you do not want to issue a command, press the **Esc key** until the worksheet reappears. The Esc key, located on the top left side of the keyboard next to the digit 1 key (see Figure 1-33), instructs VP-Planner Plus to exit command mode and return to READY mode.

Press the Esc key and the screen changes from the one in Figure 1-32 to the one in Figure 1-30. Press the Slash key once and the Down Arrow key four times and the command menu in Figure 1-32 reappears on the screen.

The Esc key allows you to *back out* of any command or entry on the input line. So if you become confused while making any kind of entry (command or data), use the Esc key to reset the current entry. When in doubt, press the Esc key.

The File Save Command (/FS)

To save a file, select the File command from the command menu. There are three ways to select the File command.

1. Press the F key for File. Each command in the command menu begins with a different letter. Therefore, the first letter uniquely identifies each command.
2. Use the Down Arrow key to move the command cursor to the word File (see Figure 1-32). With the command cursor on the word File, press the Enter key.
3. Press function key F6. Each of the first nine commands in the command menu is preceded by a digit (2 through 0) that corresponds to function keys F2 through F10. Function key F1 is permanently set aside for the online help facility.

Use the first method and press the F key as shown in Figure 1-34. This causes the **File menu** to partially move on top of the command menu and display a third-level menu. The command cursor is now active in the File menu, the topmost of the layered menus.

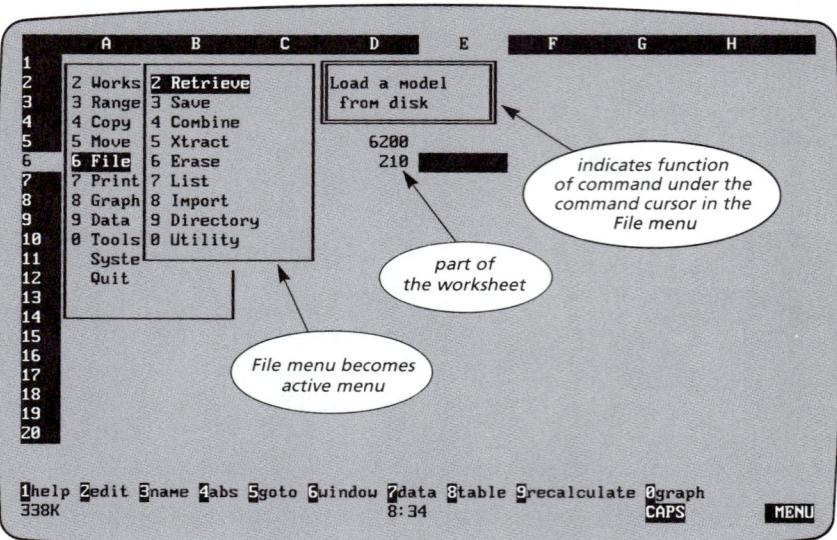

FIGURE 1-34 Typing the letter F moves the command cursor to the second-level menu.

Pressing the S key for Save causes the worksheet to reappear. The message "Enter file name: A:\" displays followed by the blinking edit cursor on the input line at the bottom of the screen. This procedure is shown in Figure 1-35.

The next step is to select a file name. Any file name will do, so long as it is eight or fewer characters in length and includes only the characters A–Z (uppercase or lowercase), 0–9, and the special characters described earlier in the Introduction to DOS. VP-Planner Plus automatically adds the file extension .WKS to the file name. This file .WKS extension stands for worksheet.

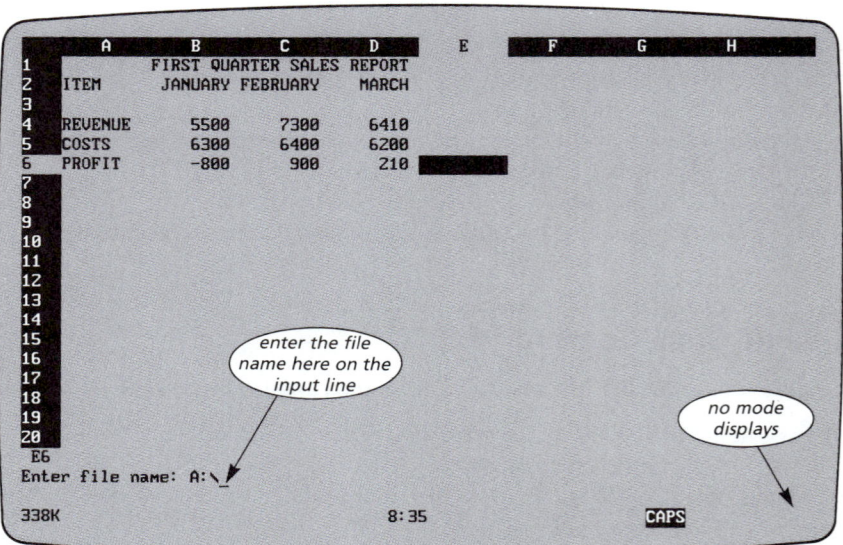

FIGURE 1-35 Typing the letter S for Save causes VP-Planner Plus to display the prompt message on the input line.

In this example, let's choose the file name PROJS-1. Type the file name PROJS-1 as shown in Figure 1-36. Next, press the Enter key. The file is stored on the A drive with the file name PROJS-1.WKS. Remember, VP-Planner Plus does not distinguish between uppercase and lowercase letters. Therefore, you can type PROJS-1 or projs-1 or ProJS-1. All three file names will be treated the same.

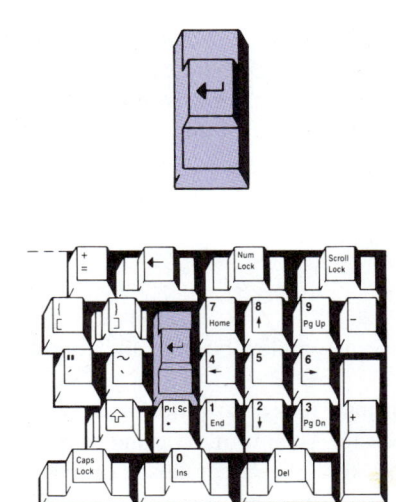

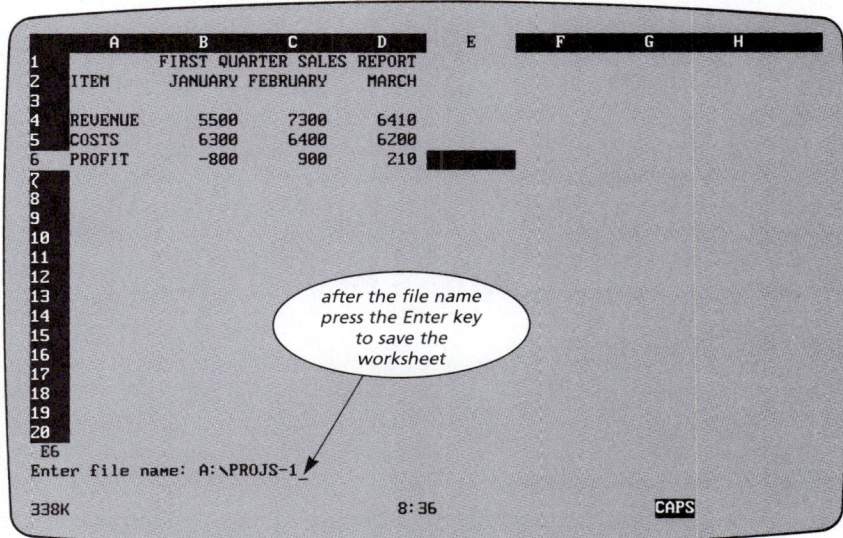

FIGURE 1-36 After you enter the file name on the input line, press the Enter key to complete the /FS command.

While VP-Planner Plus writes the worksheet on the disk, the mode changes from MENU to WAIT. The red light on the A drive also lights up to show it is in use. As soon as the writing is complete, the red light goes off and VP-Planner Plus returns to the READY mode. This is shown in Figure 1-37.

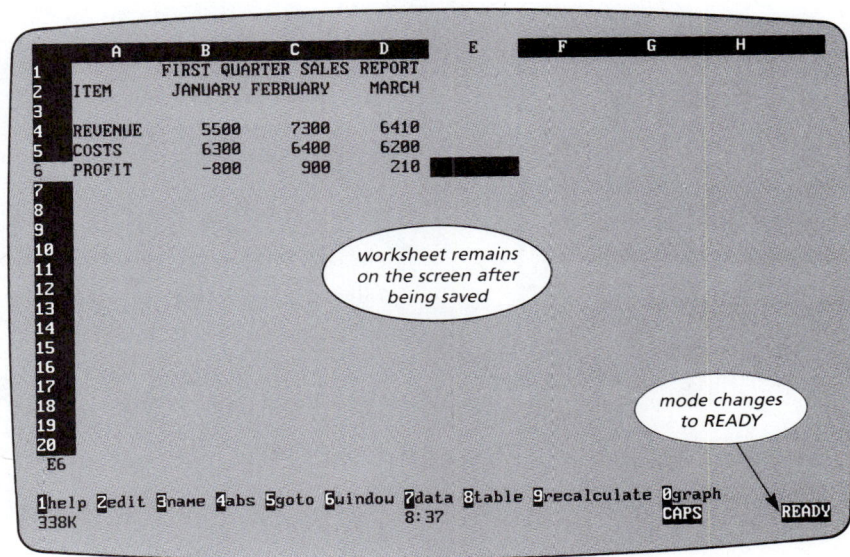

FIGURE 1-37
When the computer is finished saving the worksheet to disk, VP-Planner Plus returns to READY Mode.

Saving Worksheets to a Different Disk Drive

If you want to save the worksheet to a different drive, press the Esc key to delete the "A:\" from the prompt message "Enter file name: A:\". Next, enter the drive of your choice followed by the file name. For example, to save the worksheet on the disk in drive B, enter B:PROJS-1 in response to the prompt "Enter file name:". Do not attempt to write a worksheet to the B drive if it is unavailable.

To change the default drive permanently from A to B, enter the command /**W**orksheet **G**lobal **D**efault **D**irectory (/WGDD). That is, first type the Slash key, then type the letters WGDD. Type the letter B for drive B and press the Enter key. Next, enter the commands Update and Quit (UQ). The Update command permanently changes the default drive in the VP-Planner Plus program. The Quit command quits the Default menu. The examples in the remainder of this book use the B drive as the default drive.

PRINTING A SCREEN IMAGE OF THE WORKSHEET

T he **screen image** of the worksheet is exactly what you see on the screen, including the window borders and control panel. A printed version of the worksheet is called a **hard copy**.

Anytime you use the printer, you must be sure that it is ready. To make the printer ready, turn it off and use the platen knob to align the perforated edge of the paper with the top of the print head mechanism. Then turn the printer on.

With the printer in READY mode, hold down one of the Shift keys and press the PrtSc key. The screen image of the worksheet immediately prints on the printer. When the printer stops, eject the paper from the printer and carefully tear off the printed version of the worksheet (see Figure 1-38).

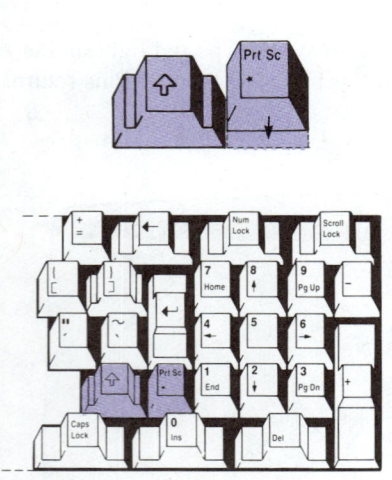

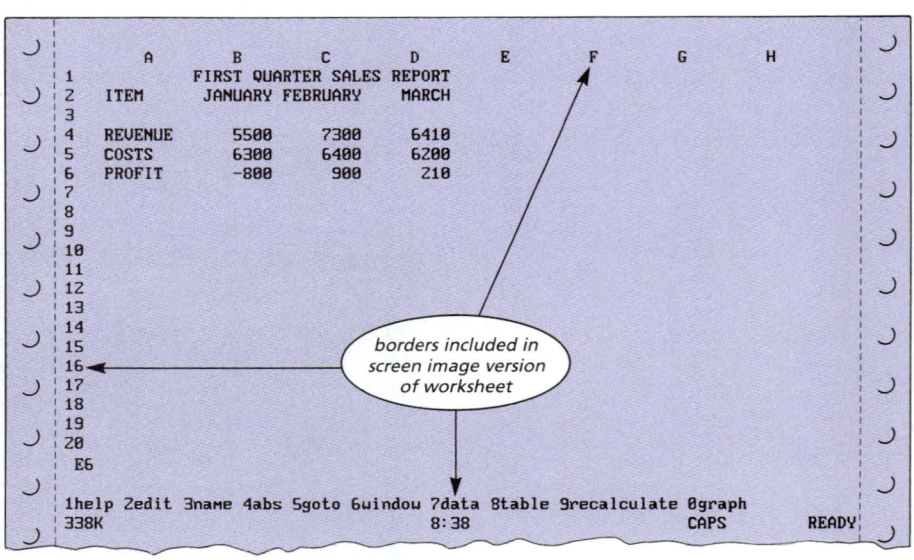

FIGURE 1-38 Hold down the Shift key and press the PrtSc key to obtain a hard copy of the worksheet.

CORRECTING ERRORS

There are five methods for correcting errors in a worksheet. The one you choose will depend on the severity of the error, and whether you notice it while typing the data on the input line or after the data is in the cell.

The error-correcting examples that follow are not part of the worksheet we are building in Project 1. However, you should carefully step through them since they are essential to building and maintaining worksheets.

Correcting Errors While the Data Is on the Input Line

Move the cell cursor to cell A5 and type the label COTTS, rather than COSTS, on the input line. This error is shown in Figure 1-39.

FIGURE 1-39
Incorrect data spotted on the input line.

To correct the error, follow Step 1 of Figure 1-40 and move the edit cursor back to position 3 on the input line by pressing the Backspace key three times. Each time you press the Backspace key, the character immediately to the left of the edit cursor is erased.

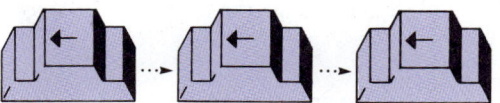

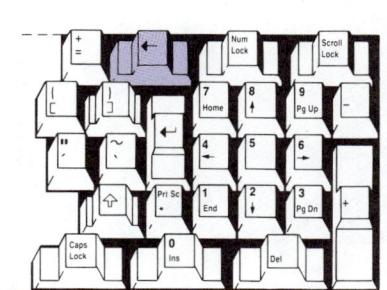

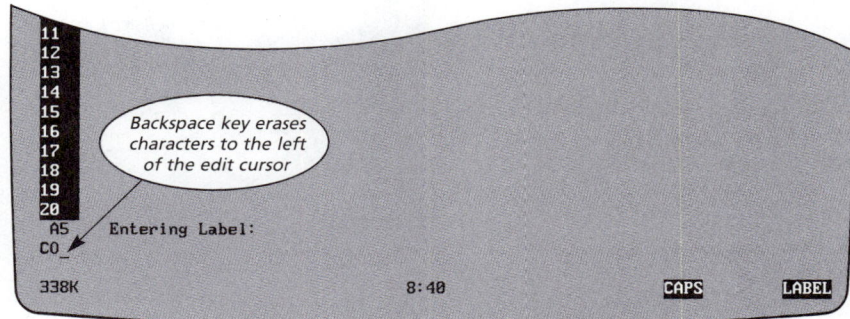

FIGURE 1-40 (Step 1 of 2) Press the Backspace key three times to erase the characters up to and including the first T in COTTS.

Then, as in Step 2 of Figure 1-40, type the correct letters STS. Now the entry is correct. Press the Right Arrow key to enter the label COSTS into cell A5.

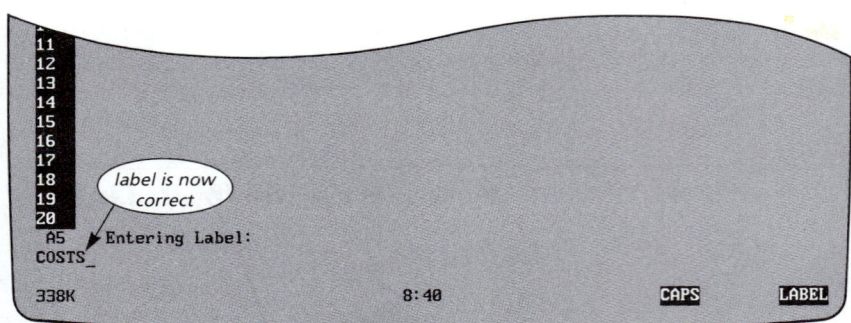

FIGURE 1-40 (Step 2 of 2)
Enter the correct characters and press the Enter key or one of the arrow keys.

In summary, if you notice an error while the label, number, or formula is on the input line, you can do one of two things. You can use the Backspace key to erase the portion in error and then type the correct characters. Or, if the error is too severe, you can press the Esc key to erase the entire entry on the input line and reenter the data item from the beginning.

Editing Data in a Cell

If you spot an error in the worksheet, move the cell cursor to the cell with the error. You then have two ways to correct the error. If the entry is short, simply type it and press the Enter key. The new entry will replace the old entry. Remember, the cell cursor must be on the cell with the error before you begin typing the correct entry.

If the entry in the cell is long and the errors are minor, using the EDIT mode may be a better choice, rather than retyping. Move the cell cursor to cell A18 and enter the label GROSS PAY incorrectly as GRSS PSY. Figure 1-41 shows the label GRSS PSY in cell A18. You will have to insert the letter O between the letters R and S in GRSS and change the letter S in PSY to the letter A.

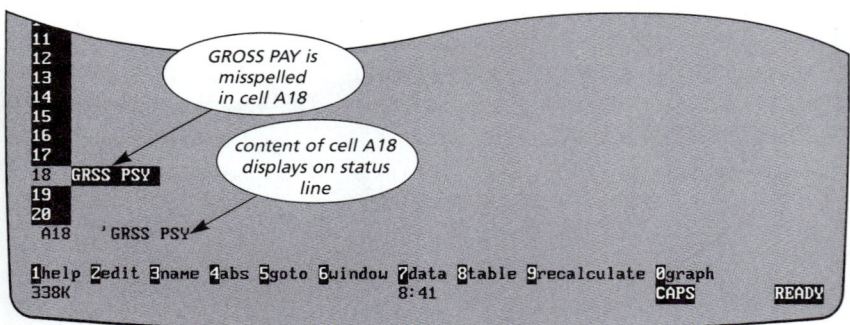

FIGURE 1-41
Error spotted in cell.

The six steps in Figure 1-42 illustrate how to use the EDIT mode to correct the entry in cell A18. As shown in Step 1, first press function key F2 to switch VP-Planner Plus to EDIT mode. The contents of cell A18 immediately display on the input line, followed by the rectangular edit cursor. The contents of the cell can now be corrected. Table 1-5 lists the edit keys available in EDIT mode and their functions.

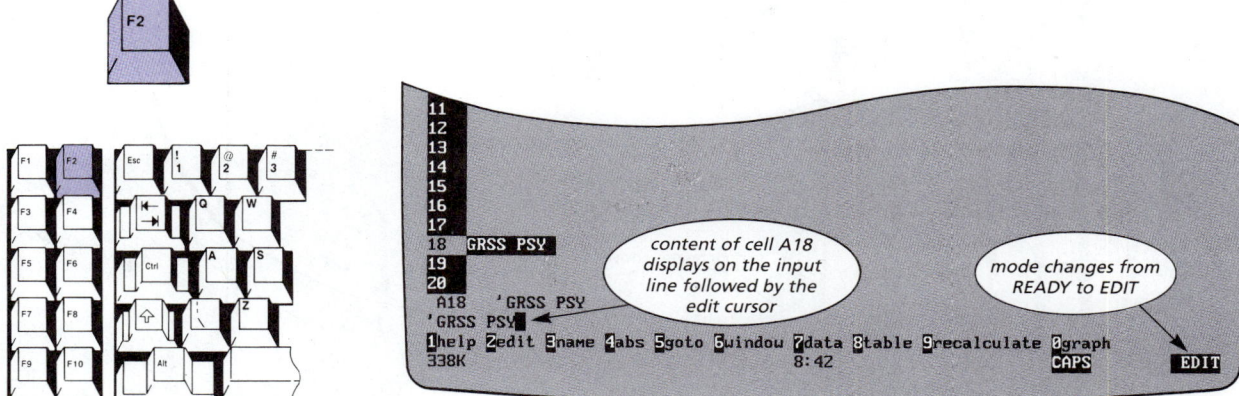

FIGURE 1-42 (Step 1 of 6) Press function key F2 to switch VP-Planner Plus to EDIT mode.

TABLE 1-5   Keys for Editing Cell Entries

KEY	FUNCTION
F2	Switches VP-Planner Plus to EDIT mode.
Enter	Completes entry. Up Arrow key or Down Arrow Key also completes an entry. Either key also moves the cell cursor in the corresponding direction.
Backspace	Erases the character immediately to the left of the edit cursor.
Del	Deletes the character under the edit cursor.
Ins	Used to switch between inserting characters and overtyping characters. In EDIT mode, characters are inserted when the cursor is a blinking rectangle. Characters are overtyped when the edit cursor is an underline.
Right Arrow	Moves the edit cursor one character to the right on the input line.
Left Arrow	Moves the edit cursor one character to the left on the input line.
End	Moves the edit cursor to the end of the entry on the input line.
Home	Moves the edit cursor to the first character in the entry on the input line.

With VP-Planner Plus in EDIT mode, the next step in changing GRSS PSY to GROSS PAY is to move the edit cursor on the input line to the leftmost S in GRSS PSY. Press the Left Arrow key six times as shown in Step 2 of Figure 1-42. Next, type the letter O. Typing the letter O "pushes" the leftmost letter S and all the letters to the right of it to the right. The O is inserted as shown in Step 3 of Figure 1-42.

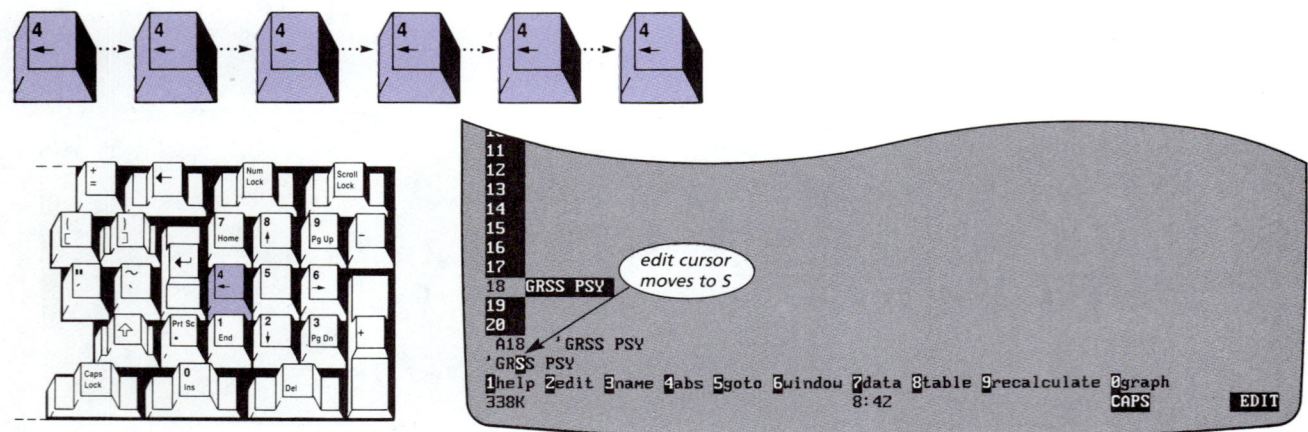

FIGURE 1-42 (Step 2 of 6) Press the Left Arrow key six times to move the edit cursor on the input line to the first S in GRSS PSY.

FIGURE 1-42 (Step 3 of 6) With the block edit cursor on the first letter S in GRSS PSY, type the letter 0.

The next step calls for moving the edit cursor to the S in PSY and changing it to the letter A. Use the Right Arrow key as shown in Step 4 of Figure 1-42. After moving the edit cursor, press the **Ins key** (Insert key) to switch from inserting characters to overtyping characters.

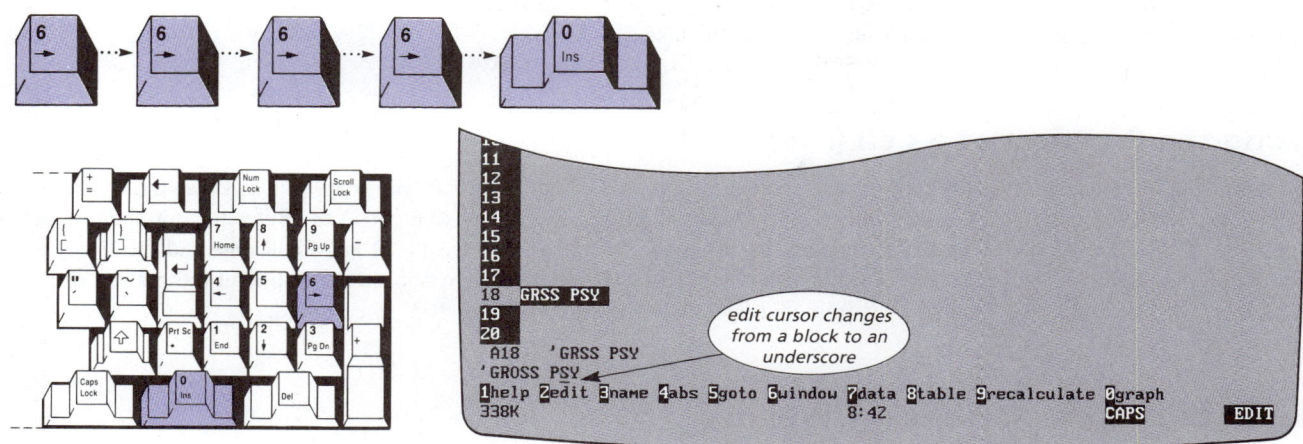

FIGURE 1-42 (Step 4 of 6) Press the Right Arrow key four times to move the edit cursor to the letter S in PSY. Press the Ins (Insert) key to switch to overtype. The edit cursor changes from a block to an underscore.

Type the letter A. The correct label GROSS PAY now resides on the input line (see Step 5 of Figure 1-42). Press the Enter key to replace GRSS PSY in cell A18 with GROSS PAY. This is illustrated in Step 6 of Figure 1-42.

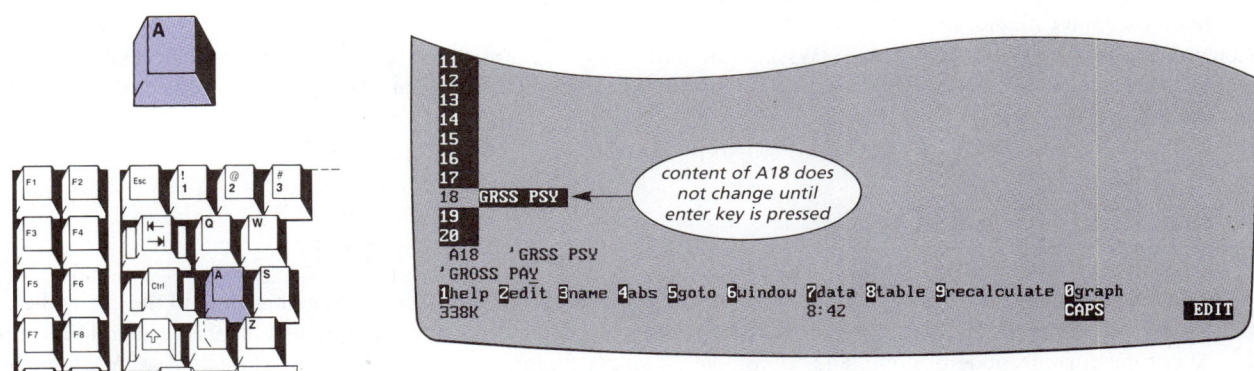

FIGURE 1-42 (Step 5 of 6) With the edit cursor on the letter S in PSY, type the letter A.

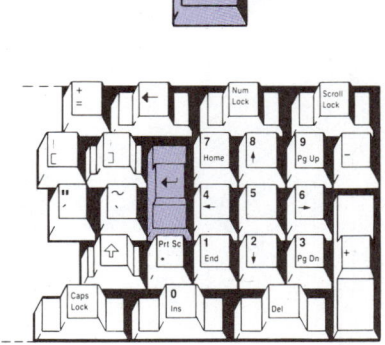

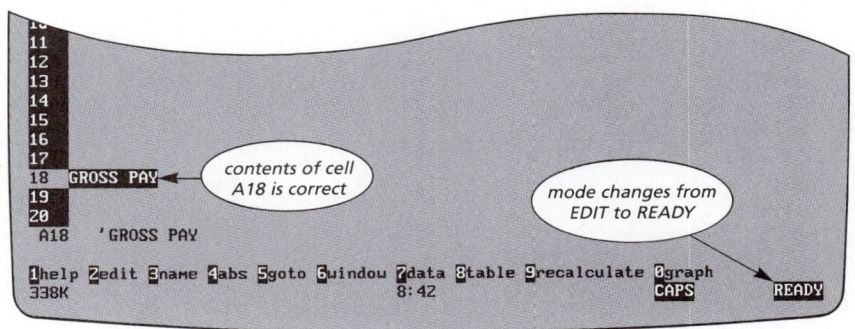

FIGURE 1-42 (Step 6 of 6) Press the Enter key to assign the edited value to cell A18.

Pay careful attention to the six steps in Figure 1-42. It is easy to make keyboard and grammatical errors. Understanding how to use the EDIT mode will make it easier to correct mistakes.

Erasing the Contents of a Cell (/RE)

It is not unusual to enter data into the wrong cell. In such a case, to correct the error, you may want to erase the contents of the cell. Let's erase the label GROSS PAY in cell A18. Make sure the cell cursor is on cell A18. Enter the command /**R**ange **E**rase (/RE). That is, press the Slash key to display the command menu. Then press the R key for Range and the E key for Erase. When the message "Select Range of Cells to be blanked: A18..A18" appears on the input line at the bottom of the screen, press the Enter key. VP-Planner Plus immediately erases the entry GROSS PAY in cell A18.

Erasing the Entire Worksheet (/WE)

Sometimes, everything goes wrong. The worksheet is such a mess that you don't know where to begin to correct it. In this case, you want to erase the entire worksheet and start over. To do this, enter the command /**W**orksheet **E**rase (/WE). That is, first type the Slash key to display the command menu. Next, enter the letters W for Worksheet and E for Erase.

Two messages display at the bottom of the screen. On the status line, the following message appears: "Modifications to this worksheet are about to be lost". On the input line appears the message: "You have asked that the worksheet be ERASED. Are you sure? (Y/N)". At this point, press the Y key and VP-Planner Plus clears all the cells in the worksheet. The /**W**orksheet **E**rase (/WE) command does not erase the worksheet PROJS-1 from disk. This command only affects the worksheet in main computer memory.

Remember that the /**W**orksheet **E**rase (/WE) command can also be a method for clearing the worksheet on the screen of its contents after you have saved it. This is especially useful when you no longer want the current worksheet displayed because you want to begin a new one.

ONLINE HELP FACILITY

At any time while you are using VP-Planner Plus, you can press function key F1 to gain access to the online help facility. When you press F1, VP-Planner Plus temporarily suspends the current activity and displays valuable information about the current mode or command. If you have a single floppy disk drive and no fixed disk drive, VP-Planner Plus will request that you place the VP-Planner program disk in the A drive when you press function key F1.

With VP-Planner Plus in READY mode, press function key F1. The help screen shown in Figure 1-43 displays. Directions are given on the help screen for accessing information on any VP-Planner Plus subject. For example, press function key F1 a second time and a table of contents appears, informing you of the screen numbers to look up for information on a given topic. To exit the help facility and return to the worksheet, press the Esc key.

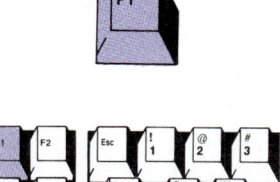

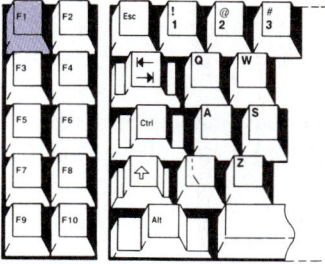

FIGURE 1-43
Press function key F1 to use the online help facility of VP-Planner Plus.

```
                          (5)  Using Help

Help is always available.  Press <F1> at any time to see a help screen
relevant to the current mode or command.  For an index of all help topics,
press <F1> twice.

Many help screens include numbers enclosed in parentheses.  These are cross
references to other help screens.  Cross references are also indicated at the
lower left of the screen.  To look at one of these references, press <F5>, type
the number, and press <ENTER>.

The lower right corner shows the next help screen.  To scan the next
screen, press <PGDN>.  For example, the topic of the next help screen after
this is "Ready Mode:" to view it, press <PGDN> or type <F5> 6 <ENTER>.

To return to previous screens you have viewed, press <PGUP> one or more
times.  To return to this screen from any other help screen, type
<F5> 5 <ENTER>.  To leave help, press <ESC>.

See also: (28) Function Keys


                                         Next Screen:
                                         (6) Ready Mode/Moving the Cursor/Quit
_____
   <F1> index   <PgDn> next   <PgUp> previous   <F5> goto   <ESC> exit_
```

use these keys for additional help

to quit the online help facility, press the Esc key

The best way to familiarize yourself with the help facility is to use it. When you have a question about how a command works in VP-Planner Plus, press F1. You may want to consider printing a hard copy of the information displayed on the screen. To print a hard copy, ready the printer, hold down one of the Shift keys, and press the PrtSc key.

QUITTING VP-PLANNER PLUS (/Q)

T o exit VP-Planner Plus and return control to DOS, do the following:

1. If you have a fixed disk system, proceed to step 2. If you loaded VP-Planner Plus from a floppy diskette, place the DOS disk in drive A.
2. Enter the /Quit command (/Q). First, press the Slash key to display the command menu. Next, type the letter Q for Quit.
3. When the message shown in Figure 1-44 displays on the input line, type the letter Y to confirm your exit from VP-Planner Plus.

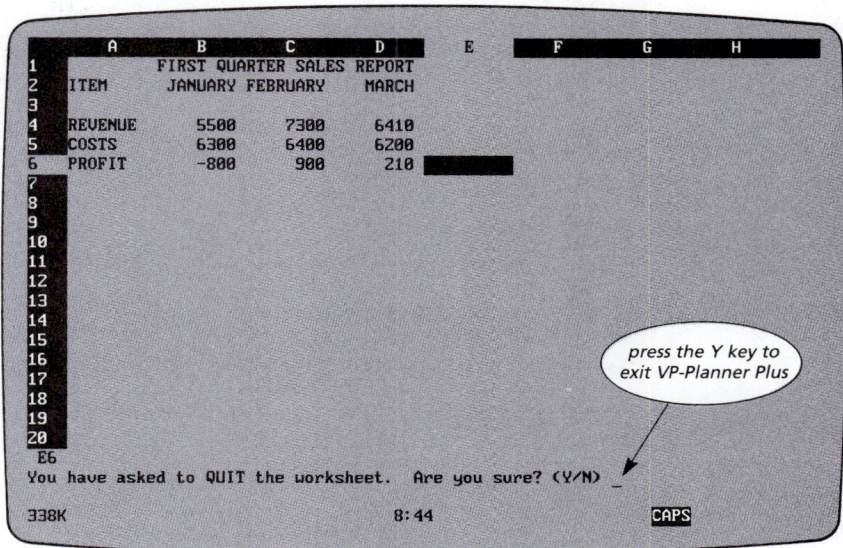

press the Y key to exit VP-Planner Plus

FIGURE 1-44 To quit VP-Planner Plus and return control to DOS, enter the command /Q and type the letter Y.

If you forgot to save the latest version of the worksheet before issuing the Quit command, the following warning displays on the status line to remind you: "Modifications to this worksheet are about to be lost." To save the worksheet, press the N key or the Esc key and save the worksheet as described earlier. If you type the letter Y when this reminder appears on the status line, you will lose the latest version of the worksheet.

PROJECT SUMMARY

In Project 1 you learned how to move the cell cursor around the worksheet, enter data into the worksheet, and save a worksheet. Each of the steps required to build the worksheet in this project is listed in the following table. Review the steps in detail to make sure you understand them.

SUMMARY OF KEYSTROKES—Project 1

STEPS	KEY(S) PRESSED	RESULTS
1	Caps Lock	Set Caps Lock on
2	→	Move the cell cursor to B1
3	FIRST QUARTER SALES REPORT ↵	Enter report heading
4	↓ ←	Move the cell cursor to A2
5	ITEM →	Enter column heading
6	"JANUARY →	Enter column heading
7	"FEBRUARY →	Enter column heading
8	"MARCH →	Enter column heading
9	↓ ↓ ← ← ← ←	Move the cell cursor to A4
10	REVENUE →	Enter row identifier
11	5500 →	Enter January revenue
12	7300 →	Enter February revenue
13	6410 →	Enter March revenue
14	F5 A5 ↵	Move the cell cursor to A5
15	COSTS →	Enter row identifier
16	6300 →	Enter January costs
17	6400 →	Enter February costs
18	6200 →	Enter March costs
19	F5 A6 ↵	Move the cell cursor to A6
20	PROFIT →	Enter row identifier
21	+ B4–B5 →	Enter January profit formula
22	+ C4–C5 →	Enter February profit formula
23	+ D4–D5 →	Enter March profit formula
24	/FS PROJS–1 ↵	Save the worksheet as PROJS-1
25	Shift - PrtSc	Print the screen image of the worksheet

The following list summarizes the material covered in Project 1.

1. The worksheet is organized in two dimensions—columns (vertical) and rows (horizontal).
2. In the border at the top of the screen, each **column** is identified by a column letter. In the border on the left side, each **row** is identified by a row number.
3. A **cell** is the intersection of a row and a column. A cell is referred to by its **cell address**, the coordinates of the intersection of a column and row.
4. The **current cell** is the cell in which data (labels, numbers, and formulas) can be entered. The current cell is identified in two ways. A reverse video rectangle called the **cell cursor** is displayed over the current cell, and the current cell address displays on the status line at the bottom of the screen.
5. The area between the borders on the screen is called a **window**.
6. The first three lines immediately below the window—status line, input line, and prompt line—are collectively called the **control panel**.
7. The **status line** is the first line below the window. It indicates the current cell address. If a value is already in the cell, the status line also shows the type of entry and its contents.
8. The second line below the window is the **input line**. It shows what you are typing as you enter data or edit cell contents.
9. The third line below the window is the **prompt line**. It displays a menu that describes the purpose of the function keys.
10. The last line below the screen is the **current-mode line**. It displays four items: the amount of main computer memory remaining for your worksheet; the time of day as maintained by DOS; status indicators; and the current mode.
11. To move the cell cursor one cell at a time use the arrow keys found on the right side of the keyboard.
12. No matter where the cell cursor is on the worksheet, if you press the Home key, the cell cursor always moves to cell A1.
13. You may use the **GOTO command** (function key F5) to move the cell cursor to any cell in the worksheet.
14. Three type of entries may be made in a cell: labels, numbers, and formulas.
15. A cell entry is a **number** or a **formula** if the first character typed is one of the following: 0 1 2 3 4 5 6 7 8 9 (@ + − . # $
16. A number or formula is also called a **value**.
17. A cell entry is a **label** if the first character is any character other than one that identifies it as a number or formula.
18. If a label begins with a letter or apostrophe, it is positioned in the cell left-justified. If a label begins with a quotation mark ("), it is positioned right-justified. If a label begins with a circumflex (^), it is centered in the cell.
19. One of the most powerful features of VP-Planner Plus is the ability to assign a formula to a cell and calculate it automatically. The result of the calculation is displayed in the cell.
20. Spreadsheet programs use the same order of operations as in algebra. Moving from left to right in a formula, the order of operations is as follows: all exponentiations (^) are completed first, then all multiplications (∗) and divisions (/), and finally all additions (+) and subtractions (−). Parentheses may be used to override the order of operations.
21. To put VP-Planner Plus in command mode, press the **Slash key (/)**. To leave command mode, press the Esc key.
22. There are three different cursors: cell cursor, edit cursor, and command cursor. The **cell cursor** moves from cell to cell in the worksheet. The **edit cursor** shows where the next character will be placed on the input line. The **command cursor** moves from command to command in the command menu.
23. If you get confused while making any kind of entry (command or data), press the **Esc key** to reset the current entry. When in doubt, press the Esc key.
24. In order to save a worksheet, enter the command /**File Save** (/FS) and the file name that you plan to call the worksheet.
25. VP-Planner Plus automatically appends the file extension .WKS (worksheet) to the file name.
26. To print the screen image of the worksheet, make sure the printer is in READY mode. Next, hold down one of the Shift keys and press the PrtSc key. After the worksheet has printed, eject the paper from the printer and carefully tear off the printed worksheet. A printed version of the worksheet is called a **hard copy**.
27. To edit the contents of a cell, press function key F2.
28. To erase the contents of a cell, move the cell cursor to the cell in question, enter the command /**Range Erase** (/RE), and press the Enter key.
29. To erase the entire worksheet, enter the command /**Worksheet Erase** (/WE) and press the Y key.
30. At any time while you are using VP-Planner Plus, you may press function key F1 to gain access to the online help facility.
31. To exit VP-Planner Plus and return control to DOS, enter the command /**Quit** (/Q). Press the Y key to confirm your exit. Before entering the Quit command, be sure that the DOS program COMMAND.COM is available to the system.

STUDENT ASSIGNMENTS

STUDENT ASSIGNMENT 1: True/False

Instructions: Circle T if the statement is true or F if the statement is false.

T F   1. The current cell address on the status line identifies the cell that the cell cursor is on in the worksheet.
T F   2. With a spreadsheet program, each column is identified by a number and each row by a letter of the alphabet.
T F   3. A cell is identified by specifying its cell address, the coordinates of the intersection of a column and a row.
T F   4. When VP-Planner Plus first begins execution, the column width is nine characters.
T F   5. One method of moving the worksheet cell cursor is by using the arrow keys on the right side of the keyboard.
T F   6. A cell entry that consists of just words or letters of the alphabet is called a label.
T F   7. When text data is entered that contains more characters than the width of the column, an error message displays.
T F   8. If a cell entry begins with a circumflex ($\wedge$), the data is right-justified in the cell.
T F   9. To move the cell cursor from cell C1 to cell A2, press the Down Arrow key one time and the Left Arrow key one time.
T F   10. Numeric data entered into a worksheet is stored right-justified in a cell.
T F   11. The GOTO command moves the cell cursor directly to a designated cell.
T F   12. Typing GOTO A1 causes the worksheet cell cursor to be positioned in cell A1.
T F   13. A formula may begin with a letter.
T F   14. When you enter a formula in a cell, the formula is evaluated and the result is displayed in the same cell on the worksheet.
T F   15. The cell cursor is at C6. The formula +C4–C5 causes the value in cell C5 to be subtracted from the value in cell C4. The answer is displayed in cell C5.

STUDENT ASSIGNMENT 2: Multiple Choice

Instructions: Circle the correct response.

1. In the border at the top of the screen, each column is identified by a _____ .
   a. number
   b. letter
   c. cursor
   d. none of the above
2. If the first character typed on the input line is the letter F, the mode on the current-mode line changes from READY to _____ .
   a. VALUE
   b. LABEL
   c. MENU
   d. EDIT
3. A cell is identified by a cell _____ .
   a. cursor
   b. address
   c. entry
   d. none of the above
4. The command /File Save (/FS) is used to _____ .
   a. load a new worksheet
   b. save a worksheet on disk
   c. suspend work on the current worksheet and return to the operating system
   d. make corrections in the current entry

5. To exit from VP-Planner Plus, _____ .
   a. type /Q for Quit and then Y
   b. type /E for Exit
   c. type /FS for Finally Stop
   d. both B and C are correct
6. Which one of the following should you press to put VP-Planner Plus in EDIT mode?
   a. function key F1
   b. function key F2
   c. function key F3
   d. function key F5
7. Which one of the following best describes the function of the Backspace key?
   a. deletes the value in the current cell
   b. deletes the character on the input line under which the edit cursor is located
   c. deletes the character to the right of the edit cursor on the input line
   d. deletes the character to the left of the edit cursor on the input line
8. Which one of the following should you press to activate the online help facility of VP-Planner Plus?
   a. function key F1
   b. function key F2
   c. function key F3
   d. function key F4

STUDENT ASSIGNMENT 3: Understanding the Worksheet

Instructions: Answer the following questions.

1. In Figure 1-45, a series of arrows points to the major components of a worksheet. Identify the various parts of the worksheet in the space provided in the figure.

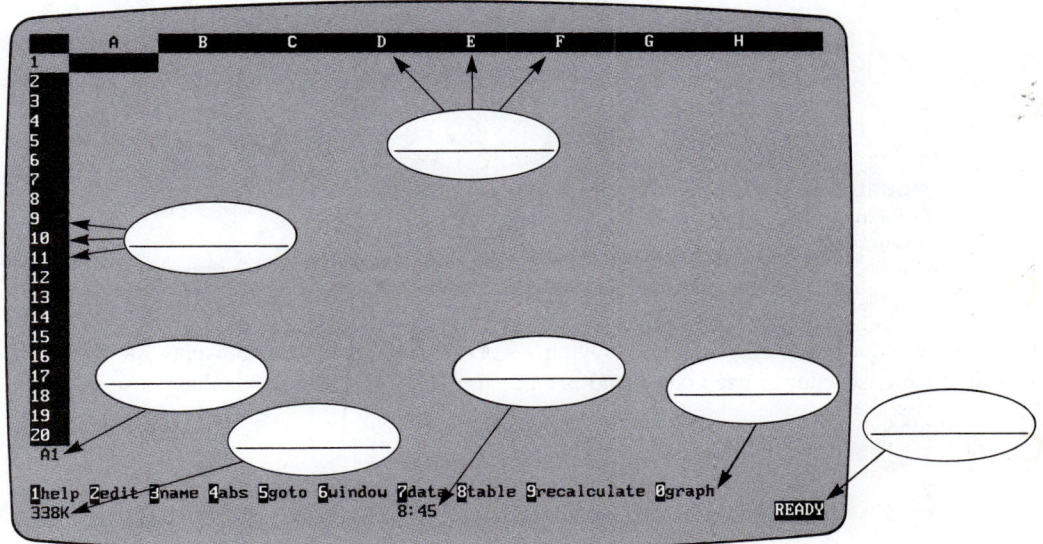

FIGURE 1-45
Problem 1 of Student Assignment 3

Student Assignment 3 (continued)

2. Explain the following entries that may be contained on the current-mode line at the bottom of the screen.

a. 343K _____

_____

b. 13:15 _____

_____

c. WAIT _____

_____

d. EDIT _____

_____

STUDENT ASSIGNMENT 4: Understanding VP-Planner Plus Commands

Instructions: Answer the following questions.

1. Use Figure 1-46 to answer the following two questions. Where is the cell cursor located in the worksheet? Which keystroke causes the display on the input line?

Cell cursor location: ___E6___

Keystroke: _____

FIGURE 1-46
Problem 1 of Student
Assignment 4

```
11
12
13
14
15
16
17
18
19
20
 E6
Enter destination cell: E6
1help 2edit 3name 4abs 5goto 6window 7data 8table 9recalculate 0graph
338K                              8:46                                    POINT
```

2. Indicate the sequence of keystrokes for saving a worksheet that causes the display shown on the input line in Figure 1-47. Assume that the first letter of each command is entered to issue the commands that cause the display.

Keystroke sequence: _____

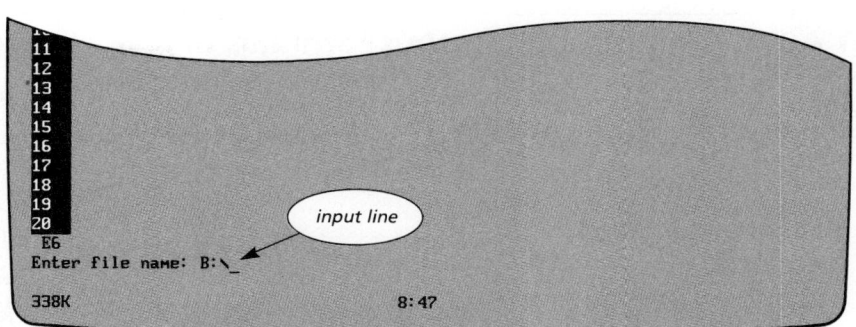

FIGURE 1-47
Problem 2 of Student
Assignment 4

3. Indicate the value assigned to the current cell caused by the entry on the input line in Figure 1-48. Assume that cell B4 contains the value 6 and cell B5 contains the value 7. Also, indicate the cell address of the cell that is assigned the value.

Value: _____

Current cell: _____

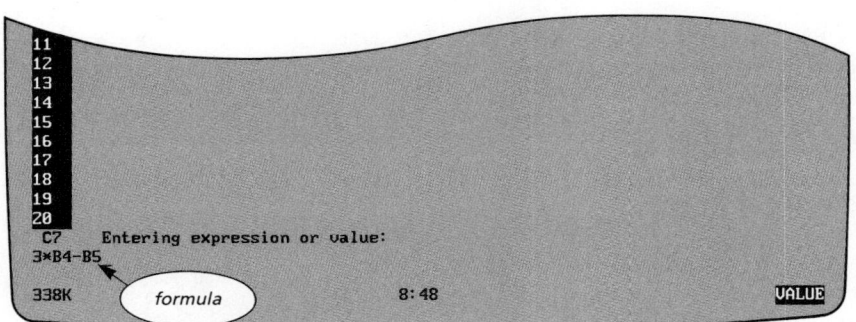

FIGURE 1-48
Problem 3 of Student
Assignment 4

4. Which keystroke causes VP-Planner Plus to display the current mode shown in Figure 1-49?

Keystroke: _____

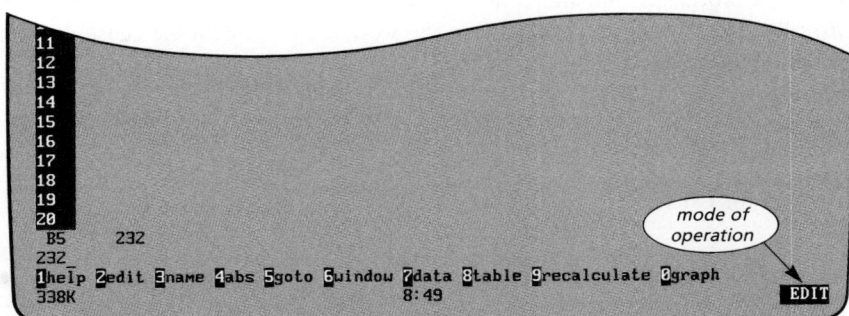

FIGURE 1-49
Problem 4 of Student
Assignment 4

STUDENT ASSIGNMENT 5: Correcting Formulas in a Worksheet

Instructions: The worksheet illustrated in Figure 1-50 contains an error in the PROFIT row for January. Analyze the entries displayed on the worksheet. Explain the cause of the error and the method of correction in the space provided below.

Cause of error: _____

_____

Method of correction: _____

_____

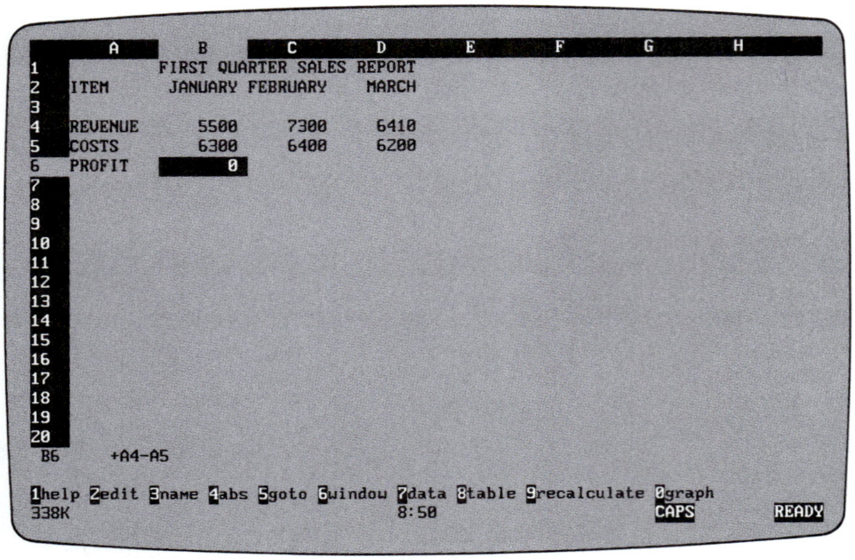

FIGURE 1-50
Student Assignment 5

STUDENT ASSIGNMENT 6: Correcting Worksheet Entries

Instructions: The worksheet illustrated in Figure 1-51 contains errors in the PROFIT row for February (cell C6) and March (cell D6). Analyze the entries displayed on the worksheet. Explain the cause of the errors for the two months and the methods of correction in the space provided below.

Cause of error in C6: _____

_____

Method of correction for C6: _____

_____

Cause of error in D6: _____

_____

Method of correction for D6: _____

_____

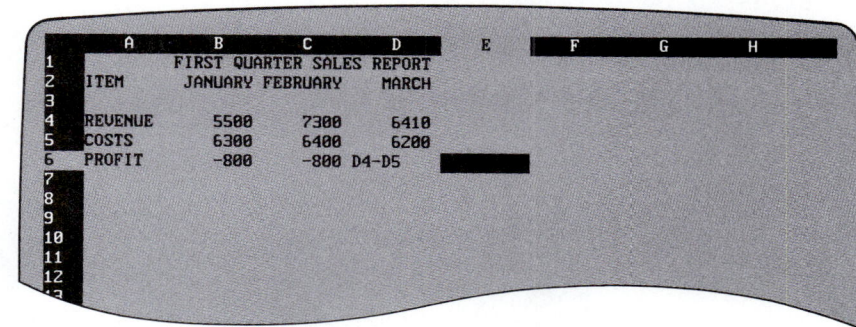

FIGURE 1-51
Student Assignment 6

STUDENT ASSIGNMENT 7: Entering Formulas

Instructions: For each worksheet below, write the formula that accomplishes the specified task and manually compute the value assigned to the specified cell.

1. See Figure 1-52. Assign to cell A20 the product of cell A18 and cell A19.

Formula: _____

Result assigned to cell A20: _____

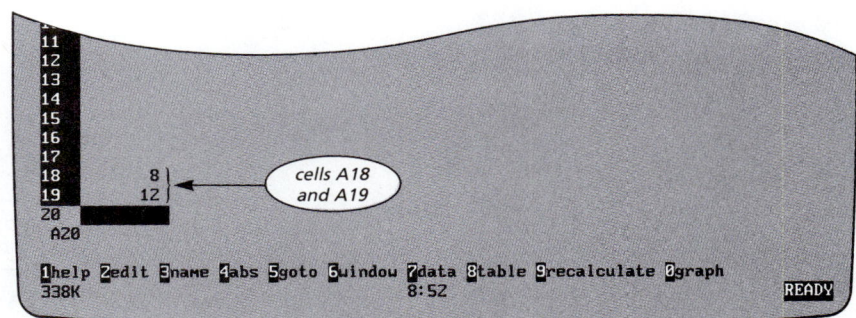

FIGURE 1-52
Problem 1 of Student
Assignment 7

2. See Figure 1-53. Assign to cell B20 the sum of cells B17, B18, and B19, minus cell A20.

Formula: _____

Result assigned to cell B20: _____

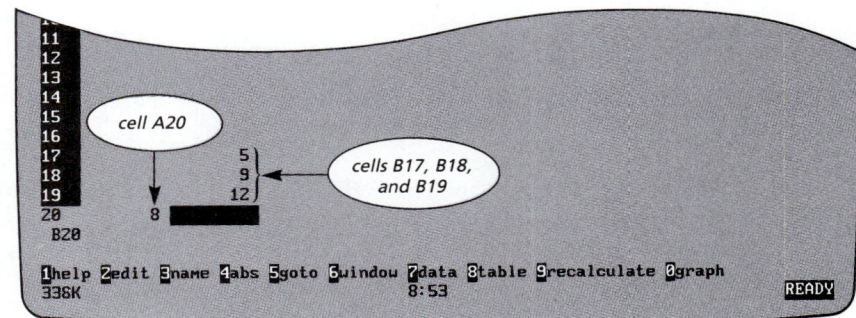

FIGURE 1-53
Problem 2 of Student
Assignment 7

Student Assignment 7 (continued)

3. See Figure 1-54. Assign to cell C20 two times the quotient of cell D19 divided by cell C19.

Formula: _____

Result assigned to cell C20: _____

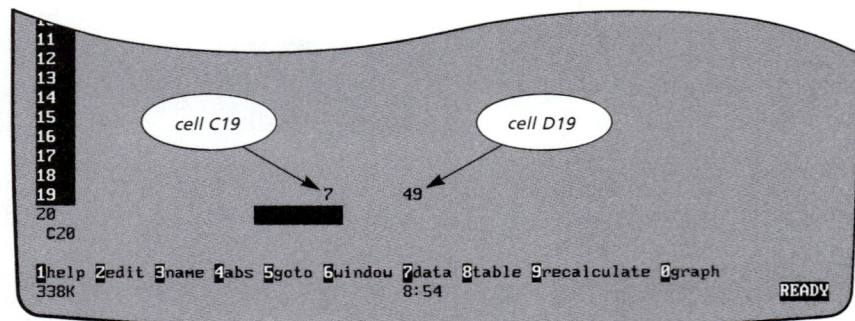

FIGURE 1-54
Problem 3 of Student
Assignment 7

4. See Figure 1-55. Assign to cell D20 the sum of cells D17 through D19 minus the sum of cells C18 and C19.

Formula: _____

Result assigned to cell D20: _____

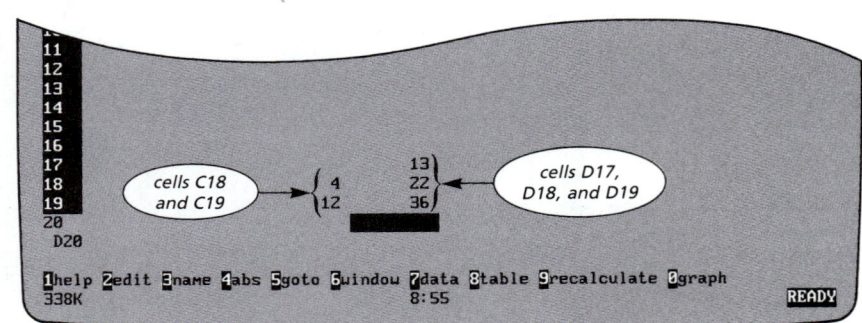

FIGURE 1-55
Problem 4 of Student
Assignment 7

STUDENT ASSIGNMENT 8: Building an Inventory Listing Worksheet

Instructions: Perform the following tasks using a personal computer.

1. Boot the computer.
2. Load VP-Planner Plus into main computer memory.
3. After reading the screen, press the Enter key.
4. Build the worksheet illustrated in Figure 1-56. The TOTAL line in row 7 contains the totals for Part A, Part B, and Part C for each of the plants (Seattle, Omaha, and Flint). For example, the total in cell B7 is the sum of the values in cells B4, B5, and B6.
5. Save the worksheet. Use the file name STUS1-8.
6. Print the screen image of the worksheet.

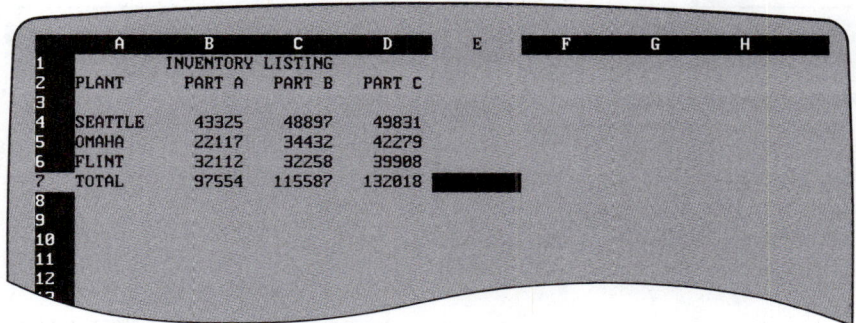

FIGURE 1-56
Student Assignment 8

STUDENT ASSIGNMENT 9: Building a Yearly Personal Expenses Comparison Worksheet

Instructions: Load VP-Planner Plus and perform the following tasks.

1. Build the worksheet illustrated in Figure 1-57. Calculate the total expenses for THIS YEAR in column C and LAST YEAR in column D by adding the values in the cells representing the rent, food, utilities, auto, insurance, and entertainment expenses.
2. Save the worksheet. Use the file name STUS1-9.
3. Print the screen image of the worksheet.

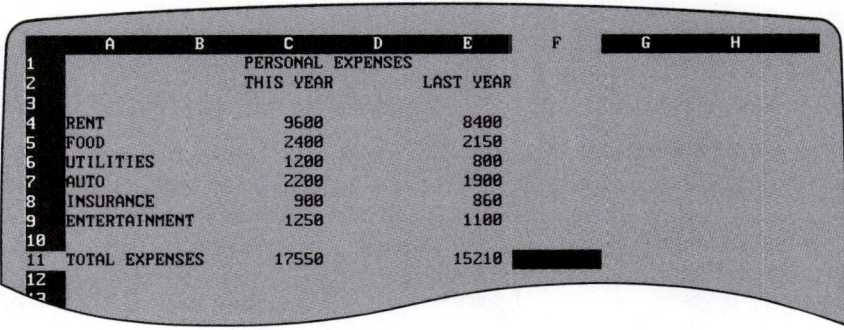

FIGURE 1-57
Student Assignment 9

STUDENT ASSIGNMENT 10: Building a Quarterly Income and Expense Worksheet

Instructions: Load VP-Planner Plus and perform the following tasks.

1. Build the worksheet illustrated in Figure 1-58. Calculate the total income in row 10 by adding the income for gas and oil, labor, and parts. Calculate the total expenses in row 17 by adding salaries, rent, and cost of goods. Calculate the net profit in row 19 by subtracting the total expenses from the total income.
2. Save the worksheet. Use the file name STUS1-10.
3. Print the screen image of the worksheet.

FIGURE 1-58
Student Assignment 10

```
          A        B        C         D        E        F       G        H
    1                       CHARLIE'S GASOLINE STATION
    2
    3                                 JAN-JUNE          JULY-DEC
    4
    5    INCOME:
    6            GAS & OIL            39764             44567
    7            LABOR                13450             15760
    8            PARTS                 4503              5623
    9
   10   TOTAL INCOME:                 57717             65950
   11
   12   EXPENSES:
   13            SALARIES             12000             12800
   14            RENT                  6500              6500
   15            COST OF GOODS        19766             21345
   16
   17   TOTAL EXPENSES:               38266             40645
   18
   19   NET PROFIT:                   19451             25305
   20
     G19

    1help 2edit 3name 4abs 5goto 6window 7data 8table 9recalculate 0graph
    370K                                      10:42                   CAPS    READY
```

STUDENT ASSIGNMENT 11: Using the Online Help Facility

Instructions: Load VP-Planner Plus and perform the following tasks.

1. With VP-Planner Plus in READY mode, press function key F1. Print the screen image.
2. Press function key F1 a second time to view the first page of the table of contents. Print the screen image.
3. Press the PgDn key to view the remainder of the table of contents. Print the image of each screen.
4. Use function key F5 to go to screens 6, 8, 9, 10, and 12. Read and print the image of each screen.
5. Press the Esc key to quit the online help facility.

STUDENT ASSIGNMENT 12: Changing Data in the Quarterly Income and Expense Worksheet

Instructions: If you did not do Student Assignment 10, do it before you begin this assignment. With the worksheet in Student Assignment 10 stored on the disk, load VP-Planner Plus and perform the following tasks.

1. Retrieve the worksheet STUS1-10 (see Figure 1-58) from disk. Use the command /File Retrieve (/FR). When the list of worksheet names displays on the screen, use the arrow keys to move the command cursor to the worksheet name STUS1-10. Press the Enter key. The worksheet illustrated in Figure 1-58 will display on the screen.
2. Make the changes to the worksheet described in Table 1-6. Use the EDIT mode of VP-Planner Plus. Recall that to use EDIT mode to change an entry in a cell, move the cell cursor to the cell and then press function key F2.

TABLE 1-6 List of Corrections to the Quarterly Income and Expense Worksheet

CELL	CURRENT CELL CONTENTS	CHANGE THE CELL CONTENTS TO
C1	CHARLIE'S GASOLINE STATION	CHUCK'S GAS STATION
D6	39764	39564
F6	44567	40592
D8	4503	45003
F8	5623	45623
D13	12000	22000
F13	12800	19765

As you edit the values in the cells containing numeric data, keep an eye on the total income, total expenses, and net profit cells. The values in these cells are based on formulas that reference the cells you are editing. You will see that each time a new value is entered into a cell referenced by a formula, VP-Planner Plus automatically recalculates a new value for the formula. It then stores the new value in the cell assigned the formula. This automatic recalculation of formulas is one of the most powerful aspects of any spreadsheet program.

After you have successfully made the changes listed in Table 1-6, the net profit for Jan-June in cell D19 should equal 49751 and the net profit for July-Dec should equal 54365.

3. Save the worksheet. Use the file name STUS1-12.

4. Print the screen image of the worksheet on the printer.

PROJECT 2

Formatting and Printing a Worksheet

Objectives

You will have mastered the material in this project when you can:

- Retrieve a worksheet from disk
- Increase the width of the columns in a worksheet
- Define a range of cells
- Format a worksheet
- Enter repeating characters into a cell using the Backslash key
- Copy one range of cells to another range of cells
- Add the contents of a range using the SUM function
- Determine a percentage
- Print a partial or complete worksheet without window borders
- Print the cell-formulas version of a worksheet
- Display the formulas assigned to cells, rather than their numeric results

The Sales Report worksheet created in Project 1 contains the revenue, costs, and profit for each of the three months of the first quarter, but it is not presented in the most readable manner. For example, as you can see in Figure 2-1, the columns are too close together and the numbers are displayed as whole numbers, even though they are dollar figures.

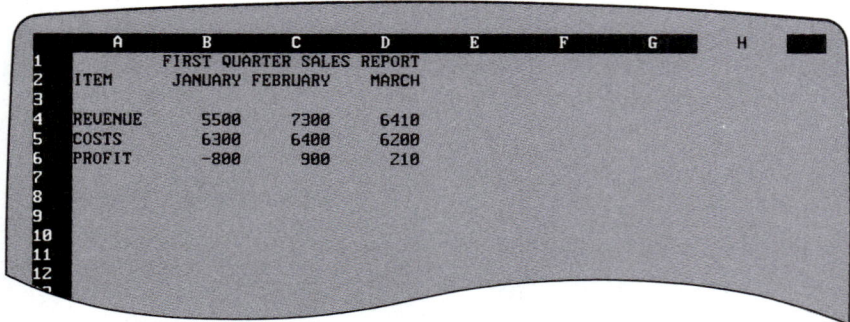

FIGURE 2-1
The worksheet we completed
in Project 1.

In this project we will use the formatting capabilities of VP-Planner Plus to make the worksheet more presentable and easier to read. We will also add summary totals for the quarter, using formulas. As shown in Figure 2-2, the total revenue in cell B12 is the sum of the revenue values for January, February, and March. The total cost in cell B13 is the sum of the cost values for January, February, and March; and the total profit in cell B14 is the sum of the profit values for January, February, and March. The percent profit in cell B15 is determined by dividing the total profit by the total revenue. After the worksheet is complete, we will print it without the window borders.

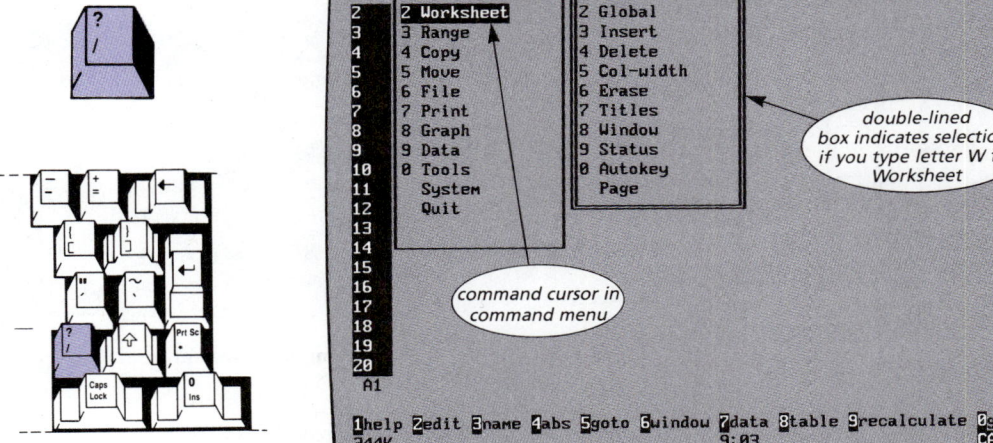

FIGURE 2-2
The worksheet we will complete in Project 2.

```
              A            B            C            D          E
 1                FIRST QUARTER SALES REPORT
 2   ITEM          JANUARY     FEBRUARY        MARCH
 3
 4   REVENUE       5500.00      7300.00      6410.00
 5   COSTS         6300.00      6400.00      6200.00
 6   PROFIT        -800.00       900.00       210.00
 7
 8   _____
 9
10   QUARTER RESULTS
11
12   TOTAL REVENUE   $19,210.00
13   TOTAL COSTS     $18,900.00
14   TOTAL PROFIT       $310.00
15   % PROFIT             1.6%
16
17
```

RETRIEVING A WORKSHEET (/FR)

Recall that at the end of Project 1, we used the Save command to store the worksheet shown in Figure 2-1 on disk under the name PROJS-1.WKS. Since Project 2 involves making modifications to this stored worksheet, we can eliminate retyping the whole worksheet, and save a lot of time, by retrieving it from disk and placing it into main computer memory.

After booting the computer and loading the VP-Planner Plus program, retrieve the worksheet PROJS-1 from the data disk. To retrieve the worksheet, enter the command /**F**ile **R**etrieve (/FR). First, press the Slash key (/) as illustrated in Figure 2-3. This causes VP-Planner Plus to enter the command mode. Next, use the Down Arrow key to move the command cursor to the word File. The result of this activity is shown in Figure 2-4 on the next page. With the command cursor on the word File, the File menu to the right of the active menu displays the commands that are available if you select the File command. To select it, press the Enter key. We also could have typed the letter F to select the File command.

```
              A         B         C         D         E         F         G         H
 1
 2    2 Worksheet      2 Global
 3    3 Range          3 Insert
 4    4 Copy           4 Delete
 5    5 Move           5 Col-width
 6    6 File           6 Erase
 7    7 Print          7 Titles
 8    8 Graph          8 Window
 9    9 Data           9 Status
10    0 Tools          0 Autokey
11      System           Page
12      Quit
13
14
15
16
17
18
19
20
A1
```

double-lined box indicates selections if you type letter W for Worksheet

command cursor in command menu

```
1help 2edit 3name 4abs 5goto 6window 7data 8table 9recalculate 0graph
344K                                    9:03                           CAPS    MENU
```

FIGURE 2-3 Step 1 of retrieving a worksheet from disk—press the Slash key (/).

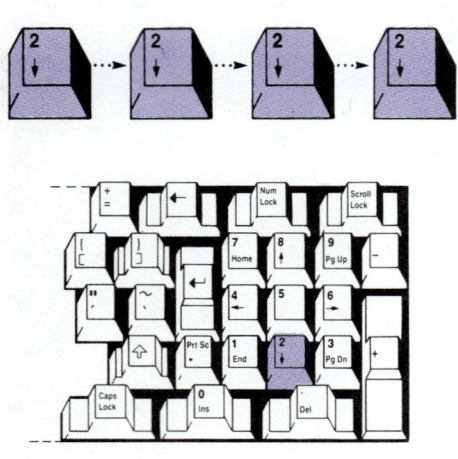

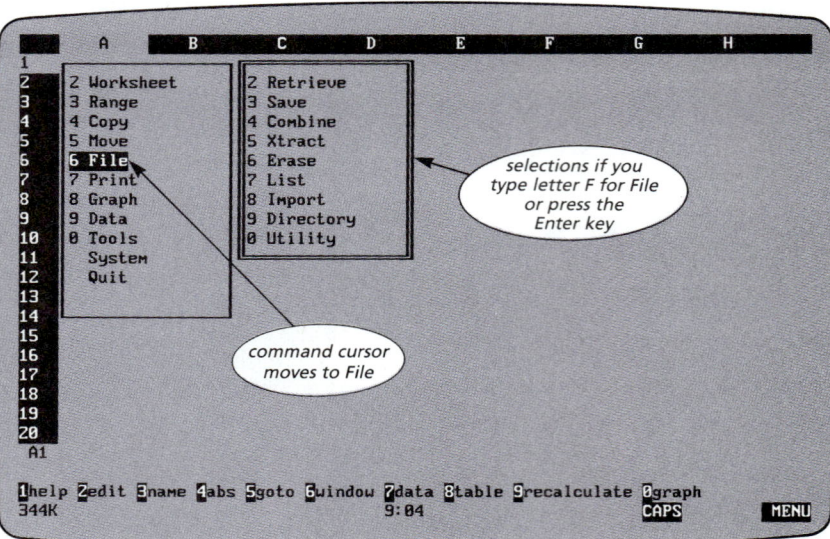

FIGURE 2-4 Step 2 of retrieving a worksheet from disk—use the arrow keys to move the command cursor to the word File in the command menu.

The command cursor is now active in the File menu as illustrated in Figure 2-5. The Retrieve command is the first command in the list. The double-lined box to the right of the file menu indicates the function of this command. With the command cursor on the Retrieve command, type the letter R for Retrieve.

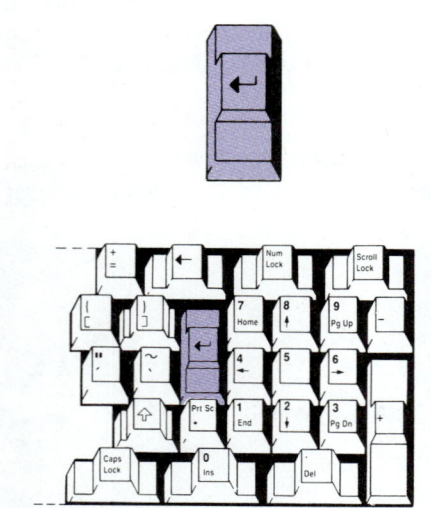

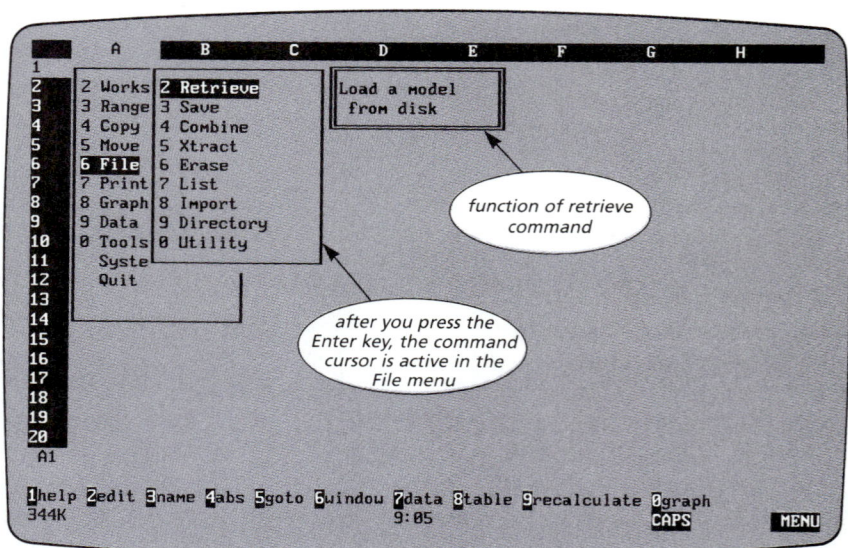

FIGURE 2-5 Step 3 of retrieving a worksheet from disk—press the Enter key.

As illustrated in Figure 2-6, VP-Planner Plus displays a boxed-in alphabetized list of the file names on the default drive that have the extension .WKS or .WK1. This helps you remember the names of the worksheets stored on the data disk. The boxed-in list includes all the worksheets you were told to save in Project 1, including PROJS-1.WKS.

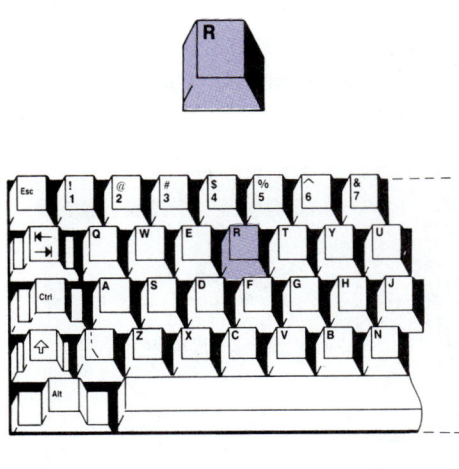

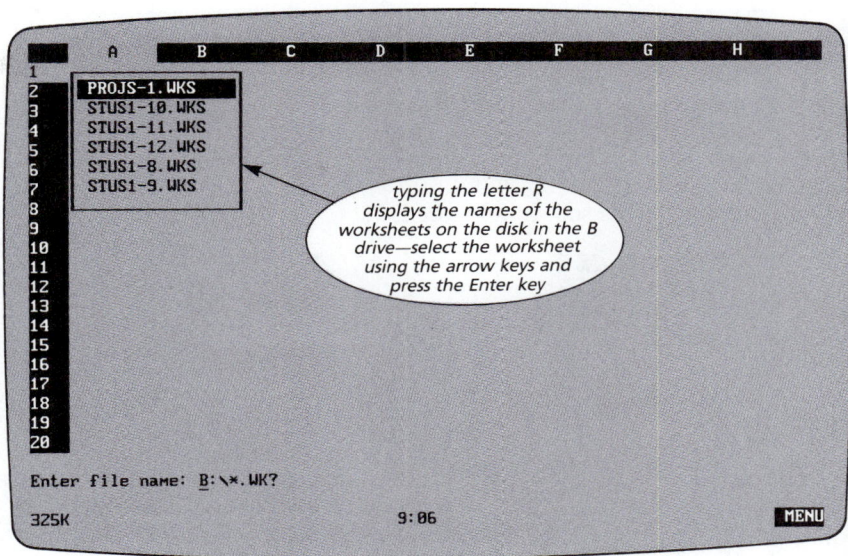

PROJS-1.WKS
STUS1-10.WKS
STUS1-11.WKS
STUS1-12.WKS
STUS1-8.WKS
STUS1-9.WKS

typing the letter R displays the names of the worksheets on the disk in the B drive—select the worksheet using the arrow keys and press the Enter key

Enter file name: B:*.WK?

325K   9:06   MENU

FIGURE 2-6 Step 4 of retrieving a worksheet from disk—type the letter R for Retrieve.

One way to select the worksheet you want to retrieve is to type PROJS-1 on the input line and press the Enter key. Better yet, because the command cursor is on the file name PROJS-1.WKS in the boxed-in list in Figure 2-6, press the Enter key. This method saves keying time. While VP-Planner Plus is accessing the worksheet, the mode indicator in the lower right corner of the screen changes to WAIT and the red light flashes on the default drive. After the worksheet is retrieved, the screen appears as shown in Figure 2-1.

According to Figure 2-2, all the new labels are in capitals. Therefore, press the Caps Lock key before modifying the worksheet.

The tasks in this project are to widen the columns, format the dollar amounts, and add the quarter results. The tasks may be completed in any sequence. Let's complete them in the following sequence:

1. Widen the columns from 9 characters to 13 characters to allow the quarter result titles and other numeric data to fit in the columns.
2. Change the numeric representations for the three months to dollars and cents—two digits to the right of the decimal place.
3. Determine the quarter results.
4. Change the percent profit to a number in percent.
5. Change the numeric representations of the quarter results to dollars and cents with a leading dollar sign.

CHANGING THE WIDTH OF THE COLUMNS

When VP-Planner Plus first executes and the blank worksheet appears on the screen, all the columns have a default width of nine characters. But you might want to change the width of the columns to make the worksheet easier to read or to ensure that entries will display properly in the cells to which they are assigned.

There are three ways to change the width of the columns in a worksheet. First, make a global change, which uniformly increases or decreases the width of all the columns in the worksheet. **Global** means the entire worksheet. Second, make a change in the width of one column at a time. Third, make a change in the width over a series of adjacent columns. We discuss the first two methods. To learn about the third alternative, press function key F1 to get the online help facility of VP-Planner Plus. When the online help facility screen appears, press function key F5 and go to screen 54. After reading or printing the screen, press the Esc key to return to the worksheet.

Changing the Width of All the Columns (/WGC)

To change the width of all the columns, enter the command /Worksheet Global Col-width (/WGC). When you press the Slash key, the command menu displays with the first command, Worksheet, highlighted as shown in Figure 2-3, and the **Worksheet menu** displays to the right of the command menu. Note that the first command in the Worksheet menu is Global. This command makes the changes to the entire worksheet. Therefore, type the letter W for Worksheet to move the command cursor to the Worksheet menu, as shown in Figure 2-7.

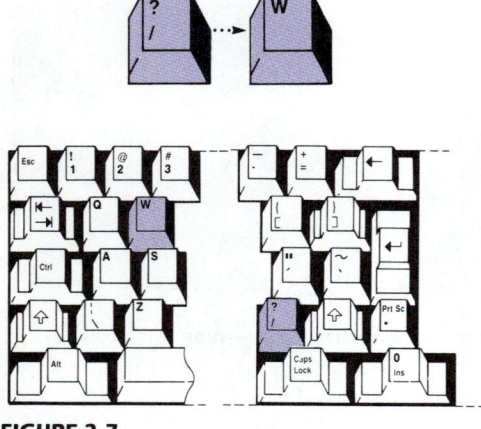

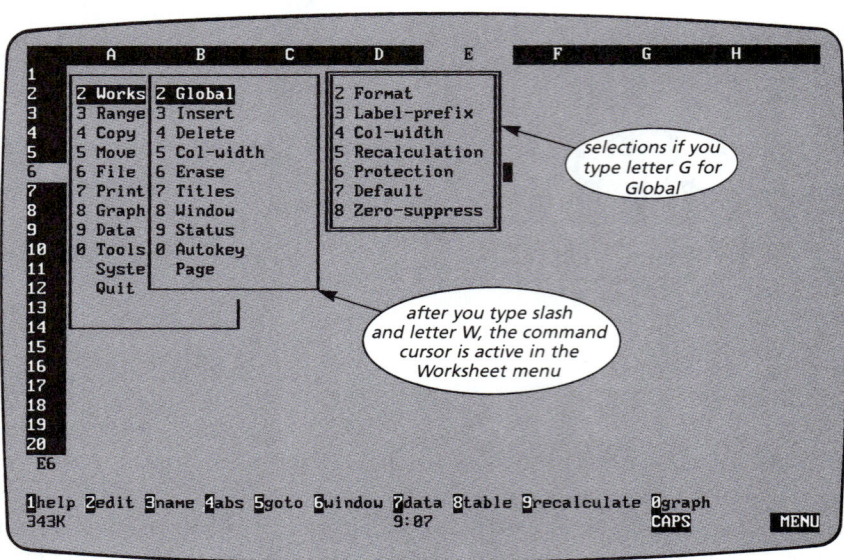

FIGURE 2-7
Step 1 of increasing the width of the columns—press the Slash key (/) and type the letter W.

Recall from Project 1 that when the menus are layered, as they are in Figure 2-7, the topmost one is active. The menu to the right in the double-lined box indicates the choice of commands if you select the Global command. The command Col-width is the one we want—the third one in the double-lined box. Type the letter G for Global. This moves the command cursor to the **Global menu**. Next, use the Down Arrow key to move the command cursor to Col-width. Now the doubled-lined box to the right of the command menu explains the purpose of the Col-width command. This procedure is illustrated in Figure 2-8.

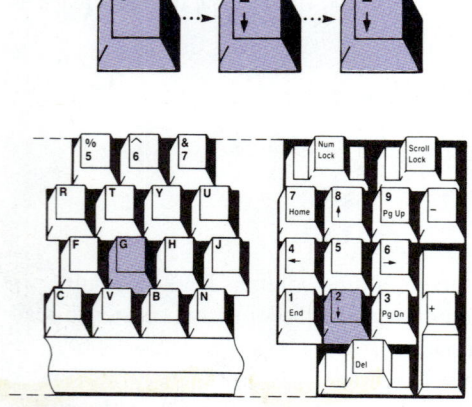

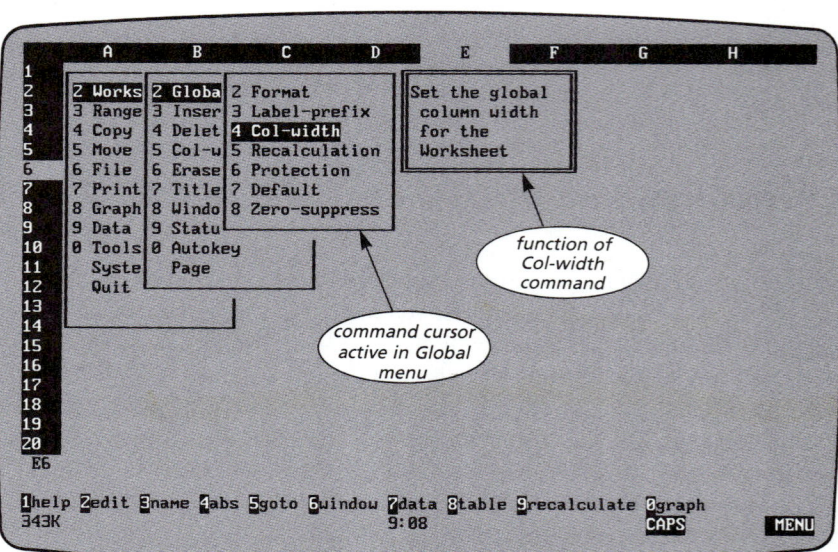

FIGURE 2-8
Step 2 of increasing the width of the columns—type the letter G and use the Down Arrow key to move the command cursor to Col-width in the Global menu.

Before typing the letter C for Col-width, note that the reverse video on each of the bottom-layered menus shows the current sequence of commands entered so far—/Worksheet Global (/WG). If you decide at the last second that you do not want to increase the width of the columns, how many times do you have to press the Esc key to *back out* of the command mode in Figure 2-8 and return to the READY mode? If your answer is three, you're right—once for the Global command, once for the Worksheet command, and once for the Slash key (/).

Now type the letter C for Col-width. The prompt message "Enter desired column width (0–240): 9" displays on the input line at the bottom of the screen. This message is illustrated on the partial screen in Figure 2-9. The numbers "0–240" define the range of valid entries. The number 9 following the colon indicates the current global (default) column width.

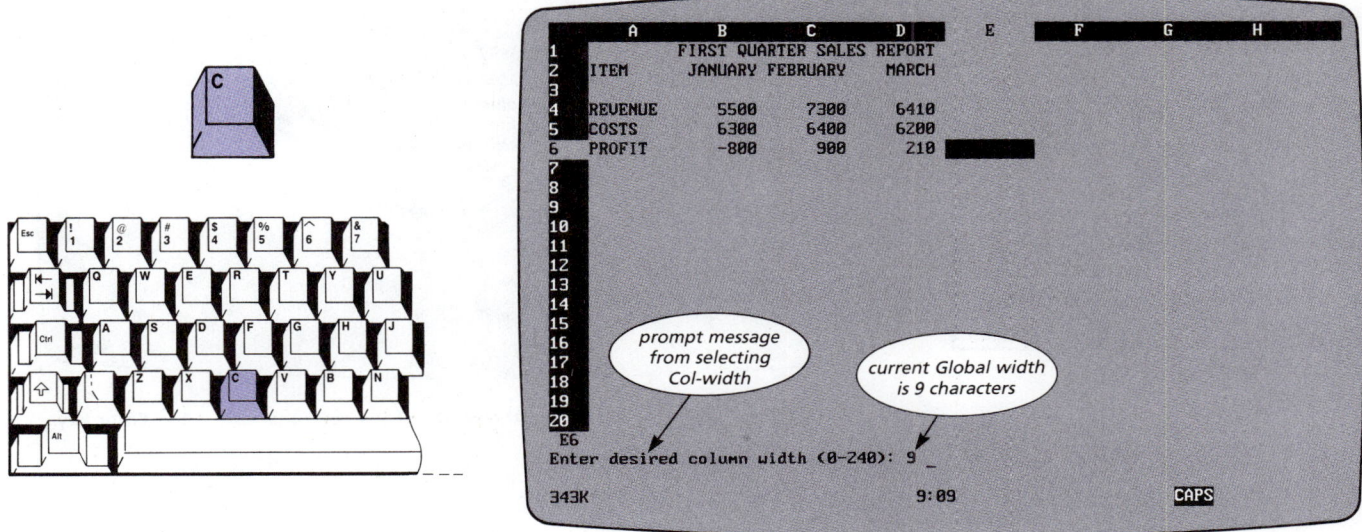

FIGURE 2-9 Step 3 of increasing the width of the columns—type the letter C.

Type the number 13 as shown in Figure 2-10, then press the Enter key. An alternative to typing the number 13 is to use the Right and Left arrow keys to increase or decrease the number on the input line.

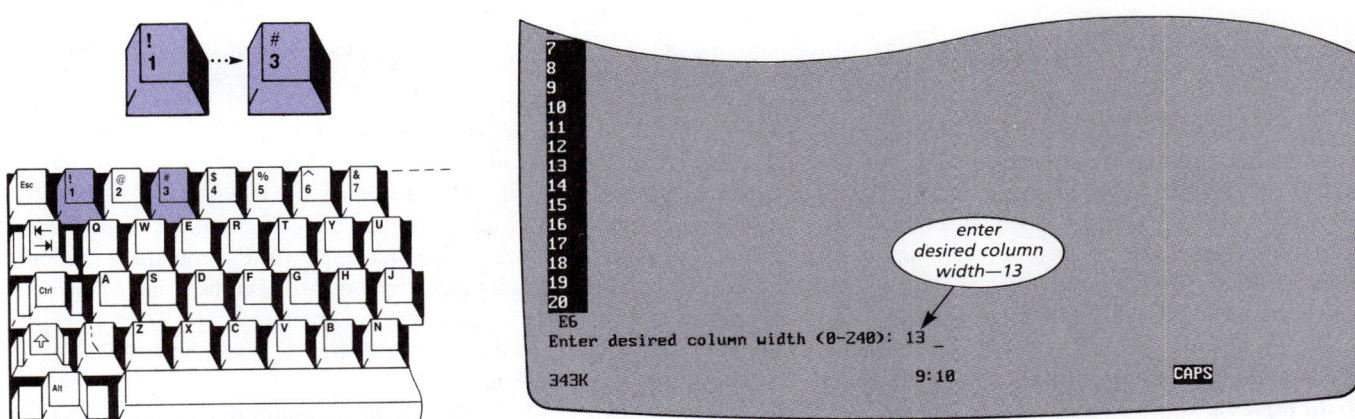

FIGURE 2-10 Step 4 of increasing the width of the columns—enter the number 13.

Figure 2-11 illustrates the worksheet with the new column width of 13 characters. Compare Figure 2-11 to Figure 2-1. Because the columns in Figure 2-11 are wider, the worksheet is easier to read. But because the columns are wider, fewer show on the screen.

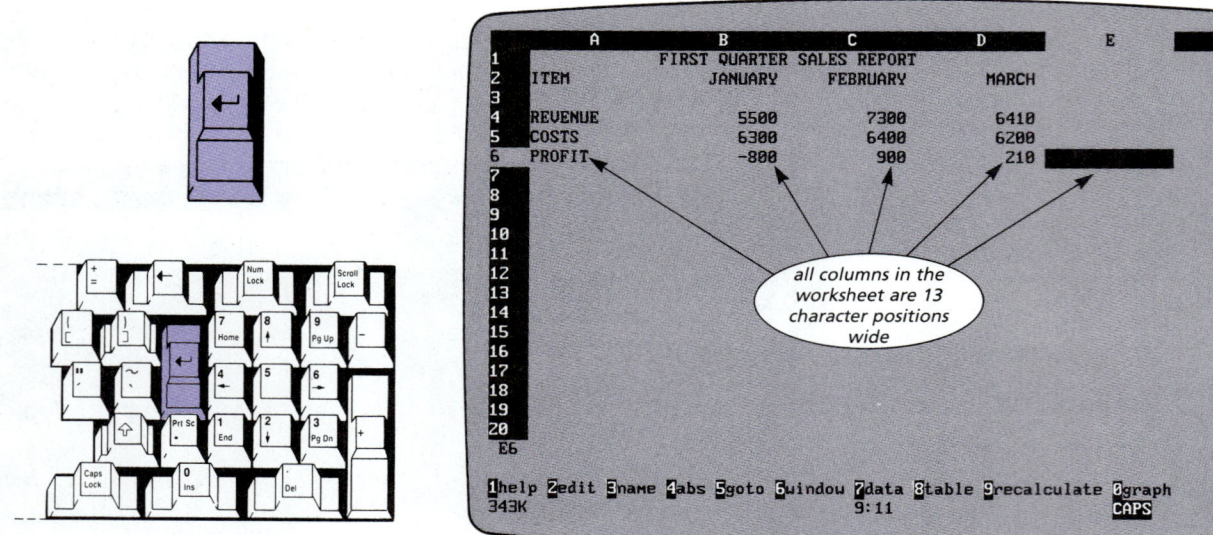

FIGURE 2-11 Step 5 of increasing the width of the columns—press the Enter key.

Changing the Width of One Column at a Time (/WCS)

You can change the width of one column at a time in the worksheet. Let's change the width of column A to 20 characters, leaving the width of the other columns at 13 characters. To change the width of column A to 20 characters, do the following:

1. Press the Home key to move the cell cursor into column A.
2. Type the command /**W**orksheet **C**ol-width **S**et (/WCS). The Slash key switches VP-Planner Plus to the command mode. The letter W selects the Worksheet command. The letter C selects the command Col-width and the letter S selects the command Set.
3. In response to the prompt message "Enter desired column width (0-240): 13" on the input line, type the number 20 and press the Enter key.

Now column A is 20 characters wide while the other columns in the worksheet are 13 characters wide. Let's change column A back to the default width of 13 characters. With the cell cursor in column A, enter the command /**W**orksheet **C**ol-width **R**eset (/WCR). This command changes column A back to the default width—13 characters.

What do you think happens if you set the width of a column to zero? If your answer is that the column becomes invisible, you're right—any entries placed in the column are hidden from view. It is not unusual to hide columns that contain confidential information, like employee salaries. Columns that are **hidden** do not display on the screen or print on the printer. Once the worksheet is printed, you can set the width of the hidden column to a value that displays the column entries.

Let's hide column A. Then we'll reset it back to 13 characters. Type the command /**W**orksheet **C**ol-width **S**et (/WCS). Type the digit zero and press the Enter key. Column A disappears from the screen.

To reset the width of column A, enter the command /**W**orksheet **C**ol-width **R**eset (/WCR). Column A displays with the same width as the other columns.

Use the GOTO command to move the cell cursor back to cell E6, where it was before we set and then reset the width of column A.

DEFINING A RANGE

Our next step is to format the monthly dollar amounts. The Format command requires you to specify the cells you want to format. For this reason, you need to understand the term *range* before using the Format command.

A **range** in VP-Planner Plus means one or more cells on which an operation can take place. A range may be a single cell, a series of adjacent cells in a row or column, or a rectangular group of adjacent cells. Hence, a range may consist of one cell or many cells. However, a range cannot be made up of cells that only run diagonally or are separated. Figure 2-12 illustrates several valid and invalid ranges of cells.

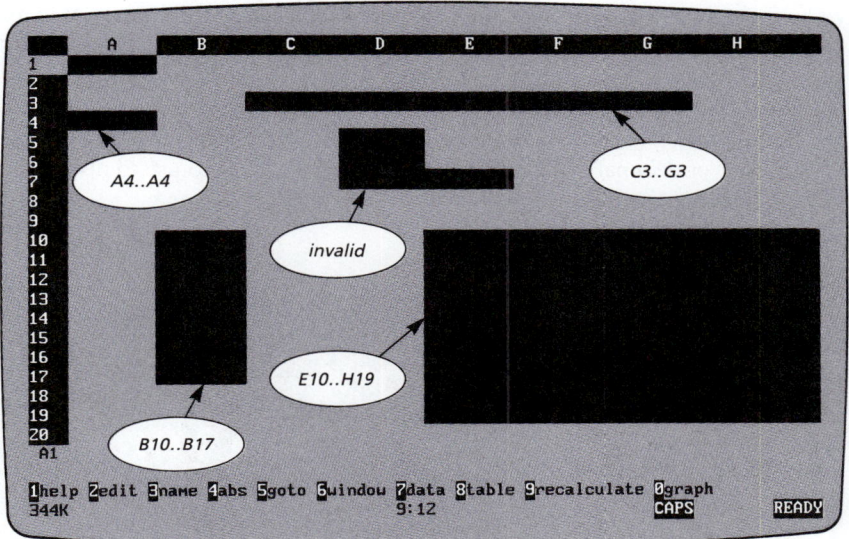

FIGURE 2-12
Valid and invalid ranges.

When you are asked by VP-Planner Plus to specify a range, you simply type the cell address for the first cell in the range, followed by a **period** (.), followed by the cell address for the last cell in the range. If a range defines a rectangular group of cells, any pair of diagonally opposite corner cells may be used to identify it. For example, the upper left cell and the lower right cell of the rectangular group of cells identify the range. Table 2-1 summarizes the ranges described in Figure 2-12.

TABLE 2-1 A Summary of the Ranges Specified in Figure 2-23

RANGE	COMMENT
A4..A4	The range is made up of one cell, A4.
C3..G3	The range is made up of five adjacent cells in row 3. The five cells are C3, D3, E3, F3, and G3.
B10..B17	The range is made up of eight adjacent cells in column B. The eight cells are B10, B11, B12, B13, B14, B15, B16, and B17.
E10..H19	The range is made up of a rectangular group of cells. The upper left cell (E10) and the lower right cell (H19) define the rectangle. The ranges H19..E10, H10..E19, and E19..H10 define the same range as E10..H19.

Now that you know how to define a range, we can move on to the next step in Project 2: formatting the numeric values in the worksheet.

FORMATTING NUMERIC VALUES

he Format command is used to control the manner in which numeric values appear in the worksheet. As shown in Figure 2-2, we want to change the numeric values in the range B4 through D6 to display as dollars and cents with two digits to the right of the decimal point.

Invoking the Format Command (/RF or /WGF)

There are two ways to invoke the Format command. First, you can use the series of commands /**W**orksheet **G**lobal **F**ormat (/WGF) to format all the cells in the worksheet the same way. Second, you can use the commands /**R**ange **F**ormat (/RF) to format just a particular range of cells. Since this project involves formatting a range rather than all the cells in the worksheet, type /RF to activate the command cursor in the Format menu as shown in Figure 2-13. The **Format menu** lists the different ways to format a range. As indicated in the double-lined box to the right, the first format type in the menu, Fixed, formats cells to a fixed number of decimal places. This is the format we want to use to display the monthly amounts to two decimal places. Therefore, type the letter F for Fixed.

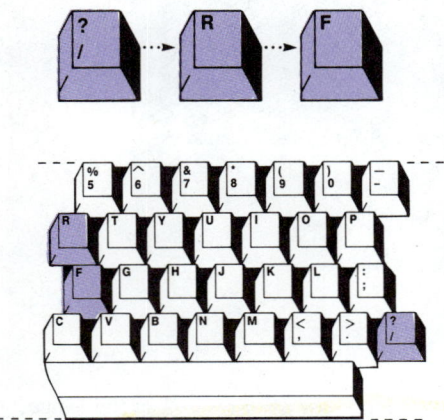

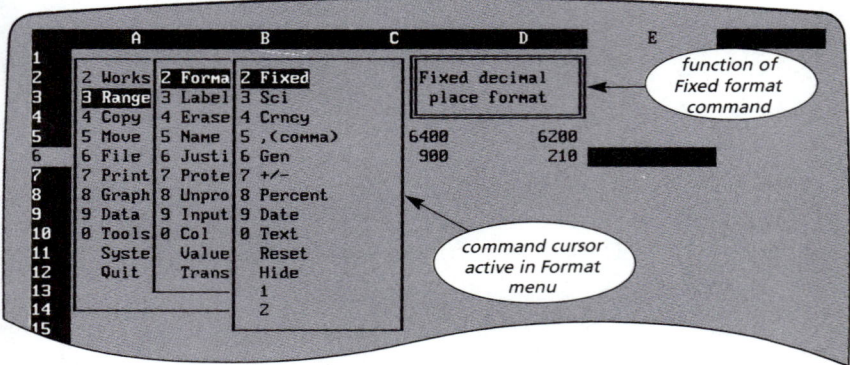

FIGURE 2-13 Step 1 of formatting a range of cells—press the Slash key (/) and type the letters R and F.

As shown in Figure 2-14, VP-Planner Plus displays the message "Enter desired decimal position: 2" on the input line at the bottom of the screen. Since most spreadsheet applications require two decimal positions, VP-Planner Plus displays 2 as the entry to save you time. Press the Enter key to enter two decimal positions. Next, VP-Planner Plus changes to POINT mode and displays the message "Select Range of Cells to be altered: E6..E6" (see Figure 2-15). The range E6..E6 displays at the end of the input line because the cell cursor is at cell E6. At this point, enter the range by typing B4.D6, or use the arrow keys to select the range. (Don't be concerned that VP-Planner Plus displays two periods between the cell address when you press the Period key once. It is the program's way of displaying a range.) Using the arrow keys to select a range is called **pointing**. Let's use the pointing method, because it requires less effort.

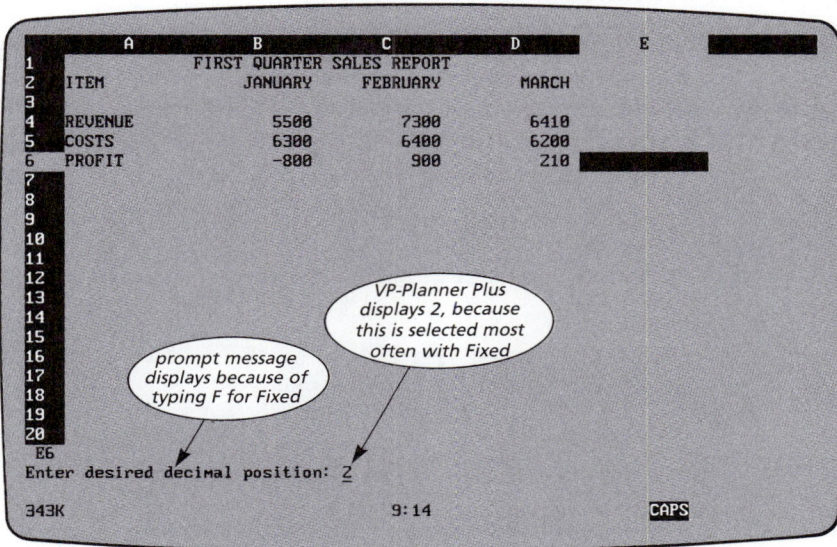

FIGURE 2-14 Step 2 of formatting a range of cells—type the letter F for Fixed and VP-Planner Plus displays a prompt message on the input line.

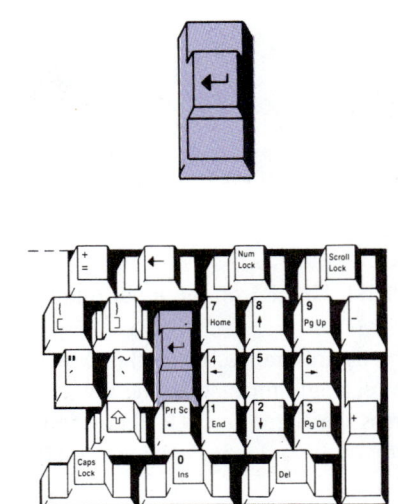

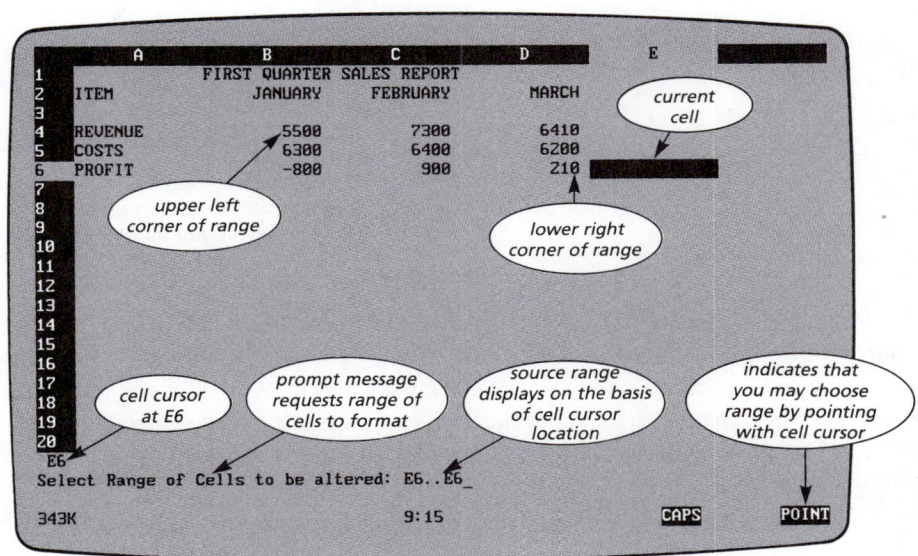

FIGURE 2-15 Step 3 of formatting a range of cells—press the Enter key to select two decimal places and VP-Planner Plus displays the prompt message on the input line, requesting the range to format.

Selecting a Range by Pointing

To select a range by pointing, first press the Backspace key (or Esc key) to change the default entry on the input line in Figure 2-15 from E6..E6 to E6. Next, use the arrow keys to move the cell cursor to B4, the upper left corner cell of the desired range. This procedure is shown in Figure 2-16.

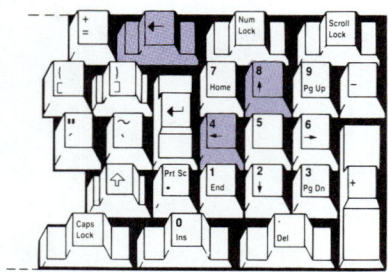

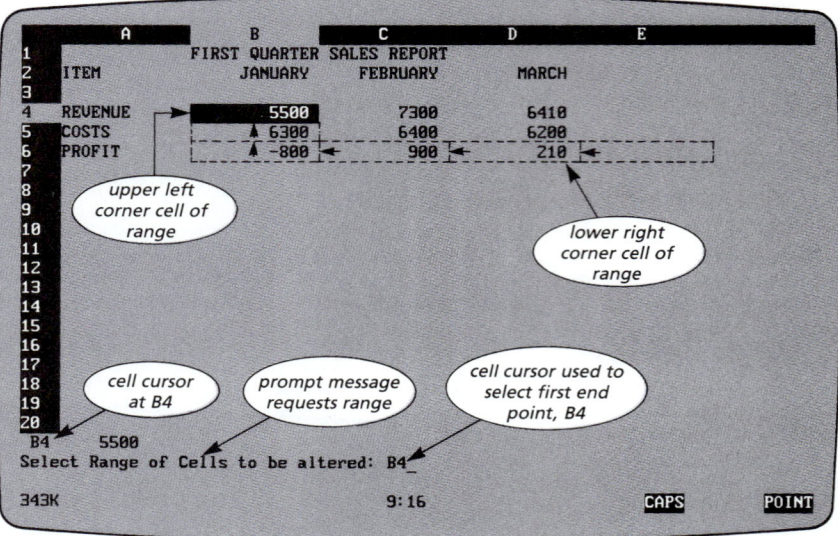

FIGURE 2-16 Step 4 of formatting a range of cells—press the Backspace key to unlock the first end point on the input line and use the arrow keys to select end point B4.

With the cell cursor at B4, press the Period key to *lock in* or *anchor* the first end point, B4. The B4 on the input line changes to B4..B4.

Now use the arrow keys to move the cell cursor to cell D6, the lower right corner of the desired range. Press the Down Arrow key twice and the Right Arrow key twice. As the cell cursor moves, a reverse video rectangle forms over the range covered. The range on the input line changes from B4..B4 to B4..D6 (see Figure 2-17). Press the Enter key. VP-Planner Plus immediately displays the monthly values in cells B4, C4, D4, B5, C5, D5, B6, C6, and D6 with two decimal places (dollars and cents). Everything else in the worksheet remains the same as shown in Figure 2-18.

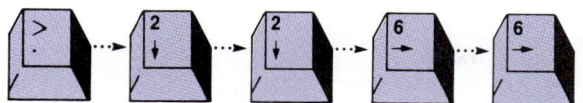

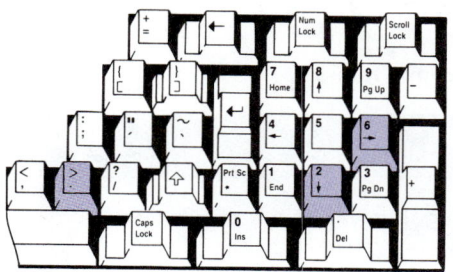

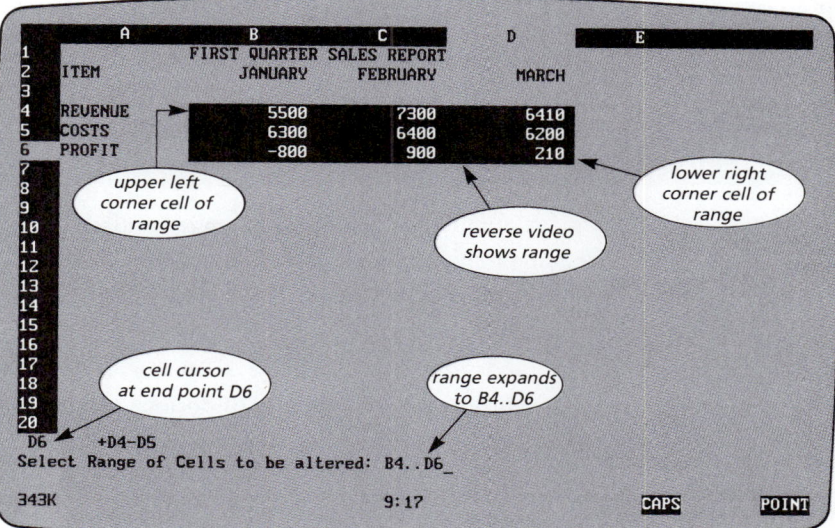

FIGURE 2-17 Step 5 of formatting a range of cells—press the Period key (.) to anchor the first end point and use the arrow keys to move the cell cursor to the opposite end point.

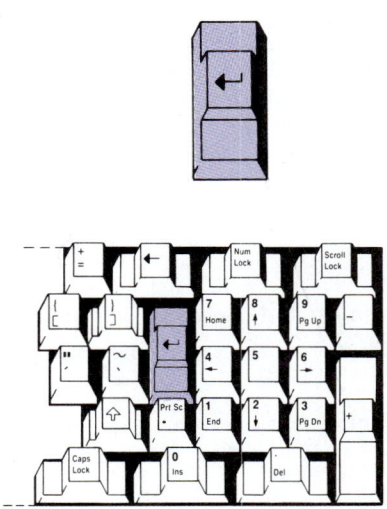

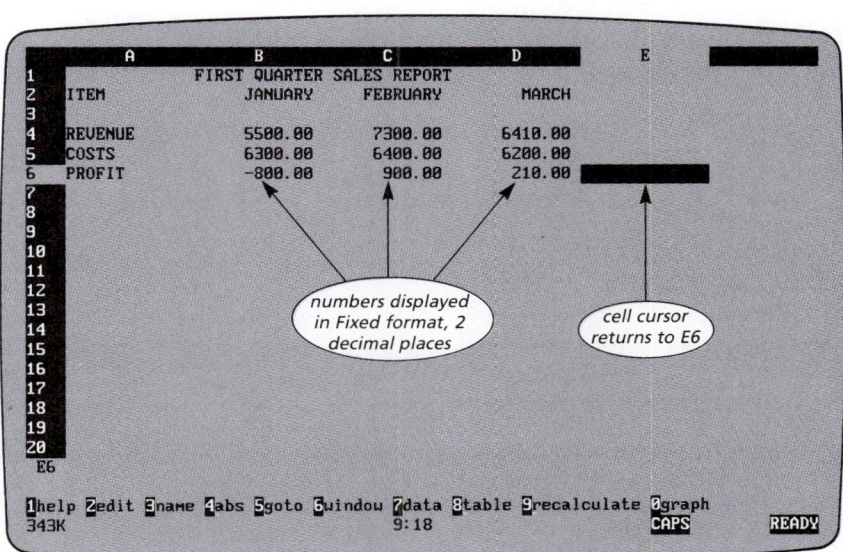

FIGURE 2-18 Step 6 of formatting a range—press the Enter key and the numbers display in Fixed format.

We could have used three other ways to describe the rectangular group of cells B4..D6 to VP-Planner Plus. B6..D4 and D4..B6 are two other ways. Can you identify the third way?

Summary of Format Commands

You can format numbers in cells in a variety of ways using the /**W**orksheet **G**lobal (/WGF) or /**R**ange **F**ormat (/RF) commands. Table 2-2 summarizes the various format options. You will find Table 2-2 helpful when you begin formatting your own worksheets. Also, remember that VP-Planner Plus rounds a number to the rightmost position if any digits are lost because of the format or number of decimal positions chosen.

TABLE 2-2   Format Types for Numeric Values in the Format Menu

MENU ITEM	DESCRIPTION
Fixed	Displays numbers to a specified number of decimal places. Negative values are displayed with a leading minus sign. Examples: 38; 0.912; –45.67.
Sci	Displays numbers in a form called **scientific notation**. The letter E stands for "times 10 to the power." Examples: 3.7E + 01; –2.345E–30.
Crncy	Crncy stands for Currency. Displays numbers preceded by a dollar sign next to the leftmost digit, with a specified number of decimal places (0–15), and uses commas to group the integer portion of the number by thousands. Negative numbers display in parentheses. Examples: $1,234.56; $0.98; $23,934,876.15; ($48.34).
, (comma)	The , (comma) is the same as the Crncy format, except the dollar sign does not display. Examples: 2,123.00; 5,456,023.34; (22,000).
Gen	Gen stands for General. This is the default format in which a number is stored when it is entered into a cell. Trailing zeros are suppressed and leading integer zeros display. Negative numbers display with a leading minus sign. Examples: 23.981; 0.563; 23401; –500.45.
+/–	Displays a single horizontal bar graph composed of plus (+) or minus (–) signs that indicate the sign of the number and the magnitude of the number. One plus or minus sign displays for each unit value. Only the integer portion of a decimal-fraction number is used. Examples: + + + + + + for 6; ––– for –3.8.
Percent	Displays numbers in percent form. Examples: 34% for 0.34; .11% for 0.0011; –13.245% for –0.13245.
Date	Used to format cells that contain a date or time.
Text	Displays formulas rather than their values. Numbers appear in General format. Examples: + B4–B5; 2∗(F5 – G3).
Reset	Resets cells back to Global format.
Hide	Prevents the display of the cell contents on the screen and when printed. To see what's in a hidden cell, move the cursor to that cell. The contents will display on the status line. (Not available for a global format.)
1 and 2	Allows you to assign your own custom formats. See the VP-Planner Plus user's manual for details.

Determining the Format Assigned to a Cell

You can determine the format assigned to a cell by the Range Format command by moving the cursor to that cell. The format displays on the status line in the lower left corner of the screen. In Figure 2-19, the cursor is at cell D6. Format F2 displays on the status line in parentheses next to the cell address. F2 is an abbreviation for the format "Fixed, 2 decimal places." Recall that we assigned this format to cell D4 in Figures 2-13 through 2-18.

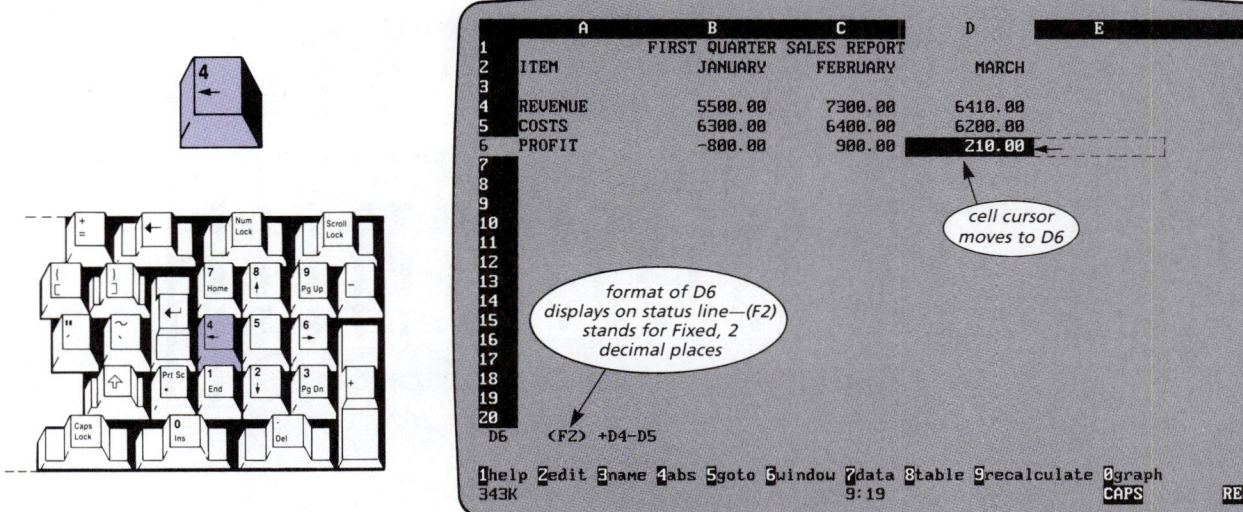

FIGURE 2-19 The format assigned to a cell displays on the status line when the cell cursor is on the cell.

REPEATING CHARACTERS IN A CELL

In Figure 2-2, row 8 contains a dashed line. We will add the dashed line to the worksheet using **repeating characters**—characters that are repeated throughout a cell.

To enter the dashed line, move the cell cursor to cell A8 using the GOTO command. Recall that function key F5 invokes the GOTO command. Next, enter the cell address A8 and press the Enter key. The cell cursor immediately moves to cell A8 as shown in Figure 2-20.

FIGURE 2-20 Moving the cell cursor to A8 and entering a repeating dash on the input line.

With the cell cursor at A8, press the Backslash key (\). The **Backslash key** signals VP-Planner Plus that the character or sequence of characters that follow it on the input line are to be repeated throughout the cell. Repeating the minus sign (-) creates the dashed line shown in Figure 2-2. Therefore, immediately after the Backslash key, press the Minus Sign key once as illustrated at the bottom of the screen in Figure 2-20.

To enter the repeating dash, press the Enter key. The dash repeats throughout cell A8 as shown in Figure 2-21. Note that the Backslash key is not included as part of the cell entry. Like the quotation mark ("), circumflex (^), and apostrophe ('), the backslash (\) is used as the first character that instructs VP-Planner Plus what to do with the characters that follow on the input line.

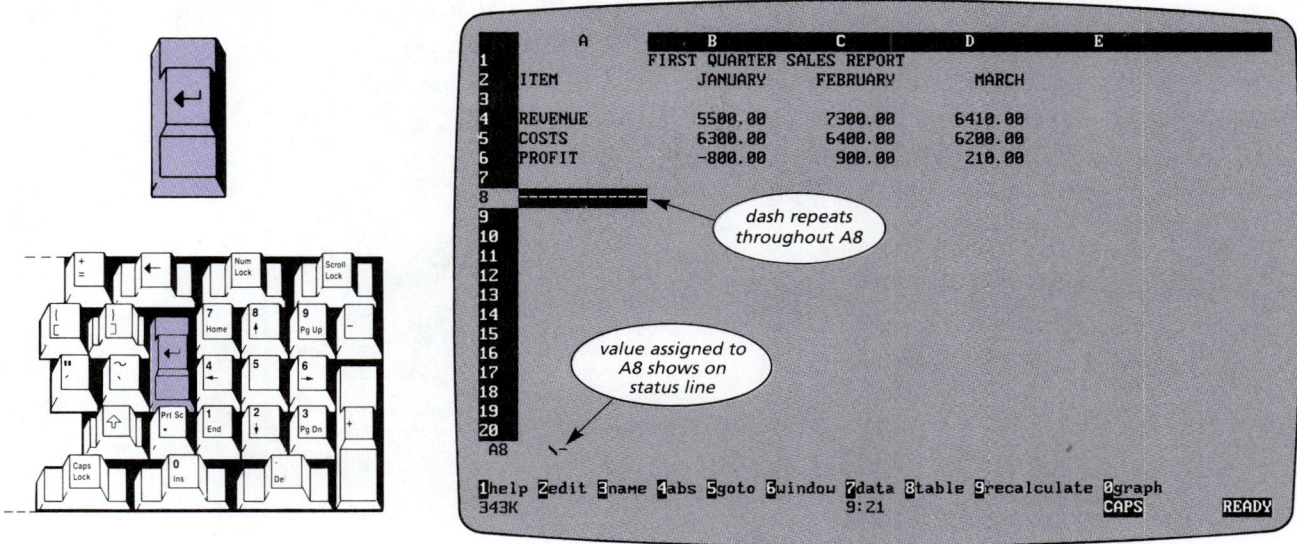

FIGURE 2-21 Press the Enter key to assign the repeating dash to cell A8.

We still need to extend the dashed line through cells B8, C8, and D8. We can move the cell cursor to each individual cell and make the same entry we made in cell A8, or we can use the Copy command. Let's use the Copy command.

REPLICATION—THE COPY COMMAND (/C)

The /Copy command (/C) is used to copy or replicate the contents of one group of cells to another group of cells. This command is one of the most useful because it can save you both time and keystrokes when you build a worksheet. We will use the Copy command to copy the dashes in cell A8 to cells B8 through D8. Type the Slash key (/) to place VP-Planner Plus in the command mode. In the command menu list, the Copy command is the third one. Type the letter C to invoke the Copy command.

Source Range

The prompt message "Source cell range: A8..A8" displays on the input line as shown in Figure 2-22. The **source range** is the range we want to copy. Since A8 is the cell that we want to copy to B8 through D8, press the Enter key.

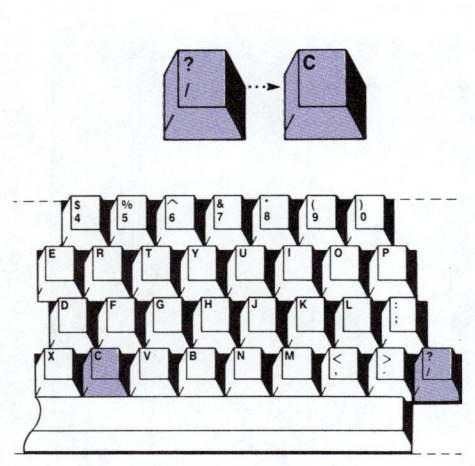
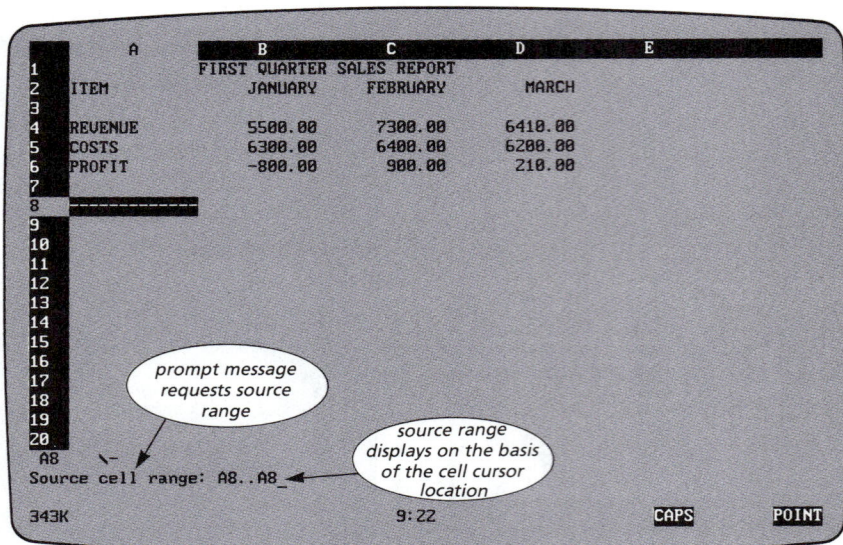

FIGURE 2-22 Step 1 of copying a range of cells—press the Slash key (/) and type the letter C for Copy.

Destination Range

After you press the Enter key, the prompt message "Destination cell range: A8" displays on the input line. This message is shown in Figure 2-23. The **destination range** is the range to which we want to copy the source range.

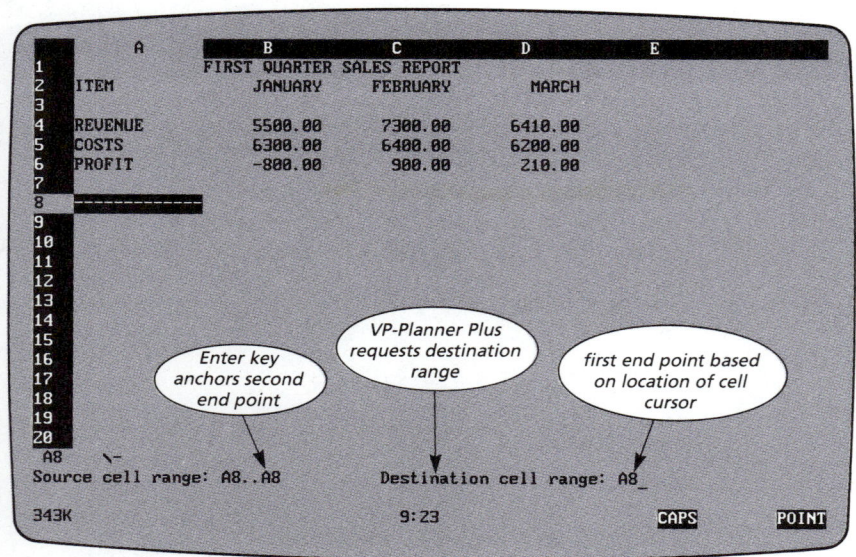

FIGURE 2-23 Step 2 of copying a range of cells—anchor the end points of the source range to copy by pressing the Enter key.

Move the cell cursor to B8, the left end point of the range to copy to (see Figure 2-24). Note that following the prompt message on the input line, the cell address is now B8, the location of the cell cursor.

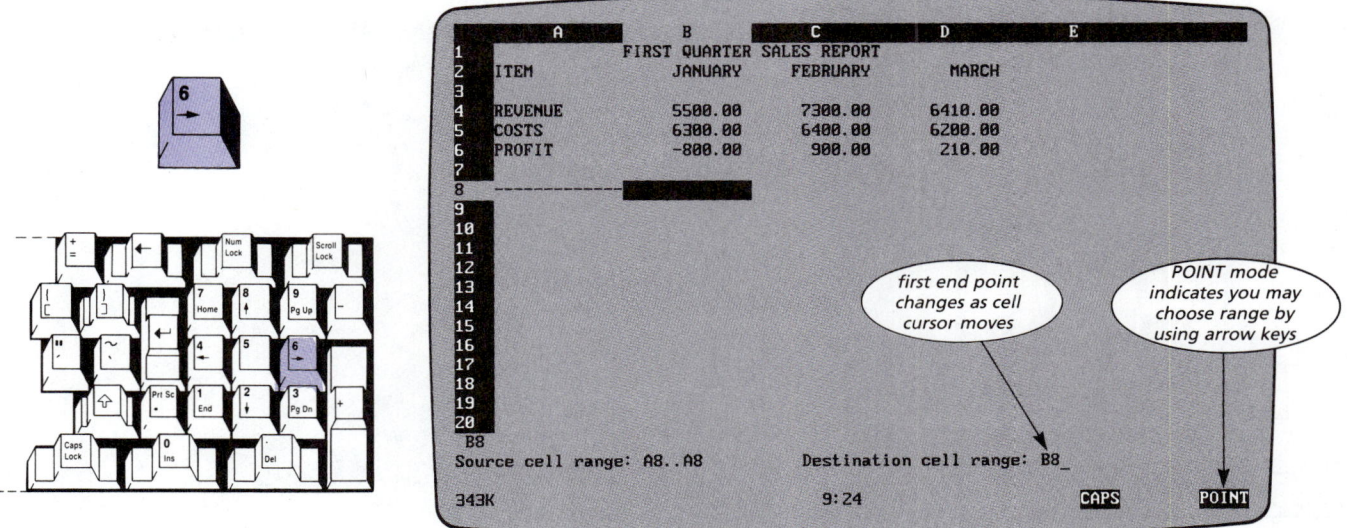

FIGURE 2-24 Step 3 of copying a range of cells—move the cell cursor to one of the end points of the destination range.

Press the Period key to anchor end point B8 and move the cell cursor to D8 as shown in Figure 2-25. Finally, press the Enter key to copy cell A8 to cells B8 through D8 (see Figure 2-26).

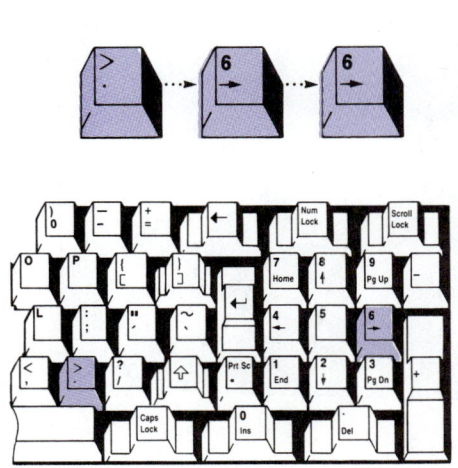
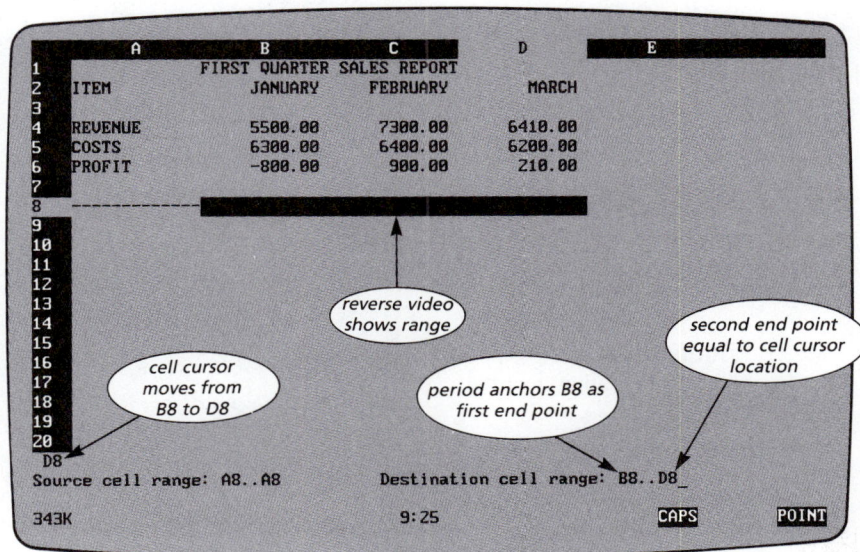

FIGURE 2-25 Step 4 of copying a range of cells—move the cell cursor to the opposite end point of the destination range.

As illustrated in Figure 2-26, the dashed line is complete and the cell cursor is back in cell A8 where it was before invoking the Copy command.

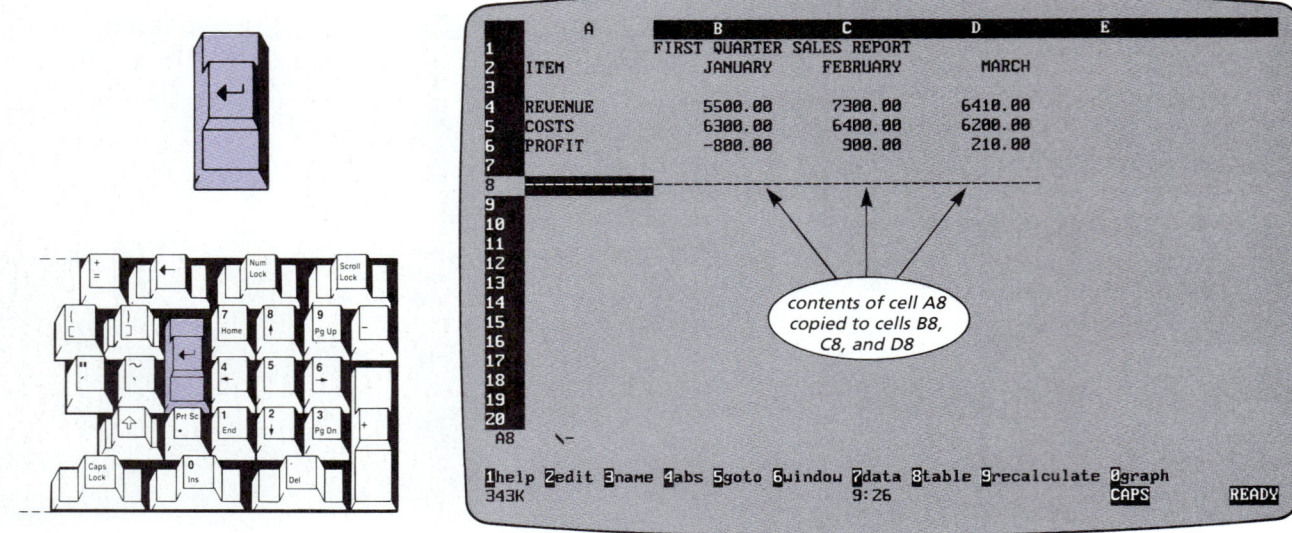

FIGURE 2-26 Step 5 of copying a range of cells—press the Enter key to complete the copy.

With the dashed line complete, move the cell cursor to A10 and begin entering the labels that identify the quarter results. First enter the label QUARTER RESULTS and press the Down Arrow key twice as shown in Figure 2-27.

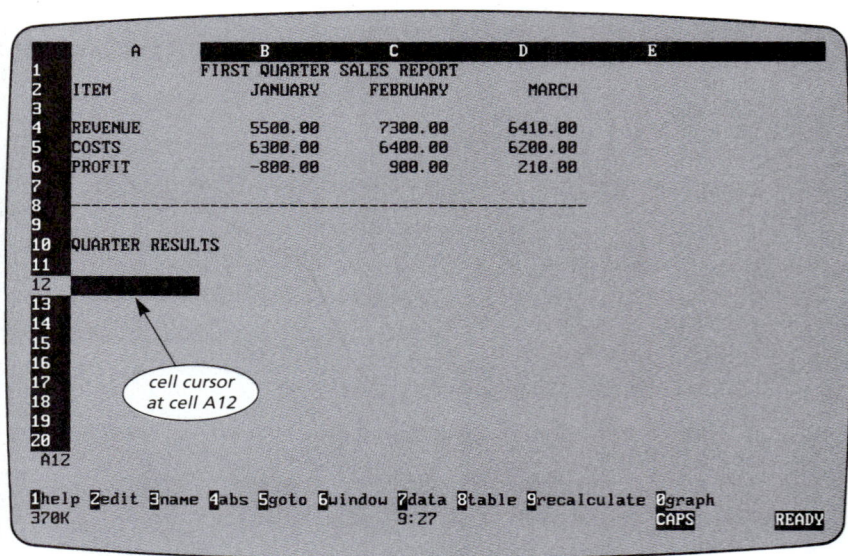

FIGURE 2-27
Step 1 of entering the total labels.

Enter the remaining labels that identify the quarter results in cells A12 through A15. Use the Down Arrow key to enter each one. After the label entries are complete, the cell cursor ends up at cell A16 as illustrated in Figure 2-28. Use the GOTO command to move the cell cursor to cell B12, the location of the next entry.

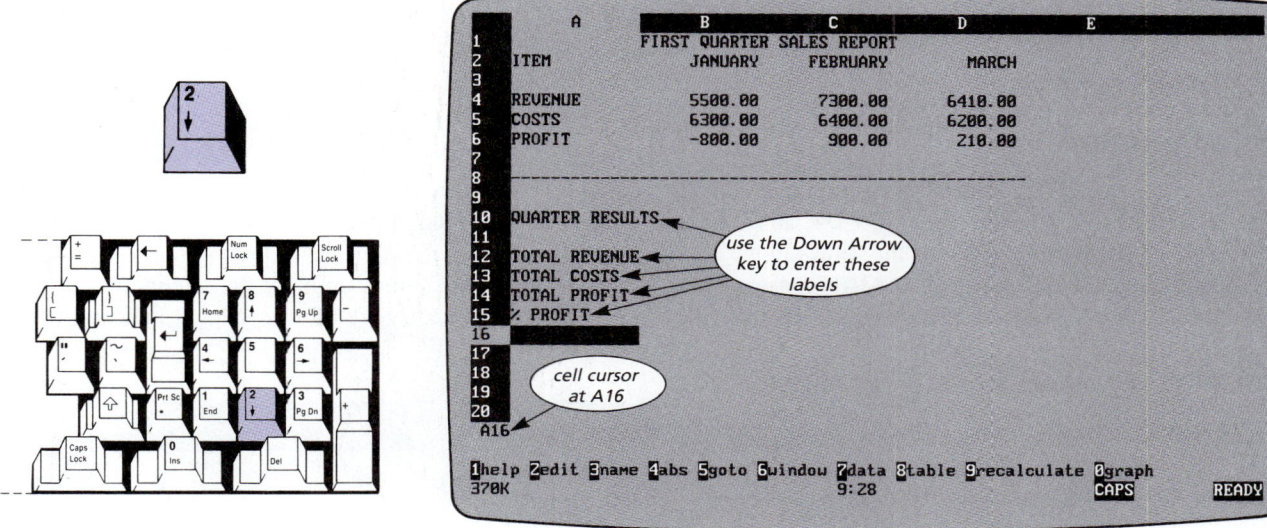

FIGURE 2-28 Step 2 of entering the total labels.

SAVING AN INTERMEDIATE COPY OF THE WORKSHEET

*I*t's good practice to save intermediate copies of your worksheet. That way, if the computer loses power or you make a serious mistake, you can always retrieve the latest copy on disk. We recommend that you save an intermediate copy of the worksheet every 50 to 75 keystrokes. It makes sense to use the Save command often, because it saves keying time later if the unexpected happens.

Before we continue with Project 2, let's save the current worksheet as PROJS-2. Recall that to save the worksheet displayed on the screen you must do the following:

1. Enter the command /**F**ile **S**ave (/FS).
2. In response to the prompt message on the input line, type the new file name, PROJS-2. As soon as you type the letter P in PROJS-2, the old file name, PROJS-1, disappears from the input line. File name PROJS-1 is on the input line because we retrieved it to begin this project and VP-Planner Plus assumes you want to save the revised worksheet under the same name.
3. Press the Enter key.

After VP-Planner Plus completes the save, the worksheet remains on the screen. You can immediately continue with the next entry.

USING BUILT-IN FUNCTIONS

VP-Planner Plus has many **built-in functions** that automatically handle calculations. These built-in functions save you a lot of time and effort because they eliminate the need to enter complex formulas. The first built-in function we will discuss is the SUM function, since it is one of the most widely used. For the remainder of the projects in this book, the term *function* will mean built-in function.

The SUM Function

In the worksheet for Project 2, the total revenue is calculated by adding the values in cells B4, C4, and D4. While the calculation can be written in cell B12 as $+B4+C4+D4$, an easier and more general method to produce the same result is to use the SUM function. The **SUM function** adds the values in the specified range.

With the cell cursor at B12, enter @SUM(B4.D4) as illustrated on the input line at the bottom of the screen in Figure 2-29. Note that the SUM function begins with the **at sign** (@). Beginning an entry with the @ symbol indicates to VP-Planner Plus that the entry is a function.

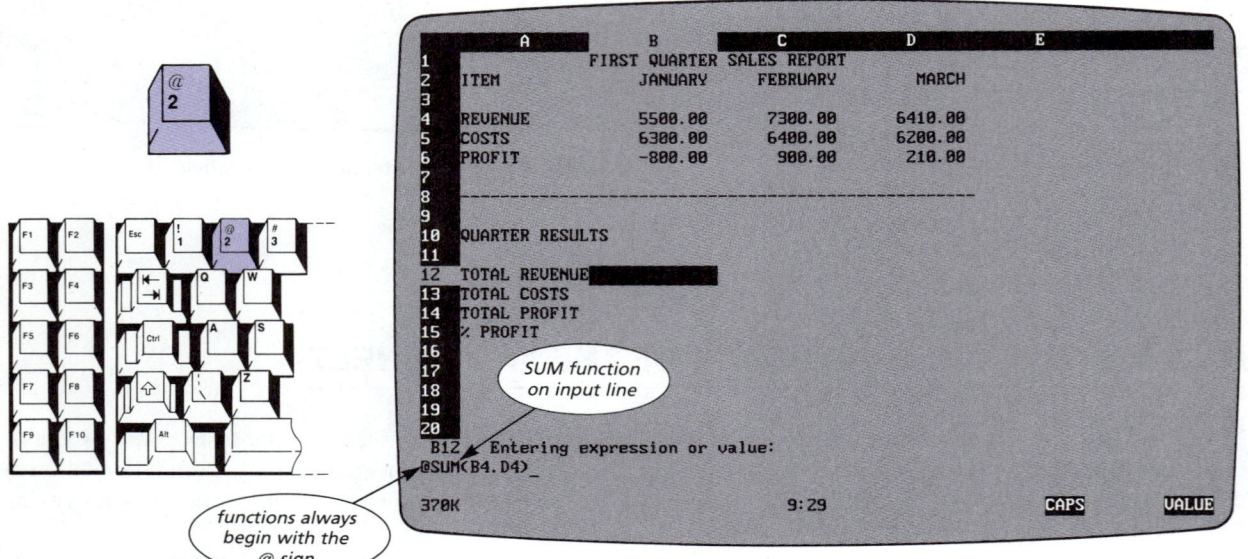

FIGURE 2-29 Entering a function on the input line.

After the @ symbol, type the function name SUM (or sum) followed by a left parenthesis. Next, enter B4.D4, the range to be added. The range can be specified either by typing the beginning and ending cells or by using the pointing feature described earlier. In this case, type the two end points of the range separated by a period (.). Finally, type the right parenthesis.

Press the Enter key as shown in Figure 2-30. As a result, VP-Planner Plus evaluates the sum of the entries in cells B4, C4, and D4 and displays the result in cell B12. Functions belong to the broader category called *formulas*. Therefore, VP-Planner Plus handles functions the same way it handles formulas—it evaluates the function and places a number in the cell. For example, in Figure 2-30, you can see on the status line that the formula @SUM(B4..D4) is assigned to cell B12. However, the value 19210 displays in cell B12 of the worksheet. The value 19210 is the sum of the numbers in cells B4, C4, and D4.

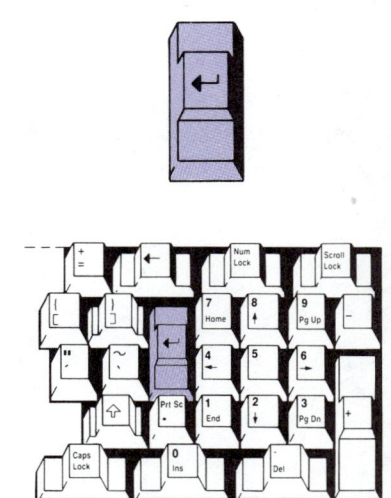

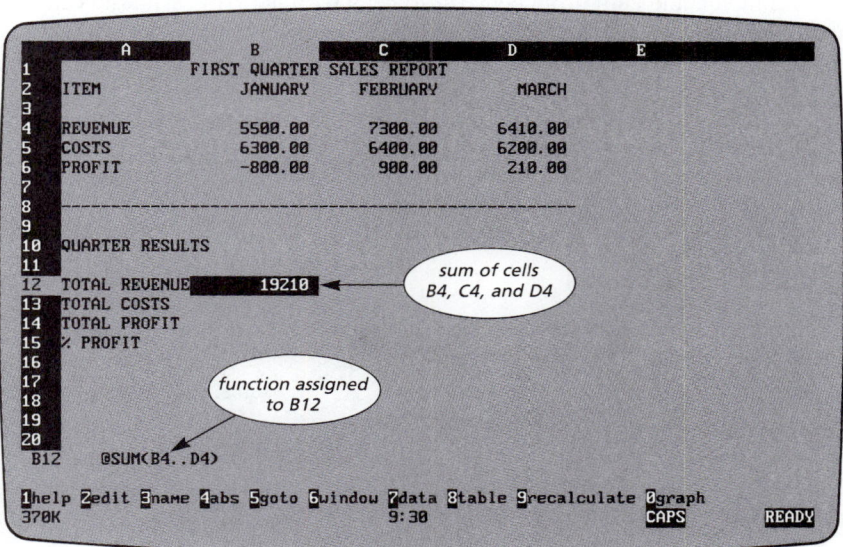

FIGURE 2-30 Press the Enter key to assign the function to B12. When a function is assigned to a cell, it is evaluated and the value displays in the cell.

Copying Functions

According to Figure 2-2, the two cells B13 and B14 require the identical function and similar ranges that we assigned to cell B12 in Figure 2-30. That is, cell B13 should contain the total costs for the quarter, or the sum of cells B5, C5, and D5. Cell B14 should contain the total profit for the quarter, or the sum of cells B6, C6, and D6. Table 2-3 illustrates the similarity between the entry in cell B12 and the entries required in cells B13 and B14.

TABLE 2-3 Three Function Entries for Cells B12, B13, and B14

CELL	FUNCTION ENTRIES
B12	@SUM(B4..D4)
B13	@SUM(B5..D5)
B14	@SUM(B6..D6)

Again, there are two methods for entering the functions in cells B13 and B14. The first method involves moving the cell cursor to B13, entering the function @SUM(B5..D5), then moving the cell cursor to B14 and entering the function @SUM(B6..D6).

The second method, the one we are going to use, involves using the Copy command. That is, copy cell B12 to cells B13 and B14. Note in Table 2-3, however, that the ranges do not agree exactly. Each cell below B12 has a range that is one row below the previous one. Fortunately, when the Copy command copies cell addresses, it adjusts them for the new position. This cell-address adjustment used by the Copy command is called **relative addressing**. In other words, after cell B12 is copied to cells B13 and B14, the contents of B13 and B14 are identical to the entries shown in Table 2-3.

Let's complete the copy from cell B12 to cells B13 and B14. With the cell cursor at B12 as shown in Figure 2-30, enter the command /Copy (/C). The prompt message "Source cell range: B12..B12" displays on the input line as shown in Figure 2-31. Since B12 is the cell that we want to copy to cells B13 and B14, press the Enter key.

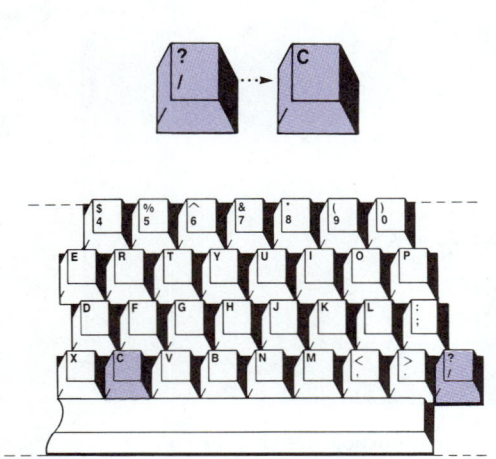

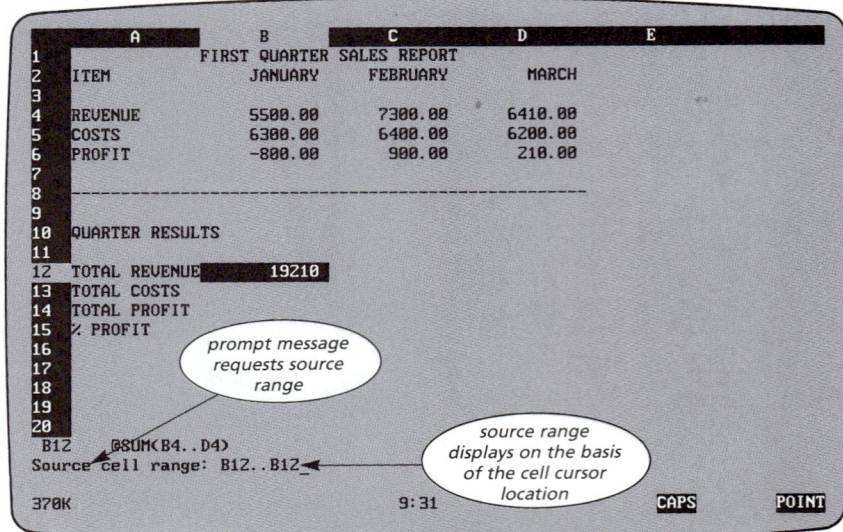

FIGURE 2-31 Step 1 of copying a function—press the Slash key (/) and type the letter C for Copy.

When we press the Enter key, the prompt message "Destination cell range: B12" displays on the input line. This message is shown in Figure 2-32. Use the Down Arrow key to move the cell cursor to B13, the topmost end point of the destination range. As shown in Figure 2-33, the cell address following the prompt message on the input line has changed from B12 to B13.

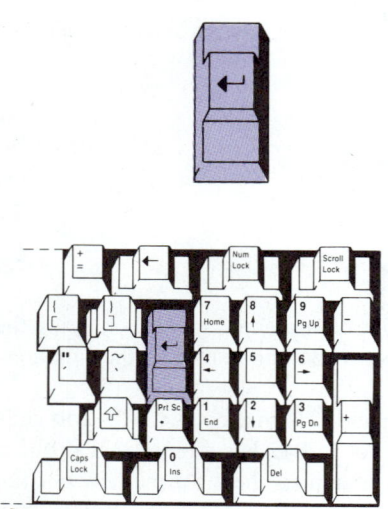

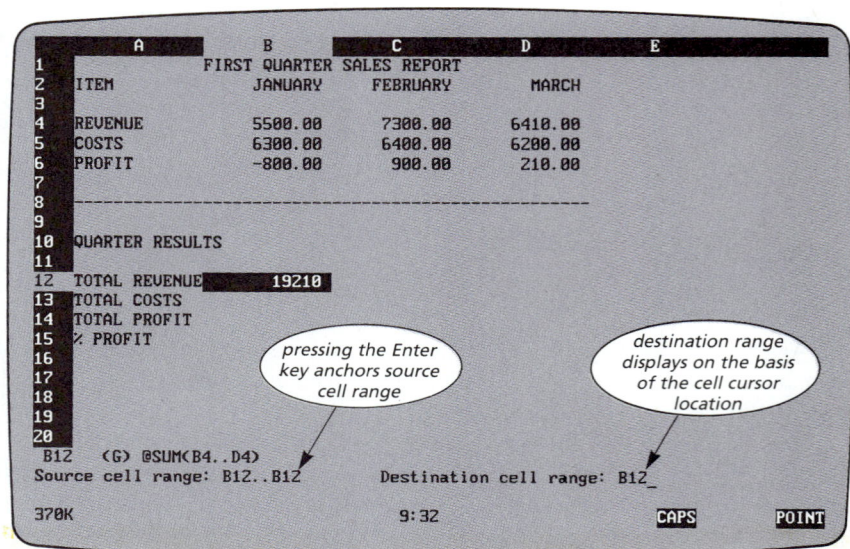

FIGURE 2-32 Step 2 of copying a function—anchor the end points of the source range of cells to copy by pressing the Enter key.

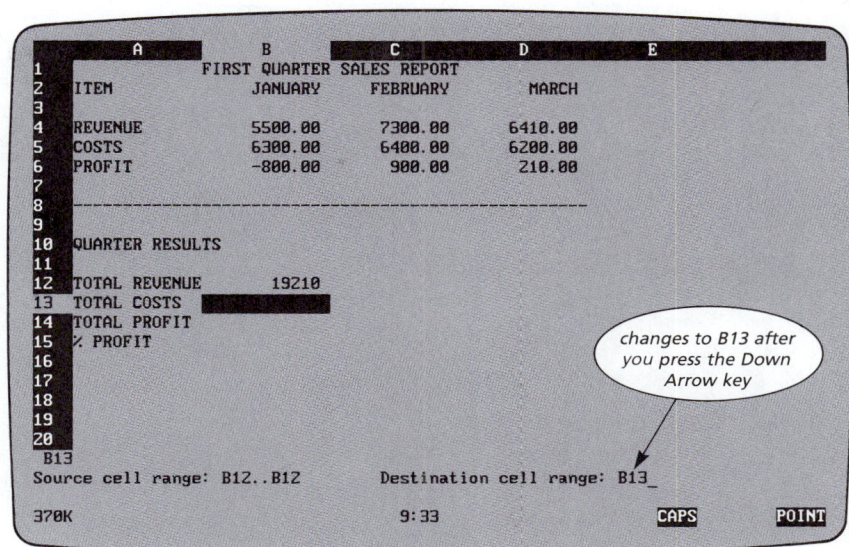

FIGURE 2-33 Step 3 of copying a function—move the cell cursor to one of the end points of the destination range.

Press the Period key to anchor the topmost end point, B13. Next, move the cell cursor to B14 as shown in Figure 2-34. Finally, press the Enter key to copy the function in cell B12 to cells B13 and B14. As illustrated in Figure 2-35 on the next page, cell B13 contains the total costs for the quarter and cell B14 contains the total profit for the quarter. The cell cursor remains at cell B12, where it was before we invoked the Copy command.

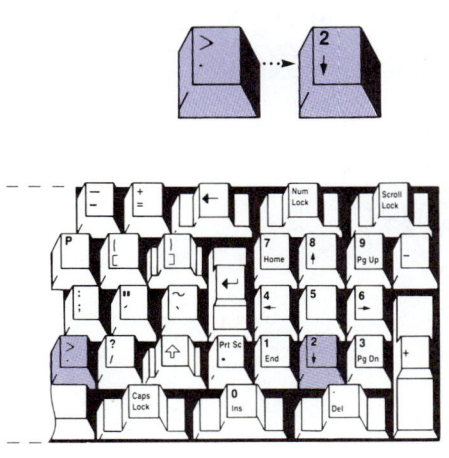

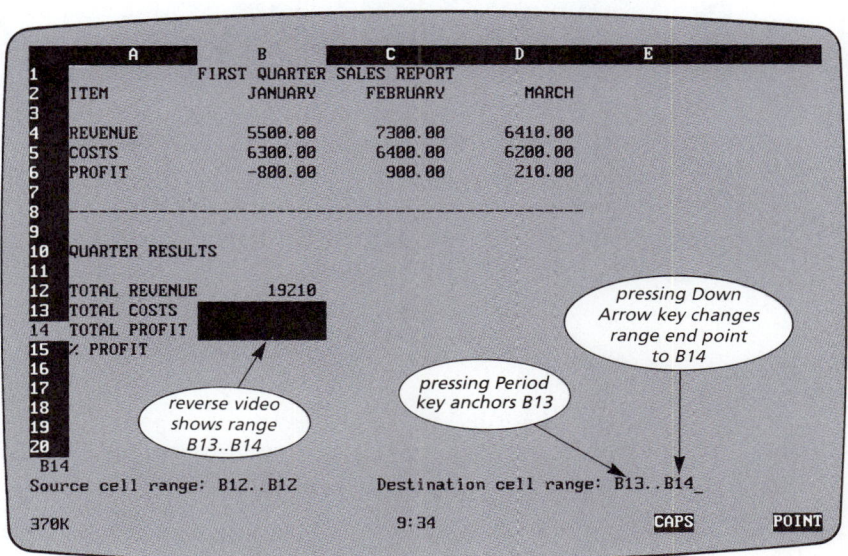

FIGURE 2-34 Step 4 of copying a function—move the cell cursor to the opposite end point of the destination range.

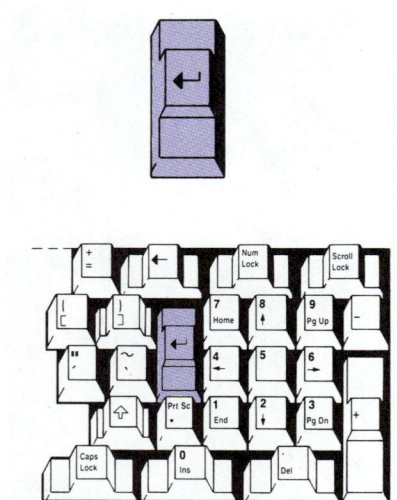

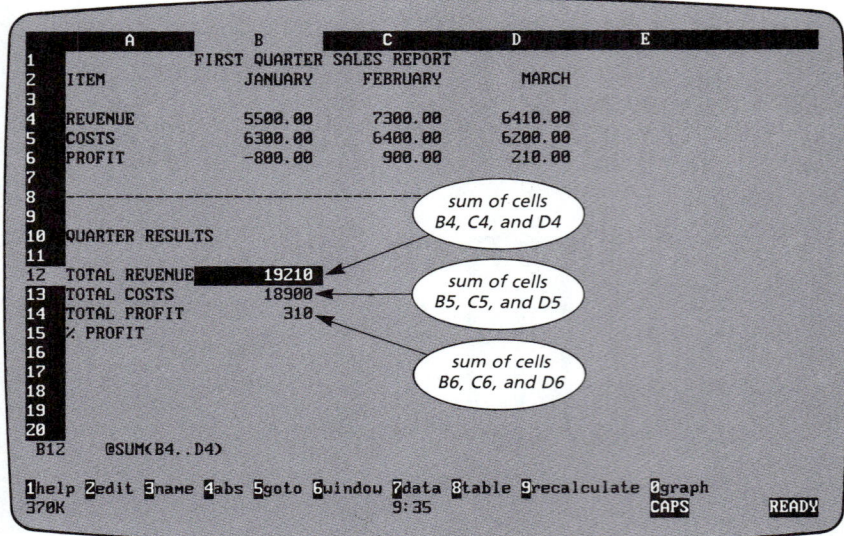

FIGURE 2-35 Step 5 of copying a function—press the Enter key to complete the copy.

Alternative Ways to Sum Cells

In Figure 2-35, the function @SUM(B4..D4) is assigned to cell B12. This function instructs VP-Planner Plus to add the values assigned to B4, C4, and D4. There are other ways that we could have written the SUM function and ended up with the same result in cell B12. These alternatives are described in Table 2-4.

TABLE 2-4 Alternative Ways to Sum Cells

FUNCTION OR STATEMENT	COMMENT
@SUM(B4..D4)	Use the range technique (B4..D4) when the cells to sum are adjacent to one another.
@SUM(B4,C4,D4)	Separate the cells by commas when the cells are non-adjacent. This alternative may also be used to complete arithmetic on the individual cells. For example, @SUM(B4,–C4,D4*4/3) is valid.
+ B4 + C4 + D4	Use the addition sign to sum the cells when the cells are non-adjacent.

DETERMINING A PERCENT VALUE

According to Figure 2-2, the percent profit appears in cell B15. The percent profit is determined by assigning a formula that divides the total profit (cell B14) by the total revenue (cell B12). Recall that the Slash key (/) represents the operation of division, provided it is not the first key typed in the READY mode and the entry is not a label.

Move the cell cursor to cell B15 and enter the formula +B14/B12 as shown on the input line in Step 1 of Figure 2-36. Next, press the Enter key. VP-Planner Plus determines the quotient of +B14/B12 and stores the result, .01613742842, in cell B15. This is shown in Step 2 of Figure 2-36.

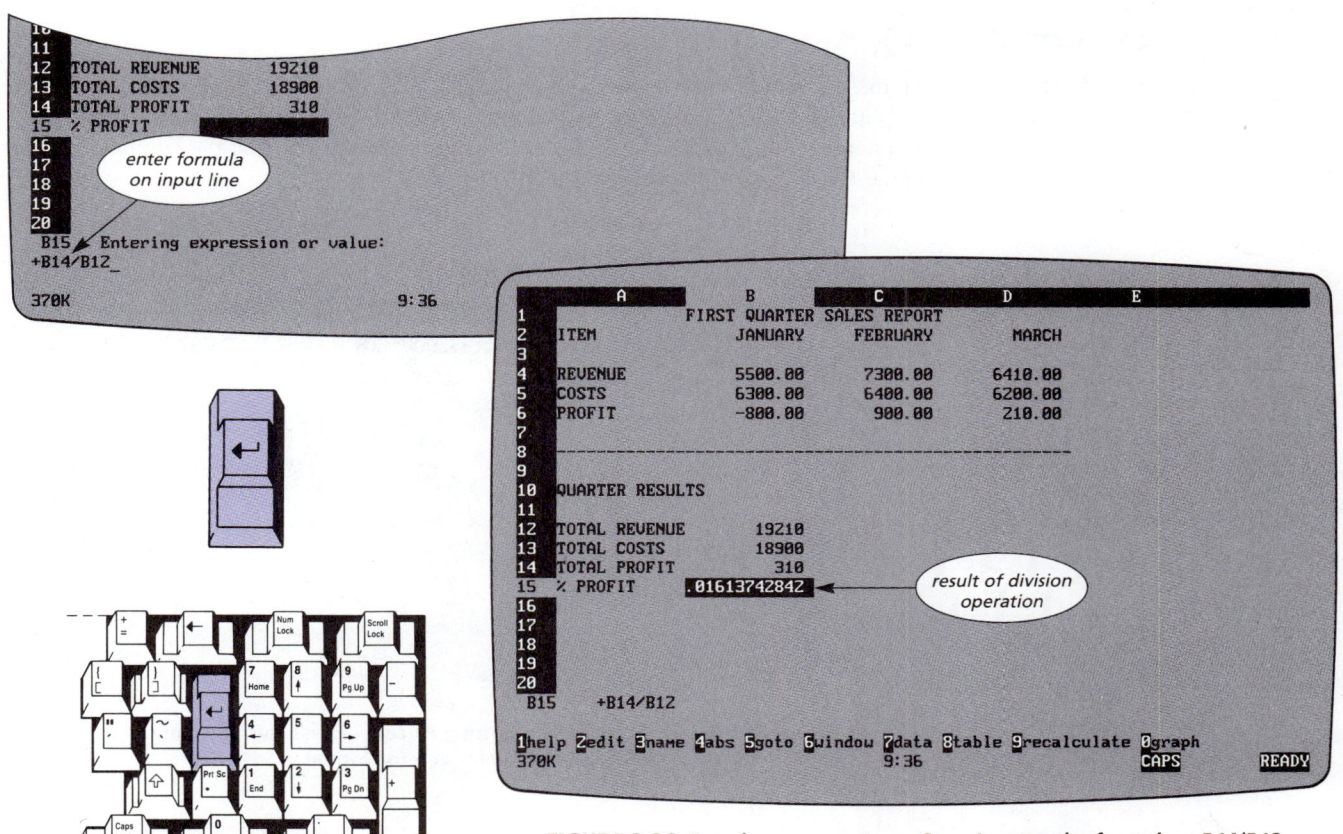

FIGURE 2-36 Entering a percentage. Step 1, enter the formula +B14/B12. Step 2, press the Enter key.

FORMATTING TO PERCENT AND CURRENCY

Although the quarter totals displayed on the worksheet in Figure 2-36 are correct, they are not in an easy-to-read format. The dollar values are displayed as whole numbers and the percentage value is displayed as a decimal fraction carried out to 11 places. In Figure 2-2, the dollar figures in the quarter results are displayed as dollars and cents with a leading dollar sign. Furthermore, the quotient in cell B15 is displayed as a percent with one decimal place. Let's complete the formatting for this project.

The Percentage Format (/RFP)

Since the cell cursor is at B15, first format the decimal fraction value to a percentage value. With the cursor on cell B15, enter the command /**R**ange **F**ormat (/RF) as illustrated in Figure 2-37. With the command cursor active in the Format menu, type the letter P to select the Percent format. Remember, you can also select the command Percent by moving the command cursor to highlight the word Percent and pressing the Enter key, or by pressing function key F8.

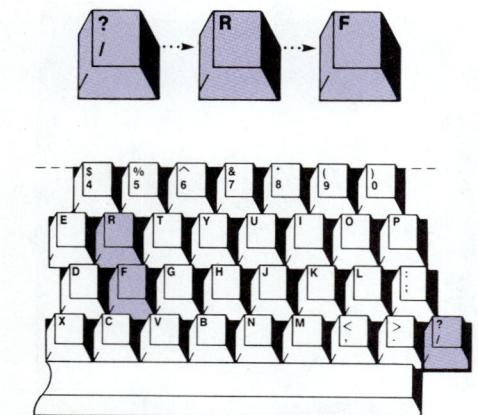
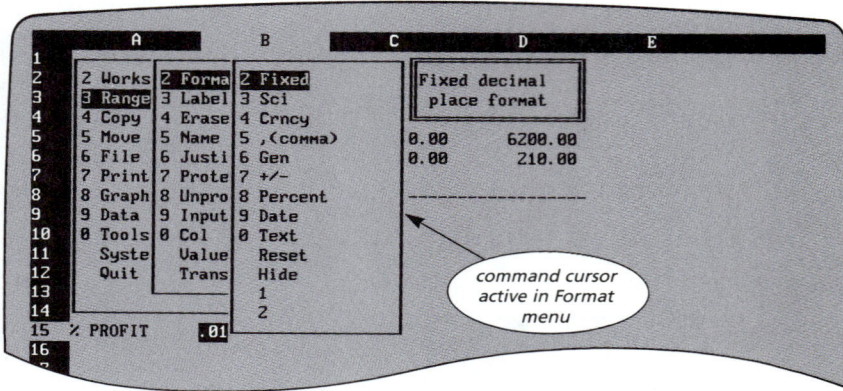

FIGURE 2-37 Step 1 of formatting Percent—press the Slash key (/), type the letter R for Range and the letter F for Format.

   When we type the letter P, VP-Planner Plus displays the prompt message "Enter desired decimal position: 2" on the input line. Type the digit 1 for one decimal position (see Figure 2-38). Next, press the Enter key. VP-Planner Plus displays the prompt message "Select Range of Cells to be altered: B15..B15" on the input line. Press the Enter key, since we want to assign this format only to cell B15. The decimal number .0613742842, assigned to cell B15 by the formula +B14/B12, now displays as 1.6%. This result is shown in Figure 2-39.

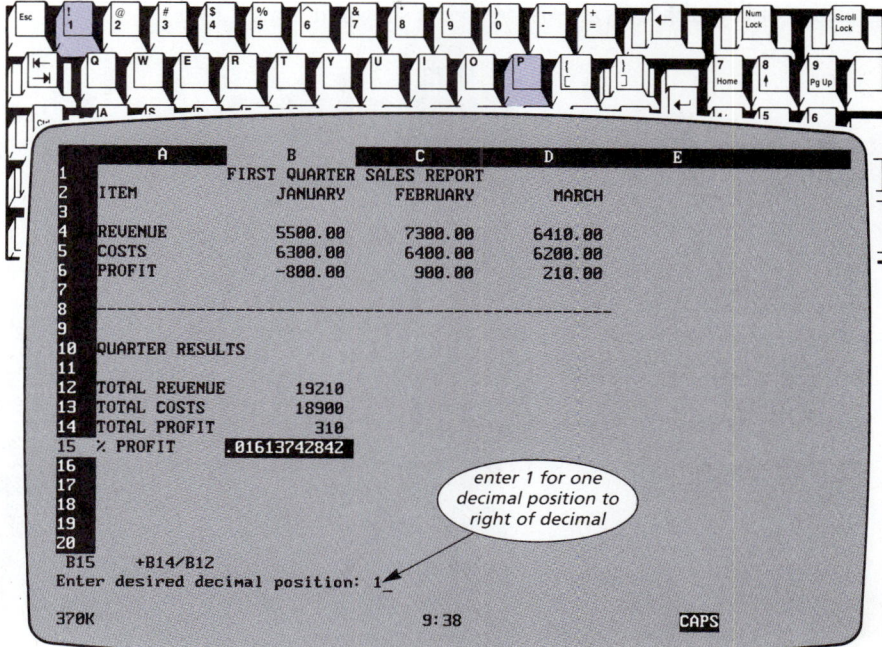

FIGURE 2-38
Step 2 of formatting Percent—type the letter P for Percent and the number 1 for decimal positions desired.

enter 1 for one decimal position to right of decimal

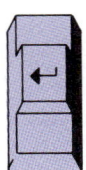

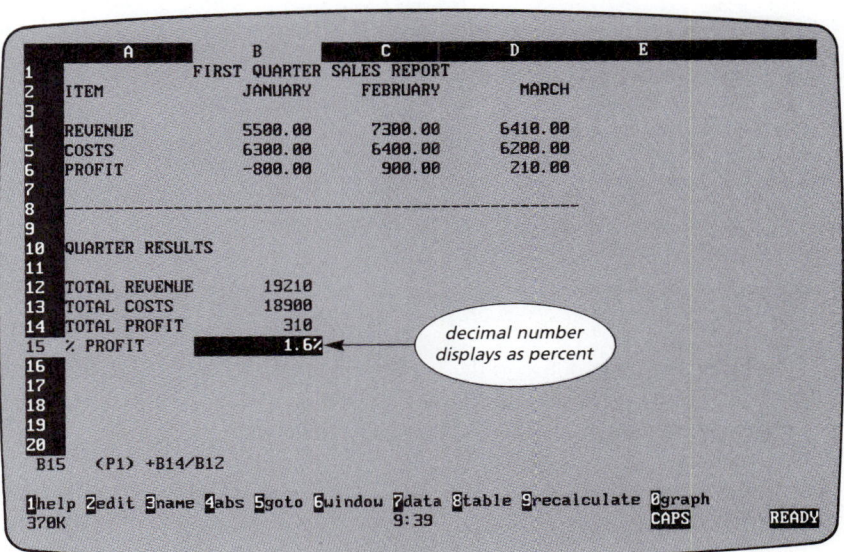

decimal number displays as percent

FIGURE 2-39 Step 3 of formatting Percent—press the Enter key, because the range of cells to be affected is only the cell where the cell cursor is.

The Currency Format (/RFC)

The next step is to format the quarter results in cells B12, B13, and B14 to dollars and cents with a leading dollar sign. Scanning the list of available formats in Table 2-2 reveals that the Crncy (Currency) format is the one that displays monetary amounts with a leading dollar sign. Move the cell cursor to cell B12 and type the command **/R**ange **F**ormat **C**rncy (/RFC). This sequence of keystrokes results in the screen shown in Figure 2-40.

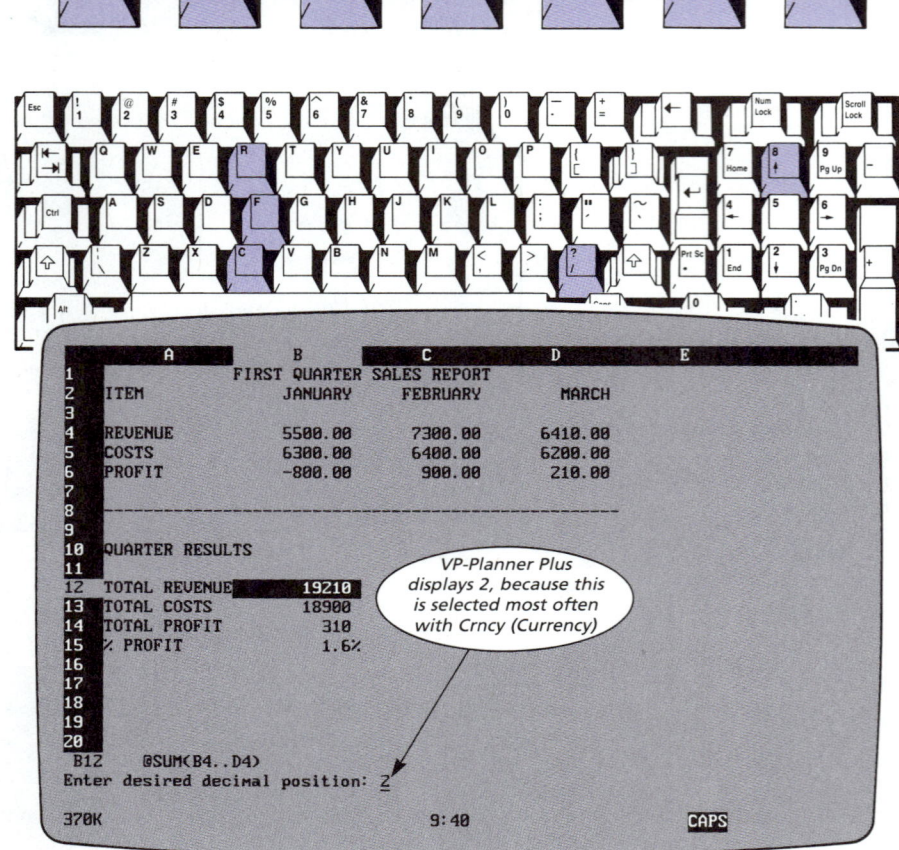

FIGURE 2-40
Step 1 of formatting Crncy—
move the cell cursor to one of
the end points of the range of
cells to be affected, press the
Slash key (/), R for Range, F for
Format, and C for Crncy.

Press the Enter key in response to the prompt message "Enter desired decimal position: 2" because the desired number of decimal positions is 2. As shown on the input line in Figure 2-41, VP-Planner Plus wants to know the range we want to assign the Crncy format. Use the pointing method to enter the range.

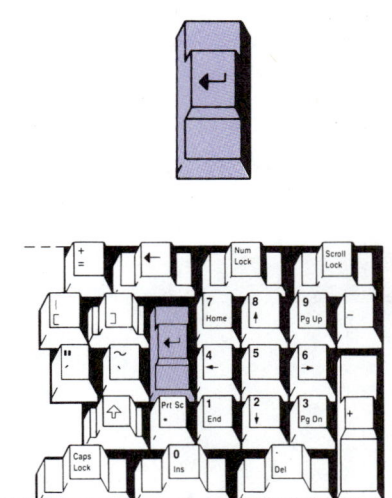

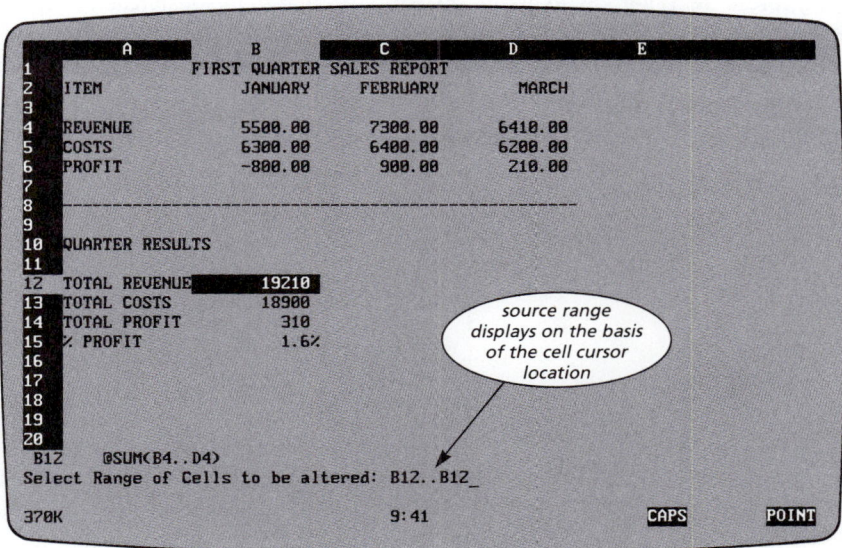

FIGURE 2-41 Step 2 of formatting Crncy—press the Enter key. This sets decimal places to 2 and displays the prompt message on the input line.

The first cell address, B12, on the input line is correct. Therefore, move the cell cursor down to B14. As the cell cursor moves, VP-Planner Plus displays the range in reverse video. Also, the second cell address on the input line changes to agree with the location of the cell cursor. With the cell cursor on B14, the range we want to assign the Crncy format to is now correct. This result is shown in Figure 2-42.

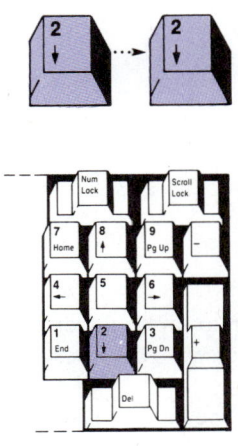

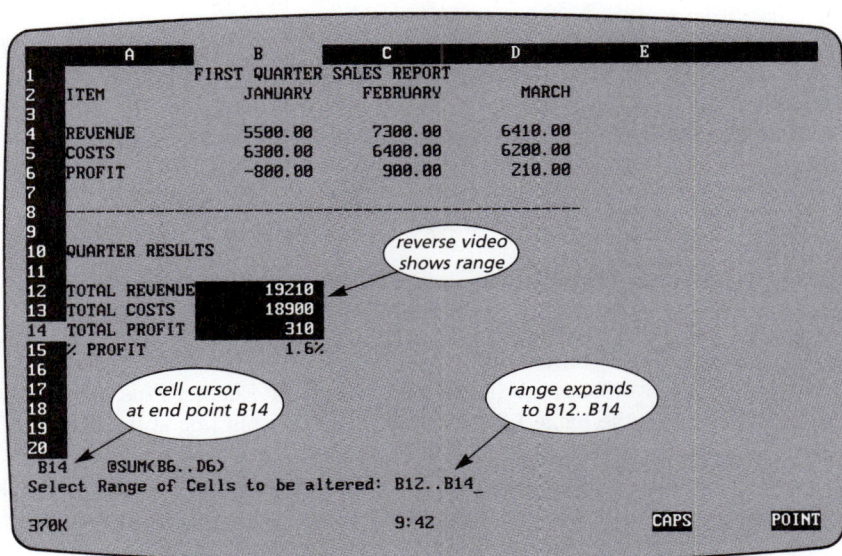

FIGURE 2-42 Step 3 of formatting Crncy—use the arrow keys to select the range of cells to be affected.

Next, press the Enter key to assign the Crncy format to the designated range, cells B12 through B14. Finally, press the Home key to move the cell cursor from cell B12 to cell A1 to prepare for the final step, printing the worksheet. Recall from Project 1 that no matter where the cell cursor is in the worksheet, it immediately moves to cell A1 when you press the Home key. The complete worksheet is shown in Figure 2-43.

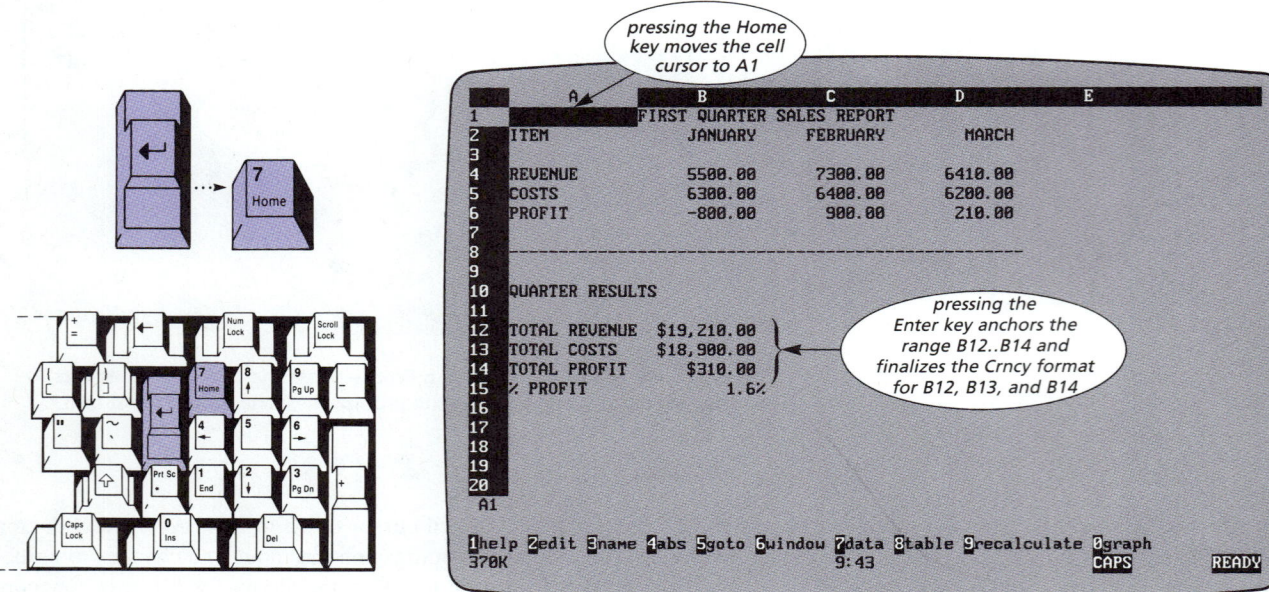

FIGURE 2-43 Step 4 of formatting Crncy—press the Enter key to lock in the range B12..B14. The worksheet is complete. Press the Home key to move the cell cursor to A1.

SAVING THE WORKSHEET A SECOND TIME

We already saved an intermediate version of the worksheet as PROJS-2.

To save the worksheet again, do the following:

1. Enter the command **/File Save** (/FS).
2. Since we saved this worksheet earlier in the session, VP-Planner Plus assumes we want to save it under the same file name. Therefore, it displays the name PROJS-2.WKS on the input line at the bottom of the screen. This saves keying time. Press the Enter key and the screen illustrated in Figure 2-44 displays.
3. The topmost menu in Figure 2-44 gives three choices—Cancel, Replace, or Backup. Type the letter R for Replace. VP-Planner Plus replaces the worksheet we saved earlier on disk with the worksheet on the screen.

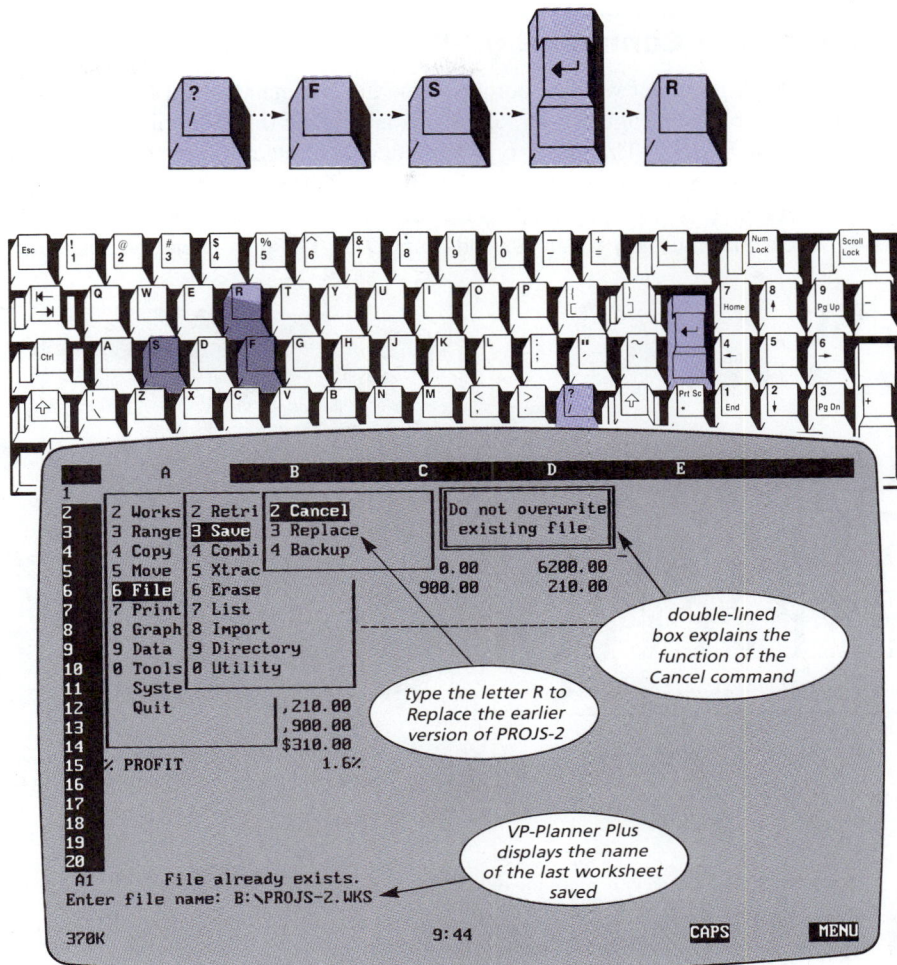

FIGURE 2-44
When a worksheet is saved a
second time under the same file
name, type the letter R to
replace the previous version
on disk.

If we had typed the letter C for Cancel rather than R for Replace, the Save command would have been terminated. If we had typed the letter B for Backup, the current worksheet would have been saved under the file name PROJS-2.BAK. In other words, typing B saves the worksheet on the screen under a different name. A worksheet stored with the extension .BAK is referred to as a **backup**. Saving a backup copy of the worksheet is another form of protection against losing all your work.

PRINTING THE WORKSHEET

*I*n Project 1, we printed the worksheet by holding down a Shift key and pressing the PrtSc key. The printed report included the window borders as well as the control panel and current-mode line. However, window borders clutter the report and make it more difficult to read. In this section, we will discuss how to print the worksheet without the window borders, how to print sections of the worksheet, and how to print the actual entries assigned to the cells in a worksheet.

The Print Printer Command (/PP)

To print the worksheet without window borders, type the command /**Print** **P**rinter (/PP). This activates the command cursor in the **Print menu** as shown in Figure 2-45. Since this is the first time we will print this report using the Print command, we must enter the range to print. Therefore, type the letter R to select Range from the Print menu. The entire worksheet is in the range A1..D15. With the cell cursor at cell A1, press the Period key to anchor A1. Next, use the arrow keys to move the cell cursor to D15. As the cell cursor moves, the reverse video enlarges to encompass the entire range. This procedure is shown in Figure 2-46. Press the Enter key to anchor end point D15. The print menu reappears as shown in Figure 2-47.

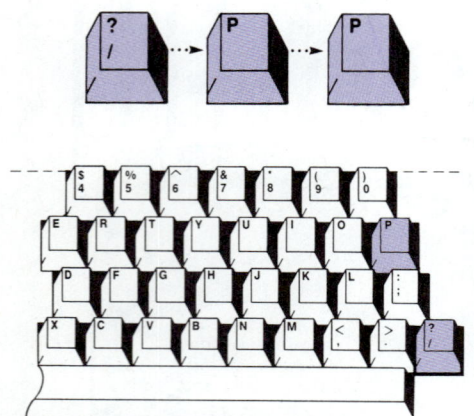

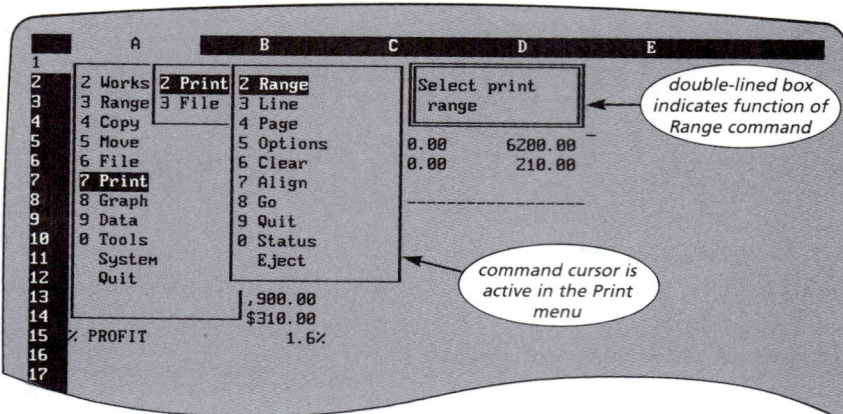

FIGURE 2-45 Step 1 of printing a worksheet using the Print command—press the Slash key (/) and type the letter P twice.

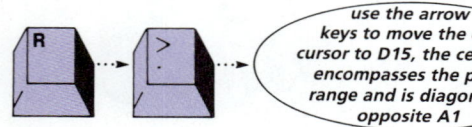

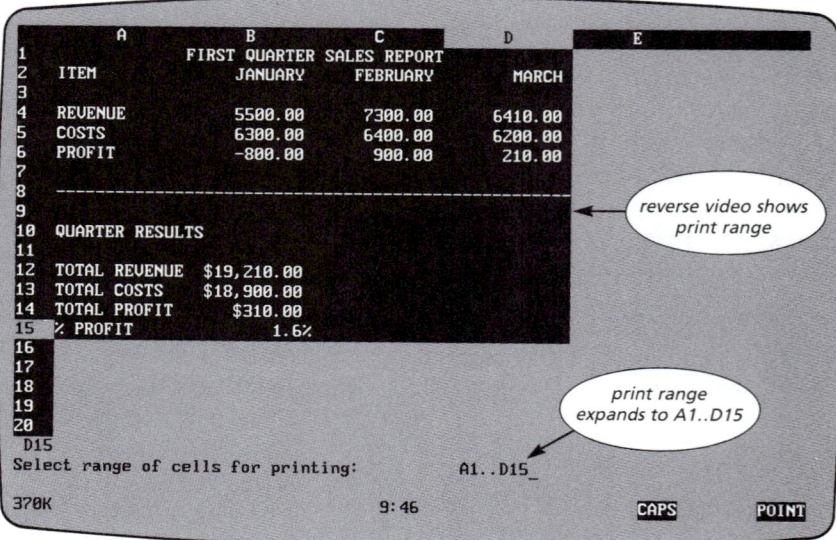

FIGURE 2-46 Step 2 of printing a worksheet using the Print command—type the letter R for Range and use the arrow keys to select the range.

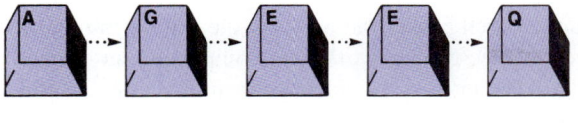

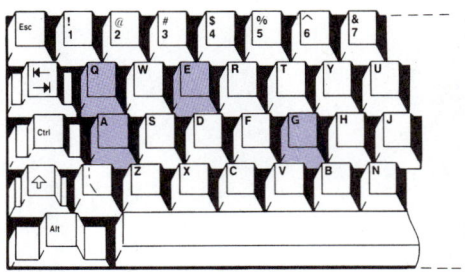

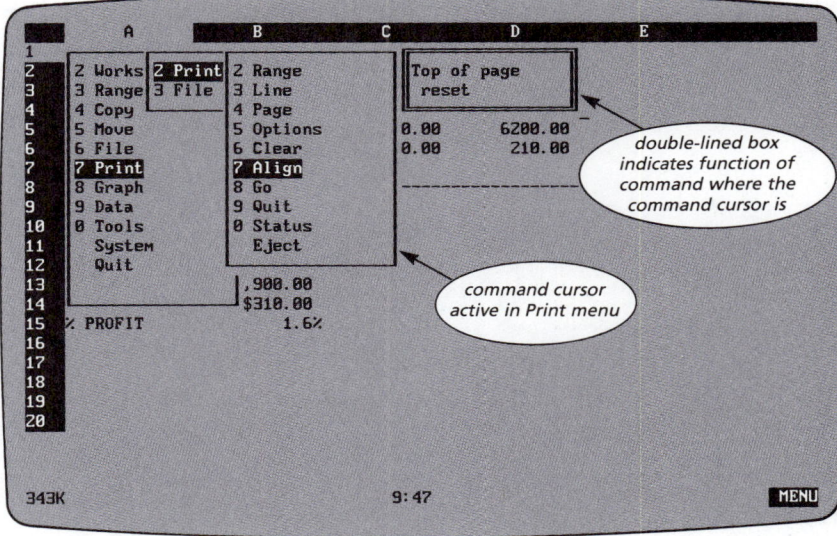

FIGURE 2-47 Step 3 of printing a worksheet using the Print command—type A for Align, G for Go, E for Eject twice, and Q for Quit.

With the printer turned off, use the platen knob on the printer to align the perforated edge of the paper with the top of the print-head mechanism. Turn the printer on.

Type the letter A for Align as shown in Figure 2-47. VP-Planner Plus has its own line counter. Invoking the Align command ensures that the program's line counter is the same as the printer's line counter, that is, that both counters are equal to zero after you turn the printer on and enter the Align command. If the two counters do not agree, the printed version of the worksheet may end up with a few inches of white space in the middle.

Next, type the letter G for Go. The printer immediately begins to print the worksheet. When the printer stops printing, type the letter E twice. Typing the letter E once invokes the Eject command, which causes the paper in the printer to move to the top of the next page. Typing the letter E a second time moves the page with the printed worksheet completely out of the printer. Carefully tear the paper just below the report at the perforated edge. The printed results are shown in Figure 2-48(a).

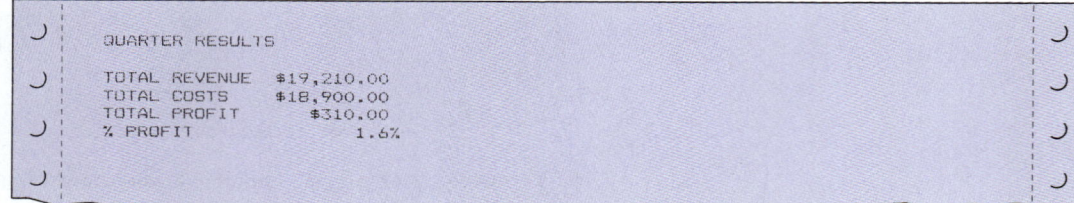

```
                FIRST QUARTER SALES REPORT
    ITEM            JANUARY       FEBRUARY       MARCH

    REVENUE          5500.00       7300.00       6410.00
    COSTS            6300.00       6400.00       6200.00
    PROFIT           -800.00        900.00        210.00

    ------------------------------------------------------

    QUARTER RESULTS

    TOTAL REVENUE   $19,210.00
    TOTAL COSTS     $18,900.00
    TOTAL PROFIT       $310.00
    % PROFIT             1.6%
```

```
    QUARTER RESULTS

    TOTAL REVENUE   $19,210.00
    TOTAL COSTS     $18,900.00
    TOTAL PROFIT       $310.00
    % PROFIT             1.6%
```

FIGURE 2-48
Complete (a) and partial
(b) printed versions of
the worksheet.

Quitting the Print Command

The Print command is one of the few commands that does not immediately return VP-Planner Plus to READY mode when the command is finished executing. To return to READY mode after the Print command is complete, type the letter Q for Quit. This Quit command clears the menus from the screen and returns VP-Planner Plus to READY mode.

Printing a Section of the Worksheet

You may not always want to print the entire worksheet. Portions of the worksheet can be printed by entering the selected range in response to the Range command. Let's assume that you want to print only the quarter results as shown in Figure 2-48(b). From Figure 2-43, you can see that the quarter results are in the range A10..B15.

To print the quarter results, enter the command /Print Printer (/PP) as shown in Figure 2-45. Next, type the letter R for Range. The screen in Figure 2-46 displays because VP-Planner Plus always remembers the last range entered for the Print command. Recall that we entered the range A1..D15 when we printed the complete worksheet earlier.

To change the range, press the Backspace key to free the end points A1 and D15 on the input line. Use the arrow keys to move the cell cursor to A10. Press the Period key (.) to anchor the upper left end point of the range containing the quarter results. Move the cell cursor to B15. At this point, the screen appears as shown in Figure 2-49. Press the Enter key to anchor the lower right end point.

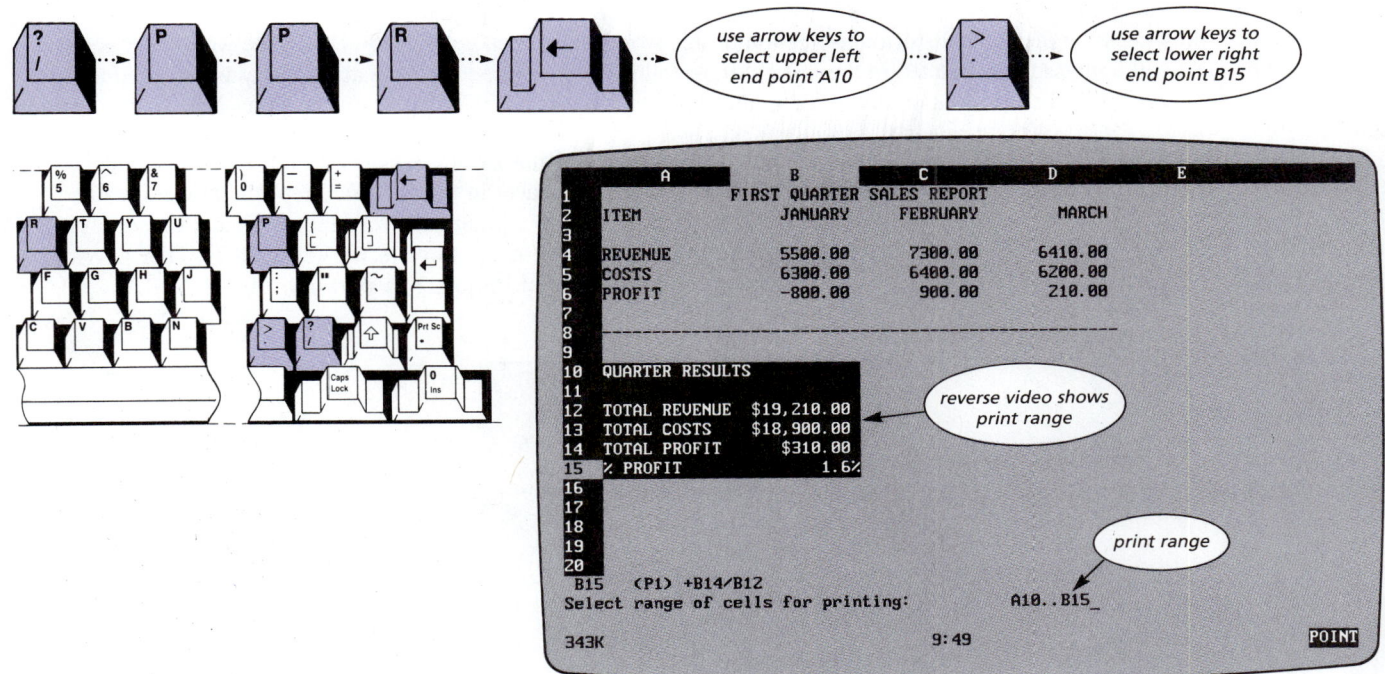

FIGURE 2-49 Printing a portion of the worksheet.

Next, make sure the paper is aligned and the printer is ready. As listed in Figure 2-47, type the letter A for Align and the letter G for Go to print the partial report. The partial report shown in Figure 2-48(b) prints on the printer. When the report is complete, type the letter E twice to eject the paper from the printer. Finally, type the letter Q for Quit to complete the Print command. The Print menu disappears and the worksheet displays on the screen as it did shown in Figure 2-43.

Printing the Cell-Formulas Version of the Worksheet (/PPOOCQAG)

Thus far, we have printed the worksheet exactly as it is on the screen. This is called the **as-is** version of the worksheet. Another variation that you can print is called the cell-formulas version. The **cell-formulas** version prints what was assigned to the cells, rather than what's in the cells. It is useful for debugging a worksheet because the formulas and functions print out, rather than the numeric results.

Figure 2-50 illustrates the printed cell-formulas version of this worksheet. Each column of cells in the worksheet appears on a new page. The cell addresses are printed in the left column, followed by any special formatting that was assigned to the cell, and the actual contents. The information displayed in the report is identical to the display on the status line for the current cell.

To print the cell-formulas version of the worksheet, type the command **/Print Printer Range** (/PPR). Enter the range A1..D15 and press the Enter key. (If we had not printed a portion of the worksheet in the previous step, the range already would have been set to A1..D15. In this case we would have skipped the Range command.) With the command cursor still active in the Print menu, enter the command **Other Options Cell-formulas Quit Align Go Eject Eject** (OOCQAGEE). With the printer in READY mode, VP-Planner Plus prints the cell-formulas version of Project 2 as shown in Figure 2-50.

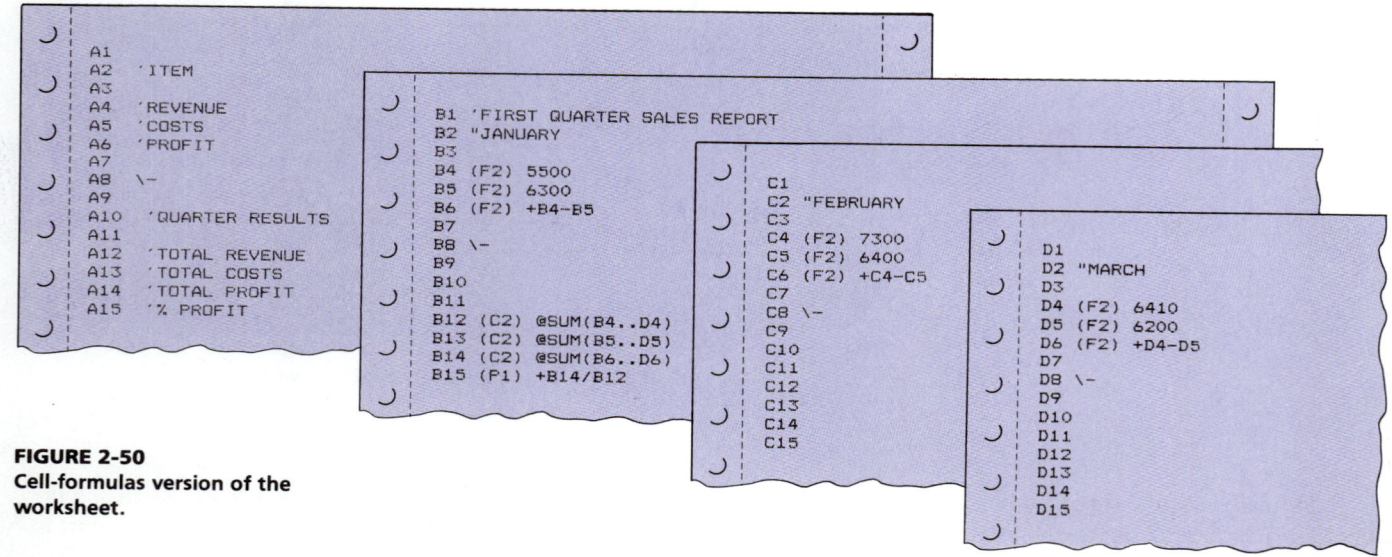

FIGURE 2-50
Cell-formulas version of the worksheet.

Once the Print command option has been set to print the cell-formulas version, VP-Planner Plus will continue to print this variation each time you use the **/Print Printer** (/PP) command until you change the print option back to as-is. Therefore, after printing the cell-formulas version, but before quitting the Print command, enter the command **Options Other As-is Quit Quit** (OOAQQ). The last Quit in the chain of commands causes VP-Planner Plus to return to READY mode. The next time you issue the Print command VP-Planner Plus will print the as-is version.

Printing a Worksheet to a File (/PF)

You can instruct VP-Planner Plus to transmit the printed version of a worksheet to a file. This can be useful if your printer is not functioning or if you prefer to print the worksheet at a later time. Use the command /**P**rint **F**ile (/PF), rather than /**P**rint **P**rinter (/PP). When you enter the command /PF, VP-Planner Plus requests a file name. After you enter the file name, the Print menu in Figure 2-47 displays. From this point on, you could select commands from the Print menu as if you were printing the worksheet directly to the printer.

Later, after quitting VP-Planner Plus, you could use the DOS command Type to display the worksheet on the screen or the DOS command Print to print the worksheet on the printer. The file extension .PRN, which stands for printer file, automatically appends to the file name you select.

Summary of Commands in the Print Menu

Table 2-5 summarizes the commands available in the Print menu.

TABLE 2-5 Commands Available in the Print Menu

COMMAND	FUNCTION
Range	Allows you to specify what part of the worksheet is printed. If no range is specified when the /PPG command is invoked, the entire worksheet is printed.
Line	Moves the paper in the printer one line.
Page	Advances the paper in the printer to the top of the next page on the basis of the program's page-length setting.
Options	Sets headers, footers, margins, page length, borders, and special printer commands. The Options menu also shows the current Print command settings.
Clear	Sets all Print command settings to their default and clears the current print-range setting.
Align	Resets the line counter for the printer.
Go	Starts printing the worksheet on the printer.
Quit	Returns VP-Planner Plus to READY mode.
Status	Displays the current Print command settings.
Eject	Advances the paper in the printer to the top of the next page on the basis of the printer's top-of-page setting.

DEBUGGING THE FORMULAS IN A WORKSHEET USING THE TEXT FORMAT

Debugging is the process of finding and correcting errors in a worksheet. When formulas are assigned to the cells in a worksheet, the cell-formulas version is a handy tool for debugging it. Recall that the cell-formulas version shows the formulas associated with a worksheet (see Figure 2-50). An alternative to printing the cell-formulas version of the worksheet is to format the worksheet to the Text type. This format allows you to see the formulas in the cells on the screen, instead of their numeric result. When the worksheet is formatted to the Text type, it is called the **text version**.

To view the text version of the worksheet, do the following:

1. Save the worksheet to disk. You must save the worksheet so that you don't lose the formats currently assigned to the cells in the worksheet.
2. Enter the command **/R**ange **F**ormat **T**ext (/RFT) and enter the range (A1..D15).

As shown in Figure 2-51, the formulas display in the cells instead of their numeric results. One problem with this procedure is that if a formula is longer than the width of the cell, a portion of it is hidden unless the adjacent cell on the right side is empty.

When you are finished viewing or printing the worksheet formatted to the Text type, retrieve from disk the original version—the one that contains the properly formatted cells.

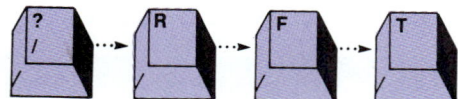

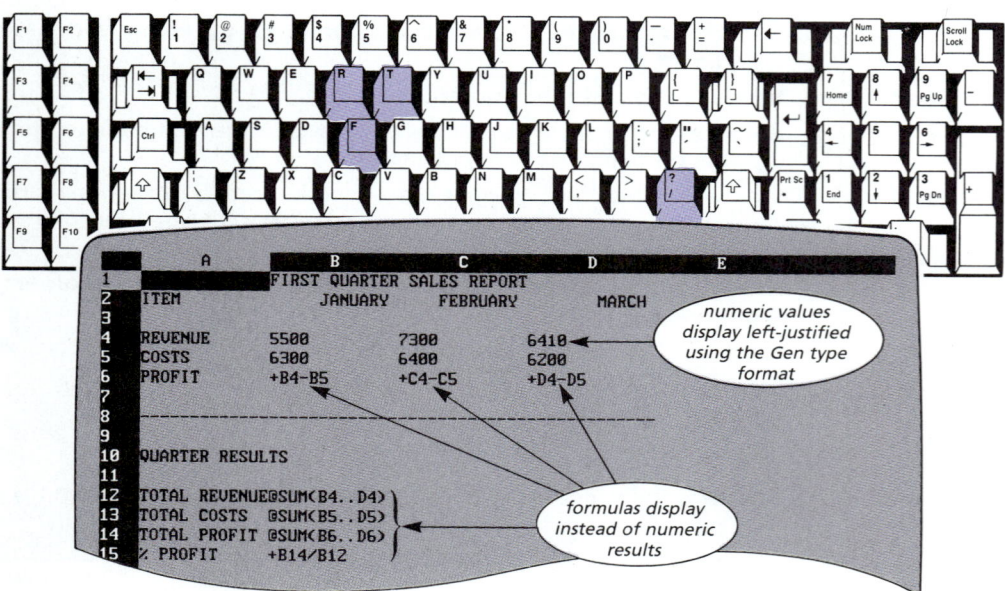

FIGURE 2-51

Display of the formulas in the cells instead of the numeric results. Use the command /Range Format Text (/RFT) and enter the range A1..D15.

PROJECT SUMMARY

*I*n Project 2 we formatted the numeric values entered in Project 1, added summaries, and formatted the summaries. Although this sequence of performing operations works well in many applications, it is not mandatory. For example, it may be more economical in terms of time and effort to enter portions of the data and then format it immediately, or it might be advisable to format the cells before entering the data into the worksheet. You will learn which sequence to choose as you gain experience with spreadsheet programs.

In Project 2 you learned how to load a worksheet, increase the size of columns, specify a range, copy cells, format a worksheet, and print a worksheet without borders. The steps for Project 2 are summarized in the table below. Review each step in the table in detail to make sure you fully understand the commands and concepts.

SUMMARY OF KEYSTROKES—Project 2

STEPS	KEY(S) PRESSED	RESULTS
1	/FR ←	Retrieve PROJS-1 from disk
2	Caps Lock	Set Caps Lock on
3	/WGC13 ←	Set column width to 13
4	/RFF ← Backspace ← ← ← ↑↑.↓↓ → → ←	Set monthly revenue, costs, and profit to a fixed format with two decimal places
5	F5 A8 ←	Move the cell cursor to A8
6	\-←	Repeat dashes in cell A8
7	/C ← → . → → ←	Copy dashes in cell A8 to cells B8, C8, and D8
8	↓↓ QUARTER RESULTS ↓↓	Enter title
9	TOTAL REVENUE ↓	Enter title
10	TOTAL COSTS ↓	Enter title
11	TOTAL PROFIT ↓	Enter title
12	% PROFIT ↓	Enter title
13	F5 B12 ←	Move the cell cursor to B12
14	/FSPROJS-2 ←	Save worksheet as PROJS-2
15	@SUM(B4.D4) ←	Enter SUM function for total revenue
16	/C ← ↓.↓ ←	Copy SUM function from cell B12 to B13 and B14
17	↓↓↓ +B14/B12 ←	Enter % profit formula
18	/RFP1 ← ←	Format decimal fraction to cell B15 to percent
19	↑↑↑/RFC ← ↓↓ ←	Set the total revenue, costs, and profit to a currency format
20	Home	Move the cell cursor to A1
21	/FS ← R	Save worksheet as PROJS-2
22	/PPRA1.D15 ← AGEEQ	Print the as-is version of the worksheet
23	/PPRA10.B15 ← AGEEQ	Print a portion of the worksheet
24	/PPRA1.D15 ← OOCQAGEE	Print the cell-formulas version of the worksheet
25	OOAQQ	Change the print option to as-is
26	/RFT A1..D15	Format the worksheet to the Text type

The following list summarizes the material covered in Project 2.

1. To retrieve a worksheet from disk, enter the command /**F**ile **R**etrieve (/FR). Use the Up and Down Arrow keys to move the command cursor in the boxed-in alphabetized list to the worksheet name you wish to retrieve and then press the Enter key.
2. To change the width of all the columns in the worksheet, type the command /**W**orksheet **G**lobal **C**ol-width (/WGC). Enter the desired column width (0–240) on the input line and press the Enter key. Enter the new width and press the Enter key.

Project Summary (continued)

3. To change the width of a specific column in the worksheet, move the cell cursor to the column in question and type the command **/Worksheet Col-width Set** (/WCS). Enter the new width and press the Enter key.

4. A column width of zero hides the column. The column does not display on the screen or print on the printer.

5. A **range** is one or more cells upon which you want to complete an operation. A range may be a single cell, a series of adjacent cells in a column or row, or a rectangular group of adjacent cells. A range cannot be made up of cells that only run diagonally or are separated.

6. To enter a range, type the cell address at one end point of the range, type a period (.) to anchor the first end point, followed by the cell address at the opposite end point of the range. If it is necessary to change the first end point after it is *anchored*, press the Backspace key.

7. If a range defines a rectangular group of cells, the two end points must be diagonally opposite corner cells of the rectangle.

8. To format a range, type the command **/Range Format** (/RF). Select the type of format you wish to use from the topmost menu. Enter the number of decimal places if required. Enter the range to be affected and press the Enter key.

9. To format the entire worksheet, type the command **/Worksheet Global Format** (/WGF). Follow the same steps described for formatting a range.

10. You can also enter a range by **pointing**. Pointing involves using the arrow keys to move the cell cursor to select the end points.

11. When you use pointing to select the range, use the Backspace key to *unlock* the end points of the range on the input line.

12. VP-Planner Plus displays the range with the end points separated by two periods (..), even though you enter only a single period (.) to anchor the first end point.

13. There are several ways to format numeric values. See Table 2-2.

14. Move the cell cursor to a cell to determine the format assigned to it. The format displays in parentheses next to the cell address on the status line at the bottom of the screen.

15. To repeat a series of characters throughout a cell, begin the entry by typing the Backslash key (\).

16. To copy a group of cells to another group of cells, type the command **/Copy** (/C). Enter the source range and then the destination range.

17. It is good practice to save a worksheet to disk after every 50 to 75 keystrokes.

18. A **built-in function** automatically handles calculations.

19. All built-in functions begin with the @ symbol.

20. The SUM function adds the contents of the range specified in parentheses.

21. When you copy a function, the Copy command adjusts the range for the new position.

22. If the Slash key (/) is the first key pressed, VP-Planner Plus switches to command mode. If the Slash key follows any character in a nonlabel entry on the input line, it represents division.

23. When you save a worksheet the second time using the same file name, VP-Planner Plus requires that you type the letter R for Replace.

24. To print the **as-is** version of the worksheet without borders, type the command **/Print Printer** (/PP). If the range has not yet been established from a previous printout of the worksheet, you must enter the range to print. With the printer off, use the platen knob to align the perforated edge of the paper with the top of the print head mechanism. Turn the printer on. Type the letter A for Align and the letter G for Go. After the worksheet is printed, type the letter E (for Eject) twice. Carefully remove the printed version of the worksheet from the printer. Finally, type the letter Q for Quit.

25. To print a section of the worksheet, enter the command **/Print Printer Range** (/PPR). Use the Backspace key to *unlock* the range. Enter the desired range and continue with the steps just outlined.

26. To print the **cell-formulas** version of the worksheet, type the command **/Print Printer Other Options Cell-formulas Quit Align Go Eject Eject** (/PPOOCQAGEE). It is important to change the print option back to as-is, so that future printouts will print the as-is version rather than the cell-formulas version.

27. To print the worksheet to a file, use the command **/Print File** (/PF). Later, after you have quit VP-Planner Plus, you may use the DOS command TYPE to display the worksheet on the screen or the DOS command PRINT to print the worksheet on the printer.

28. To display formulas assigned to cells rather than their numeric result, assign the Text type format to the cells in the worksheet.

STUDENT ASSIGNMENTS

STUDENT ASSIGNMENT 1: True/False

Instructions: Circle T if the statement is true or F if the statement is false.

T F   1. With the /**F**ile **R**etrieve (/FR) command, you are required to type the name of the worksheet you want loaded into main computer memory on the input line.

T F   2. The command /**W**orksheet **G**lobal **C**ol-width (/WGC) is used to set the width of all the columns in the worksheet.

T F   3. If you want to *back out* of the command /FR, press the Esc key three times.

T F   4. When using the /**R**ange **F**ormat command (/RF), entire columns can be formatted; however, entire rows cannot be formatted.

T F   5. For a rectangular group of cells, you must enter the cell addresses of two opposite corners to define the range.

T F   6. A range can be made up of one cell.

T F   7. If you decide to use the pointing method when VP-Planner Plus requests a range, press the Tab key to *unlock* the first end point, if necessary.

T F   8. A range can be referenced by an entry such as B4.D6.

T F   9. With the format Fixed, negative numbers display in parentheses.

T F 10. When in POINT mode, anchor the first cell end point by moving the cell cursor to it and pressing the Period key.

T F 11. The type of format assigned to a cell displays on the current-mode line at the bottom of the screen when the cell cursor is on the cell.

T F 12. If the Backslash key (\) is the first character typed on the input line, the characters that follow will repeat throughout the cell when you press the Enter key or one of the arrow keys.

T F 13. The command /**C**opy (/C) is used to copy the contents of a range to another range of cells.

T F 14. If the function @SUM(B4.D4) is assigned to cell A20, A20 will be equal to the sum of the contents of cells B4, C4, and D4.

T F 15. It is not possible to copy a single cell to a group of cells.

T F 16. If the function @SUM(B4.B8) assigns a value of 10 to cell B9, and B9 is copied to C9, C9 will be equal to 10.

T F 17. If you save a worksheet a second time, you cannot use the same file name originally assigned to the worksheet.

T F 18. The Align command on the Print menu is used to align the cells on the screen.

STUDENT ASSIGNMENT 2: Multiple Choice

Instructions: Circle the correct response.

1. Which of the following is the correct command for retrieving the worksheet PROJS-1.WKS stored on the disk in the default drive?
   a. /FRPROJS-1 ↵
   b. /WRPROJS-1 ↵
   c. /CPROJS-1 ↵
   d. none of these

2. When the /**W**orksheet **G**lobal command (/WG) is used, it means that _____ .
   a. only a single cell will be affected
   b. only a single column will be affected
   c. only a single row will be affected
   d. the entire worksheet will be affected

3. Which one of the following is a valid range of cells?
   a. B2,D2
   b. B2:D2
   c. B2.D2
   d. both b and c are correct

4. The format Currency with two decimal places causes 5000 to display as:
   a. $5,000.00
   b. 5000.00
   c. 5,000.00
   d. $5000.00

Student Assignment 2 (continued)

5. Which one of the following causes the data in cells B4, C4, and D4 to be added together?
   a. @SUM(B4.D4)   c. @SUM(B4:D4)
   b. @ADD(B4.D4)   d. @SUM(B4 C4 D4)
6. Which one of the following correctly identifies the range of the rectangular group of cells with corner cells at A10, A18, D10, and D18?
   a. A10.D18   c. D18.A10
   b. A18.D10   d. all of these
7. Which one of the following characters instructs VP-Planner Plus to repeat the characters that follow in the current cell?
   a. circumflex (^)   c. apostrophe (')
   b. quotation mark (")   d. backslash (\)
8. A listing on the printer of what was entered into each cell of a worksheet is called a _____ version of the worksheet.
   a. cell-formulas   c. formatted
   b. as-is   d. content

STUDENT ASSIGNMENT 3: Understanding Ranges

Instructions: At the top of the next page, list all the possible ranges for each of the designated areas in Figure 2-52. For example, one range that identifies the first group of cells is A1..B3. There are three other ways to identify this first group of cells.

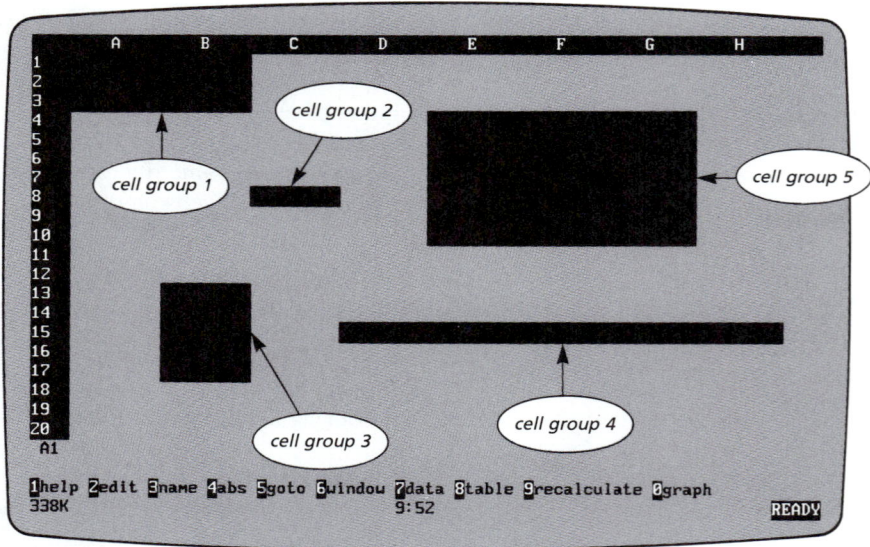

FIGURE 2-52
Student Assignment 3

Cell group 1: _____   _____   _____   _____

Cell group 2: _____

Cell group 3: _____   _____

Cell group 4: _____   _____

Cell group 5: _____   _____   _____   _____

STUDENT ASSIGNMENT 4: Understanding Formats

Instructions: Using Table 2-1, fill in the *Results In* column of Table 2-5 below. Assume that the column width of each cell is 10 characters. Use the character b to indicate positions containing the blank character. As examples, the first two problems in Table 2-5 are complete.

TABLE 2-5   **Determining the Value of a Number Based on a Given Format**

PROBLEM	CELL CONTENTS	FORMAT TO	DECIMAL PLACES	RESULTS IN
1	25	Fixed	1	bbbbb25.0b
2	1.26	Crncy	2	bbbb$1.26b
3	5000	,(comma)	2	_____
4	3.87	Fixed	0	_____
5	.137	Percent	2	_____
6	5	+/−	Not reqd.	_____
7	−45.87	, (comma)	3	_____
8	9523.6	Gen	Not reqd.	_____
9	25	Percent	2	_____
10	.16	Fixed	2	_____
11	109234	Crncy	0	_____
12	2357.85	Sci	1	_____
13	1903.4	Crncy	2	_____
14	23.56	Hide	Not reqd.	_____
15	−34.95	Crncy	2	_____

STUDENT ASSIGNMENT 5: Correcting the Range in a Worksheet

Instructions: The worksheet illustrated in Figure 2-53 contains errors in cells B12 through B15. Analyze the entries displayed on the worksheet. Explain the cause of the errors and the method of correction in the space provided below.

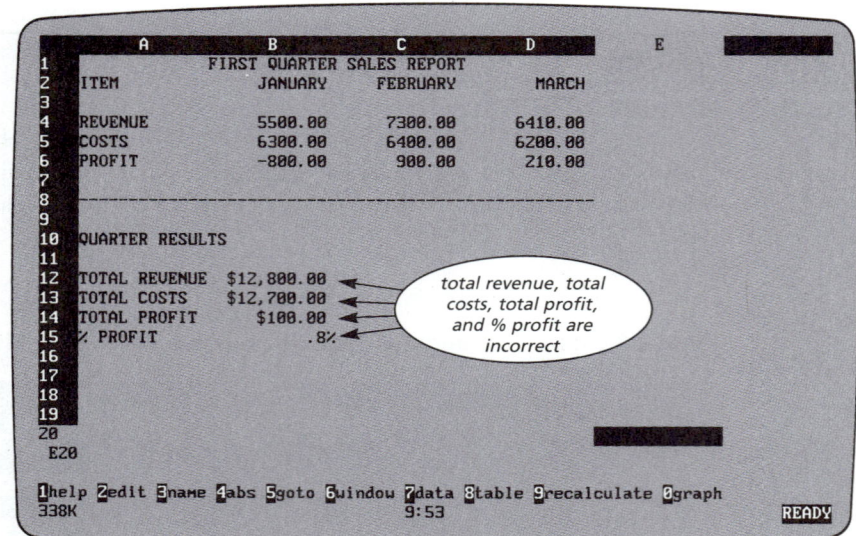

FIGURE 2-53
Student Assignment 5

Cause of error: _____

_____

Method of correction for cell B12: _____

_____

Method of correction for cells B13, B14, and B15: _____

_____

_____

STUDENT ASSIGNMENT 6: Correcting Functions in a Worksheet

Instructions: The worksheet illustrated in Figure 2-54 contains invalid function entries in cells B12, B13, and B14. The invalid entries in these cells cause the diagnostic message ERR to display in cell B15. Analyze the entries displayed on the worksheet. Explain the cause of the errors and the method of correction in the space provided below.

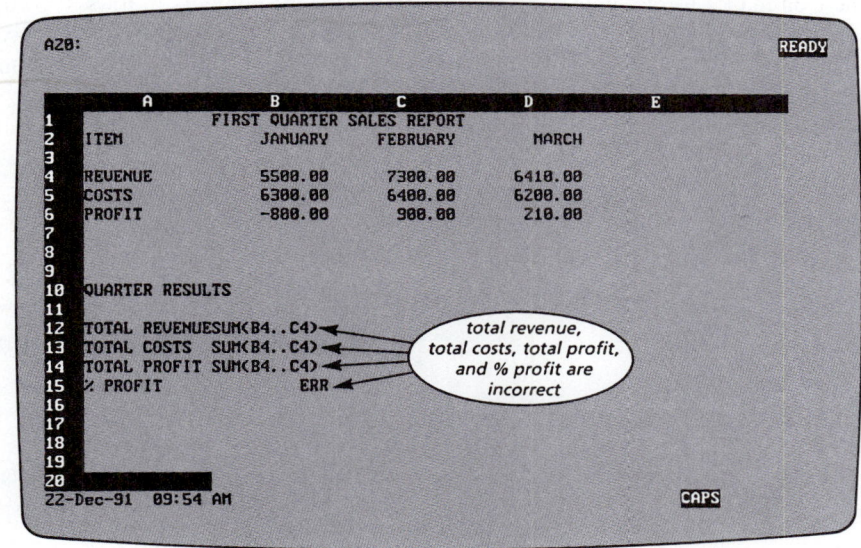

FIGURE 2-54
Student Assignment 6

Cause of error: _____

_____

Method of correction for cell B12: _____

_____

Method of correction for cells B13, B14, and B15: _____

_____

_____

STUDENT ASSIGNMENT 7: Modifying an Inventory Worksheet

Instructions: Load VP-Planner Plus and perform the following tasks.

1. Load the worksheet that was created in Project 1, Student Assignment 8. This worksheet is illustrated in Figure 2-55(a).
2. Perform the following modifications:
   a. Use the Comma (,) format with zero decimal places for the numbers in rows 4, 5, 6, and 7.
   b. Include the inventory total in the worksheet, as illustrated in Figure 2-55(b). The inventory total consists of a total for each plant (B13..B16). For example, the total for Seattle is the sum of cells B4 through D4. Separate the inventory total from the other values by a double line (use the equal sign).
   c. Use the Comma (,) format with zero decimal places for the inventory totals.
3. Save the modified worksheet. Use the file name STUS2-7.
4. Print the entire worksheet on the printer using the /**P**rint **P**rinter (/PP) command.
5. Print only the inventory totals in the range A11..B16.
6. Print the worksheet after formatting all the cells to the Text type.

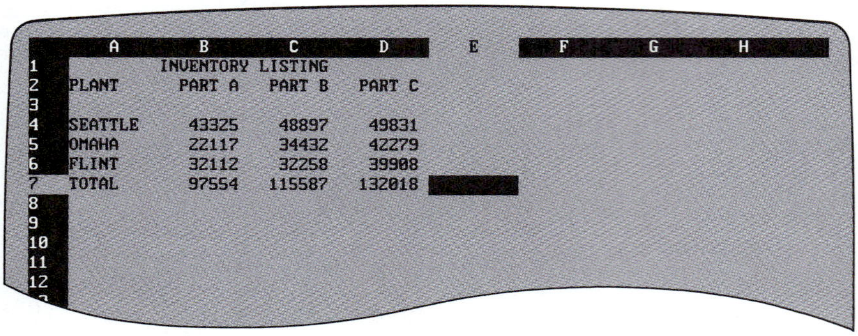

(a)

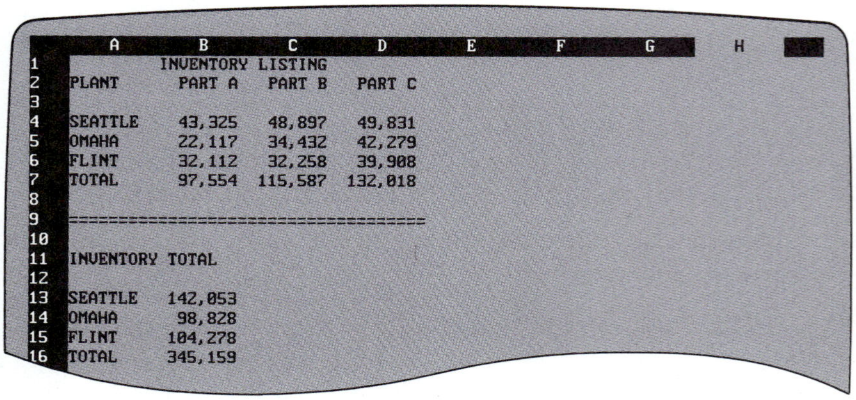

FIGURE 2-55(a) & (b)
Student Assignment 7 Worksheet before (a) and after (b) modification.

(b)

STUDENT ASSIGNMENT 8: Building an Employee Payroll Comparison Worksheet

Instructions: Load VP-Planner Plus and perform the following tasks.

1. Build the worksheet illustrated in Figure 2-56. Change the width of all the columns to 14 characters. The totals displayed in row 9 of the worksheet are the sum of the salaried personnel in column B and the hourly personnel in column C. The store totals (B15..B18) are the sum of the salaried personnel and the hourly personnel for each store. The total in B20 is the sum of the store totals.
2. Save the worksheet. Use the file name STUS2-8.
3. Print the as-is and cell-formulas versions of this worksheet.
4. Print the portion of the worksheet in the range A1..C9.

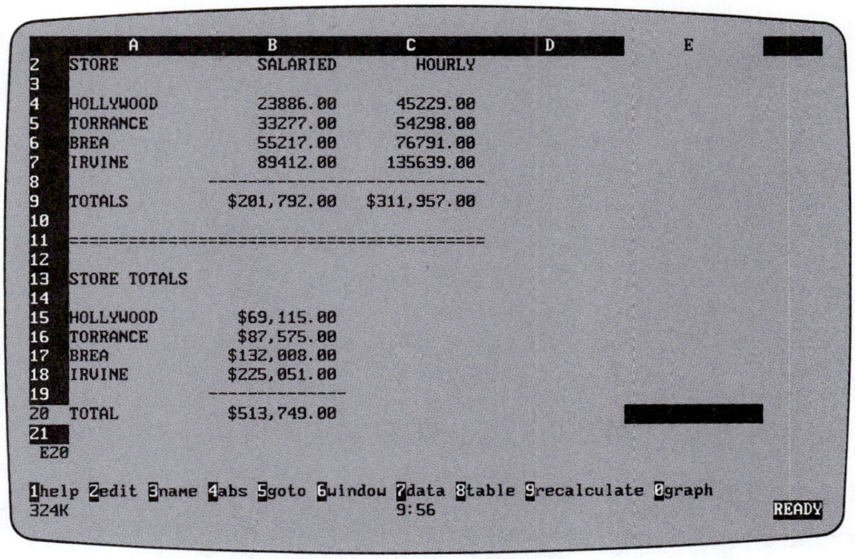

```
            A              B              C              D         E
 2  STORE           SALARIED        HOURLY
 3
 4  HOLLYWOOD       23886.00        45229.00
 5  TORRANCE        33277.00        54298.00
 6  BREA            55217.00        76791.00
 7  IRVINE          89412.00       135639.00
 8                  ------------    ------------
 9  TOTALS          $201,792.00    $311,957.00
10
11                  ========================================
12
13  STORE TOTALS
14
15  HOLLYWOOD       $69,115.00
16  TORRANCE        $87,575.00
17  BREA           $132,008.00
18  IRVINE         $225,051.00
19                  ------------
20  TOTAL          $513,749.00
21
     E20

 1help 2edit 3name 4abs 5goto 6window 7data 8table 9recalculate 0graph
324K                              9:56                            READY
```

FIGURE 2-56
Student Assignment 8

STUDENT ASSIGNMENT 9: Building a Monthly Expense Worksheet

Instructions: Load VP-Planner Plus and perform the following tasks.

1. Build the worksheet illustrated in Figure 2-57. Change the width of all the columns to 15 character positions. The variances in column D of the worksheet are obtained by subtracting the actual expenses from the budgeted expenses. In the summary portion of the worksheet, the percentage of budget used (C17) is obtained by dividing the total actual amount (C15) by the total budgeted amount.
2. Save the worksheet. Use the file name STUS2-9.
3. Print the as-is and cell-formulas versions of this worksheet.
4. Print the portion of the worksheet in the range A3..B8.
5. Print the worksheet after formatting all the cells to the Text type.

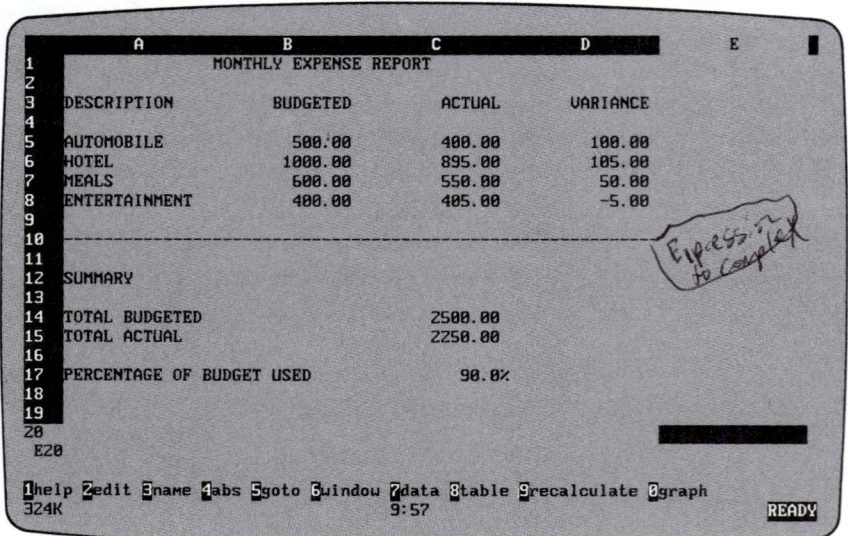

FIGURE 2-57
Student Assignment 9

STUDENT ASSIGNMENT 10: Building a Monthly Sales Analysis Worksheet

Instructions: Load VP-Planner Plus and perform the following tasks.

1. Build the worksheet illustrated in Figure 2-58. Change the width of all the columns to 12 characters. Then change the width of column A to 14 positions. Center all the column headings using the circumflex (^). The net sales in column D of the worksheet is determined by subtracting the sales returns in column C from the sales amount in column B. The above/below quota amount in column F is obtained by subtracting the sales quota in column E from the net sales in column D. In the summary section of the worksheet, the totals for each group are obtained by adding the values for each salesperson. The percent of quota sold is obtained by dividing the total net sales amount by the total sales quota amount.
2. Save the worksheet. Use the file name STUS2-10.
3. Print the as-is and cell-formulas versions of this worksheet.
4. Print the portion of the worksheet in the range A1..F9.
5. Print the worksheet after formatting all the cells to the Text type.

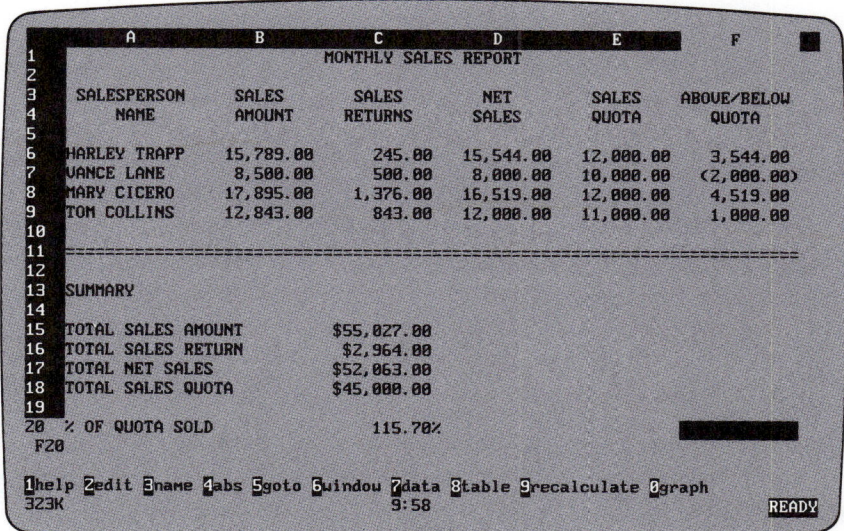

FIGURE 2-58
Student Assignment 10

STUDENT ASSIGNMENT 11: Changing Data in the Monthly Expense Worksheet

Instructions: Load VP-Planner Plus and perform the following tasks.

1. Retrieve the worksheet STUS2-9 from disk. The worksheet is illustrated in Figure 2-57.
2. Decrement each of the four values in the ACTUAL column by $30.00 until the percentage of budget used is as close as possible to 80%. All four values must be decremented the same number of times. You should end up with a percentage of budget used equal to 80.4%.
3. After successfully modifying the worksheet, print it on the printer.
4. Save the modified worksheet. Use the file name STUS2-11.

STUDENT ASSIGNMENT 12: Changing Data in the Monthly Sales Analysis Worksheet

Instructions: Load VP-Planner Plus and perform the following tasks.

1. Retrieve the worksheet STUS2-10 from disk. The worksheet is illustrated in Figure 2-58.
2. Increment each of the four values in the sales quota column by $1000.00 until the percent of quota sold in cell C20 is below, yet as close as possible to 100%. All four values must be incremented the same number of times. The percent of quota sold should be equal to 98.23%.
3. Decrement each of the four values in the sales returns column by $100.00 until the percent of quota sold in cell C20 is below, yet as close as possible to 100%. All four values must be decremented the same number of times. Your worksheet is correct when the percent of quota sold is equal to 99.74%.
4. After successfully modifying the worksheet, print it on the printer.
5. Save the modified worksheet. Use the file name STUS2-12.

PROJECT 3

Enhancing Your Worksheet

Objectives

You will have mastered the material in this project when you can:

- Display today's date and time in a worksheet using the NOW function.
- Move a group of rows or columns to another area of the worksheet.
- Insert and delete rows and columns.
- Freeze the horizontal and vertical titles.
- Enter percentage values using the percent sign (%).
- Copy absolute cell addresses.
- Employ the pointing method to enter a range to be summed.
- Increase the margins of the line printed on the printer.

- Print a worksheet in condensed mode.
- Switch between manual and automatic recalculation of a worksheet.
- Change the default settings.
- Change the VP-Planner Plus screen to make it look like the Lotus 1-2-3 screen.
- Undo and redo previously executed commands using the Undo and Redo keys.
- Copy, erase, list, and rename files on disk.
- Temporarily exit VP-Planner Plus and return control to DOS.

*I*n the first two projects you learned to build, save, retrieve, format, copy, and print worksheets. In this project we continue to emphasize these topics and discuss some new ones. We especially want to examine the Copy command in greater detail. The ability to copy one range to another range is one of the most powerful features of a spreadsheet program.

The new topics in this project teach you to insert and delete rows and columns in a worksheet and move the contents of a range to another range. In general, they make the job of creating, saving, and printing a worksheet easier.

Finally, this project illustrates using VP-Planner Plus to answer **what-if questions**, like "What if the marketing expenses decrease 3%—how would the decrease affect net income for the first quarter of the year?" This capability of quickly analyzing the effect of changing values in a worksheet is important in making business decisions. To illustrate answering what-if questions, we will prepare the quarterly budget report shown in Figure 3-1.

```
              A            B            C            D            E
 1   Quarterly Report - January through March                    12/22/91
 2   Prepared by SAS                                              10:01 am
 3
 4
 5   ITEM              JANUARY     FEBRUARY        MARCH   QUARTER TOTAL
 6   ==================================================================
 7
 8   REVENUE
 9      Sales Revenue  232,897.95   432,989.76   765,998.61   1,431,886.32
10      Other Revenue    1,232.93    3,265.81     2,145.99       6,644.73
11
12      Total Revenue  234,130.88   436,255.57   768,144.60   1,438,531.05
13
14   EXPENSES
15      Manufacturing   88,969.73   165,777.12   291,894.95     546,641.80
16      Research        25,754.40    47,988.11    84,495.91     158,238.42
17      Marketing       37,460.94    69,800.89   122,903.14     230,164.97
18      Administrative  39,802.25    74,163.45   130,584.58     244,550.28
19      Fulfillment     18,730.47    34,900.45    61,451.57     115,082.48
20
21      Total Expenses 210,717.79   392,630.01   691,330.14   1,294,677.95
22
23   NET INCOME         23,413.09    43,625.56    76,814.46     143,853.10
24
25   Budget % Values
26
27      Manufacturing             38%
28      Research                  11%
29      Marketing                 16%
30      Administrative            17%
31      Fulfillment                8%
```

FIGURE 3-1
The worksheet we will build in Project 3.

The worksheet in Figure 3-1 contains a company's budgeted revenue and expenses for the quarterly period of January through March. In addition, this worksheet includes the quarter total for all revenues and budgeted expenses. The total revenues for each month and the quarter total in row 12 are determined by adding the corresponding sales revenue and other revenue.

Each of the budgeted expenses—manufacturing, research, marketing, administrative, and fulfillment—is determined by taking a percentage of the total revenue. The budget percent values are located in rows 27–31 as follows:

1. The manufacturing expense is 38% of the total revenue.
2. The research expense is 11% of the total revenue.
3. The marketing expense is 16% of the total revenue.
4. The administrative expense is 17% of the total revenue.
5. The fulfillment expense is 8% of the total revenue.

The total expenses for each month in row 21 of Figure 3-1 are determined by adding all the corresponding budgeted expenses together. The net income for each month in row 23 is determined by subtracting the corresponding total expenses from the total revenue. Finally, the quarter totals in the far right column are determined by summing the monthly values in each row.

Begin this project by booting the computer and loading VP-Planner Plus. When the copyright message appears, press the Esc key to erase the message. An empty worksheet appears on the screen. All the columns in the empty worksheet are nine characters wide. This default width is not enough to hold some of the larger numbers in the worksheet we plan to build. Therefore, let's change the width of the columns.

VARYING THE WIDTH OF THE COLUMNS

*I*n the worksheet shown in Figure 3-1, column A is 17 characters wide, columns B through D are 14 characters wide, and column E is 16 characters wide. You select a column width setting on the basis of the longest column entry and the general appearance of the worksheet. Change the widths of the columns in the following manner:

1. Enter the /**W**orksheet **G**lobal **C**ol-width (/WGC) command to change the width of all the columns to 14 characters. Change the number on the input line from 9 to 14 by pressing the Right Arrow key five times followed by the Enter key as shown in Figure 3-2. You may also enter the number 14 in response to the prompt message on the input line and press the Enter key. The Global command is used to change the width of all the cells in the worksheet to 14 characters because that is the desired width of most of the columns for this project.

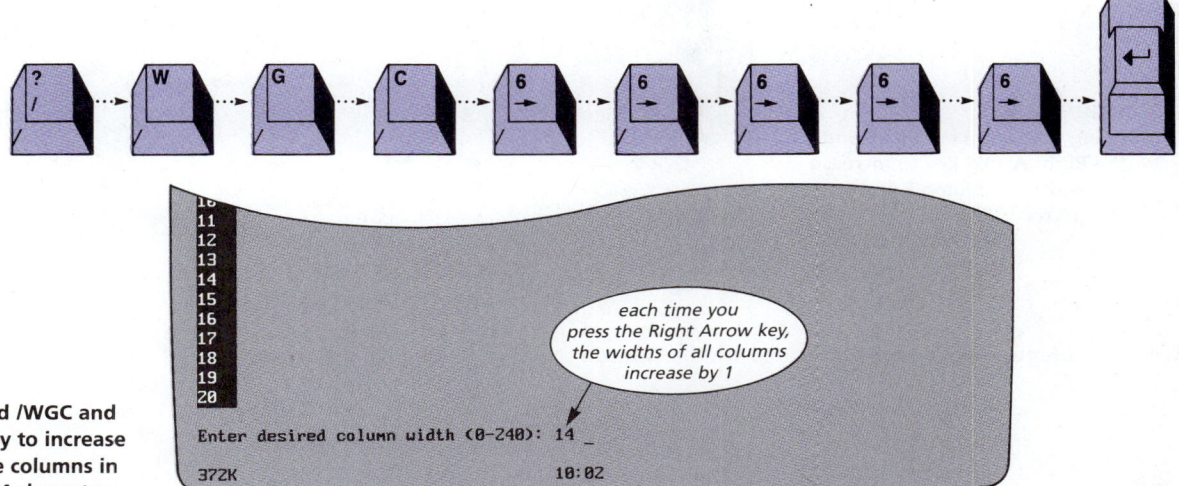

FIGURE 3-2
Using the command /WGC and the Right Arrow key to increase the width of all the columns in the worksheet to 14 characters.

2. With the cell cursor on A1, enter the command /Worksheet Col-width Set (/WCS) to change the width of column A to 17 characters. Again, press the Right Arrow key three times to change the number 14 to 17 on the input line. To complete the command, press the Enter key as shown in Figure 3-3.

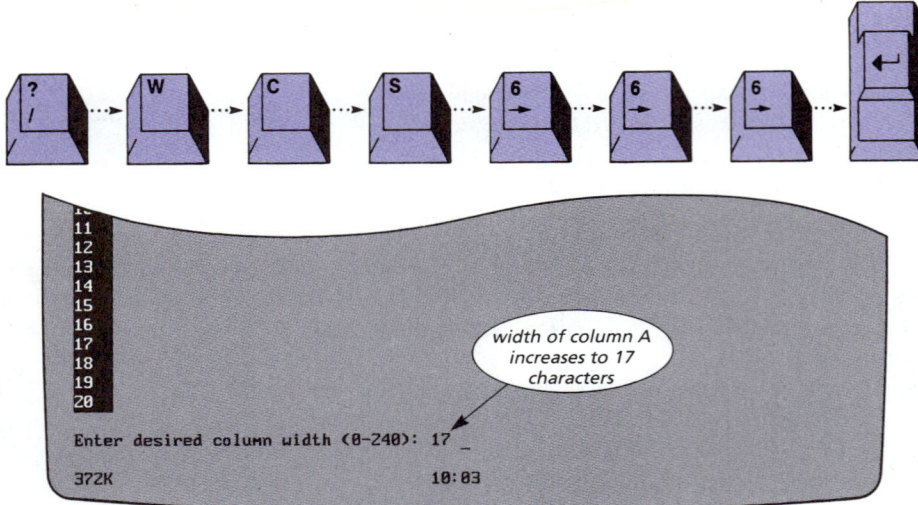

FIGURE 3-3
Using the command /WCS and the Right Arrow key to increase the width of column A to 17 characters.

3. Move the cell cursor to E1 and enter the command /Worksheet Col-width Set (/WCS) to change the width of column E to 16 characters. This is shown in Figure 3-4.

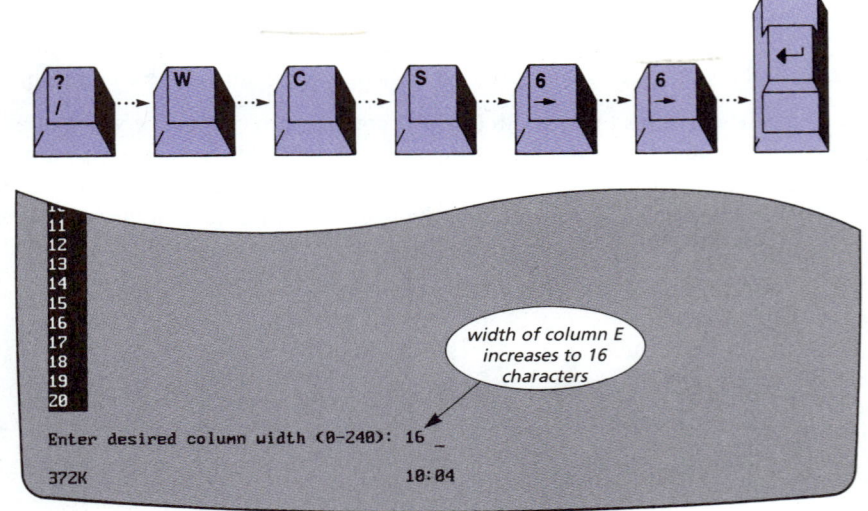

FIGURE 3-4
Using the command /WCS and the Right Arrow key to increase the width of column E to 16 characters.

With the columns set to their designated widths, we can move on to the next step, formatting the worksheet globally.

FORMATTING THE WORKSHEET GLOBALLY (/WGF)

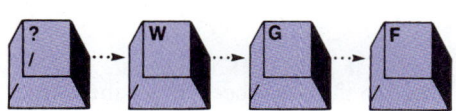

n Project 2, we formatted the numbers after we entered the data. In some cases, especially when developing a large worksheet, you should consider issuing a global format before entering any data. This formats the numbers as you enter them, which makes them easier to read. The way to do this is to choose the format that is common to most of the cells. In choosing the format, don't count the empty cells or the ones with labels, because a numeric format does not affect them.

You can see from Figure 3-1 that, except for the budget percent values and the date and time, all the numbers appear as decimal numbers with two places of accuracy. These numbers also use the comma to group the integer portion by thousands. If you refer to Table 2-2 in Project 2, you will see that the required format corresponds to the Comma (,) type. Therefore, use this format for all the cells in the worksheet.

To invoke the Global Format command, enter the command /Worksheet Global Format (/WGF). This is shown in Figure 3-5. With the command cursor active in the Format menu, press the Comma key (,). The prompt message "Enter default decimal position: 2" displays on the input line (see Figure 3-6). Since we are working with dollars and cents, we want two decimal places to display. Therefore, press the Enter key.

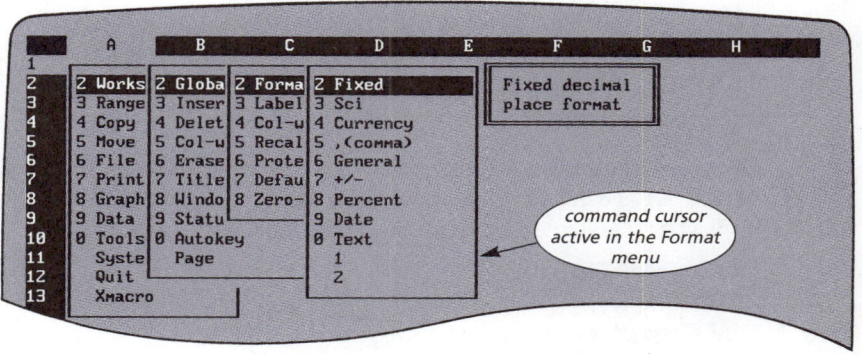

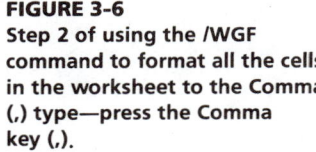

FIGURE 3-5
Step 1 of using the /WGF command to format all the cells in the worksheet to the Comma (,) type—press the Slash key (/) and type the letters W, G, and F.

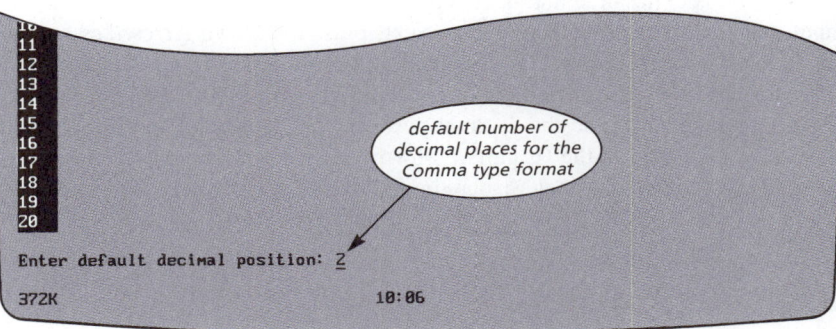

FIGURE 3-6
Step 2 of using the /WGF command to format all the cells in the worksheet to the Comma (,) type—press the Comma key (,).

The empty worksheet shown in Figure 3-7 displays. You can see that the columns are wider than nine characters. However, there is no indication of the Comma format we assigned to all the cells. The format will appear as we enter data, because VP-Planner Plus will automatically use the Comma format for any number entered into a cell.

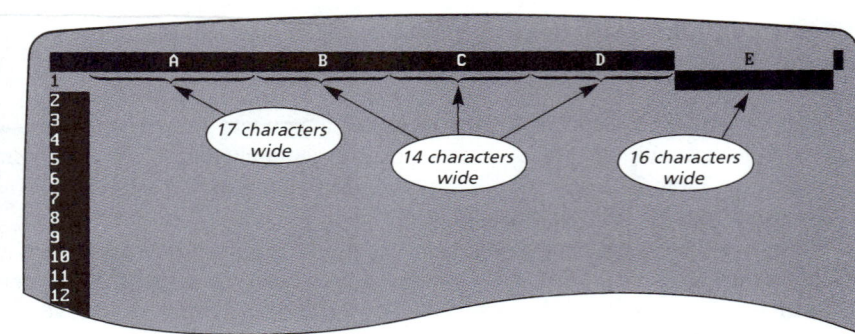

FIGURE 3-7
Step 3 of using the /WGF command to format all the cells in the worksheet to the Comma (,) type—press the Enter key.

DISPLAYING THE DATE AND TIME

ith the column widths and the global format set, the next step is to enter the data into the worksheet. Enter the titles in cells A1 and A2 as you learned in Project 1. Cells E1 and E2 require today's date and time. Both values can be displayed by assigning each cell the NOW function.

The NOW Function

The NOW function uses the current DOS date and time to determine the number of days since December 31, 1899. It displays the value in the assigned cell as a decimal number. For this project assume that the DOS date is December 22, 1991 and the time is approximately 10:08 am. For the NOW function to display the correct value, it is important that you check the accuracy of the system date and system time. Recall that in the Introduction to DOS, you learned how to set the system time and system date.

To complete the time and date entries in the worksheet, move the cell cursor to E1 and enter the NOW function on the input line as illustrated in Figure 3-8. Next, press the Down Arrow key and enter the same function in E2. Use the Up Arrow key to enter the function in E2. This places the cell cursor in E1 as shown in Figure 3-9. The value 33,594.42 in cells E1 and E2 represents the number of days since December 31, 1899. The integer portion of the number (33,594) represents the number of complete days, and the decimal portion (.42) represents the first 10 hours of December 22, 1991. Note that the two entries are displayed in the Comma (,) format, the one we assigned earlier to the entire worksheet. The next step is to format the date and time so that they display in a more meaningful way.

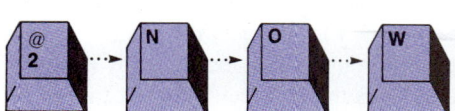

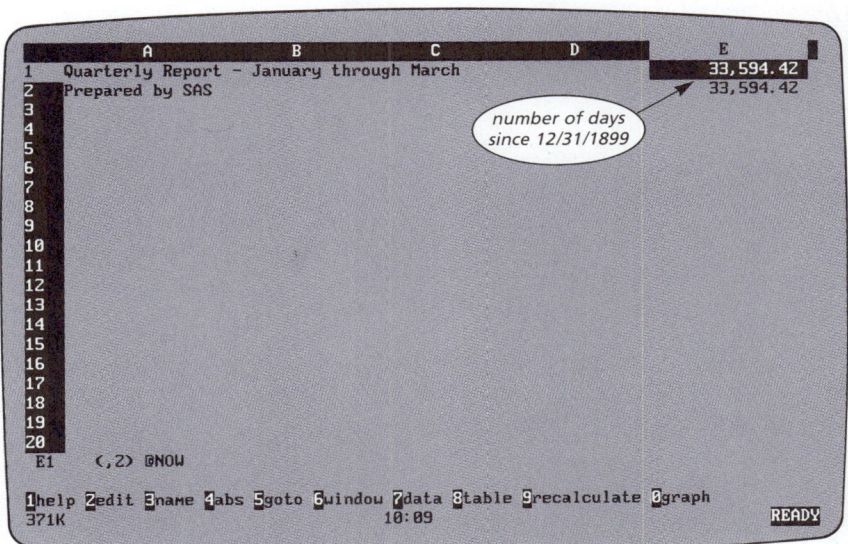

FIGURE 3-8
Entering the NOW function on the input line with the cell cursor at E1.

FIGURE 3-9
The NOW function assigned to cells E1 and E2.

Formatting the Date (/RFD)

In Figure 3-9, the cell cursor is at E1. To format the date, enter the command /**R**ange **F**ormat **D**ate (/RFD) as shown in Figure 3-10. With the command cursor active in the **Date menu**, select the fourth date format (M/D/Y). To select the desired format, move the command cursor down to the fourth one in the menu and press the Enter key. VP-Planner Plus responds by displaying the prompt message "Select Range of cells to be altered: E1..E1" on the input line. E1 is the only cell we want to format, so press the Enter key. The date immediately changes in cell E1 to 12/22/91 as shown in Figure 3-11.

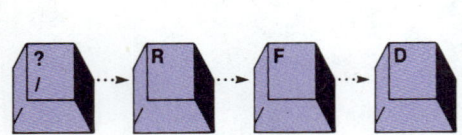

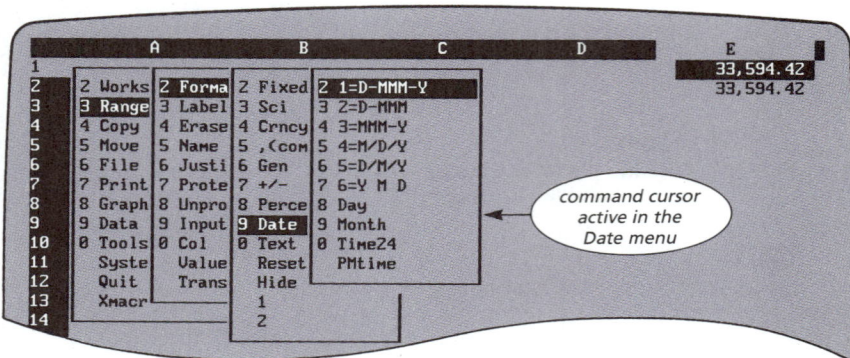

FIGURE 3-10
Formatting the date in cell E1.

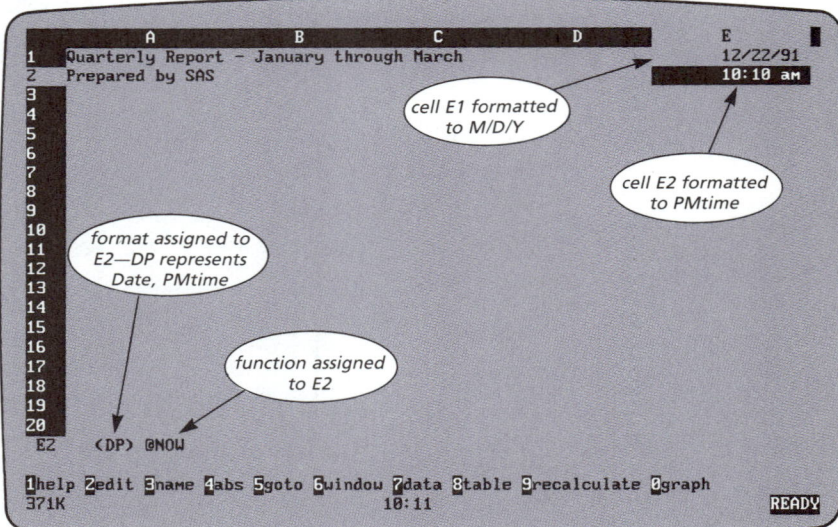

FIGURE 3-11
Date and time displayed in cells
E1 and E2—10:10 am on
December 22, 1991.

Formatting the Time (/RFD)

Move the cell cursor to E2. To format the time, enter the same command as for the date—/**R**ange **F**ormat **D**ate (/RFD). This is shown in Figure 3-10. There are two time formats at the bottom of the rightmost menu. Select the one named PMtime by typing the letter P. Press the Enter key and the time in E2 displays as 10:10 am (see Figure 3-11).

Updating the Time—Recalculation

The time displayed on the current-mode line at the bottom of the screen updates every minute while VP-Planner Plus is in READY mode. However, the time displayed in a cell, as in E2, only updates when you enter a numeric value into a cell. Any numeric entry causes VP-Planner Plus to recalculate all the formulas and functions in the worksheet automatically.

If you are not entering any numeric values and want to instruct VP-Planner Plus to recalculate all formulas and functions, press function key F9. As indicated on the prompt line at the bottom of the screen, the F9 key instructs VP-Planner Plus to recalculate. Pressing F9 updates the time as illustrated in Figure 3-12.

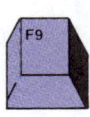
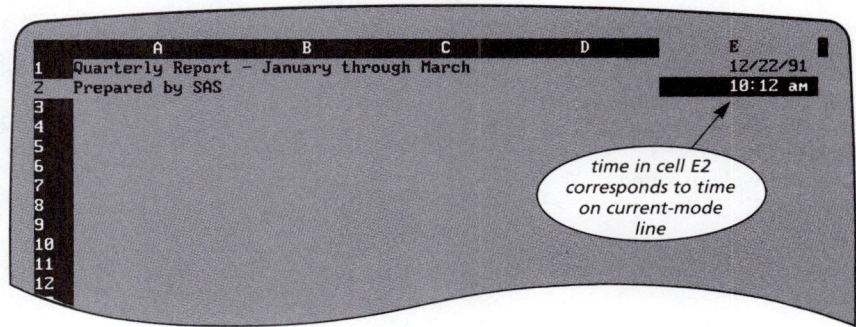

time in cell E2 corresponds to time on current-mode line

FIGURE 3-12
Press function key F9 to manually update the time in cell E2.

Date and Time Formats

Table 3-1 summarizes the date and time formats available in VP-Planner Plus. Use this table to select formats when you want to display the date and time in a worksheet.

TABLE 3-1   Date and Time Formats
(Assume the DOS date is December 22, 1991 and the time is 3:12 PM.)

FORMAT NUMBER	FORMAT TYPE	FORMAT CODE ON STATUS LINE	DATE OR TIME DISPLAYED
1	D-MMM-Y	D1	22-Dec-91
2	D-MMM	D2	22-Dec
3	MMM-Y	D3	Dec-91
4	M/D/Y	D4	12/22/91
5	D/M/Y	D5	22/12/91
6	Y M D	D6	91 12 22
D	Day	DD	Sunday
M	Month	DM	December
T	Time24	DT	15:12
P	PMtime	DP	3:12 pm

ENTERING THE QUARTERLY BUDGET LABELS

With the date and time formatted, we can enter the column headings, group titles, and row identifiers. Move the cell cursor to A5. Since the column headings consist of capital letters, press the Caps Lock key before entering them. Left-justify the first column heading and right-justify the rest. Recall that to right-justify a label, begin the label with a quotation mark ("). The worksheet with the column headings is shown in Figure 3-13.

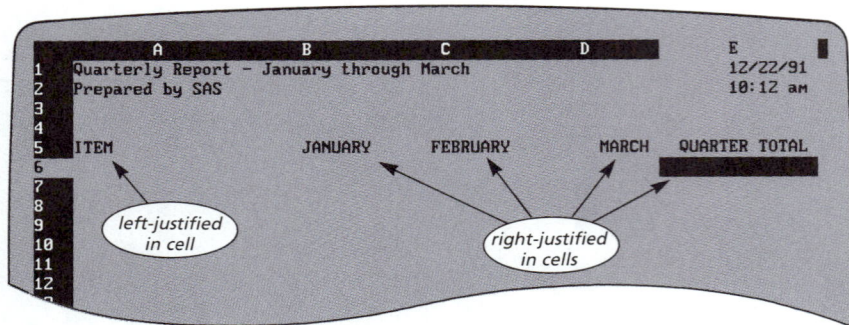

FIGURE 3-13
Column headings entered into row 5.

After completing the column headings, move the cell cursor to A6. Use the Backslash key (\) to repeat the equal sign (=) throughout cell A6. Next, use the command /Copy (/C) to copy the contents of cell A6 to cells B6 through E6. The result is a double-dashed line in row 6 as illustrated in Figure 3-14.

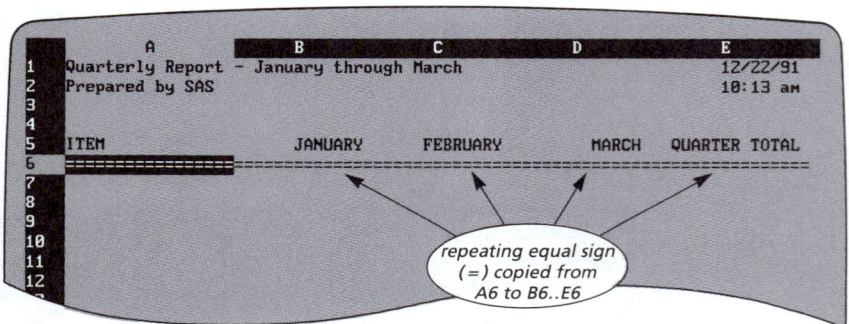

FIGURE 3-14
Column headings underlined.

Once the column headings are complete, begin entering the group titles and row identifiers that are shown on the left side of Figure 3-1. All the labels are left-justified. The group subtitles are indented by two spaces to make the worksheet easier to read. Since most of the remaining labels are in lower-case letters, press the Caps Lock key to toggle off capital letters after entering the group title REVENUE in cell A8.

Do not enter the two subtitles Marketing and Administrative under the group title EXPENSES. We will add these subtitles shortly.

Figure 3-15 shows the group titles and row identifiers up to row 24. Note in Figure 3-15 that with the cell cursor in A24 the window has moved down four rows, displaying rows 5 through 24 rather than rows 1 through 20. Once the cell cursor moves past row 20, the window begins to move down. The same applies when the cell cursor moves beyond the last column on the screen.

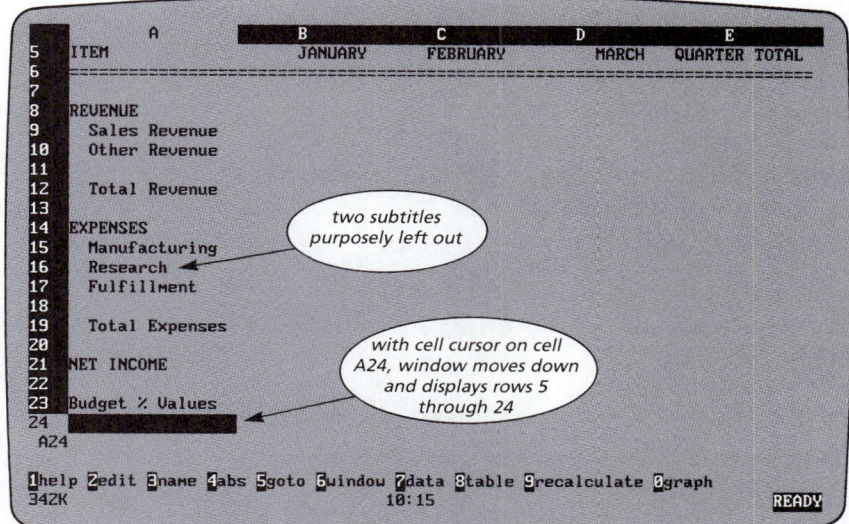

FIGURE 3-15
Group titles and subtitles entered.

INSERTING AND DELETING ROWS AND COLUMNS

 t is not unusual to forget to include rows or columns of data when building a worksheet, or to include too many rows or columns. VP-Planner Plus is forgiving. It has commands to insert or delete as many rows or columns as required. Furthermore, you can do this at any time, even after a worksheet is well under way.

The Insert Command (/WI)

The command /Worksheet Insert (/WI) is used to insert empty rows or columns anywhere in the worksheet. To make room for the new rows, VP-Planner Plus simply opens up the worksheet by *pushing down* the rows below the insertion point. If you are inserting columns, those to the right of the insertion point are *pushed* to the right. More importantly, if the *pushed* rows or columns include any formulas, VP-Planner Plus adjusts the cell references to the new locations.

Remember that we purposely left out the two subtitles Marketing and Administrative from the group title EXPENSES (compare Figure 3-15 to Figure 3-1). Let's insert—open up—two blank rows in the worksheet so that we can add the two subtitles. According to Figure 3-1, the two subtitles belong immediately before Fulfillment in cell A17. Therefore, move the cell cursor to A17. To complete a row insert, always position the cell cursor on the first row you want *pushed* down. This is shown in Figure 3-16. For a row insert, the column location of the cell cursor is not important.

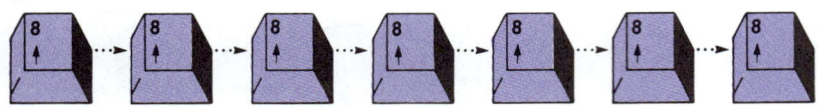

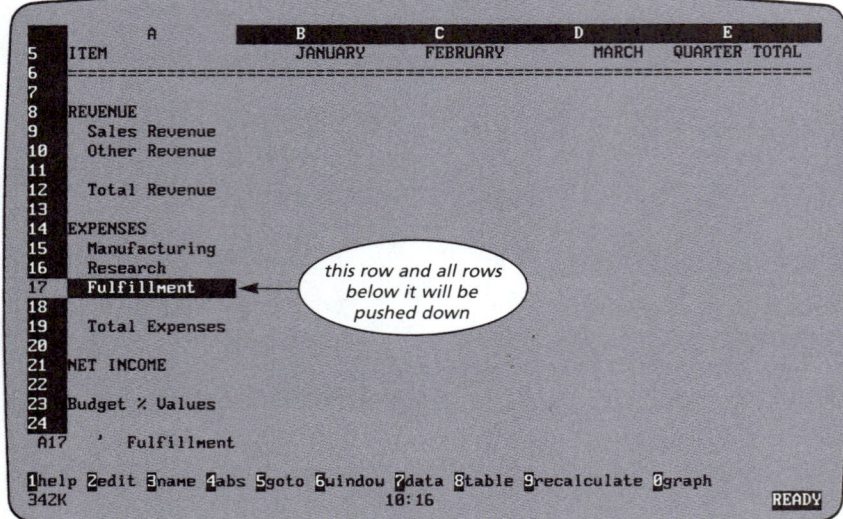

FIGURE 3-16
Step 1 of using the /WI command to insert rows—move the cell cursor to A17, the first row you want *pushed* down.

Enter the command /Worksheet Insert (/WI) as shown in Figure 3-17. With the command cursor active in the **Insert menu**, type the letter R for Row. VP-Planner Plus immediately responds on the input line at the bottom of the screen with the prompt message, "Select range of rows to insert: A17..A17." You want to add two new rows, A17 and A18. Therefore, use the Down Arrow key to increase the range on the input line from A17..A17 to A17..A18. This is illustrated in Figure 3-18.

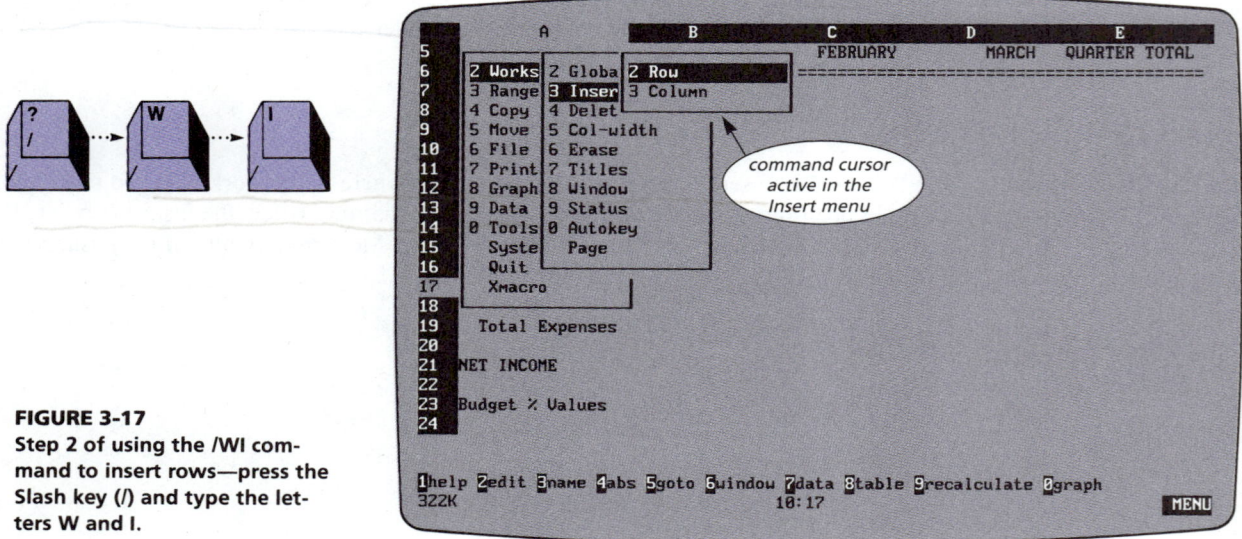

FIGURE 3-17
Step 2 of using the /WI command to insert rows—press the Slash key (/) and type the letters W and I.

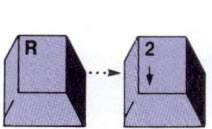

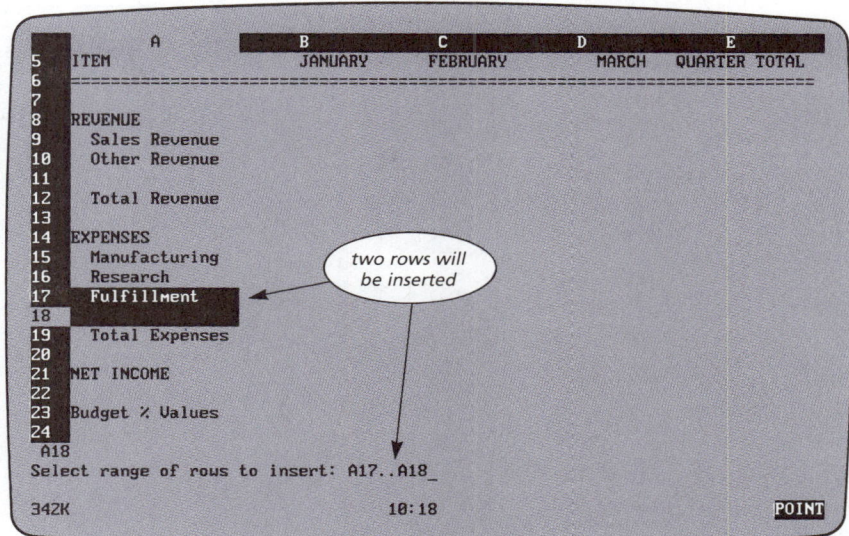

FIGURE 3-18
Step 3 of using the /WI command to insert rows—type the letter R for Row and use the Down Arrow key to select the number of rows you want to insert.

Press the Enter key and the worksheet *pushes down* all the rows beginning with row 17—the first row in the range A17..A18. This leaves rows 17 and 18 empty as shown in Figure 3-19. Enter the subtitle Marketing in cell A17 and the subtitle Administrative in cell A18. This results in the worksheet shown in Figure 3-20 on the next page.

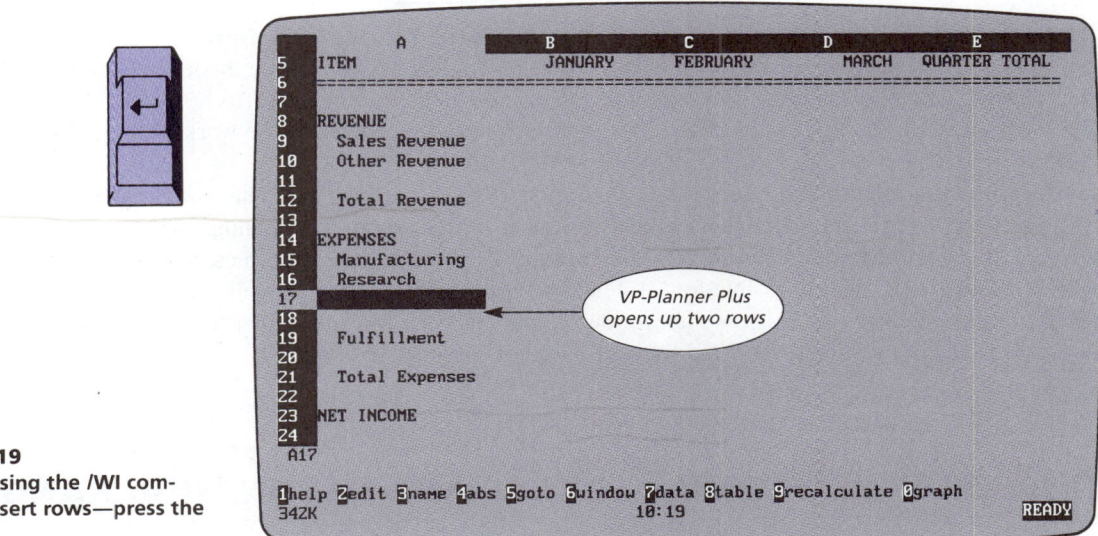

FIGURE 3-19
Step 4 of using the /WI command to insert rows—press the Enter key.

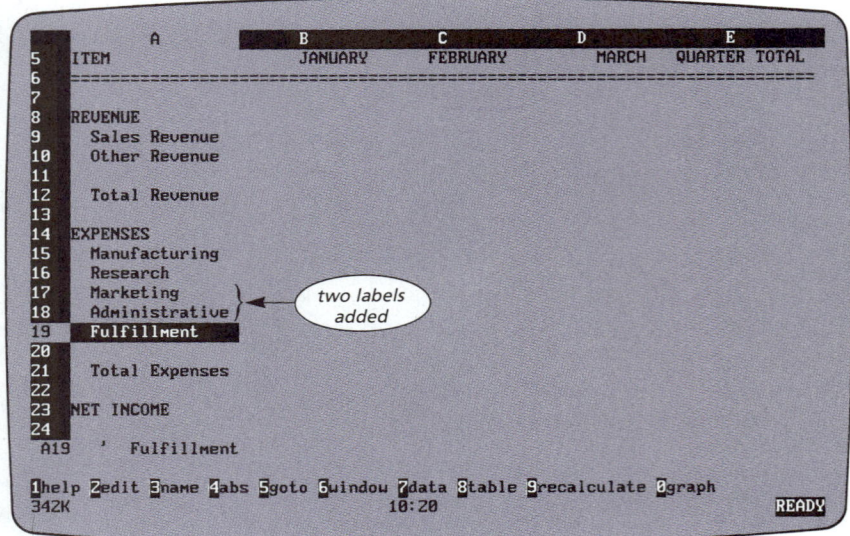

FIGURE 3-20
The two subtitles inserted into the worksheet.

The Delete Command (/WD)

You can delete unwanted rows or columns from a worksheet by using the command /**W**orksheet **D**elete (/WD). Let's delete rows 17 and 18 in Figure 3-20. After deleting these two rows, we will reinsert them using use the command /**W**orksheet **I**nsert (/WI).

With the cell cursor on cell A17, enter the command /**W**orksheet **D**elete (/WD). Next, type the letter R to instruct VP-Planner Plus to delete rows rather than columns. To delete columns we would type the letter C. When VP-Planner Plus requests the range to delete, press the Down Arrow key to change the range from A17..A17 to A17..A18. Press the Enter key. VP-Planner Plus immediately *closes up* the worksheet—rows 17 and 18 disappear. The worksheet appears as it did earlier in Figure 3-16.

Be careful when you use the Worksheet Delete command. You do not want to delete rows or columns that are part of a range used in a formula or function elsewhere in the worksheet without carefully weighing the consequences. If any formula references a cell in a deleted row or column, VP-Planner Plus displays the diagnostic message ERR in the cell assigned the formula. ERR means that it was impossible for VP-Planner Plus to complete the computation.

Before moving on, reinsert the two rows above row 17 and enter the row identifiers (Marketing and Administrative). Follow the keystroke sequence just described and shown in Figures 3-16 through 3-20.

COPYING CELLS WITH EQUAL SOURCE AND DESTINATION RANGES

We are not yet finished with the labels. We need to enter the subtitles in cells A27 through A31 (see Figure 3-1). These subtitles are the same as the ones entered earlier in cells A15 through A19. Therefore, we can use the Copy command to copy the contents of cells A15 through A19 to A27 through A31.

As shown in Figure 3-20, the cursor is at cell A19, one of the end points of the source range. Enter the command /**C**opy (/C). On the input line, the first end point of the source cell range (A19) is already anchored. Use the Up Arrow key to select the range A19..A15. Press the Enter key. Next, select the destination range by moving the cell cursor to A27 as shown in Figure 3-21. Press the Enter key to conclude the Copy command (see Figure 3-22).

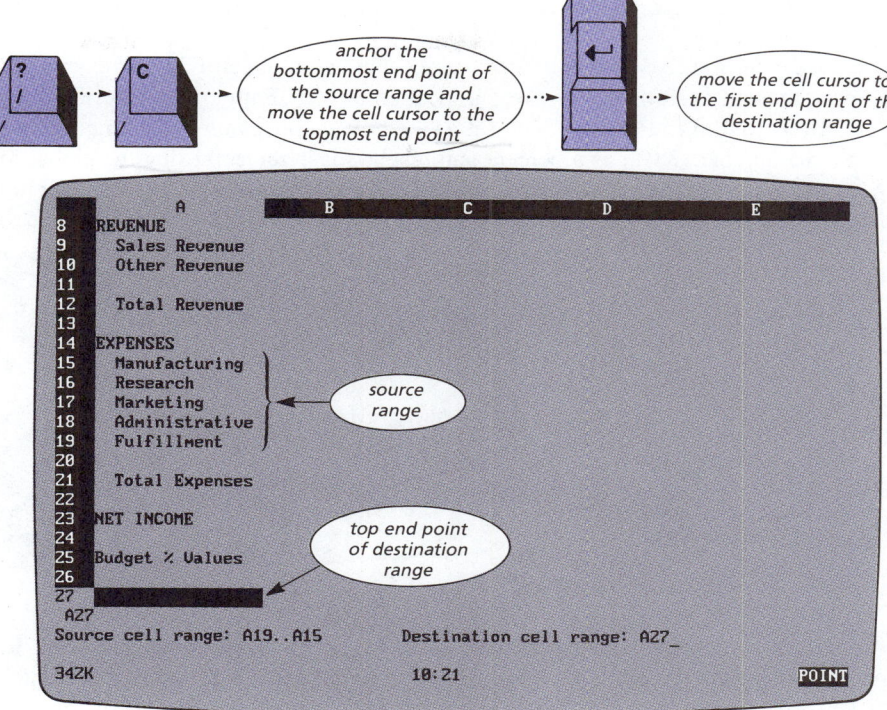

FIGURE 3-21
Step 1 of using the /C command to copy—press the Slash key (/), type the letter C, select the source range, press the Enter key, and move the cell cursor to A27.

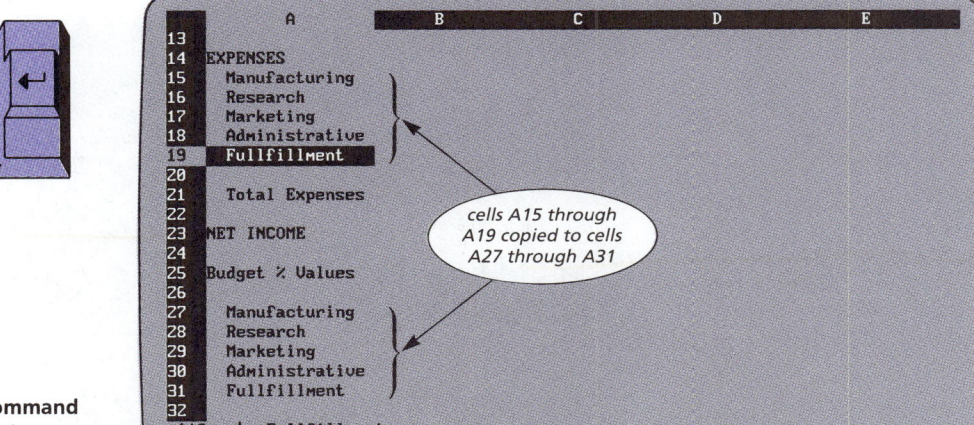

FIGURE 3-22
Step 2 of using the /C command to copy—press the Enter key. The source range (A15..A19) is copied to the destination range (A27..A31).

As shown in Figure 3-22, the source range (A15..A19) and the destination range (A27..A31) are identical. Two important points to note about copying the range A15..A19:

1. We selected the source range by entering A19..A15. Remember that the range A19..A15 is the same as A15..A19.
2. When both the source and destination ranges are the same size, it is not necessary to anchor the second end point of the destination range. VP-Planner Plus only needs to know the upper left end point, in this case A27. VP-Planner Plus copies the five cells in the source range beginning at cell A27. It always copies below the upper left end point.

ENTERING NUMBERS WITH A PERCENT SIGN

Next we enter the five budget percent values that begin in cell B27 and extend through cell B31. Use the arrow keys to move the cell cursor from its present location to B27. Rather than entering the percent value as a decimal number (.38), as we did in Project 2, enter it as a whole number followed immediately by a percent sign (%). VP-Planner Plus accepts the number (38%) as a percent and displays it in the cell using the global format assigned earlier to the worksheet. After we enter the five budget percent values, the worksheet appears as shown in Figure 3-23.

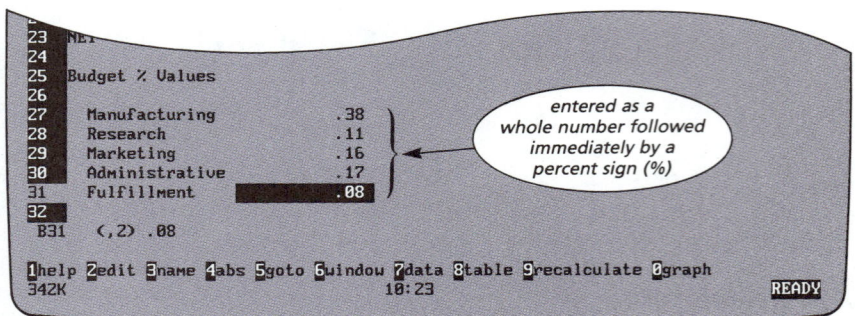

FIGURE 3-23
The five budget percent values in cells B27 through B31.

To format the five budget percent values to the Percent format, enter the command **/R**ange **F**ormat **P**ercent (/RFP). When VP-Planner Plus displays the prompt message "Enter desired decimal position: 2" on the input line, type the digit zero and press the Enter key. The prompt message "Select range of cells to be altered: B31..B31" displays on the input line. Enter the range B31..B27. The first end point (B31) is anchored. Use the Up Arrow key to move the cell cursor to B27. The range on the input line now reads B31..B27. Press the Enter key. The five budget percent values display in percent form as shown in Figure 3-24.

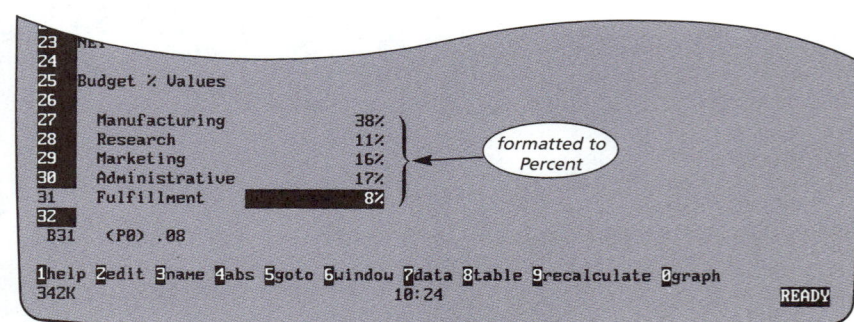

FIGURE 3-24
The five budget percent values in cells B27 through B31 formatted to the Percent type.

FREEZING THE TITLES

The worksheet for this project extends beyond the size of the window. When you move the cell cursor down or to the right, the title and column and row identifiers disappear off the screen. This makes it difficult to remember where to enter the data. To alleviate this problem, VP-Planner Plus allows you to "freeze the titles" so that they remain on the screen no matter where you move the cell cursor. The title and column headings are called the **horizontal titles** and the row identifiers are called the **vertical titles**.

The Titles Command (/WT)

To freeze the titles in this worksheet, press the Home key so that most of the titles are visible on the screen. Next, use the GOTO command to move the cursor to cell B7. The horizontal titles are just above cell B7 and the vertical titles are just to the left of cell B7. Enter the command /**W**orksheet **T**itles (/WT) as shown in Figure 3-25. With the command cursor active in the **Titles menu**, type the letter B for Both. This keeps the titles visible regardless of where you move the cell cursor, as shown in Figure 3-26.

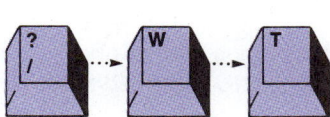

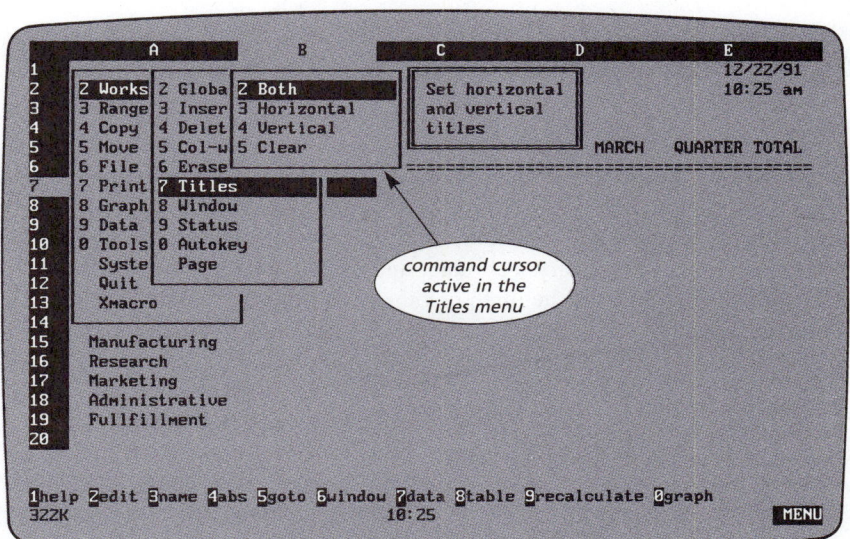

FIGURE 3-25
Step 1 of freezing both the horizontal and vertical titles—press the Slash key (/) and type the letters W and T.

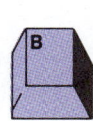

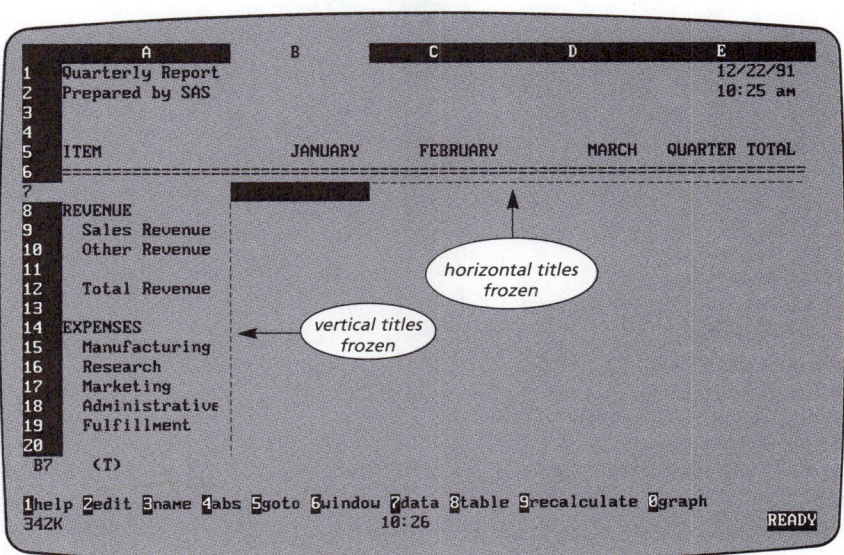

FIGURE 3-26
Step 2 of freezing both the horizontal and vertical titles—type the letter B to freeze both.

Unfreezing the Titles (/WTC)

Once you specify a title area, you cannot move the cell cursor into this area of the worksheet using the keys on the numeric keypad. If you want to make a change to the titles after freezing them, you must "unfreeze" them. To unfreeze the titles, enter the command /**W**orksheet **T**itles **C**lear (/WTC). Once the titles are unfrozen, you can move the cell cursor anywhere on the worksheet, including the title area, to make your desired changes. To refreeze the titles, move the cell cursor to the cell just below the horizontal titles and just to the right of the vertical titles. Next, enter the command /**W**orksheet **T**itles **B**oth (/WTB).

MOVING THE CONTENTS OF CELLS (/M)

The command /**M**ove (/M) moves the contents of a cell or range of cells to a different location in the worksheet. To illustrate the use of this command, let's make a mistake by entering the sales revenue (232897.95, 432989.76, and 765998.61) that belongs in cells B9 through E9 into cells B7 through E7—two rows above its location according to Figure 3-1. This type of error is common, especially when you're not careful about cell cursor placement.

The sales revenues for January, February, and March are 232,897.95, 432,989.76, and 765,998.61. The quarter total is the sum of the sales revenue for the three months. Enter the three numbers in cells B7, C7, and D7. Use the Right Arrow key after typing each number on the input line. With the cell cursor in E7, enter the function @SUM(B7..D7). VP-Planner Plus evaluates the function and stores the number 1,431,886.32 in E7 (232,897.95 + 432,989.76 + 765,998.61). The values in cells C7, D7, and E7 are shown in Figure 3-27. Note that with the cell cursor at F7, the row identifiers in column A display along with columns C, D, E, and F. However, column B does not display.

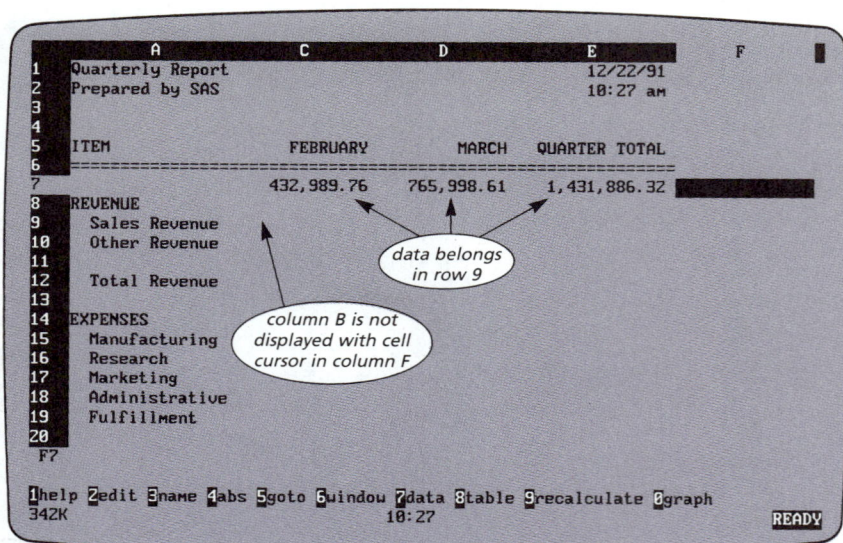

FIGURE 3-27
The sales revenue data entered into the wrong row.

As indicated earlier, the data we just entered in row 7 belongs in row 9. Let's correct the mistake and move the data from row 7 to row 9. With the cell cursor on F7, enter the command /**M**ove (/M). VP-Planner Plus displays the message "Range to be moved: F7..F7" on the input line. Press the Backspace key to *unlock* the first end point. Move the cell cursor to E7 and press the Period key. Next, move the cell cursor to B7. The range to be moved is shown in Figure 3-28. Press the Enter key to lock in the range to be moved.

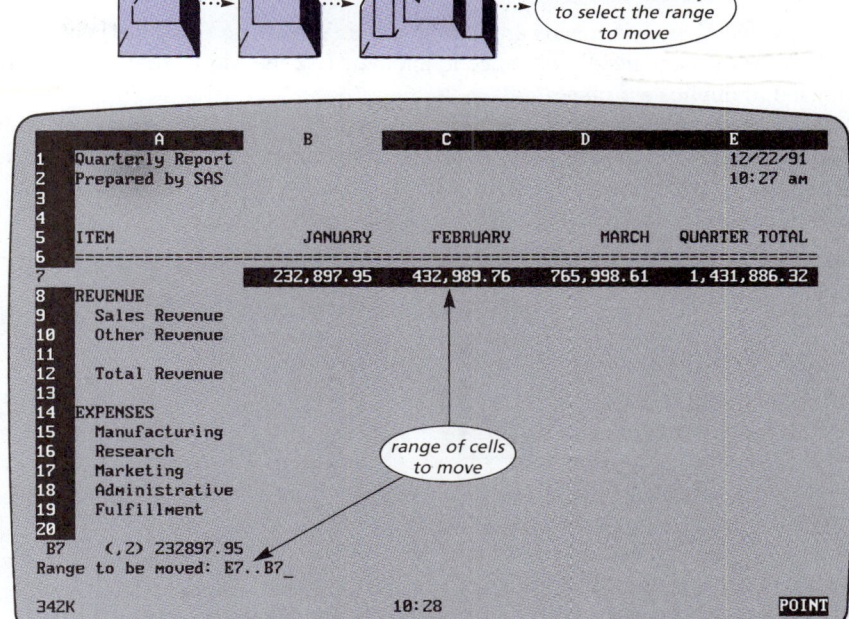

FIGURE 3-28
Step 1 of using the /M command to move data from one range to another—press the Slash key (/), type the letter M, and select the range of cells to move.

VP-Planner Plus displays a second message—Destination: F7—on the input line. Move the cell cursor to E9. Press the Period key to anchor the first end point. Move the cell cursor to B9 as shown in Figure 3-29. To complete the command, press the Enter key. Move the cell cursor to cell B10.

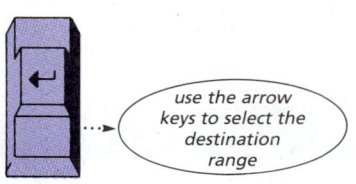

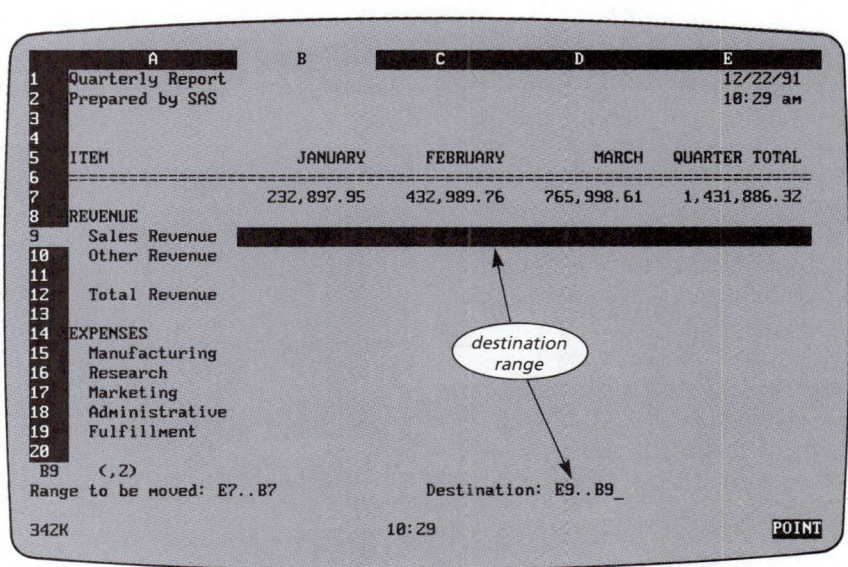

FIGURE 3-29
Step 2 of using the /M command to move data from one range to another—press the Enter key to lock in the range to move and select the destination range.

Figure 3-30 illustrates the result of moving the contents of cells B7 through E7 to B9 through E9. Here are some points regarding the Move command:

1. The Move and Copy commands are not the same. Where the Copy command copies one range to another, the Move command moves the contents of one range to another. Use the Move command to rearrange your worksheet. Use the Copy command to duplicate a range.
2. When you move a range containing a formula or function that references cell addresses, the referenced cell addresses are not changed relative to the new position, unless they refer to cells within the moved range. This was the case with the function in cell E7. Recall that we assigned the function @SUM(B7..D7) to cell E7. Following the Move command, the function assigned to cell E9 reads @SUM(B9..D9).

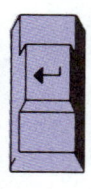

FIGURE 3-30
Step 3 of using the /M command to move data from one range to another—press the Enter key.

DISPLAYING FORMULAS AND FUNCTIONS IN THE CELLS (/RFT)

The next step in this project is to enter the other revenue in cells B10 through D10. Enter the three values for January, February, and March as described in Figure 3-1. Leave the quarter total in column E alone for now. The monthly total revenue in row 12 is equal to the sum of the corresponding monthly revenues in rows 9 and 10. Therefore, assign cell B12 the function @SUM(B9..B10). This is illustrated in Figure 3-31.

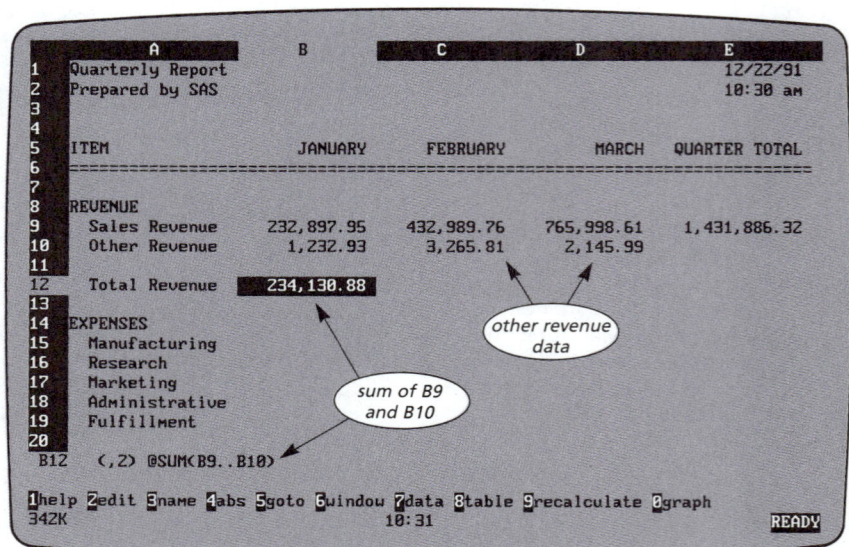

FIGURE 3-31
Other revenue and formula for January total revenue entered into worksheet.

Use the /Copy (/C) command to copy the SUM function in cell B12 to cells C12 and C13. Remember, the Copy command adjusts the cell references in the function so that it adds the contents of the cells above the cell the SUM function is copied to. Once the Copy command has been entered, VP-Planner Plus requires the source cell range and the destination cell range on the input line. In this case the source cell range is B12 and the destination cell range is C12..D12. The correct entries are shown on the input line in Figure 3-32. To complete the copy, press the Enter key. The result of the copy is shown in cells C12 and D12 in Figure 3-33.

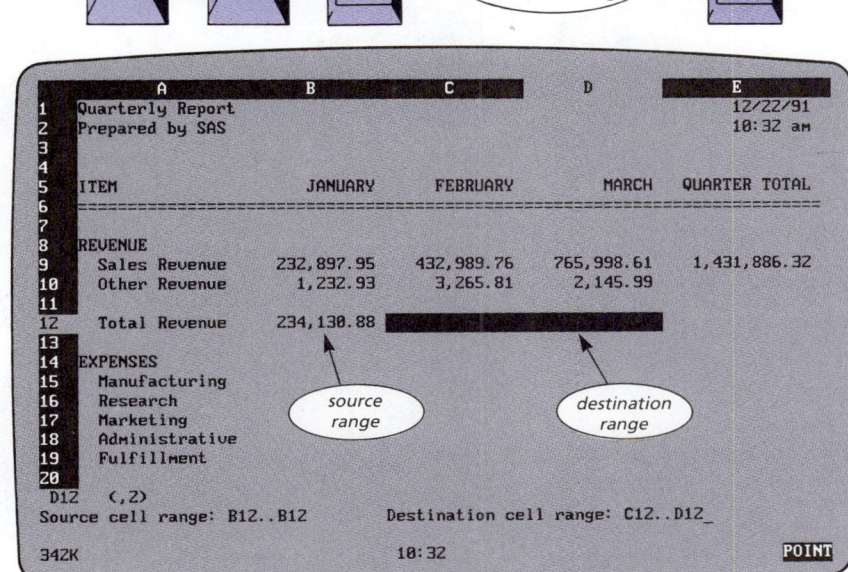

FIGURE 3-32
Using the /C command to copy cell B12 to C12 and D12—press the Slash key (/), type the letter C, press the Enter key to select the source range, use the arrow keys to select the destination range, and press the Enter key.

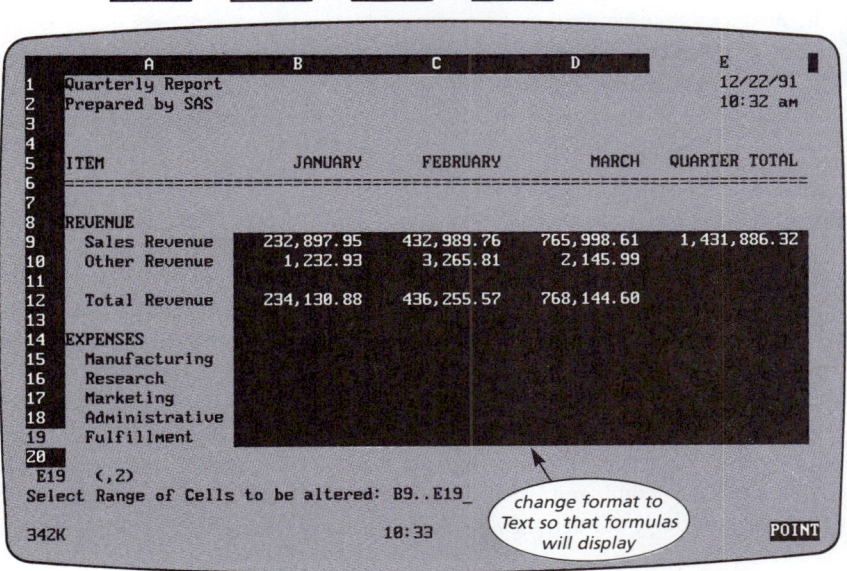

FIGURE 3-33
Step 1 of using the /RFT command to format cells B9..E19 to the Text type—press the Slash key (/), type the letters R, F, and T, and select the range B9..E19.

When entering or copying formulas, it is often useful to view them in the cells, instead of their numeric result. Therefore, to illustrate what is actually copied, let's change the format from Comma (,) to Text for the range B9..E19 in the worksheet. Remember from Project 2 that the Text format instructs VP-Planner Plus to display the formula assigned to a cell, rather than the numeric result.

Enter the command **/R**ange **F**ormat **T**ext (/RFT). VP-Planner Plus responds with the prompt message "Select Range of Cells to be altered: B12..B12" on the input line. Enter the range B9..E19 as shown in Figure 3-33 and press the Enter key. The functions in the worksheet (cells E9, B12, C12, and D12) now display in their respective cells. The numeric entries display left-justified using the Gen type format. This is shown in Figure 3-34. Later, we will reassign the Comma (,) format to the range B9..E19.

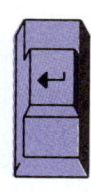

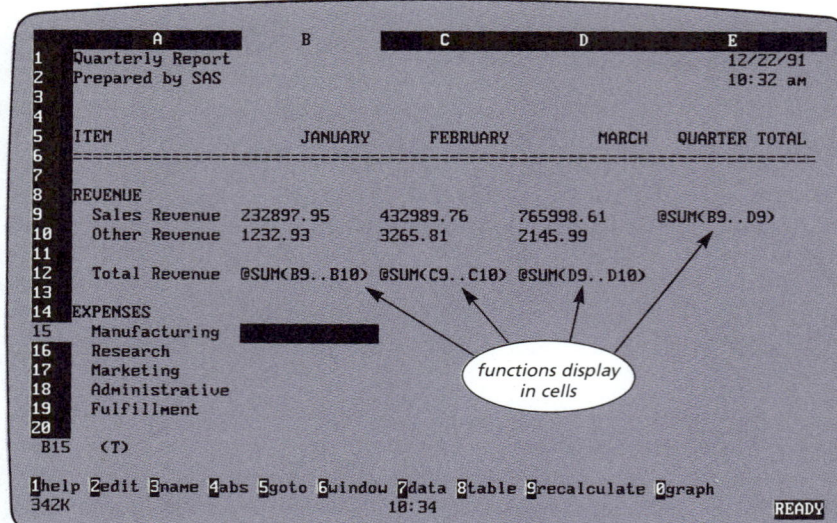

FIGURE 3-34
Step 2 of using the /RFT command to format cells B9..E19 to the Text type—press the Enter key.

ABSOLUTE VERSUS RELATIVE ADDRESSING

The next step is to determine the five monthly budgeted expenses in the rectangular group of cells B15 through D19. Each of these budgeted expenses is equal to the corresponding budgeted percent (cells B27 through B31) times the monthly total revenue (cells B12 through D12). The formulas for each of the cells in this range are similar. They differ in that the total revenue varies by the month (column) and the budgeted percent value varies by the type of expense (row).

Relative Addressing

It would be great if we could enter the formula +B27*B12 once in cell B15 (January budgeted manufacturing expense) and then copy this formula to the remaining cells in the rectangular group B15 through D19. However, we know that when a formula with relative addresses, like B27 and B12, is copied across a row or down a column, VP-Planner Plus automatically adjusts the cell references in the formula as it copies to reflect its new location.

Specifying cells in a formula using relative addressing has worked well in the previous examples of copying formulas, but it won't work here because the five budgeted percent values are all located in one column and the monthly total revenues are all located in one row. For example, if we copy +B27*B12 in cell B15 to cell C15, then cell C15 equals +C27*C12. This adjustment by the Copy command is because B27 and B12 are relative addresses. The C12 is okay, because it represents the total revenue for February, but cell C27 is blank. What we need here is for VP-Planner Plus to maintain cell B27 as it copies across the first row.

Absolute and Mixed Cell Addressing

VP-Planner Plus has the ability to keep a cell, a column, or a row constant when it copies a formula or function by using a technique called **absolute addressing**. To specify an absolute address in a formula, add a dollar sign ($) to the beginning of the column name, row name, or both.

For example, $B$27 is an absolute address and B27 is a relative address. Both reference the same cell. The difference shows when they are copied. A formula using $B$27 instructs VP-Planner Plus to use the same cell (B27) as it copies the formula to a new location. A formula using B27 instructs VP-Planner Plus to adjust the cell reference as it copies. Table 3-2 gives some additional examples of absolute addressing. A cell address with one dollar sign before either the column or the row is called a **mixed cell address**—one is relative, the other is absolute.

TABLE 3-2   Absolute Addressing

CELL ADDRESS	MEANING
$A$22	Both column and row reference remains the same when this cell address is copied.
A$22	The column reference changes when you copy this cell address to another column. The row reference does not change—it is absolute.
$A22	The row reference changes when you copy this cell address to another row. The column reference does not change—it is absolute.
A22	Both column and row references are relative. When copied to another row and column, both the row and column in the cell address are adjusted to reflect the new location.

Copying Formulas with Mixed Cell Addresses

With the cell cursor at B15, the next step is to enter the formula $B27*B$12. Because B15 was in the range we formatted to Text earlier, the formula displays in the cell, rather than the value. This is shown in Figure 3-35. Note that it is not necessary to enter the formula $B27*B$12 with a leading plus sign because, in this case, the $ indicates that the entry is a formula or a number. The cell reference $B27 (budgeted manufacturing % value) means that the row reference (27) changes when you copy

it to a new row, but the column reference (B) remains constant through all columns in the destination range. The cell reference B$12 (January expenses) in the formula means that the column reference (B) changes when you copy it to a new column, but the row reference (12) remains constant through all rows in the destination range. Let's copy the formula $B27*B$12 in cell B15 to the rectangular group of cells B15 through D19.

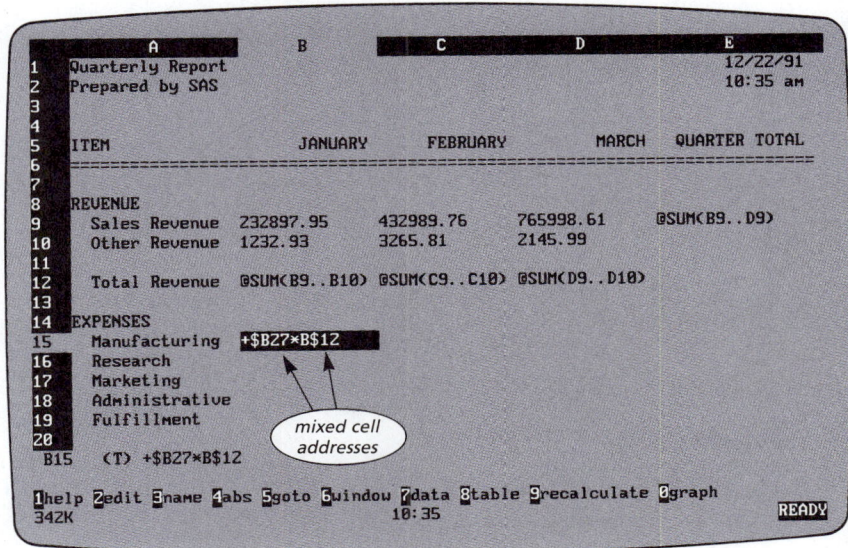

FIGURE 3-35
Formula with mixed cell addresses entered into cell B15.

The cell cursor is at B15 as shown in Figure 3-35. Enter the command /Copy (/C). When the prompt message "Source cell range: B15..B15" displays on the input line, press the Enter key. When the message "Destination cell range: B15..B15" displays on the input line, use the arrow keys to select the range B15..D19. This is shown in Figure 3-36. Note that cell B15 is copied on top of itself, because B15 is one of the end points of the destination range.

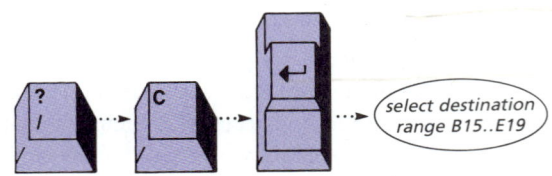

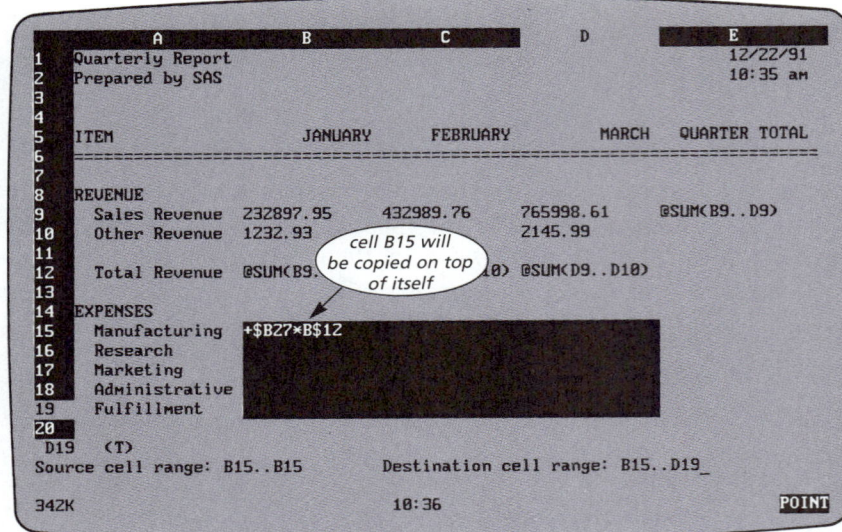

FIGURE 3-36
Step 1 of using the /C command to copy cell B15 to the range B15..D19—press the Slash key (/), type the letter C, press the Enter key, and select the destination range.

Press the Enter key. The Copy command copies the formula in cell B15 to the rectangular group of cells B15 through D19 as shown in Figure 3-37. Take a few minutes to study the formulas in Figure 3-37. You should begin to see the significance

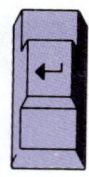

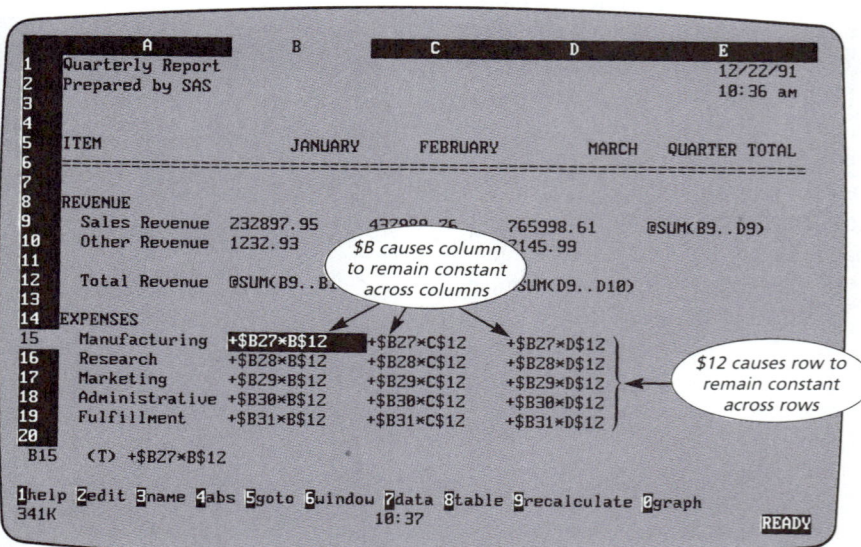

FIGURE 3-37
Step 2 of using the /C command to copy cell B15 to the range B15..D19—press the Enter key.

of mixed cell addressing. For example, every aspect of the five formulas in cells B15 through B19 is identical, except for the row in the first cell reference (budgeted % value). Also note, in columns C and D, that the column in the second cell reference (monthly total revenue) changes based on the column the formula is in.

Switching from Text Format to the Comma Format

Let's change cells B9 through E19 from the Text format back to the Comma format. Recall that we switched the format of these cells from Comma to Text so that we could view the formulas in the cells. To change the format, move the cell cursor to the lower left end point (B19) of the range B19..E9. Enter the command /**R**ange **F**ormat **,** (/RF,).

Press the Enter key when the prompt message "Enter default decimal position: 2" displays on the input line. Finally, when VP-Planner Plus requests the range, use the arrow keys to select the rectangular group of cells B19..E9. Press the Enter key. The results of the formulas, rather than the formulas themselves, display in the cells. This is shown in Figure 3-38.

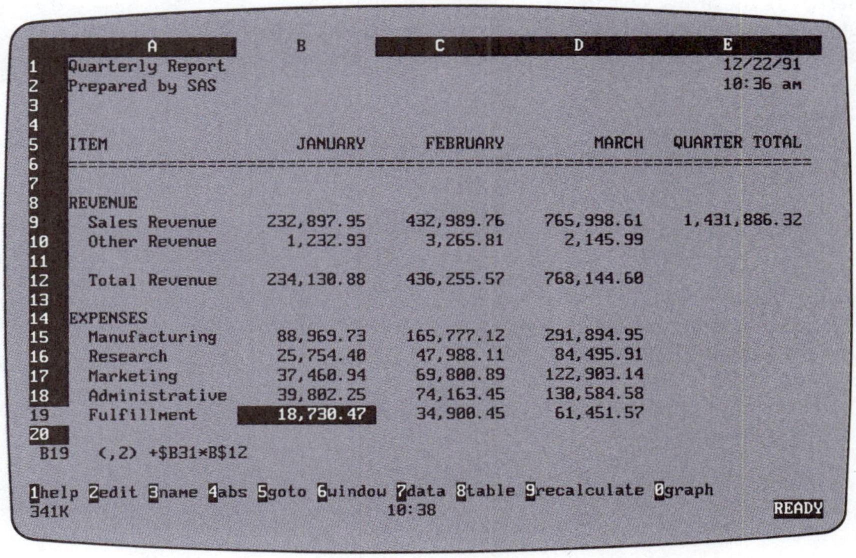

FIGURE 3-38
Range B9..E19 reformatted to the Comma (,) type.

POINTING TO A RANGE OF CELLS TO SUM

The total expenses for January (cell B21) are determined by adding the five monthly budgeted expenses in cells B15 through B19. The total expenses for February (C21) and March (D21) are found in the same way.

To sum the five monthly budgeted expenses for January, move the cell cursor to B21 and begin entering the SUM function. For this entry, let's apply the pointing method to enter the range to sum. Enter @sum(on the input line. Remember that function names can be entered in lowercase. After typing the open parenthesis, use the Up Arrow key to move the cell cursor to B15, the topmost end point of the range to sum.

As the cell cursor moves upward, VP-Planner Plus changes the cell address following the open parenthesis on the input line. When the cell cursor reaches B15, press the Period key (.) to lock in the first end point of the range to sum as shown in Figure 3-39. Next, use the Down Arrow key to move the cell cursor to B19 (see Figure 3-40). To complete the entry, press the Close Parenthesis key and the Enter key. As shown in cell B21 of Figure 3-41, VP-Planner Plus displays the sum (210,717.79) of the five January budgeted expenses stored in cells B15 through B19.

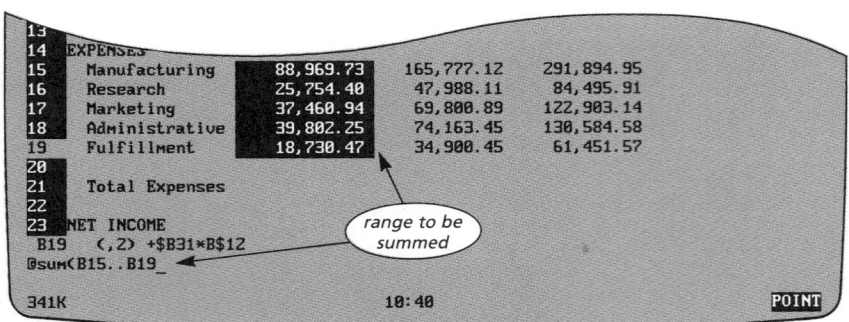

FIGURE 3-39
Step 1 of entering the SUM function using the pointing method—after the open parenthesis, use the arrow keys to select the first end point of the range.

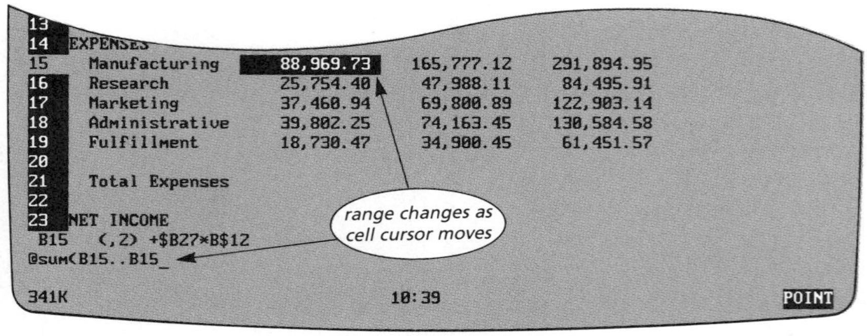

FIGURE 3-40
Step 2 of entering the SUM function using the pointing method—press the Period key (.), use the arrow keys to select the second end point of the range, type the Close Parenthesis key, and press the Enter key.

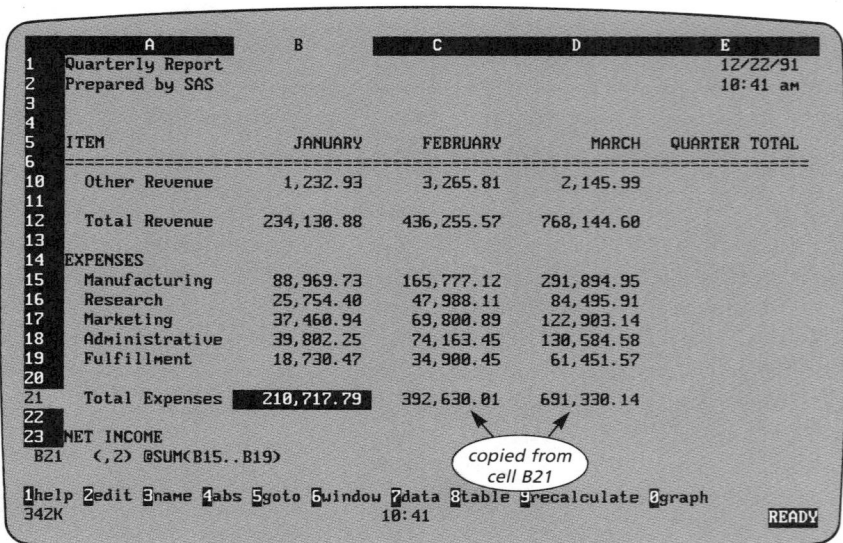

FIGURE 3-41
SUM function in cell B21 copied to cells C21 and D21.

Pointing versus Entering a Range of Cells

The pointing method used to enter the range for the SUM function in cell B21 saves keying time. Anytime you need to enter a range, you may use the arrow keys to point to it. Alternatively, you may type the cell addresses. Once you begin typing a cell address, VP-Planner Plus is no longer in POINT mode.

Copying the Total Expenses and Net Income for Each Month

The next step in this project is to determine the total expenses for February and March. To accomplish this task, copy the function in cell B21 to cells C21 and D21. Type the command /Copy (/C). After entering the source range (B21) press the Enter key. Next, select the destination range (C21..D21) and press the Enter key. Figure 3-41 shows the result of copying cell B21 to cells C21 and D21.

We can now determine the net income for each month in row 23 by subtracting the total expenses for each month in row 21 from the total revenue for each month in row 12. Move the cell cursor to B23 and enter the formula +B12–B21. Copy this formula to cells C23 and D23. The result of entering the formula in cell B23 and copying it to C23 and D23 is shown in Figure 3-42.

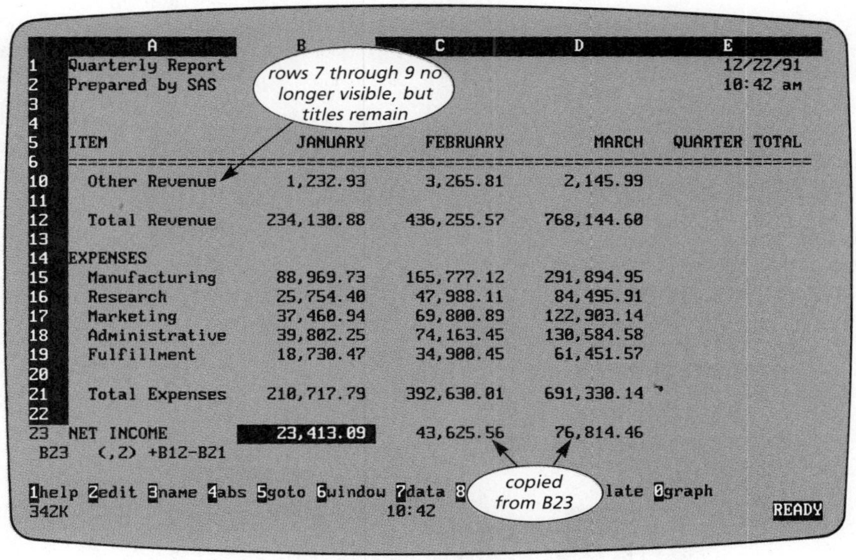

FIGURE 3-42
Formula in cell B23 copied to
cells C23 and D23.

Summing Empty Cells and Labels

One more step and the worksheet is complete. We need to determine the quarter totals in column E. Use the GOTO command to move the cell cursor to the quarter total in cell E9. Since cell E9 is not on the screen (see Figure 3-42), the GOTO command causes the window to move so that cell E9 is positioned in the upper left corner, just below and to the right of the titles.

Recall that we determined the quarter total for the sales revenue after we entered the monthly sales revenue (see Figure 3-30). The functions required for all the row entries (E10, E12, E15 through E19, E21, and E23) are identical to the function in cell E9. Therefore, let's copy the function in cell E9 to these cells.

Unfortunately, the cells in the destination range are not contiguous, that is, connected. For example, in the range E10 through E23, the function is not needed in E11, E13, E14, E20, and E22. We have three choices here: (1) use the copy command several times and copy the function in E9 to E10, E12, E15 through E19, E21, and E23; (2) enter the function manually in each required cell; or (3) copy the function to the range E10 through E23. If we select the third method, we have to use the command **/R**ange **E**rase (/RE) to erase the function from E11, E13, E14, E20, and E22, the cells in which the function is not required. Let's use the third method.

With the cell cursor on E9, enter the command **/C**opy (/C). When VP-Planner Plus displays the prompt message "Source cell range: E9..E9," press the Enter key. For the destination range, leave E9 anchored as the first end point and use the Down Arrow key to move the cell cursor to E23. This is shown in Figure 3-43. Press the Enter key and the function in cell E9 is copied to the cells in the range E9..E23 (see Figure 3-44).

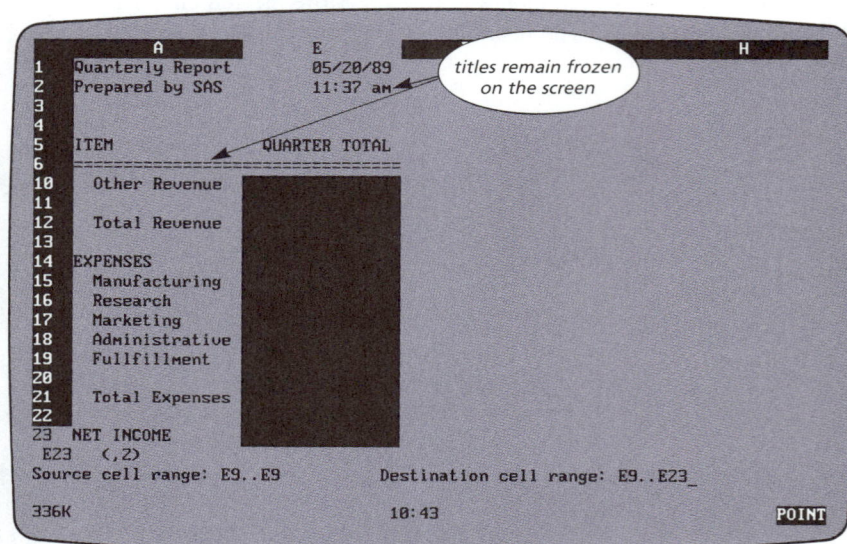

FIGURE 3-43
Step 1 of using the /C command to copy cell E9 to the range E9..E23—press the Slash key (/), type the letter C, press the Enter key, and select the destination range.

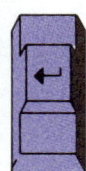
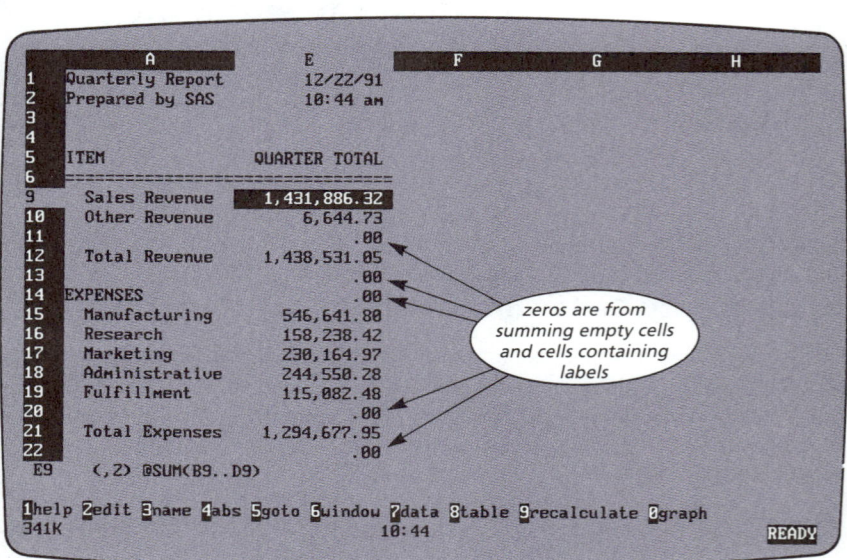

FIGURE 3-44
Step 2 of using the /C command to copy cell E9 to the range E9..E23—press the Enter key.

Notice the zeros in cells E11, E13, E14, E20, and E22. The formula in cell E11 reads @SUM(B11..D11). VP-Planner Plus considers empty cells and cells with labels to be equal to zero when they are referenced in a formula or function. Since cells B11, C11, and D11 are empty, the SUM function assigned to E11 produces the zero display. We need to erase the functions in the cells displaying zero. Recall from Project 1 that the command /**R**ange **E**rase (/RE) erases the contents of a cell. Use this command to erase the zeros in cells E11, E13, E14, E20, and E22.

After the zeros in column E are erased, use the command /**W**orksheet **T**itles **C**lear (/WTC) to unfreeze the titles. Finally, press the Home key to move the cell cursor to A1. The worksheet is complete as shown in Figure 3-45.

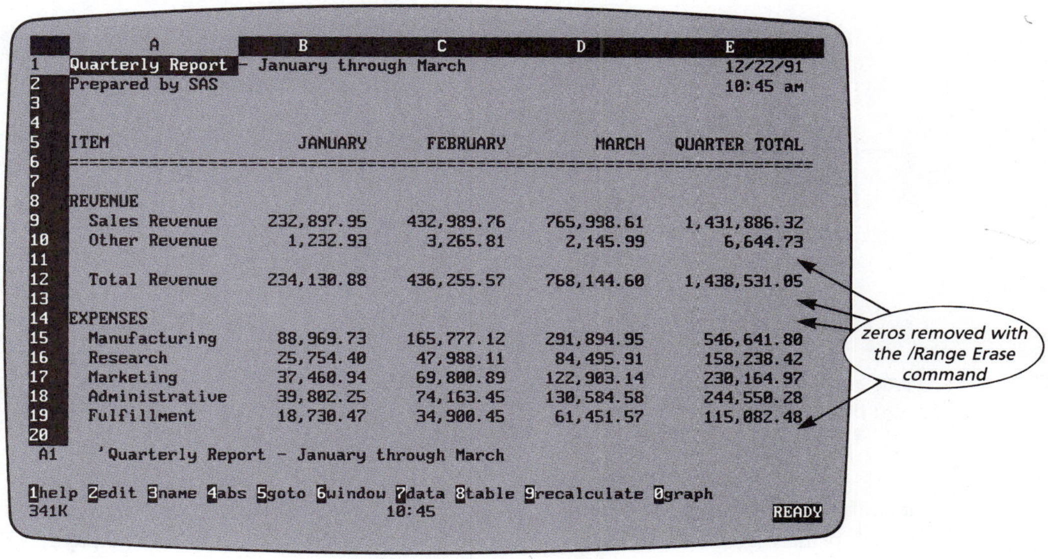

FIGURE 3-45
The completed worksheet.

SAVING AND PRINTING THE WORKSHEET

Save the worksheet on disk so that you can retrieve and use it later. Use the command /**F**ile **S**ave (/FS) and the file name PROJS-3. As we discussed in Project 2, when you create a large worksheet such as this one, it is prudent to save the worksheet periodically—every 50 to 75 keystrokes. Then, if there should be an inadvertent loss of power to the computer or other unforeseen mishap, you will not lose the whole worksheet.

Printing the Worksheet (/PP)

After saving the worksheet as PROJS-3, obtain a hard copy by printing the worksheet on the printer. Recall from Project 2, that to print the worksheet you use the command /**P**rint **P**rinter (/PP). This command activates the command cursor in the Printer menu (see Figure 3-46). Type the letter R for Range. The cell cursor is at one end point of the range we wish to print, A1. Use the arrow keys to move the cell cursor to E31. Press the Enter key to anchor the second end point.

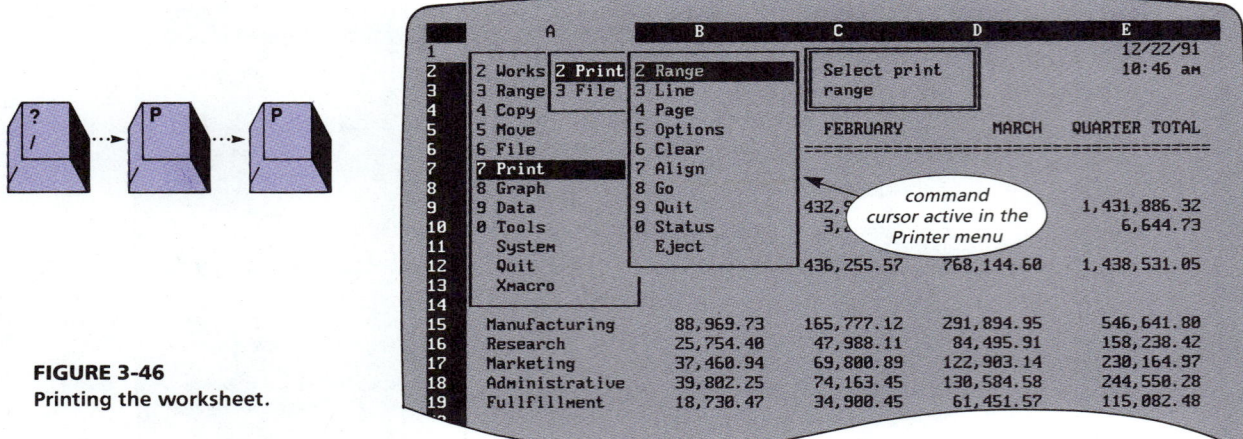

FIGURE 3-46
Printing the worksheet.

Next, check the printer to be sure it is in READY mode. Type the letter A for Align and the letter G for Go. The worksheet prints on the printer as shown in Figure 3-47. Because it is too wide to fit on one page, VP-Planner Plus automatically prints as many columns as it can on one page and prints the remaining ones on the following pages.

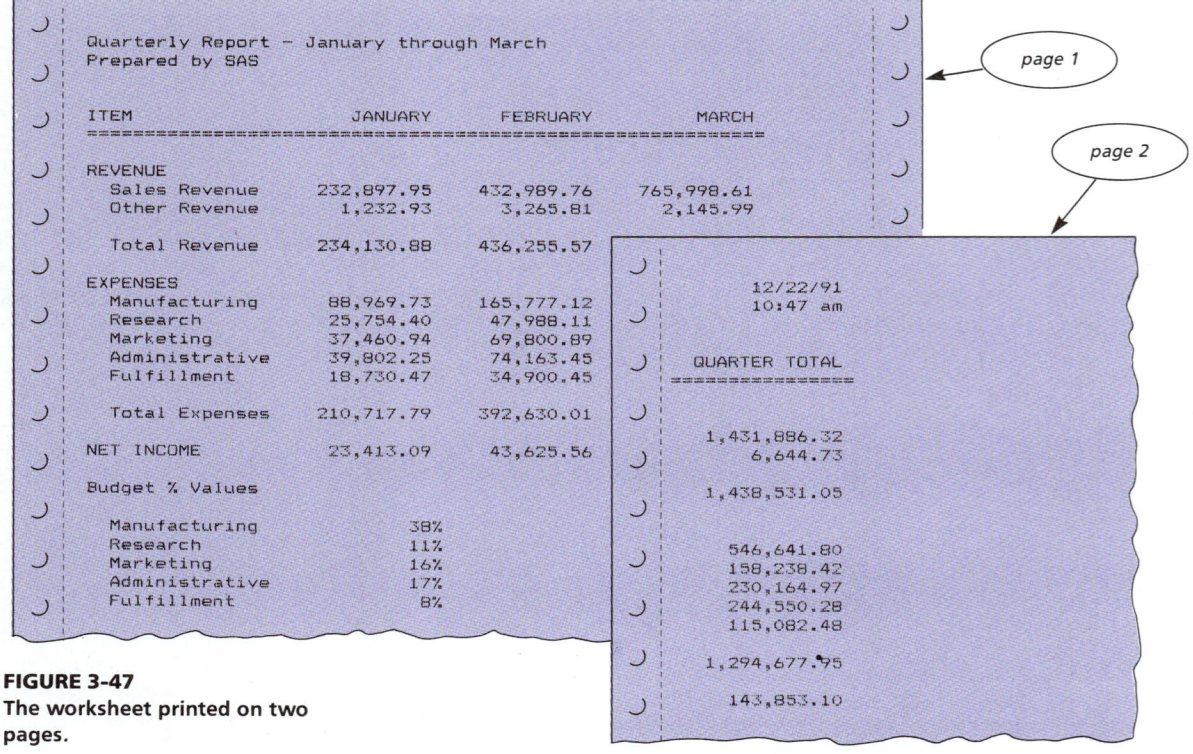

FIGURE 3-47
The worksheet printed on two pages.

Obviously, the multipage hard copy version of the worksheet is not in the most readable form. One way to fix the problem is to cut and paste the two pages together. This technique is often used for very large worksheets. If all the columns containing information in the worksheet fit on the screen, there is another alternative. Reduce the width of the left and right margins to allow more characters to fit on a line.

Changing the Printer Margin Settings (/PPOM)

Because all the columns in the Quarterly Report worksheet fit on the screen, we can print the worksheet on one page by decreasing the margins used by VP-Planner Plus. This way there will be more room to print across the page. VP-Planner Plus has default margins of four characters from the left edge of the paper and 76 characters from the right edge of the paper. With these margins you can print up to 72 characters across each line. We want to decrease the two margins so that more characters will fit on each line.

To change the printer margins, be sure the Print menu is on the screen. Next, type the letter O for Options. The **Printer Options menu** shown in Figure 3-48 displays on the screen. This menu shows you all the current printer settings. It is like a checklist. The word "none" indicates that nothing has been selected. The letter X designates the choice of two or more possible settings. The other entries on the menu are self-explanatory. You may change any of these settings while the Printer Options menu is on the screen.

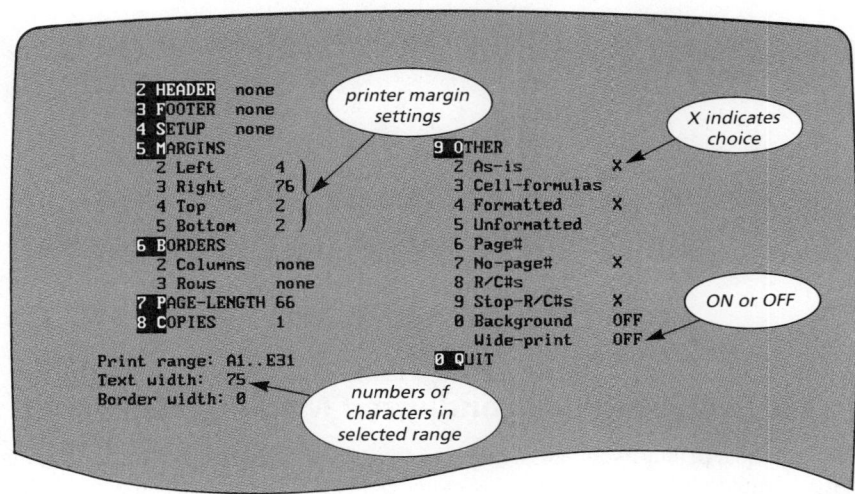

FIGURE 3-48
The Printer Options menu.

Let's continue with the task of changing the printer margins. In the lower left corner of the Printer Options menu in Figure 3-48, you can see that the print range (A1..E31) requires exactly 75 characters. Therefore, we need to decrease the left and right margins by a total of three characters. Type the letter M to select MARGINS. Press the Enter key. The command cursor is now active in the subtitles under MARGINS. Type the letter L for Left margin. At the bottom of the screen, VP-Planner Plus displays the prompt message "Enter left margin (0 - 74): 4". Type the number 3 and press the Enter key. Select MARGINS again and set the right margin to 78. To return to the Print menu, type the letter Q to quit the Print Options menu.

With the Print menu on the screen (see Figure 3-46), type the letters A for Align and G for Go. The Quarterly Report worksheet prints on one page as shown in Figure 3-49. Type the letter E for Eject twice to move the printed worksheet out of the printer. To quit the Print menu, type Q for Quit.

```
Quarterly Report - January through March            12/22/91
Prepared by SAS                                     10:49 am


ITEM                JANUARY       FEBRUARY        MARCH   QUARTER TOTAL
================================================================================

REVENUE
   Sales Revenue    232,897.95    432,989.76   765,998.61    1,431,886.32
   Other Revenue     1,232.93      3,265.81     2,145.99        6,644.73

   Total Revenue    234,130.88    436,255.57   768,144.60    1,438,531.05

EXPENSES
   Manufacturing     88,969.73    165,777.12   291,894.95      546,641.80
   Research          25,754.40     47,988.11    84,495.91      158,238.42
   Marketing         37,460.94     69,800.89   122,903.14      230,164.97
   Administrative    39,802.25     74,163.45   130,584.58      244,550.28
   Fulfillment       18,730.47     34,900.45    61,451.57      115,082.48

   Total Expenses   210,717.79    392,630.01   691,330.14    1,294,677.95

NET INCOME           23,413.09     43,625.56    76,814.46      143,853.10

Budget % Values

   Manufacturing        38%
   Research             11%
   Marketing            16%
   Administrative       17%
   Fulfillment           8%
```

FIGURE 3-49 The worksheet printed on one page after changing the printer margins.

Printing the Worksheet in Condensed Mode (/PPOS)

If you have a graphics printer, you can print more than 80 characters per line by printing the worksheet in condensed mode. The **condensed mode** allows nearly twice as many characters to fit across the page. To print a worksheet in the condensed mode, do the following:

1. Enter the command /**P**rint **P**rinter **O**ptions Setup (/PPOS). See the Printer Options menu in Figure 3-48. Enter the code \015 and press the Enter key.
2. With the Printer Options menu on the screen, enter the command **M**argins **R**ight. Type in a right margin of 140. Press the Enter key and type the letter Q to quit the Printer Options menu.
3. Select the range to print and follow the usual steps for printing the worksheet.

If the printer does not print in condensed mode, check the printer manual to be sure the current dip switch settings on the printer allow for it. You may have to change these settings. If you continue to experience problems, check the printer manual to be sure that code \015 instructs the printer to print in condensed mode. This code works for most printers. To change VP-Planner Plus back to the normal print mode, redo the three steps above, except enter the code \018 in step 1 and a right margin of 76 in step 2.

Other Printer Options (/PPO)

There are other printer options in Figure 3-48 that can enhance your worksheet. Table 3-3 summarizes some of the more important ones. For additional information on all the printer options, use the online help facility of VP-Planner Plus (press function key F1). Once the online help facility appears on the screen, press function key F5 to go to screens 70 and 71. When you are finished, press the Esc key to return to the worksheet.

TABLE 3-3 Printer Options

OPTION	DEFAULT SETTING	PURPOSE
HEADER	none	Print a message at the top of every page of the worksheet.
FOOTER	none	Print a message at the bottom of every page of the worksheet.
SETUP	none	Send commands to the printer, for example, to print the worksheet in condensed mode.
MARGINS	Left 4 Right 76 Top 2 Bottom 2	Set the margins.
BORDERS	none	Print specified columns and rows on every page.
PAGE-LENGTH	66	Set printed lines per page.
COPIES	1	Set the number of copies of the worksheet to be printed.
OTHER		See Figure 3-48.
QUIT		Return to the Print menu.

Under the option OTHER in Figure 3-48, there are three settings you should note. As-is versus Cell-formulas allows you to print the formulas as described in Project 2. Page# versus No-Page# allows you to page a printed worksheet. Wide-print versus Normal-print allows you to print a worksheet with many columns sideways on the printer so that it is easier to read. Here again the letter X indicates the choice from a group of possible selections. ON or OFF are self-explanatory.

The options you set with the /Print Printer Options (/PPO) command are saved with the worksheet and stay in effect when you retrieve it. So remember, if you change any of the printer options and you want the changes to stay with the worksheet, be sure to save the worksheet after you finish printing it. That way you won't have to change the options the next time you retrieve the worksheet.

If you use the command /Worksheet Erase (/WE) to clear the worksheet on the screen or restart VP-Planner Plus, the printer options revert back to the default settings shown in Figure 3-48.

WHAT-IF QUESTIONS

A powerful feature of VP-Planner Plus is the ability to answer what-if questions. Quick responses to these questions are invaluable when making business decisions. Using a spreadsheet program to answer what-if questions is called performing **what-if analyses** or **sensitivity analyses**.

A what-if question for the worksheet in Project 3 might be, "What if the manufacturing budgeted percentage is decreased from 38% to 35%—how would this affect the total expenses and net income?" To answer questions like this, you need only change a single value in the worksheet. The recalculation feature of VP-Planner Plus answers the question immediately by displaying new values in any cells with formulas or functions that reference the changed cell.

Let's change the manufacturing budgeted percentage from 38% to 35% (see Figure 3-50). In the "before change" screen in Figure 3-50, the manufacturing budgeted percentage is 38%. After the change is made, the manufacturing budgeted percentage is 35%. When we make the change, all the formulas are immediately recalculated. This process generally requires less than one second, depending on how many calculations must be performed.

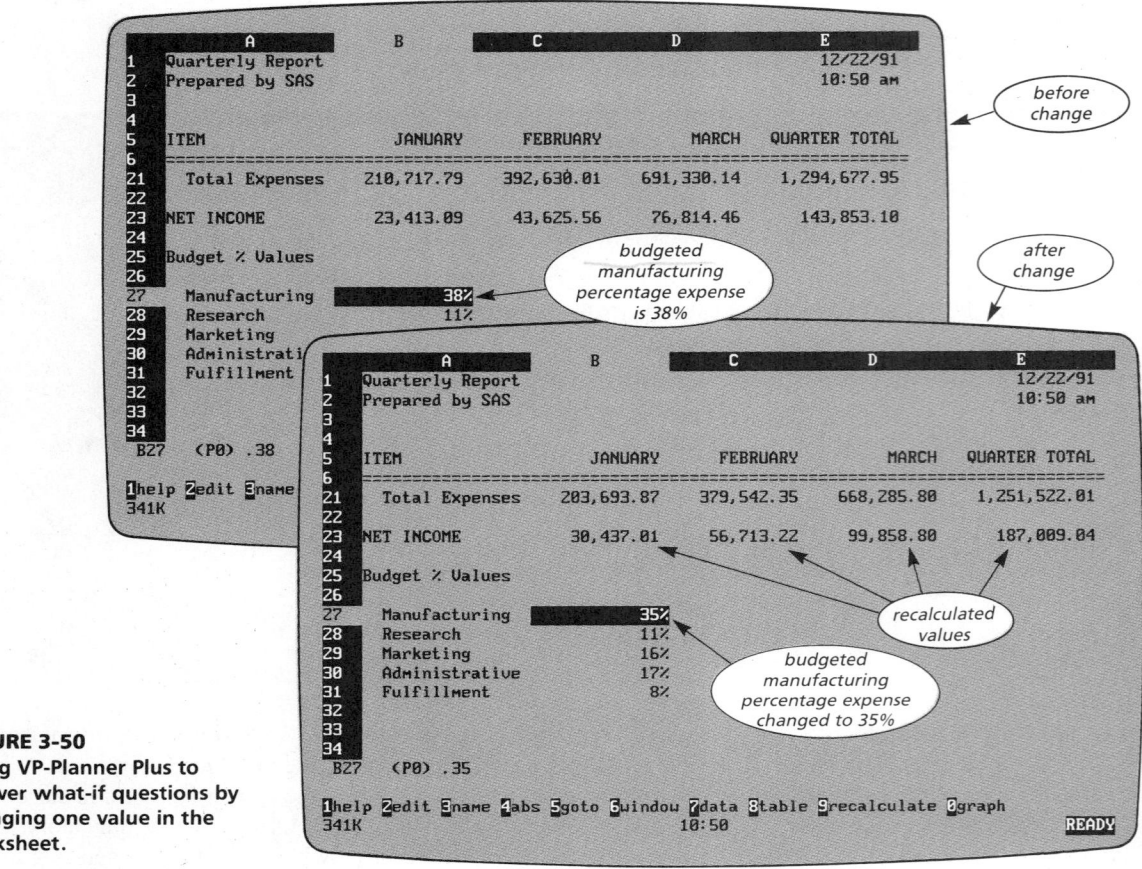

FIGURE 3-50
Using VP-Planner Plus to answer what-if questions by changing one value in the worksheet.

As soon as the 35% replaces the 38% in cell B27, the new expenses and new net income values can be examined (see the "after change" screen in Figure 3-50). By changing the value in B27 from 38% to 35%, the total January expenses decrease from 210,717.79 to 203,693.87, and the January net income increases from 23,413.09 to 30,437.01. The February and March figures change the same way. The quarter total expenses decrease from 1,294,677.95 to 1,251,522.01, and the quarter net income increases from 143,853.11 to 187,009.04. Thus, if the budgeted manufacturing expenses are reduced, it is clear that net income increases.

As shown in the "after change" screen in Figure 3-51, you can change more than one percentage. Let's change all the percentages. The new calculations display immediately.

In Figure 3-51, we ask the question, "What if we change all the budgeted percent values to the following: Manufacturing (35%); Research (10%); Marketing (18%); Administrative (14%); Fulfillment (6%)—how would these changes affect the total expenses and the net income?" By merely changing the five values on the worksheet, all formulas are automatically recalculated to provide the answer to this question.

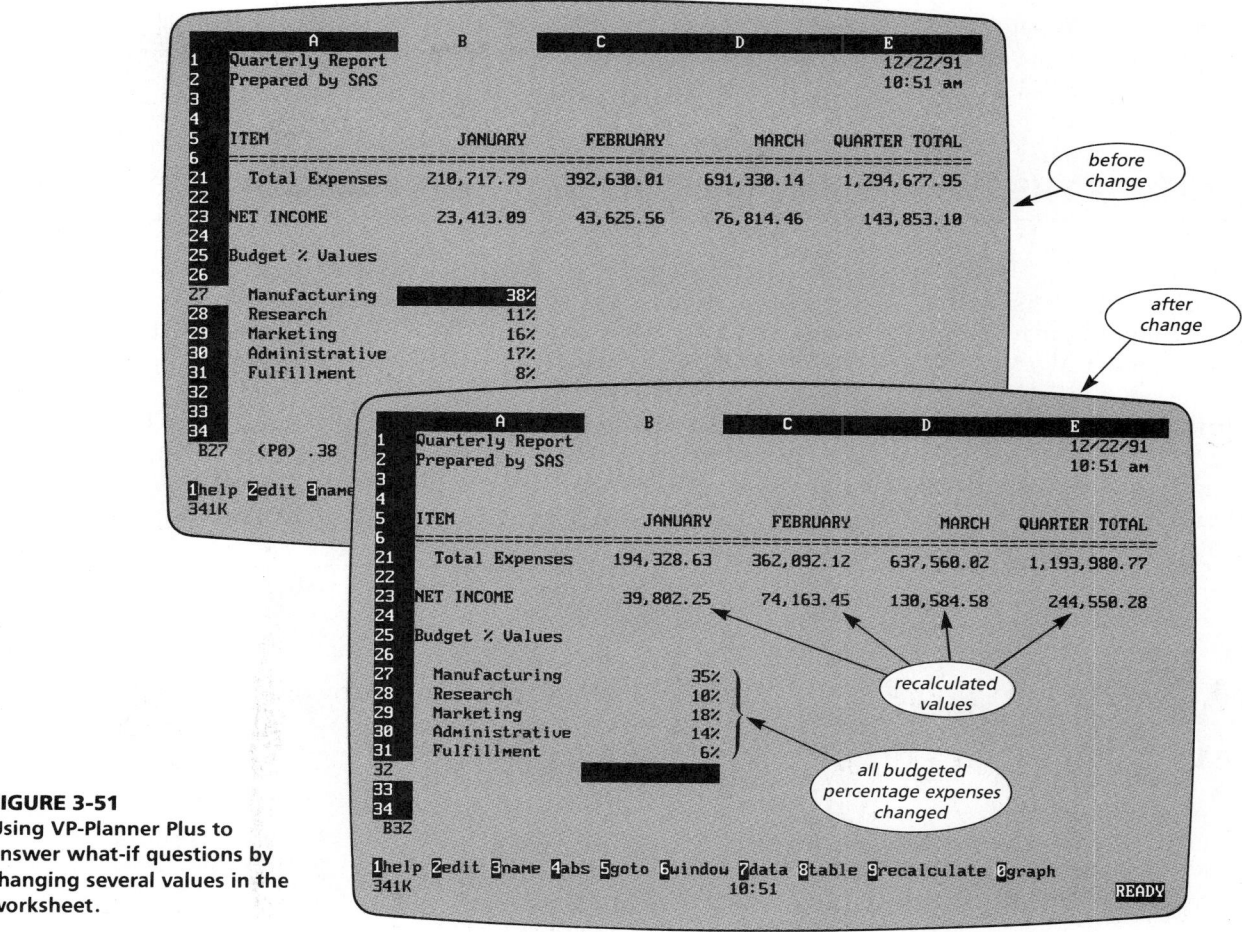

FIGURE 3-51
Using VP-Planner Plus to answer what-if questions by changing several values in the worksheet.

Manual versus Automatic Recalculation (/WGR)

Each time you enter a number in the worksheet, VP-Planner Plus automatically recalculates all formulas and functions in the background, unless you change this feature. **Background recalculation** means that all recalculations are completed between keystrokes, rather than locking up the keyboard until all recalculations are complete, as most other spreadsheet programs do. Background recalculation saves a lot of time, especially as a worksheet grows in size. This form of recalculation makes Release 2 of VP-Planner Plus one of the fastest spreadsheet programs on the market.

An alternative to automatic recalculation is manual recalculation. With **manual recalculation**, VP-Planner Plus only recalculates after you tell it to do so. To change recalculation from automatic to manual, enter the command **/W**orksheet **G**lobal **R**ecalculate (/WGR). With the command cursor active in the **Recalculate menu**, type the letter M for Manual. Then recalculation of formulas takes place *only* after you press function key F9. To change back to automatic recalculation, use the same command but type the letter A for Automatic rather than M for Manual.

When you save a worksheet, the current recalculation mode is saved along with it. For an explanation of the other types of recalculation available with VP-Planner Plus, press function key F1. Once the online help facility menu appears on the screen, press function key F5 and go to screen 39. When you are finished with the online help facility, press the Esc key to return to your worksheet.

CHANGING THE WORKSHEET DEFAULT SETTINGS (/WGD)

VP-Planner Plus comes with default settings. We have already discussed some of the more obvious ones—column width is nine characters, format is General, and recalculation of formulas is Automatic. Some of the default settings, like the format, can be changed for a range or for the entire worksheet. When you make a change to the entire worksheet using the command /**W**orksheet **G**lobal (/WG), the change is saved with the worksheet when you issue the /**F**ile **S**ave (/FS) command.

There is another group of default settings that affect all worksheets created or retrieved during the current session, until you quit VP-Planner Plus. To view or change these settings, type the command /**W**orksheet **G**lobal **D**efault (/WGD). This command displays the **Global Default menu** shown in Figure 3-52. Then use the arrow keys, function keys, or first letters to select features to change.

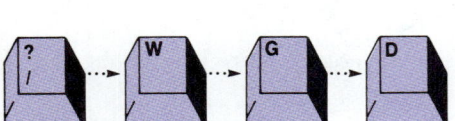

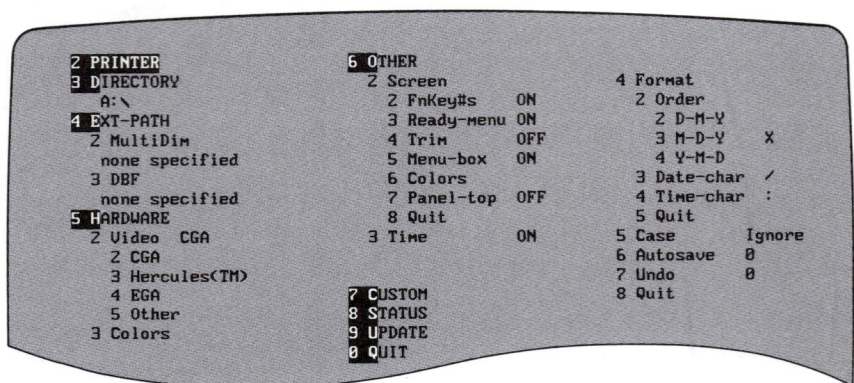

FIGURE 3-52
The Global Default menu. To display this menu, enter the command /WGD.

Once you pick the desired settings, you have the choice of saving the changes for the current session or saving them permanently. To save the changes for the current session, type the letter Q for Quit. To save the changes permanently, type the letters U for Update and then Q for Quit. If you typed the letter U for update, the new settings become the defaults for the current and future VP-Planner Plus sessions. Table 3-4 describes some of the more important features you can change by typing the command /WGD.

TABLE 3-4 Important Global Defaults

FEATURE	DESCRIPTION
PRINTER	Sets printer options. Printer options set using /PPO for individual worksheets override global default printer settings.
OTHER Screen	Changes the screen to make it look like a Lotus 1-2-3 screen. If you have a color/ graphics adapter and color screen, selects background and foreground colors.
OTHER Undo	Activates the Undo and Redo keys.
OTHER Autosave	Saves the worksheet automatically every specified number of minutes.
DIRECTORY	Changes the default directory.

Some of the settings go beyond the scope of this book. For an explanation of the other features you may change using the /WGD command, press function key F1. Once the online help facility menu appears on the screen, press function key F5 and go to screens 41–43. To quit the online help facility, press the Esc key.

CHANGING THE SCREEN SO THAT IT LOOKS LIKE THE LOTUS 1-2-3 SCREEN

Release 2 of VP-Planner Plus and Release 2 of Lotus 1-2-3 work the same way. The concepts and commands presented in this book are nearly identical for both spreadsheet programs. For this reason, it is often said that VP-Planner Plus is a "1-2-3 look-alike" or a "1-2-3 clone." Once you master one, you will have mastered the other.

The only differences between the two spreadsheet programs are the location of the control panel; the contents of the current-mode line; and the lack of pop-up menus and a prompt line in Lotus 1-2-3. Through the command /**W**orksheet **G**lobal **D**efault (/WGD), you can turn the pop-up menus and function key prompt line off and display the control panel at the top of the screen to make it look like a Lotus 1-2-3 screen. Listed below are the steps for changing the default screen settings. We recommend that you step through these commands on your computer.

1. Enter the command /**W**orksheet **G**lobal **D**efault (/WGD). The Global Default menu in Figure 3-52 appears on the screen.
2. Type the letters O for OTHER and S for Screen. This makes the command cursor active in the middle column under OTHER Screen (see Figure 3-52). The commands under OTHER Screen act like switches. If you type a letter that corresponds to one of the commands in the column, VP-Planner Plus toggles it on when it is off, and off when it is on.
3. With the command cursor active in the OTHER Screen portion of the Global Default menu, enter the following series of commands:
   a. Type the letter F for FnKey#s. The default setting is on. This command turns off the function key numbers that precede each command in the command menu.
   b. Type R for Ready-menu. The default setting is on. This command turns off the prompt line that identifies the function keys when VP-Planner Plus is in READY mode.
   c. Type the letter P for Panel-top. The default setting is off. This command displays the control panel at the top of the screen, rather than at the bottom.
   d. Type the letter M for Menu-box. The default setting is on. This command turns off the pop-up menus. When the pop-up menus are turned off, the command menus display on the input and prompt lines of the control panel.
   e. Type the letter Q to quit the Screen command.
4. If you want to change to the Lotus 1-2-3 screen permanently, type the letters U for Update and then Q for quit. When you quit the Global Default menu, VP-Planner Plus returns to READY mode.

After you enter the series of commands in steps 1 through 4, the VP-Planner Plus screen appears almost identical to the Lotus 1-2-3 screen as shown in Figure 3-53. When you press the Slash key, the command menu displays on the input line and prompt line of the control panel at the top of the screen as shown in Figure 3-54.

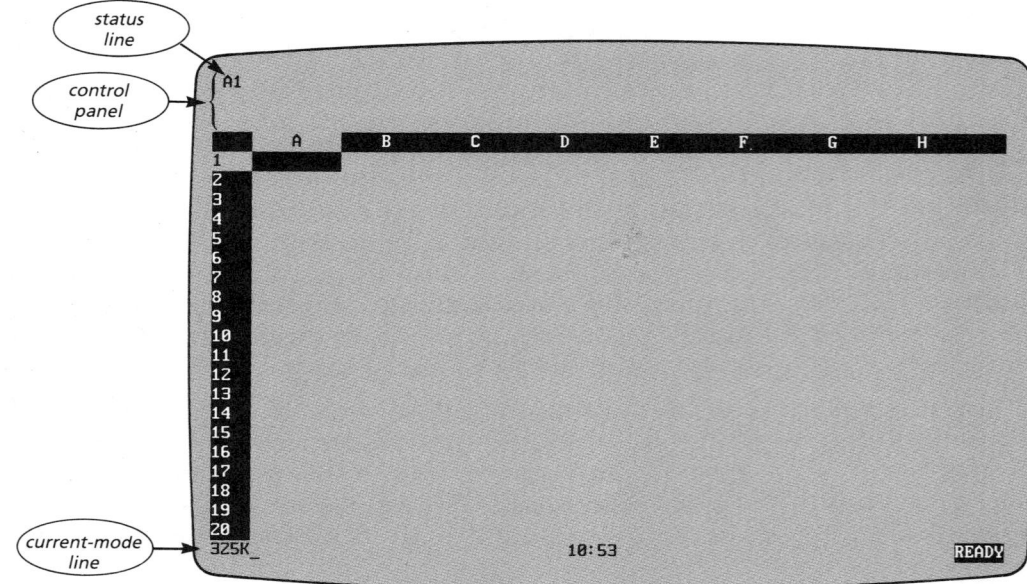

FIGURE 3-53
The Lotus 1-2-3 look-alike screen. To modify the normal VP-Planner Plus screen to look like the Lotus 1-2-3 screen, use the command /WGD.

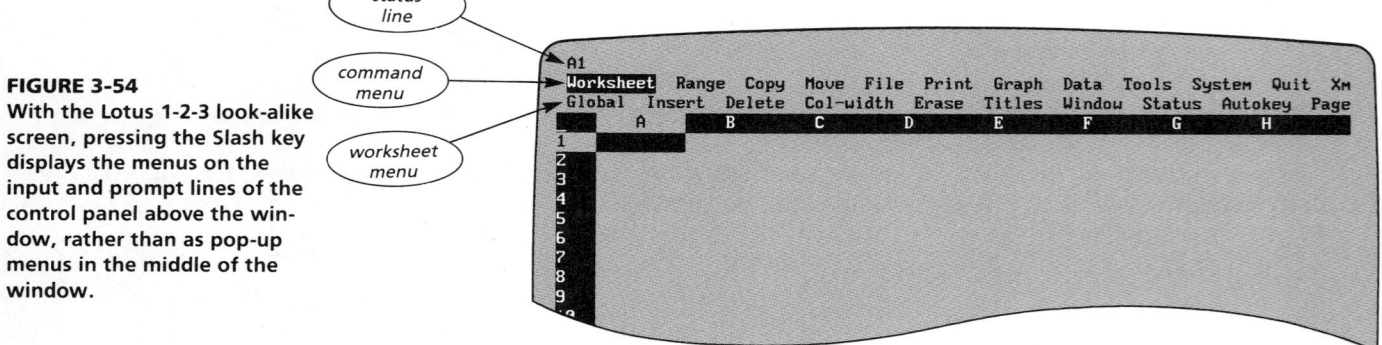

FIGURE 3-54
With the Lotus 1-2-3 look-alike screen, pressing the Slash key displays the menus on the input and prompt lines of the control panel above the window, rather than as pop-up menus in the middle of the window.

To change the Lotus 1-2-3 look-alike screen back to the normal VP-Planner Plus screen, simply reenter the commands listed in steps 1 through 4 on the previous page.

Note that the mode, which displays in Lotus 1-2-3 as part of the status line, cannot be moved from the bottom to the top of the screen. Furthermore, there is no way to erase the amount of main computer memory that displays in the lower left corner of the current-mode line.

THE UNDO AND REDO KEYS

*T*hrough the Global Default options menu you can instruct VP-Planner Plus to save the prior commands and contents of cells as you make changes to your worksheet. If you make a mistake, like accidentally erasing the worksheet with the Worksheet Erase command, you can press the Undo key (hold down the Alt key and press the function key F2) to back out the last command you entered. Each time you press the Undo key, it backs out another command. You can continue backing out until you reach the bottom of the list. If you back out too far, press the Redo key (hold down the Alt key and press function key F3) to reexecute the last command undone.

To activate the Undo and Redo keys, enter the command /**W**orksheet **G**lobal **D**efault **O**ther **U**ndo (/WGDOU). In response to the prompt message "Enter size of UNDO buffer in Kbytes (0 - 63): 0" on the input line, enter a value that corresponds to the amount of work you plan to do. A value of 10 is sufficient for most worksheets. A value of zero deactivates the Undo and Redo keys. After entering a value between 1 and 63, press the Enter key and quit the Global Default menu. You can now back out of previous commands.

This ability to switch back and forth between different versions of your worksheet is useful not only for correcting mistakes but also for what-if analyses.

INTERACTING WITH DOS

*U*p to this point, we have used the File command to save and retrieve worksheets from disk. This command may also be used to carry out several other file management functions normally done at the DOS level. Table 3-5 summarizes the major file management commands available in VP-Planner Plus.

TABLE 3-5   File Management Commands

COMMAND	FUNCTION	DUPLICATE DOS COMMAND
/FE	Erases a file from disk.	ERASE or DEL
/FUR	Renames a file on disk.	RENAME
/FUC	Copies a file on disk.	COPY
/FLO	Lists the names of all the files on disk.	DIR

Other DOS commands and programs can be executed by placing VP-Planner Plus and your worksheet in a wait state. A **wait state** means that VP-Planner Plus has given up control to another program, like DOS, but still resides in main computer memory. To leave VP-Planner Plus temporarily, enter the command /**S**ystem (/S). (If you do not have a fixed disk, place the DOS disk in the A drive before entering the /S command.)

You can use the System command to leave VP-Planner Plus to format a disk. Once the disk is formatted, you can return to VP-Planner Plus and the worksheet by typing the command Exit in response to the DOS prompt. One word of advice—save your worksheet before using the System command, especially if you plan to load and execute an application program through DOS.

PROJECT SUMMARY

*I*n this project you learned a variety of ways to enhance a worksheet and simplify the steps of building, formatting, and printing large worksheets. You were introduced to the capabilities of VP-Planner Plus to answer what-if questions. Finally, you learned how to change the default settings and interact with DOS through VP-Planner Plus.

Each of the steps required to build the worksheet in Project 3 is listed in the following table.

SUMMARY OF KEYSTROKES—Project 3

STEPS	KEY(S) PRESSED	STEPS	KEY(S) PRESSED
1	/WGC → → → → → → ↵	30	/RFP0 ← ↑ ↑ ↑ ↑ ↵
2	/WCS17 ↵	31	(Home) (F5) B7 ↵
3	→ → → → /WCS16 ↵	32	/WTB
4	/WGF, ↵	33	232897.95 → 432989.76 → 765998.61 →
5	← ← ← ← Quarterly Report – January through March↓	34	@SUM(B7.D7) →
6	Prepared by SAS ↵	35	/M (Backspace) ← . ← ← ← ← ↓ ↓ ← . ← ← ← ← ↵
7	(F5) E1 ↵ @now↓	36	↓ ↓ ↓ ← ← ← ← ←
8	@now↑	37	1232.93 → 3265.81 → 2145.99↓ ↓ ← ←
9	/RFD↓ ↓ ↓ ← ↵	38	@SUM(B9.B10) ↵
10	↓/RFDP ↵	39	/C ↵ → . → ↵
11	(F5) A5 ↵ (Caps Lock)	40	/RFTB9.E19 ↵
12	ITEM → "JANUARY →	41	↓ ↓ ↓ $B27*B$12 ↵
13	"FEBRUARY → "MARCH →	42	/C ↵ . ↓ ↓ ↓ ↓ → → ↵
14	"QUARTER TOTAL ↵	43	(F5) B19 ↵ /RF, ← B19.E9 ↵
15	(F5) A6 ↵ \ = ↵	44	↓ ↓ @SUM(↑ ↑ ↑ ↑ ↑ ↑ . ↓ ↓ ↓ ↓) ↵
16	/C ↵ → . → → → ↵	45	/C ↵ → . → ↵
17	↓ ↓ REVENUE↓ (Caps Lock)	46	↓ ↓ + B12–B21 ↵
18	' Sales Revenue↓' Other Revenue↓ ↓	47	/C ↵ → . → ↵
19	' Total Revenue↓ ↓	48	(F5) E9 ↵
20	EXPENSES↓' Manufacturing↓	49	/C ← E9.E23 ↵
21	' Research↓' Fulfillment↓ ↓	50	↓ ↓ /RE ↵
22	' Total Expenses↓ ↓ NET INCOME↓ ↓	51	↓ ↓ /RE↓ ↵
23	Budget % Values↓	52	↓ ↓ ↓ ↓ ↓ ↓ /RE ↵
24	(F5) A17 ↵	53	↓ ↓ /RE ↵
25	/WIR↓ ↵	54	/WTC (Home)
26	' Marketing↓' Administrative↓	55	/FS PROJS-3 ↵
27	/CA15.A19 ↵ A27 ↵	56	/PPRA1.E31 ↵
28	(F5) B27 ↵	57	OML3 ↵ MR78 ↵ Q
29	38%↓ 11%↓ 16%↓ 17%↓ 8% ↵	58	AGEEQ

The following list summarizes the material covered in Project 3.

1. After setting the column width for the entire worksheet, use the command /Worksheet Col-width Set (/WCS) to set the width of individual columns requiring a different width.
2. Use the command /Worksheet Global Format (/WGF) to format all the cells in the worksheet to the same type.
3. To display the date and time as a decimal number, use the NOW function. The whole number portion is the number of complete days since December 31, 1899. The decimal portion represents today's time.
4. Use the command /Range Format Date (/RFD) to format today's date and time. See Table 3-1 for a summary of the date and time formats.
5. The time stored in a cell is updated only after you make a numeric entry into the worksheet or after you press function key F9.
6. To insert rows or columns into a worksheet, move the cell cursor to the point of insertion and enter the command /Worksheet Insert (/WI). Type the letter R to insert rows or the letter C to insert columns. Use the arrow keys to select how many rows or columns you want to insert.
7. To delete rows or columns from a worksheet, move the cell cursor to one of the end points of the range you plan to delete. Enter the command /Worksheet Delete (/WD). Type the letter R to delete rows or the letter C to delete columns. Use the arrow keys to select how many rows or columns you want to delete.
8. Enter a percentage value in percent form by appending a percent sign (%) to the right of the number.
9. To freeze the titles so that they remain on the screen as you move the cell cursor around the worksheet, use the command /Worksheet Titles (/WT). You then have the choice of freezing horizontal (row) titles, vertical (column) titles, or both. Use the same command to unfreeze the titles.
10. To move a range to another range, use the command /Move (/M).
11. With respect to the Copy command, a cell address with no dollar sign ($) is a relative address. A cell address with a dollar sign appended to the front of both the column name and row number is an absolute address. A cell address with a dollar sign added to the front of the column name or to the front of the row number is a mixed cell address.
12. When entering a formula or function, you may use the arrow keys to point to the range.
13. It is valid to copy a cell to itself. This is necessary when you copy the end point of the destination range.
14. An empty cell or a cell with a label has a numeric value of zero.
15. Use the command /Print Printer Option (/PPO) to change the printer default settings.
16. Any change to the printer default settings is saved with the worksheet.
17. The ability to answer what-if questions is a powerful and important feature of VP-Planner Plus.
18. Once a worksheet is complete, you can enter new values into cells. Formulas and functions that reference the modified cells are immediately recalculated, thus giving new results.
19. Use the command /Worksheet Global Recalculation (/WGR) to change from automatic to manual recalculation.
20. To change the default settings for the worksheet, use the command /Worksheet Global Default (/WGD).
21. Default settings changed with the command /WGD remain in force for the entire session, until you quit VP-Planner Plus.
22. To permanently change the default settings, type the letter U for Update before quitting the Global Default menu.
23. VP-Planner Plus is a "Lotus 1-2-3 clone." The concepts and commands for the two spreadsheet programs are nearly identical. To modify the VP-Planner Plus screen so that it looks like a Lotus 1-2-3 screen, use the command /Worksheet Global Default Other Screen (/WGDOS). With the command cursor active in the OTHER Screen portion of the Global Default menu, type the letters FRPMQQ.
24. Through the Global Default options menu you can instruct VP-Planner Plus to save the prior commands and contents of cells as you make changes to your worksheet. Then you can use the Undo and Redo keys to go back and forth between previous commands and entries.
25. The File command may be used to rename files, list the names of the files on disk, copy files, and delete files.
26. The System command allows you to temporarily place VP-Planner Plus in a wait state and return control to DOS. Once control returns to DOS, you may execute DOS commands. To return to VP-Planner Plus, enter the command Exit.

STUDENT ASSIGNMENTS

STUDENT ASSIGNMENT 1: True/False

Instructions: Circle T if the statement is true or F if the statement is false.

T F   1. The /Worksheet Global Format (/WGF) command requires that you enter a range in the worksheet to be affected.
T F   2. Use the NOW function to display the date and time as a decimal number.
T F   3. The time displayed in a cell is automatically updated every minute.
T F   4. You can format the cell assigned the NOW function to display today's name (i.e., Sunday, Monday, etc.).
T F   5. When you insert rows in a worksheet, VP-Planner Plus *pushes up* the rows above the point of insertion to open up the worksheet.
T F   6. A percentage value, like 5.3%, can be entered exactly as 5.3% on the input line.
T F   7. The range B10..B15 is the same as B15..B10.
T (F)   8. When using the /Worksheet Title (/WT) command, the title and column headings are called vertical titles.
T F   9. Use the command /Worksheet Title Reset (/WTR) to unfreeze the titles.
T F 10. Use the /Move (/M) command to move the contents of a cell or range of cells to a different location in the worksheet.
T F 11. When numbers are displayed using the Text format, they display left-justified in the cells.
T F 12. D23 is a relative address and $D$23 is an absolute address.
T F 13. You cannot use the arrow keys to select the range for the SUM function.
T F 14. If a cell within the range summed by the SUM function contains a label, VP-Planner Plus displays an error message.
T F 15. It is possible to print multiple copies of a worksheet by entering the command /Print Printer Align Go (/PPAG) once.
T F 16. Even a worksheet with no formulas or functions can be used to answer what-if questions.
T F 17. Manual recalculation means that you must tell VP-Planner Plus when to recalculate formulas by pressing function key F9.
T F 18. The System command is identical to the Quit command, except that the Quit command reminds you to save your worksheet.
T F 19. To permanently change the default settings of VP-Planner Plus, type the letter U for Update before quitting the modified default-setting screen.
T F 20. The command /File (/F) can be used to copy, erase, and rename worksheets on disk.

STUDENT ASSIGNMENT 2: Multiple Choice

Instructions: Circle the correct response.

1. Which one of the following functions is used to display the time?
   a. TODAY   b. TIME (c.) NOW   d. CLOCK
2. Which one of the following commands is used to delete rows or columns from a worksheet?
   (a.) /Worksheet Delete (/WD)   c. /Worksheet Label (/WL)
   b. /Worksheet Erase (/WE)   d. /Worksheet Unprotect (/WU)
3. Which one of the following is an absolute address?
   a. G45   b. !G!45 (c.) $B$45   d. #G#45
4. If cell B14 is assigned the label TEN, then the function @SUM(B10..B14) in cell C25 considers B14 to be equal to
   _____ .
   a. 10   b. 0   c. an undefined number   d. 3
5. The command /Print Printer Options (/PPO) may be used to change _____ .
   (a.) the margins   c. to printing sideways
   b. the number of copies printed   d. all of these
6. The /File (/F) command can be used to _____ .
   a. format disks   c. erase worksheets from disk
   b. rename worksheets   d. both b and c

7. The command /Worksheet Global Default (/WGD) can be used to _____ .
   a. select screen colors
   b. select cell-formula printing
   c. display the date on the current-mode line
   d. save the worksheet automatically every 50 to 75 keystrokes
8. The command /Move (/M) results in the same change to the worksheet as _____ .
   a. /Worksheet Erase (/WE)
   b. /Copy (/C)
   c. /Worksheet Insert (/WI)
   d. none of these

STUDENT ASSIGNMENT 3: Understanding Absolute, Mixed, and Relative Addressing

Instructions: Fill in the correct answers.

1. Write cell B1 as a relative address, absolute address, mixed address with the row varying, and mixed address with the column varying.

Relative address: _____   Mixed, row varying: _____

Absolute address: _____   Mixed, column varying: _____

2. In Figure 3-55, write the formula for cell B8 that multiplies cell B1 times the sum of cells B4, B5, and B6. Write the formula so that when it is copied to cells C8 and D8, cell B1 remains absolute. Verify your formula by checking it with the values found in cells B8, C8, and D8 in Figure 3-55.

Formula for cell B8: _____

	A	B	C	D	E	F	G	H	
1		3	5	7					
2									
3									
4	2	5	2	1	16	16			
5	3	7	3	5	30	45			
6	5	8	7	8	46	115			
7									
8		60	36	42					
9									
10		60	60	98					
11									
12									

FIGURE 3-55
Student Assignment 3

3. In Figure 3-55, write the formula for cell E4 that multiplies cell A4 times the sum of cells B4, C4, and D4. Write the formula so that when it is copied to cells E5 and E6, cell A4 remains absolute. Verify your formula by checking it with the values found in cells E4, E5, and E6 in Figure 3-55.

Formula for cell E4: _____

4. In Figure 3-55, write the formula for cell B10 that multiplies cell B1 times the sum of cells B4, B5, and B6. Write the formula so that when it is copied to cells C10 and D10, VP-Planner Plus adjusts all the cell addresses according to the new location. Verify your formula by checking it with the values found in cells B10, C10, and D10 in Figure 3-55.

Formula for cell B10: _____

5. In Figure 3-55, write the formula for cell F4 that multiplies cell A4 times the sum of cells B4, C4, and D4. Write the formula so that when it is copied to cells F5 and F6, VP-Planner Plus adjusts all the cell addresses according to the new location. Verify your formula by checking it with the values found in cells F4, F5, and F6 in Figure 3-55.

Formula for cell F4: _____

STUDENT ASSIGNMENT 4: Writing VP-Planner Plus Commands

Instructions: Write the VP-Planner Plus command to accomplish the task in each of the problems below. Write the command up to the point where you enter the range or type the letter Q to quit the command.

1. Delete columns A, B, and C. Assume the cell cursor is at A1.

   Command: _____

2. Insert three rows between rows 5 and 6. Assume the cell cursor is at A6.

   Command: _____

3. Move the range of cells A12..C15 to F14..H17. Assume the cell cursor is at A12.

   Command: _____

4. Freeze the vertical and horizontal titles. Assume that the cell cursor is immediately below and to the right of the titles.

   Command: _____

5. Return control to DOS temporarily.

   Command: _____

6. Change the default directory to the B drive permanently.

   Command: _____

7. Change the screen so that it looks like the Lotus 1-2-3 screen.

   Command: _____

8. Change the left print margin to 1 and the right print margin to 79 for the current worksheet only.

   Command: _____

9. Change to print in condensed mode with a right margin of 140.

   Command: _____

10. Change VP-Planner Plus from automatic to manual recalculation. Change it back to automatic recalculation.

   Command: _____

STUDENT ASSIGNMENT 5: Correcting the Range in a Worksheet

Instructions: The worksheet illustrated in Figure 3-56 contains errors in cells E9 through E21. Analyze the entries displayed on the worksheet. Explain the cause of the errors and the method of correction in the space provided below.

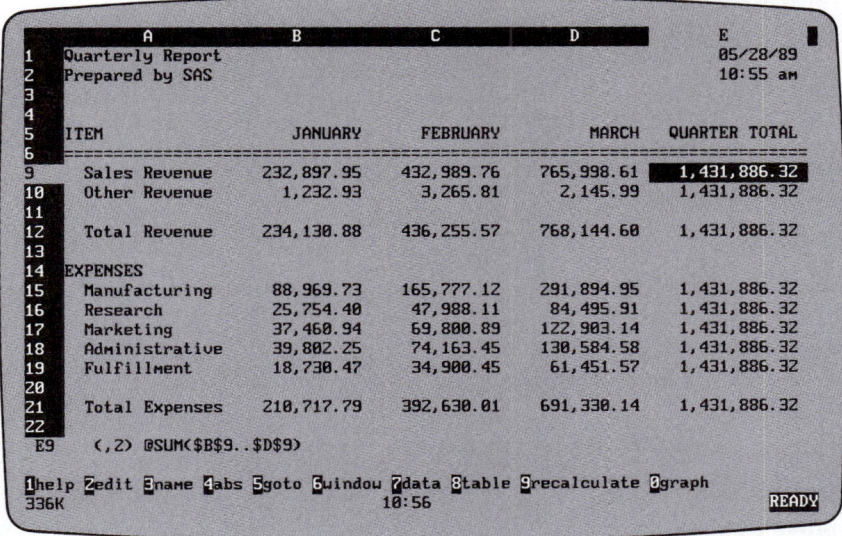

FIGURE 3-56
Student Assignment 5

Cause of errors: _____

_____

Method of correction for cell E9: _____

_____

Method of correction for cells E10 through E21: _____

_____

_____

STUDENT ASSIGNMENT 6: Correcting Errors in a Worksheet

Instructions: The worksheet illustrated in Figure 3-57 contains errors in the range B15..E23. The formulas used in the range B15..E23 are the same as in Project 3. Analyze the entries displayed on the worksheet. Explain the cause of the errors and the method of correction in the space provided below. (Hint: Check the cells that are referenced in the range B15..E23.)

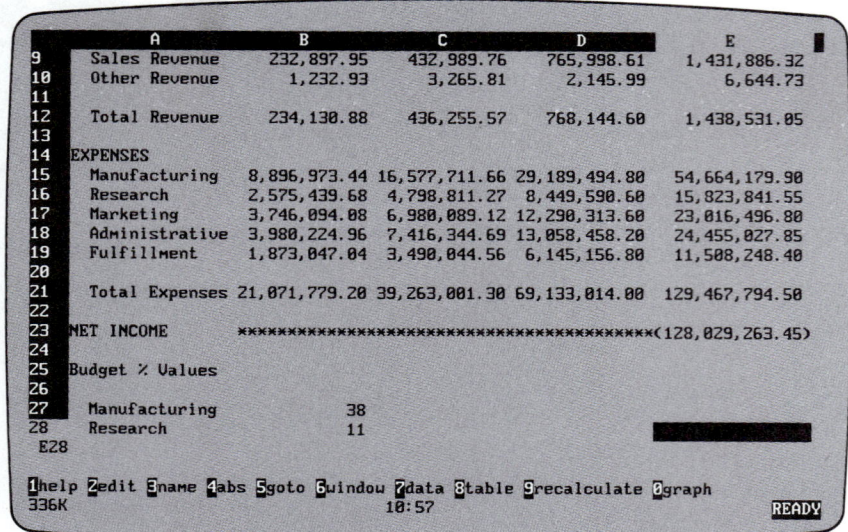

FIGURE 3-57
Student Assignment 6

Cause of errors: _____

_____

Method of correction: _____

_____

STUDENT ASSIGNMENT 7: Building a Projected Price Increase Worksheet

Instructions: Load VP-Planner Plus and perform the following tasks.

1. Build the worksheet illustrated in Figure 3-58. Increase the width of columns B through E to 14 characters. Enter the title, column headings, model numbers, and corresponding current prices. The entries in the columns labeled 10% INCREASE, 15% INCREASE, and 20% INCREASE are determined from formulas. Multiply one plus the percent specified in the column heading by the current price. For example, assign C8 the formula 1.10*B8. To determine the total current price in cell B18, enter a formula that adds the products of the on-hand column and the corresponding current price. Copy this total formula in cell B18 to cells C18 through E18 to determine the totals in the remaining columns.

```
            A           B           C           D           E         F
 1                              VIDEOLAND                          22-Dec
 2                PROJECTED PRICE INCREASES FOR NEXT QUARTER       10:57 am
 3
 4        MODEL         CURRENT        10%         15%         20%
 5        NUMBER        PRICE       INCREASE    INCREASE    INCREASE  ON HAND
 6        ================================================================
 7
 8        VCR-101       250.00       275.00      287.50      300.00     12
 9        VCR-201       295.00       324.50      339.25      354.00     23
10        VCR-325       350.00       385.00      402.50      420.00      8
11        VCR-500       495.00       544.50      569.25      594.00     17
12        VCR-750       600.00       660.00      690.00      720.00     16
13        VCR-800       675.00       742.50      776.25      810.00     25
14        VCR-825       700.00       770.00      805.00      840.00     41
15        VCR-900       750.00       825.00      862.50      900.00     19
16        VCR-990       800.00       880.00      920.00      960.00      7
17
18        TOTAL      $96,025.00  $105,627.50 $110,428.75 $115,230.00
19
20
   F20

    1help 2edit 3name 4abs 5goto 6window 7data 8table 9recalculate 0graph
    336K                              10:58                           READY
```

FIGURE 3-58
Student Assignment 7

2. Save the worksheet as STUS3-7.
3. Print the worksheet in the condensed mode.
4. Print the cell-formulas version of the worksheet.   /PPOOCQAGEE
5. Print only the first 18 rows of the model number and current price columns.
6. Print the worksheet after formatting all the cells to the Text type.   /RFT

(handwritten, circled) ✗ Start Look

STUDENT ASSIGNMENT 8: Building a Payroll Analysis Worksheet

Instructions: Load VP-Planner Plus and perform the following tasks.

1. Build the worksheet illustrated in Figure 3-59. Change the width of all the columns in the worksheet to 14 characters. Enter the title, column headings, row identifiers, employee names, and corresponding current hourly pay rate. Use the sum function to determine the totals called for in cells B18 through B20. Use the NOW function to display the date and time in cells E19 and E20. Finally, enter the proposed percent increase and hours per week in cells B15 and B16. Enter the following formulas once and copy them to complete the remainder of the worksheet:
   a. Cell C8—current weekly pay = hours per week × current hourly pay rate
   b. Cell D8—proposed hourly pay rate = current hourly pay rate × (1 + proposed percent increase)
   c. Cell E8—proposed weekly pay = hours per week × proposed hourly pay rate

Format the numbers in rows 8 through 12 to the Fixed type with two decimal places. Format the totals in rows 18 through 20 to the Crncy type with two decimal places.

```
             A                 B           C          D          E
 1                      PAYROLL ANALYSIS REPORT
 2
 3                           CURRENT     CURRENT    PROPOSED    PROPOSED
 4                           HOURLY      WEEKLY     HOURLY      WEEKLY
 5    EMPLOYEE NAME          PAY RATE       PAY     PAY RATE       PAY
 6    ==================================================================
 7
 8    BAKER, MARY A.            7.00      280.00       7.35     294.00
 9    DAVIS, STEPHEN D.         9.00      360.00       9.45     378.00
10    LONG, CLARENCE R.         8.00      320.00       8.40     336.00
11    MONROE, JAMES L.         10.00      400.00      10.50     420.00
12    CHANG, JUSTIN M.          5.00      200.00       5.25     210.00
13    ------------------------------------------------------------------
14
15    PROPOSED % INCREASE          5%
16    HOURS PER WEEK              40
17
18    TOTAL PROPOSED PAY    $1,638.00
19    TOTAL CURRENT PAY     $1,560.00                          91 12 22
20    AMOUNT OF INCREASE       $78.00                          10:59 am
 E1

 1help 2edit 3name 4abs 5goto 6window 7data 8table 9recalculate 0graph
 337K                                      10:59                         READY
```

FIGURE 3-59
Student Assignment 8

2. Save the worksheet as STUS3-8.   *(handwritten)* / P PO S 015/1080
3. Print the worksheet in condensed mode.
4. Print only the range A1..C13.
5. Answer the following what-if questions. Print the worksheet for each question.
   a. What is the total proposed pay if the proposed percent increase is changed to 10%?
   b. What is the total proposed pay if the proposed percent increase is changed to 7.5%?

STUDENT ASSIGNMENT 9: Building a Book Income Worksheet

Instructions: Load VP-Planner Plus and perform the following tasks.

1. Change the screen so that it looks like the Lotus 1-2-3 screen (see Figures 3-53 and 3-54).
2. Build the worksheet illustrated in Figure 3-60. Set column A to a width of 18 characters and columns B through E to a width of 14 characters. The calculations for each author are determined as follows:
   a. The royalty in column C is the net sales of the book multiplied by the author's royalty percentage in cell B30 or B31.
   b. The manufacturing costs in column D are the net sales of the book multiplied by the manufacturing budgeted percent in cell B35.
   c. The net income in column E for each book is determined by subtracting the royalty and manufacturing costs from the net sales.
   d. The report totals in rows 25 and 26 are the sum of the individual book titles for each author.

```
                 A              B              C            D          E
 1                            BOOK INCOME REPORT
 2   ------------------------------------------------------  ------------------
 3   AUTHOR:        HANSEN
 4
 5   BOOK TITLE         NET SALES      ROYALTY     MANU. COSTS  NET INCOME
 6
 7   Fury in the Sky    122,356.61     15,906.36    32,179.79    74,270.46
 8   Night Crawler      543,667.92     70,676.83   142,984.66   330,006.43
 9   White Feathers     885,443.91    115,107.71   232,871.75   537,464.45
10
11   ------------------------------------------------------------------------
12   AUTHOR:        MERRIT
13
14   BOOK TITLE         NET SALES      ROYALTY     MANU. COSTS  NET INCOME
15
16   The Sharp Beak     553,889.04     74,775.02   145,672.82   333,441.20
17   Webbed Intrigue    657,443.25     88,754.84   172,907.57   395,780.84
18   Information Blight 956,441.89    129,119.66   251,544.22   575,778.02
19
20   ------------------------------------------------------------------------
21   REPORT TOTALS
22
23   AUTHOR             NET SALES      ROYALTY     MANU. COSTS  NET INCOME
24
25   Hansen           1,551,468.44    201,690.90   408,036.20   941,741.34
26   Merrit           2,167,774.18    292,649.51   570,124.61 1,305,000.06
27
28   ========================================================================
29   Royalty:
30   Hansen                            13.0%
31   Merrit                            13.5%
32
33
34   Manufacturing Cost                                        Dec-91
35   All books:                        26.3%                   10:00 am
36
```

FIGURE 3-60
Student Assignment 9

3. Save the worksheet. Use the file name STUS3-9.
4. Print the worksheet.
5. Print only the range A3..E9.
6. Print the worksheet after formatting all the cells to the Text type.
7. Change the screen back to the normal VP-Planner Plus screen.

STUDENT ASSIGNMENT 10: Building a Salary Budget Worksheet

Instructions: Load VP-Planner Plus and perform the following tasks.

1. Build the worksheet illustrated in Figure 3-61. Change the width of all the columns in the worksheet to 15 characters. Then change the width of column A to 20 characters. Enter the title, column headings, row titles, date, time, and current salary for full- and part-time employees. Determine the projected salaries in column C by using the salary increase in cell B27 and the current salaries in column B. Determine the salaries by department by multiplying the total salaries in row 12 by the corresponding sales allocation percent value in the range B21..B24. Use the SUM function to determine the annual totals in column D.

```
              A                   B                C                D
 1  SALARY BUDGET - CURRENT AND PROJECTED SALARIES           12/22/91
 2  PREPARED BY ACCOUNTING                                   10:00 am
 3
 4
 5                            CURRENT          PROJECTED
 6  SALARY TYPE               JAN - JUNE       JULY - DEC     ANNUAL TOTAL
 7  ==================================================================
 8
 9  FULL TIME                 1,250,500.00     1,313,025.00   2,563,525.00
10  PART TIME                   750,500.00       788,025.00   1,538,525.00
11
12  TOTAL SALARIES            2,001,000.00     2,101,050.00   4,102,050.00
13
14  SALARIES BY DEPARTMENT
15      Accounting              200,100.00       210,105.00     410,205.00
16      Production              600,300.00       630,315.00   1,230,615.00
17      Sales                   500,250.00       525,262.50   1,025,512.50
18      Distribution            700,350.00       735,367.50   1,435,717.50
19
20  SALES ALLOCATION % VALUES
21      Accounting                    10%
22      Production                    30%
23      Sales                         25%
24      Distribution                  35%
25
26
27  SALARY INCREASE %                  5%
28
29
```

FIGURE 3-61
Student Assignment 10

2. Save the worksheet using the file name STUS3-10.
3. Print the worksheet.
4. Print the portion of the worksheet in the range A14..D18.

(handwritten notes in top margin)
10 89/10
1.3
88.7

90.
19 99
100/10
1.4
98.4

(handwritten) Print each one

STUDENT ASSIGNMENT 11: Changing Manufacturing Costs and Royalty Rates in the Book Income Worksheet

Instructions: Load VP-Planner Plus and perform the following tasks.

1. Change the screen so that it looks like the Lotus 1-2-3 screen (see Figures 3-53 and 3-54).
2. Retrieve the worksheet STUS3-9 from disk. The worksheet is illustrated in Figure 3-60.
3. Answer the following what-if questions. Print the worksheet for each question. Each question is independent of the others.
   a. If the manufacturing percentage cost in cell B35 is reduced from 26.3% to 24.7%, what is the net income from all of Hansen's books? *(handwritten)* 24.7 1.6
   b. If Merrit's royalty percentage in cell B31 is changed from 13.5% to 14.8%, what would be the royalty amount for the book *Webbed Intrigue*?
    c. If Hansen's royalty percentage in cell B30 is reduced from 13% to 12.5%, Merrit's royalty percentage is increased from 13.5% to 14.1%, and the manufacturing percentage costs are reduced from 26.3% to 25%, what would be the net incomes for Hansen and Merrit?
4. Change the screen back to the normal VP-Planner Plus screen. *(handwritten)* 1.3

STUDENT ASSIGNMENT 12: Changing Sales Allocation Percent Values and Salary Increase Percent in the Salary Budget Worksheet

Instructions: Load VP-Planner Plus and perform the following tasks.

1. Change the screen so that it looks like the Lotus 1-2-3 screen (see Figures 3-53 and 3-54).
2. Retrieve the worksheet STUS3-10 from disk. The worksheet is illustrated in Figure 3-61.
3. Answer the following what-if questions. Print the worksheet for each question. Each question is independent of the other.
   a. If the four sales allocation percent values in the range B21..B24 are each decreased by 1% and the salary increase in cell B27 is changed from 5% to 4%, what are the annual totals in the Salary Budget worksheet?
   b. If the salary increase percent is cut in half, what would be the total projected salaries?
4. Change the screen back to the normal VP-Planner Plus screen.

(handwritten) 5 to 4

PROJECT 4

Building Worksheets with Functions and Macros

Objectives

You will have mastered the material in this project when you can:

- Assign a name to a range and refer to the range in a formula using the assigned name.
- Apply the elementary statistical functions AVG, COUNT, MAX, MIN, STD, and VAR.
- Determine the monthly payment of a loan using the financial function PMT.
- Enter a series of numbers into a range using the Data Fill command.
- Employ the IF function to enter one value or another in a cell on the basis of a condition.
- Determine the present value of an annuity using the financial function PV.
- Determine the future value of an investment using the financial function FV.
- Build a data table to perform what-if analyses.
- Store keystrokes as a macro and execute the macro.
- Write programlike macros to automate your worksheet.
- Divide the screen into multiple windows.
- Protect and unprotect cells.

*I*n this project we will develop two worksheets, Project 4A and Project 4B. The worksheet for Project 4A, shown in Figure 4-1, is a grading report that displays a row of information for each student enrolled in DP 101. The student information includes a student identification number, three test scores, a test score total, and total percent correct. At the bottom of the worksheet is summary information for each test and all three tests grouped together. The summary includes the number of students that took the test, the highest and lowest test scores, the average test score, standard deviation, and variance. The **standard deviation** is a statistic used to measure the dispersion of test scores. The **variance** is used to make additional statistical inferences about the test scores.

FIGURE 4-1
The grading report we will build in Project 4A.

	A	B	C	D	E	F
1	DP 101		Grading Report			22-Dec-91
2						
3		Test 1	Test 2	Test 3	Total	Percent
4	Student	139	142	150	431	Correct
5	=========	=====	=====	=====	=====	=======
6	1035	121	127	142	390	90.5
7	1074	114	113	132	359	83.3
8	1265	79	97	101	277	64.3
9	1345	85	106	95	286	66.4
10	1392	127	124	120	371	86.1
11	3167	101	120	109	330	76.6
12	3382	110	104	120	334	77.5
13	3597	92	104	100	296	68.7
14	4126	105	100	96	301	69.8
15	5619	125	135	143	403	93.5
16	7561	112	130	123	365	84.7
17						
18	Count	11	11	11	11	
19	Lowest Grade	79	97	95	277	
20	Highest Grade	127	135	143	403	
21	Average Score	106.5	114.5	116.5	337.5	
22	Std Deviation	15.2	12.6	16.8	41.4	
23	Variance	230.2	159.0	282.8	1711.2	
24						
25						

Project 4B has three parts. The first part is shown in Figure 4-2. This worksheet determines the monthly payment and an amortization table for a car loan. An **amortization table** shows the beginning and ending balances and the amount of payment that applies to the principal and interest for each period. This type of worksheet can be very useful if you are planning to take out a loan and want to see the effects of increasing the down payment, changing the interest rate, or changing the length of time it takes to pay off the loan.

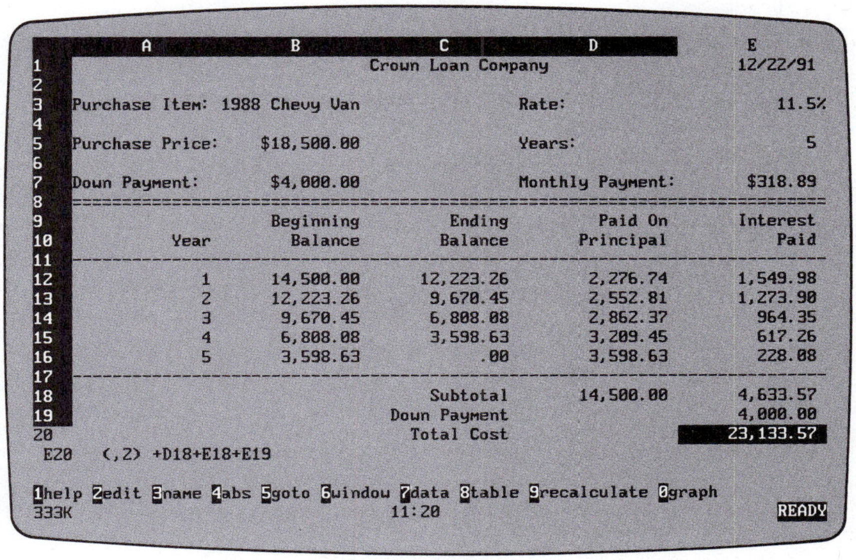

FIGURE 4-2
The monthly payment and amortization table we will build for the Crown Loan Company in Part 1 of Project 4B.

The second part of this worksheet is shown in Figure 4-3. Here we use a data table to analyze the effect of different interest rates on the monthly payment and total amount paid for the car loan. A **data table** is an area of the worksheet set up to contain answers to what-if questions. By using a data table you can automate your what-if questions and organize the answers returned by VP-Planner Plus into a table. For example, the data table in Figure 4-3 displays the monthly payments and total cost of the loan for interest rates that vary between 8.5% and 15% in increments of 0.5%.

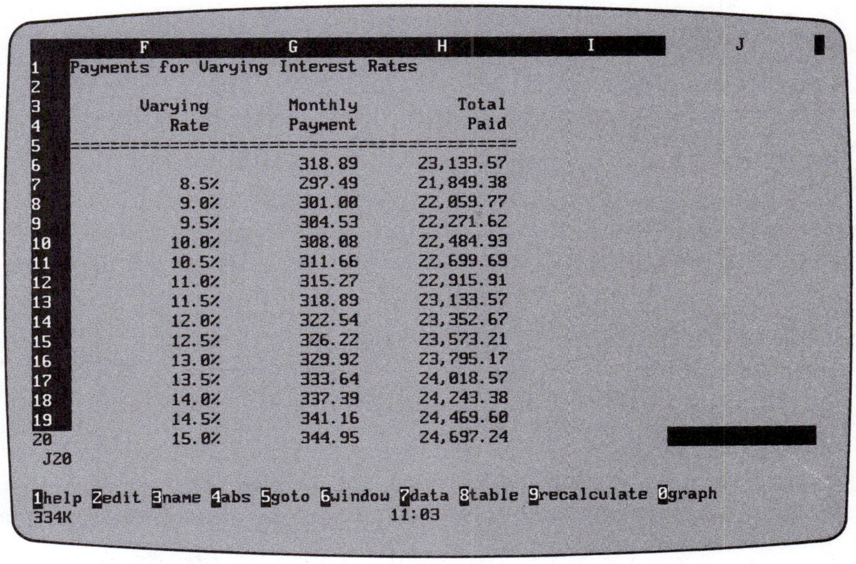

FIGURE 4-3
The data table we will build for the Crown Loan Company in Part 2 of Project 4B.

The third part of Project 4B involves writing the four macros shown in Figure 4-4. A **macro** is a series of keystrokes or instructions that are stored in a cell or a range of cells associated with that particular worksheet. They are executed by pressing only two keys: the Alt key and the single letter macro name. Macros save you time and effort. For example, they allow you to store a complex sequence of commands in a cell. Later you can execute the macro (stored commands) as often as you want by simply typing its name.

```
              A              B              C              D              E
22                      Crown Loan Company Worksheet Macros
23
24   Macro                      Macro Name      Function
25   ================            ==========      ============================
26   /FS~R                       \S              Saves worksheet under same name
27
28   /PPAGEEQ                    \P              Prints worksheet
29
30   /PPOOCQAGOOAQEEQ            \C              Print cell-formulas version
31
32
33   {HOME}                      \D              Accept loan information
34   {GOTO}B3~/RE~                               --Clear cell B3
35   {DOWN}{DOWN}/RE~                            --Clear cell B5
36   {DOWN}{DOWN}/RE~                            --Clear cell B7
37   {GOTO}E3~/RE~                               --Clear cell E3
38   {DOWN}{DOWN}/RE~                            --Clear cell E5
39   {HOME}                                      --Move to cell A1
40   /XLPurchase Item:~B3~                       --Accept purchase item
41   /XNPurchase Price:~B5~                      --Accept purchase price
42   /XNDown Payment:~B7~                        --Accept down payment
43   /XNInterest Rate in %:~E3~                  --Accept interest rate
44   /XNTime in Years:~E5~                       --Accept time in years
45   {HOME}                                      --Move to cell A1
46   /XQ                                         --End of macro
47
```

FIGURE 4-4 The four macros we will build for the Crown Loan Company in Part 3 of Project 4B.

When executed, the macro in cell A26 of Figure 4-4 saves the worksheet. The one in cell A28 prints the worksheet on the basis of the previously defined range. The macro in cell A30 prints the cell-formulas version of the worksheet on the basis of the previously defined range. The multicell macro in the range A33..A46 is a type of computer program. When it executes, it automatically clears the cells containing the loan information in Figure 4-2, requests new loan data on the input line, and displays the new loan information.

PROJECT 4A—ANALYZING STUDENT TEST SCORES

Begin Project 4A with an empty worksheet and the cell cursor at A1, the home position. The first step is to change the widths of the columns in the worksheet. Set the width of column A to 13 characters, so that the row identifier "Std Deviation" fits in cell A22 (see Figure 4-1). Change the width of the rest of the columns in the worksheet from 9 to 11 characters so that all the student information fits across the screen. To change the columns to the desired widths, do the following:

1. Enter the command /**W**orksheet **G**lobal **C**ol-width (/WGC). Change the default width on the input line from 9 to 11 and press the Enter key.
2. With the cell cursor at A1, enter the command /**W**orksheet **C**ol-width **S**et (/WCS). Change the number 11 on the input line to 13 and press the Enter key.

If you reverse steps 1 and 2, the results will still be the same. That is, you can change the width of column A first and then change the width of the rest of the columns. The command /WGC affects only those columns that were not previously changed by the /WCS command.

The next step is to add the titles and student data to the worksheet. Enter the course number, worksheet title, date, column headings, maximum possible points for each test, student number, test scores, and summary identifiers as specified in Figure 4-1. Note that the numbers in column A identify the students in the class and are not used in any computations. Therefore, enter these numbers with a leading apostrophe (_'_). After entering the last row identifier in cell A23, press the Home key. The first 20 rows display as shown in Figure 4-5.

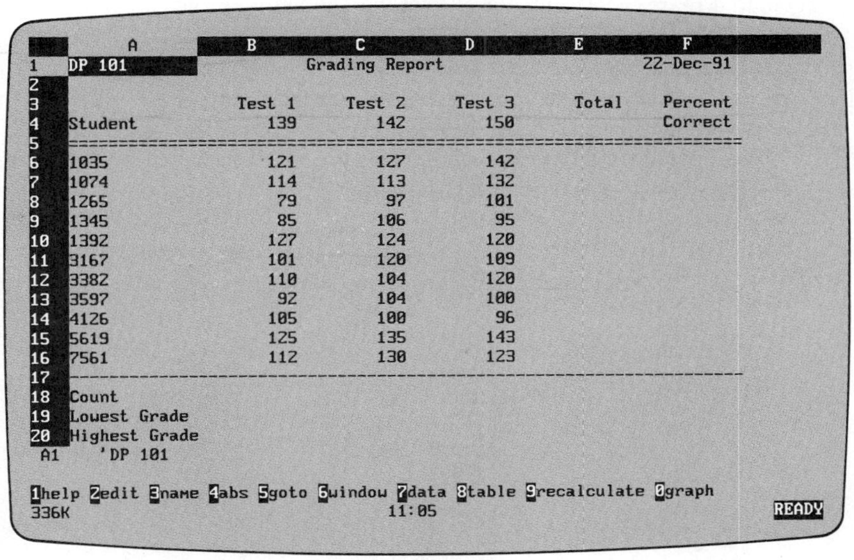

FIGURE 4-5
Labels and student data
entered into the grading report.

With the student data in the worksheet, we can determine the totals and summaries. Let's start with the maximum number of points for all three tests in cell E4. Use the GOTO command to move the cell cursor from cell A1 to cell E4 and enter the function @SUM(B4..D4). The range B4..D4 contains the maximum possible points for each test.

The SUM function in cell E4 is the same one required in the range E6..E16 to determine the total number of points received by each student. Hence, use the Copy command to copy cell E4 to the range E6..E16. With the cell cursor at E4, enter the command /Copy (/C), press the Enter key to lock in the source range, and use the Down Arrow key and Period key to select the destination range E6..E16. Press the Enter key. The total number of points received by each student displays in the range E6..E16 (see Figure 4-6).

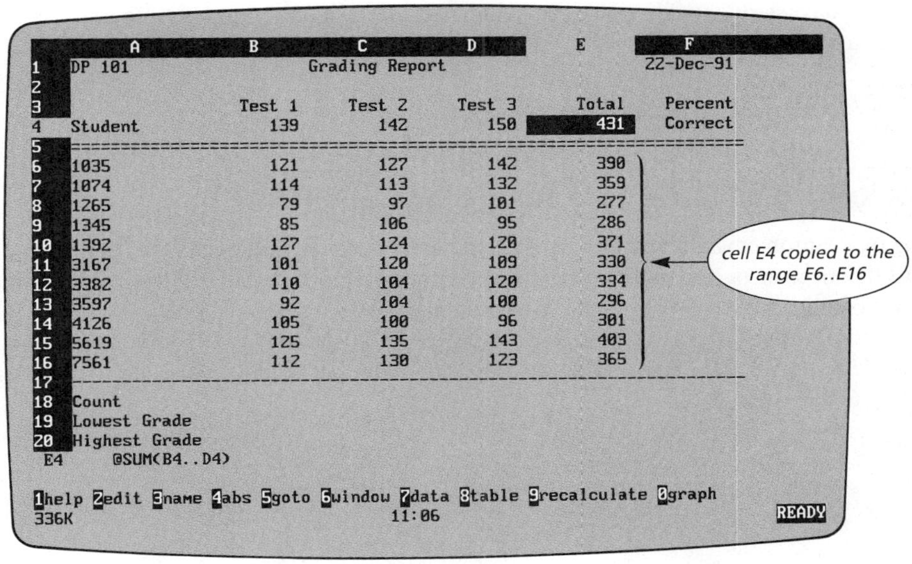

FIGURE 4-6
Student test totals entered into
column E of the grading report.

Once the total number of points received by each student is part of the worksheet, we can determine the total percent-correct in column F. Move the cell cursor to F6 and enter the formula +E6/$E$4*100. The numerator in this formula, cell E6, is equal to the total number of points for the first student. The denominator, cell E4, is equal to the maximum number of points for the three tests. Multiplying the quotient +E6/$E$4 by 100 converts the ratio to a percent value. We use this procedure to display a percent value rather than formatting it in the Percent type because the column heading already indicates that the values in column E are in percent. Recall that the Percent type adds a percent sign (%) to the right side of the number.

Copy cell F6 to the range F7..F16. Note that we use the dollar sign ($) character in the denominator of the formula in cell E6 to make cell E4 an absolute cell address. Therefore, when we copy the formula in cell F6, the relative address E6 in the numerator changes based on the new location and the absolute address $E$4 in the denominator stays the same.

Format the percent correct in column F to the Fixed type with one decimal place. Enter the command /Range Format Fixed (/RFF). Select one decimal position and press the Enter key. Enter the range F6..F16 and press the Enter key. The worksheet with each student's percent correct formatted to the Fixed type with one decimal place is illustrated in Figure 4-7.

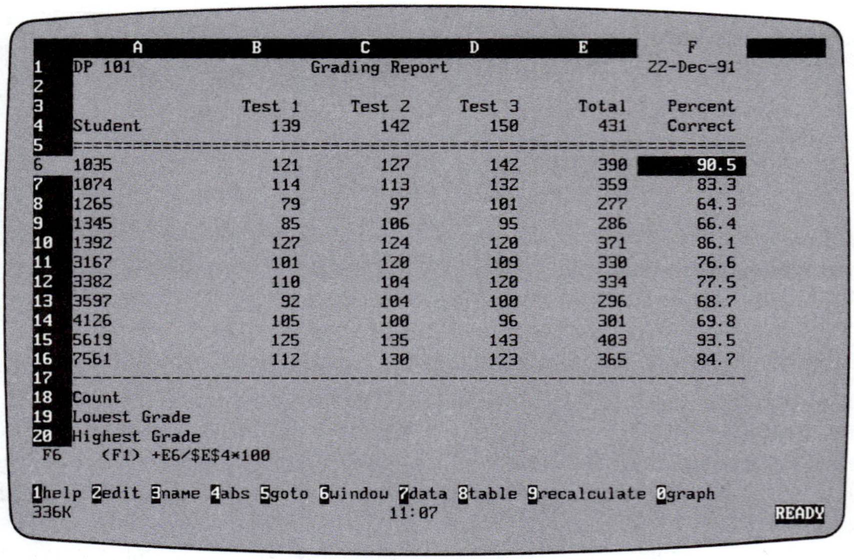

FIGURE 4-7
Total percent correct for each student formatted to the Fixed type with one decimal position.

	A	B	C	D	E	F	
1	DP 101		Grading Report			22-Dec-91	
2							
3		Test 1	Test 2	Test 3	Total	Percent	
4	Student	139	142	150	431	Correct	
5							
6	1035	121	127	142	390	90.5	
7	1074	114	113	132	359	83.3	
8	1265	79	97	101	277	64.3	
9	1345	85	106	95	286	66.4	
10	1392	127	124	120	371	86.1	
11	3167	101	120	109	330	76.6	
12	3382	110	104	120	334	77.5	
13	3597	92	104	100	296	68.7	
14	4126	105	100	96	301	69.8	
15	5619	125	135	143	403	93.5	
16	7561	112	130	123	365	84.7	
17							
18	Count						
19	Lowest Grade						
20	Highest Grade						

```
F6      (F1) +E6/$E$4*100

1help 2edit 3name 4abs 5goto 6window 7data 8table 9recalculate 0graph
336K                              11:07                              READY
```

The next step is to determine the summaries in rows 18 through 23. To make the job of entering these summaries easier, we need to discuss range names.

Assigning a Name to a Range of Cells (/RNC)

One of the problems with using a range is remembering the end points that define it. The problem becomes more difficult as worksheets grow in size and the same range is referred to repeatedly. This is the situation in the summary rows at the bottom of the grading report. For example, each summary item for Test 1 in cells B18 through B23 reference the same range, B6..B16. To make it easier to refer to the range, VP-Planner Plus allows you to assign a name to it. You may then use the name to reference the range, rather than the cell addresses of the end points. Let's assign the name TEST1 to the range B6..B16.

Move the cell cursor to B6, one of the end points of the range B6..B16. Enter the command /Range Name (/RN) as shown in Figure 4-8. With the command cursor active in the **Range Name** menu, type the letter C for Create. VP-Planner Plus responds with the prompt message "Enter name:" on the input line (see Figure 4-9). Enter the name TEST1 and press the Enter key. The prompt message "Enter range:" immediately displays on the input line. Use the arrow keys to select the range B6..B16 as shown in Figure 4-9. Press the Enter key. The range name TEST1 can now be used in place of B6..B16.

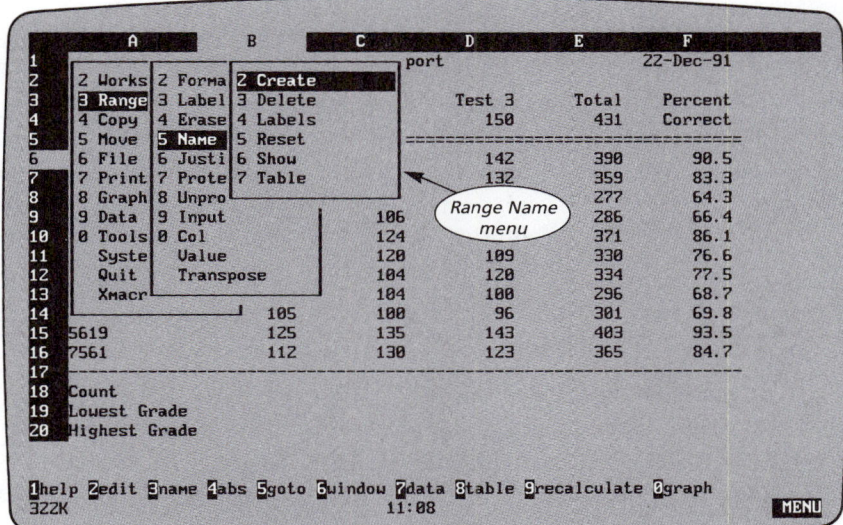

FIGURE 4-8
The display after entering the command /Range Name (/RN).

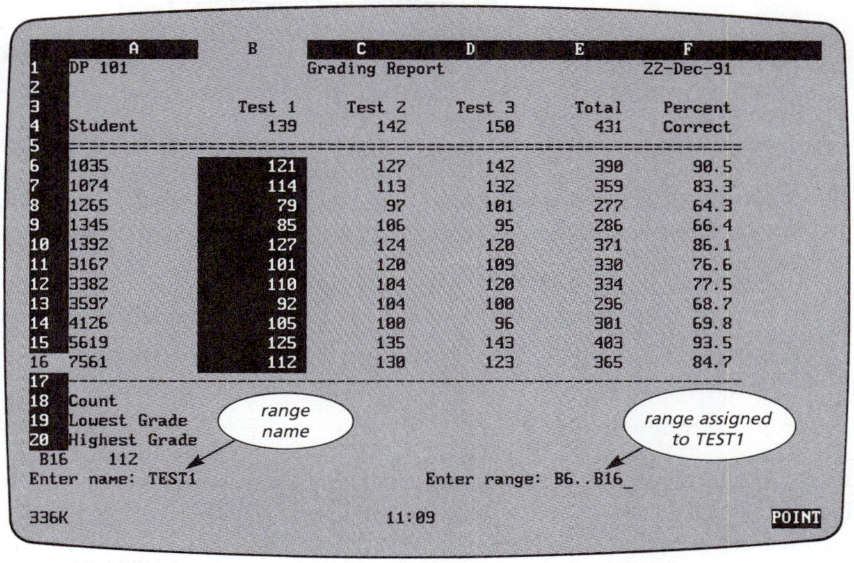

FIGURE 4-9
Range name TEST1 assigned to the range B6..B16.

As shown in the Range Name menu in Figure 4-8, there are several Range Name commands. These commands are summarized in Table 4-1.

TABLE 4-1   Summary of the Range Name Commands

COMMAND	KEYSTROKES	FUNCTION
Create	/RNC	Assigns a name to a range. The name can be no longer than 16 characters.
Delete	/RND	Deletes the specified range name.
Labels	/RNL	Assigns the label in the current cell as a name to the cell above, below, to the right, or to the left of the current cell.
Reset	/RNR	Deletes range names associated with the worksheet.
Show	/RNS	Displays all the range names associated with a worksheet. You may also press function key F3 to display the range names when VP-Planner Plus is in POINT mode.
Table	/RNT	Places the list of range names in the worksheet beginning at the location of the cell cursor.

Statistical Functions—AVG, COUNT, MIN, MAX, STD, and VAR

VP-Planner Plus has several statistical functions that return values that are handy for evaluating a group of numbers, like the test scores in the grading report. The statistical functions are summarized in Table 4-2.

TABLE 4-2   Statistical Functions

FUNCTION	FUNCTION VALUE
AVG(R)	Returns the average of the numbers in range R by summing the nonempty cells and dividing by the number of nonempty cells. Labels are treated as zeros.
COUNT(R)	Returns the number of cells that are not empty in range R.
MAX(R)	Returns the largest number in range R.
MIN(R)	Returns the smallest number in range R.
STD(R)	Returns the standard deviation of the numbers in range R.
SUM(R)	Returns the sum of the numbers in range R.
VAR(R)	Returns the variance of the numbers in range R.

In the grading report, cell B18 displays the number of students that received a grade for Test 1. This value can be obtained by using the COUNT function. With the cell cursor at B18, enter the function @COUNT(TEST1). VP-Planner Plus immediately displays the value 11—the number of students that received a grade for Test 1. This is shown in Figure 4-10. Remember, the range name TEST1 is equal to the range B6..B16.

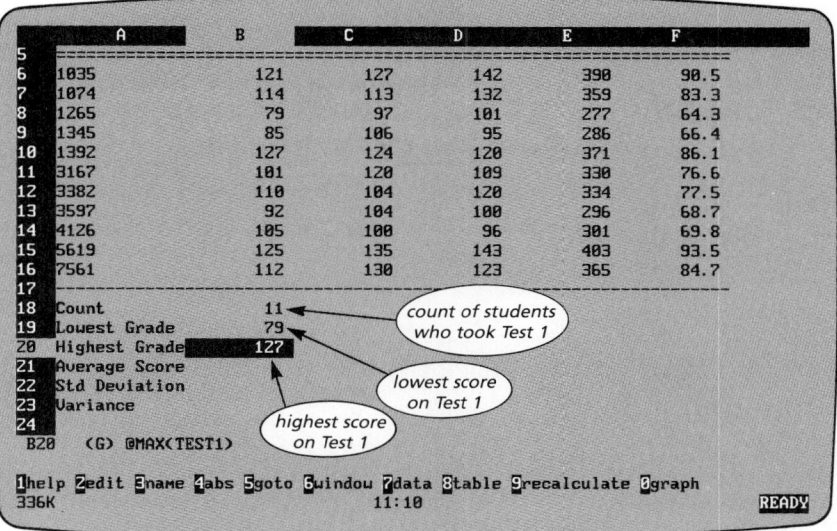

FIGURE 4-10
COUNT, MIN, and MAX functions entered into the grading report for Test 1.

In cells B19 and B20, the grading report contains the lowest score and the highest score received on Test 1. Student 1265 received the lowest score—79. Student 1392 received the highest score—127. To display the lowest score obtained on Test 1, enter the function @MIN(TEST1) in cell B19. To display the highest score, enter the function @MAX(TEST1) in cell B20. The results of entering these functions are shown in cells B19 and B20 in Figure 4-10.

The next step is to determine the average of the scores received on Test 1. Enter the function @AVG(TEST1) in cell B21. As illustrated in Figure 4-11, the average score for Test 1 in cell B21 is 106.454545. VP-Planner Plus arrives at this value by summing the scores for Test 1 and dividing by the number of non-empty cells in the range B6..B16.

```
         A           B           C           D           E           F
5    ====================================================================
6    1035          121         127         142         390         90.5
7    1074          114         113         132         359         83.3
8    1265           79          97         101         277         64.3
9    1345           85         106          95         286         66.4
10   1392          127         124         120         371         86.1
11   3167          101         120         109         330         76.6
12   3382          110         104         120         334         77.5
13   3597           92         104         100         296         68.7
14   4126          105         100          96         301         69.8
15   5619          125         135         143         403         93.5
16   7561          112         130         123         365         84.7
17   --------------------------------------------------------------------
18   Count          11                            average score
19   Lowest Grade   79                              for Test 1
20   Highest Grade 127
21   Average Score106.454545                  standard deviation
22   Std Deviation15.1739228                       for Test 1
23   Variance      230.247934
24                                            variance for
     B23    (G) @VAR(TEST1)                      Test 1

     1help 2edit 3name 4abs 5goto 6window 7data 8table 9recalculate 0graph
     336K                           11:11                              READY
```

FIGURE 4-11
STD and VAR functions entered into the grading report for Test 1.

The last two summary lines require us to use the functions STD and VAR. As indicated in Table 4-2, the STD function returns the standard deviation and the VAR function returns the variance. To complete the summary lines for Test 1, enter the functions @STD(TEST1) in cell B22 and @VAR(TEST1) in cell B23. The results are shown in Figure 4-11.

The same six functions that are used to summarize the results for Test 1 are required for Test 2, Test 3, and the sum of the test scores for each student in column E. With the cell cursor at B23, enter the command /**C**opy (/**C**). Copy the source range B23..B18 to the destination range C23..E18.

As the functions in column B are copied to the new locations in columns C, D, and E, VP-Planner Plus adjusts the range TEST1 (B6..B16) to C6..C16 for Test 2, D6..D16 for Test 3, and E6..E16 for the sum of the test scores in column E.

To complete the worksheet, format the last three rows in the worksheet to the Fixed type with one decimal place. With the cell cursor at B23, enter the command /**R**ange **F**ormat **F**ixed (/**RFF**). In response to the prompt message "Enter desired decimal position: 2" on the input line, type the digit 1 and press the Enter key. Next, VP-Planner Plus displays the prompt message "Select Range of Cells to be altered: B23..B23." Use the arrow keys to select the range B23..E21 and press the Enter key. The complete grading report is shown in Figure 4-1.

Saving and Printing the Worksheet

To save the grading report worksheet to disk, enter the command /**F**ile **S**ave (/**FS**). In response to the prompt message on the input line, enter the file name PROJS-4A and press the Enter key.

To obtain a printed version of the worksheet, follow these steps:

1. Make sure the printer is in READY mode.
2. Press the Home key to move the cell cursor to A1.
3. Enter the command /**P**rint **P**rinter **R**ange (/**PPR**) and select the range A1..F23.
4. Type the letters A for Align and G for Go.
5. After the worksheet prints on the printer, type the letter E for Eject twice. Recall that the Eject command moves the paper through the printer to the top of the next page.
6. Type the letter Q to quit the /PP command and carefully remove the grading report from the printer.

Erasing the Worksheet from Main Computer Memory (/WE)

After saving and printing the grading report, we can erase it from main computer memory so that we can begin Project 4B. Recall from Project 1, that to erase the current worksheet, enter the command /**W**orksheet **E**rase (/**WE**). When the prompt message "Are you sure? (Y/N)" appears on the input line at the bottom of the screen, type the letter Y. VP-Planner Plus responds by clearing all the cells in the worksheet and changing all the settings to their default values.

PROJECT 4B—DETERMINING THE MONTHLY PAYMENT FOR A CAR LOAN

With the grading report worksheet cleared from main computer memory, we can begin entering Project 4B. The car loan payment worksheet is shown in Figures 4-2, 4-3, and 4-4. It is by far the most complex worksheet undertaken thus far. For this reason, use the divide and conquer strategy to build it. This strategy involves completing a section of the worksheet and testing it before moving on to the next section. Let's divide the worksheet into five sections:

1. Determine the monthly payment on a five-year loan for a 1988 Chevy Van with a sticker price of $18,500.00, down payment of $4,000.00, at an interest rate of 11.5%—range A1..E7 in Figure 4-2.
2. Display the amortization schedule—range A8..E20 in Figure 4-2.
3. Generate the data table—range F1..H20 in Figure 4-3.
4. Create the simple macros—range A22..E30 in Figure 4-4.
5. Create the multicell macro—range A33..E46 in Figure 4-4.

The first step in determining the car loan payment is to change the column widths. Set the width of column D to 16 characters so that the label "Monthly Payment:" will fit in D7. Set the width of the rest of the column widths in the worksheet to 15 characters. To change the widths of the columns, do the following:

1. With the cell cursor at A1, enter the command /**W**orksheet **G**lobal **C**ol-width (/WGC). Change the default value 9 on the input line to 15 and press the Enter key.
2. Move the cell cursor to D1 and enter the command /**W**orksheet **C**ol-width **S**et (/WCS) to change the width of column D to 16 characters. Press the Right Arrow key to change the value 15 on the input line to 16. Press the Enter key.

With the column widths set, enter the worksheet title, date, the six cell titles and the five data items in the range A1..E7 (see Figure 4-12). Assign cell E1 the TODAY function, rather than the NOW function. The TODAY function returns the same value as the NOW function, except that it truncates the decimal portion and returns a whole number.

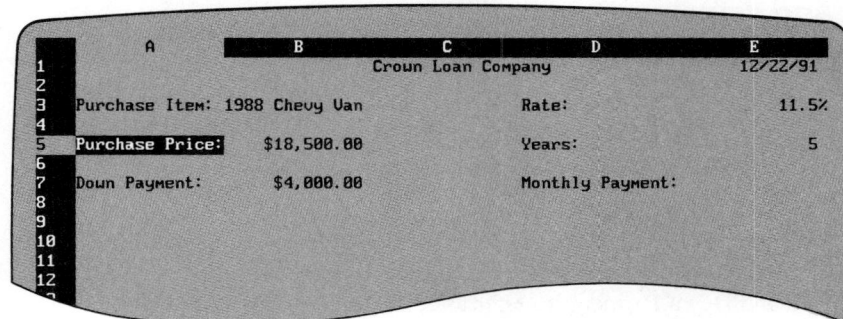

FIGURE 4-12
Labels and data entered into the Crown Loan Company worksheet.

Use the command /**R**ange **F**ormat (/RF) to change the format of the cells assigned numeric data in the range A1..E7 as follows:

1. Cell E1 to the M/D/Y type.
2. Cells B5, B7, and E7 to the Crncy type with two decimal positions.
3. Cell E3 to the Percent type with one decimal position.

The formatted worksheet with the cell cursor at A5 is shown in Figure 4-12.

Assigning a Label Name to an Adjacent Cell (/RNL)

In Project 4A we used the command /**R**ange **N**ame **C**reate (/RNC) to assign the name TEST1 to the range B6..B16. Later, when we built the summary lines, we used the name TEST1 several times in functions to reference the range B6..B16 because the name TEST1 is easier to remember than the range B6..B16. Another advantage of using range names is that they make it easier to remember what the range represents in the worksheet. This is especially helpful when working with complex formulas or functions.

The function for determining the monthly payment in cell E7 uses the purchase price (B5), down payment (B7), rate (E3), and years (E5). Let's name each of these cells. In this case, we'll use a second technique for assigning names to the individual cells. Rather than typing in a new name for each cell, use the adjacent cell title—the label located immediately to the left of each cell you want to name. For example, use the label Purchase Price: in cell A5 to name cell B5.

With the cell cursor at A5, enter the command /**R**ange **N**ame **L**abel (/RNL). This is shown in Figure 4-13. By entering the command Label, we instruct VP-Planner Plus to use a label in the worksheet as the name, rather than to create a new name. With the command cursor active in the **Range Name Label** menu, type the letter R for Right. Note that this command allows us to assign any adjacent cell to the label name. Typing the letter R tells VP-Planner Plus that we want to assign the cell to the right of the label name.

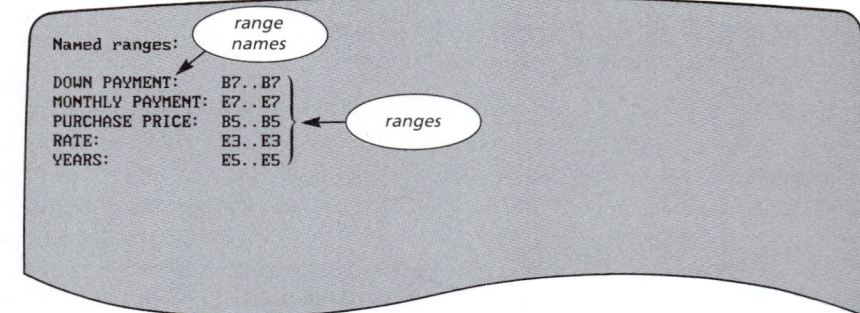

FIGURE 4-13
Display after entering the command /Range Name Label (/RNL).

Next, VP-Planner Plus requests that we enter the range containing the labels that we wish to assign to the cells to the right. Use the Down Arrow key to select the range A5..A7. Press the Enter key. We can now use the name Purchase Price: to refer to cell B5 and Down Payment: to refer to cell B7.

Name cells E3, E5, and E7 in a similar fashion. Move the cell cursor to D3. Enter the command /**R**ange **N**ame **L**abel (/RNL). Type the letter R for Right, select the range D3..D7, and press the Enter key. We can now use Rate: to refer to cell E3, Years: to refer to cell E5, and Monthly Payment: to refer to cell E7.

To verify that the names have been assigned properly, enter the command /**R**ange **N**ame **S**how (/RNS). This command lists all the range names and their corresponding ranges, as shown in Figure 4-14. To return to the worksheet, press any key.

```
                                  range
            Named ranges:         names

            DOWN PAYMENT:    B7..B7
            MONTHLY PAYMENT: E7..E7
            PURCHASE PRICE:  B5..B5        ranges
            RATE:            E3..E3
            YEARS:           E5..E5
```

FIGURE 4-14
Display of the range names and corresponding ranges after entering the command /Range Name Show (/RNS).

Two points to remember about the /RNL command: first, if a label in a cell is subsequently changed, the old label remains the name of the range; and second, only the first 16 characters of the label can be used as the name.

Determining the Loan Payment—PMT

VP-Planner Plus has several financial functions that save you from writing out long complicated formulas. One of the most important of these is the PMT function. This function determines the payment of a loan on the basis of the amount of the loan (principal), the interest rate (interest), and the length of time required to pay the loan back (term). If the term is in months, the PMT function returns the monthly payment. The PMT function is written in the following form:

@PMT(principal,interest,term)

To display the monthly payment of the car loan in cell E7, move the cell cursor to E7 and enter the following function:

@PMT($Purchase Price:–$Down Payment:,$Rate:/12,$Years:*12)

The first argument ($Purchase Price:–$Down Payment:) is the principal. The second argument ($Rate:/12) is the interest rate charged by the Crown Loan Company compounded monthly. The third argument ($Years:*12) is the number of months required to pay back the loan. As illustrated in cell E7 of Figure 4-15, it will cost $318.89 per month for 5 years to purchase the 1988 Chevy Van with a sticker price of $18,500.00, down payment of $4,000.00, at an annual interest rate of 11.5%.

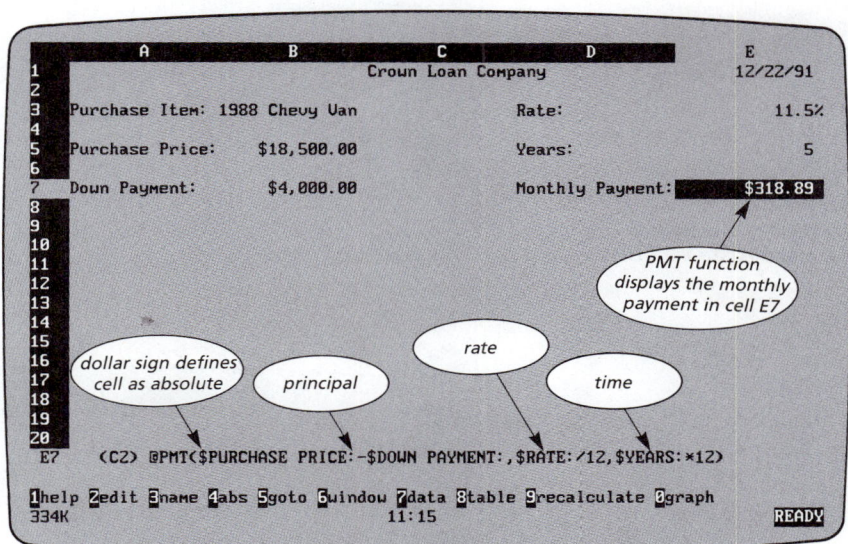

FIGURE 4-15
The PMT function entered into cell E7.

Note that we preceded all the names in the function arguments with a dollar sign ($). This is necessary because the function will be copied to another part of the worksheet later, and we want the cell references to remain the same.

Remember, VP-Planner Plus automatically recalculates all functions and formulas in a worksheet when a number is changed. If we change the purchase price, the amount of the down payment, the interest rate, the number of years, or any combination of these, VP-Planner Plus immediately adjusts the monthly payment displayed in cell E7.

The Data Fill Feature (/DF)

The next step is to add the amortization table in cells A8..E16 (see Figure 4-2). Enter the double underline in row 8, the column headings in rows 9 and 10, and the single underline in row 11.

In the range A12..A16, the series of numbers 1 though 5 represent the years. We can enter these numbers one at a time or we can use the Data Fill command. The Data Fill command allows us to quickly enter a series of numbers into a range using a specified increment or decrement. In this case, we want to enter a series of numbers in the range A12..A16 that begins with 1, increments by 1, and ends with 5.

With the cell cursor at A12, enter the command /**D**ata **F**ill (/DF). In response to the prompt message "Enter data fill range: A12" on the input line, press the Period key to anchor the first end point, A12. Use the Down Arrow key to move the cell cursor to the second end point (A16) and press the Enter key. Next, VP-Planner Plus requests that we enter the start, increment, and stop values. In response to the prompt messages on the input line, enter a start value of 1, an increment value of 1, and a stop value of 9999. The length of the range (five cells) will terminate the Data Fill command before it reaches the stop value 9999. The three entries are shown on the input line in Figure 4-16. Press the Enter key and the range A12..A16 is filled with the series of numbers 1 through 5. This is shown in Figure 4-17.

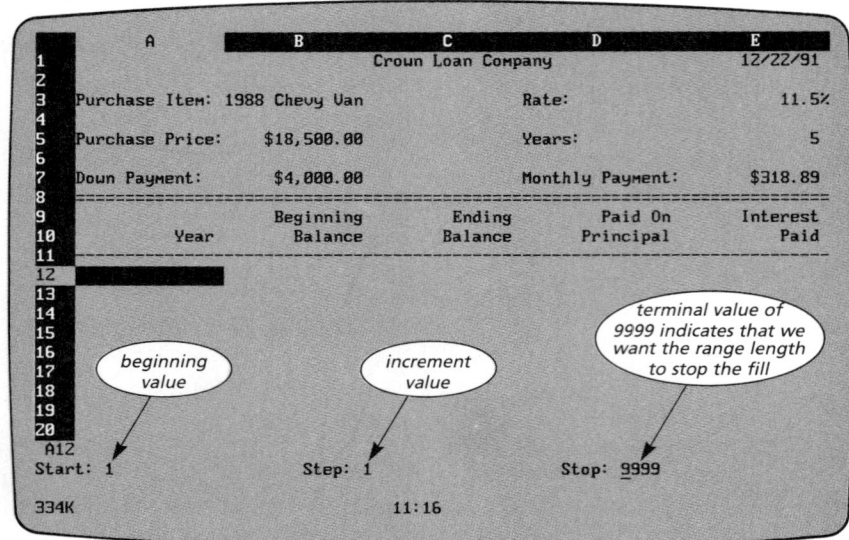

FIGURE 4-16
The display due to entering the command /**D**ata **F**ill (/DF).

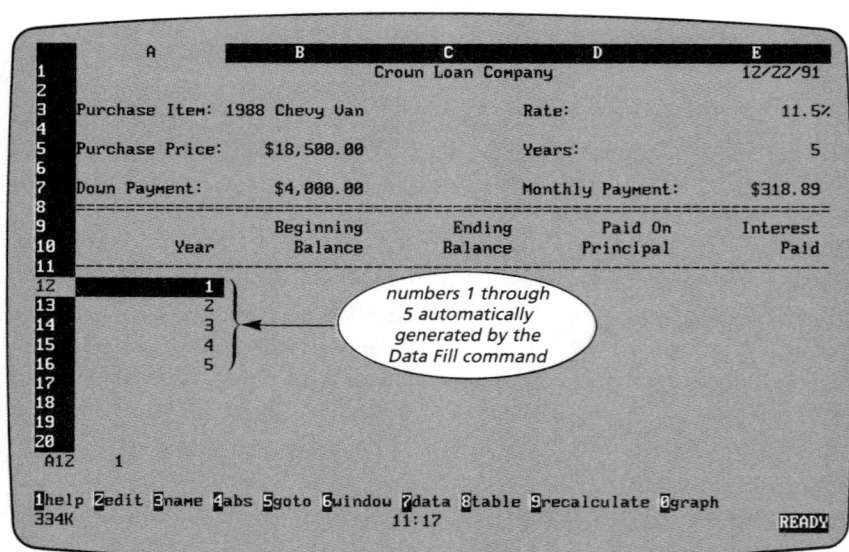

FIGURE 4-17
The display after using the Data Fill command.

Move the cell cursor to B12 and enter the beginning balance for year 1. This value is equal to the amount of the loan—+ Purchase Price:−Down Payment: or (+B5–B7).

Before we enter any more values in the amortization table, format cells B12 through E20 to the Comma (,) type with two decimal positions. The Comma (,) type with two decimal positions displays the numbers in the form of dollar and cents. Although labels will be part of the range (B12..E20), recall that a numeric format is only used if a numeric value is stored in the cell. Enter the command **/R**ange **F**ormat **,** (/RF,). Press the Enter key to select two decimal positions. Enter the range B12..E20 and press the Enter key.

Determining the Yearly Ending Balance—PV

Another important financial function is the PV function. This function returns the present value of an annuity. An **annuity** is a series of fixed payments made at the end of each of a fixed number of terms at a fixed interest rate. This function can be used to determine how much the borrower of the car loan still owes at the end of each year (C12..C16).

The general form of the PV function is:

@PV(payment,interest,term)

Use this function to determine the ending balance after the first year (C12) by using a term equal to the number of months the borrower must still make payments. For example, if the loan is for five years (60 months, therefore 60 payments), as it is in Figure 4-18, then the borrower still owes 48 payments after the first year. After the second year, the number of payments remaining is 36, and so on.

The entry for cell C12 that determines the ending balance reads as follows:

@PV($Monthly Payment:, $RATE:/12, 12*($YEARS:–A12))

The first argument, $Monthly Payment:, refers to cell E7, the monthly payment. The second argument, $RATE:/12, refers to the interest rate in cell E5. The third argument, 12*($YEARS:–A12), indicates the number of monthly payments that still must be made—48 after the first year. Note that each name in the three arguments of the PV function for cell C12 is preceded by a dollar sign ($). This tells VP-Planner Plus to treat these cell references as absolute. That is, when we copy the PV function in cell C12 to cells C13 through C16, the cell references in the arguments will not be adjusted.

Making Decisions—The IF Function

If we assign the PV function just described to cell C12 and copy it to cells C13 through C16, the ending balances for each year of a five-year loan will display properly as illustrated in Figure 4-2. If the loan is for a period of time less than five years, the ending balances displayed for the years beyond the time the loan is due are invalid. For example, if a loan is taken out for three years, the ending balance for years four and five in the amortization table should be zero. However, the PV function will display negative values even though the loan has already been paid off.

What we need here is a way to assign the PV function to the range C12..C16 as long as the corresponding year in the range A12..A16 is less than or equal to the number of years in cell E5, which contains the number of years of the loan. If the corresponding year in column A is greater than the number of years in cell E5, we need to assign C12 through C16 the value zero. VP-Planner Plus has a function that can handle this type of decision making. It is called the IF function.

The IF function is useful when the value you want assigned to a cell is dependent on a condition. A **condition** is made up of two expressions and a relation. Each **expression** may be a cell, a function, or a formula.

The general form of the IF function is:

@IF(condition,true,false)

The argument **true** is the value you want to assign to the cell when the condition is true. The argument **false** is the value you want to assign to the cell when the condition is false. For example, assume the IF function @IF(A1 = A2,C3 + D4,C3-D4) is assigned to cell B12. If the value assigned to A1 is equal to the value assigned to A2, then the sum of the values in C3 and D4 is assigned to B12. If the value assigned to A1 does not equal the value assigned to A2, then B12 is assigned the difference between the values in C3 and D4.

Valid relations and examples of their use in IF functions are shown in Table 4-3.

TABLE 4-3 Valid Relational Operators and Their Use in Conditions

RELATIONAL OPERATOR	MEANING	EXAMPLE
=	Equal to	@IF(A5 = B7,A22–A3,G5^E3)
<	Less than	@IF(E12/D5 < 6,A15,B13–5)
>	Greater than	@IF(@SUM(A1..A5) > 100,1,0)
< =	Less than or equal to	@IF(A12 < = $YEARS,A4÷D5,1)
> =	Greater than or equal to	@IF(@NOW > = 30000,H15,J12)
< >	Not equal to	@IF(5 < >F6,''Valid'',''Invalid'')

Logical operators like NOT, AND, and OR may also be used to write a **compound condition**—two or more conditions in the same IF function. A summary of the logical operators is given in Table 4-4.

TABLE 4-4 Valid Logical Operators and Their Use in Conditions

LOGICAL OPERATOR	MEANING	EXAMPLE
#NOT#	The compound condition is true if, and only if, the simple condition is false.	@IF(#NOT#($A$2 = A6),2,4)
#AND#	The compound condition is true if, and only if, both simple conditions are true.	@IF($J6 = R$4#AND#G5–S2 > D2, D4÷D6,T3/D2)
#OR#	The compound condition is true if, and only if, either simple condition is true, or both simple conditions are true.	@IF(A1 > $PRINCIPAL#OR#B7 = E4, ''Contact'',''OK'')

By using the IF function, we can assign the PV function or zero as the ending balance to cells C12 through C16. Enter the following IF function in cell C12:

@IF(A12 < = $Years:,@PV($Monthly Payment:,$Rate:/12,12÷($Years:–A12)),0)

If the condition A12 < = $Years: is true, then C12 is assigned the PV function. If the condition is false, then C12 is assigned the value zero. Use the command /Copy (/C) to copy cell C12 to the range C13..C16. The results of this copy are shown in Figure 4-18.

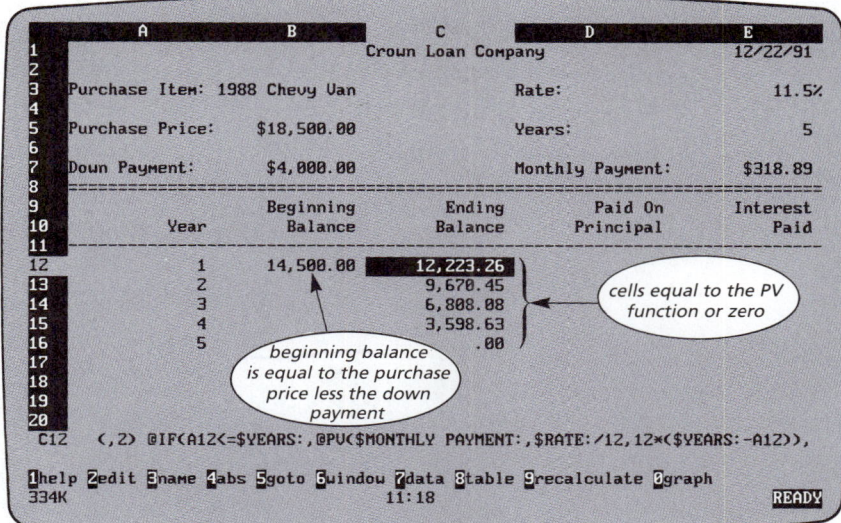

FIGURE 4-18
The IF function entered into cell
A12 and copied to the range
C13..C16.

Let's go back now and complete the entries in the beginning balance column, cells B13 through B16. The beginning balance in B13 is equal to the ending balance in cell C12. Therefore, enter +C12 in cell B13 and copy this cell to B14 through B16. The beginning balance for each year in cells A12 through A16 displays as shown in Figure 4-19.

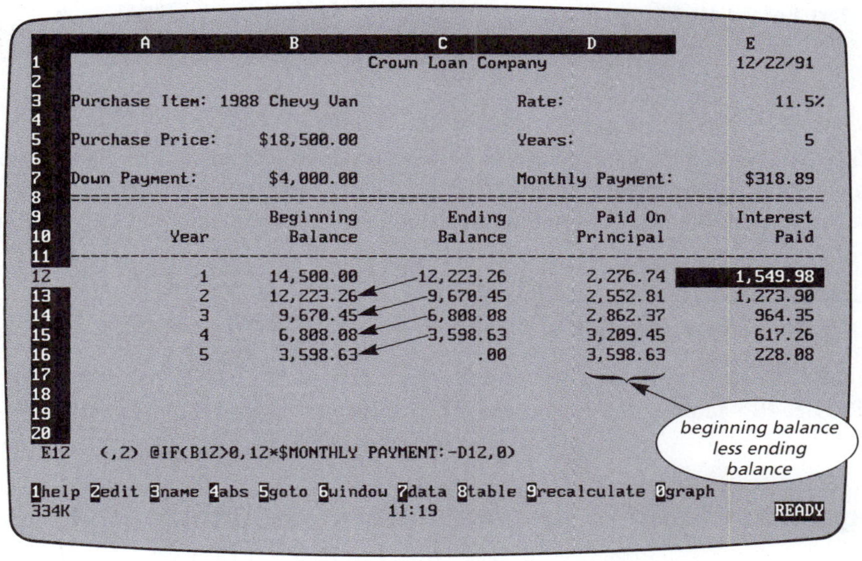

FIGURE 4-19
The amortization table filled in.

The total amount paid on the principal each year in column D is determined by subtracting the ending balance from the beginning balance. Enter the formula +B12–C12 in cell D12. Copy cell D12 to cells D13 through D16. This is shown in Figure 4-19.

The total amount of interest paid each year by the lender to the borrower in column E is equal to 12 times the monthly payment in cell E7 less the amount paid on the principal. Here again, use the IF function because the loan may be for less than five years. Interest is paid in any year in which the beginning balance is greater than zero. Therefore, in cell E12, enter the IF function @IF(B12>0,12*$Monthly Payment:–D12,0). Copy cell E12 to cells E13 through E16. The interest paid each year for a loan of $14,500.00 at 11.5% for 5 years is shown in column E of the worksheet in Figure 4-19.

To complete the amortization table, add the single underline in row 17 and the labels that identify the totals in cells C18 through C20. In cell D18, enter the SUM function @SUM(D12..D16). Note that this agrees with the original amount of the loan, $14,500.00. In cell E18, enter the SUM function @SUM(E12..E16). Cell E18 displays the total interest paid for the loan, $4,633.57. In cell E19, enter the name +Down Payment:. Cell E19 displays $4,000.00, the amount in cell B7. Finally, in cell E20, enter the formula +D18+E18+E19. Cell E20 displays the total amount paid for the 1988 Chevy Van. This is shown in Figure 4-20.

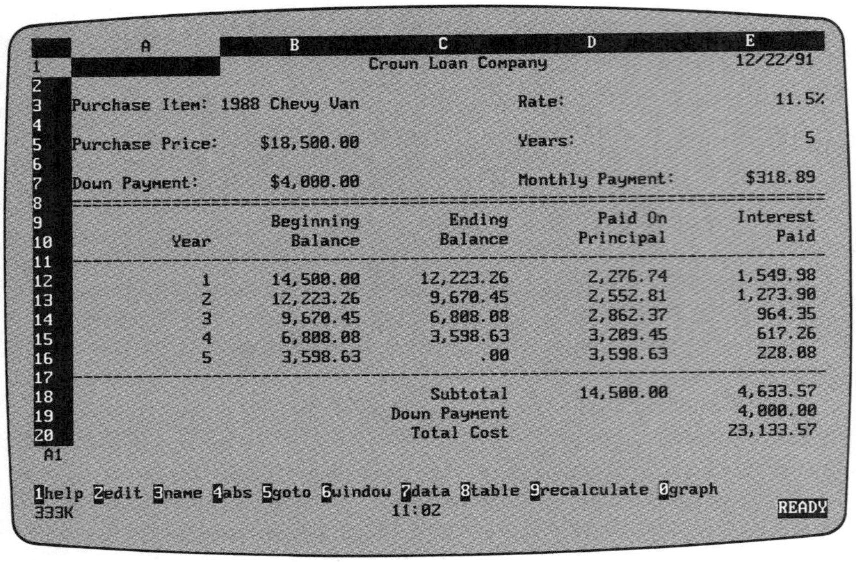

	A	B	C	D	E
1			Crown Loan Company		12/22/91
2					
3	Purchase Item:	1988 Chevy Van		Rate:	11.5%
4					
5	Purchase Price:	$18,500.00		Years:	5
6					
7	Down Payment:	$4,000.00		Monthly Payment:	$318.89
8	==========	==========	==========	==========	==========
9		Beginning	Ending	Paid On	Interest
10	Year	Balance	Balance	Principal	Paid
11	----------	----------	----------	----------	----------
12	1	14,500.00	12,223.26	2,276.74	1,549.98
13	2	12,223.26	9,670.45	2,552.81	1,273.90
14	3	9,670.45	6,808.08	2,862.37	964.35
15	4	6,808.08	3,598.63	3,209.45	617.26
16	5	3,598.63	.00	3,598.63	228.08
17	----------	----------	----------	----------	----------
18			Subtotal	14,500.00	4,633.57
19			Down Payment		4,000.00
20			Total Cost		23,133.57

A1

1help 2edit 3name 4abs 5goto 6window 7data 8table 9recalculate 0graph
333K 11:02 READY

FIGURE 4-20
Part 1 of Project 4B complete.

With the amortization table complete, try various combinations of loan data to evaluate the what-if capabilities of VP-Planner Plus. If you change the purchase price (B5), down payment (B7), interest rate (E3), time (E5) or any combination of these values, VP-Planner Plus will immediately change the monthly payment and the numbers in the amortization table.

Saving the Worksheet

Before we continue with Project 4B, save the worksheet as PROJS-4B. Enter the command /File Save (/FS). Enter the file name PROJS-4B and press the Enter key. The worksheet is saved on the default drive.

Using a Data Table to Answer What-If Questions (/DT)

The next step is to build the data table at the right-hand side of the amortization table (see Figure 4-3). As described earlier, a data table has one purpose—it organizes the answers to what-if questions into a table. We have already seen that if a value is changed in a cell referenced elsewhere in a formula, VP-Planner Plus immediately recalculates and stores the new value in the cell assigned the formula. You may want to compare the results of the formula for several different values, but it would be unwieldy to write down or remember all the answers to the what-if questions. This is where a data table comes in handy.

Data tables are built in an unused area of the worksheet. You may vary one or two values and display the results of the specified formulas in table form. Figure 4-21 illustrates the makeup of a data table.

In Project 4B, the data table shows the impact of changing interest rates on the monthly payment and the total cost of the loan. The interest rates range from 8.5% to 15% in increments of 0.5%. Therefore, in this data table we are varying one value, the interest rate (E3). We are interested in its impact on two formulas: the monthly payment (E7) and the total cost (E20).

(a) data table with one value varying

THIS CELL MUST BE EMPTY	FORMULA-1 FORMULA-2 . . . FORMULA-k
Value-1	
Value-2	
Value-3	
Value-4	VP-Planner Plus places results of formulas here on the basis of the values in the left-hand column.
⏐	
Value-n	

(b) data table with two values varying

ASSIGN FORMULA TO THIS CELL	VALUE-2a VALUE-2b . . . VALUE-2k
Value-1a	
Value-1b	
Value-1c	
Value-1d	VP-Planner Plus places results of the formula in the upper left corner cell here on the basis of the two corresponding values.
⏐	
Value-1n	

FIGURE 4-21
General forms of a data table with one value varying (a) and two values varying (b).

To construct the data table, enter the headings in the range F1..H5 as described in Figure 4-3. Next, move the cell cursor to F7 and use the command **/D**ata **F**ill (/DF) to enter the varying interest rates. Select the range F7..F20. Use a start value of 8.5%, an increment value of 0.5%, and a stop value of 9999. After pressing the Enter key, the range F7..F20 contains the varying interest rates. Format the interest rates to the Percent type with one decimal position (see Figure 4-22).

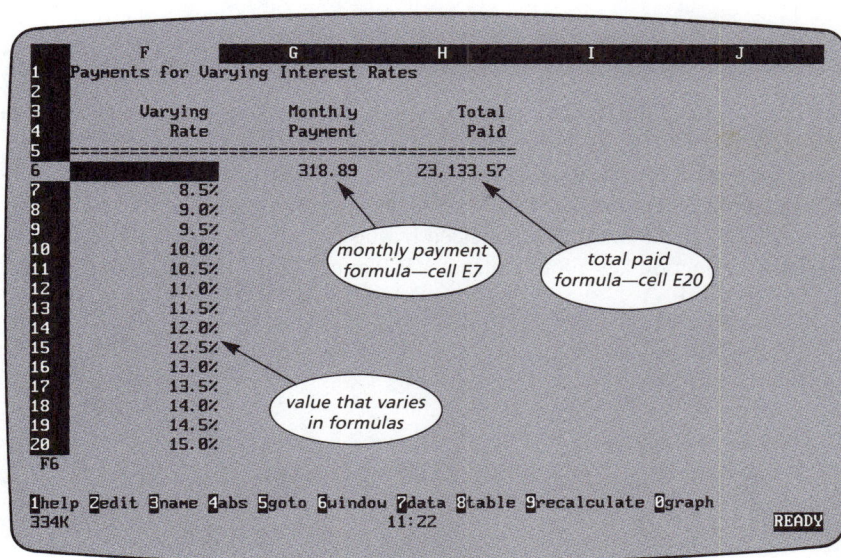

FIGURE 4-22
Monthly payment formula, total paid formula, and varying interest rates entered into the worksheet in preparation for applying a data table in the range F6..H20.

In cell G6 enter +E7, the cell with the monthly payment formula. In cell H6 enter +E20, the cell with the total cost of the loan formula. Format the range G6..H20 to the Comma (,) type with two decimal positions. Move the cell cursor to F6. The range F1..H20 of the worksheet is shown in Figure 4-22.

To define the data table, enter the command /**D**ata Table **1**-variable (/DT1). VP-Planner Plus responds by displaying the prompt message "Enter data table range: F6" on the input line. Press the Period key to anchor F6 as one of the end points. Use the arrow keys to move the cell cursor to H20 and press the Enter key. (Note that the data table itself does not include the headings above F6.) VP-Planner Plus responds with the prompt message "Enter input cell: F6" on the input line. The **input cell** is defined as the cell in the worksheet that contains the value we want to vary. For this data table, we want to vary the interest rate in cell E3 (also called Rate:). Therefore, enter the name Rate: in response to the prompt message on the input line and press the Enter key.

The data table, in the range F6..H20, immediately fills with monthly payments and total loan costs for the corresponding varying interest rates, as shown in Figure 4-23. Look over the table. Note how it allows you to compare the monthly payments and total loan costs for different interest rates. For example, at 10%, the monthly payment on the loan of $14,500.00 for 5 years is $308.08. At 10.5%, the monthly payment is $311.66 for the same loan. The two numbers at the top of the table, in cells G6 and H6, are the same as the monthly payment and total cost displayed in cells E7 and E20.

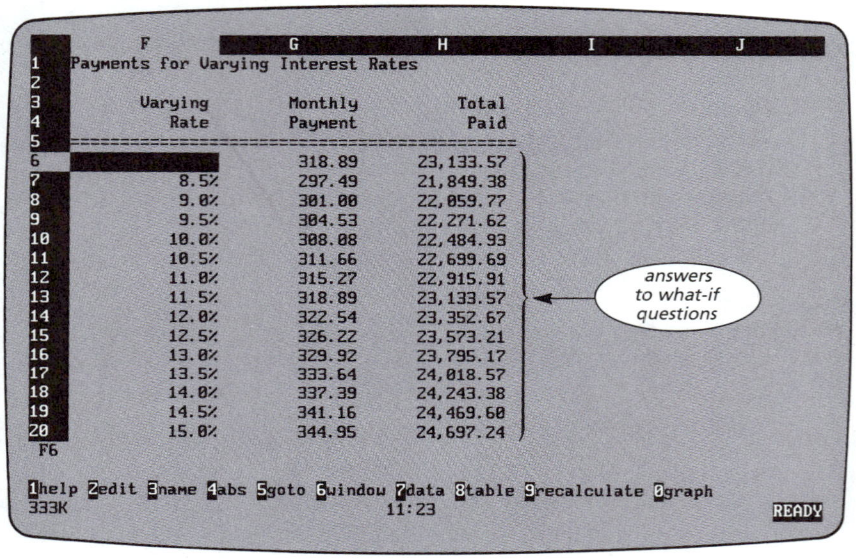

FIGURE 4-23
Data table in the range F6..H20 filled with answers to what-if questions regarding varying interest rates.

Here are some important points to remember about data tables:

1. You can have only one active data table in a worksheet. If you want to move or establish a new data table, use the command /**Data Table Res**et (/DTR) to deactivate the current data table.
2. For a data table with one varying value, the cell in the upper left corner of the table (F6) must be empty. With two values varying, assign the formula you want to analyze to the upper left corner cell of the table (see Figure 4-21).
3. If you change any value in a cell referenced by the formula that is part of the data table but does not vary in the data table, you must press function key F8 to instruct VP-Planner Plus to recalculate the data table values.

MACROS

A **macro** is a series of keystrokes entered into a cell or a range of cells. The macro is assigned a name using the command /**R**ange **N**ame **C**reate (/RNC). Later, when you enter the macro name, the keystrokes stored in the cell or range of cells execute one after another, as if you entered each keystroke manually at the keyboard. A macro can be as simple as the series of keystrokes required to save a worksheet or as complex as a sophisticated computer program.

Whether simple or complex, macros save time and help remove the drudgery associated with building and using a worksheet. You should consider using a macro when you find yourself typing the same keystrokes over and over again; when the series of keystrokes required is difficult to remember; or if you want to automate the use of the worksheet.

Designing a Simple Macro

In Project 2, we suggested that you save your worksheet every 50 to 75 keystrokes. If you follow this suggestion, you will be entering the series of keystrokes shown in Table 4-5 often. This is an excellent example of how a macro can save you time and effort.

TABLE 4-5   Series of Keystrokes for Saving a Worksheet Under the Same File Name

KEYSTROKE	PURPOSE
/	Switch VP-Planner Plus to command mode.
F	Select File command.
S	Select Save command.
←	Save worksheet under the same file name.
R	Replace the worksheet on disk.

One of the keystrokes in Table 4-5 is the Enter key(←). In a macro, we use the **tilde character** (˜) to represent the Enter key. Therefore, /FS˜R represents the series of keystrokes in Table 4-5.

After determining the makeup of the macro, the next step is to move the cell cursor to a cell in an unused area of the worksheet. According to Figure 4-4, the macros for this project are to be placed below the amortization table. Hence, use the GOTO command and move the cell cursor to A22.

Documenting Macros

We recommend that all macros be documented, even the simple ones. *Documenting* a macro means writing a comment off to the side of the cell or range containing the macro. The comment explains the purpose of the macro, and if it is complex, how it works. To document this macro, as well as the other macros in this worksheet, first enter the macro title and column headings in cells A22 through E25 (see Figure 4-4).

Entering and Naming a Macro

Move the cell cursor to A26 and enter the macro '/FS˜R. It is important that you begin the macro with an apostrophe (') or one of the other characters that defines the entry as a label (^, "). If you don't begin the macro with an apostrophe, VP-Planner Plus immediately switches to the command mode because the Slash key (/) is the first character entered.

With the macro assigned to A26, enter the command /**R**ange **N**ame **C**reate (/RNC) and assign the name \S to cell A26. A macro name must consist of two characters. The first character is the **backslash** (\). The second character is a letter. Choose the letter S for the name of the macro because it **S**aves the worksheet.

Complete the documentation in cells C26 and D26. Figure 4-24 illustrates the \S macro in cell A26 and the corresponding documentation.

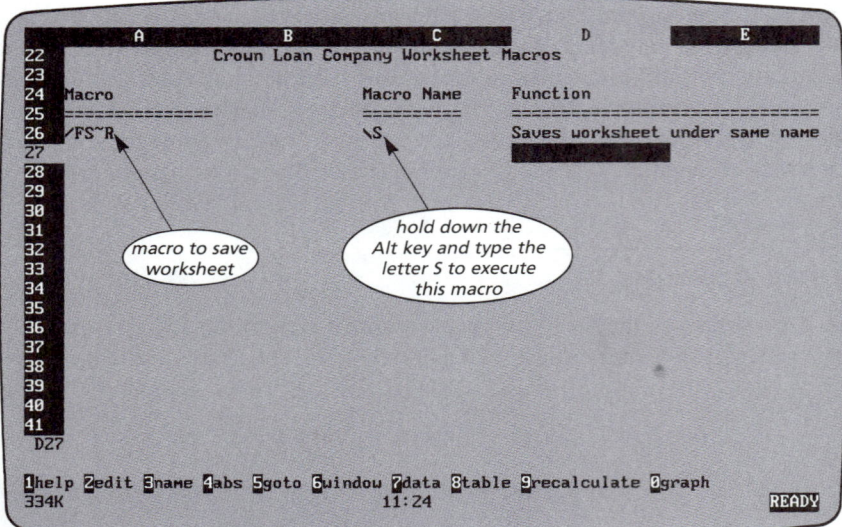

FIGURE 4-24
The macro \S entered into cell A26 and documented in cells C26 and D26.

Invoking a Macro

After entering the macro '/FS~R in cell A26 and naming it \S, execute it by holding down the Alt key and pressing the letter S. VP-Planner Plus automatically executes the series of keystrokes in cell A26 and saves the worksheet. Note that the \S macro is part of the worksheet that is saved. Hence, the macro will be available the next time we load the worksheet into main computer memory.

Adding More Macros to the Worksheet

When VP-Planner Plus executes a macro, it starts at the specified cell. After executing the keystrokes in this cell, it inspects the adjacent cells. First it checks the cell below, then the cell to the right. If they are empty, the macro terminates. If they are not empty, VP-Planner Plus considers the nonempty cell to be part of the macro and executes its contents. Hence, VP-Planner Plus is finished executing a macro when the cells below and to the right are empty. It is for this reason that when you add additional macros to a worksheet, make sure that there is at least one empty cell between each macro.

With this rule in mind, enter the macro /PPAGEEQ in cell A28 and /PPOOCQAGOOAQEEQ in cell A30. Also enter the corresponding documentation in cells C28 through D30. This is shown in Figure 4-25. Use the command /**R**ange Name Create (/RNC) and assign the names \P to cell A28 and \C to cell A30.

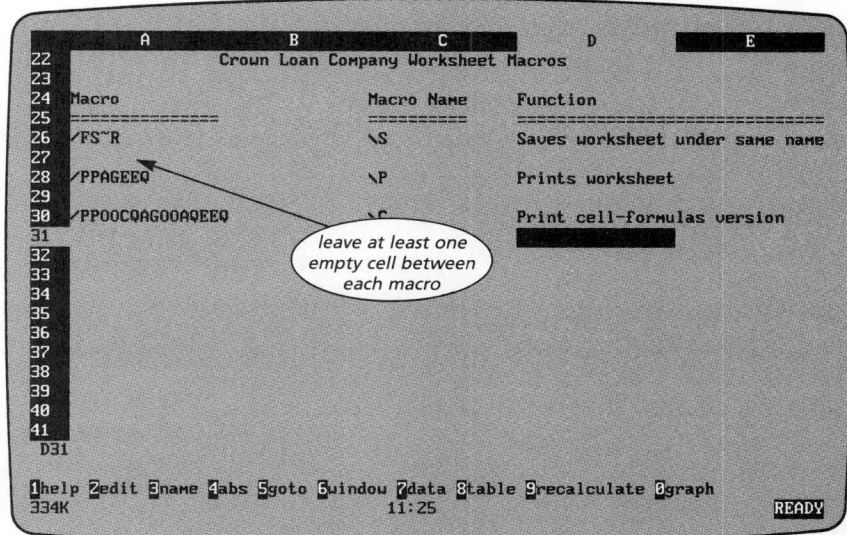

FIGURE 4-25
The macros \P and \C entered into cells A28 and A30 and documented in the range C28..D30.

The \P macro in cell A28 prints the worksheet on the basis of the previous printer range setting. It also ejects the paper in the printer and quits the Print command. Build a print macro like this one when you expect to print the worksheet often.

To prepare to execute the \P macro, use the /**P**rint **P**rinter **R**ange (/PPR) command to set the range to A1..E20. After pressing the Enter key, press the O key for Printer Options to check the text width. Since the text width is 76, adjust the margins so that the width of the range (A1..E20) fits across the page. With the Printer Options menu on the screen, type ML2 and press the Enter key. Next, type MR78 and press the Enter key. Finally, type the letter Q twice, once to quit the Printer Options menu and once to quit the Print menu. Invoke the \S macro again to save the print range permanently.

Now, imagine you are the loan officer for the Crown Loan Company. A customer comes in and requests information on the 1988 Chevy Van we discussed earlier. With the monthly payment and the amortization table on the screen, you can print a copy of the loan information and pass it to the customer. First, make sure the printer is ready. Next, hold down the Alt key and press the letter P. The monthly payment and amortization table shown in Figure 4-20 print on the printer.

The \C macro in cell A30 prints the cell-formulas version of the worksheet according to the previously defined printer range. After printing the as-is version of the range A1..E20, hold down the Alt key and press the C key. This invokes the \C macro. Note that after the printer is done printing the cell-formulas version, the macro resets the print setting to the as-is version.

Guarding Against Macro Catastrophes

Take care when applying macros to a worksheet. If you enter the wrong letter, forget the tilde (˜) when required, place macros in adjacent cells, or transpose characters in a macro, serious damage in the form of lost data can occur. For this reason we recommend you save the worksheet before executing a macro for the first time.

You should also use the **STEP mode** of VP-Planner Plus to test the macro. The STEP mode allows you to watch VP-Planner Plus execute the macro keystroke by keystroke just as if you entered the keystrokes one at a time at the keyboard. Let's execute the \S macro again using the STEP mode. To place VP-Planner Plus in STEP mode, hold down the Alt key and press function key F1. Next, invoke the \S macro by holding down the Alt key and pressing the S key. Now press any key on the keyboard to execute the next keystroke in the macro. When you press any key, a counter displays next to the word STEP at the bottom of the screen on the current-mode line. This counter indicates the number of keystrokes executed thus far in the macro.

If you encounter an error while in STEP mode, you could terminate the macro by holding down the Ctrl key and pressing the Break key. This combination of keys terminates the macro immediately. You may then edit the macro and execute it once again using STEP mode. Continue in this fashion until the macro is doing exactly what you intend it to do. To quit the STEP mode, hold down the Alt key and press function key F1. This process of finding and correcting errors in a macro is called **debugging**.

/X Macro Commands and Macro Words

The final step in Project 4B is to enter the macro that extends from cell A33 through A46. Before entering this macro, we need to discuss macro commands and macro words. **Macro commands** are used to write programs that can guide you or another user of the worksheet through complex tasks, like accepting data into various cells. Some of the macro commands are listed in Table 4-6. For a complete list of the macro commands, press function key F1 and go to screen 142 of the online help facility. After reading or printing the screen, press the Esc key to return to the worksheet.

TABLE 4-6   Macro Commands

COMMAND	EXAMPLE	EXPLANATION
/XC	/XCBONUS˜	Executes the macro beginning at the cell named BONUS. Saves the return cell address—the one below the cell containing /XCBONUS˜. The return cell address is used by the /XR command.
/XG	/XGB10˜	Executes the macro beginning at a specified cell.
/XI	/XIB10< =40˜/XCREG˜	Executes the macro at the cell named REG if B10 contains a value less than or equal to 40; otherwise it executes the macro in the cell below.
/XL	/XLPurchase Item:˜B3˜	Displays a prompt message on the input line, accepts a label, and assigns it to cell B3.
/XN	/XNPurchase Price:˜B5˜	Displays a prompt message on the input line, accepts a number, and assigns it to cell B5.
/XQ	/XQ	Ends the execution of a macro.
/XR	/XR	Returns control to the cell below the corresponding /XC.

Macro words are used to handle special circumstances in a macro, like moving the cell cursor from one cell to another. Except for the tilde (˜), which represents the Enter key, all macro words are enclosed in curly braces { }. The important macro words are listed in Table 4-7. For a complete list of the macro words, load VP-Planner Plus, press function key F1, and go to screens 143 through 145. After reading or printing the screens, press the Esc key to return to the worksheet.

TABLE 4-7   Macro Words That Represent Special Keys on the Keyboard

CATEGORY	MACRO WORD
Cursor movement	{UP} {DOWN} {RIGHT} {LEFT} {PGUP} {PGDN} {HOME} {END} {BACKSPACE} {DEL} {ESC} {INS} {TAB}
Function keys	{EDIT} {NAME} {ABS} {GOTO} {WINDOW} {QUERY} {TABLE} {CALC} {GRAPH}
Enter key	˜
Interaction	{?}

The cursor movement macro words in Table 4-7 move the cursor, as if you pressed the key named within the curly braces. The function key macro words operate the same as pressing one of the function keys, as specified at the bottom of the screen on the prompt line. The macro word {?} makes the macro pause and wait for keyboard input from the user. For example, the macro /FR{?}˜ may be used to retrieve a worksheet from disk. The macro word {?} following /FR tells the macro to pause and wait for the user to select a file name. When you press the Enter key after entering the file name, the macro resumes execution and accepts the name entered on the input line.

Interactive Macros

The macro defined in cells A33 through A46 in Figure 4-4 automates the entry of the loan data in cells B3, B5, B7, E3, and E5 in Figure 4-2. The instructions in cells A34 through A39 clear the cells that contain the loan data. The instructions in cells A40 through A44 prompts the user to enter the loan data. Each /XL and /XN command displays a prompt message and halts the execution of the macro until the user responds by entering a value on the input line. /XQ in cell A46 terminates the macro.

Enter the macro and documentation in the range A33..D46 as shown in Figure 4-4. Use the command /Range Name Create (/RNC) and assign cell A33 the macro name \D. Note that it is not necessary to assign the range A33..A46 to the macro name \D, since a macro executes downward until it comes across an empty cell. Invoke the \D macro and reenter the loan data for the 1988 Chevy Van shown in Figure 4-20. In a step-by-step fashion, Table 4-8 explains how the \D macro works. Use Table 4-8 to step through the macro activity when you execute it.

TABLE 4-8   Step-by-Step Explanation of the \D Macro in the Range A33..A46

STEP	CELL	ENTRY	FUNCTION
1	A33	{HOME}	Move the cell cursor to A1.
2	A34	{GOTO}B3~/RE~	Move the cell cursor to B3 and erase the contents.
3	A35	{DOWN}{DOWN}/RE~	Move the cell cursor to B5 and erase the contents.
4	A36	{DOWN}{DOWN}/RE~	Move the cell cursor to B7 and erase the contents.
5	A37	{GOTO}E3~/RE~	Move the cell cursor to E3 and erase the contents.
6	A38	{DOWN}{DOWN}/RE~	Move the cell cursor to E5 and erase the contents.
7	A39	{HOME}	Move the cell cursor to A1.
8	A40	/XLPurchase Item:~B3~	Accept the purchase item (1988 Chevy Van) and assign it to cell B3.
9	A41	/XNPurchase Price:~B5~	Accept the purchase price (18500) and assign it to cell B5.
10	A42	/XNDown Payment :~B7~	Accept the down payment (4000) and assign it to cell B7.
11	A43	/XNInterest Rate in %:~E3~	Accept the interest rate (11.5) and assign it to cell E3.
12	A44	/XNTime in Years:~E5~	Accept the time (5) and assign it to cell E5.
13	A45	{HOME}	Move the cell cursor to A1.
14	A46	/XQ	Quit the macro.

WINDOWS (/WW)

When you have a large worksheet like the one in Project 4B, it is helpful to view two or more parts of the worksheet at one time. VP-Planner Plus lets you divide the screen into two to six windows. For example, by dividing the screen into two windows, you can view the \D macro in cells A33..A46 and the cells (A1..E7) that are affected by this macro at the same time.

To show multiple windows, press the Home key and use the arrow keys to move the cell cursor to A8. Enter the command /Worksheet Window Horizontal (/WWH). The rows above row 8 display in the top window and rows 8 through 19 display in the lower window.

Immediately after a window split, the cell cursor is active in the window above or to the right of the split. You can move the cell cursor from window to window by pressing function key F6. Press function key F6 and use the PgDn and Down Arrow keys to move the cell cursor to A44. As shown in Figure 4-26, the top window shows the cells that are modified by the \D macro located in the lower window.

Press function key F6 to move the cell cursor to the top window. Execute the \D macro a second time. Step through the macro in the lower window and watch the cells change in the top window.

It is important to understand that the entire worksheet is available through any window. If you make a change to a cell in one window, the change will show up in any other window.

Figure 4-27 shows the screen divided into three windows. Each window contains one of the three parts of Project 4B. The third window was added by moving the cell cursor in the lower window to C33 and entering the command /**W**orksheet **W**indow **V**ertical (/WWV). With the three windows on the screen, press function key F6 several times. Each time you press it, it moves counterclockwise to the next window. Table 4-9 summarizes the window commands available when you enter the command /**W**orksheet **W**indow (/WW).

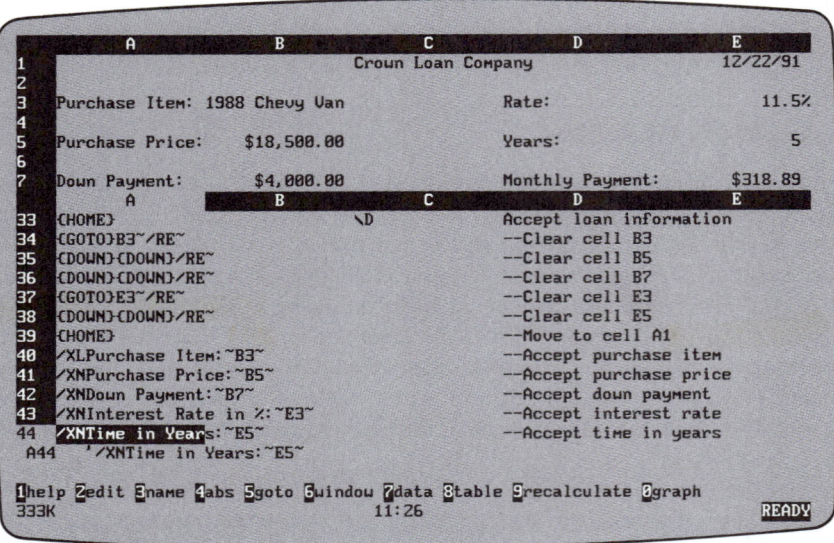

FIGURE 4-26 The screen divided into two windows.

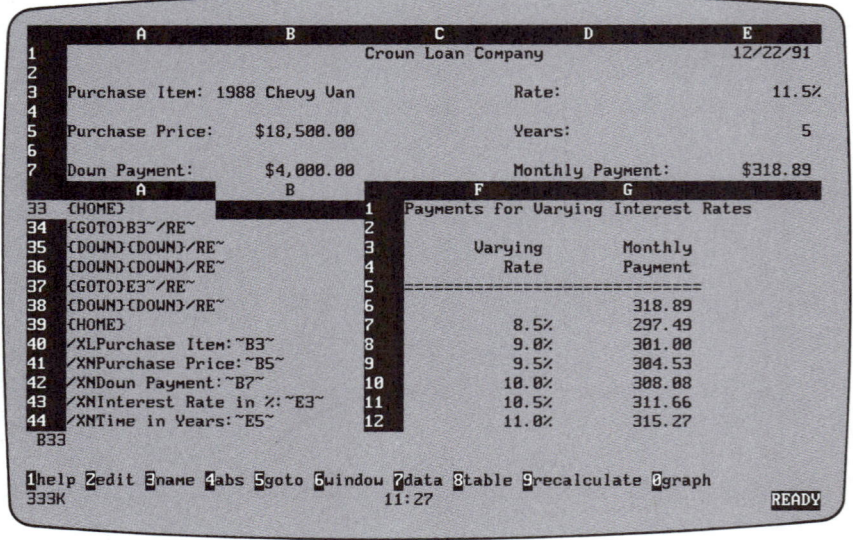

FIGURE 4-27
The screen divided into three windows.

TABLE 4-9 Summary of the Worksheet Window Commands

COMMAND	KEYSTROKES	FUNCTION
Horizontal	/WWH	Splits the screen or window from side to side.
Vertical	/WWV	Splits the screen or window from top to bottom.
Sync	/WWS	Causes windows that are aligned horizontally or vertically to scroll together.
Unsync	/WWU	Causes each window to scroll independently.
Clear	/WWC	Returns the screen to a single window.

Synchronizing Windows (/WWS)

If you look closely at the three windows in Figure 4-27, you'll notice that they are not **synchronized**, that is, the same row numbers and column letters are not aligned in all three windows. Each window scrolls independent of the other windows. To synchronize the windows, enter the command /**W**orksheet **W**indow **S**ync (/WWS). **Vertical synchronization** (up-and-down movement) requires that the windows have their upper left corners lined up horizontally and that each window contains the same number of rows. **Horizontal synchronization** (left-and-right movement) requires that the windows have their upper left corners lined up vertically and that each window contains the same number of columns.

Clearing the Windows (/WWC)

To return to the normal worksheet display with one window, enter the command /**W**orksheet **W**indow **C**lear (/WWC). This command switches the screen from multiple windows back to one window.

CELL PROTECTION (/WGPE)

C ells are either protected or unprotected. When you create a new worksheet, all cells are unprotected. **Unprotected cells** are cells whose values may be changed at any time, but **protected cells** cannot be changed. If a cell is protected and the user attempts to change its value, the computer beeps and VP-Planner Plus displays the error message "Protected cell" on the status line.

Once the worksheet has been fully tested and displays the correct results, you should protect the cells that you don't want changed by mistake. You should protect cells that contain information that will not change or is unlikely to change, cells that contain macros, and cells whose values are determined by formulas. In the case of Project 4B, we want to protect all the cells in the worksheet except for B3, B5, B7, E3, E5, and the data table in the range G6..H20.

The first step in protecting cells is to protect all the cells in the worksheet. Once all the cells are protected, we can be selective and "unprotect" those that we want to change. To protect all the cells in the worksheet, enter the command /**W**orksheet **G**lobal **P**rotection **E**nable (/WGPE).

Next, move the cell cursor to B3. Enter the command /**R**ange **U**nprot (/RU). Press the Enter key when VP-Planner Plus requests the range to unprotect. Do the same for cells B5, B7, E3, and E5. Finally, move the cell cursor to G7 and unprotect the range G7..H20, which contains the data table information.

You can check whether a cell is unprotected by moving the cell cursor to the cell in question. The letter U will display on the status line if the cell is unprotected. If you mistakenly unprotect the wrong cell, you may protect it by using the command /**R**ange **P**rotect (/RP). This command is meaningless unless global protection has been enabled (turned on).

If for some reason you need to modify the cells that are in a protected area, such as the macros, disable (turn off) global protection by using the command /**W**orksheet **G**lobal **P**rotection **D**isable (/WGPD). Once you are finished modifying the cells, enable (turn on) global protection. The worksheet will be protected exactly as it was before you disabled (turned off) global protection.

Saving and Printing the Worksheet

To save the Crown Loan Company worksheet to disk with the cells protected, invoke the \S macro by holding down the Alt key and pressing the S key.

To obtain a printed version of the worksheet, do the following:

1. Enter the command /**P**rint **P**rinter **R**ange (/PPR) and select the range A1..H46.
2. Type the letter Q to quit the Print menu.
3. Invoke the \P macro by holding down the Alt key and pressing the P key.

VP-Planner Plus prints the three parts of the worksheet on separate pages. After the printer stops, carefully remove the Crown Loan Company worksheet from the printer. The complete worksheet is shown in Figures 4-2, 4-3, and 4-4.

OBTAINING A SUMMARY OF ALL THE VP-PLANNER PLUS FUNCTIONS

VP-Planner Plus has over 100 useful functions. We have discussed the most widely used ones. You may find the others to be useful in certain situations. For a complete listing and description of the functions available, load VP-Planner Plus, press function key F1, and go to screens 18 through 27. Print each screen using the Shift and PrtSc keys. After you are finished, press the Esc key to return to the worksheet.

PROJECT SUMMARY

In Project 4 we developed two worksheets. Project 4A introduced you to statistical functions and range names. Project 4B taught you how to use the TODAY, IF, PMT, and PV functions, the data fill feature, data tables, and macros. You also learned how to protect cells in the worksheet and how to use multiple windows to see different parts of the worksheet at the same time.

Each of the steps required to build the worksheets in Projects 4A and 4B is listed in the following tables.

SUMMARY OF KEYSTROKES—Project 4A

STEPS	KEY(S) PRESSED	STEPS	KEY(S) PRESSED
1	/WGC → → ↵	18	[F5]A16 ← '7561 → 112 → 130 → 123 ↵
2	/WCS → → ↵	19	[F5]A17 ← \ – ← /C ← . → → → → → ↵
3	DP 101 → → Grading Report → → →	20	↓ Count ↓ Lowest Grade ↓ Highest Grade ↓ Average Score ↓ Std Deviation ↓ Variation ↵
4	@NOW ← /RFD1 ↵	21	[F5]E4 ← @SUM(B4.D4) ↵
5	[F5]B3 ← "Test 1 → "Test 2 → "Test 3 → "Total → "Percent ↵	22	/C ← E6.E16 ↵
6	[F5]A4 ← Student → 139 → 142 → 150 → → "Correct ↵	23	[F5]F6 ← + E6/$E$4∗100 ↵
7	[F5]A5 ← \ = ← /C ← . → → → → → → ↵	24	/C ← F6.F16 ↵
8	↓ '1035 → 121 → 127 → 142 ↵	25	/RFF1 ← F6.F16 ↵
9	[F5]A7 ← '1074 → 114 → 113 → 132 ↵	26	[F5]B6 ← /RNCTEST1 ← B6.B16 ↵
10	[F5]A8 ← '1265 → 79 → 97 → 101 ↵	27	[F5]B18 ← @COUNT(TEST1) ↓ @MIN(TEST1) ↓ @MAX(TEST1) ↓
11	[F5]A9 ← '1345 → 85 → 106 → 95 ↵	28	@AVG(TEST1) ↓ @STD(TEST1) ↓ @VAR(TEST1) ↵
12	[F5]A10 ← '1392 → 127 → 124 → 120 ↵	29	/CB18.B23 ← C18.E23 ↵
13	[F5]A11 ← '3167 → 101 → 120 → 109 ↵	30	/RFF1 ← ↑ ↑ → → → → ↵
14	[F5]A12 ← '3382 → 110 → 104 → 120 ↵	31	/FSPROJS-4A ↵
15	[F5]A13 ← '3597 → 92 → 104 → 100 ↵	32	[Home] /PPRA1.F23 ↵
16	[F5]A14 ← '4126 → 105 → 100 → 96 ↵	33	AGEEQ
17	[F5]A15 ← '5619 → 125 → 135 → 143 ↵	34	/WEY

SUMMARY OF KEYSTROKES—Project 4B

STEPS	KEY(S) PRESSED	STEPS	KEY(S) PRESSED
1	/WGC15↵	40	F5 A22↵ → Crown Loan Company Worksheet Macros↵
2	→ → → /WCS16↵	41	F5 A24↵ Macro → → Macro Name → Function↓
3	← Crown Loan Company → →	42	\ = → \ = ← ← ========== ← ← \ = ↓
4	@TODAY ↵ /RFD4↵	43	'/FS˜R → → '\S → Saves worksheet under same name ↵
5	F5 A3↵ Purchase Item:↓↓Purchase Price: ↓↓Down Payment:↵	44	← ← ← /RNC\S↵ ↵
6	F5 D3↵ Rate:↓↓Years:↓↓Monthly Payment:↵	45	Alt S
7	F5 B3↵ '1988 Chevy Van↓↓18500↓↓4000↵ /RFC↵.↑↑↵	46	↓↓'/PPAGEEQ → → '\P → Prints worksheet ↵
8	F5 E3↵ 11.5% ↵ /RFPI↵ ← ↓↓5↓↓/RFC↵ ↵	47	← ← ← /RNC\P↵ ↵
9	F5 A5↵ /RNLR.↓↓ ↵	48	↓↓'/PPOOCQAGOOAQEEQ → → '\C → Prints cell-formulas version ↵
10	F5 D3↵ /RNLR.↓↓↓↓ ↵	49	← ← ← /RNC\C↵ ↵
11	F5 E7↵ @PMT($Purchase Price:–$Down Payment:,$Rate:/12,$Years:*12) ↵	50	/PPRA1.E20↵ OML2↵ MR78↵ QQ
12	F5 A8↵ \ = ↵ /C ↵ . → → → → → ↵	51	Alt P
13	F5 B9↵ ''Beginning → ''Ending → ''Paid On → ''Interest↓	52	Alt C
14	''Paid ← ''Principal ← ''Balance ← ''Balance ← ''Year↓	53	↓↓↓{HOME} → → '\D → Accept loan information ↵
15	\ - ↵ /C ↵ . → → → → → ↵	54	← ← ← /RNC\D↵ ↵
16	↓/DF.↓↓↓↓↓ ↵ 1↵ ↵ ↵	55	↓{GOTO}B3˜/RE˜ → → → '--Clear cell B3 ↵
17	→ + Purchase Price:–Down Payment: ↵	56	F5 A35↵ {DOWN}{DOWN}/RE˜ → → → '--Clear cell B5 ↵
18	/RF,↵ B12.E20↵	57	F5 A36↵ /CA35↵ A36↵ → → → '--Clear cell B7 ↵
19	→ @IF(A12 < = $YEARS:,@PV($Monthly Payment:,$Rate:/12,12*($Years:–A12)),0) ↵	58	F5 A37↵ {GOTO}E3˜/RE˜ → → → '--Clear cell E3 ↵
20	/C↵.↓↓↓↓ ↵	59	F5 A38↵ {DOWN}{DOWN}/RE˜ → → → '--Clear cell E5 ↵
21	↓← + C12↵/C↵.↓↓↓ ↵	60	F5 A39↵ {HOME} → → → '--Move to cell A1 ↵
22	F5 D12↵ + B12–C12↵/C↵.↓↓↓↓ ↵	61	F5 A40↵ '/XLPurchase Item:˜B3˜ → → → '--Accept purchase item ↵
23	→ @IF(B12 > 0,12*$Monthly Payment:–D12,0) ↵/C↵.↓↓↓↓ ↵	62	F5 A41↵ '/XNPurchase Price:˜B5˜ → → → '--Accept purchase price ↵
24	F5 A17↵ \ - ↵ /C↵ . → → → → → ↵	63	F5 A42↵ '/XNDown Payment:˜B7˜ → → → '--Accept down payment ↵
25	F5 C18↵ ''Subtotal↓''Down Payment↓ ''Total Cost ↵	64	F5 A43↵ '/XNInterest Rate in %:˜E3˜ → → → ' --Accept interest rate ↵
26	F5 D18↵ @SUM(D12.D16) →	65	F5 A44↵ '/XNTime in Years:˜E5˜ → → → '--Accept time in years ↵
27	@SUM(E12.E16)↓	66	F5 A45↵ {HOME} → → → '--Move to cell A1 ↵
28	+ Down Payment:↓	67	F5 A46↵ '/XQ → → → '--End of macro ↵
29	+ D18 + E18 + E19 ↵	68	Alt D1988 Chevy Van ↵ 18500↵ 4000↵ 11.5%↵ 5↵
30	/FSPROJS-4B ↵	69	/WGPE
31	F5 F1↵ Payments for Varying Interest Rates↓↓	70	→ ↓↓/RU↵
32	''Varying → ''Monthly → ''Total↓	71	↓↓/RU↵
33	''Paid ← ''Payment ← ''Rate↓	72	↓↓/RU↵
34	\ = → \ = → \ = ↓	73	F5 E3↵ /RU↵
35	F5 F7↵ /DFF7.F20↵ 8.5%↵ 0.5%↵ ↵	74	↓↓/RU↵
36	/RFP1↵ F7.F20↵	75	F5 G7↵ /RUG7.H20↵ Home
37	↑ → + E7 → + E20↵	76	Alt S
38	/RF,↵ G6.H20↵	77	/PPRA1.H46↵ Q
39	/DT1H6.F20↵ Rate: ↵	78	Alt P

Project Summary (continued)

The following list summarizes the material covered in Project 4:

1. If you plan to reference a range often, assign a name to it. To name a range, use the command /**R**ange **N**ame **C**reate (/RNC).
2. The Range Name command allows you to create range names, delete range names, assign labels as range names, show all range names, clear all range names, and insert the list of range names in the worksheet. See Table 4-1.
3. VP-Planner Plus has several statistical functions, like AVG, COUNT, MAX, MIN, STD, and VAR. See Table 4-2.
4. The command /**R**ange **N**ame **L**abel (/RNL) allows you to assign a label in a cell as the name of the cell immediately above, below, to the right, or to the left.
5. The PMT function determines the payment of a loan on the basis of the amount of the loan (principal), the interest rate (interest), and the length of time required to pay the loan back (term). The general form of the PMT function is @PMT(principal,interest,term).
6. The command /**D**ata **F**ill (/DF) allows you to quickly enter a series of numbers into a range using a specified increment or decrement.
7. The PV function can be used to return the amount the borrower still owes at the end of a period at any time during the life of a loan. The general form of the PV function is @PV(payment,interest,term).
8. The general form of the IF function is @IF(condition,true,false). When the IF function is assigned to a cell, the value displayed will depend on the condition. If the condition is true, the cell is assigned the true value. If the condition is false, the cell is assigned the false value.
9. The true and false values in an IF function may be a number, label (in quotation marks), function, or formula.
10. A condition is made up of two expressions and a relation. Each expression may be a number, label (in quotation marks), function, or formula. See Table 4-3 for a list of the valid relations.
11. A compound condition is one that includes a logical operator like #AND#, #OR#, and #NOT#. See Table 4-4 for examples.
12. A data table is used to automate asking what-if questions and organize the values returned by VP-Planner Plus.
13. A data table may have one value or two varying values. See Figure 4-21.
14. A **macro** is a series of keystrokes entered into a cell or range of cells. The macro is assigned a name using the command /**R**ange **N**ame **C**reate (/RNC).
15. A macro name begins with the backslash (\) character followed immediately by a letter.
16. If you have more than one macro associated with a worksheet, each macro should be separated by an empty cell.
17. The tilde character (˜) is used to represent the Enter key in a macro.
18. All macros should be documented.
19. To invoke a macro, hold down the Alt key and type the single letter name of the macro.
20. A poorly designed macro can damage a worksheet. Before you execute a new macro, save the worksheet. To test a macro, place VP-Planner Plus in STEP mode, hold down the Alt key, and press function key F1. When you are finished testing the macro, hold down the Alt key and press function key F1 to toggle the STEP mode off.
21. If you encounter an error in a macro while in STEP mode, hold down the Ctrl key and press the Break key to stop the macro.
22. /X macro commands are used to write programs. See Table 4-6.
23. Macro words represent special keys, like the cursor movement and function keys. See Table 4-7.
24. VP-Planner Plus allows you to divide the screen into two to six windows for viewing different parts of the worksheet at the same time. Use the command /**W**orksheet **W**indow (/WW). See Table 4-9.
25. To protect cells in a worksheet that you do not want the user to change, enter the command /**W**orksheet **G**lobal **P**rotection **E**nable (/WGPE). Once all the cells in the worksheet are protected, use the command /**R**ange **U**nprot (/RU) to unprotect the cells you want the user to be able to change. If you unprotect the wrong cell, use the command /**R**ange **P**rotect (/RP) to protect it.
26. To correct the values in protected cells, enter the command /**W**orksheet **G**lobal **P**rotection **D**isable (/WGPD). After the cells are corrected, enable (turn on) global protection. VP-Planner Plus remembers the cells you unprotected earlier.

STUDENT ASSIGNMENTS

STUDENT ASSIGNMENT 1: True/False

Instructions: Circle T if the statement is true or F if the statement is false.

T F   1. A data table allows you to automate what-if questions.
T F   2. The @COUNT(R) function returns the largest number in the range R.
T F   3. You may assign a single cell to a name using the /Range Name Create (/RNC) command.
T F   4. If there are seven cells in range R and five of the cells have a value of 10 and two of the cells are empty, then the function @AVG(R) returns a value of 50.
T F   5. The command /Worksheet Erase (/WE) may be used to erase the contents of a single cell without affecting the remaining cells in the worksheet.
T F   6. The @TODAY function returns a whole number equal to the number of days since December 31, 1899 on the basis of the system date.
T F   7. The command /Range Name Label (/RNL) is used to name a cell that contains a label.
T F   8. The PMT function may be used to determine the monthly payment on a loan.
T F   9. To fill a range from top to bottom with the sequence of numbers 5, 4, 3, 2, and 1, use the /Data Fill (/DF) command with a start value of 5, a step value of 1, and a stop value of 1.
T F 10. The IF function is used to assign one value or another to a cell on the basis of a condition that may be true, false, or both true and false.
T F 11. The logical operator #AND# requires both conditions to be true for the compound condition to be true.
T F 12. You may vary one or two values in a data table.
T F 13. VP-Planner Plus recalculates the values in a data table when you press function key F9.
T F 14. To invoke a macro, hold down the Ctrl key and type the letter that names the macro.
T F 15. To name a macro, use the /Range Name Create (/RNC) command.
T F 16. The STEP mode is used to enter a macro into a cell.
T F 17. Each macro should be separated by at least one empty cell.
T F 18. To protect cells in the worksheet, global protection must be enabled (turned on).
T F 19. The /Worksheet Window (/WW) command allows you to divide the screen into two to six windows.
T F 20. The /X macro commands allow you to write programs.

STUDENT ASSIGNMENT 2: Multiple Choice

Instructions: Circle the correct response.

1. Which one of the following allows you to assign a name to one or more adjacent cells?
   a. /Range Name Create (/RNC)   c. /Range Name Label (/RNL)
   b. /Worksheet Name Create (/WNC)   d. /Range Name Show (/RNS)
2. Which one of the following functions returns the average of the numbers in a range?
   a. AVG b. COUNT c. MAX d. MIN
3. Which one of the following functions returns the payment on a loan?
   a. TERM b. PMT c. PV d. RATE
4. Which one of the following functions is used to assign one value or another value to a cell on the basis of a condition?
   a. CHOOSE b. FALSE c. IF d. TRUE
5. Which one of the following is used to instruct VP-Planner Plus to terminate the Data Fill command?
   a. The last cell in the selected range terminates the command.
   b. The STOP parameter terminates the command.
   c. Either a or b can terminate the command.
   d. None of the above.

Student Assignment 2 (continued)

6. Which one of the following relations is used to represent not equal to?
   a. <   b. >   c. <>   d. none of these
7. In a data table, you may vary up to _____ values.
   a. one   b. two   c. three   d. four
8. Which one of the following characters represents the Enter key in a macro?
   a. backslash (\)   b. curly braces ({})   c. circumflex (^)   d. tilde (˜)

STUDENT ASSIGNMENT 3: Understanding Functions

Instructions: Fill in the correct answers.

1. Write a function that will count the nonempty cells in the range B10..B50.

Function: _____

2. Write a function that will find the average of the nonempty cells in the range A12..E12.

Function: _____

3. Write a function that will display the largest value in the range D1..D13.

Function: _____

4. Write a function that will determine the monthly payment on a loan of $85,000, over a period of 30 years, at an interest rate of 9.9% compounded monthly.

Function: _____

5. The cell cursor is at F15. Write a function that assigns the value zero or 1 to cell F15. Assign zero to cell F15 if the value in cell A12 is less than the value in cell B15. Assign 1 to cell F15 if the value in A12 is not less than the value in cell B15.

Function: _____

6. The cell cursor is at F15. Write a function that assigns the value Credit OK or Credit Not OK to cell F15. Assign the label Credit OK if the value in cell A1 is equal to the value in cell B1 or the value of cell C12 is greater than 500. If both conditions are false, assign the label Credit Not OK.

Function: _____

7. When there are multiple logical operators in a compound condition, VP-Planner Plus determines the truth value of each simple condition. It then evaluates the logical operators, left to right, in the following order: #NOT#, #AND#, #OR#. Determine the truth value of the compound conditions below, given the following: $E1 = 300$ $F1 = 500$ $G1 = 1$
$H1 = 50$ $I1 = 40$

   a. E1<400#OR#G1=1   Truth value: _____

   b. F1<300#AND#I1<50#OR#G1=2   Truth value: _____

   c. #NOT#(F1>600)#OR#G1=0#AND#I1=40   Truth value: _____

   d. E1+F1=800#AND#H1*4/10=30   Truth value: _____

STUDENT ASSIGNMENT 4: Understanding Macros

Instructions: Fill in the correct answers.

1. Describe the function of each of the following macros.
   a. /FS~R/QY

   Function of macro: _____

   b. /RE~

   Function of macro: _____

   c. /RFC2~{?}~

   Function of macro: _____

   d. /C~{?}~

   Function of macro: _____

   e. /PPOML2~MR78~Q

   Function of macro: _____

   f. /PPR{?}~AGEEQ

   Function of macro: _____

   g. {DOWN}{DOWN}/RE~

   Function of macro: _____

   h. /DF{?}~1~2~~

   Function of macro: _____

2. Describe the function of each of the following macro commands and macro words.
   a. tilde (~)   Function: _____   f. {GOTO}   Function: _____

   b. curly braces ({})   Function: _____   g. {UP}   Function: _____

   c. /XN   Function: _____   h. /XQ   Function: _____

   d. {?}   Function: _____   i. /XI   Function: _____

   e. {HOME}   Function: _____   j. {ESC}   Function: _____

STUDENT ASSIGNMENT 5: Using the Data Fill Command

Instructions: Enter the worksheet illustrated in Figure 4-28. The worksheet is a multiplication table. Change the global width of the columns to 6 characters. Use the Data Fill command twice, once to enter the numbers 1 to 18 in column A, and once to enter the numbers 2 to 22 by 2 in row 1. Enter the formula +$A3*B$1 in cell B3. Copy the formula to the range B3..L20.

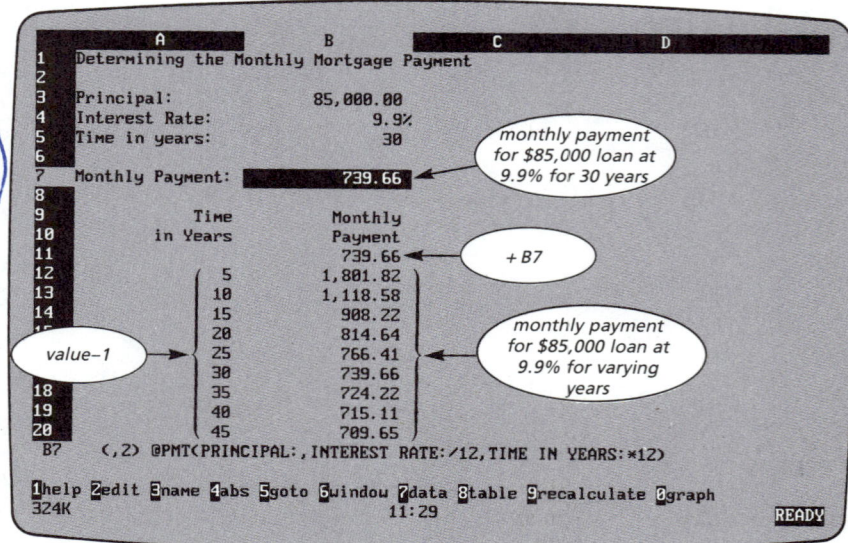

FIGURE 4-28
Student Assignment 5

Save the worksheet as STUS4-5. Print the as-is version of the worksheet. Format all the cells in the worksheet to the Text type and print the worksheet.

STUDENT ASSIGNMENT 6: Using the Data Table Command

Instructions: Create the following worksheets.

1. The worksheet illustrated in Figure 4-29 contains a data table with one value (time) varying. At the top of the worksheet, the PMT function is used to determine the monthly mortgage payment for a loan of $85,000.00 at 9.9% annual interest for 30 years. The data table indicates the monthly payment for the same loan for different terms (5 years, 10 years, 15 years, etc.).

FIGURE 4-29
Student Assignment 6A

Do the following to create the worksheet in Figure 4-29:

a. Increase the global column width to 17.

b. Format the entire worksheet to the Comma (,) type with two decimal places.

c. Enter the labels and numeric values in the range A1 through B5 and in cell A7. Format cell B4 to the Percent type with one decimal position. Format cell B5 to the Fixed type with zero decimal positions.

d. Use the Range Name Label command to assign the labels in cells A3 through A7 to B3 through B7.

e. Assign the PMT function shown on the input line in Figure 4-29 to cell B7.

f. Enter the labels in the range A9..B10.

g. Use the Data Fill command to enter the multiples of five shown in the range A12..A20. Format A12..A20 to the Fixed type with zero decimal positions.

h. Assign cell B11 the formula +B7.

i. Use the command /Data Fill 1 (/DF1) to create a data table in the range A11..B20. Use B5 (time in years) as the input cell.

j. After the data table displays, save the worksheet using the file name STUS4-6A.

k. Print the worksheet.

l. Select and enter several other sets of numbers into cells B3, B4, and B5. When necessary, use function key F8 to reset the data table.

2. The worksheet illustrated in Figure 4-30 contains a data table with two values varying. It also uses the FV function in cell B7 to determine the future value of a fund. The FV function tells you how much money you will have in a fund if you pay a fixed payment and earn a fixed interest rate over a period of time.

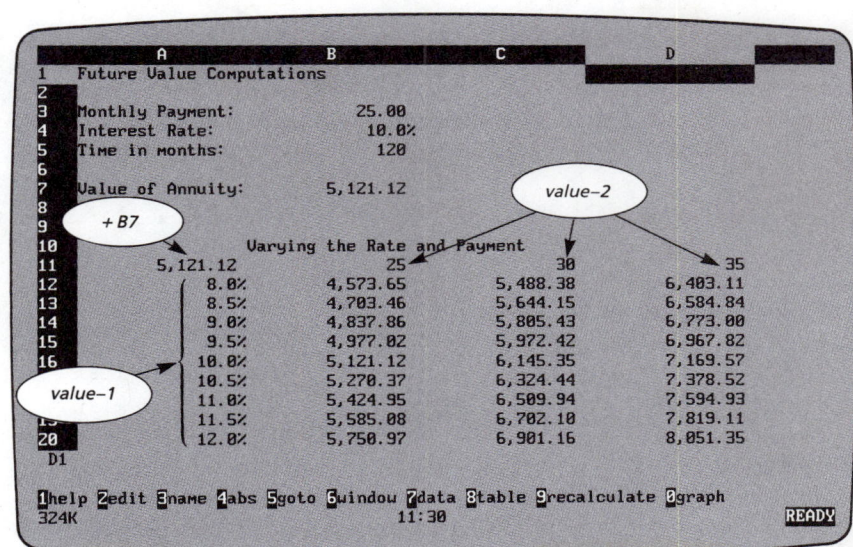

FIGURE 4-30
Student Assignment 6B

The data table describes the future values for varying interest rates and varying monthly payments. For example, if you invest $35.00 per month instead of $25.00 per month and if the interest rate is 11.5%, then you will have $7,819.11 rather than $5,585.08 at the end of 10 years.

Do the following to create the worksheet in Figure 4-30:

a. Increase the global column width to 17.

b. Enter the labels and numeric values in the range A1 through B5 and in cell A7.

c. Assign the FV function @FV(B3,B4/12,B5) to cell B7 to determine the future value of a fund in which you invest $25.00 per month at 10% interest, compounded monthly, for 10 years (120 months).

d. Use the Data Fill command to build the percent values in the range A12..A20. Assign +B7 to cell A11.

e. With the cell cursor at A11, enter the command /Data Table 2 (/DT2). Enter the data table range A11..D20.

f. Enter an input cell-1 value of B4 and an input cell-2 value of B3. Press the Enter key. The data table should fill as shown in Figure 4-30.

Student Assignment 6 (continued)

g. Save the worksheet using the file name STUS4-6B.
h. Print the worksheet.
i. Change the format of the worksheet to the Text type and print it.
j. Try several different investment combinations in cells B3, B4, and B5. Use function key F8 to instruct VP-Planner Plus to recalculate the data table if you change the value in cell B5.

STUDENT ASSIGNMENT 7: Building a Weekly Payroll Worksheet

Instructions: Load VP-Planner Plus and perform the following tasks.

1. Build the worksheet illustrated in Figure 4-31. For each employee, use the following formulas to determine the gross pay in column E, federal tax in column F, state tax in column G, and net pay in column H:
    a. If Hours ≤ 40, then Gross Pay = Rate * Hours, otherwise Gross Pay = Rate * Hours + 0.5 * Rate * (Hours – 40).
    b. If (Gross Pay – Dependents * 38.46) > 0, then Federal Tax = 20% * (Gross Pay – Dependents * 38.46), otherwise Federal Tax = 0.
    c. State Tax = 3.2% * Gross Pay.
    d. Net Pay = Gross Pay – (Federal Tax + State Tax).

```
        A         B        C        D        E        F        G        H
 1                          Payroll File List                      22-Dec
 2
 3                                           Gross   Federal   State     Net
 4   Employee    Rate    Hours    Dep.        Pay      Tax      Tax      Pay
 5   ================================================================
 6   Col, Joan   12.50   40.00      2       500.00    84.62    16.00   399.38
 7   Fiel, Don   18.00   32.00      4       576.00    84.43    18.43   473.14
 8   Dit, Lisa   13.00   48.50      0       685.75   137.15    21.94   526.66
 9   Snow, Joe    4.50   52.00      1       261.00    44.51     8.35   208.14
10   Hi, Frank    3.35    8.00      8        26.80      .00      .86    25.94
11   Bri, Edie   10.40   40.00      3       416.00    60.12    13.31   342.56
12
13   Total Gross Pay =====>        2465.55
14   Total Federal Tax ===>         410.83
15   Total State Tax =====>          78.90
16   Total Net Pay =======>       1,975.82
17
18
19
```

FIGURE 4-31
Student Assignment 7

2. Use the Range Name Create command to name cells B6, C6, and D6 so that you can use the variable names described in step 1 when you enter the formulas in cells E6, F6, G6, and H6.
3. Protect all the cells in the worksheet except those in the range C6..C11.
4. Save the worksheet as STUS4-7.
5. Print the worksheet.
6. Print the cell-formulas version of the worksheet.
7. Print the worksheet after formatting all the cells to the Text type.

STUDENT ASSIGNMENT 8: Building a Future Value Worksheet

Instructions: Load VP-Planner Plus and perform the following tasks.

1. Build the worksheet illustrated in Figure 4-32. Set column A to a width of 16 characters and the rest of the columns to a width of 15 characters. Use the Range Name Label command to name B3, B5, E3, and E5. Use the label to the right of each cell in Figure 4-32 as the label name. Determine the future value in cell E5 from the function @FV($Monthly Payment:, $Rate:/12,12*$Time:).

   Determine the values in the table in rows 10 through 19 as follows:

   a. Use the Data Fill command to create the series of numbers in the range A10..A19.
   b. Assign the function @IF(A10< =$Time:,@FV($Monthly Payment:,$Rate:/12,12*A10),0) to B10 and copy B10 to B11..B19.
   c. Assign the function @IF(A10< =$Time:,12*A10*$Monthly Payment:,0) to C10 and copy C10 to C11..C19.
   d. Assign the formula +B10-C10 to D10 and copy D10 to D11..D19.

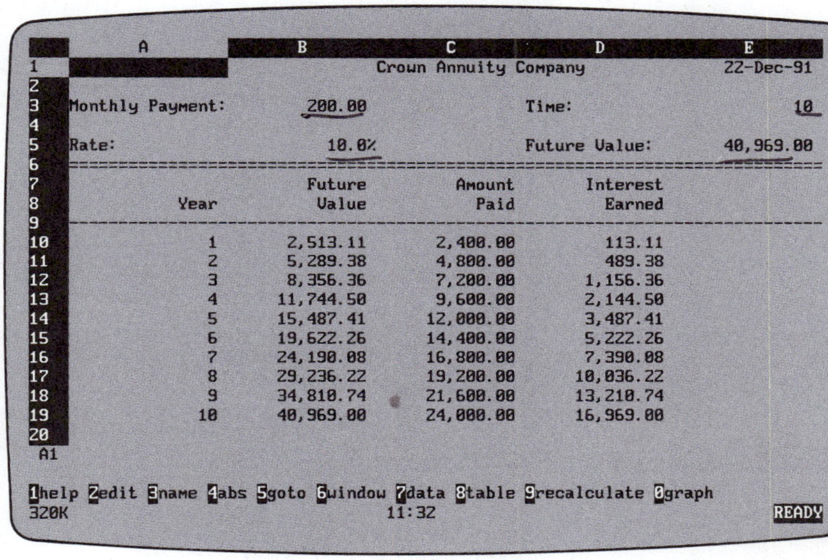

	A	B	C	D	E
1			Crown Annuity Company		22-Dec-91
2					
3	Monthly Payment:	200.00		Time:	10
4					
5	Rate:	10.0%		Future Value:	40,969.00
6	========	========	========	========	========
7		Future	Amount	Interest	
8	Year	Value	Paid	Earned	
9	--------	--------	--------	--------	--------
10	1	2,513.11	2,400.00	113.11	
11	2	5,289.38	4,800.00	489.38	
12	3	8,356.36	7,200.00	1,156.36	
13	4	11,744.50	9,600.00	2,144.50	
14	5	15,487.41	12,000.00	3,487.41	
15	6	19,622.26	14,400.00	5,222.26	
16	7	24,190.08	16,800.00	7,390.08	
17	8	29,236.22	19,200.00	10,036.22	
18	9	34,810.74	21,600.00	13,210.74	
19	10	40,969.00	24,000.00	16,969.00	
20					

A1

1help 2edit 3name 4abs 5goto 6window 7data 8table 9recalculate 0graph
320K 11:32 READY

FIGURE 4-32
Student Assignment 8

2. Save the worksheet. Use the file name STUS4-8.
3. Determine the future value for the following: monthly payment, 500; rate of interest, 11.5%; time in years, 10.
4. Print the worksheet with the future value for the data described in step 3.
5. Print only the range A1..E5 with the future value for the data described in step 3.

STUDENT ASSIGNMENT 9: Building a Data Table for the Future Value Worksheet

Instructions: Load VP-Planner Plus and perform the following tasks.

1. Load STUS4-8, the future value worksheet, which you created in Student Assignment 8. This worksheet is illustrated in Figure 4-32.
2. Add the data table shown in Figure 4-33. Do the following to complete the data table:
   a. Use the Data Fill command to enter the series of numbers 8.5% to 14.5% in increments of 0.5% in the range F8..F20.
   b. Assign +E5 (future value) to cell G7.
   c. Assign the formula +Future Value:−Time:*12*Monthly Payment: to cell H7.
   d. Use the command /Data Table 1 (/DT1) to establish the range F7..H20 as a data table.
   e. Enter an input cell value of B5, the interest rate.

```
            F             G             H             I         J
1   Future Values for Varying Interest Rates
2
3
4          Varying        Future        Interest
5           Rate          Value         Earned
6   ===========================================================
7                        40,969.00     16,969.00
8           8.5%         37,627.68     13,627.68
9           9.0%         38,702.86     14,702.86
10          9.5%         39,816.14     15,816.14
11         10.0%         40,969.00     16,969.00
12         10.5%         42,162.96     18,162.96
13         11.0%         43,399.63     19,399.63
14         11.5%         44,680.65     20,680.65
15         12.0%         46,007.74     22,007.74
16         12.5%         47,382.70     23,382.70
17         13.0%         48,807.38     24,807.38
18         13.5%         50,283.74     26,283.74
19         14.0%         51,813.78     27,813.78
20         14.5%         53,399.61     29,399.61
   J1

   1help 2edit 3name 4abs 5goto 6window 7data 8table 9recalculate 0graph
   321K                                  11:33                      READY
```

FIGURE 4-33
Student Assignment 9

3. Save the worksheet using the file name STUS4-9.
4. Print the data table (F1..H20).
5. Determine the future value for the following: monthly payment, 1000; rate of interest, 10.5%; time in years, 8.
6. Press function key F8 to recalculate the data table.
7. Print the complete worksheet (A1..H20) with the future value for the data described in step 5.

STUDENT ASSIGNMENT 10: Building Macros for the Future Value Worksheet

Instructions: Load VP-Planner Plus and perform the following tasks.

1. Load STUS4-9, the future value worksheet, which was created in Student Assignments 8 and 9. This worksheet is illustrated in Figures 4-32 and 4-33.
2. Enter the four macros shown in Figure 4-34.

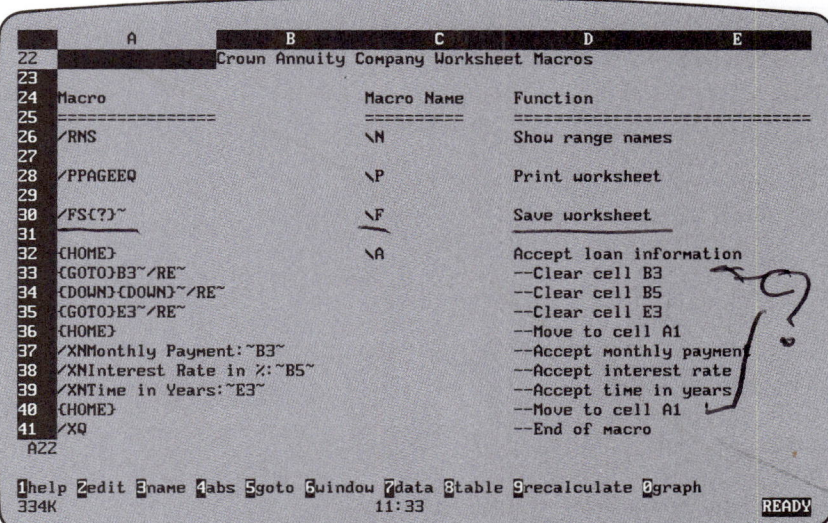

```
                A            B             C            D            E
22                     Crown Annuity Company Worksheet Macros
23
24  Macro                         Macro Name   Function
25  ===============               ==========   ==================================
26  /RNS                              \N        Show range names
27
28  /PPAGEEQ                          \P        Print worksheet
29
30  /FS{?}~                           \F        Save worksheet
31                                             _____
32  {HOME}                            \A        Accept loan information
33  {GOTO}B3~/RE~                               --Clear cell B3
34  {DOWN}{DOWN}~/RE~                           --Clear cell B5
35  {GOTO}E3~/RE~                               --Clear cell E3
36  {HOME}                                      --Move to cell A1
37  /XNMonthly Payment:~B3~                     --Accept monthly payment
38  /XNInterest Rate in %:~B5~                  --Accept interest rate
39  /XNTime in Years:~E3~                       --Accept time in years
40  {HOME}                                      --Move to cell A1
41  /XQ                                         --End of macro
   A22
1help 2edit 3name 4abs 5goto 6window 7data 8table 9recalculate 0graph
334K                                    11:33                        READY
```

FIGURE 4-34
Student Assignment 10

3. Change the printer range to A1..E19.
4. Use the STEP mode to test each macro. For the \S macro, use the file name STUS4-10. For the \A macro, use the following data: monthly payment, 350; rate of interest, 8%; time in years, 7.
5. Enable cell protection for the worksheet. Unprotect cells B3, B5, E3, and the range G8..H20.
6. Press function key F8 to recalculate the data table.
7. Use the \S command to save the worksheet a second time.
8. Print the complete worksheet (A1..H41) with the future value for the data described in step 4.

STUDENT ASSIGNMENT 11: Building Macros for the Weekly Payroll Worksheet

Instructions: Load VP-Planner Plus and perform the following tasks.

1. Load STUS4-7, the weekly payroll worksheet, which was created in Student Assignment 7. This worksheet is illustrated in Figure 4-31.
2. Disable all protection and add macros that will do the following:
   a. Save the worksheet under the file name entered by the user (\S).
   b. Print the range A1..H16 (\P).
   c. Erase the current hours worked and accept the new hours worked (\A).
3. Enable cell protection for the worksheet. Unprotect cells C6..C11.
4. Use the STEP mode to test each macro. For the save macro, use the file name STUS4-11. For the accept hours worked macro, enter the following hours worked: Col, Joan—36.5; Fiel, Don—42.5; Dit, Lisa—53.5; Snow, Joe—40; Hi, Frank—40; Bri, Edie—61.5.
5. Use the save macro to save the worksheet a second time. Use the file name STUS4-11.
6. Print the worksheet (A1..H16) for the data described in step 4.

PROJECT 5

Graphing with VP-Planner Plus

Objectives

You will have mastered the material in this project when you can:

- Create a pie chart.
- Create a line graph.
- Create a multiple-line graph.
- Create a scatter graph.
- Create a simple bar graph.
- Create a side-by-side bar graph.
- Create a stacked-bar graph.
- Create an XY graph.
- Assign multiple graphs to the same worksheet.
- Dress up a graph by adding titles and legends.
- Save a graph as a PIC file.
- Save a worksheet with the graph specifications.
- Print a graph.
- View the current graph and graphs saved on disk.

A s we have seen in the previous four projects, a worksheet is a powerful tool for analyzing data. Sometimes, however, the message you are trying to convey gets lost in the rows and columns of numbers. This is where the graphics capability of VP-Planner Plus comes in handy. With only a little effort, you can have VP-Planner Plus create, display, and print a graph of the data in your worksheet and get your message across in a dramatic pictorial fashion. With the Graph command, you can select a pie chart, a line graph, a variety of bar graphs, an XY graph, or a scatter graph. We will study these types of graphs in this project.

To display or print graphs, your computer must have a graphics adapter. If it does not have one, it will beep at you when you try to display a graph. The initial VP-Planner Plus graphics adapter setting is CGA. If you have another type of graphics board, like Hercules or EGA, use the command /**W**orksheet **G**lobal **D**efault **H**ardware **V**ideo (/WGDHV) to change the setting. Screen 43 of the online help facility describes the Video settings available with VP-Planner Plus.

We will use the year-end sales analysis worksheet shown in Figure 5-1 to illustrate all the graphs except the XY graph. The worksheet in Figure 5-1 includes the quarter sales for each of six cities in which King's Computer Outlet has a store. Total sales for each quarter and the year are displayed in row 13. The total sales for each of the six cities are displayed in column F.

FIGURE 5-1
The year-end sales analysis report we will use to illustrate graphing with VP-Planner Plus.

	A	B	C	D	E	F
1			King's Computer Outlet			22-Dec-91
2			Year-End Sales Analysis			
3						Total
4	City	Quarter 1	Quarter 2	Quarter 3	Quarter 4	Sales
5	===					
6	Chicago	40,135	52,345	38,764	22,908	154,152
7	New York	48,812	42,761	34,499	56,123	182,195
8	Atlanta	12,769	15,278	19,265	17,326	64,638
9	Dallas	38,713	29,023	34,786	23,417	125,939
10	Boston	34,215	42,864	38,142	45,375	160,596
11	Los Angeles	52,912	63,182	57,505	55,832	229,431
12						
13	Total	227,556	245,453	222,961	220,981	916,951
14						

Before going any further, let's build the worksheet shown in Figure 5-1. As a guide, we will follow the first 23 steps in the list of keystrokes given in the Project Summary section at the end of this project.

THE GRAPH COMMAND (/G)

With the worksheet in Figure 5-1 in main computer memory, the first step in drawing a graph is to enter the command /Graph (/G). The **Graph menu** shown in Figure 5-2 displays on the screen. The functions of the commands listed in the Graph menu are described in Table 5-1.

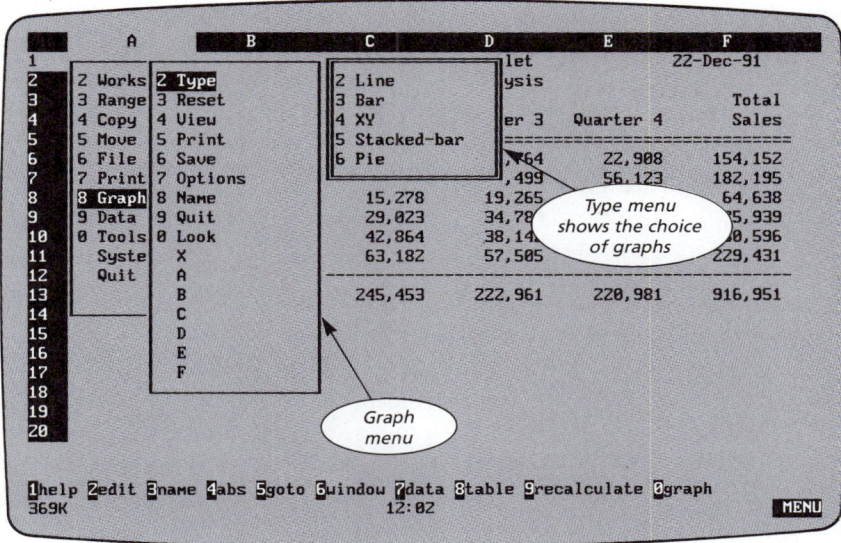

FIGURE 5-2
The Graph menu of VP-Planner Plus—enter the command /Graph (/G).

TABLE 5-1   Commands Available in the Graph Menu

COMMAND	FUNCTION
Type	Allows you to select the type of graph you want to display—Line, Bar, XY, Stacked-bar, Pie.
Reset	Clears the current graph specifications.
View	Displays the current graph.
Print	Prints the current graph on the printer.
Save	Saves the current graph to disk. VP-Planner Plus automatically adds the extension .PIC, rather than .WKS.
Options	Allows you to define titles or labels for the X and Y axes and for the top of the graph.
Name	Allows you to save a set of graph specifications by name. In this way you can have several different graphs associated with the same worksheet.
Quit	Quits the Graph command.
Look	Allows you to view graphs saved as PIC files.
X	Defines a range of labels for the X axis for a line or bar graph. Also defines a range of labels to describe each piece of a pie chart. In an XY graph the X range is assigned the X coordinates.
ABCDEF	Allows you to define up to six Y-axis data ranges. For example, in a multiple-line graph each data range is represented by a line.

PIE CHARTS (/GTP)

A pie chart is used to show how 100% of an amount is divided. Let's create the pie chart in Figure 5-3. This pie chart shows the percentage of total annual sales for each of the six cities where King's Computer Outlet has a store. The total annual sales for each of the six stores are in the range F6..F11 of the worksheet in Figure 5-4.

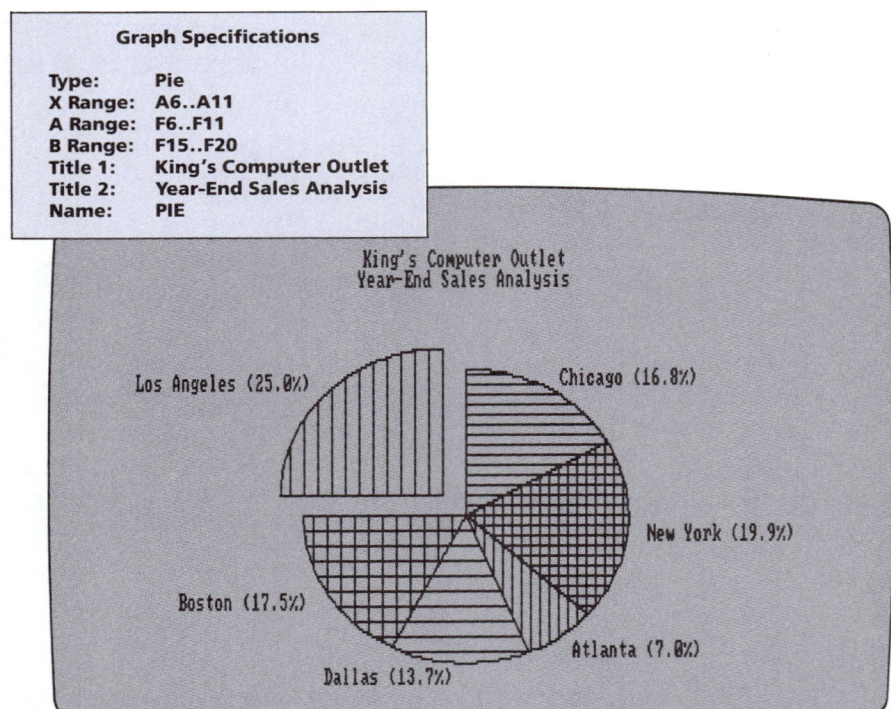

Graph Specifications

Type:	Pie
X Range:	A6..A11
A Range:	F6..F11
B Range:	F15..F20
Title 1:	King's Computer Outlet
Title 2:	Year-End Sales Analysis
Name:	PIE

FIGURE 5-3
Pie graph with titles, shading, and "exploded" segment showing the annual sales for each of the six cities in the worksheet in Figure 5-1.

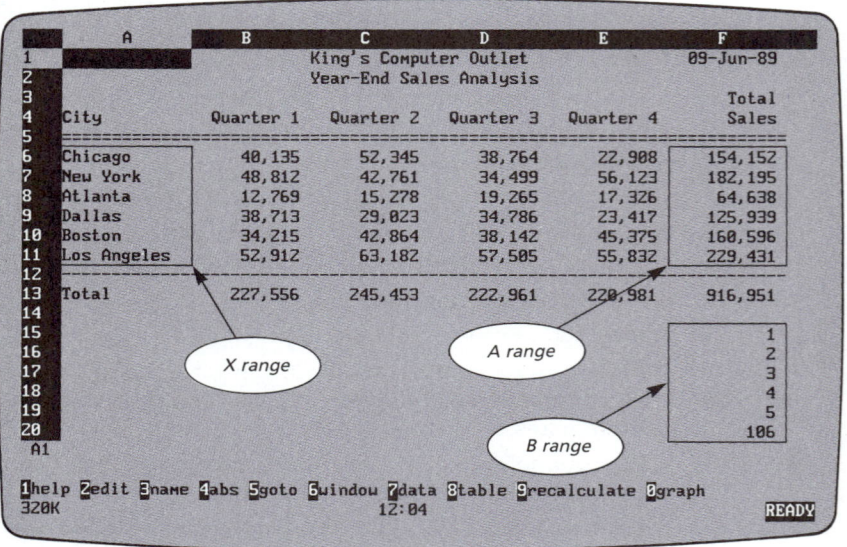

FIGURE 5-4
Ranges specified in the worksheet for the pie graph in Figure 5-3.

To create any graph using VP-Planner Plus, you need to enter the type of graph, the ranges in the worksheet to graph, graph titles, and graph options. Collectively, these are called the **graph specifications**.

With the Graph menu on the screen (see Figure 5-2), enter the command **Type Pie (TP)**. This command tells VP-Planner Plus that you want to create a pie chart as the current graph. The **current graph** is the one that displays when you enter the command /Graph View (/GV).

Selecting the A Range

After we type the letter P for Pie, the command cursor returns to the Graph menu, the menu that begins with the command Type in Figure 5-2. For a pie chart, you can select only one data range to graph, and it must be assigned as the A range. As shown in Figure 5-4, assign the annual sales for each city (F6..F11) as the A range. Type the letter A. VP-Planner Plus responds by displaying the prompt message "Enter data range: A1" on the input line. Enter the range F6..F11 and press the Enter key.

Selecting the X Range

The X range is used to identify each "slice" or segment of the pie. We must select a range that can identify the cells in the A range. Since the A range is equal to the annual sales for each of the six cities, select the names of the cities (A6..A11) to identify each segment of the pie. With the command cursor in the Graph menu, type the letter X. VP-Planner Plus responds by displaying the prompt message "Enter label range: A1" on the input line. Enter the range A6.A11 and press the Enter key.

After we define the A range and X range, VP-Planner Plus has enough information to draw a *primitive* pie chart, one that shows the characteristics assigned thus far. With the command cursor in the Graph menu, type the letter V for View and the primitive pie chart in Figure 5-5 displays on the screen. After viewing it, press any key on the keyboard to return to the Graph menu. Once a range has been assigned you may view the pie chart at any time and make changes if you feel it is not being drawn the way you want it.

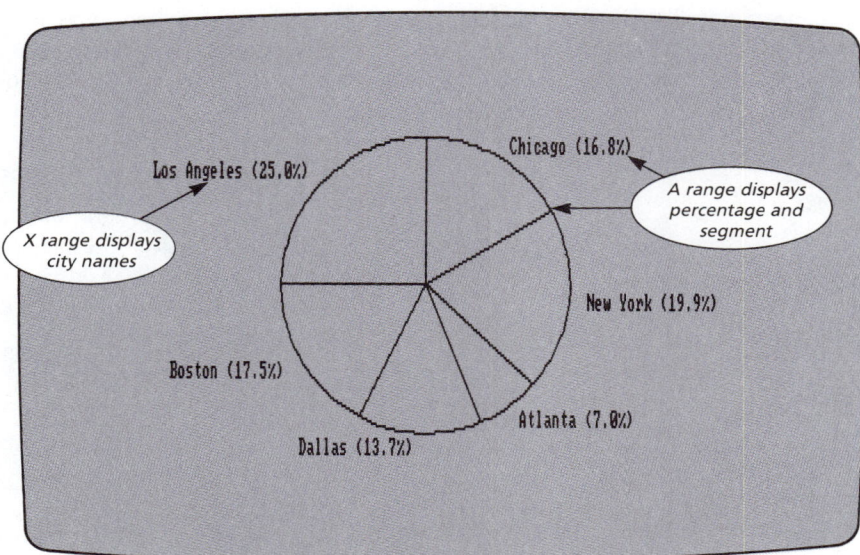

Graph Specifications

Type: Pie
X Range: A6..A11
A Range: F6..F11

FIGURE 5-5
Primitive pie chart with no titles or shading. Shows the proportion of annual sales contributed by each city in the form of a "slice of the pie."

It is the A range that causes the pie in Figure 5-5 to be divided into segments. Each segment is proportionate to the annual sales for each city. The A range is also responsible for the percentage value displayed within parentheses outside each segment. The city names outside each segment of the pie are the labels assigned as the X range.

In certain instances, you may want to assign the same group of cells to both the A and X ranges. When both ranges are assigned the same group of cells, the values in the A range that determine the size of each segment of the pie are also used to identify (label) each segment.

Selecting the B Range

The B range is used to "dress up" the pie chart and make it more presentable and easier to read. Through the use of the B range, you can create segment shading and "explode" a pie chart. An **exploded pie chart** is one in which one or more segments are offset or slightly removed from the main portion of the pie so that they stand out (see Figure 5-3).

The B range is usually set up off to the side or below the worksheet. To shade and explode the pie chart in Figure 5-5 so that it looks more like Figure 5-3, you need six adjacent cells for the B range, one for each pie segment. In each cell, enter a code number between 0 and 7. Each code represents a different type of shading. A code of zero instructs VP-Planner Plus to leave the corresponding segment of the pie chart unshaded.

Let's use the range F15..F20 to enter the code numbers. The first of the six cells, F15, will refer to the first entry in the A range, Chicago. The last of the six cells will refer to the last entry in the A range, Los Angeles.

To enter the shading codes, first quit the Graph menu by typing the letter Q. Use function key F5 to move the cell cursor to F15. Enter the shading codes 1 through 5 in the range F15..F19. To explode one or more segments of the pie chart, add 100 to the shading values. Explode the segment representing Los Angeles by entering the number 106, rather than 6, in cell F20. The six shading codes are shown in the range F15..F20 in Figure 5-4.

Select the range F15..F20 by entering the command /Graph **B** (/GB). Enter the range F15..F20 and press the Enter key. Press the V key to view the pie chart. The pie chart (without titles) displays as shown in Figure 5-3. The pie chart is complete. However, we still have to add graph titles. After viewing the pie chart, press any key to redisplay the Graph menu.

Adding a Title to the Pie Chart

To add the graph titles above the pie chart in Figure 5-3, type the letter O for Options. This causes the **Graph Options menu** shown in Figure 5-6 to display. With the Graph Options menu on the screen, type the letter T for Titles. You are allowed two title lines—First Line and Second Line—of up to 39 characters each. Type the letter F for First Line. Enter the title—King's Computer Outlet—and press the Enter key. Type the letters T for Titles and S for Second Line. Enter the second line of the title—Year-End Sales Analysis—and press the Enter key.

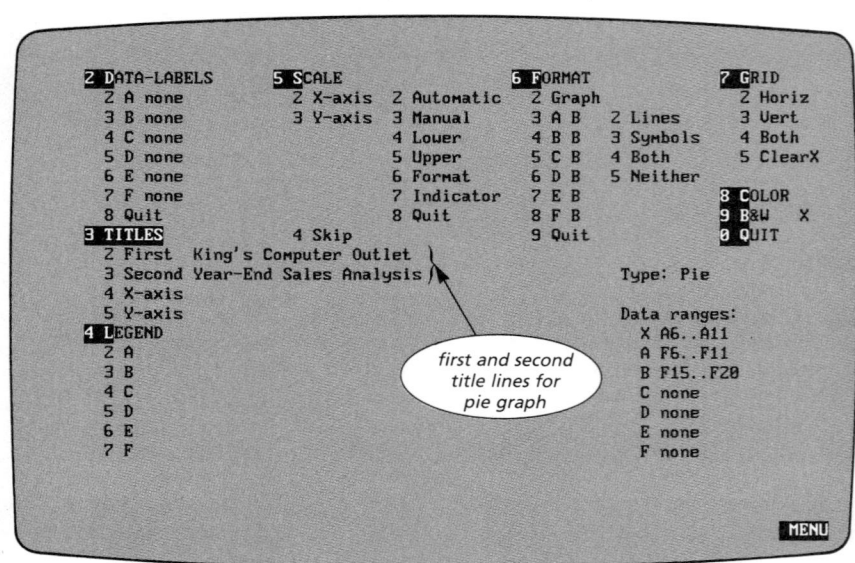

FIGURE 5-6
The Graph Options menu shows all the pie chart specifications associated with the worksheet in Figure 5-4.

To quit the Graph Options menu, type the letter Q for Quit. VP-Planner Plus returns to the Graph menu. The graph specifications for the pie chart in Figure 5-3 are complete. Type the letter V for View and VP-Planner Plus displays the pie chart with titles as shown in Figure 5-3. To terminate the View command, press any key on the keyboard and the Graph menu redisplays on the screen.

If the title you plan to use for a graph is identical to one in the worksheet, you can press the Backslash (\) key followed by the cell address in place of the title. For example, we could have entered \C1 for the first title and \C2 for the second title, since the titles are identical to the worksheet titles in cells C1 and C2 (see Figure 5-4). To check if any cells in the worksheet contain an acceptable title for the graph, hold down the Shift key when the Graph Options menu is on the screen and VP-Planner Plus will display the worksheet.

Naming the Pie Chart

With the command cursor in the Graph menu and the pie chart complete, our next step is to name the graph specifications. That way we can develop a new graph from the same worksheet and still have the pie chart specifications stored away to view and modify at a later time. To assign a name to the graph specifications, type the letter N for Name. The **Graph Name menu** shown in Figure 5-7 displays on the screen. Type the letter C for Create. VP-Planner Plus displays the prompt message "Enter name:" on the input line. Enter the name PIE for pie chart and press the Enter key. After assigning the name, VP-Planner Plus returns control to the Graph menu.

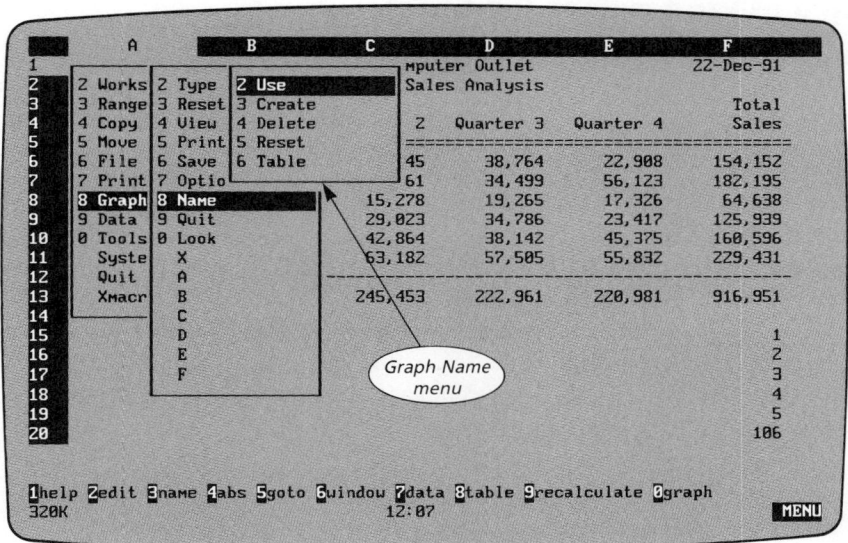

FIGURE 5-7
The Graph Name Menu display after entering the command /Graph Name (/GN).

The graph specifications, described in the Graph Options menu in Figure 5-6, are now stored under the name PIE. Graph names, like PIE, can be up to 16 characters long and should be as descriptive as possible. Table 5-2 summarizes the commands available in the Graph Name menu.

TABLE 5-2   **Summary of the Graph Name Commands**

COMMAND	KEYSTROKES	FUNCTION
Use	/GNU	Lists the directory of graph names associated with the current worksheet. Assigns the selected named set of graph specifications as the current graph and displays the graph.
Create	/GNC	Names the current graph specifications.
Delete	/GND	Deletes the named set of graph specifications.
Reset	/GNR	Deletes all graph names and their specifications.
Table	/GNT	Places the list of graph names in the worksheet beginning at the location of the cell cursor.

Saving and Printing the Pie Chart

When you assign a name, like PIE, to the current set of graph specifications using the /GNC command, they are not saved on disk. To save the named graph specifications you must save the worksheet itself using the File Save command. When the /FS command is used, both the current graph settings and any named graph specifications are saved with the worksheet. To complete the save, first type the letter Q to quit the Graph menu. When the worksheet reappears on the screen, enter the command /File Save (/FS). When the file name PROJS-5A appears on the input line, press the Enter key. Finally, type the letter R for Replace.

Later, when you retrieve the worksheet, the pie chart specifications will be available and you can display or print the pie chart at any time. If you retrieve the worksheet and decide to change any of the pie chart specifications, you must save the worksheet again or the latest changes will be lost.

To obtain a hard copy of the pie chart, enter the command /Graph Print (/GP). When you enter this command, VP-Planner Plus displays the pie chart on the screen and then transmits it to the printer. You may also obtain a hard copy of the pie chart by displaying it, using the View command and printing the contents of the screen by holding down one of the Shift keys and pressing the PrtSc key.

The Effect of What-If Analyses on the Pie Chart

Once you have assigned the pie chart specifications to the worksheet, any values changed in the worksheet will show up in the pie chart the next time it is drawn. For example, quit the Graph menu and change the sales amount for Quarter 1 for Chicago in cell B6 from 40,135 to 45,550.

With the worksheet on the screen, press the F10 key to view the pie chart. As indicated on the prompt line, function key F10 displays the current graph. When the worksheet is displayed on the screen, it is quicker to press the F10 key to display the current graph than it is to enter the command /GV. Compare the displayed pie chart to the one in Figure 5-3. Note that the segments representing all six cities have changed because of the change to the first quarter sales for Chicago. After viewing the pie chart, press any key on the keyboard to return to the worksheet. Before continuing with this project, change the sales amount for Chicago in cell B6 back to 40,135.

PIC Files

You can save a copy of the current graph that is independent of the worksheet. This is often referred to as a "snapshot" of the graph. To do this, enter the command /**G**raph **S**ave (/GS). In response to the prompt message on the input line, enter the file name PIES-5A and press the Enter key. The pie chart (not the worksheet) is saved to disk under the name PIES-5A with the extension .PIC (picture). We call the file a **PIC file**. It is important to remember that PIC files are independent of the worksheet and, therefore, do not include changes made to the worksheet after the PIC file is saved.

To display a PIC file on the screen, enter the command /**G**raph **L**ook (/GL) and select the one you want from the list of PIC file names displayed on the screen. PIC files display faster using the Look command than the current graph does using the View command.

LINE GRAPHS (/GTL)

Line graphs are used to show trends. For example, a line graph can show pictorially whether sales increased or decreased during quarters of the year. The lines are drawn on X and Y axes. You can have from one to six lines in the graph. Each line represents a different data range in the worksheet. We will create two line graphs, one with a single data range and another with six data ranges.

First we will create a line graph with a single data range that shows the trend of the total sales for the four quarters (see Figure 5-8). Begin by resetting the current graph specifications associated with PROJS-5A. That is, clear the pie chart—the current graph—to begin the line graph because the specifications are different. With the Graph menu on the screen, type the letter R for Reset.

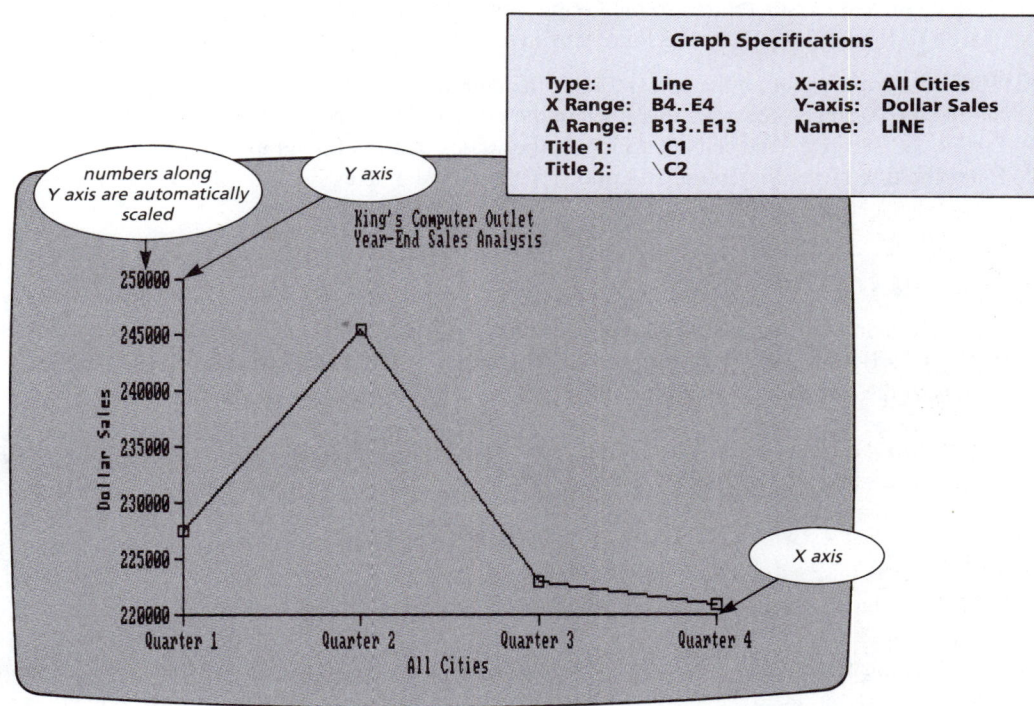

Graph Specifications

Type:	Line	X-axis:	All Cities
X Range:	B4..E4	Y-axis:	Dollar Sales
A Range:	B13..E13	Name:	LINE
Title 1:	\C1		
Title 2:	\C2		

FIGURE 5-8
Line graph showing the trend in quarterly sales.

The **Graph Reset menu** shown in Figure 5-9 displays on the screen. Note that the graph specifications can be reset on an individual basis (X, A, B, C, D, E, F) or for the entire graph (Graph). In this case, reset all the graph specifications. With the command cursor in the Graph Reset menu, type the letter G for Graph. The pie chart is no longer the current graph. Remember, however, that the pie chart specifications are stored under the name PIE and can be accessed at any time using the Graph Name Use command (see Table 5-2).

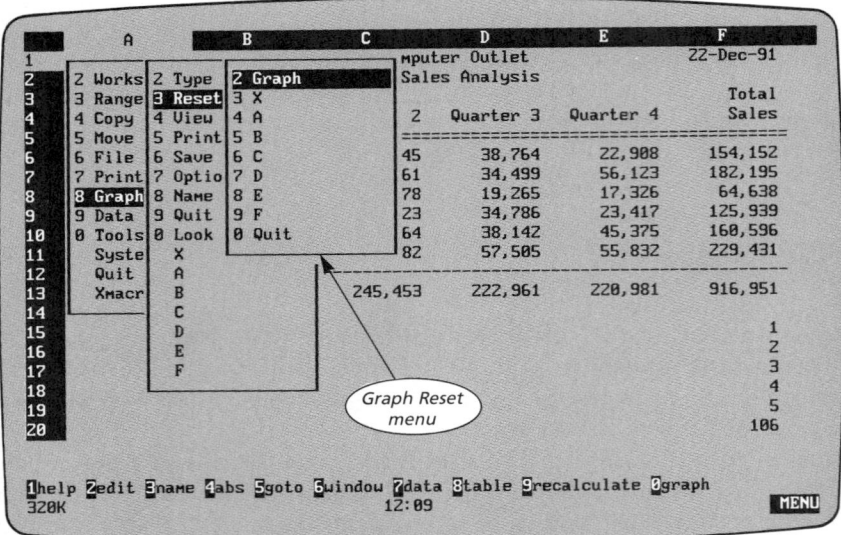

FIGURE 5-9
The Graph Reset menu—enter the command /Graph Reset (/GR).

The command cursor returns to the Graph menu after resetting the graph specifications. We can now proceed to build the line graph in Figure 5-8. There are four steps involved:

1. With the Graph menu on the screen, enter the command **T**ype **L**ine (TL).
2. Define the X range—the cells that contain the desired labels for the X axis.
3. Define the A range—the cells that include the values that the line graph will represent.
4. Enter the title of the line graph and titles for the X and Y axes.

Selecting the X Range

With the command cursor in the Graph menu, type the letter X and assign the range B4..E4 to the X range. As shown in Figure 5-10, cells B4 through E4 contain the labels Quarter 1, Quarter 2, Quarter 3, and Quarter 4. These labels display along the X axis in the line graph (see Figure 5-8).

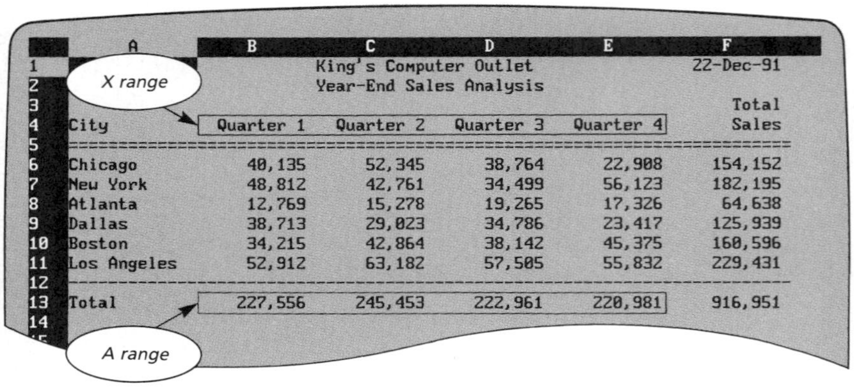

FIGURE 5-10
Range specifications for line graph in Figure 5-8.

Selecting the A Range

The next step is to select the A range. Assign to the A range the cells that include the values the line graph is to represent. This is also called the **Y-axis data range**. With the command cursor in the Graph menu, type the letter A and enter the range B13..E13. The desired A range is shown in the worksheet in Figure 5-10.

Adding Titles to the Line Graph

You can add three different titles to the line graph: (1) line graph title (you are allowed two of these); (2) X-axis title; (3) Y-axis title. Let's add the same line graph title used for the pie chart. For the X axis use the title All Cities. For the Y axis use the title Dollar Sales.

  To add these titles, type the letter O for Options while the Graph menu is on the screen. The Graph Options menu shown in Figure 5-11 displays without the title entries. Type the letters T for Titles and F for First. Enter \C1 and press the Enter key. \C1 instructs VP-Planner Plus to use the label assigned to cell C1 in the worksheet as the first title. Next, type the letters T and S to enter the second title. Enter \C2 and press the Enter key. The label in cell C2 serves as the second title.

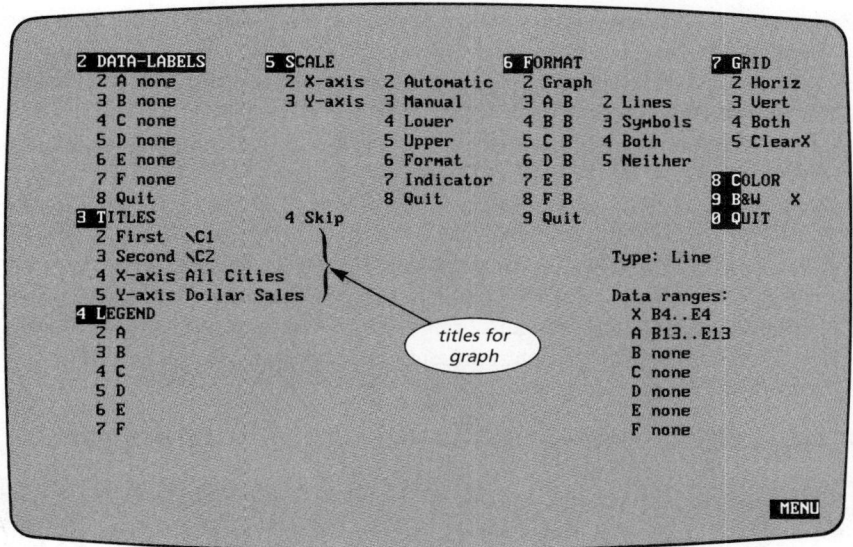

FIGURE 5-11
Graph Options menu allows you to enter a title for the line graph and titles for the X and Y axis.

  Enter the X-axis title by typing the letters T and X and the label All Cities. Press the Enter key. Enter the Y-axis title by typing the letters T and Y and the label Dollar Sales. Press the Enter key. The title entries are shown in Figure 5-11. Finally, type the letter Q to quit the Graph Options menu.

Viewing the Line Graph

With the command cursor in the Graph menu, type the letter V for View. The line graph in Figure 5-8 displays. Note that VP-Planner Plus automatically scales the numeric labels along the Y axis on the basis of the numbers in the A range. The small squares that the line graph passes through represent the points whose coordinates are the corresponding values in the X and A ranges.

You can see from Figure 5-8 that the line graph is useful for showing a trend. The line graph clearly shows that sales for King's Computer Outlet increased significantly during the second quarter and then fell sharply in the third quarter. Finally, there was a slight drop in sales during the fourth quarter. Here again, if you change any numeric values in the worksheet, the line graph will show the latest values the next time you invoke the View command.

After viewing the graph, press any key to redisplay the Graph menu.

Naming the Line Graph

With the line graph complete and the command cursor active in the Graph menu, type the letters N for Name and C for Create. When VP-Planner Plus requests the graph name, enter the name LINE and press the Enter key. The line graph specifications shown in the Graph Options menu in Figure 5-11 are stored under the name LINE.

Saving and Printing the Line Graph

To save the named graph specifications (LINE) with the worksheet to disk, type the letter Q to quit the Graph menu. Enter the command /File Save (/FS). Press the Enter key when the file name PROJS-5A appears on the input line. Type the letter R for Replace to rewrite the file to disk. Now there are two sets of graph specifications associated with PROJS-5A—PIE and LINE. The line graph continues to be the current graph.

Make a hard copy of the line graph in the same manner described for the pie chart. That is, with the command cursor in the Graph menu, type the letter P for Print. VP-Planner Plus displays the line graph on the screen and then sends it to the printer. When the printing activity is complete, the Graph menu reappears on the screen.

Multiple-Line Graphs

VP-Planner Plus allows up to six Y-axis data ranges (A–F) and the range of corresponding labels (X) to be assigned to a line graph. When more than one data range is assigned to a line graph, it is called a **multiple-line graph**. The multiple-line graph in Figure 5-12 includes six lines, each representing the four quarterly sales for one of the six cities in the worksheet. Multiple-line graphs like this one are used not only to show trends, but also to compare one range of data to another.

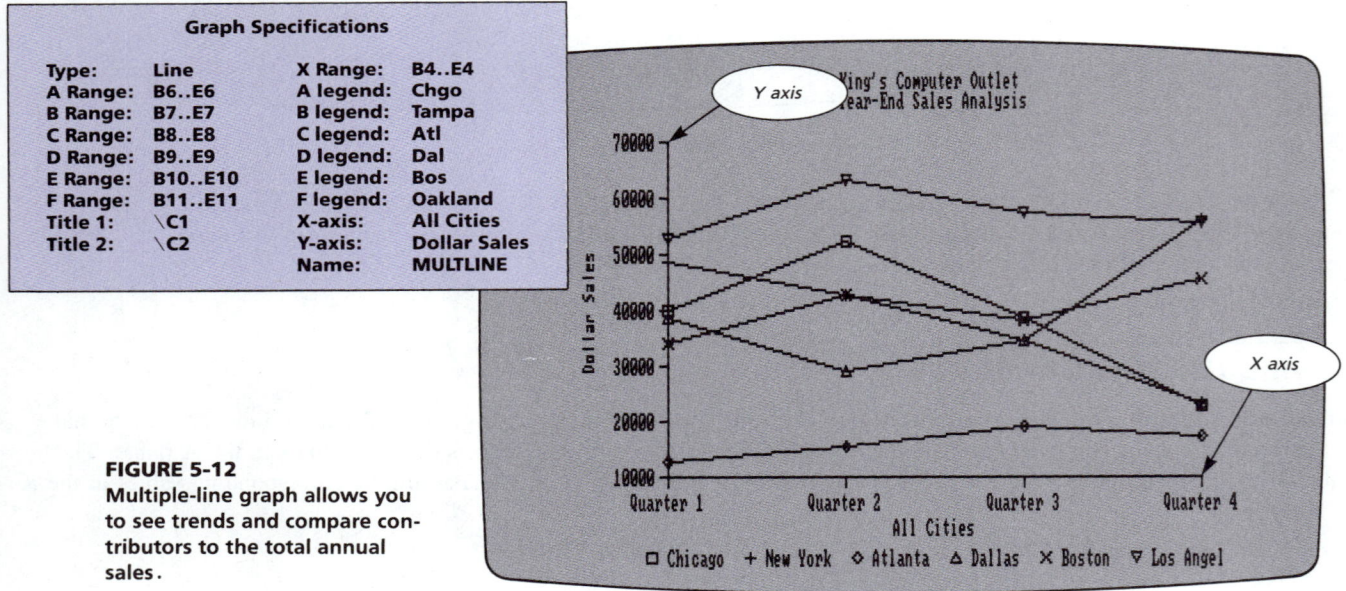

Graph Specifications

Type:	Line	X Range:	B4..E4
A Range:	B6..E6	A legend:	Chgo
B Range:	B7..E7	B legend:	Tampa
C Range:	B8..E8	C legend:	Atl
D Range:	B9..E9	D legend:	Dal
E Range:	B10..E10	E legend:	Bos
F Range:	B11..E11	F legend:	Oakland
Title 1:	\C1	X-axis:	All Cities
Title 2:	\C2	Y-axis:	Dollar Sales
		Name:	MULTLINE

FIGURE 5-12
Multiple-line graph allows you to see trends and compare contributors to the total annual sales.

The multiple-line graph in Figure 5-12 uses the same titles, X range, and graph type as the line graph in Figure 5-8, the current graph associated with the worksheet. Therefore, rather than resetting the current graph specifications, modify them.

With the command cursor active in the Graph menu, assign to the six data ranges A through F the quarterly sales of the six cities shown in Figure 5-13. Type the letter A for the A range. Enter the range B6..E6 and press the Enter key. Follow the same procedure for the other five ranges—assign the B range B7..E7, the C range B8..E8, the D range B9..E9, the E range B10..E10, and the F range B11..E11. After entering the ranges, type the letter O for Options. The data ranges should be the same as those shown in the lower right corner of the Graph Options menu in Figure 5-14.

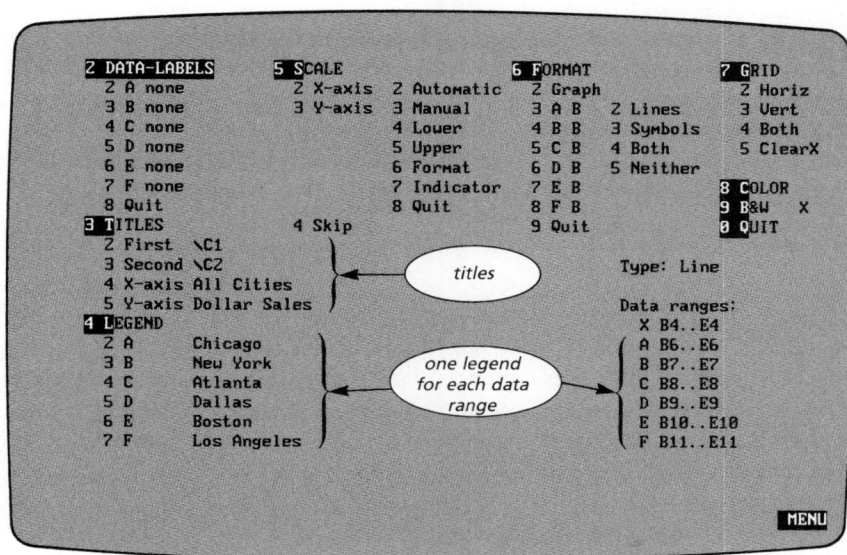

FIGURE 5-13
Multiple-line graph range specifications.

```
        X range      B           C           D           E           F
1                         King's Computer Outlet            22-Dec-91
2       A range           Year-End Sales Analysis
3                                                                Total
4  City                Quarter 1   Quarter 2   Quarter 3   Quarter 4   Sales
5       B range      ================================================
6  Ch                   40,135      52,345      38,764      22,908    154,152
7  New         C range  48,812      42,761      34,499      56,123    182,195
8                       12,769      15,278      19,265      17,326     64,638
9  Dallas               38,713      29,023      34,786      23,417    125,939
10 B      D range       34,215      42,864      38,142      45,375    160,596
11 L                    52,912      63,182      57,505      55,832    229,431
12
13     E range         227,556     245,453     222,961     220,981    916,951
14
15
16     F range
17
18
19
20
A20

1help 2edit 3name 4abs 5goto 6window 7data 8table 9recalculate 0graph
336K_                          12:10                                READY
```

FIGURE 5-14
Graph Options menu with titles and legends entered for multiple-line graph.

Assigning Legends to the Data Ranges

Before quitting the Graph Options menu, we need to enter **legends** that help identify each of the six lines that are drawn in the multiple-line graph. Without legends, the multiple-line graph is useless because we cannot identify the lines.

In Figure 5-14, the legend fields are located in the lower left corner of the Graph Options menu. To enter the legend that identifies the A range, type the letters L for Legend and A for A range. From Figure 5-13 we can determine that the A range was assigned the quarterly sales for Chicago (B6..E6). Therefore, enter the label Chicago or \A6 in response to the prompt message "Enter legend:" on the input line. Assign the corresponding city names as the legends for the B through F ranges.

Note that the Graph Options menu shows all the graph specifications selected for the multiple-line graph. It indicates the type of graph, the X range, A–F data ranges, the titles, and the legends. To quit the Graph Options menu, type the letter Q.

Viewing the Multiple-Line Graph

Next, type the letter V for View and the multiple-line graph illustrated in Figure 5-12 displays on the screen. The six lines in the graph show the trend in quarterly sales for each of the six cities. The graph also allows us to compare the sales for the six cities. To identify the line that represents a particular city, scan the legends at the bottom of the graph in Figure 5-12. Before each city name is a special character called a **symbol**, like the square for Chicago. The line that passes through the square in the graph represents Chicago's four quarterly sales. After viewing the multiple-line graph, press any key to return control to the Graph menu.

Naming the Multiple-Line Graph

To assign a name to the multiple-line graph specifications, type the letters N for Name and C for Create. When VP-Planner Plus requests the graph name, enter the name MULTLINE and press the Enter key. The multiple-line graph specifications shown in the Graph Options menu in Figure 5-14 are stored under the name MULTLINE.

There are now three graphs associated with the worksheet—PIE, LINE, and MULTLINE. However, there is only one current graph. At this point, the current graph is the multiple-line graph, because it is the last one created.

Saving and Printing the Multiple-Line Graph

Type Q to quit the Graph menu. The worksheet in Figure 5-1 reappears on the screen. Save the worksheet. This ensures that the graph specifications under the name MULTLINE are saved with the worksheet on disk. Enter the command /File Save (/FS). When the file name PROJS-5A appears on the input line, press the Enter key. Type the letter R to replace the old version of PROJS-5A with the new one.

After saving the worksheet, enter the command /Graph Print (/GP) to print the multiple-line graph. VP-Planner Plus displays the graph on the screen and sends it to the printer. When the printer is finished, the Graph menu redisplays on the screen.

Scatter Graphs

A **scatter graph** displays the points (symbols) in a graph without any connecting lines. Sometimes a scatter graph is better able to illustrate what a multiple-line graph is attempting to show. To create the scatter graph shown in Figure 5-15, we need only instruct VP-Planner Plus not to connect the symbols with lines in the multiple-line graph. Remember, the multiple-line graph is still the current graph.

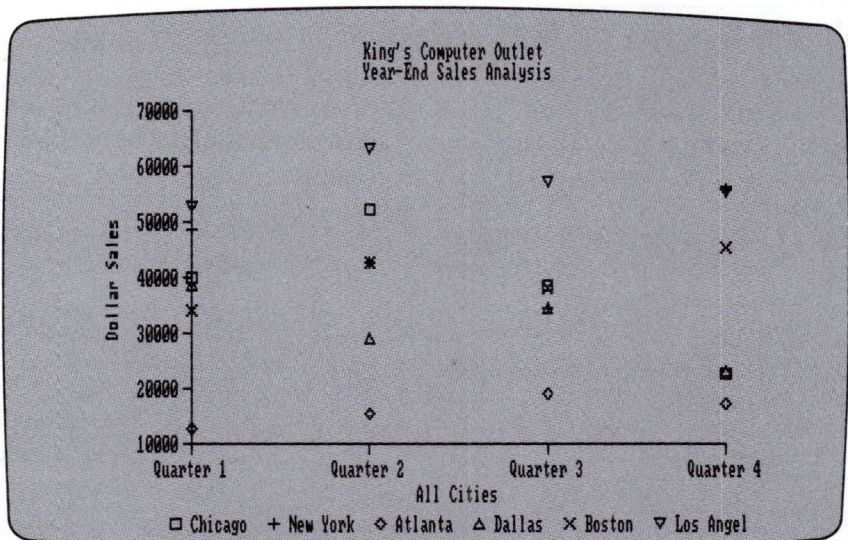

FIGURE 5-15
The scatter graph is an alternative to the multiple-line graph.

Changing the Multiple-Line Graph to a Scatter Graph   With the Graph menu on the screen, type the letter O for Options. The Graph Options menu displays as shown in Figure 5-14. The default setting for the Format command at the top of the Graph Options menu is Both. This means that both lines and symbols are displayed for the current multiple-line graph. Change this to Symbols so that only the symbols are displayed. Type the letters F for Format, G for all the lines in the Graph, and S for Symbols. Finally, type the letter Q twice, once to quit the Format section of the Graph Options menu and once to quit the Graph Options menu.

Viewing the Scatter Graph   Type the letter V and the original multiple-line graph (see Figure 5-12) displays as a scatter graph (Figure 5-15). Here again, the symbols are identified by the legends displayed below the scatter graph. Press any key to redisplay the Graph menu.

Naming, Saving, and Printing the Scatter Graph   To assign a name to the scatter graph specifications, type the letters N for Name and C for Create. When VP-Planner Plus requests the graph name, enter the name SCATTER and press the Enter key. Type the letter Q to quit the Graph menu and save the worksheet to disk using the File Save command. Now there are four graphs associated with the worksheet—PIE, LINE, MULTLINE, and SCATTER.

To print the scatter graph, enter the command /**Graph Print** (/GP). After the graph prints on the printer, the Graph menu automatically reappears on the screen.

BAR GRAPHS (/GTB) or (/GTS)

The **bar graph** is the most popular business graphic. It is used to show trends and comparisons. The bar graph is similar to a line graph, except that a bar rather than a point on a line represents the Y-axis value for each X-axis value. Unlike the line graph that shows a continuous transition from one point to the next, the bar graph emphasizes the magnitude of the value it represents.

We will discuss three types of bar graphs: simple bar graphs, side-by-side bar graphs, and stacked-bar graphs. The following examples change the preceding line graphs to bar graphs. The range settings, titles, and legends remain the same.

Simple Bar Graphs (/GTB)

A **simple bar graph** has a single bar for each value in the X range. The graph specifications for a bar graph are similar to those for a line graph. Let's create the bar graph in Figure 5-16. It is a bar graph of the same data used earlier for the line graph shown in Figure 5-8. Recall that the line graph showed the trend in total sales for the four quarters.

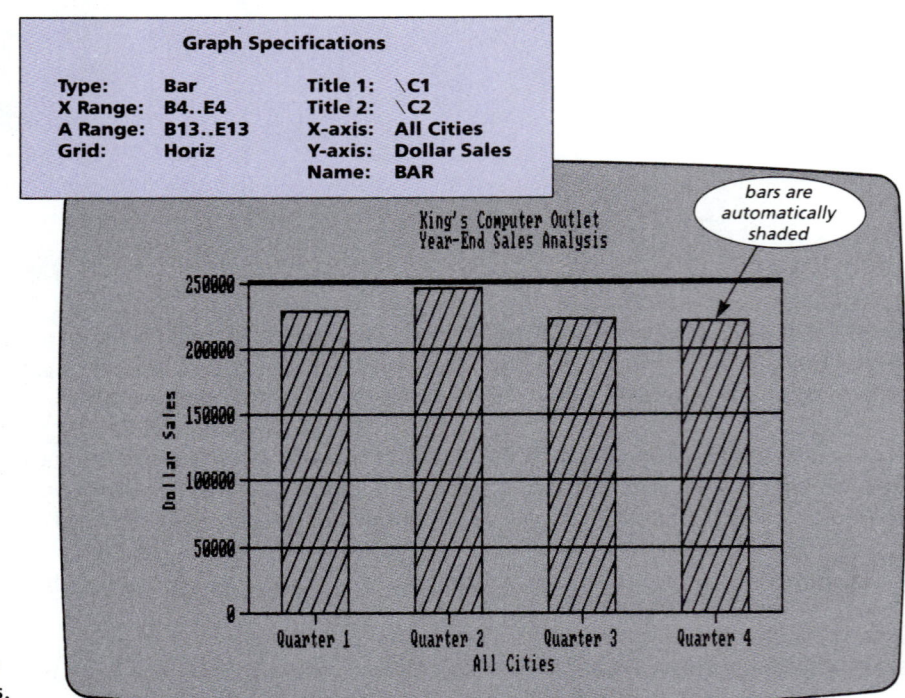

Graph Specifications

Type:	Bar	Title 1:	\C1
X Range:	B4..E4	Title 2:	\C2
A Range:	B13..E13	X-axis:	All Cities
Grid:	Horiz	Y-axis:	Dollar Sales
		Name:	BAR

bars are automatically shaded

FIGURE 5-16
A simple bar chart is useful for comparing and showing trends.

Using a Named Graph   The first step in creating the bar graph is to assign the line graph specifications stored under the graph name LINE as the current graph. Therefore, with the Graph menu on the screen, type the letters N for Name and U for Use. VP-Planner Plus displays an alphabetized list of all the graph names associated with worksheet PROJS-5A—LINE, MULTLINE, PIE, and SCATTER. With the command cursor on the name LINE, press the Enter key. The line graph in Figure 5-8 immediately displays on the screen. Press any key on the keyboard and the Graph menu reappears. The graph specifications for the line graph (LINE) shown in Figure 5-11 now represent the current graph.

Changing the Line Graph to a Bar Graph   With the Graph menu on the screen, type the letters T for Type and B for Bar. The current graph is now a bar graph, rather than a line graph. To improve the appearance of the bar graph and make it easier to read, add a horizontal grid. Type the letter O for Options. With the Graph Options menu displayed (see Figure 5-11), type the letters G for Grid and H for Horizontal. Quit the Graph Options menu by typing the letter Q.

Viewing the Simple Bar Graph   Type the letter V for View. The simple bar graph shown in Figure 5-16 displays on the screen. Note that it gives a more static view of the total sales for each quarter as compared to the line graph in Figure 5-8. The horizontal grid in the simple bar graph makes it easier to recognize the magnitude of the bars that are not adjacent to the Y axis. After viewing the graph, press any key on the keyboard. The Graph menu reappears on the screen.

Naming, Saving, and Printing the Simple Bar Graph   To name the simple bar graph, type the letters N for Name and C for Create. Enter the graph name BAR and press the Enter key. Type the letter Q to quit the Graph menu. Use the command /File Save (/FS) to save the worksheet to disk. Press the Enter key when the file name PROJS-5A appears on the input line. Next, press the letter R to replace PROJS-5A on disk with the latest version. Now there are five graphs associated with the worksheet—PIE, LINE, MULTLINE, SCATTER, and BAR.

Print the simple bar graph by entering the command /Graph Print (/GP). After the graph prints on the printer, the Graph menu reappears on the screen.

Side-by-Side Bar Graphs (/GTB)

Like a line graph, a bar graph can have from one to six independent bars (data ranges) for each value in the X range. When a bar graph has more than one bar per X value, we call it a **side-by-side bar graph** (see Figure 5-17). This type of graph is primarily used to compare data. For example, you might want to compare the sales in each quarter for Los Angeles to the sales of the rest of the cities.

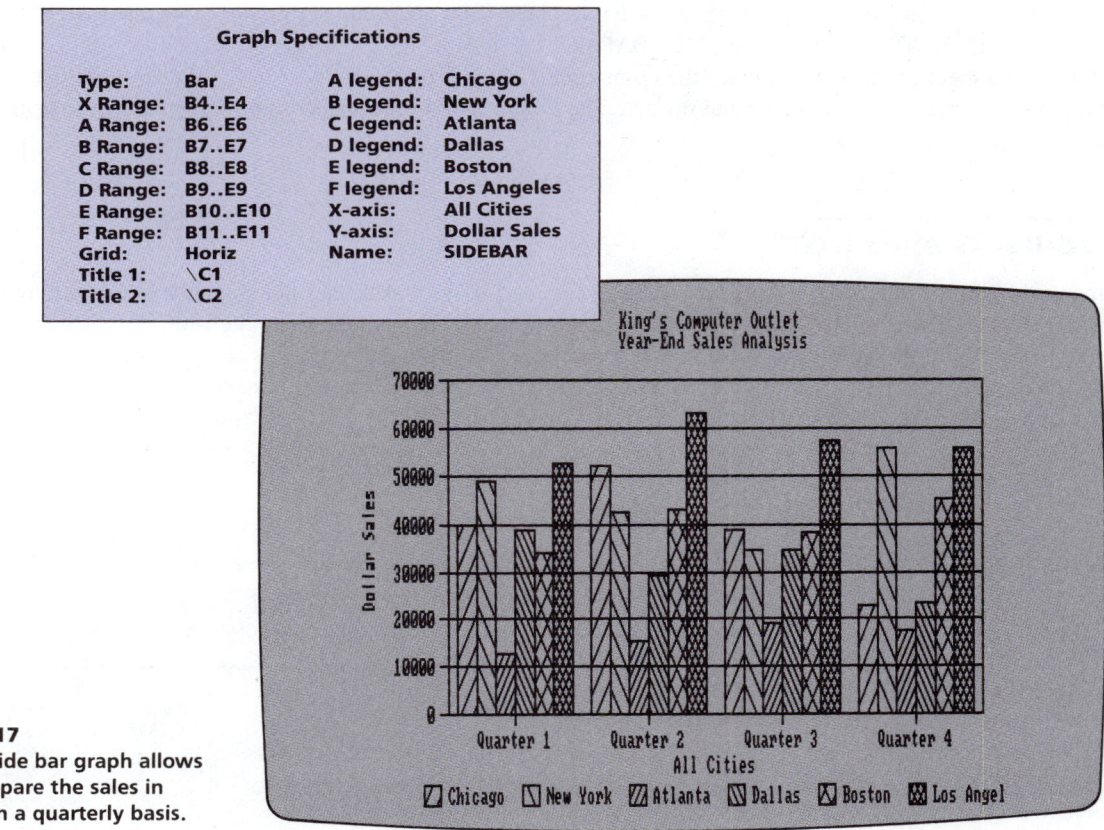

Graph Specifications

Type:	**Bar**	**A legend:**	**Chicago**
X Range:	**B4..E4**	**B legend:**	**New York**
A Range:	**B6..E6**	**C legend:**	**Atlanta**
B Range:	**B7..E7**	**D legend:**	**Dallas**
C Range:	**B8..E8**	**E legend:**	**Boston**
D Range:	**B9..E9**	**F legend:**	**Los Angeles**
E Range:	**B10..E10**	**X-axis:**	**All Cities**
F Range:	**B11..E11**	**Y-axis:**	**Dollar Sales**
Grid:	**Horiz**	**Name:**	**SIDEBAR**
Title 1:	**\C1**		
Title 2:	**\C2**		

FIGURE 5-17
A side-by-side bar graph allows you to compare the sales in each city on a quarterly basis.

Using a Named Graph   To create a side-by-side bar graph, let's assign the graph name MULTLINE as the current graph. With the command cursor in the Graph menu, type the letters N for Name and U for Use. When the list of named graphs display on the screen, enter the name MULTLINE and press the Enter key. The multiple-line graph in Figure 5-12 displays on the screen and is assigned to the worksheet as the current graph. Press any key to redisplay the Graph menu.

Changing the Multiple-Line Graph to a Side-by-Side Bar Graph   Change the current graph from a multiple-line graph to a side-by-side bar graph by typing the letters T for Type and B for Bar. All the other graph specifications (A–F ranges, titles, and legends) remain the same. Add the horizontal grid, as we did earlier with the simple bar graph, by typing the letters O for Options, G for Grid, and H for Horizontal. Quit the Graph Options menu by typing the letter Q.

Viewing the Side-by-Side Bar Graph   Type the letter V for View. The side-by-side bar graph shown in Figure 5-17 displays on the screen. The different shading that you see for each bar (data range) is automatically done by VP-Planner Plus. The legends below the graph indicate which shaded bar corresponds to which city. Compare Figure 5-17 to Figure 5-12. The side-by-side bar graph is much easier to interpret than the multiple-line graph. For example, it is clear that Los Angeles had the greatest sales during the first three quarters. For the fourth quarter, Los Angeles had about the same sales as New York. After viewing the graph, press any key to redisplay the Graph menu.

Naming, Saving, and Printing the Side-by-Side Bar Graph   With the Graph menu on the screen, type the letters N for Name and C for Create to name the side-by-side bar graph. Enter the graph name SIDEBAR and press the Enter key. Next, type the letter Q to quit the Graph menu.

Use the command **/File Save** (**/FS**) to save the worksheet to disk. Press the Enter key when the file name PROJS-5A appears on the input line. Finally, type the letter R for Replace. Now there are six graphs associated with the worksheet—PIE, LINE, MULTLINE, SCATTER, BAR, and SIDEBAR.

With the worksheet on the screen, enter the command **/Graph Print** (**/GP**) to print the side-by-side bar graph. The graph is displayed on the screen and printed on the printer. The Graph menu redisplays on the screen after the printing activity is complete.

Stacked-Bar Graphs (/GTS)

One of the problems with the side-by-side bar graph in Figure 5-17 is that it does not show the combined total sales for the six cities for any quarter. An alternative graph to consider is the stacked-bar graph. A **stacked-bar graph** has a single bar for every value in the X range (see Figure 5-18). Each bar is made up of shaded segments. Each segment or piece of the total bar represents an element (city) as a distinct contributor. Together, the stacked segments make up a single bar that shows the cumulative amount (total quarterly sales) of all elements for each value in the X range (quarter).

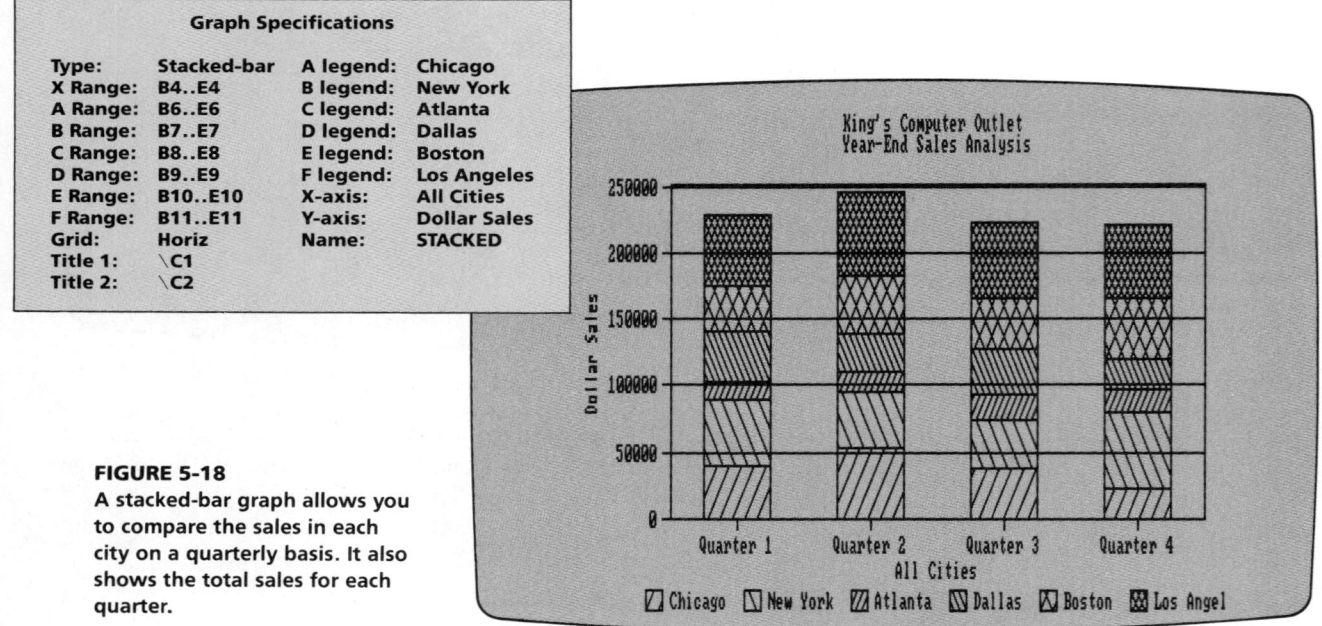

Graph Specifications			
Type:	**Stacked-bar**	**A legend:**	**Chicago**
X Range:	**B4..E4**	**B legend:**	**New York**
A Range:	**B6..E6**	**C legend:**	**Atlanta**
B Range:	**B7..E7**	**D legend:**	**Dallas**
C Range:	**B8..E8**	**E legend:**	**Boston**
D Range:	**B9..E9**	**F legend:**	**Los Angeles**
E Range:	**B10..E10**	**X-axis:**	**All Cities**
F Range:	**B11..E11**	**Y-axis:**	**Dollar Sales**
Grid:	**Horiz**	**Name:**	**STACKED**
Title 1:	**\C1**		
Title 2:	**\C2**		

FIGURE 5-18
A stacked-bar graph allows you to compare the sales in each city on a quarterly basis. It also shows the total sales for each quarter.

Changing the Side-by-Side Bar Graph to a Stacked-Bar Graph   The side-by-side bar graph is still the current graph associated with the worksheet. Therefore, let's modify it to display the stacked-bar graph shown in Figure 5-18. With the Graph menu on the screen, enter the command **Type Stacked-bar (TS)**. This command changes the side-by-side graph to a stacked-bar graph. All the other graph specifications (A-F ranges, titles, horizontal grid, and legends) remain the same.

Viewing the Stacked-Bar Graph   Type the letter V for View. The stacked-bar graph shown in Figure 5-18 displays on the screen. Compare Figure 5-18 to Figure 5-17. Notice how the stacked-bar graph shows both the quarterly contributions of each city and the total sales for each quarter. The stacked-bar graph is an effective way of showing trends and contributions from all segments, while still showing a total for each quarter.

Naming, Saving, and Printing the Stacked-Bar Graph   With the stacked-bar graph still on the screen, press any key to redisplay the Graph menu. Type the letters N for Name and C for Create to name the stacked-bar graph. Enter the graph name STACKED and press the Enter key. Quit the Graph menu by typing the letter Q.

Save the worksheet to disk. Enter the command /**File Save (/FS)**. Press the Enter key when the file name PROJS-5A appears on the input line. Press the letter R for Replace. Now there are seven graphs associated with the worksheet—PIE, LINE, MULTLINE, SCATTER, BAR, SIDEBAR, and STACKED.

Print the stacked-bar graph by entering the command /**Graph Print (/GP)**. When the printer is done printing the graph, type the letter Q to quit the Graph menu.

ADDITIONAL GRAPH OPTIONS (/GO)

 Three graph options that we did not cover in this project are the Data-Labels, Scale, and Color/B&W commands.

Data-Labels (/GOD)

Data-labels are used to explicitly label a bar or a point in a graph. Select the actual values in the range that the bar or point represents. VP-Planner Plus then positions the labels near the corresponding points or bars in the graph (see Figure 5-19).

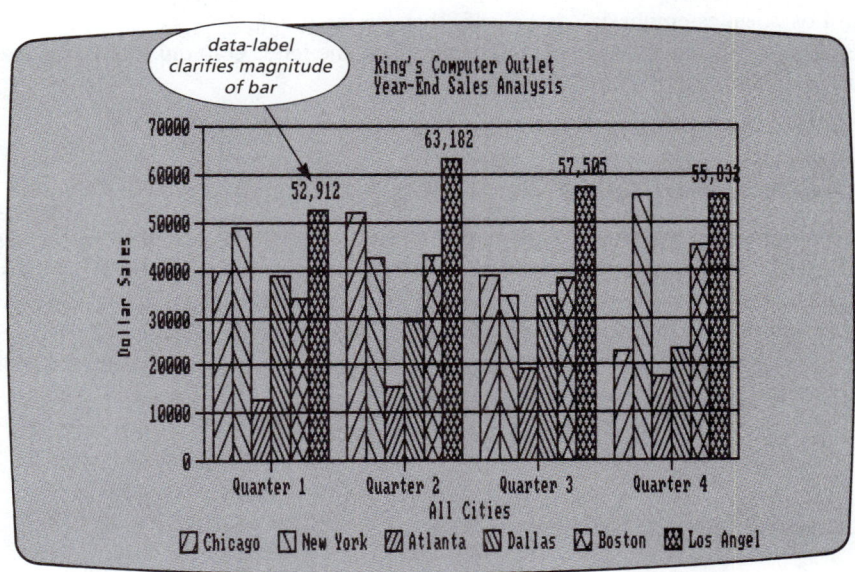

FIGURE 5-19
Data-labels are useful for clarifying and emphasizing various segments of the graph.

To illustrate the use of data-labels, make the SIDEBAR graph specifications the current graph by entering the command **/Graph Name Use** (/GNU). When the alphabetized list of named graphs display on the screen (see Figure 5-20), use the Down Arrow key to select SIDEBAR and press the Enter key. VP-Planner Plus immediately displays the side-by-side bar graph shown in Figure 5-17. Press any key on the keyboard and the Graph menu reappears on the screen.

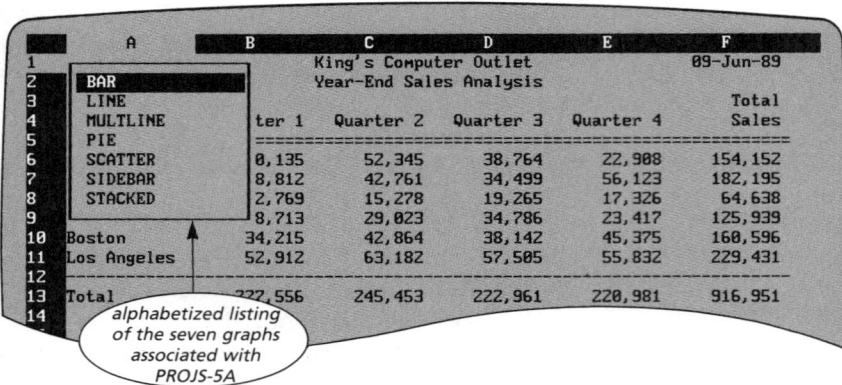

FIGURE 5-20
Directory of named graphs associated with the worksheet PROJS-5A—enter the command /Graph Name Use (/GNU).

Let's emphasize the four bars in Figure 5-17 that represent the quarterly sales for Los Angeles by displaying the actual quarterly sales above each corresponding bar. Enter the command **Options Data-Labels** (OD). This command causes the Graph Options menu to display and the command cursor to be active in the upper left-hand corner in the Data-Labels portion of the menu (see Figure 5-14). Note that data-labels can be assigned to any of the six data ranges, A through F.

Type the letter F to select the F range because it was assigned the range representing the four quarterly sales for Los Angeles. The worksheet reappears on the screen and VP-Planner Plus responds with the prompt message "Enter data label range: A1". Type the range B11..E11 and press the Enter key. The range B11..E11 contains the four quarterly sales for Los Angeles. Therefore, we are selecting the same range for the F data-label that we selected earlier for the F range.

After we press the Enter key, VP-Planner Plus prompts us to enter the desired position of the data-labels in the graph. A response to this prompt is only possible for line and XY graphs. For simple and side-by-side bar graphs, VP-Planner Plus automatically positions data-labels above each bar. Hence, press the Enter key. Next, type the letter Q twice, once to quit the Data-Labels section of the Graph Options menu and once to quit the Graph Options menu. Finally, type the letter V for View. The modified side-by-side bar graph in Figure 5-19 displays on the screen. Notice how the data-labels above the four bars representing Los Angeles emphasize and clarify them in the graph.

Press any key to redisplay the Graph menu. Type the letter Q to quit the Graph menu. The worksheet in Figure 5-1 displays on the screen.

Scale Command (/GOS)

The Scale command in the Graph Options menu (see Figure 5-14) is used to set the scales on the X and Y axes automatically or manually. The default setting is automatic. With automatic scaling, VP-Planner Plus adjusts the graph to include all points in each data range. If you set the graph scales to manual, you must specify the upper and lower limits on the Y axis in line and bar graphs, and the X and Y axes in XY graphs. (The pie chart is not affected by the Scale command.) It is possible to set one axis to automatic scaling and the other to manual scaling. You may also use this command to format the numbers that mark the X and Y axes.

Color/B&W Commands (/GOC or /GOB)

The Color command in the Graph Options menu (see Figure 5-14) eliminates the crosshatch patterns from bar and stacked-bar graphs. Alternatively, the B&W command causes the bar and stacked-bar graphs to have crosshatched patterns. The B&W command is the default setting. The Color and B&W commands are mutually exclusive. Neither command affects the patterns in a pie chart.

XY GRAPHS (/GTX)

XY graphs differ from the graphs we have discussed thus far. Rather than graphing the magnitude of a value at a fixed point on the X axis, an XY graph plots points of the form (x,y), where x is the X-axis coordinate and y is the Y-axis coordinate. Adjacent points are connected by a line to form the graph (see Figure 5-21). The XY graph is the type of graph used to plot mathematical functions.

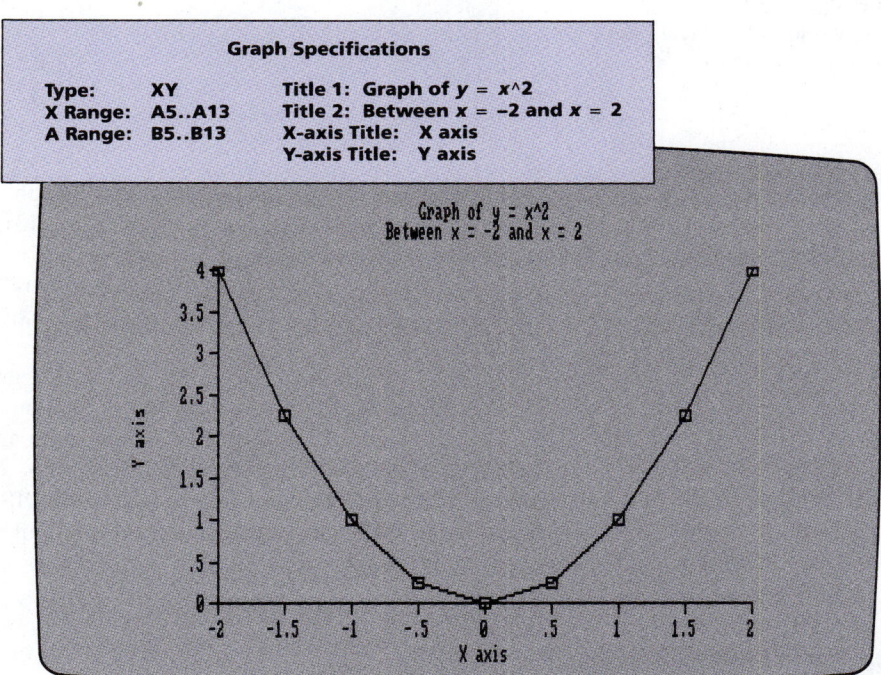

FIGURE 5-21
The XY graph is useful for plotting mathematical functions.

In an XY graph, both the X and Y axes are automatically scaled relative to the low and high values, so that all (x,y) points display and the graph fits on the screen. You can switch to manual scaling and scale either the X or Y axis yourself (use the Scale command).

To illustrate an XY graph, we will use the worksheet in Figure 5-22. As the title indicates, this worksheet includes a table of x and y coordinates for the function $y = x^2$. The x coordinates are in the range A5..A13. They begin at –2 and end at 2 in increments of 0.5. The x coordinates are formed in the worksheet by using the Data Fill command. The y coordinates are determined by assigning the formula +A5^2 to cell B5 and then copying B5 to the range B6..B13. Enter the worksheet in Figure 5-22 by following the first seven steps in the second list of keystrokes in the Project Summary section.

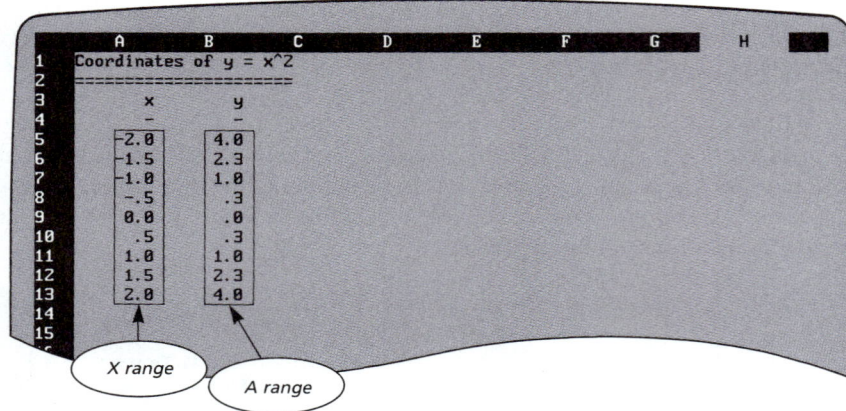

FIGURE 5-22
The worksheet we will use to plot the function y = x².

To plot the function $y = x^2$ in the form of an XY graph, enter the command /**Graph T**ype **XY** (/GTX). Next, type the letter X to define the X range. Assign the X range the x coordinates (cells A5 through A13). Type the letter A to define the A range. Assign the A range the y coordinates (cells B5 through B13).

To complete the XY graph, let's dress it up using the Graph Options menu. Assign "Graph of y = x^2" to the first line of the title and assign "Between x = –2 and x = 2" to the second line. Label the X axis as "X axis" and the Y axis as "Y axis". Type the letter Q to quit the Graph Options menu.

With the command cursor in the Graph menu, type the letter V for View. The XY graph shown in Figure 5-21 displays on the screen. Note that the Y axis is displayed to the far left side passing through –2 on the X axis, rather than in the standard mathematical style of passing through zero on the X axis. To return to the Graph menu after viewing the graph, press any key on the keyboard.

Finally, quit the Graph menu and save the worksheet shown in Figure 5-22 as PROJS-5B. Print the XY graph in Figure 5-21 by entering the command /**Graph P**rint (/GP). Type the letter Q twice, once to quit the Graph menu and once to quit VP-Planner Plus. Finally, type the letter Y to confirm your exit from VP-Planner Plus.

PROJECT SUMMARY

*I*n this project, we created several graphs. Each of the steps required to build the worksheets and graphs is listed in the following two tables.

SUMMARY OF KEYSTROKES—PROJS-5A   (Figure 5-1) and Associated Graphs

STEPS	KEY(S) PRESSED	STEPS	KEY(S) PRESSED
1	/WGC12 ↵ (Build worksheet)	42	V
2	/WCS13 ↵	43	↵NCLINE ↵Q
3	→ → King's Computer Outlet↓	44	/FS ↵R
4	Year-End Sales Analysis → → → ↑	45	/GP
5	@TODAY ↵/RFD1 ↵	46	AB6.E6 ↵ (Build multiple-line graph)
6	↓↓"Total ↵	47	BB7.E7 ↵
7	F5 A4 ↵City → "Quarter 1 → "Quarter 2 →	48	CB8.E8 ↵
8	"Quarter 3 → "Quarter 4 → "Sales ↵	49	DB9.E9 ↵
9	F5 A5 ↵\ = ↵/C ↵. → → → → → → ↵	50	EB10.E10 ↵
10	↓Chicago → 40135 → 52345 → 38764 → 22908 ↵	51	FB11.E11 ↵
11	F5 A7 ↵New York → 48812 → 42761 → 34499 → 56123 ↵	52	OLAChicago ↵LBNew York ↵LCAtlanta ↵
12	F5 A8 ↵Atlanta → 12769 → 15278 → 19265 → 17326 ↵	53	LDDallas ↵LEBoston ↵LFLos Angeles ↵Q
13	F5 A9 ↵Dallas → 38713 → 29023 → 34786 → 23417 ↵	54	V
14	F5 A10 ↵Boston → 34215 → 42864 → 38142 → 45375 ↵	55	↵NCMULTLINE ↵Q
15	F5 A11 ↵Los Angeles → 52912 → 63182 → 57505 → 55832 ↵	56	/FS ↵R
16	F5 A12 ↵\-↵/C ↵. → → → → → → ↵	57	/GP
17	F5 F6 ↵@SUM(B6.E6) ↵	58	OFGSQQ (Build scatter graph)
18	/C ↵.↓↓↓↓↓ ↵	59	V
19	F5 A13 ↵Total →	60	↵NCSCATTER ↵Q
20	@SUM(B6.B11) ↵	61	/FS ↵R
21	/C ↵. → → → → → ↵	62	/GP
22	/RF,0 ↵A6.F13 ↵ Home	63	NULINE ↵ (Build simple bar graph)
23	/FSPROJS-5A ↵	64	↵TB
24	/GTP (Build pie chart)	65	OGHQ
25	AF6.F11 ↵	66	V
26	XA6.A11 ↵Q	67	↵NCBAR ↵Q
27	F5 F15 ↵1↓2↓3↓4↓5↓106 ↵	68	/FS ↵R
28	/GBF15.F20 ↵	69	/GP
29	OTFKing's Computer Outlet ↵	70	NUMULTLINE ↵ (Build side-by-side bar graph)
30	TSYear-End Sales Analysis ↵Q	71	↵TB
31	V	72	OGHQ
32	↵NCPIE ↵	73	V
33	/FS ↵R	74	↵NCSIDEBAR ↵Q
34	/GP	75	/FS ↵R
35	SPIES-5A ↵	76	/GP
36	RG (Build line graph)	77	TS (Build stacked-bar graph)
37	TL	78	V
38	XB4.E4 ↵	79	↵NCSTACKED ↵Q
39	AB13.E13 ↵	80	/FS ↵R
40	OTF\C1 ↵TS\C2 ↵	81	/GP
41	TXAll Cities ↵TYDollar Sales ↵Q	82	Q

Project Summary (continued)

SUMMARY OF KEYSTROKES—PROJS-5B

STEPS	KEY(S) PRESSED	STEPS	KEY(S) PRESSED
1	/WEY	10	AB5.B13 ↵
2	Coordinates of y = x^2↓	11	OTFGraph of y = x^2 ↵
3	=======================↓	12	TSBetween x = –2 and x = 2 ↵
4	"x → "y↓"–←"–↓	13	TXX axis ↵
5	/DFA5.A13 ↵ –2 ↵ 0.5 ↵ ↵	14	TYY axis ↵Q
6	→ +A5^2 ↵ /C ↵ B6.B13 ↵	15	V
7	/RFF1 ↵ A5.B13 ↵	16	↵Q/FSPROJS-5B ↵
8	/GTX (Start XY graph)	17	/GPQ
9	XA5.A13 ↵	18	/QY

The following list summarizes the material covered in Project 5:

1. VP-Planner Plus allows you to create, display, and print a graph of the data in your worksheet and get your message across in a dramatic pictorial fashion.
2. The first step in drawing a graph is to enter the command /**G**raph (/G). This command activates the command cursor in the **Graph menu**.
3. A **pie chart** is used to show how 100% of an amount is divided.
4. With a pie chart, you are allowed only three ranges. The A range specifies the data that is used to segment the pie. The X range is assigned the range of labels that identify the segments. The B range is used to shade and explode segments of the pie chart.
5. Through the Graph Options menu, you can assign two title lines of 39 characters each to identify the graph. Except on the pie chart, you may also add titles of up to 39 characters each for the X axis and Y axis. Titles may be entered by keying in the title or by keying in a cell address preceded by a backslash (\).
6. When numbers are changed in a worksheet, the current graph will reflect the changes the next time it is displayed.
7. You may obtain a hard copy of the current graph by using the Print or View commands in the Graph menu. The Print command displays the graph on the screen and then sends it to the printer. With the View command, hold down the Shift key and press the PrtSc key.
8. The command /**G**raph **N**ame **C**reate (/GNC) can be used to store the current graph specifications under a name. This allows you to have more than one set of graph specifications associated with a worksheet. To assign a named set of graph specifications as the current graph, use the command /**G**raph **N**ame **U**se (/GNU).
9. To save any named graph specifications to disk, you must save the worksheet. Use the /**F**ile **S**ave (/FS) command.
10. The command /**G**raph **R**eset (/GR) allows you to reset all the current graph specifications or any individual ones.
11. You can save a copy of the current graph that is independent of the worksheet. This "snapshot" of the graph is called a **PIC file** because VP-Planner Plus saves the graph with the file extension .PIC. To view PIC files, use the Look command in the Graph menu.
12. **Line graphs** are used to show trends. You may have from one to six lines drawn in the graph. Each line represents a different data range (A through F) in the worksheet.
13. In a line graph, assign the labels for the X axis to the X range and assign the data ranges to the A through F ranges.
14. When more than one line is assigned to a line graph, it is called a **multiple-line graph**. Multiple-line graphs are used to show trends and comparisons.
15. To identify the lines in a multiple-line graph, use the Legends command in the Graph Options menu.

16. A **scatter graph** displays the points in a graph without any connecting lines.
17. To create a scatter graph, follow the steps for a multiple-line graph. Next, through the Graph Options menu, use the Format Graph Symbols command to draw the symbols and delete the connecting lines.
18. A **bar graph** is used to show trends and comparisons.
19. A **simple bar graph** has a single bar (A range) for each value in the X range.
20. To add a horizontal grid to a graph, display the Graph Options menu and type the letters G for Grid and H for Horizontal.
21. A **side-by-side bar graph** is used to compare multiple data ranges. A side-by-side bar graph may have up to six bars per X range value.
22. A **stacked-bar** graph shows one bar per X range value. However, the bar shows both the sum of the parts and the individual contributors.
23. VP-Planner Plus automatically scales the Y axis for bar and line graphs and the X and Y axes for XY graphs. If you prefer to set the scales manually, use the Scale command in the Graph Options menu.
24. The Color and B&W commands in the Graph Options menu are used to turn the shading of bar graphs on and off.
25. Data-labels are used to explicitly label a bar or point in a graph. You may label any of the six data ranges A through F.
26. **XY graphs** are used to plot mathematical functions. In an XY graph the X range is assigned the X-axis values and the A range is assigned the Y-axis values.

STUDENT ASSIGNMENTS

STUDENT ASSIGNMENT 1: True/False

Instructions: Circle T if the statement is true or F if the statement is false.

T F   1. A pie chart is used to show a trend.
T F   2. The Save command in the Graph Options menu saves the worksheet.
T F   3. A PIC file contains a worksheet.
T F   4. The Look command in the Options menu is used to display PIC files.
T F   5. A pie chart can have from one to six data ranges.
T F   6. The B range is used to shade the segments of a pie chart.
T F   7. A line graph can have from one to six lines.
T F   8. To store the graph specifications assigned to a worksheet under a name, save the worksheet using the Save command in the Graph menu.
T F   9. Multiple-line graphs are used to show trends and comparisons.
T F 10. If the title for a graph is the same as a label in a cell of the corresponding worksheet, enter the cell address preceded by a circumflex (^) for the title.
T F 11. Legends are used to identify the bars and lines in a graph.
T F 12. Data-labels are used to clarify a bar or a point in a graph.
T F 13. A scatter graph shows a random sample of points in the graph.
T F 14. Side-by-side bar graphs are used to compare data ranges for the same period.
T F 15. A stacked-bar graph differs from a side-by-side bar graph in that it shows the combined total of the contributors.
T F 16. VP-Planner Plus automatically scales the axes in a graph unless you use the Scale command in the Graph Options menu.
T F 17. The XY command in the Graph Type menu is used to display a bar graph.
T F 18. The Reset command in the Graph Options menu allows you to reset individual graph specifications, like the ranges A through F.
T F 19. There can be only one current graph assigned to a worksheet.
T F 20. The Graph Retrieve command is used to assign a named graph as the current graph.

STUDENT ASSIGNMENT 2: Multiple Choice

Instructions: Circle the correct response.

1. Which of the following types of graphs can you draw with VP-Planner Plus?
   a. line   b. bar   c. pie   d. XY   e. all of these
2. Which of the following ranges are meaningless for a pie chart?
   a. X   b. A   c. B   d. C through F
3. A pie chart is used to show _____ .
   a. how 100% of an amount is divided   c. how two or more data ranges compare
   b. trends   d. none of these
4. A side-by-side bar graph can have up to _____ bars per value in the X range.
   a. 3   b. 5   c. 6   d. 8
5. Data-labels are used to _____ .
   a. assign a title to the graph   c. clarify points and bars in a graph
   b. define which bar or line belongs to which data range   d. scale the X and Y axes
6. To explode a segment of a pie chart, add _____ to the corresponding cell in the _____ range.
   a. 10, C   b. 100, B   c. 1000, A   d. none of these
7. In a stacked-bar graph each bar shows _____ .
   a. the total amount for a label in the X range   c. none of these
   b. the contribution of each participant   d. both a and b
8. Which one of the following commands in the Graph menu displays the current graph?
   a. View   b. Print   c. Save   d. both a and b

STUDENT ASSIGNMENT 3: Understanding Graph Commands

Instructions: Describe the function of each of the following commands. Refer to Figures 5-2, 5-6, and 5-9.

a. /G _____   i. /GS _____
b. /GRG _____   j. /GV _____
c. /GNU _____   k. /GP _____
d. /GO _____   l. /GND _____
e. /GTB _____   m. /GTS _____
f. /GTP _____   n. /GNC _____
g. /GOTF _____   o. /GOL _____
h. /GRXQ _____   p. /GOD _____

STUDENT ASSIGNMENT 4: Understanding the Graph Options

Instructions: Describe the purpose of the following titled sections in the Graph Options menu (see Figure 5-6).

a. DATA-LABELS

   Purpose: _____

b. TITLES

   Purpose: _____

c. LEGEND

   Purpose: _____

d. SCALE

   Purpose: _____

e. FORMAT

   Purpose: _____

f. GRID

   Purpose: _____

g. COLOR

   Purpose: _____

h. B&W

   Purpose: _____

i. QUIT

   Purpose: _____

STUDENT ASSIGNMENT 5: Drawing a Pie Chart

Instructions: Load VP-Planner Plus. Retrieve the worksheet PROJS-2 built in Project 2 (see Figure 2-2).

Draw a pie chart that shows the revenue contribution for each month to the total quarterly revenue in the first quarter sales report. The pie chart should resemble the one shown in Figure 5-23. Use the following graph specifications:

Type = Pie	A range = B4..D4	Title 1 = \B1
X range = B2..D2	B range = E4..E6	Title 2 = TOTAL REVENUE
	(explode the February revenue)	

Print the worksheet and the pie chart. Save the worksheet with the graph specifications as STUS5-5.

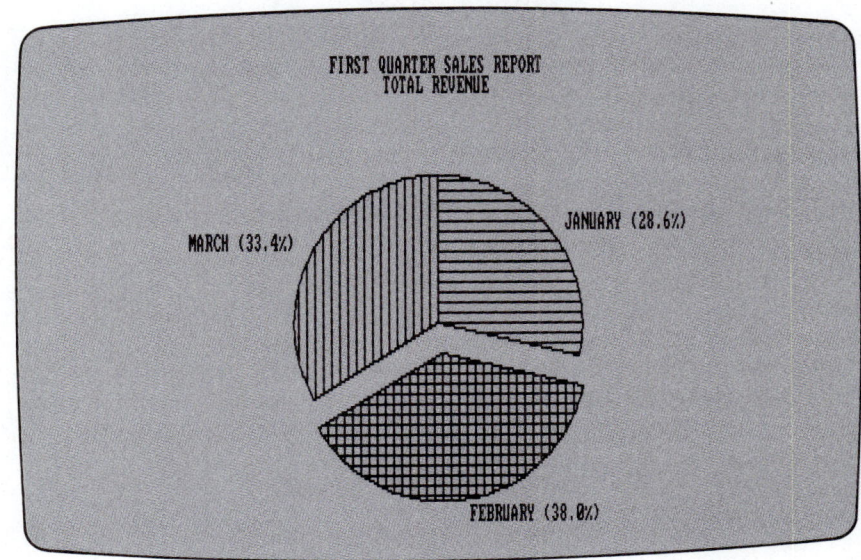

FIGURE 5-23
Student Assignment 5

STUDENT ASSIGNMENT 6: Drawing a Multiple-Line Graph and Side-by-Side Bar Graph

Instructions: Load VP-Planner Plus. Retrieve the worksheet PROJS-2 built in Project 2 (see Figure 2-2).

Draw a multiple-line graph and a side-by-side bar graph that show the trends in the revenue, costs, and profit of the first quarter sales report. The multiple-line graph should resemble the one shown in Figure 5-24. The side-by-side bar graph should resemble the one shown in Figure 5-25. Name the multiple-line graph MULTLINE and the side-by-side bar graph SIDEBAR.

Use the following graph specifications:

Type = Line   Title 1 = \B1
X range = B2..D2   Y axis title = Dollars
A range = B4..D4   A legend = \A4
B range = B5..D5   B legend = \A5
C range = B6..D6   C legend = \A6

For the side-by-side bar graph, change the Type to Bar. Print the worksheet and the two graphs. Save the worksheet as STUS5-6.

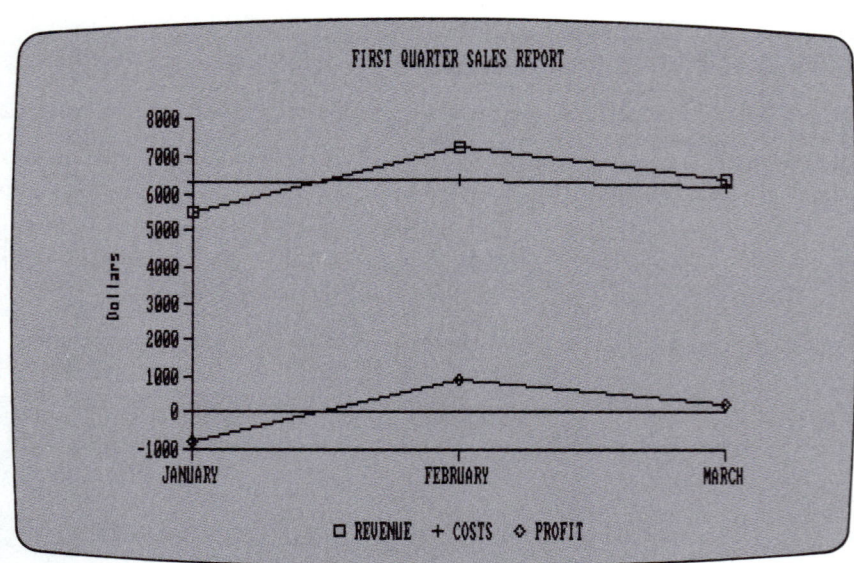

FIGURE 5-24
Student Assignment 6A

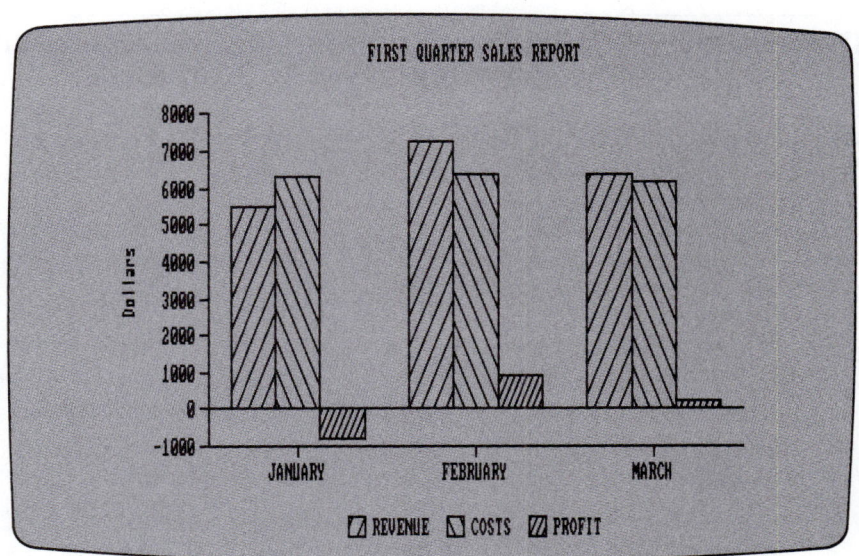

FIGURE 5-25
Student Assignment 6B

STUDENT ASSIGNMENT 7: Drawing a Stacked-Bar Graph

Instructions: Load VP-Planner Plus. Retrieve the worksheet PROJS-3 built in Project 3 (see Figure 3-1).

Draw a stacked-bar graph that shows the individual contributions of each expense category and the total estimated expenses for each of the three months. The stacked-bar graph should resemble the one shown in Figure 5-26.

Use the following graph specifications:

Type = Stacked-bar
X range = B5..D5
A range = B15..D15
B range = B16..D16
C range = B17..D17
D range = B18..D18
E range = B19..D19
Title 1 = \A1
Title 2 = Estimated Expenses
Y axis title = Dollars
A legend = Mfg.
B legend = Research
C legend = Mktg.
D legend = Adm.
E legend = Fulfillment
Grid = Horizontal

Print the stacked-bar graph and worksheet. Save the worksheet with the stacked-bar graph specifications as STUS5-7.

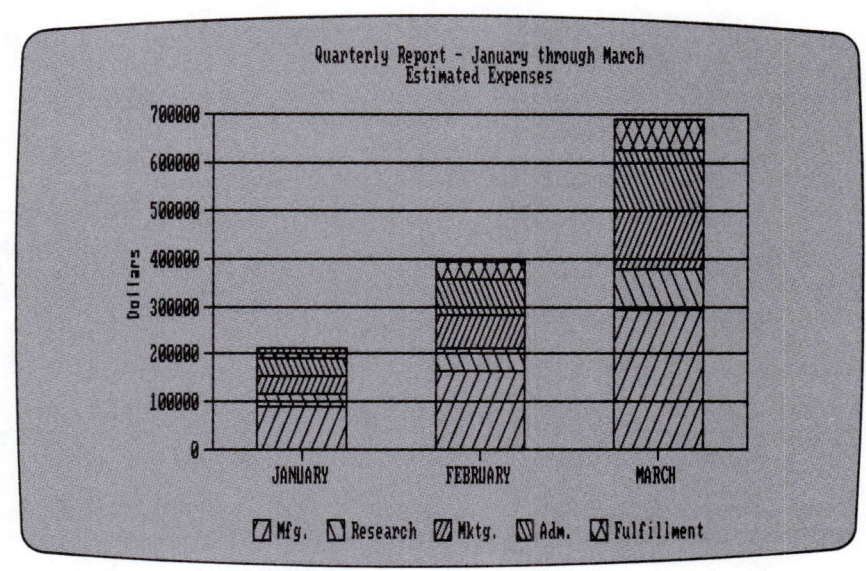

FIGURE 5-26 Student Assignment 7

STUDENT ASSIGNMENT 8: Building a Table of Coordinates and Drawing the Corresponding XY Graph

Instructions: Load VP-Planner Plus. Build the table of coordinates for the function $y = 2x^3 + 6x^2 - 18x + 6$ shown in Figure 5-27 and draw the corresponding XY graph shown in Figure 5-28.

For the worksheet use the Data Fill command to build the column of X coordinates in the range A6..A20. Start with –5, increment by 0.5, and stop at 9999. Assign the formula $2*A6^3 + 6*A6^2 - 18*A6 + 6$ to B6. Copy B6 to the range B7..B20. Format the range A6..B20 to the Fixed type with 1 decimal position.

```
         A           B        C        D        E        F        G        H
1    Coordinates of y = 2x^3 + 6x^2 - 18x + 6
2    =============================================
3
4            x           y
5            -           -
6          -5.0        -4.0
7          -4.5        26.3
8          -4.0        46.0
9          -3.5        56.8
10         -3.0        60.0
11         -2.5        57.3
12         -2.0        50.0
13         -1.5        39.8
14         -1.0        28.0
15          -.5        16.3
16          0.0         6.0
17           .5        -1.3
18          1.0        -4.0
19          1.5         -.8
20          2.0        10.0
A3

1help 2edit 3name 4abs 5goto 6window 7data 8table 9recalculate 0graph
336K                                       12:24                      READY
```

FIGURE 5-27
Student Assignment 8 worksheet.

For the XY graph (see Figure 5-28), use the following graph specifications:

Type = XY
X range = A6..A20
A range = B6..B20
Title 1 = Graph of y = 2x^3 + 6x^2 – 18x + 6
X axis title = X axis
Y axis title = Y axis

Print the XY graph and worksheet. Save the worksheet with the XY graph specifications as STUS5-8.

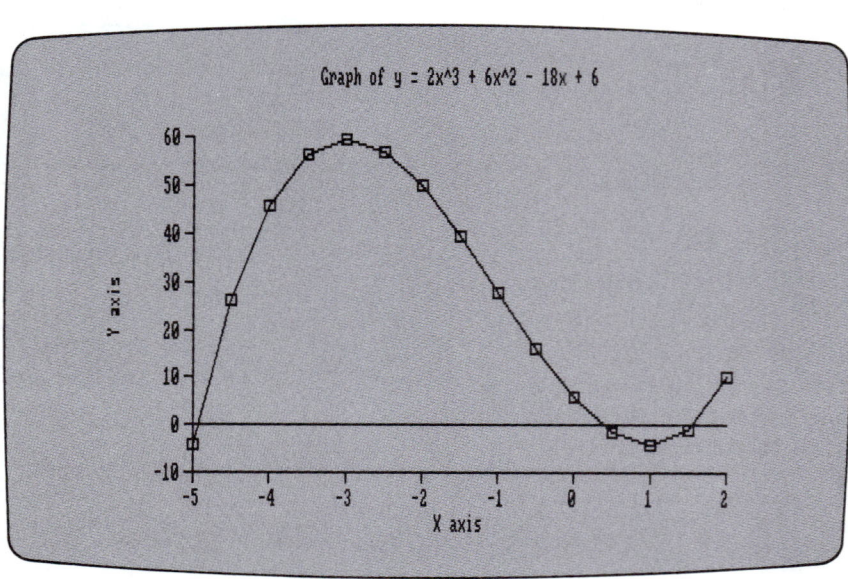

FIGURE 5-28
Student Assignment 8 XY graph.

PROJECT 6

Sorting and Querying a Worksheet Database

Objectives

You will have mastered the material in this project when you can:

■ Define the terms database, DBMS, field, field name, and record.
■ Differentiate between records in ascending and descending sequence.
■ Sort a database on the basis of a primary key.
■ Sort a database on the basis of both primary and secondary keys.
■ Establish criteria for selecting records in a database.
■ Find records in a database that match specified criteria.
■ Extract records from a database that match specified criteria.
■ Apply the database functions to generate information about the database.
■ Utilize the lookup functions to select values from a list or a table.

*I*n this project we discuss some of the database capabilities of VP-Planner Plus. A **database** is an organized collection of data. For example, a telephone book, a grade book, and a list of company employees are databases. In these cases, the data related to a person is called a **record**, and the data items that make up a record are called **fields**. In a telephone book database, the fields are name, address, and telephone number.

A worksheet's row and column structure can easily be used to organize and store a database (see Figure 6-1). Each row of a worksheet can be used to store a record and each column can store a field. Furthermore, a row of column headings at the top of the worksheet can be used as **field names** to identify each field.

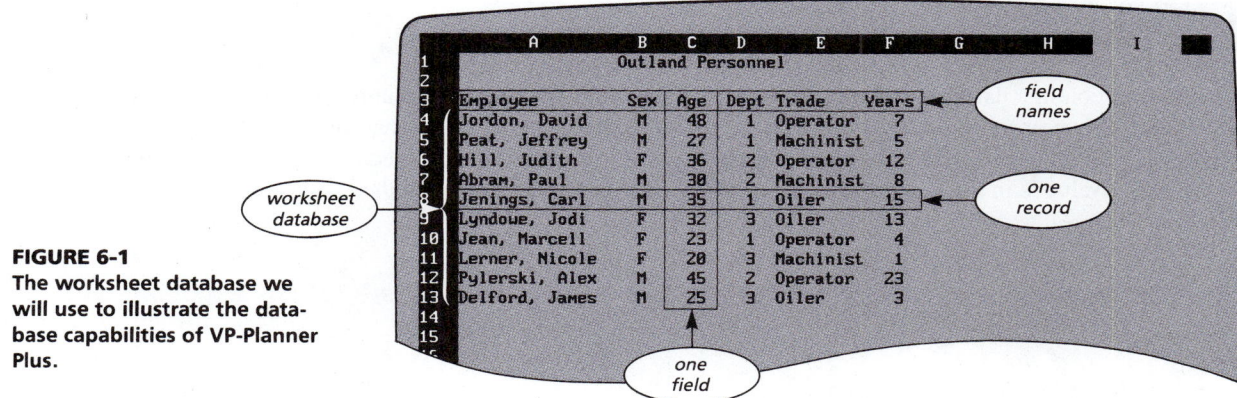

FIGURE 6-1
The worksheet database we will use to illustrate the database capabilities of VP-Planner Plus.

A **database management system (DBMS)** is a software package that is used to create a database and store, access, sort, and make additions, deletions, and changes to that database. Although somewhat limited by the number of records that can be stored, VP-Planner Plus is capable of carrying out all the DBMS functions. In many ways, we have already used VP-Planner Plus as a database management system when we built, formatted, and enhanced our worksheets in the earlier projects.

In this project, we will focus on the two functions of a DBMS that we have not yet discussed—sorting and accessing records. We will also discuss the special database and table lookup functions available with VP-Planner Plus. For the remainder of this project, the term database will mean worksheet database.

The database for this project is illustrated on the previous page in Figure 6-1. It consists of 10 personnel records. Each record represents an employee for the Outland Company. The names, columns, types, and sizes of the fields are described in Table 6-1. Since the database is visible on the screen, it is important that it be readable. Therefore, most of the field sizes (column widths) in Table 6-1 are determined from the column headings (field names) and not the maximum length of the data as is the case with most database management systems. For example, column E represents the Trade field, which has a width of nine characters because the longest trade designation is machinist (nine characters). Column F, which represents the years of seniority, is five characters wide because the field name Years is five letters long. The column headings in the row immediately above the first record (row 3) play an important role in the database commands issued to VP-Planner Plus.

TABLE 6-1   Field Descriptions for the Outland Personnel Database

FIELD NAME	COLUMN	TYPE OF DATA	SIZE
Employee	A	Label	16
Sex	B	Label	5
Age	C	Numeric	5
Dept	D	Label	6
Trade	E	Label	9
Years	F	Numeric	5

Build the database shown in Figure 6-1 by following the steps listed in the first table of the Project Summary section at the end of this project on page 233.

SORTING A DATABASE

The information in a database is easier to work with and more meaningful if the records are arranged in sequence on the basis of one or more fields. Arranging the records in sequence is called **sorting**. Figure 6-2 illustrates the difference between unsorted data and the same data in ascending and descending sequence. Data that is in sequence from lowest to highest in value is in **ascending sequence**. Data that is in sequence from highest to lowest in value is in **descending sequence**.

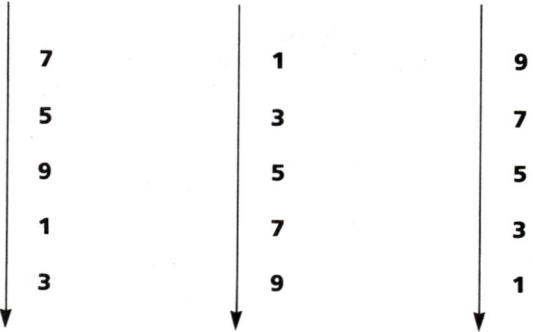

FIGURE 6-2
Data in various sequences.

data in no particular sequence

data in ascending sequence

data in descending sequence

The Sort Menu (/DS)

To sort a database, enter the command /**D**ata **S**ort (/DS). The **Sort menu** in Figure 6-3 displays. The commands available in the Sort menu are described in Table 6-2.

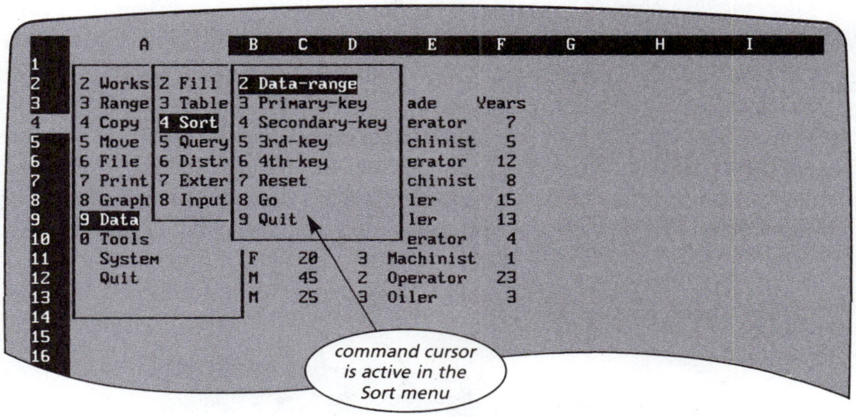

FIGURE 6-3
Step 1 of using the Sort command—enter the command /Data Sort (/DS) and the sort menu displays.

TABLE 6-2   Commands Available in the Sort Menu

COMMAND	FUNCTION
Data-range	Prompts you to specify the range of the database to sort.
Primary-key	Prompts you to enter the field (column) you wish to sort the records on and the sequence.
Secondary-key	Prompts you to enter a second field (column) you wish to sort on within the primary-key field, and the sequence for the secondary-key field. Used to "break ties" on the primary-key field.
3rd-key	Prompts you to enter a third field (column) you wish to sort on within the secondary-key field, and the sequence for the third-key field. Used to "break ties" on the primary-key field and secondary-key field.
4th-key	Prompts you to enter a fourth field (column) you wish to sort on within the third-key field, and the sequence for the fourth-key field. Used to "break ties" on the primary-key field, secondary-key field, and third-key field.
Reset	Clears all sort settings.
Go	Causes the database to be sorted on the basis of the sort settings.
Quit	Quits the Data command and returns control to READY mode.

To illustrate the use of the Data Sort command, we will first sort the database in Figure 6-1 into ascending sequence on the basis of the employee name field (column A). Next, we will sort the same database on years of seniority (column F) within the sex code (column B). That is, the sex code will be the primary-key field and years of seniority will be the secondary-key field.

Sorting the Records by Employee Name

With the command cursor active in the Sort menu (see Figure 6-3), do the following:

1. Enter the data range.
2. Enter the primary-key field.
3. Enter the Go command.

To enter the data range, type the letter D for Data-range. The **data range** defines the fields and records to be sorted in the database. The data range almost always encompasses *all* the fields in *all* the records below the column headings, although it can be made up of fewer records or fewer fields. Be aware, however, that if you do not select all the fields (columns) in the database, the unselected fields will not remain with the records they belong to and the data will get mixed up.

When you type the letter D for Data-range, VP-Planner Plus responds by displaying the database and a prompt message on the input line. Press the Backspace key to unlock the first end point on the input line. Use the arrow keys to select the range A4..F13 as shown in Figure 6-4. Press the Enter key and the Sort menu shown in Figure 6-3 reappears on the screen.

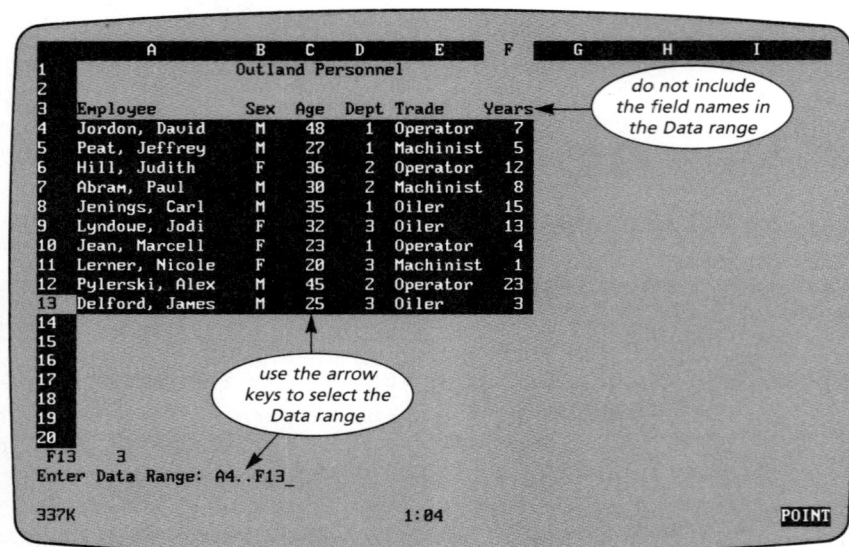

FIGURE 6-4
Step 2 of using the Sort command—enter the Data range. The Data range usually encompasses all the fields in all the records of the database.

The next step is to enter the primary-key field. With the Sort menu on the screen, type the letter P for Primary-key. VP-Planner Plus responds by displaying a prompt message on the input line requesting that we enter the primary key. Since column A is the employee name field, move the cell cursor to column A and press the Enter key. As shown in Figure 6-5, a second prompt message requesting the desired sequence of the sort appears on the input line. Type the letter A for ascending sequence and press the Enter key.

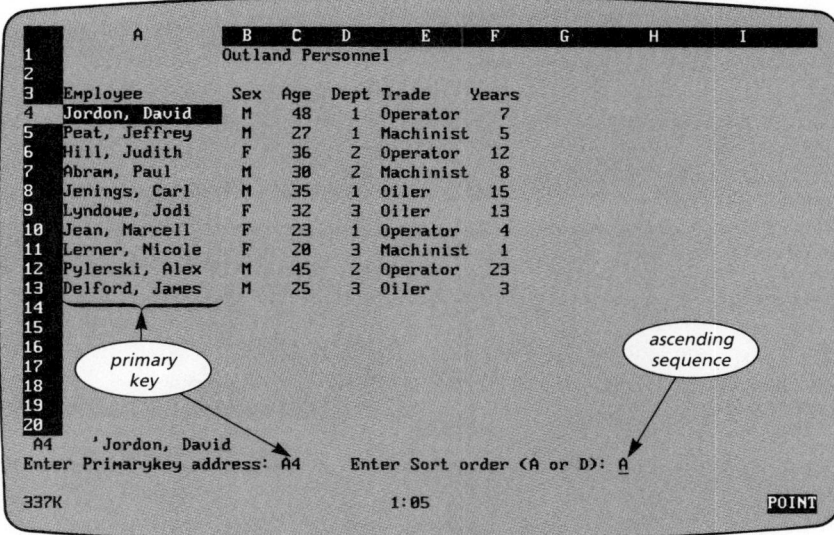

FIGURE 6-5
Step 3 of using the Sort command—enter the primary key and desired sequence for sorting the worksheet database by employee name.

To complete the sort, type the letter G for Go. VP-Planner Plus sorts the records and displays them in ascending sequence according to employee name. Following the completion of the Go command, control returns to READY mode as shown in Figure 6-6. Whereas the records in Figure 6-1 are in no particular sequence, the same records in Figure 6-6 are now in ascending sequence by employee name.

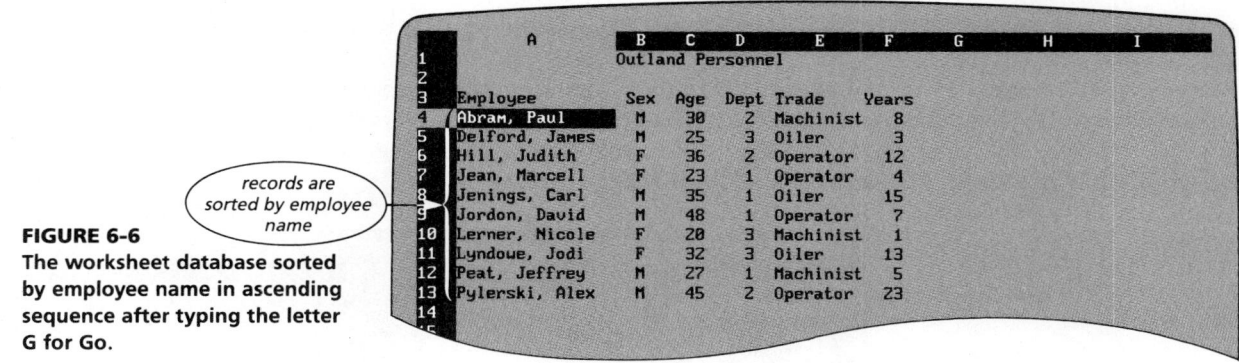

FIGURE 6-6
The worksheet database sorted by employee name in ascending sequence after typing the letter G for Go.

To complete this portion of the project, save and print a hard copy of the sorted database. Save the database using the file name PROJS-6A. Print the database using the same procedures we used in the previous projects.

Sorting the Records by Years of Seniority within Sex Code

In this example, we will use two sort keys. Our goal is to order the records so that the secondary-key field, years of seniority (column F), is ordered in descending sequence within the primary-key field, sex code (column B). Sort the primary-key field into ascending sequence. The female with the most years of seniority will be at the top of the list, and the male with the least seniority will be at the bottom of the list. This nested sorting always assumes that the primary key field contains duplicate values.

To start this portion of the project, load the original database PROJS-6 (see Figure 6-1) into main computer memory and enter the command /**D**ata **S**ort (/DS). With the command cursor active in the Sort menu (see Figure 6-3), type the letter D for Data-range. Next, select all the records in the database (A4..F13) as shown in Figure 6-4. Press the Enter key and the Sort menu shown in Figure 6-3 reappears on the screen.

After the data range is set, enter the primary-key field. To accomplish this, type the letter P for Primary-key. Move the cell cursor to column B (sex code) and press the Enter key. Type the letter A for ascending sequence. The primary-key field selections are shown on the input line in Figure 6-7. Press the Enter key to finalize the primary-key selections.

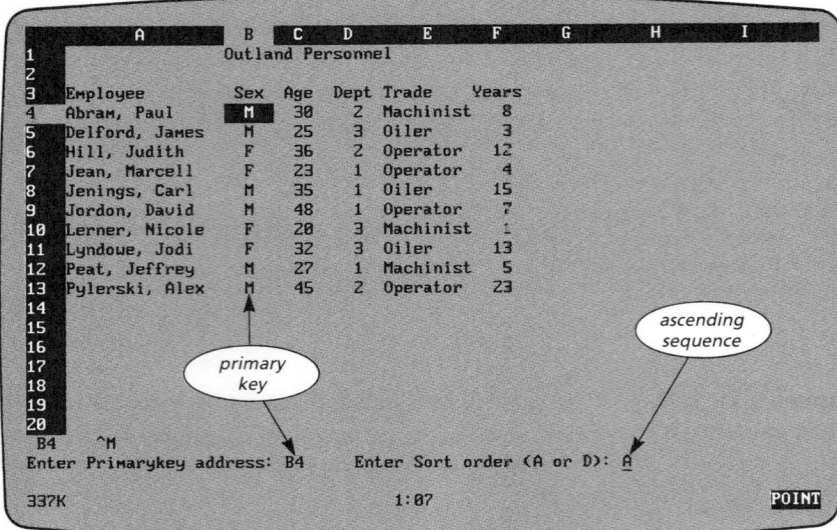

FIGURE 6-7
Entering the primary key and desired sequence for sorting the worksheet database by years of seniority within sex code.

Type the letter S for Secondary-key. VP-Planner Plus responds by displaying a prompt message on the input line requesting the secondary key. Move the cell cursor to column F, the one that contains the years of seniority, and press the Enter key. In response to the second prompt message on the input line, leave the D for descending sequence. The secondary-key field selections are shown in Figure 6-8. Press the Enter key.

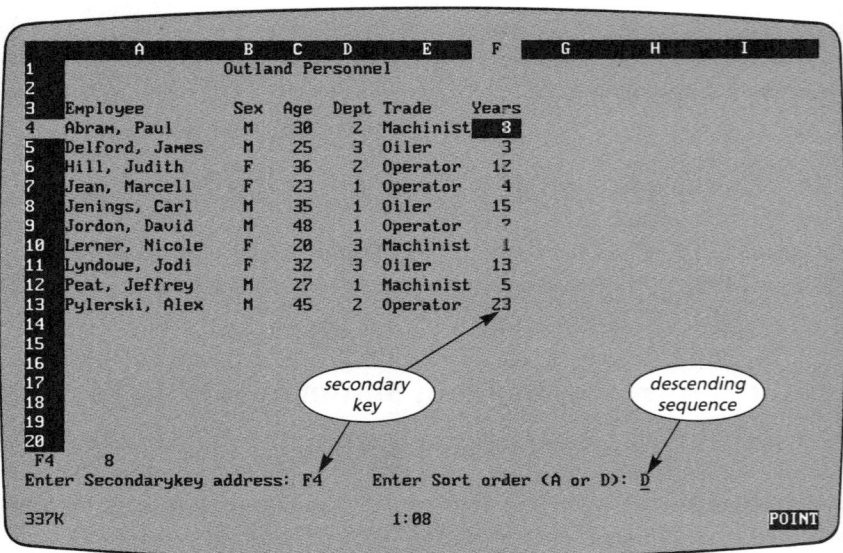

FIGURE 6-8
Entering the secondary key and desired sequence for sorting the worksheet database by years of seniority within sex code.

To complete the sort, type the letter G for Go. VP-Planner Plus sorts the records and places them in ascending sequence according to the sex-code field in column B. Within the sex code, the records are in descending sequence according to the years of seniority in column F. This is shown in Figure 6-9. Following the completion of the Go command, VP-Planner Plus displays the sorted records and returns to READY mode.

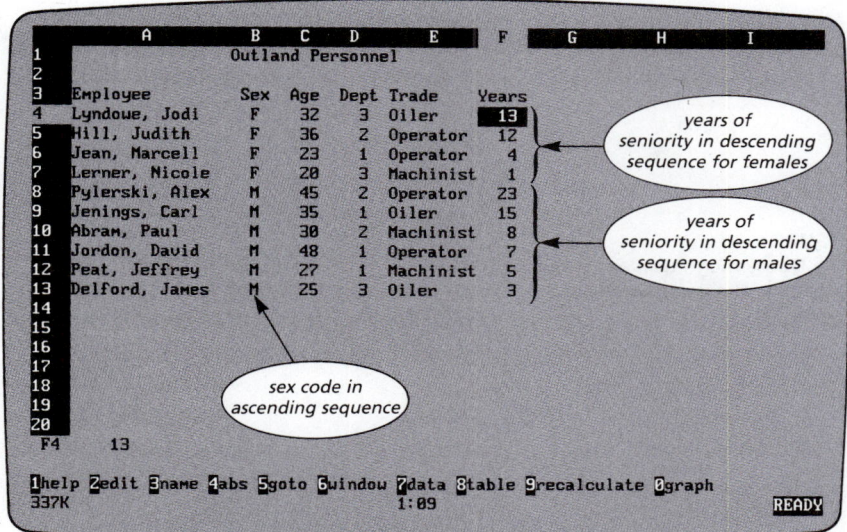

FIGURE 6-9
The worksheet database sorted by years of seniority within sex code.

Save and print a hard copy of the sorted database. Use the file name PROJS-6B.

QUERYING A DATABASE

One of the most powerful aspects of a DBMS is its ability to select records from a database that match specified criteria. This activity is called **querying a database**. Records that match the criteria can be highlighted, copied to another part of the worksheet, or deleted. If a record meets the specified criteria, we say that it *passed the test*. If a record does not meet the specific criteria, we say that it *flunked the test*.

The Query Menu (/DQ)

To query a database, enter the command /**D**ata **Q**uery (/DQ). This is shown in Figure 6-10. The topmost menu is called the **Query menu**. The function of each of the Query commands is described in Table 6-3.

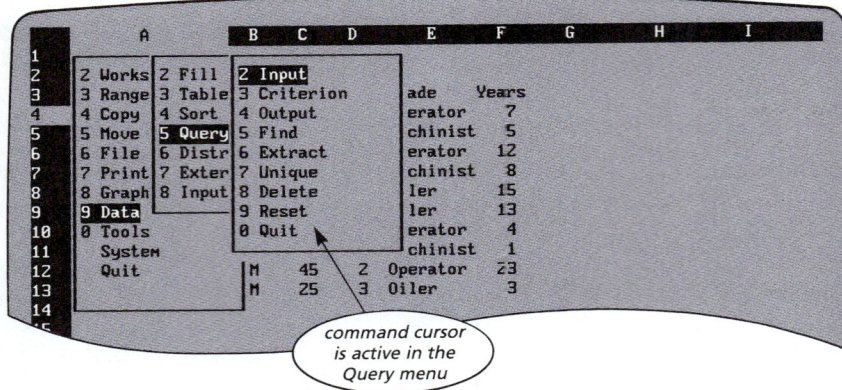

FIGURE 6-10
The Query menu displays when you enter the command /Data Query (/DQ).

command cursor is active in the Query menu

TABLE 6-3 Commands Available in the Query Menu

COMMAND	FUNCTION
Input	Prompts you to enter the range of the database to be queried. Usually the entire database is selected.
Criterion	Prompts you to enter the range of cells that includes the conditions for record selection. The conditions are entered into the worksheet off to the side or below the database.
Output	Prompts you to enter a range of cells to which records can be copied. The Output range is defined in the worksheet off to the side or below the database.
Find	Moves the cell cursor to the first record in the database that passes the test. The cell cursor moves one record at a time as you press the Up Arrow or Down Arrow keys. When you invoke the Find command, the cell cursor extends to include the entire record. Pressing the Esc key or Enter key cancels the search.
Extract	Copies all selected records from the database to the Output range. The records that pass the test are selected from the database. Records that flunk the test are not copied to the Output range.
Unique	Same as the Extract command, except that it copies only the first of any duplicate records.
Delete	Deletes all records from the database that pass the test.
Reset	Resets the Input, Output, and Criterion settings.
Quit	Quits the Data command and returns control to READY mode.

The Find Command (/DQF)

The Find command is used to search for records in the database that meet certain criteria. The command highlights the first record in the database that passes the test and continues to highlight records that pass the test as you press the Up and Down Arrow keys. If no more records pass the test in the direction you are searching, the computer beeps at you and the last record meeting the criteria remains highlighted.

With the database (PROJS-6) in Figure 6-1 in main computer memory, let's search for records representing males who work in department 2 (Sex = M AND Dept = 2). To complete the search, do the following:

1. Choose an unused area off to the side of the database and set up the criteria.
2. Type the command /**D**ata **Q**uery (/DQ) and enter the Input range.
3. Enter the Criterion range.
4. Type the letter F for Find.

The first step in setting up the Criterion range is to select an unused area of the worksheet. Let's begin the Criterion range at cell H3. Next, copy the names of those fields (column headings) that we are basing the search on to this area. That is, copy cell B3 (Sex) to cell H3 and cell D3 (Dept) to cell I3. You can bypass the Copy command and enter the field names through the keyboard, but the field names in the Criterion range must agree with the field names in the database, or the search won't work properly. To ensure that they are the same, it's best to use the Copy command.

An alternative to using the Copy command to set up the field names in the Criterion range is to assign cell H3 the formula +B3 and cell I3 the formula +D3. However, be aware that when you use formulas to assign a label to a cell, you lose right-justification and centering. Even so, the labels are considered to be identical. A positive result of using the formula method instead of the Copy command is that if you change a field name in the database, the corresponding field name in the Criterion range will change automatically.

Under each field name in the Criterion range, enter the value for which you want to search. In our example, we want to search for males who work in department 2. Therefore, enter the letter M in cell H4. (VP-Planner Plus considers lowercase m and uppercase M to be the same in a Criterion range. If you want VP-Planner Plus to distinguish between uppercase and lower-case letters, enter the command /WGDOCM.) In cell I4, enter the label 2 (^2 or "2 or '2). These entries for the Criterion range are shown in Figure 6-11. Note that the Criterion range must contain at least two rows—the field names in the first row and the criteria in the second row.

FIGURE 6-11
Step 1 of using the Find command—enter the criteria in unused cells off to the side of the database before issuing the Data Query command.

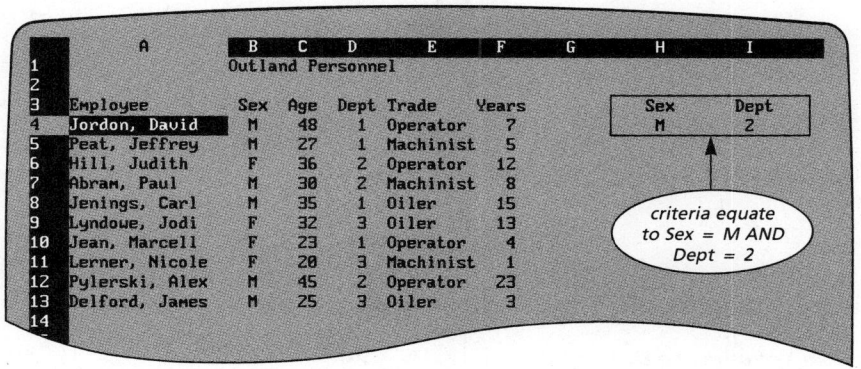

After building the Criterion range, enter the command /Data Query (/DQ). The Query menu displays as shown in Figure 6-10. Type the letter I for Input and use the arrow keys to select the entire database (A3..F13). This is shown in Figure 6-12. Note that the field names in row 3 must be included in the Input range. Press the Enter key.

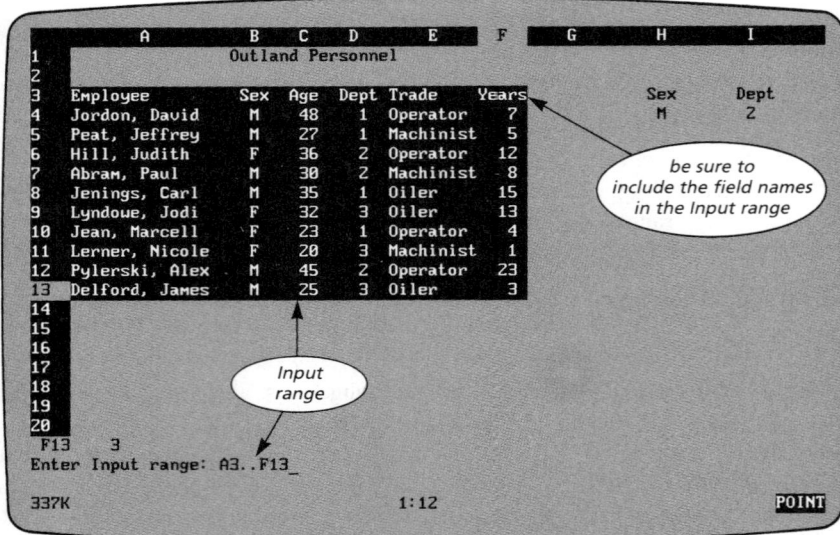

FIGURE 6-12
Step 2 of using the Find command—enter the command /Data Query Input (/DQI). Enter the Input range, which should encompass all the fields in all the records of the database, including the field names at the top.

Earlier, we set up the Criterion range (H3..I4). Now we must select it. Therefore, type the letter C for Criterion. Select the range H3..I4 as illustrated in Figure 6-13 and press the Enter key.

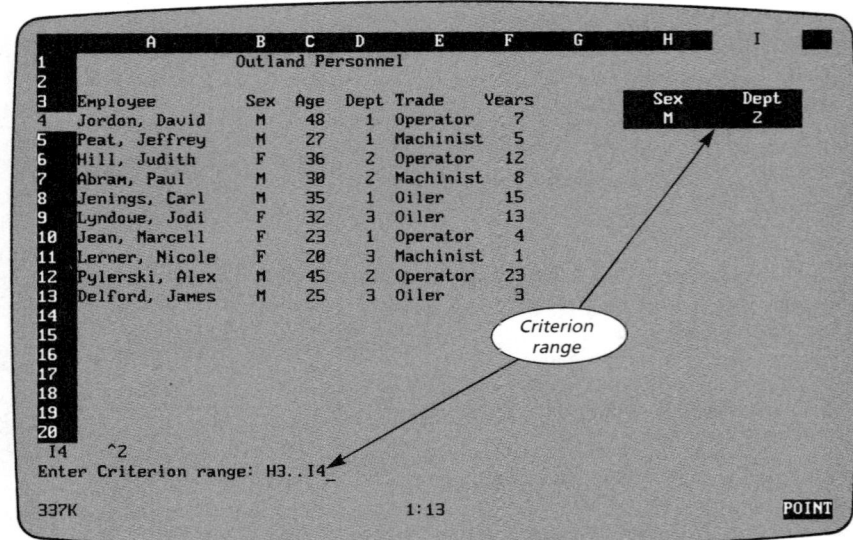

FIGURE 6-13
Step 3 of using the Find command—select the Criterion range.

Next, type the letter F for Find. As shown in the top screen of Figure 6-14, the first record that passes the test (Sex = M AND Dept = 2) is highlighted. Press the Down Arrow key and the next record that passes the test is highlighted. This is shown in the lower screen in Figure 6-14. If we press the Down Arrow key again, the computer will beep at us because there are no more records that pass the test below the highlighted one. If we press the Up Arrow key, the previous record that passed the test is highlighted again.

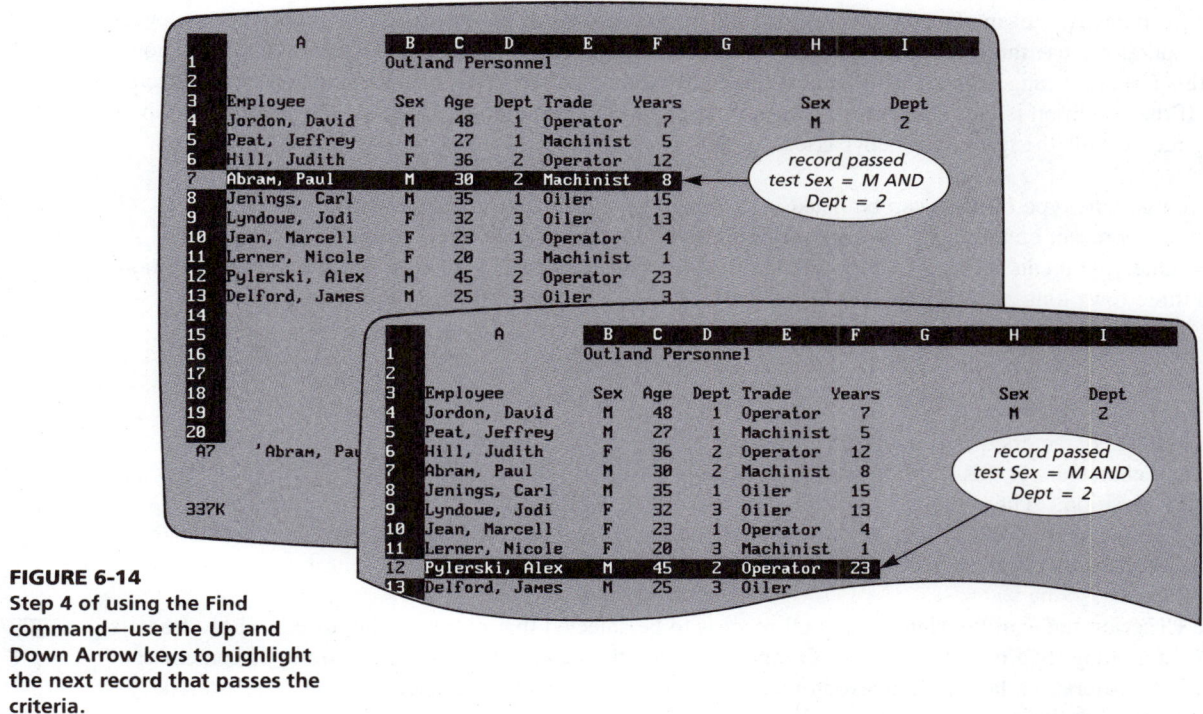

FIGURE 6-14
Step 4 of using the Find command—use the Up and Down Arrow keys to highlight the next record that passes the criteria.

After typing the letter F to invoke the Find command, we can move the elongated cursor to the very first record by pressing the Home key. We can move it to the last record by pressing the End key. These two keys allow us to start the search at the top or the bottom of the database. To terminate the Find command, press the Enter key to return to the Data Query menu or the Esc key to return to READY mode.

While the Find command is still active, we can edit the record that is highlighted. Use the Right Arrow and Left Arrow keys to move from one field to another. Because the entire record is highlighted, the cursor does not move to the different fields when we use the arrow keys. However, we can determine the field location of the cell cursor because the contents of the cell will display at the bottom of the screen on the status line. When the contents of the field we want to change display on the status line, we can retype the contents or use function key F2 to edit them. If we decide the original values were correct before pressing the Enter key to complete the change, we can press the Esc key to discard the change and return to READY mode.

To complete this portion of this project, save and print the database and criteria. Use the file name PROJS-6C.

More About the Criterion Range

The way you set up the Criterion range determines which records pass the test when you use the Find command. The following paragraphs describe several different examples of valid field names and logical expressions within a Criterion range.

No Conditions   If the Criterion range contains no values below the field names, all the records pass the test. For example, if you use the Criterion range at the right, then all the records in the Input range pass the test and the Find command highlights every record in the Input range, one at a time.

Sex	Trade

Conditions with Labels   The values below the field names in the Criterion range can be labels, numbers, or formulas. For example, if you want to select all the records in the database that represent employees who are operators, use the criteria at the right. In this example Operator is a label. If you use the Find command, this Criterion range causes VP-Planner Plus to use the condition Trade = Operator to evaluate each record. If the condition is true, the record passes the test and it is highlighted. If Trade does not equal Operator, the record fails the test and it is bypassed.

Trade
Operator

More than one type of trade can be listed in the Criterion range. For example, if you want to select records that represent employees who are operators or employees who are oilers (Trade = Operator OR Trade = Oiler), you can set up a Criterion range with the entries at the right. In this example, the Criterion range is three rows long.

Trade
Operator
Oiler

The global characters question mark (?) and asterisk (*) can be used within labels. The asterisk (*) means "any characters at this position and all remaining positions." The question mark (?) means "any character at this position." These global characters are also called **wild-card characters**. For example, the Criterion range at the right causes all records whose trade begins with the letter O to be selected. In our database, records with the trade of oiler or operator pass the test. The remaining records fail the test.

Trade
O*

The Criterion range at the right causes all records to be selected that represent employees whose trade is five characters long, begins with the letter O, and ends with the letters er. With regard to the placement of wild-card characters in a label, the question mark (?) can be used in any character position. The asterisk (*) can only be used at the end of a label.

Trade
O??er

Labels can also be preceded by the following characters: $ for a substring search; > for a greater than match; < for a less than match; and ˜ to exclude a match. The tilde (˜) can precede the greater than sign (>), less than sign (<), or dollar sign ($). For example, ˜>F means "not greater than F." To select the records representing employees that work in any department other than department 3, you may use the criteria at the right. Note that the department numbers in our database are labels, not numbers. Special characters like the tilde (˜) can only precede labels.

Dept
˜3

To search for all employees whose first name is Carl, enter the criteria in the entries at the right. Since the $ indicates a numeric entry, you must precede it with a label prefix character (') when using it as the first character for a substring search. That is, the previous condition under the field name Employee should be entered as '$Carl. In this case the string of characters Carl is called a **substring**. Note that the $ instructs VP-Planner Plus to search throughout the Employee field for the substring that follows the $. Hence, if the substring Carl is any part of the last name or first name of an employee, the corresponding record passes the test.

Employee
$Carl

Another way to select records in the database that represent males is to enter the criteria at the right. Since the letter M is greater than the letter F, all male employee records in the Input range pass the test and are selected. All female employee records fail the test and are bypassed. Preceding the code F with a tilde (˜) is another option for selecting males.

Sex
>F

Table 6-4 summarizes the special symbols that may be used with labels in a Criterion range.

TABLE 6-4   Summary of Special Symbols That Can Be Used with Labels in a Criterion Range.

SYMBOL	MEANING	EXAMPLE
*	Any characters at this position and all remaining positions	Tr*
?	Any character at this position	M??T
$	Substring search	$TV
~	Not	~F
>	Greater than match	>IN
<	Less than match	<TED

Conditions with Numbers   If you want to select records that represent employees who are 30 years old, enter the criteria at the right. In this example, VP-Planner Plus uses the expression Age = 30 to determine if each record passes the test when the Find command is used. It is invalid to begin a number with any of the special characters described earlier for labels, like *, ?, >, <, and ~.

Age
30

Conditions with Formulas   Formula criteria are entered into the Criterion range beginning with a plus sign (+). The plus sign is followed by the address of the cell of the first record immediately below the specified field name in the Input range. The cell address is followed by a relational operator and the value to which to compare the field name. (See Table 4-3 in Project 4 for a list of the valid relational operators.) If you wanted to select all records that represent employees who are older than 25, use the criterion at the right.

Age
+ C4 > 25

The cell address C4 is the first cell in the database below the field name Age (see Figure 6-14). Since C4 is a relative cell address, VP-Planner Plus adjusts the row as it goes through the database, passing and flunking records. Hence, when you invoke the Find command, cell address C4 is only used to evaluate the first record. Thereafter, the 4 in C4 is adjusted to 5, 6, and so on, as each record in the database is evaluated.

In the previous example, the formula + C4 > 25 was shown in the cell below the field name Age. Actually, when a condition containing a formula is assigned to the cell, 0 or 1 displays. The number displayed in the cell assigned the formula + C4 > 25 depends on the value in cell C4. If it is greater than 25, then 1 (true) displays. If C4 contains a value less than or equal to 25, then 0 (false) displays. You can use the command **/R**ange **F**ormat **T**ext (/RFT) to display the formula in the Criterion range, rather than the numeric value 0 or 1.

Compound conditions may be formed by using the logical operators #AND#, #OR#, and #NOT#. (See Table 4-4 in Project 4 for an explanation of their meaning.) In the example at the right, all records are selected that meet the criteria Age < 37 AND Years ≥ 10. Note that the compound condition may include fields that are not directly under the field name. In this case, C4 refers to the Age field and F4 refers to the Years field.

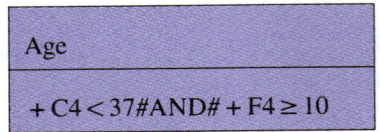

Mixing Conditions with Formulas and Labels   If the criteria require both a label and a formula, use multiple field names. For example, if you wanted to find all records in the employee database that represent operators with more than 10 years of seniority (Trade = Operator AND Years > 10), use the criteria at the right.

Trade	Years
Operator	+ F4 > 10

To select records that meet the criteria Trade = Operator OR Years > 10, use the entry at the right. Because the expressions Operator and + F4 > 10 are in different rows, VP-Planner Plus selects records that represent employees who are operators or have more than 10 years of seniority.

Trade	Years
Operator	+ F4 > 10

The Extract Command (/DQE)

The Extract command copies data from the records that pass the test to the designated fields in the Output range. The Output range is a group of cells off to the side or below the database. The first row of the Output range includes duplicates of the field names in the Input range that you want to extract. This command is very powerful because it allows you to build a database that is a subset of the original one. The subset database can be printed, saved as a new database, or queried like any other database.

Again, consider the employee database in Figure 6-1. Assume that your manager wants you to generate a list of all those employees who meet the following criteria:

Age ≥ 27 AND NOT(Dept = 3) AND Years < 10

In the list, include the employee name, department, and sex code of all the records that pass the test.

To complete the extract, do the following:

1. Choose an area off to the side of the database and set up the criteria.
2. Choose an area below the database and set up an area to receive the extracted results.
3. Invoke the command /**Data Query** (/DQ) and enter the Input range.
4. Enter the Criterion range.
5. Enter the Output range.
6. Type the letter E for Extract.

The criteria for this query involve three fields—Age, Dept, and Years. Use the cells in the range G3 through I4 for the Criterion range. Copy the three field names Age, Dept, and Years from the database in row 3 to cells G3, H3, and I3. The first condition in the previously stated criteria is Age ≥ 27. Therefore, in cell G4, enter the formula + C4 ≥ 27. This is shown in Figure 6-15. (Cells G4 through I4 have been formatted to the Text type so that the formulas display, rather than the numeric values 0 or 1.) The second condition is NOT(Dept = 3). Therefore, in cell H4, enter ~3. The condition for the third field is Years < 10. In cell I4, enter + F4 < 10.

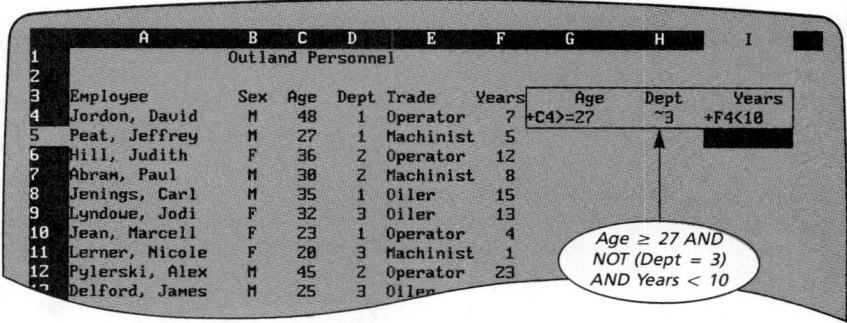

FIGURE 6-15
Step 1 of using the Extract command—enter the criteria in unused cells off to the side of the database.

The next step is to set up the Output range. This involves copying the names of the fields at the top of the database (row 3) to an area below the database. Since we want to extract the employee name, department, and sex code, copy the three field names to row 16 as illustrated in Figure 6-16.

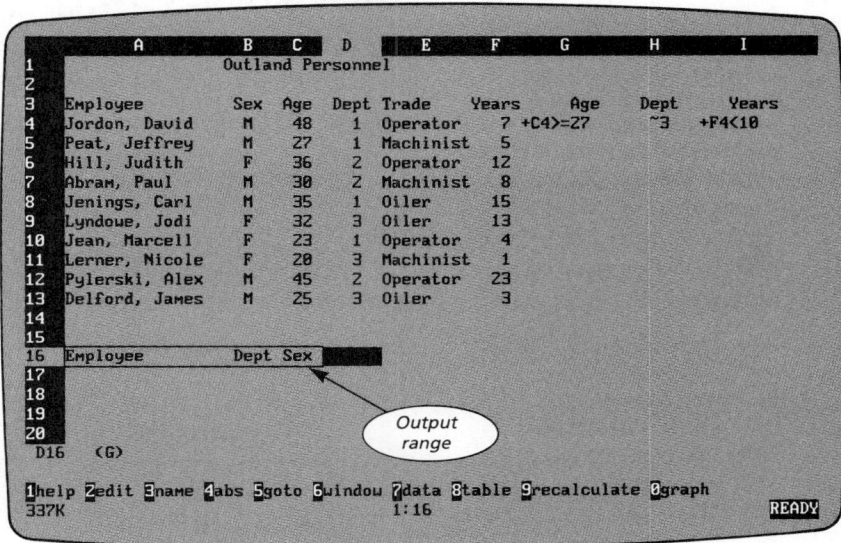

FIGURE 6-16
Step 2 of using the Extract command—enter the field names for the Output range below the database.

Enter the command /Data Query (/DQ). The Query menu shown in Figure 6-10 displays on the screen. Type the letter I for Input. Use the arrow keys to select the entire database, including the field names in row 3 (A3..F13). The Input range is shown in Figure 6-17. Press the Enter key.

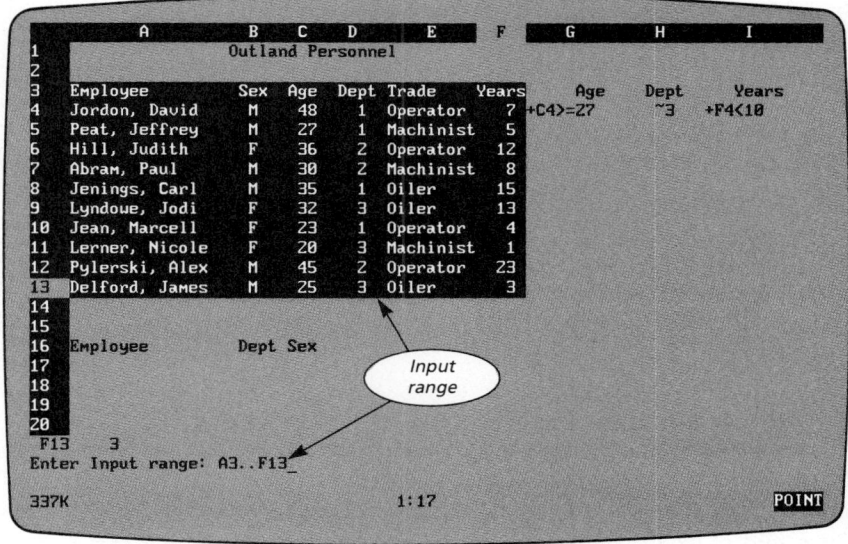

FIGURE 6-17
Step 3 of using the Extract command—enter the command /Data Query (/DQ) and enter the Input range. The Input range usually encompasses all the fields in all the records of the database, including the field names.

With the command cursor in the Query menu, type the letter C for Criterion. Select the Criterion range G3..I4 as shown in Figure 6-18. Press the Enter key. Now type the letter O for Output. Select the range A16..C16 (see Figure 6-19). Press the Enter key.

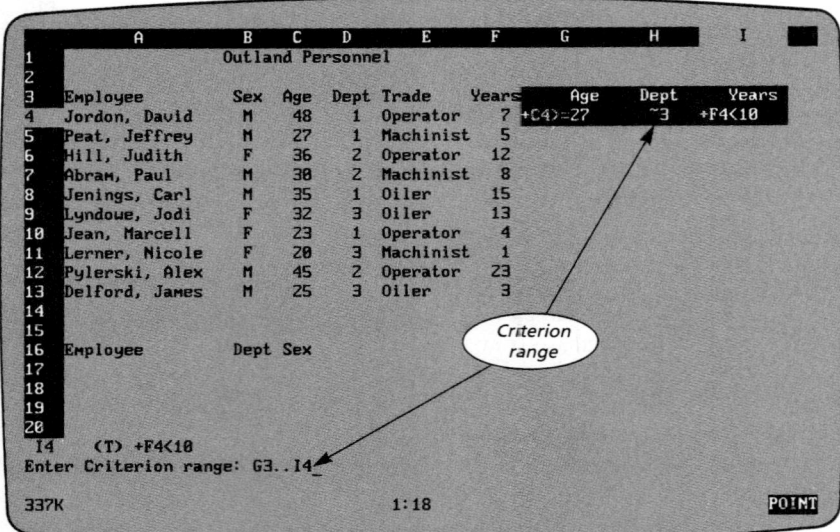

FIGURE 6-18
Step 4 of using the Extract command—enter the Criterion range.

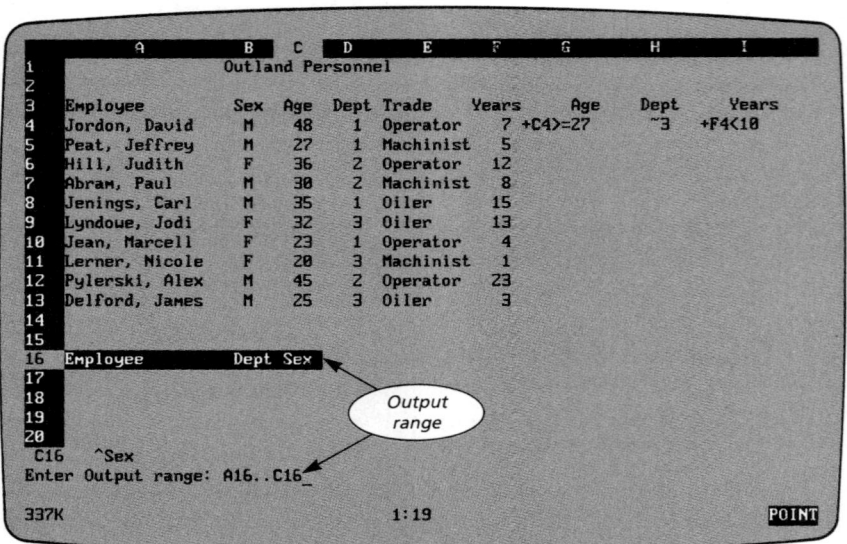

FIGURE 6-19
Step 5 of using the Extract command—enter the Output range.

After the Input, Criterion, and Output ranges are set, type the letter E for Extract. This causes VP-Planner Plus to select the records that meet the criteria specified in the range A3..I4. For each record selected, it copies the employee name, department, and sex code to the next available row beneath the Output range. Type the letter Q to Quit the Data Query command. The results of the extract display below the database as shown in Figure 6-20. Save and print the database, criteria, and records extracted. To save the database, use the file name PROJS-6D.

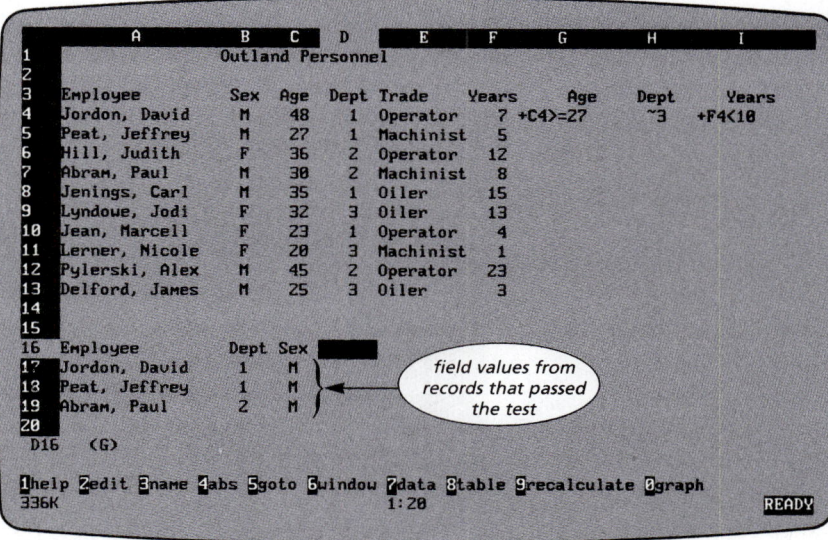

FIGURE 6-20
Step 6 of using the Extract command—invoke the Extract command. Specified fields are displayed in the Output range from the records that pass the test Age ≥ 27 AND NOT(Dept = 3) AND Years < 10.

In the previous example, we defined the Output range to be the row containing the field names (A16..C16). When the Output range is defined in this fashion, any number of records can be extracted from the database. The alternative is to define a rectangular Output range. In this case, if more records are extracted than rows in the Output range, VP-Planner Plus displays the diagnostic message "Output Range Full."

THE DATABASE FUNCTIONS

P-Planner Plus has seven functions for evaluating numeric data in the database. The functions, which are similar to the statistical functions discussed in Project 4, are described in Table 6-5.

TABLE 6-5 Database Statistical Functions

FUNCTION	FUNCTION VALUE
DAVG(I,O,C)	Returns the average of the numbers in the Offset column (O) in the Input range (I) that meet the criterion (C).
DCOUNT(I,O,C)	Returns the number of nonempty cells in the Offset column (O) in the Input range (I) that meet the criterion (C).
DMAX(I,O,C)	Returns the largest number in the Offset column (O) in the Input range (I) that meet the criterion (C).
DMIN(I,O,C)	Returns the smallest number in the Offset column (O) in the Input range (I) that meet the criterion (C).
DSTD(I,O,C)	Returns the standard deviation of the numbers in the Offset column (O) in the Input range (I) that meet the criterion (C).
DSUM(I,O,C)	Returns the sum of the numbers in the Offset column (O) in the Input range (I) that meet the criterion (C).
DVAR(I,O,C)	Returns the variance of the numbers in the Offset column (O) in the Input range (I) that meet the criterion (C).

The purpose of these functions is to return a statistic, like the average, on the values in the column of the records that meet the specified criteria. For example, with the database in Figure 6-1 in main computer memory, let's compute the average age of the male employees and the average age of the female employees.

The first step is to set up the criteria for each average. For the average age of females, use the criteria shown in cells H3 and H4 in Figure 6-21. Likewise, for the average age of males, use the criteria shown in cells I3 and I4. Next, enter the labels that identify the averages. This is shown in cells A16 and A17 in Figure 6-21.

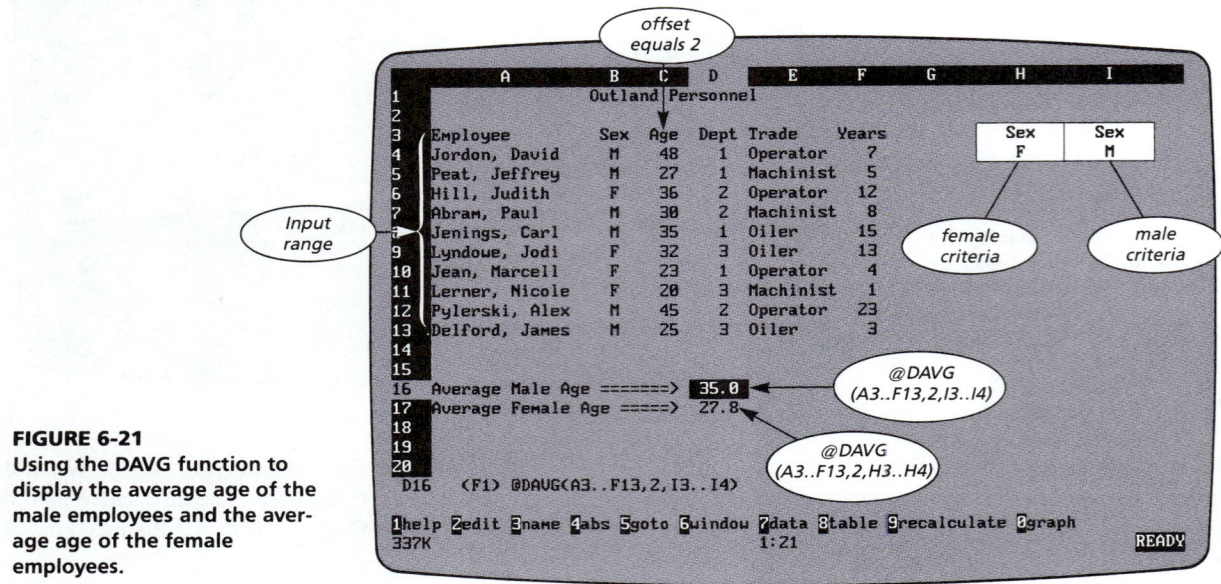

FIGURE 6-21
Using the DAVG function to display the average age of the male employees and the average age of the female employees.

We can now assign the DAVG function to cells D16 and D17. This function has three arguments—Input range, offset, and Criterion range. Since the arguments in the function define the ranges, this function does not require that the ranges be defined through the Data Query command.

Set the Input range to the entire database (A3..F13). The **offset** argument defines the field in the database to be used in the computation. The offset of the leftmost field (Employee) is 0. The offset of the Sex field is 1. The offset of the Age field is 2, and so on. Hence, use the value 2 for the offset argument in the DAVG function. The third argument is the range of cells that make up the criteria—H3..H4 for females and I3..I4 for the males.

With the cell cursor at D16, enter the function @DAVG(A3..F13,2,I3..I4). This causes the average age of the male employees to display in cell D16. Press the Down Arrow key and enter the function @DAVG(A3..F13,2,H3..H4). This function causes the average age of the female employees to display in cell D17. Format cells D16 and D17 to the Fixed type with one decimal position. The effect of entering these two functions and formatting the results is shown in Figure 6-21. To complete this portion of the project, save and print the database, criteria, and averages. Save the database using the file name PROJS-6E.

THE LOOKUP FUNCTIONS

hree functions that we have not discussed are the CHOOSE, VLOOKUP, and HLOOKUP functions. These three functions are called **lookup functions** because they allow you to look up values in a list or a table that is part of the worksheet.

The CHOOSE Function

The CHOOSE function selects a value from a list on the basis of an index. The general form of the CHOOSE function is @CHOOSE(x,y0,y1,y2,...,yn), where the value of x determines the value in the list (y0, y1, y2, ..., yn) to store in the cell. If x equals 0, the first value (y0) is stored in the cell. If x equals 1, the second value (y1) is stored in the cell, and so on. The list can contain values, quoted strings, cell addresses, formulas, range names, or a combination of these.

Consider the partial worksheet in Figure 6-22. The table in the range E1..E7 contains costs. B1 is assigned the index that determines the value in the list that the function returns. The CHOOSE function is assigned to cell B3. It is entered as follows: @CHOOSE(B1,0,E2,E3,E4,E5 + .02,E6*.95,E7,.46). Since B1 is equal to 3, the CHOOSE function returns the fourth value in the list—the value of cell E4.

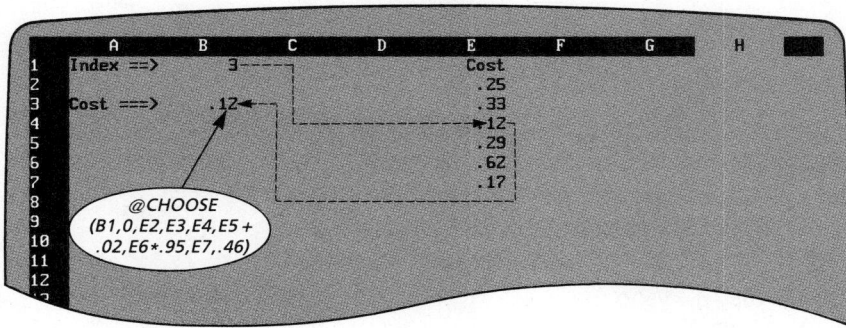

FIGURE 6-22
Using the CHOOSE function to select a value from the list of arguments following the index.

If we change the value of B1 to some other number between 0 and 7, the function will store a different value in B3. If the value in B1 exceeds the number of items in the list, the diagnostic message ERR is assigned to B3. Note that an index value of zero in cell B1 causes the CHOOSE function to assign zero to B3. If cell B1 is assigned a value of 7, the function returns the value .46 from the list and stores it in cell B3.

The VLOOKUP and HLOOKUP Functions

The VLOOKUP and HLOOKUP functions are useful for looking up values in tables, like tax tables, discount tables, and part tables. The general form of the VLOOKUP function is @VLOOKUP(x,range,offset). The first argument, x, is called the **search argument**. It is compared to values in the leftmost column of the multiple-column table defined by the second argument, range. The leftmost column of the range is called the **range column**. Offset defines the column from which a value is returned when a hit is made in the range column. A **hit** occurs when a value is found in the range column that is closest to but not greater than the search argument x.

The offset in the VLOOKUP function can be zero, positive, or negative. The offset value of the range column is zero. A positive offset causes a value to be selected from a column to the right of the range column. A negative offset causes a value to be selected from a column to the left of the range column.

While the VLOOKUP function looks up values in a table arranged vertically, the HLOOKUP function looks up values in a table arranged horizontally. Vertical tables are used more often than horizontal tables.

Consider the top screen in Figure 6-23. Column B contains a list of student test scores. A grade scale table is in the range F5..G9. Look up the corresponding letter grade in the grade scale table for each student test score and assign it to the appropriate cell in column D. For example, a test score of 78 returns the letter grade C; a test score of 99 returns the letter grade A. To look up the letter grades for the student test scores, enter the function @VLOOKUP(B5,$F$5..$G$9,1) in cell D5, the location of the letter grade for student number 1035.

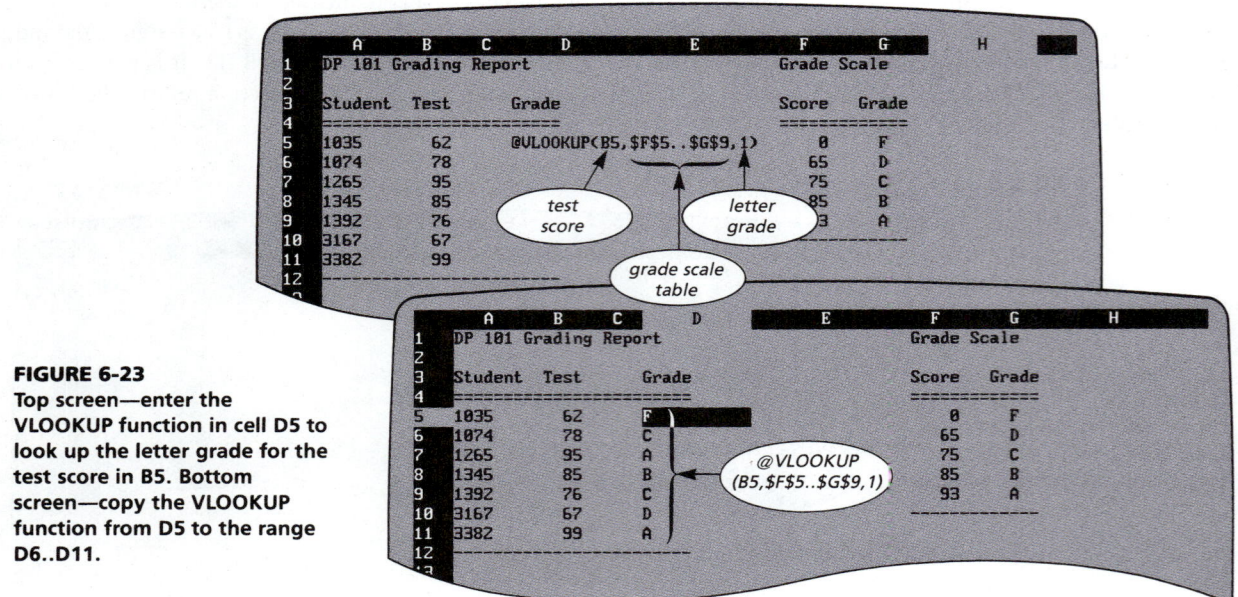

FIGURE 6-23
Top screen—enter the VLOOKUP function in cell D5 to look up the letter grade for the test score in B5. Bottom screen—copy the VLOOKUP function from D5 to the range D6..D11.

The first argument in the VLOOKUP function is cell B5, the test score for student number 1035. The second argument, $F$5..$G$9, defines the grade scale table. The third argument, 1, is the offset. It instructs VP-Planner Plus to assign the corresponding value in the grade scale table that is located one column to the right of the range column—column F.

Copy the VLOOKUP function in cell D5 to the range D6..D11. As the copy takes place, the first argument in the VLOOKUP function, B5, is adjusted to B6, B7, B8, and so on. The result of copying the VLOOKUP function is shown in the lower screen in Figure 6-23. In this case, the VLOOKUP function in cells D5 through D11 returns the letter grades that correspond to the student test scores.

PROJECT SUMMARY

In this project you learned how to sort and query a worksheet database. We sorted the database in two different ways, first by employee name and then by years of seniority within sex code.

Querying a database involves searching for records that meet a specified criteria. The selected records can be highlighted or extracted.

Powerful database functions can be used to generate information about the database. In this project you were introduced to the lookup functions. These functions are used to return a value from a list or table.

Each of the steps required to build and manipulate the worksheet database presented in Project 6 is listed in the following tables.

SUMMARY OF KEYSTROKES—PROJS-6 (Figure 6-1)

STEPS	KEY(S) PRESSED	STEPS	KEY(S) PRESSED
1	/WCS16 ←	13	(F5) A4 ← Jordon, David → ^M → 48 → ^1 → Operator → 7 ←
2	→ /WCS5 ←	14	(F5) A5 ← Peat, Jeffrey → ^M → 27 → ^1 → Machinist → 5 ←
3	→ /WCS5 ←	15	(F5) A6 ← Hill, Judith → ^F → 36 → ^2 → Operator → 12 ←
4	→ /WCS6 ←	16	(F5) A7 ← Abram, Paul → ^M → 30 → ^2 → Machinist → 8 ←
5	→ → /WCS5 ←	17	(F5) A8 ← Jenings, Carl → ^M → 35 → ^1 → Oiler → 15 ←
6	(F5) B1 ← Outland Personnel ↓	18	(F5) A9 ← Lyndowe, Jodi → ^F → 32 → ^3 → Oiler → 13 ←
7	↓ ← Employee →	19	(F5) A10 ← Jean, Marcell → ^F → 23 → ^1 → Operator → 4 ←
8	^Sex →	20	(F5) A11 ← Lerner, Nicole → ^F → 20 → ^3 → Machinist → 1 ←
9	''Age →	21	(F5) A12 ← Pylerski, Alex → ^M → 45 → ^2 → Operator → 23 ←
10	^Dept →	22	(F5) A13 ← Delford, James → ^M → 25 → ^3 → Oiler → 3 ←
11	Trade →	23	/FSPROJS-6 ←
12	''Years ←		

SUMMARY OF KEYSTROKES
Sorting PROJS-6 by
Employee Name
(Figure 6-6)

STEPS	KEY(S) PRESSED
1	/FRPROJS-6 ←
2	/DS
3	DA4.F13 ←
4	PA4 ← A ←
5	G
6	/PPRA1.F13 ← AGEEQ
7	/FSPROJS-6A ←

SUMMARY OF KEYSTROKES
Sorting PROJS-6
by Years of Seniority
within Sex Code
(Figure 6-9)

STEPS	KEY(S) PRESSED
1	/FRPROJS-6 ←
2	/DS
3	DA4.F13 ←
4	PB4 ← A ←
5	SF4 ← ←
6	G
7	/PPRA1.F13 ← AGEEQ
8	/FSPROJS-6B ←

SUMMARY OF KEYSTROKES
Finding Records in PROJS-6
That Meet the Criteria
Sex = M AND Dept = 2
(Figure 6-14)

STEPS	KEY(S) PRESSED	STEPS	KEY(S) PRESSED
1	/FRPROJS-6 ←	7	CH3.I4 ←
2	(F5) B3 ← /C ← H3 ←	8	F
3	(F5) D3 ← /C ← I3 ←	9	(Esc)
4	(F5) H4 ← ^M → ^2 ←	10	/PPRA1.I13 ← OMR77 ← QAGEEQ
5	/DQ	11	/FSPROJS-6C ←
6	IA3.F13 ←		

SUMMARY OF KEYSTROKES
Extracting Records from PROJS-6 That Meet the Criteria Age ≥ 27 AND NOT (Dept = 3) AND Years < 10 (Figure 6-20)

STEPS	KEY(S) PRESSED	STEPS	KEY(S) PRESSED
1	/FRPROJS-6 ↵	9	[F5]B3 ↵/C ↵ C16 ↵
2	[F5]C3 ↵/C ↵ G3 ↵	10	/DQ
3	→ /C ↵ H3 ↵	11	IA3.F13 ↵
4	→ → /C ↵ I3 ↵	12	CG3.I4 ↵
5	→ ↓ +C4>27 → ^ ˜3 → +F4<10 ↵	13	OA16.C16 ↵
6	/RFT ← ← ↵	14	EQ
7	[F5]A3 ↵/C ↵ A16 ↵	15	/PPRA1.I20 ↵ OMR77 ↵ QAGEEQ
8	[F5]D3 ↵/C ↵ B16 ↵	16	/FSPROJS-6D ↵

SUMMARY OF KEYSTROKES
Using the Database Function DAVG with PROJS-6 (Figure 6-21)

STEPS	KEY(S) PRESSED
1	/FRPROJS-6 ↵
2	[F5]B3 ↵/C ↵ H3.I3 ↵
3	[F5]H4 ↵ ^F → ^M ↵
4	[F5]A16 ↵ Average Male Age =======> ↓
5	Average Female Age =====> ↵
6	[F5]D16 ↵ @DAVG(A3.F13,2,I3.I4) ↓
7	@DAVG(A3.F13,2,H3.H4) ↑
8	/RFF1 ↵ ↓ ↵
9	/FSPROJS-6E ↵
10	/PPRA1.I17 ↵ AGEEQ

The following list summarizes the material covered in Project 6:

1. A **database** is an organized collection of data.
2. The data related to a person, place, or thing is called a **record**.
3. The data items that make up a record are called **fields**.
4. Each row in a worksheet can be used to store a record.
5. Each column in a worksheet can be used to store a field.
6. The row immediately above the first record contains the field names.
7. A **database management system (DBMS)** is a software package that is used to create a database and store, access, sort, and make additions, deletions, and changes to that database.
8. **Sorting** rearranges the records in a database in a particular sequence on the basis of one or more fields.
9. Data that is in sequence from lowest to highest is in **ascending sequence**.
10. Data that is in sequence from highest to lowest is in **descending sequence**.
11. To sort a database, enter the command /**D**ata **S**ort (/DS). Enter the data range and the sort keys. To complete the sort, enter the Go command.
12. The data range for a sort is usually all the records in the database. Never include the field names in the data range.
13. A sort key, like the primary key, is assigned a column and a sort sequence.
14. Selecting records in a database on the basis of a specified criteria is called **querying a database**. Records that match the criteria can be highlighted, copied to another part of the worksheet, or deleted.
15. To query a database, enter the command /**D**ata **Q**uery (/DQ).
16. Before you enter the Data Query command, the criteria should be present in the worksheet. If you use an Output range, the field names for the Output range should also be present in the worksheet.
17. The Find command highlights records that pass the criteria.
18. To apply the Find command to a database, use the Data Query command to define the Input range and Criterion range. Finally, type the letter F for Find.
19. The criteria used to pass records include the field names and the values that the field names are compared to. Field names can be compared to labels, numbers, and formulas.

20. Global or wild-card characters are allowed in labels in the criteria. The two valid wild-card characters are the asterisk (*), which means "any characters in this position and all remaining positions," and the question mark (?), which means "any character at this position." The question mark (?) can be used anywhere in the label. The asterisk (*) can only be used at the end of a label.

21. Special characters, like $, ~, >, and <, can precede labels in the criteria.

22. The criteria can include the logical operators AND, OR, and NOT.

23. The Extract command is used to copy selected records from the database to the Output range.

24. VP-Planner Plus includes database statistical functions to generate information about the database.

25. The lookup functions, CHOOSE, VLOOKUP, and HLOOKUP allow you to look up values in a list or table that is part of the worksheet.

STUDENT ASSIGNMENTS   STUDENT ASSIGNMENT 1: True/False

Instructions: Circle T if the statement is true or F if the statement is false.

T F   1. A database is a collection of data consisting of fields and records.

T F   2. A database management system is a worksheet.

T F   3. The series of numbers 1, 3, 4, 5, 6 is in descending sequence.

T F   4. The Reset command in the Sort menu resets the database back to its original sequence.

T F   5. In a sort operation, the secondary-key field has a lower priority than the primary-key field.

T F   6. A sort key is identified by any cell in the column containing the field you wish to sort by.

T F   7. To query a database, you must first select unused cells off to the side or below the database and set up the criteria.

T F   8. The Find command copies selected records to the Output range.

T F   9. The Criterion range must contain at least two rows and two columns.

T F   10. A Criterion range consisting of field names and empty cells below the field names will cause all the records in the database to be selected.

T F   11. The wild-card character asterisk (*) may only be used at the front of a label that is part of the criteria.

T F   12. The tilde (~) is used to negate a condition in the Criterion range.

T F   13. It is not required that the field names in the Output range be the same as the field names in the Input range.

T F   14. The database functions require that you define the Input range and Criterion range by invoking the Data Query command.

T F   15. The Offset column is relative to the rightmost field in the Input range.

T F   16. The DAVG function returns the average number of records in the database.

T F   17. The Offset column in the VLOOKUP function cannot be negative.

T F   18. An Offset column value of zero causes the VLOOKUP function to return the value in the range column that is closest to but not greater than the search argument.

T F   19. The VLOOKUP and HLOOKUP functions are the same, except that VLOOKUP verifies the search of the table and HLOOKUP does not.

T F   20. The CHOOSE function is used to select a value from a list on the basis of an index.

STUDENT ASSIGNMENT 2: Multiple Choice

Instructions: Circle the correct response.

1. Which one of the following series of numbers is in descending sequence?
   a. 1, 2, 3, 4, 5   b. 5, 4, 3, 2, 1   c. 1, 3, 5, 3, 1   d. none of these

2. Which one of the following commands in the Query menu is used to highlight records?
   a. Find   b. Extract   c. Unique   d. Criterion

Student Assignment 2 (continued)

3. To properly execute the Find command, the _____ and _____ ranges must be set.
   a. Input, Output   b. Input, Criterion   c. Data-range, Output   d. Data-range, Criterion
4. Which one of the following characters represent "any characters in this position?"
   a. tilde (~)   b. number sign (#)   c. asterisk (*)   d. question mark (?)
5. To copy all records that satisfy the criteria to the Output range, use the _____ command.
   a. Find   b. Extract   c. Delete   d. Output
6. Which one of the following database functions returns the number of nonempty cells in the Offset column (O) of the records in the Input range (I) that meet the Criterion range (C)?
   a. DMAX(I,O,C)   b. DAVG(I,O,C)   c. DCOUNT(I,O,C)   d. DVAR(I,O,C)
7. If a database has four fields, the rightmost column has an Offset value of _____ .
   a. 0   b. 3   c. 4   d. 5
8. Which one of the following functions is used to search a columnar table?
   a. CHOOSE   b. VLOOKUP   c. HLOOKUP   d. both b and c

STUDENT ASSIGNMENT 3: Understanding Sorting

Instructions: Rewrite the order of the seven records in the database listed in Table 6-6 on the basis of the problems that follow. Treat each problem independently.

1. Sort the database into descending sequence by division.
2. Sort the database by district within division. Both sort keys are to be in ascending sequence.
3. Sort the database by department within district within division. All three sort keys are to be in ascending sequence.
4. Sort the database into descending sequence by cost.
5. Sort the database by department within district within division. All three sort keys are to be in descending sequence.

TABLE 6-6   Student Assignment 3

DIVISION	DISTRICT	DEPARTMENT	COST
2	1	2	1.21
1	2	2	2.22
2	1	3	1.57
1	2	1	3.56
1	1	1	1.11
2	1	1	1.45
1	2	3	2.10

STUDENT ASSIGNMENT 4: Understanding Criteria

Instructions: Write the criteria required to select records from the database in Figure 6-1 according to the problems listed below. So that you can better understand what is required for this assignment, we have answered the first problem.

1. Select records that represent male employees who are less than 25 years old.

   Criteria: _Sex_____   _Age_____

   _M_____   _+C4<25_

2. Select records that represent employees whose trade is machinist or oiler.

   Criteria: _____

   _____

   _____

3. Select records that represent employees whose last names begin with P or who work in department 2.

   Criteria: _____   _____

   _____   _____

   _____   _____

4. Select records that represent female employees who are at least 30 years old and have at least 10 years of seniority.

   Criteria: _____   _____

   _____   _____

   _____   _____

5. Select records that represent employees whose first name is Alex.

   Criteria: ________

   ____

6. Select records that represent male machinist employees who are at least 28 years old and whose last names begin with P.

   Criteria: ________ ________ ________ ________

   ________ ________ ________ ________

STUDENT ASSIGNMENT 5: Understanding Database and Lookup Functions

Instructions: Load VP-Planner Plus and perform the following tasks.

1. Consider Figure 6-21. Write a database function and the criteria that will assign to the current cell the number of years of seniority for the female employee with the maximum years of seniority. Use a Criterion range of I3..I4.
2. Consider Figure 6-21. Write a database function and the criteria that will assign to the current cell the average years of seniority of the male employees. Use a Criterion range of I3..I4.
3. Consider Figure 6-21. Write a database function and the criteria that will assign to the current cell the sum of the ages of the female employees. Use a Criterion range of I3..I4.
4. Consider Figure 6-21. Write a database function and the criteria that will assign to the current cell the average years of seniority for both the male and female employees. Use a Criterion range of I3..I4.
5. Consider Figure 6-22. Use the CHOOSE function to assign cell B3 twelve times the cost in column E. Select the cost in column E on the basis of the index value in cell B1.
6. Consider the VLOOKUP function in the upper screen in Figure 6-23. Complete the following problems independently and write down the results displayed in column D:
   a. Decrease all test scores in column B by 10 points.
   b. Increase all test scores in column B by 10 points.
   c. Reset the test scores in column B to their original values and change the offset argument in the VLOOKUP function to zero.

STUDENT ASSIGNMENT 6: Building and Sorting a Database of Prospective Programmers

Instructions: Load VP-Planner Plus and perform the following tasks.

1. Build the database illustrated in Figure 6-24. Use the field sizes listed in Table 6-7.

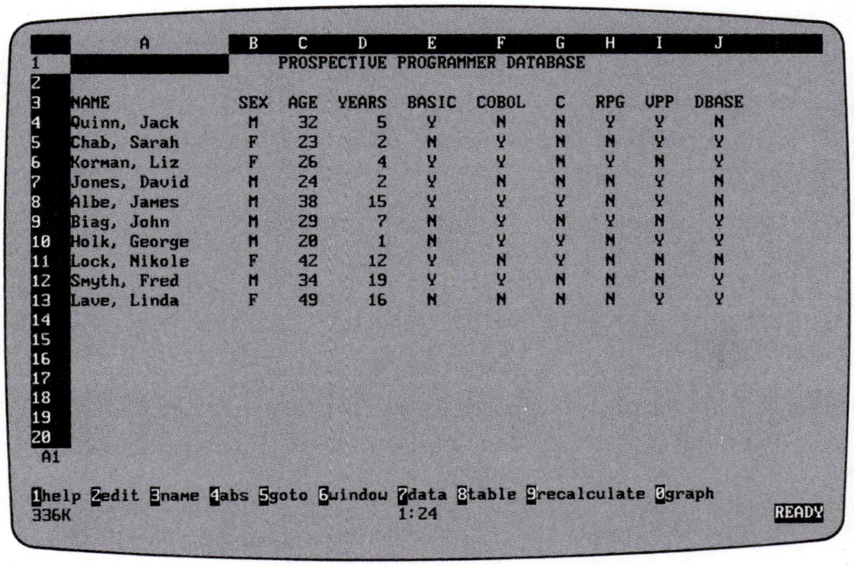

PROSPECTIVE PROGRAMMER DATABASE

NAME	SEX	AGE	YEARS	BASIC	COBOL	C	RPG	VPP	DBASE
Quinn, Jack	M	32	5	Y	N	N	Y	Y	N
Chab, Sarah	F	23	2	N	Y	N	N	Y	Y
Korman, Liz	F	26	4	Y	Y	N	Y	N	Y
Jones, David	M	24	2	Y	N	N	N	Y	N
Albe, James	M	38	15	Y	Y	Y	N	Y	N
Biag, John	M	29	7	N	Y	N	Y	N	Y
Holk, George	M	20	1	N	Y	Y	N	Y	Y
Lock, Nikole	F	42	12	Y	N	Y	N	N	N
Smyth, Fred	M	34	19	Y	Y	N	N	N	Y
Lave, Linda	F	49	16	N	N	N	N	Y	Y

FIGURE 6-24 Student Assignment 6

TABLE 6-7 Field Descriptions for the Prospective Programmer Database

FIELD NAME	COLUMN	TYPE OF DATA	SIZE
Name	A	Label	16
Sex	B	Label	5
Age	C	Numeric	5
Years	D	Numeric	7
BASIC	E	Label	7
COBOL	F	Label	7
C	G	Label	5
RPG	H	Label	5
VPP	I	Label	5
DBASE	J	Label	7

2. Save and print the database. Use the file name STUS6-6.

3. Sort the records in the database into ascending sequence by name. Print the sorted version.

4. Sort the records in the database by age within sex. Select descending sequence for the sex code and ascending sequence for the age. Print the sorted version.

STUDENT ASSIGNMENT 7: Finding Records in the Prospective Programmer Database

Instructions: Load VP-Planner Plus and perform the following tasks.

1. Load the database created in Student Assignment 6 (STUS6-6). This worksheet is illustrated in Figure 6-24.

2. For the Criterion range, copy row 3 (A3..J3) to row 15 (A15..J15).

3. In columns E through J of the database, the letter Y indicates that a prospective programmer knows the language or software package identified by the field name. The letter N indicates no experience with the language or software package. Find records that meet the following criteria. Treat each set of criteria in problems a through e separately.

   a. Find all records that represent prospective programmers who are female and can program in COBOL.

   b. Find all records that represent prospective programmers who can program in BASIC and RPG and use VPP.

   c. Find all records that represent prospective male programmers who are at least 26 years old and can use DBASE.

   d. Find all records that represent prospective programmers who know COBOL and DBASE.

   e. Find all records that represent prospective programmers who know at least one programming language and can use VPP or DBASE.

   f. All prospective programmers who did not know DBASE were sent to a seminar on the software package. Use the Find command to locate the records of these programmers and change the entries from the letter N to the letter Y under the field name DBASE. Save and print the database and the accompanying Criterion range. Use the file name STUS6-7.

STUDENT ASSIGNMENT 8: Extracting Records from the Prospective Programmer Database

Instructions: Load VP-Planner Plus and perform the following tasks.

1. Load the database created in Student Assignment 6 (STUS6-6). This worksheet is illustrated in Figure 6-24.

2. For the Criterion range, copy row 3 (A3..J3) to row 15 (A15..J15). For the Output range, copy the field names NAME, SEX, and AGE (A3..C3) to K3..M3. Change the widths of column K to 16, column L to 5, and column M to 5. Extract the three fields from the records that meet the criteria in problems a through e. Treat each extraction separately. Print the worksheet after each extraction.

   a. Extract from records that represent prospective programmers who are female.

   b. Extract from records that represent prospective programmers who can program in COBOL and RPG.

   c. Extract from records that represent prospective male programmers who are at least 24 years old and can use VPP.

   d. Extract from records that represent prospective programmers who know COBOL and DBASE.

   e. Extract from records that represent prospective programmers who do not know how to use any programming language.

3. Save the database with the Criterion range specified in 2e. Use the file name STUS6-8.

STUDENT ASSIGNMENT 9: Property Tax Rate Table Lookup

Instructions: Load VP-Planner Plus and perform the following tasks to build the worksheet shown in Figure 6-25. This worksheet uses the VLOOKUP function in cell C5 to look up the tax rate in the tax table in columns F and G. The VLOOKUP function employs cell C3 as the search argument. From the tax rate, the tax amount due in cell C7 can be determined.

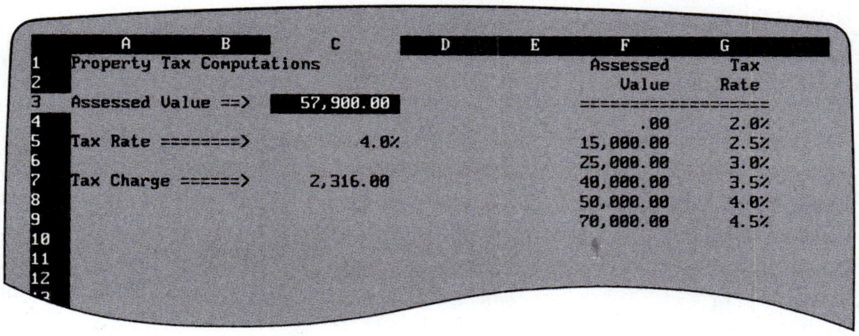

FIGURE 6-25
Student Assignment 9

1. Change the widths of column A to 11, column C to 13, and column F to 10. Leave the widths of the remaining columns at 9 characters.

2. Enter the title, column headings, and row identifiers.

3. Format cells C3 and C7 and range F4..F9 to the Comma (,) type with two decimal positions. Format cell C5 and range G4..G9 to the Percent type with one decimal position.

4. Enter the table values in the range F4..G9.

5. Assign the function @VLOOKUP(C3,F4..G9,1) to cell C5.

6. Assign the formula +C3*C5 to cell C7. This cell displays the tax amount due.

7. Test the worksheet to ensure that the VLOOKUP function is working properly.

8. Use the command /**W**orksheet **G**lobal **P**rotection **E**nable (/WGPE) to enable (turn on) cell protection. Unprotect cell C3.

9. Save the worksheet. Use the file name STUS6-9.

10. Determine the tax rate and tax charge for the following assessed valuations: $10,980.00; $25,000.00; $350,450.00; $48,560.00; and $57,900.00. Remember that commas (,) are not allowed in a numeric entry. Print the worksheet for each assessed valuation.

VP-Planner PLUS Index

Absolute addressing, VP117
AND logical operator, VP160
Apostrophe with labels, VP10
Arrow keys, VP6
Arthmetic operator, VP18
As is version, VP82
Ascending sequence, VP214
AVG function, VP152, VP153

Backup copy, VP77
Bar graphs, VP197–201
Built-in functions, VP66, VP67–70
B&W command, VP203

Cell(s), VP4
 assigning formulas to VP18
 displaying formulas in, VP114–116
 editing data in, VP28–32
 erasing contents of, VP32
 format assigned to, VP59
 moving contents of, VP112–114
 naming adjacent, VP155–156
 positioning labels, VP10
 protecting, VP171
 repeating characters in, VP60–61

 summing empty, VP121–123
Cell address, VP4
 absolute versus relative, VP116–119
Cell cursor, VP4, VP6, VP15–17
Cell-formulas version, VP82
CHOOSE function, VP231
Circumflex with labels, VP10
Color command, VP203
Column(s), VP4
 changing width of, VP49–52, VP97–98
 deleting and inserting, VP105–108
Command cursor, VP22
Command menu, VP22–23
Command mode
 escaping from, VP23
Condensed mode, printing in, VP126
Conditions, VP159–160
Control panel, VP5, VP131
Copy command, VP61–70
 Move command vs., VP114
COUNT function, VP152–153
Criterion range, VP223–226
Current cell address, VP4
Current graph, VP187

Current-mode line, VP5

Database, VP213–235
 querying, VP219–229
 sorting, VP214–219
 statistical functions, VP229–230
Data Fill command, VP157–159
Data Find command, VP221–226
Data labels, VP201–202
Data Query menu, VP220
Data range, VP196, VP216–217
Data Sort menu, VP215
Data table, VP147
 what-if questions and, VP162–164
Date display, VP100–103
DBMS, VP213
Debugging, VP82, VP84, VP167
Default drive, changing, VP26
Default settings, changing, VP130–131
Delete command, VP108
Descending sequence, VP214
Destination cell range, VP62
DOS, interacting with, VP133

Erasing cell or worksheet, VP32

Errors, VP84
 correcting, VP27–32
 in macros, VP167
Exploded pie chart, VP188
Extract command, VP226–229

Field(s), VP213
File(s), saving, VP23–25, VP133
File menu, VP24
Find command, VP221–226
Format menu, VP54
Formatting, VP46–86
 date and time, VP102
 defining range, VP53
 globally, VP99–100, VP110
 numeric values, VP54–57
 percentages, VP72–73
Formulas, VP66
 absolute addresses, VP117
 debugging, VP84
 displaying in cells, VP114–116
 entering, VP17–21
 mixed cell addresses, VP117–119
 order of operations, VP21
 relative addresses, VP116
Freezing titles, VP110–111
Function(s)
 AVG, VP152, VP153
 CHOOSE, VP231
 COUNT, VP152–153
 database, VP229–230
 FV, VP179, VP181–183
 IF, VP159–161
 lookup, VP230–232
 MAX, VP152, VP153
 MIN, VP152, VP153
 NOW, 100–101
 PV, VP159, VP160
 statistical, VP152–154
 STD, VP152–153
 SUM, VP66–67, VP152
 summary of, VP171
 VAR, VP152–VP153
 VLOOKUP, VP231–232

Global change, VP49
Global Default menu, VP130
Global formatting, VP99–100, VP110
Global menu, VP49–50
GOTO command, VP15–17
Graph menu, VP185–206
 bar, VP197–201
 line, VP191–197
 options, VP201–203
 pie chart, VP186–191
 XY, VP203–204

Graph Name menu, VP189–190
Graph Options menu, VP188
Graph Reset menu, VP192
Graph specifications, VP187

Hard copy, VP26
Help facility, VP32
HLOOKUP function, VP231
Horizontal synchronization, VP171
Horizontal titles, VP110–111

IF function, VP159–161

Input line, VP5
Insert command, VP105–108
Interactive macros, VP169

Label, VP6–13
Left-justified labels, VP8
Legends, VP196
Line graphs, VP191–197, VP198
Lookup functions, VP230–232
Lotus 1-2-3 screen, VP131–132

Macro(s), VP148, VP165–169
Macro commands, VP168–169
Macro words, VP168–169
Margins, printer, VP125–126
MAX function, VP152, VP153
Memory, VP5, VP132, VP154
Menu(s), VP22–23
MIN function, VP152, VP153
Mixed cell address, VP117
Move command, VP112–114
Multiple-line graphs, VP194–197, VP200

NOT logical operator, VP160
NOW function, VP100–101
Numbers, VP13–15, VP18

Offset argument, VP230
Order of operations, VP21
OR logical operator, VP160

Percent values, VP71, VP72–73, VP110
PIC files, VP191
Pie chart, VP186–191
Pointing, VP54–57, VP112
Pop-up menus, VP23
Primary-key, sorting on, VP216
Print menu, VP78
Printing, VP77–83
 in condensed mode, VP126
 default settings, VP130
 to a file, VP83
Printer Options menu, VP125–126
PRN file extension, VP83
Prompt line, VP5
Protected cells, VP171

Querying a database, VP219–229
Query menu, VP220
Quitting, VP21, VP33–34
Quotation mark, labels beginning with, VP10

Range Name Label menu, VP156
Range Name menu, VP151–152
Range of cells, VP53
 naming, VP150–152
 pointing to, VP54–57
 pointing vs. entering, VP121
 printing, VP80–81
 to sum, VP119–123
Recalculate menu, VP129–130
Record, VP213
Redo key, VP130, VP133
Relative addressing, VP67, VP116
Repeating characters, VP60–61
Right arrow key, VP6
Right-justified labels, VP10
Rows, VP4, VP104
 deleting and inserting, VP105–108

Saving, VP21–26
 automatically, VP130

intermediate copy, VP65
 macro for, VP165–166
Scale command, VP202
Scatter graphs, VP196–197
Screen image, VP4
 Lotus 1-2-3, VP131–132
 printing, VP26
 windows, VP169–171
Search argument, VP231
Secondary-key, sorting on, VP217–218
Sensitivity analyses, VP127–130
Side-by-side bar graph, VP199–200, VP201
Simple bar graphs, VP198–199
Sorting database, VP214–219
Sort menu, VP215
Source cell range, VP62
Stacked-bar graph, VP200–201
Status line, VP5, VP19, VP132
STEP mode, VP167
Substring search, VP224
SUM function, VP66, VP119–123
Synchronized windows, VP171
System command, VP133

Table, range name, VP152
Text version, VP84
Tilde character, VP165
Time display, VP100–103
Titles
 entering, VP7–8
 freezing, VP110–111
 horizontal, VP110
 subtitles, VP108–109
 unfreezing, VP112
 vertical, VP110
TODAY function, VP155

Undo key, VP130, VP133
Unprotected cells, VP171

VALUE mode, VP14
VAR function, VP152, VP153
Vertical synchronization, VP171
Vertical titles, VP110–111
VLOOKUP function, VP231–232

WAIT mode, VP133, VP24
Wait state, VP133
What-if analyses, VP96, VP127–130, VP162–164
 pie charts and, VP190
Whole numbers, VP13–14
Wild-card characters, VP224
Windows, VP4, VP169–171
WKS file extension, VP24
Worksheet
 database, VP213–235
 default settings, VP130–131
 erasing, VP32
 formatting, VP46–86
 organization of, VP4
 printing, VP77–83
 printing to a file, VP83
 retrieving, VP47–49
 saving, VP21–26, VP76–77
Worksheet menu, VP50

X range, in graphs, VP187–188, VP192
XY graphs, VP203–204

Y-axis data range, VP193